RAINMAKER

RAINMAKER

The Saga of Jeff Beck, Wall Street's Mad Dog

ANTHONY BIANCO

Random House   New York

*Grateful acknowledgment is made to the following for permission to reprint previously
published material:*
EMI MUSIC PUBLISHING: Excerpts from "One Fine Day" by Gerry Goffin and Carole King.
Copyright © 1963 by Screen Gems–EMI Music, Inc. All rights reserved. International
copyright secured. Reprinted by permission of EMI Music Publishing.
THE PUTNAM PUBLISHING GROUP: Excerpts from *Agent of Influence* by David Aaron.
Copyright © 1989 by D. L. Aaron & Co., Inc. Reprinted by permission of The Putnam
Publishing Group.
TWENTIETH CENTURY FOX FILM CORPORATION: Excerpts from the screenplay of *Wall Street*,
written by Stanley Weiser and Oliver Stone. *Wall Street* © 1987 Twentieth Century Fox
Film Corporation. All rights reserved. Reprinted by permission.
WARNER/CHAPPELL MUSIC, INC.: Excerpts from "Like a Rolling Stone" by Bob Dylan.
Copyright © 1965 by Warner Brothers, Inc. All rights reserved. Reprinted by permission of
Warner/Chappell Music, Inc.

Library of Congress Cataloging-in-Publication Data
Bianco, Anthony.
Rainmaker: the saga of Jeff Beck, Wall Street's mad dog/by Anthony Bianco.
p.   cm.
Includes index.
ISBN 0-394-57023-5
1. Beck, Jeffrey P.   2. Stockbrokers—United States—Biography.
I. Title.
HG4928.5.B53   1991
332.6′2′092—dc20
[B]   88-42821

For my parents, who for as long as I can remember have had the grace and the wisdom to encourage me to think for myself

You say you never compromise
With the mystery tramp but now you realize
He's not selling any alibis
As you stare into the vacuum of his eyes
And say, "Do you want to make a deal?"
How does it feel?
How does it feel?
To be on your own
With no direction home
Like a complete unknown.

—from "Like a Rolling Stone," Bob Dylan (1965)

So sacred is the office [of rainmaker] that the holder thereof is put to death before old age and infirmity creep on, lest his demise from natural causes should bring distress on the tribe. But so honoured a life and death are not always the lot of the rain-maker . . . When people believe that a man has power to make the rain to fall, the sun to shine, the winds to blow, the thunders to roll, and the fruits of the earth to grow, they are also apt to attribute drought and death to his negligence or evil magic. Thus, the Banjars of West Africa beat the chief in times of drought till the weather changes, and the tribes on the Upper Nile rip up the abdomen of the rain-king, in which he is supposed to keep the storms.

Encyclopedia of Religion (1954)

RAINMAKER

The Legend of the Mad Dog

Over the years, Jeff Beck told me many stories about his military exploits. Here is his complete Vietnam saga:

I never thought much about Vietnam until 1968, when I was a senior at Florida State. I'd always figured the war would be over by the time I graduated so I tested out of all these math and science courses. I was smart but I was stupid. I graduated a semester and a half early, just as they were doing away with graduate-school deferments. I thought about going to Canada. Anyone with half a brain did. That didn't last long, though. They shoot deserters in times of war, you know. So I kept asking my stepfather to use his influence with his son-in-law, Richard Stone, who was a U.S. senator, but he wouldn't do it. He wanted to see me dead. And my mother! I remember the day she told me that some of her friends had sons who were over in Vietnam and that they really enjoyed it over there. Can you believe that shit? "Having a great time in 'Nam, wish you were here."

Instead of waiting around to be drafted, I enlisted. I could have gone over as a regular army second lieutenant in infantry, but the kill rate was like 95 percent. I wanted to get out of infantry and into intelligence. So I took all these tests and they found out that I fit the classic profile of Special Forces guys—driven achievers motivated by anger. I had a very high IQ and was off the charts on anger. But I rated high on trustworthiness and goal accomplishment, too. When they said they wanted to send me to ranger school, I said why not? If I'm going to be in the army, I might as well go all the way. After ranger school, I went to jump school at Fort Bragg and jungle school in the Panama Canal Zone. I did well in training with my peers. I was gung ho at it, a regular Boy Scout. You had to be or you'd never make it through. Then I went to Fort Halliburton, where I finally got shifted out of the infantry into intelligence. By the time we shipped out to Vietnam five months later, I had qualified for my green beret.

Before I left, I tried to patch things up with my mother and stepfather. They had a dinner for me, a reconciliation dinner, at their apartment in Miami. It was a big fancy place. They always made me wear a tie for dinner there, but I'd had it with that Mickey Mouse shit. I was wearing my old football jersey when I got there in my 1957 Mercury with no floorboards in the back. What a great car! We called it "the Cuban Border Patrol car." It was backfiring like crazy, smoke was pouring out from underneath. Their maid met me at the door of the apartment and said, "I wouldn't go in looking like that." I turned around and left. I'm shipping out to 'Nam and they're all worried about a fucking tie.

I was attached to the Fifth Special Forces, First Army. I was hoping to watch the war from the terrace of the Caravelle Hotel in Saigon, but it didn't quite work out that way. Vietnam was a big shock initially. A couple of guys I came over with bought it early. At first, I was with MACV [Military Assistance Command, Vietnam], advising a South Vietnamese battalion for about two months. I was billeted in Saigon but I was rarely there. I had to go into battle with these guys but a lot of them didn't want to fight. I treed a South Vietnamese colonel, sent him right up in a tree with my M-16 because he was too chickenshit to fight. I was reprimanded for that one. It was on or around that event that people started calling me Mad Dog.

After MACV, I went to Fifth Special Forces headquarters in Nhatrang on the South China Sea. The Special Forces is broken down into certain strike forces. My unit assignment was always mobile air strike force. For twelve and a half months I was attached to a special topsecret "dark" unit of mobile air. Mobile air meant dropping from planes, but in Vietnam it also meant taking A teams into enemy areas for reconnaissance. That's what I did. I led an A team with the rank of second lieutenant. There were eight guys in an A team—a couple of Kit Carsons [scouts who were former Vietcong], a few explosives experts, a medic, a radio man. We went deep into Laos and Cambodia. We blew up a lot of people and a lot of things—medical and ammo dumps, underground bunkers. A couple times we had to find POW camps and spring somebody. On those kinds of missions, we did a lot of closequarter kills, slitting guards' throats and shit.

This was very lonely stuff. No speaking, no smoking. You had combat paint all over you. We tried to look like trees. I remember on the Ho

Chi Minh Trail once a North Vietnamese unit came and pissed on the trees right next to us. They were so close you could smell their urine. That was close. Sometimes we'd miss a rendezvous point and get separated. Once we lost four guys for a month. That was the longest time. We finally found them drawn and quartered and hanging from trees. Let me tell you, it was a long walk back to camp that day.

After six months of heavy combat, the fear is gone and you're just part of the jungle. I started carrying a big Bowie knife. It was sharp enough to take someone's head off. I threw away my M-16 and started carrying an enemy AK-47 because it was a better weapon. I also carried two canteens, a packet of rice, four or five grenades, plastic explosives, a detonator, twenty ammo clips, a .45. I got my food wherever I could find it. I lived like the dinks did. I survived. When my thirteen months was up, I reenlisted. I was totally into it, barely human any more. I hardly ever slept because when I closed my eyes I saw myself floating facedown in the Mekong River. I stopped wearing my flak jacket and my helmet. America seemed as far away as Mars. I stopped even thinking about getting back.

I was a captain now, with a two-hundred-man company. I always led from the front. One day about halfway through my second tour I was with a platoon in the Ia Drang [Valley]—I can't tell you exactly where —when we were ambushed by what seemed like a whole battalion. By the time we fell back and got some cover, I'd lost about half my men. The wounded were lying all over, screaming for help. But they had us pinned down tight. We couldn't do anything but listen to them die all night long, the poor fuckers. By the next morning, you could hear just a few guys moaning. We got the radio working and I called in the F-16s. We were at close quarters and right in the thick jungle so they dropped a big load of napalm to take away the enemy's cover. Everything was burning—trees, bodies, rocks. The fucking ground was on fire! The smell of charred flesh was unbelievable. If there's hell on earth, man, this was it.

They had us pinned down for four days, four days without food or sleep—a combat eternity. Every few hours a sniper would pick off someone else. By the time they finally got us the fuck out of there, there were only eight guys still alive, including me. Everybody was wounded. I was lucky, though. All I got was a bullet in the right wrist and it was deflected by my watch, which probably saved my hand. They loaded us in a helicopter and the major in charge told the pilot to take us to some army hospital in the jungle. I'd heard a lot of horror stories about army *doctors so I told him to take us to the navy hospital at Cam Ranh Bay. He refused, and after four days of hell I was in no mood to debate. He was a real stuffed shirt, West Point guy. I gave him one more chance and he was stupid enough not to take it. I used the butt end of my AK-47 to rearrange his face for him. Those navy doctors were pretty good but two of my men didn't make it. That left only six of us.*

They gave me a Silver Star for bravery and court-martialed me at the same time. I was in a jail cell for three weeks, looking at twenty years' hard labor. I got a good lawyer, a guy I'd grown up with in Florida— Brian DeGarmo. He was a great guy, but was later killed in a freak accident and never made it back. The trial was in a sealed courtroom at command headquarters in Saigon. We went before a three-man tribunal of commanding officers. They acquitted me on a two-to-one vote. I had extenuating circumstances going for me. I was honorably discharged and they sent me to the Presidio in San Francisco, where the army shrinks tried to put my head back together.

Or so Beck claimed.

Prologue

When I met Jeff Beck for the first time, in 1983, he was thirty-seven years old and running the mergers and acquisitions department at Oppenheimer & Company, a midsized investment bank that was more profitable than important. At thirty, I'd worked as a business reporter for five years and was well into my second year of covering the Wall Street beat for *Business Week*. Although Beck wasn't even mentioned in the short article I wrote about Oppenheimer, he intrigued me right from the start. The great bull market of the 1980s was just beginning to reach full throttle, and Beck seemed to embody the manic exuberance of the times to a greater extent than anyone else I had met in my Wall Street travels or would meet over the remainder of that tumultuous decade.

Nothing about Jeffrey Paul Beck's looks was particularly striking. He looked a bit older than his years, in part because his sandy hair was flecked with gray at the temples and was thinning on top. Although he carried extra weight around the midsection, the remnants of youthful athleticism were apparent in a powerful upper torso, of which he seemed inordinately proud. At five foot nine and about 180 pounds (this being the midpoint of a thirty-pound range within which his weight fluctuated with the rhythm of his deals), Beck was an average-sized man with an outsized presence. He didn't dominate a roomful of people so much as agitate it, like a flame under a pan of water. Beck's one indisputably commanding feature was his voice, a marvelously flexible instrument that was easily adaptable to the many classic American dialects—Wolfman Jack hipster, drawling Southern sheriff, hard-bitten marine sergeant, sly gangster—with which he flavored his speech. Unadorned, his voice was an accentless baritone that rose to deafening volume when he was angry or, as was more often the case, feigning anger. It was almost impossible to outshout Beck, though fortunately he was not by nature a shouter. Yet for all his raucous physicality, Beck projected good-natured amiability rather than temperamental menace. He had a broad, open face with a strong chin, an expressive mouth, and full cheeks that dimpled when he laughed. The only discordant element in the general merriment of Beck's features was his eyes, weak and wary behind horn-rimmed glasses. I once told Beck that he had the eyes of a border guard. He liked the sound of that.

Beck had a congenital irreverence that, like a psychological sixth toe, prevented his personality from being shoehorned into an official role. Imagine a Jewish John Belushi wearing a thousand-dollar suit and sitting in a neat, elegantly appointed office with his feet propped on the desk. *Something* had to happen. Beck hovered perpetually on the edge of explosion. He might say or do anything. Once I was listening to an impassioned Beck soliloquy on the unappreciated greatness of his M & A group at Oppenheimer when he bounded to the doorway of his office and bellowed down the hallway: "Hey, Sanzo, don't forget to take your lithium, man." (John Sanzo, as it turned out, not only wasn't on lithium but was the most solidly professional banker in the department—a fact that, to Beck's way of thinking, qualified Sanzo as the most deserving butt of his humor.) None of his better-known M & A peers—Felix Rohatyn, Joe Flom, Bruce Wasserstein—came close to matching the exuberant theatricality of Beck, who was aptly cast in a cameo role as a deal man in the 1987 film *Wall Street.* Beck self-promoted with a vengeance, big-dealing it in Hermès ties and suspenders, exhaling clouds of tough-guy talk with his Cuban-cigar smoke, making urgent long-distance phone calls from the backseats of limousines speeding to the airport on his way to the latest battleground of the Big Deal. "Rock and roll!" he'd shout amid the frenzy of a deal. "Lock and load."

As a reporter, I found it tough not to like a guy like Beck, if only because he made the public-relations people assigned to him very, very nervous. While other investment bankers presented themselves as sober statesmen of high finance engaged in safeguarding American capitalism, Beck offered himself as a tour guide to a carnival funhouse known as Wall Street. The world might know Felix Rohatyn as an accomplished, even dignified, personage, but when Beck paraded this financial savant past the mirrors of his skewed perception it was hard to see him as anything but a dwarf with a pin-sized head and an enormous butt. I added Beck to the list of the dozen or so Wall Street dealers whom I spoke with regularly and quoted occasionally, though rarely by name. Beck preferred this arrangement, as did most M & A men. Gradually, he and I became friends, though not without residual unease on my part. In the past I'd always steered clear of personal relationships with professional sources for fear of compromising my objectivity or seeming to. But Beck simply left me no choice. It was his nature to relentlessly personalize his dealings. In all the relationships he struck up, the middle ground quite quickly disappeared: You were his friend or, by definition, you were his enemy. I chose to be his friend, and in time became, in Beck's own description, his "confessor."

As it happened, I'd met Beck just as his career was taking off. In mid-1983, he'd assisted at his first billion-dollar deal, advising Esmark Company on its acquisition of Norton Simon. Within a year, Beck had brokered the sale of Esmark to Beatrice Companies for $2.8 billion. A few months later, he had put himself in the middle of a $1 billion buyout of Northwest Industries. Plucky, audacious little Oppenheimer & Company was grabbing headlines away from Morgan Stanley & Company and the other old-line houses that had imperiously ruled investment banking for most of the twentieth century. I'd always been a sucker for underdog stories, and in late 1984 I wrote for *Business Week* the first full-fledged profile of Beck. The article was favorable, even flattering, but I might as well have laid a curse on Beck's head. Within months of its publication, the Northwest Industries deal collapsed and long-festering resentments within Oppenheimer exploded into open conflict. Beck left in mid-1985, vowing never to return to Wall Street; at his suggestion we began collaborating on an exposé of the deal world, to be based on his own experiences. However, our book project was shelved almost before it began when, in late 1985, Beck decided to take a job at Drexel Burnham Lambert. His lifetime exile from the Street had lasted all of four months.

Within weeks of joining Drexel, Beck was celebrating a deal that was the biggest of his career and one of the most important of the takeover era: the $8.2 billion leveraged buyout of Beatrice. Yes, this was the same Beatrice that had just acquired Esmark, which in turn had recently acquired Norton Simon. The object of these deals—$12 billion worth—done in less than three years had been to make a fortune by building one of America's largest food companies. With the leveraged buyout of Beatrice, the object now became to make a fortune by dismantling one of America's largest food companies. A crazy logic drove this epic trio of deals, and Beck was its master. A few months after Esmark had been acquired by Beatrice, Beck had bet Donald Kelly, the former chief executive officer of Esmark, $250,000 and breakfast in Rio de Janeiro or dinner in Paris that within a year Kelly would displace his displacer and become CEO of Beatrice. One year later—to the very day—Beatrice did in fact agree to a buyout led by Kelly, who annoyed Beck no end by refusing to pay off on the bet.

The Beatrice deal was a spectacular comeback for Beck, whose personal fee of $4.5 million comfortably exceeded the fee paid his old firm. But Beck continued to insist that he was fed up with Wall Street and intended to retire from dealing at the earliest opportunity to collaborate with me on a book. By the summer of 1987, I'd finally succeeded in prodding Beck into action on the book front. The actor Michael Douglas introduced him to Lynn Nesbit, a prominent literary agent. While Nesbit quickly agreed to represent us, our search for a publisher was protracted not only by the vagaries of Beck's schedule but by his tactical obsessiveness. He tried to stage-manage our book sale as meticulously as if it had been a billion-dollar deal. Although Beck had set a $1 million advance as his goal, we settled for considerably less in reaching a preliminary agreement with Random House in the fall.

Before we actually signed with Random House, though, Beck insisted that our relationship as coauthors be defined in the form of a legal agreement. Inexplicably, three months passed before Beck's lawyer sent me a ten-page document that was labeled "COLLABORATION AGREEMENT" but that, in reality, was an employment contract obligating me to work exclusively for Beck until the manuscript was accepted by a publisher. The contract gave Beck the unilateral right to fire me and included an onerous confidentiality clause that, as far as I could tell, obligated me until the end of time not to disclose anything about Beck or our relationship. The contract stipulated, in fact, that the provisions of the confidentiality clause "shall survive the termination or expiration of this agreement for any reason whatsoever."

I had to hire my own lawyer, who set about the task of trying to transform indentured servitude into a true collaboration agreement. For every point of disagreement resolved, Beck raised a new reservation and sent his lawyer back to the drawing board. Instead of preparing to leave Drexel as planned, Beck put himself into the middle of a major takeover battle. Weeks of delay turned into months of equivocating. Finally, Peter Osnos of Random House suggested that Beck content himself with being the book's subject and leave the writing to me. Although Beck would lose any element of control over the book—the Random House agreement was redrawn to eliminate him wholly—he seemed relieved by Osnos's suggestion, which would enable him to remain at Drexel while fulfilling his promise to me to collaborate on a book. While he quickly agreed in principle to extend his full cooperation, he reserved final judgment. "Let me think about it for a week," he said.

When the week had expired, I tried for days to get him on the telephone. Finally, I reached him at Drexel one afternoon. "I'm leaning toward yes," he said. "But let me think about it overnight."

Some final restraint snapped within me. Two years of mounting frustration found voice in a single word—*"No!"*—followed by an ultimatum. I told him that I was going to leave *Business Week* and write a book that had nothing whatsoever to do with him unless he decided right then and there to cooperate. He agreed—on one condition: that he get a share of the proceeds from any sale of the film rights to the book. I had to laugh. *This* was a deal man, right to the bitter end. Thinking that this concession would assure Beck's participation throughout any rough times ahead, I agreed to split the film rights with him. The collaboration agreement drawn up by our lawyers was discarded unsigned, the useless product of thousands of dollars' worth of legal advice. Two and a half years after Beck and I ostensibly had begun working on a book together, I signed with Random House. Beck was not a party to the contract; he holds no power over this book save the power of suggestion.

From the outset of our collaboration Beck had repeatedly warned me of his penchant for exaggeration, a not uncommon trait among deal men. I must admit, though, that I began work on this book not realizing the extent to which Beck had gone beyond exaggeration into outright fabrication in telling me the story of his life. He told me repeatedly that he'd played big-time college football, that he'd fought in Vietnam as a captain in the U.S. Special Forces and that he'd assembled a vast private empire of businesses that had made him a billionaire several times over. As it turned out, none of this was true. He'd made it all up. He lied. The Jeff Beck I thought I knew turned out to be as wholly invented a character as any Hollywood hero. In the end, though, I would realize as well that this compulsive liar's peculiarly excruciating fate was to be a man more honest than the times in which he lived.

*   *   *

Jeff Beck's Wall Street career was a product of an era in which the rich got richer to an extent rarely equalled in American history. The top 1 percent of the U.S. population saw its after-tax share of the national income rise from 7 percent in the late 1970s to 11 percent by 1990; meanwhile, the share of the bottom two-fifths of Americans declined proportionally.

So many huge new fortunes were amassed in the 1980s that the word "millionaire" not only lost much of its ring but also changed its meaning. A net worth of a million dollars no longer made much of an impression. A 1980s millionaire was someone whose *annual income* topped one million dollars. Beck met this standard handily, as his pay rose over the magic million mark in 1984 and stayed there for the rest of the decade. By decade's end, too, Beck ranked among the hundred thousand Americans who'd amassed a net worth of at least $10 million —"decamillionaires," these fortunate folks were called. Amazingly, they were more numerous in 1989 than regular millionaires had been in 1960. The millionaire élite of 1960, moreover, included two of Beck's closest relatives—his stepfather and his uncle—and although Beck inherited none of their wealth, the fact that he'd come from money was a critical psychological component of his drive to amass a fortune of his own, a drive that brought him to Wall Street in its early-1970s period of unfashionability. As money and money-making were glorified in the Reagan years, Beck's pursuit of wealth and the social status derived from it flowered into full-fledged mania.

Beck was not alone in his intoxication with affluence. In New York City especially, the nouveaux riches celebrated themselves with an opulence and faux-aristocratic elitism not seen since the so-called Gilded Age of the late nineteenth century. After getting married for the third time, to Margo Preston, a blue-blooded former debutante, Beck plunged into Manhattan's glittering "Nouvelle Society" scene with a fervor that exceeded even his ample resources. He and Margo spent as much money to decorate his Upper East Side apartment— nearly half a million dollars—as he did to buy it, and then pumped another million into a country estate. Beck learned to ride and built a stable of a half-dozen thoroughbred jumpers, buying a new one to mark each of his major M & A triumphs. He hired a French governess to tend to his daughter and a chauffeur to drive him around town in his Mercedes 500 SL sedan. He tipped his way into favored treatment at The Four Seasons, Manhattan's quintessential power-deal-making restaurant, and spent thousands upon thousands of dollars every six months on the choicest accommodations at one of the world's great luxury hotels, the Hôtel du Cap d'Antibes on the Côte d'Azur. And yet all of this somehow wasn't enough. Beck began claiming that he was half owner of the Hôtel du Cap and placing bids on great works of art that were beyond his means, extricating himself just before closing from transactions that collectively could have bankrupted him.

In his financial brinksmanship, too, Beck was in synch with his times, for the prosperity of the Reagan era rested on the shaky foundation of wishful thinking masquerading as patriotic optimism. In contrast to the Gilded Age, which marked the nation's passage from an old-fashioned mercantilist to a modern industrial economy, the 1980s were a time of modest economic growth. The wealth explosion of the Reagan years was not, primarily, the result of leaps in industrial output and productivity but of a sharp upward revaluation of the nation's storehouse of existing assets through the medium of high finance—through Wall Street, the world capital of capital, which enriched itself in the 1980s as never before. To the extent that this revaluation resulted from a taming of the high inflation of the 1970s (an achievement rooted more in the dour realism of Paul Volcker, chairman of the Federal Reserve Board, than in the sunny conservatism of Ronald Reagan), it was broadly beneficial, justifiably unleashing one of history's greatest bull markets. However, the value of things financial kept rising, far beyond what the economic fundamentals warranted, propelled upward in defiance of the gravity of common sense by accounting gimmickry, massive increases in indebtedness, and a hot-air mix of ideology and mythology that served the interests of the power brokers of Washington no less than the moguls of Wall Street.

How could policies manifestly designed for the disproportionate benefit of the few and advanced at great risk to the majority prevail for so long? The short answer is that Jeff Beck was hardly the only American who spent the Reagan years sheathed in escapist fantasy. American historians have charted a broad societal shift over the course of the twentieth century, from a Puritan ethic of self-control rooted in the values of production to a new consumer ethic of personal pleasure. With the consolidation of mass entertainment, mass communications, and mass spectator sports, national hero worship was transferred from what scholar Leo Lowenthal dubbed "idols of production" to "idols of consumption." The idol of production was "inner-directed, aggressive, and driven, admired for his achievements and hard work." The idol of consumption, on the other hand, was "outer-directed, passive, and lucky, admired for his good looks and for pleasing others." In the person of Ronald Reagan, former Hollywood screen star, TV personality, and longtime pitchman for General Electric, the idol of consumption was finally graduated to the Oval Office. During his presidency, Reagan's ultimate achievement was often described, even by his supporters, as the ephemeron of "making America feel good about itself again." To a populace unable to reconcile its aspirations with the harsh reality of America's declining affluence and international might, Reagan offered the absolution of fantasy as faith.

Reagan's exemption from truth extended beyond politics to his personal history, which he improvised to fit according to the circumstances of the moment. Like Jeff Beck, Reagan at times resorted to outright fabrication, especially about his life during wartime. Astoundingly, Reagan once told Israeli prime minister Yitzhak Shamir that he had seen firsthand the devastation wrought by the Holocaust as a member of an army film crew that filmed the liberation of the concentration camps. "From then on," Reagan said, "I was concerned for the Jewish people." The fact was, though, that Reagan never left the United States during World War II and indeed lived at home with his wife throughout his four years in uniform. As time went on, the White House spin doctors became brazen in dismissing questions about contradictions between Reagan's claims and the truth. When, for example, a reporter asked why the president had cited a nonexistent British law in arguing against gun control, his press secretary responded testily, "It made the point, didn't it?"

As a Wall Street investment banker, Beck worked within a distinctive mythological tradition nearly as old as Republican conservatism. The most illuminating of Wall Street's many truisms is this: Stocks aren't bought, they're sold. Like middlemen of all kinds, the dealers of Wall Street are primarily devoted to moving merchandise, in this case securities. But what Wall Street really sells is the future, or rather the hope of a more prosperous future attained not through the drudgery of hard labor but through enlightened investment—a century-old sales pitch that meshed seamlessly with the relentless supply-side boosterism of the Reagan era.

On old Wall Street the commercial realities of securities dealing were obscured by the mystique of social class. For a century, investment banking was ruled by an oligopoly of a dozen elite firms headed by the ultra-WASPy House of Morgan and dedicated to exclusivity in every facet of their affairs. The gentleman bankers of old Wall Street styled themselves not stockjobbing brokers but lordly and discreet counselors to the largest corporations in the land. Disdaining competition and self-promotion as flip sides of the same base coin, the gentleman bankers relied on their reputations and social connections to bring in business. While the influence of J. P. Morgan was unequaled, the ideal of the gentleman banker was most artfully realized in the early years of this century in the figure of Otto Kahn, who could be seen on Sunday mornings on Fifth Avenue "strolling with his dachshunds in his tall silk hat and silver-handled cane," as Stephen Birmingham observed in *Our Crowd*. "One marveled at the polished tips of his shoes below his spats, the perfection of his mohair gloves, the inevitable large pearl stickpin in his tie, placed just above the V in his velvet-collared Chesterfield."

Not until the 1970s did the combination of inflation and deregulation cause the old oligarchy to collapse. Stripped of the gilt-edged wrapping of social class, Wall Street sought to repackage its sales pitch as logic; employing an army of analysts to sift and organize information into reports. But because markets are as susceptible to the madness of crowds as to rational argument, they are essentially unknowable, except perhaps in retrospect. Thus, the business of the new Wall Street revolved around people capable of transforming argument into prophecy, people who could convince others that they could foretell the future course of prices—though, of course, the word "prophecy" was not included in the Street's official lexicon. The euphemism of choice was "feel"—as in "So-and-So has a great feel for the market." Feel is intuition laced with inspiration and dipped in luck. Feel comes and goes as it pleases, and is easily mistaken for genius.

As the gentleman banker receded into the mists of history, a radically different breed of Wall Street man emerged to preeminence: the rainmaker. Competition supplanted collusion on the new Wall Street, endangering the very existence of every investment bank and brokerage. Many of the oldest didn't outlast the 1970s. Those houses that survived to thrive as never before in the 1980s were reinvented through the offices of a relative handful of rainmakers. As water was the first need of primitive man, profit was life to Wall Street man; the rainmaker was able to create profit from a seemingly cloudless sky. His magic was a product not of class but of charisma and conviction. The rainmaker was the broker apotheosized as shaman, a self-invented medicine man of money, possessed of such powers of persuasion that he could conjure up large securities transactions and even whole new financial markets, beginning with little more than his own faith that it could be done. The ultimate Wall Street rainmaker was Michael Milken, who created the junk-bond market under the auspices of Drexel Burnham Lambert and, in defiance of the basic laws of competitive dynamics, maintained it as his personal preserve even as it grew to more than $200 billion. In the long, prosaic history of working for a living, there had never been anyone like Milken. In 1987, his peak year, Drexel paid Milken $550 million—more than Boeing, Procter & Gamble, or Kraft made.

Unlike Milken, most of the great rainmakers of the 1980s were, like Beck, mergers and acquisitions bankers. In the self-serving mythology of the M & A man, the attributes of the gentleman banker were turned inside out, creating a fierce and cunning warrior where once was a refined clubman. M & A men even invented their own macho lingo, replete with hyperbolic metaphors of violence: "scorched earth," "poison pills," "Saturday night specials," "shark repellents," "bear hugs." All this highly publicized martial sound and fury signified nothing more than the skillful self-promotion of professional opportunists. While undeniably ferocious in their pursuit of fees, M & A men never fought to the death. They never even really lost. A corporation that lost a takeover battle disappeared, but its M & A advisers got immensely larger fees than they would have had their client maintained its independence. At bottom the M & A business was a hustle—an extraordinarily lucrative one. With the possible exception of narcotics dealers, Wall Street's M & A men were the highest-paid, most powerful commercial middlemen in Reagan's America—and all their activies were legal, or theoretically so, anyway.

For all the theatricality of his performance in the role of M & A man, in the end what most decisively set Beck apart from his Wall Street peers was that he not only knew it was all a con, but said so repeatedly to me and other reporters even while he was playing his part to the hilt. While many M & A men tried to ennoble their fee-grubbing with Reaganesque musings about how the great 1980s takeover wave was restoring the entrepreneurial vigor of corporate America, in Beck's blunt-spoken definition 1980s-style deal making turned on "the manipulation of marginal personalities by marginal personalities." As much as he wanted to be liked by his fellow M & A men, Beck was unable to play by their self-serving rules. When he saw

conspiratorial winks and nods, his reflex response was—at times literally—a mad dog's howl. He was fiercely protective of his clients, even
when safeguarding their interests meant antagonizing other deal men.
In an era of rampant lawlessness in high finance, Beck was never so
much as accused of a crime, though he did not lack for temptation.
Over the years, he came into close contact with many of the most
infamous Wall Streeters of the era—Ivan Boesky, Marty Siegel, Dennis Levine—and was both friend and colleague to Milken. Beck made
many enemies, too, but mostly for the right reasons. For on Wall
Street during the Reagan years, incomplicity was a far greater offense
to the powers that be than deceit was.

On January 22, 1990, more than four years after Beck and I had begun
collaborating on the story of his life, *The Wall Street Journal* terminated what was left of the deal man's investment-banking career with
a front-page article headlined "TOP DEAL MAKER LEAVES A TRAIL OF
DECEPTION IN WALL STREET RISE. " Although this rambling exposé was
one of the longest *Journal* articles on the 1980s, the gist of it was
contained in two paragraphs:

> A reporter's investigation into the star deal maker's career reveals that
> much of Mr. Beck's "past" has been created from whole cloth, the prod-
> uct, friends and business associates say, of the banker's active fantasy life.
> Army records and his first wife's family confirm that he never served in the
> special forces, never fought in Vietnam, never, in fact, came closer to
> combat than the Army reserves. Nor, apparently, is there any basis for Mr.
> Beck's repeated claims to associates over the years that he stood to inherit a
> family fortune he variously estimated at between $100 million and $2.5
> billion, or that he owned a "small empire" of private businesses, as a major
> magazine once reported [a reference to my 1984 article on Beck in *Busi-
> ness Week*].
> Confronted with evidence of his deceptions over lunch at a Manhattan
> restaurant, Mr. Beck first looks away, then stares at the ceiling for a mo-
> ment. Under the table, his left leg begins rapidly bobbing. A thin mist falls
> over his eyes. "I can't talk about it," he says after a long silence. But he
> does, though his answers amount to riddles wrapped in questions, wrapped
> in lies. His explanation, broadly hinted at, is that for 20 years he has led a
> double life as an intelligence agent.

Like Beck's own Legend of the Mad Dog, the *Journal* story was a
spellbinding mélange of fact and fiction that had the effect of obscur-

ing rather than revealing the real Jeff Beck. The article's basic flaw was
that it didn't go nearly far enough in unmasking Beck, who, by the end
of the 1980s, was living a life of deceit so absolute that in effect his
true personality had been turned inside out. Beck's Vietnam Hero and
Billionaire personas were merely subsidiary fantasies created to provide
relief from the psychic pain of more fundamental evasions. As generation after generation of small-town American misfits has flocked to
Hollywood seeking to reinvent themselves in grander form, so Beck
escaped to Wall Street, where he made himself into the business-world
equivalent of the Star: the M & A Man. This was a triumph of sheer
will, for he created the character of Mad Dog the M & A Man in
complete contradiction to his basic nature. The real Jeff Beck was not
a gregarious natural promoter, not the irreverent provocateur whom I
first met, but an insecure, analytical introvert for whom every board
meeting, every episode of deal theater was preceded by an agony of
ambivalent introspection—an unpretentious, almost tender man who
was driven not by greed or even by ambition in any usual sense but by
a desperate, perhaps pathological need to please others.

For the real Jeff Beck, making millions of dollars a year doing billions of dollars of deals was not a dream come true but a waking
nightmare of self-betrayal. Over the seven years that I've known him,
I've watched his mood swing from ecstatic absorption in his latest
maneuverings to utter disillusionment after a deal ended. Whether it
ended in success didn't seem to matter much; defeat only had the
effect of deepening his postpartum malaise. But then along would
come another deal, another billion-dollar fix of combat and intrigue,
followed by more anguished talk of leaving Wall Street and New York
City—soon, always soon—and living "like a real human being" somewhere, somehow. Over and over turned this self-destructive cycle as
the deals got bigger and wilder with every passing year. Beck was like a
convict who'd lived so long in prison that he couldn't bring himself to
go home when his sentence expired.

In time I realized that when Beck said he was addicted to deal
making what he really meant was that he was addicted to the persona
of M & A wizard that he'd created and inhabited. He could not
relinquish the controls of his smoke-and-mirrors machine without admitting to the truth of who he really was, and this he just could not
bring himself to do, even as the growing contradiction between his
public and private selves pushed him to what he would later describe
as "the edge of madness." Instead Beck lied and deceived as never

before, augmenting his basic identity as Rainmaker with Vietnam
Hero and Billionaire while the decade of the Big Lie climbed peaks of
destructive delusion in Washington and on Wall Street.

To the extent that Beck was seeking stronger pain relief through
ever more extravagant fantasy, his lies were symptoms of a loss of self-
control that at times did indeed border on madness. Even at his worst,
though, I believe that Beck never wholly lost the ability to distinguish
his fictions from reality. He was never so self-deluded that he believed
his own myth à la Reagan, Milken, or Donald Trump, who to the very
end of his masquerade kept trying to recast ruination as triumph ("I
am the king of cash," Trump proclaimed while hurriedly liquidating
assets in a vain attempt to keep from defaulting on his loans). In fact, I
would go further and say that Beck not only knew that he was lying
but that, paradoxically, part of his purpose in lying was to be forced
into admitting the truth. Almost congenitally unable to reveal himself,
he needed someone to force self-revelation on him, someone whose
professional duty it was to attempt to separate fact from fiction—a
reporter, namely me. And so it was that Beck suggested collaborating
on a book and began calling me his confessor, while laying on me the
biggest, most fully rendered lies of his entire career as a fabulist.

Until I began taking notes in 1985 at the Hôtel du Cap, Beck's
Vietnam repertoire consisted of cryptic allusions and brief anecdotes
that he'd made use of mainly as a romantic ploy. It was principally
with me in mind that he began to develop these sketchy elements into
a full-blown antiheroic persona. Like a screenwriter, he had the ability
to absorb a mass of knowledge about a complex subject and craft from
it an absorbing, convincing tale. And like an actor, he was capable of
bringing an imaginary character fully to life in the telling. I not only
believed him, I admired him and sympathized with him.

It was largely for my "benefit," too, that Beck inflated what had
been mere passing hints at private wealth into a multibillion-dollar
secret corporate empire and bestowed a name upon his imaginary colossus. He called it Rosebud. As Beck well knew, there is no more
famous invitation to investigation than "Rosebud," which is the last,
dying word of Charles Foster Kane, the mogul protagonist of Orson
Welles's masterpiece, *Citizen Kane.* In the movie, a reporter assigned
the task of making sense of Kane's haunted, unhappy life focuses his
quest on deciphering the meaning of that deathbed utterance. The
reporter never does figure out that *Rosebud* was the sled with which
Kane was playing on the last happy day of his boyhood, the day his

parents sent him away to be schooled in preparation for the vast fortune he would inherit. In Welles's hands, *Rosebud* becomes a poignant symbol of a life irreparably warped by emotional deprivation in
childhood.

While I recognized that Beck was providing me with a clue, an
indirect invitation to search his distant past, I was slow to act on it. For
one thing, our book project began not as autobiography but as an
account of Beck's deal-making adventures. For another, until I began
digging into his personal history I had no reason to doubt his veracity.
To the contrary, my early reporting on the transactions in which he'd
been involved suggested that he was not only truthful but unusually
candid for a deal man. Because initially Beck's tales of Vietnam and
Rosebud were not germane to the book, I could allow myself the
luxury of belief without having to verify them. Beck shrewdly played to
my reporter's frustration at being unable to cut through the public-
relations pabulum, the disinformation, and the silence through which
the mighty obscure their exercise of power. Beck presented himself as
the ultimate insider, as a man who'd penetrated through the many-
layered worlds of finance and government to the deepest, darkest point
of connection between private capital and public power. As he spun
his larger-than-life tales, I felt I was at last getting a glimpse of these
secret inner workings. Jeff Beck was a reporter's fantasy come to life.
He proved no less intriguing when, eighteen months into my research,
I finally discovered his Rosebud on a three-by-five index card in the
Allegheny County Court House in Pittsburgh.

The causes and consequences of the great takeover explosion of the
1980s no doubt will remain a subject of academic and political controversy for years to come. The macroeconomic issues around which this
debate revolves are not my subject here, except as they are refracted
through the prism of Beck's own story. If this book is about the making and unmaking of a 1980s rainmaker, it is also the saga of one man's
agonized odyssey of self-discovery. In this latter aspect, I believe it to
be a tale happily ended. By the time this book went to press at the end
of 1990, Beck had attained a depth of self-understanding and an emotional honesty that few of us will ever reach.

However, given his long-standing penchant for fiction, a comment
on methodology is in order. During my research, Beck allowed me
unsupervised access to a dozen cartons of records, letters, and memos
that dated from the very beginning of his Wall Street career and, to

my surprise, even contained many of his income-tax statements. It was characteristic of Beck's openness in most matters that he didn't know for sure what the cartons contained. I have spent countless hours with Beck over the last five years, spending numerous weekends at his country house and three times accompanying him on long trips. I believe that I know Beck as well as I've ever known anyone. The degree of access he provided me is unusual and was much appreciated. I also made exhaustive searches of all applicable public records. In addition to spending hundreds of hours talking with Beck, I interviewed more than 140 of his friends, colleagues, rivals, and relatives. In those few instances where my account is based wholly on Beck's recollections, I have made explicit the attribution.

In mid-1988, I flew to the island of Sardinia in the Mediterranean to interview Beck, who was hiding out at a resort in Porto Cervo with his new flame, a Hollywood television reporter named Cynthia Allison. After a few days Beck grew bored and rented a private jet to take us to France and the Hôtel du Cap d'Antibes. Allison seemed utterly infatuated with Beck and, as she listened to our interviews, grew concerned that I was not going to portray Jeff as she knew him to be (in fact, she'd only known him for a few months). One sunny afternoon, the three of us were lying around Beck's private cabana at the Hôtel du Cap. Beck was relating the details of a particularly nasty takeover battle and I was taking notes.

After his narrative had taken a theatrically savage turn, Allison turned to me and said: "You know, Jeff really is a very nice man."

Beck cut her off. "Nice?" he roared. "Nice," he snorted derisively. "You don't know who you're dealing with here. You have no idea! I'm a fucking killer."

In my opinion, Allison was a lot closer to the mark than Beck was himself. Even after seven years of association with Beck, there remains much about him that defies my understanding and perhaps his own as well. But despite all the grief that he has inflicted on himself and on the people closest to him, I am certain Jeff Beck is a good-hearted person. I wish him well. That is my bias, and this is his story.

1

History has stuck Charles "Bebe" Rebozo with a thankless cameo role as Richard Nixon's Florida vacation buddy. But Rebozo, a wealthy Miami businessman, really wasn't such a bad guy. He was, for example, a most indulgent uncle. When his niece, Tina, reached high-school age in the early 1960s, Bebe allowed her free run of his beachfront estate on Biscayne Bay. Bebe's place became a weekend rendezvous point for the coolest of the tenth-grade girls and guys from nearby Coral Gables High School. Tina's friends would arrive in twos and threes around noon on Saturday and cut through Bebe's backyard to the beach for some serious water-skiing. The best skier of the group was a funny, skinny kid named Jeff Beck. Although Beck could do all the usual one-ski, rope-behind-the-back stuff, his forte was clown-dancing on the skittery edge of control, lurching to and fro until it seemed he just had to take a tumble. But he never did, he never got wet—though every now and then he would zig when he should have zagged, and end up standing on the beach in his skis, a sheepish smile on his face.

Beck lived with his parents and his older sister, Judy, in a three-bedroom house on Santa Maria Drive, with a pool out back. It was a nice house but nothing fancy by the standards of Coral Gables. The Becks were middle-class all the way. Lou Beck, Jeff's father, sold paper wholesale on commission. Though it was a decent living, there wasn't a lot of money left over for such indulgences as country-club memberships or private schools or European vacations. A lot of Gables kids got cars when they turned sixteen, but not Judy or Jeff. The Beck kids had so many friends that they really didn't need a car of their own. Jeff especially was a veritable mogul of popularity, his lofty place in the youth society of Coral Gables confirmed by one indisputable fact: He was a Chink—a member, that is, of the high-school fraternity Ching Tang.

Founded at Coral Gables High School (then known as Ponce De Leon High) sometime in the mid-1930s, Ching Tang was modeled after a frat in Cleveland, Ohio, and brought south by one of the thousands of families who abandoned the North during the Depression years for the promised land of Florida. Although many of its members mistakenly believed that Ching Tang was Chinese for "Onward and upward," the frat's official motto, the name in fact had been plucked out of the air by joining the names of two unrelated Chinese deities. Chinks were unquestionably the coolest of the cool, cooler by a mile than Stags, Counts, Saxons, or Decallions. The coolness was a matter of selectivity; Ching Tang was the only one of the seven frats at Gables High to require unanimous approval of all new pledges. Of the 2,800 students at the high school in 1961, only forty boys were deemed worthy of Chinkhood. While other frats were basically cliques of jocks or rich kids or hard-asses, Ching Tang set only one criterion for admission: popularity. All the way through school, Beck always had been one of the most popular kids in his class, even though his performance on the athletic field and in the classroom had never been much above average. Beck didn't care. It was enough that the other kids considered him smart. Proving it by getting good grades was superfluous. When it came time to enter Coral Gables High, he found that he didn't even have to apply to Ching Tang. Such was Beck's popularity that the leaders of Ching Tang considered him the one sophomore they just had to have.

In most of America, fraternities are synonymous with college. But fraternal organizations flourished in the junior highs and high schools of Florida, taking deep root in the state's mania for social definition. Florida was sparsely populated until after World War I, when refugees from New York, Boston, Cleveland, and the other cold-weather capitals of the North began arriving in ever-larger waves. Real-estate developers built whole new cities and suburbs to accommodate the flow of transplanted northerners, many of whom were well-to-do. Prosperous newcomers found that their money traveled but that the social status derived from it didn't, so, in the boom towns and instant suburbs of the new Florida, the newcomers founded organizations with selective admissions policies intended to reinvest affluence with social status. By the mid-1940s, high-school frats had become such a pervasive annoyance to parents whose kids were excluded that the Florida legislature passed a law banning them. In Coral Gables and other affluent communities, school authorities conformed to the letter but not the spirit of the law, and the frats continued to flourish though shorn of official sanction.

Nowhere in Florida did club mania reign more intensely than in Coral Gables, which in its way was as pure an expression of the American genius for fantasy as commerce as Disneyland, Las Vegas, or Wall Street. There could be no more fitting hometown for a future M & A rainmaker than the Gables, which was conjured up from a few thousand acres of farmland during the great Florida land boom of the 1920s by a promoter whose optimism was matched only by the extravagance of his hype. His name was George Merrick; in a sense he would be Beck's first mentor in the art of rainmaking. Merrick was gripped by a vision. He saw his family's 160-acre farm on the outskirts of Miami as the nucleus of an ideal community, a model suburb dedicated to careful planning and the highest architectural standards, and free of the urban blight that had already begun to plague Miami. He envisioned Coral Gables (named after a local limestone that Merrick's father had mistaken for coral) not as another winter playground for the wealthy like Palm Beach and Miami Beach, but as a place where the middle-class American could take up year-round residence amid tropical splendor—"a new and modern city in the only American tropics . . . wherein nothing should be unlovely."

Lou and Ida Beck moved to Coral Gables from Pittsburgh in 1946 with their two kids in tow—Judy, who was seven, and Jeff, not yet one. The Becks' new hometown might not have qualified as the "American Riviera" that Merrick had envisioned, but it was blessed by an average annual temperature of 75.7 degrees and its pleasingly designed homes were generously spaced along broad streets shaded by black-olive and ficus trees. The city's eighteen thousand residents had their choice of seven country clubs and four golf courses. Coral Gables wasn't the "Athens of the South," but the University of Miami had developed into a major university and the city's high school was nationally known for academic and athletic excellence. In the early 1960s, Coral Gables High was one of only sixteen high schools with twenty semifinalists in the National Merit Scholarship tests, and its football team was chosen national champion in a poll. Born into the vanguard of the postwar baby boom, Beck came of age in a teen paradise of middle-class affluence in the twilight of the national innocence, in the years before the Beatles, Vietnam, the assassinations, and the drug epidemic.

During those years, Beck was by his own description "rocking and rolling, twisting and shouting"—usually at the dance parties, with live bands, that Ching Tang specialized in throwing at the homes of indulgent or conveniently absent parents. Like most of his fellow Chinks, Beck had a very steady girlfriend, Jenny McGlannan, who belonged to Junior Girls, the most exclusive of the Gables' three sororities. Jenny was tall, blond, and Catholic, and Beck was absolutely crazy about her almost from the moment he met her in the fall of 1961. Sometimes on a Saturday night Jeff and Jenny would opt out of their social scene to be alone. Jeff would put on a coat and tie, borrow his mother's beige Thunderbird, and take Jenny to an old-fashioned Italian restaurant downtown, with dim lights and a strolling troubadour. Beck usually requested the lush ballad "Deep Purple." Jenny saved the empty wine bottles from these nights and put them on a shelf in her room. From the sorrowful complexity of his middle age, Beck would look back on 1962 as the best year of his life. He was as happy then as he could be.

In the whole time they went out together, Jenny never once met Jeff's parents, never even went to his house. Meanwhile, Jeff practically lived at the McGlannans'. Even when Jenny wasn't home, he'd come over and hang out with her younger brother, Mickey, who regarded Jeff almost as an older brother, or spend hours talking to her mother. "I couldn't have been any fonder of Jeff had he been my own son," Mrs. McGlannan recalled. Jeff even got on well with Mr. McGlannan, a big, gruff commercial-airline pilot. Beck spent so much time at the McGlannans' that he kept his record collection there. Mrs. McGlannan didn't mind, since Jeff preferred the high-minded, earnest folk songs of the Kingston Trio and Peter, Paul and Mary to the raucous dance-party rock and roll that dominated the record charts. Jeff sat on the couch in the living room for hours, with Jenny or alone, chain-smoking cigarettes, listening over and over again to his favorite song, a Joan Baez ballad about the rain falling somewhere long ago and far away. . . .

BECK LOUIS		
Q S No 530	June 1916	Larc R S G*
Q S No 66	Mar 1918	Larc R S G
Q S No 65	May 1918	Embezzlement
Q S No 66	May 1918	Larc R S G

* R S G stands for "receiving stolen goods."

Q S No 67	May 1918	Conspiracy
Q S No 905	Nov 1923	Misd (liquor)
Q S No 694	Nov 1923	Misd (check)
Q S No 296	Nov 1934	Misd (lottery)
Q S No 143	June 1936	Misd (lottery)
Q S No 534	Sept 1938	Misd (lottery)
Q S No 538	Nov 1938	Misd (lottery)

If Lou Beck, the Pittsburgh-born son of immigrants, had compiled a record of great success, his biographers would no doubt have made much of the symbolic significance of his birthdate: January 1, 1900. As it turned out, though, the fact that Lou had arrived on a day seemingly momentous with promise did nothing more than add a touch of poignancy to his failure, as itemized above on a notecard on file at the county courthouse in Pittsburgh. Lou was born on "the Hill," a slum district predominantly inhabited by Jews, who'd begun pouring into Pittsburgh by the thousands in the 1880s and 1890s from Russia and Eastern Europe. Among them were Jacob and Martha Beck, who came from Russia. Lou was the third of their four sons.

The Pittsburgh of Lou Beck's youth was Steeltown, U.S.A., at its full fiery glory, a city of massive factories, roaring blast furnaces, belching smokestacks—and vast economic disparity. At the turn of the century more of America's wealthiest families hailed from Pittsburgh than any city except New York. The huge fortunes of the Carnegies, the Mellons, the Pitcairns, and lesser moguls were derived not only from their enterprise but from the underpaid toil of many thousands of immigrant laborers in an era before the minimum wage and the pension plan. And those workers were the lucky ones. As a rule, the big steel companies wouldn't hire Jews even for the most menial and dangerous jobs, of which they had plenty. The only major industry in Pittsburgh that employed Jews in number was stogie making, which itself was largely Jewish-owned. Stogies, which were made by rolling a fiber filler in tobacco leaves, were cheaper than fine cigars and exploded quite nicely in dozens of early silent-film comedies. For his three dollars a week, a stogie stripper or roller spent eighty hours amid choking clouds of tobacco dust.

By the time Lou Beck reached working age, employment opportunities for unskilled Jews hadn't broadened much beyond stogie making. Lou was a clever, energetic kid, but he didn't much care for schoolwork and wasn't about to toil for slave wages in some sweatshop. Even before he was graduated from high school, Beck had slipped into the criminal subculture of the Hill. He was only sixteen when he was arrested for the first time, on a misdemeanor charge of receiving stolen goods. Two years later, he was arrested twice for larceny, embezzlement, and conspiracy and packed off to jail for a few months. Incarceration apparently set Beck straight for a while. He landed a job selling paper products wholesale and kept his nose clean during the Roaring Twenties, with the exception of an arrest in 1923, during Prohibition, for writing a bad check in a liquor deal. Beck was thirty-five when he finally took as his wife a petite and strikingly beautiful blond girl by the name of Ida Roman.

Ida's father, Morris, was a skilled machinist and one of the few Jews of his generation able to make a living in steel, modest though it was. Morris and Lena Roman, Orthodox Jews, kept a strict kosher household that was increasingly riven by conflict as their four pretty daughters reached adolescence. Ida was only sixteen and beneath the age of legal consent in Pennsylvania when she eloped to West Virginia with William Harris, a twenty-one-year-old shoe salesman. Somehow Ida made peace with her parents, for upon her return to Pittsburgh she moved back into the Romans' little house in the East Liberty district, with her new husband in tow.

The marriage of Ida Roman and Bill Harris was a match made somewhere short of heaven. She was pretty and flirtatious and he was the jealous type. They fought constantly. One night about six months after their wedding, Bill picked up a fork and jammed it into Ida's arm, leaving a bruise that lasted for weeks and drawing a bit of blood. A few months later, Mr. and Mrs. Harris were walking home after a night on the town when they bumped into a former boyfriend of Ida's. "Hello," he said, infuriating Bill, who apparently didn't believe that Ida knew the man at all. When they went to bed that night, he started choking Ida, who awoke the next morning with bruises on her neck and red blotches on her forehead. Ida was placed under the care of a doctor. Late one night about ten months into their marriage, Harris left for good after vowing "to murder everybody in this God damned house." He contented himself with hurling his wife to the floor, and went home to his mother. Ida, still a minor, was granted an uncontested divorce in 1931.

Ida met Lou Beck in a candy store in 1935. According to family legend, it was love at first sight. They married quickly and moved into their own apartment not far from the Romans' place. It's possible,

though unlikely, that Ida didn't know that her new husband had recently been arrested for running an illegal lottery, which, in any event,
was a petty offense. Of the many criminal rackets that flourished in
Pittsburgh during the Depression, the numbers was one of the most
benign. It was administered by specialist gangsters who, as a rule, did
not traffic in narcotics, prostitution, protection, or the other rough
rackets; moreover, it was tightly, if unofficially, regulated by city hall.
Soon after the game's introduction in the 1920s, playing a number was
as easy as buying a newspaper. Numbers dealers were especially prevalent in impoverished neighborhoods like the Hill, which by this time
was predominantly black, for they accepted bets as low as a penny, and
the game was simple, requiring only the selection of a three-digit number. Most commonly, the day's winning number was derived from the
last three digits of the daily results from the New York Stock Exchange, though racetrack results were sometimes used, too. While the
odds against winning—or "hitting," in the parlance of the game—
were 1,000 to 1, numbers wagering was so popular that dealers found
they could pay off at 700 or 600 to 1 and still generate plenty of
business. Numbers writers camped out in taverns, cigar stores, cafete-
rias, and anywhere else people congregated, with the possible exception of church. By 1929, there were thought to be as many as five
thousand people working the numbers racket, collectively pulling in at
least $5 million a year.

While much of this mighty flow of small change came out of the
pockets of citizens who could least afford the loss, the numbers racket
also functioned as the lifeline of Pittsburgh's black community in the
hardest of hard times. Numbers baron Gus Greenlee was not only the
most powerful man on the Hill but perhaps the most revered as well.
Instead of consuming his profits through lavish living, Greenlee invested in all sorts of legitimate businesses, mostly on the Hill. Greenlee
built the all-black Pittsburgh Crawfords into one of the finest baseball
teams of its time and sponsored the career of John Henry Lewis, the
first black American light-heavyweight champion of the world. In an
era when banks wouldn't make mortgage loans to blacks, Greenlee
acted as banker to the Hill, providing not only funds for real estate but
start-up capital for neighborhood businesses and college loans. No
gangster was more a godfather than was Gus Greenlee.

The hub of Greenlee's operation was the Crawford Grill, a first-rate
jazz club on lower Wylie Avenue. The classiest nightspot on the Hill,
the Crawford attracted a racially mixed crowd, though whites were

definitely a minority. Seated at the bar, Greenlee received visitors and offered counsel. Lou Beck was a regular patron of the Crawford Grill and was well known throughout the Hill as a friend of the proprietor. As Dr. Charles Greenlee, Gus's younger brother, recalled, "It was very unusual for a white man to be accepted on the Hill at that time. But everybody was made to understand that Lou Beck was all right and that meant a lot." Beck made use of Greenlee's sponsorship to run his own modest franchise on the Hill, the city's most active numbers district. Although Beck apparently didn't work directly for Greenlee, he undoubtedly was required to give him a slice of his profits.

To appease the righteous citizenry, city hall every now and then announced a crackdown on the numbers and hauled low-level bookies by the dozen before police magistrates, many of whom were themselves on the take. As a rule, numbers violators would be fined $50—a "license fee," it was called—and would be back on the street before nightfall. However, the politics of the numbers became perilously volatile after 1934, when a reformist mayor took office and launched a crackdown, occasioning Beck's first arrest. Arrested again in 1936, Lou again paid his $50 and went back to his corner. But when Beck was arrested once more, in 1938, the law came down on him with a vengeance. Apparently, Beck's prosecution was prompted by his violation of the first commandment of numbers dealing: Always pay a hitter. According to the court filings, on June 22, 1938, two players came into Cephus Ford's Wylie Avenue hangout, the Sports Center, and laid bets amounting to $1.48 on the number 032. Ford laid the bets off on Beck, his "banker." The day's odds were fixed by Greenlee and the city's other numbers barons at 700 to 1. When 032 hit the next afternoon, Beck was unable to come up with the $1,035 he owed the two hitters. A month later Beck, Ford and an associate were rounded up by the police and indicted for operating an illegal lottery.

Despite his prompt conviction and stiff eighteen-month sentence, the case against Beck was really quite shaky, resting heavily on Ford's testimony. It's possible, in fact, that the whole thing was a frame-up. Known as the most often arrested man in Pittsburgh, Ford was the Hill's most notorious stool pigeon. According to Frank Bolden, who wrote for the Pittsburgh *Courier*, the city's leading black newspaper in the 1930s, Ford was arrested at least 119 times but wasn't once convicted—thanks to his willingness to testify for the prosecution against one and all. In the eyes of Greenlee, Harris, and their friends, Ford was beneath contempt. "Cephus Ford would have testified that he was white and he was one of the blackest men I ever saw," said Dr. Greenlee.

Beck kept appealing until he finally succeeded in getting his case out of Pittsburgh and before the Superior Court of Pennsylvania. In late 1939, more than a year after his arrest, Beck's conviction was reluctantly overturned on a procedural error. "Unfortunately, the trial judge in submitting the case to the jury inadvertently failed to direct its attention to the fact that Ford was an accomplice," the Superior Court judge concluded in granting Beck's request for a new trial. The district attorney decided to let the matter drop. And why not? There was no need to retry Beck. He'd gotten the message. As the lone white bookie in a black neighborhood, Beck had been treading dangerously from the outset. He couldn't prosper without stirring resentment among Hill dwellers and if, in fact, he did so poorly that he couldn't cover a thousand-dollar double hit, Greenlee could only conclude that his protégé was reckless and undercapitalized and likely to cause him further embarrassment at a time when he could least afford it. By the late 1930s, a new generation of bookies—many of whom were white, Italian, and violent—was nibbling away at the fringes of Greenlee's turf. In one way or another, Beck's continued involvement had become inconvenient to the powers that be.

Had Beck's conviction not been overturned he would have been behind bars when his first child, Judith, was born in 1940. Chastened by his narrow escape from doing time—again—Lou apparently got out of the numbers game for good. In any event, he managed to stay on the right side of the law until 1946, when, just a few months after Jeff's birth on March 8, he moved his family south to a new start in Coral Gables.

In Florida, Lou Beck completed his transformation from petty hood to clean-living family man. He involved himself not in making book but in making boxes, landing sales jobs at a succession of paper-wholesaling firms in the Miami area. By the standards of most of America, not to mention the Hill, Lou was a good provider. But if his family had all it needed, Ida had much less than she wanted. Not content with affluence, Ida aspired to wealth, to "deluxe accommodations," as she put it. Long after Victor Posner, the flamboyantly wealthy Miami Beach financier, had been discredited as one of the most unprincipled and destructive of modern corporate raiders, Ida continued to drop his name, though she knew him only slightly. While Lou put in a full day's work, he just didn't have the single-minded drive required to build a corporation from scratch or take one over. He would rather go home at a reasonable hour and see his kids than chase a buck from morning to midnight. Lou was sixty years old before he finally succumbed to Ida's prodding and started his own paper-wholesaling firm, the Beck Sales Co.

While Ida's materialism was rooted in the material deprivations of her youth on the Hill, it no doubt was aggravated by envy of her younger sister, Agnes, who'd married Joseph Katz, a man destined for a share of the big money. The son of poor Russian immigrants who settled on the Hill, Katz went to work as a young boy. By the time he was fourteen, Joe had set up a print shop in the family garage and begun printing handbills, graduation cards, invitations, and anything else he could persuade people to order as he went door to door. It was 1926 and the numbers were beginning to catch on. A precociously enterprising boy, Katz fitted the rudimentary booklets in which numbers writers recorded bets with carbon paper in a way that produced three copies instead of two for each slip written. Thanks to this innovation, the Katz print shop became the sole supplier of booklets to the burgeoning gambling empire of Gus Greenlee, according to Charles Greenlee. While making numbers booklets wasn't illegal, neither was it respectable. When the authorized history of Katz's business career was published, it would omit any mention of Greenlee and the numbers booklets.

It seems likely that Lou Beck and Joe Katz met even before they married the Roman sisters. In addition to their ties to Greenlee, both men worked as paper salesmen. But while Beck was content to toil as an employee, Katz set up his own company, which bought overruns, seconds, and closeouts directly from paper mills and sold the stuff to printing plants throughout Pennsylvania, Ohio, and West Virginia. It wasn't much more than a living. In 1942, though, Katz devised a letter-writing kit for servicemen. At $1.95 apiece, the kits were a hit in Pittsburgh; Katz quickly took the product national. By the war's end, Katz had amassed sufficient capital to move into the manufacture of gift wrap; in 1945, he set up the Papercraft Corporation with $10,000. Instead of making flat sheets of gift wrap for sale in department stores, Katz rolled his paper on cardboard cores and put it on display in the new self-service discount chain stores. Sales soared in 1951 when Katz hit upon the idea of putting three rolls together in one "bargain package" that sold for ninety-eight cents, which was considerably more than the same amount of paper would have fetched in standard flat-sheet form. Katz was on his way.

By the time Katz sold shares in Papercraft to the public in 1958, the company's revenues topped $7 million a year and its Kaycrest line was the biggest-selling gift-wrap brand in the country. The initial public offering made Katz a millionaire at forty-six. He would accumulate many millions more as Papercraft expanded and diversified into a major corporation, listed on the New York Stock Exchange. Joe and Agnes began buying art and made frequent trips to New York—where they kept an apartment at the Pierre Hotel—and Europe to add to a collection that included works by Renoir, Picasso, Dali, and Utrillo. The Katzes joined with an English branch of the famed Rothschild family to restore a ruined fifteenth-century synagogue in Jerusalem and also financed a seven-acre park—the Agnes and Joseph Katz Recreation Park—in the heart of the city's old quarter. Closer to home, the University of Pittsburgh christened the Joseph M. Katz Graduate School of Business in appreciation of a $10 million bequest from the gift-wrap mogul and his wife.

While Ida would regularly fly north to visit Agnes and her two other sisters, Lou very rarely returned to Pittsburgh, and not once did the Becks visit the city as a family. In addition to his seeming reluctance to return to a place filled with reminders of a past he was trying to live down, Lou bore a grudge against Joe Katz—and not just for inflaming his wife's resentment over her comparatively impecunious lot in life. Since their parents rarely so much as mentioned their life before Coral Gables, neither Judy nor Jeff was ever entirely clear on what had transpired between their father and Uncle Joe back in Pittsburgh. But as a result of the occasional barbed comment and pointed allusion, Judy and Jeff both grew up believing that part of the reason that the Katzes were rich and the Becks weren't was that Uncle Joe had double-crossed their father long ago. As Beck family legend had it, Lou had provided some of the funds on which Papercraft was founded. Although Lou went to work at the company believing that he'd invested in it as a partner, Katz later supposedly insisted that he'd merely borrowed money from his brother-in-law and hadn't cut him in on a piece of the ownership. While Lou could have sued, it would have been his word against Katz's, and what chance would he have in court with his criminal record?

As a boy, Jeff identified so strongly with his father that he grew up hating his Uncle Joe without knowing exactly why, though Katz's overbearing, pompous manner would have been excuse enough. Lou was an indulgent, doting father who was idolized equally by Judy and Jeff. "Everybody liked him," Judy recalled. "He didn't have an enemy in the world." Like many men to whom fatherhood comes late in life, Lou was incapable of administering punishment. His forte was play-time. One of Jeff's earliest memories was laughing himself silly as his dad danced a mock ballet around the living room. "My father was open and funny and generous and he taught me to be that way," Jeff said.

Yet the Beck home was not a happy one. For one thing, Lou and Ida must have lived in continual fear of being found out by their children, who grew up knowing nothing of their mother's first marriage nor of their father's criminal history. When he was still a little boy, Jeff was alarmed one day by the sight of two policemen standing in the hallway talking to his dad, who looked mortified, though apparently the visit was merely a routine check. Easygoing and deferential, Lou lived out his last decades in Coral Gables in a posture of perpetual atonement, which his wife exploited. Having been raised in a Spartan household, mistreated at sixteen by her first husband, disgraced by the lawbreak-ing of her second husband, and eclipsed by a younger sister who was altogether too nice to resent, Ida came to assume an attitude of perpet-ual aggrievement. Although Ida's complaints tended to be as vague as they were incessant, her basic gripe against Jeff was cruelly specific and oft-repeated. For as long as he could remember, Jeff was told by his mother that she hadn't planned on having another child after Judy, that he was "a mistake." Lou Beck might reasonably have hoped that twenty years of clean living would earn him absolution for the trans-gressions he'd committed in Pittsburgh. But how could a son ever please a mother who begrudged him his very existence?

Ida took upon herself the role of family disciplinarian. Although she was not inclined to spare the rod, she was altogether too idiosyncratic in applying it. As Jeff recalled, his mother would do something devious in the name of discipline and then concoct elaborate rationalizations that twisted reality into more pleasing, benign shapes in the name of maternal love. To a little boy, it was painfully bewildering. Which was real: his mother's dubious actions or the good intentions she so often professed in explaining them away? Left to fend for himself by a kindly but ineffectual father, Jeff began rebelling at an early age, sum-moning the strength to resist Ida from wherever he could find it— from his friends at school, the occasional teacher, his sister's first husband and, most of all, from his own imagination. Jeff spent hours on end alone in his room, involuntarily at first, in punishment for one act of defiance or another, and by choice as he got older and developed the habit of introspection. He'd make an appearance at dinnertime and then disappear for hours on end, escaping through his imagination into alternate realities. At night he'd prop a chair up against his door and rig the screen on his bedroom window to allow for quick escape. "Every day I went to sleep with fear and woke up with fear," Beck said. "I just never knew what my mother might try on me next."

When he hit his teens, Jeff increasingly sought refuge in the company of his peers, whose friendship he cultivated assiduously. In his ninth-grade set, he was the one who most often took the risk of sneaking his parents' car out at night, taking half a dozen buddies from the Bucks, his junior-high frat, on joyrides that at times took them all the way to Fort Lauderdale. Ida never caught him with her car but did break up the New Year's Eve party Jeff held during his sophomore year at Coral Gables High. Knowing that his parents were going out early, Beck volunteered his house for the traditional Ching Tang bash. His friends, who were hiding out back, poured in as soon as his parents left. The sinks were still being filled with ice when Ida walked in the front door to retrieve something she'd forgotten. Jeff rushed to his mother, ready with excuses that he never got a chance to use. Ida Beck, all five feet and one hundred pounds of her, split her son's lip with a punch to the chin. By the time Jeff hit the floor, the party was over in more ways than one.

After finishing tenth grade, Jeff was so desperate to put miles between himself and his mother that he pleaded with his father to send him away to school. He got his wish, though he had second thoughts as the date of his departure drew near and he contemplated life without Jenny and the Chinks. For reasons Jeff never fathomed, his parents decided to send him to Perkiomen School, an obscure, second-rate prep school in the heart of Pennsylvania Dutch country near Philadelphia. In preparation for Perkiomen, Beck studied *The Catcher in the Rye*, which proved even more apt than he'd feared. Perkiomen did indeed occupy a position in prepdom equivalent to that of the fictional Pencey Prep in J. D. Salinger's classic novel of adolescent alienation. After getting the boot from three more prestigious prep schools, Holden Caulfield ends up at Pencey in Agerstown, Pennsylvania, where the headmaster tells him that life is a game to be played by the rules. "Game my ass," Holden muses. "Some game. If you get on the side where all the hotshots are, then it's a game all right—I'll admit that. But if you get on the *other* side, where there aren't any hotshots, then what's a game about it? Nothing." Beck, who shared Holden's feeling of being an outsider forced to play an insider's game, underlined that passage in his copy of *The Catcher in the Rye* and also this sentence, which he believed would have been improved by dropping the qualifier: "All mothers are slightly insane."

The Perkiomen campus covers a few acres on the outskirts of the drab little town of Pennsburg. It's an old school, founded in 1875, and rather quaint in a mossy, red-brick sort of way. Perkiomen had been a nonsectarian Protestant school for most of its history; Beck was one of the few Jews enrolled. Most of his classmates were day students from the immediate area. Compared to party-time Coral Gables, life at Perkiomen was as austere as a monastery: chapel first thing every morning and lights out at ten P.M. sharp. Jeff was instantly miserable. He wrote or called Jenny almost every day. He also exchanged Holdenesque letters with Steve Ernst, a fellow Chink who'd been sent away to military school in Indiana. Just before Thanksgiving, Jeff called his parents to plead with them for permission to return home for the holidays but was told to wait until Christmas. Jeff was so upset that he hung up on his father. It was the last time that they talked.

A few weeks after Thanksgiving Ida telephoned Jeff at school and told him his father had had a heart attack a few days before. "Why didn't you tell me?" he screamed at his mother. Without bothering to inform the school office, Beck immediately headed to the bus station. In Allentown, he caught a plane south. But by the time he touched down in Miami, his father was dead, at the age of sixty-two. At home, Jeff found his mother nearly hysterical with what he recognized in retrospect as a mixture of grief and guilt. Right after the funeral Ida took Jeff aside and told him, apparently by way of justifying her own failings as a parent and wife, that his father had been a criminal in Pittsburgh. As proof, she offered some heartfelt letters Lou had written mentioning his jail time. Silently, Jeff leafed through the letters as shame and rage welled up in him until he felt as if he would explode. He simply could not process this new information: The likable, soft-spoken guy who played catch with him and took him, just him, on long drives and who at times sheltered him from the worst of his mother's machinations—this man, his father, was a crook? Unthinkable! And if, somehow, it was true, why would his mother tell him now, with his father's corpse not even cold in the ground? What new torture was she inflicting on him? When would it ever stop?

Beck coped with this awful new trauma in the same way that he'd survived boyhood: by retreating into the private sanctuary of his mind. "Imagine your hero was your father, and then you find out that he wasn't one and at the point of ultimate grief—his death," Beck told me as I was finishing this book. "I was shocked into a state of almost irreparable silence about who I was, who I wanted to be, and who I could be." Unable to admit to the truth about his father, Jeff willed him to disappear. He never again discussed his father's past with his mother or anyone else and made no effort to learn the details of his lawbreaking in Pittsburgh. For the next twenty-eight years, he admitted the truth about Lou to no one, burying his secret so deep inside that he even ceased to publicly acknowledge his father's existence. "When Jeff talked about his childhood, his father was always the man who wasn't there," said Margo Preston, Jeff's third wife. Try as he might, though, Jeff could not purge his father's transgressions from his memory. They survived in his heart and mind as his very own *Rosebud*. For years to come, Jeff would live in fear not only that his secret would be discovered but that he would begin to see in himself the symptoms of incipient criminality, part of his father's genetic legacy.

As a teenager, Jeff transformed the conflicting emotions produced by his father's sudden demise and discrediting into a homogenized outpouring of anger that he aimed at his remaining parent like the stream from a high-pressure fire hose. Much as he railed against his mother, though, Jeff did not disown her. He didn't even leave home after his father's funeral, spending the remaining weeks of the most miserable Christmas vacation of his life alone with Ida in the house on Santa Maria Drive. Like many of his fellow baby boomers, he craved independence but wasn't willing to purchase it at the cost of flipping burgers or pumping gas to earn his own living. In Jeff's case, his rebellion was also constrained by psychological forces even more powerful than economic insecurity. Jeff was bound to his mother by a relationship so perversely ambivalent and enduringly destructive that it was best understood as the emotional equivalent of a death embrace. Beck would spend much of his adult life struggling to reconcile his compulsion to defy his mother with his equally powerful need to please her and somehow force from her the affection that should have been his by right of birth.

For all her foibles, Ida was a very forceful woman and Jeff had been shaped in her image to such an extent that his resentment of her amounted virtually to self-loathing. Not long after Lou died, Jeff announced that his goal in life was to become a millionaire before he was thirty. Judy was not impressed, teasing, "Oh, shut up and do your push-ups, Jeff." But Ida encouraged her son in his precocious materialism as she encouraged him in nothing else. Like his mother, too, Jeff early on began applying his intelligence primarily to the manipulation of other people's thoughts and emotions. While engineering his popularity at school with great purposefulness, at home he learned how to manipulate the manipulator. Stamped on the memory of Lon Fellenz, who'd known Beck ever since grade school, is an image from the summer of 1963, the summer after Lou's death. Fellenz drove up on his motorcycle to find an elegantly attired Ida out in her front yard wrestling with a lawn mover that wouldn't start. Jeff was leaning casually against a fence a few yards away, offering offhand advice between sips from a bottle of Coke. Fellenz had to laugh. There was something oddly timeless about this tableau, like a Norman Rockwell painting turned inside out. Fellenz had a feeling that if he'd left and come back in a few years, he would have found Jeff and his mother still out in the yard, stubbornly luxuriating in impasse.

2

A year after his father's funeral, Beck flew home from Perkiomen School to attend what was for him another mournful ceremony: his mother's remarriage. After Lou's death, Ida had taken over her husband's paper-wholesaling business and managed it so capably that even Jeff had to admit his mother seemed better at business than his father had ever been. Ida managed to hang on to Lou's best customers, many of whom she'd gotten to know over the years, yet was less inclined than her softhearted husband had been to make concessions to deadbeat accounts. As a result, the profitability of the Beck Sales Company actually rose after Ida took charge, even as its revenues declined modestly. The widow Beck could afford to keep the T-bird and the nice house on Santa Maria Drive, but if Ida was going to come into serious money, she was going to have to marry it. Ida was fifty-two; with her blond beauty still intact she looked much younger.

Ida met William D. Singer at a party in Coral Gables in the summer of 1963. Singer was sixty-three and had lost his wife of more than forty years to cancer just a few months before. They began seeing each other immediately and were married the following March, in a small family ceremony at Singer's very large apartment. Singer, who'd made millions in the burger business, was such a prominent citizen that his remarriage was covered as a news event in Miami. "HAMBURGER KING PICKS A QUEEN," read the headline on *The Miami Herald*'s story, which contained this obligingly hokey quote from the bride: "No matter how fancy dinner might have been, both Judy and Jeff always clamored for hamburgers."

Jeff nearly gagged on that. Sure, Holden Caulfield had some rough times, with his brother dying of leukemia and all, but he probably never had to read something quite so phony about himself in the newspaper. It was enough to make Jeff wish he were back at Perki-

omen. He'd come home for the wedding only because his mother
would have had a fit if he'd refused, and a guy could only take so many
dramas. Jeff witnessed the ceremony in sullen silence and fled to the
McGlannans' house immediately afterward, boycotting the reception.
He felt as if his mother had dishonored his father's memory by remar-
rying with unseemly haste a man who in almost every way was Lou
Beck's opposite—worse, a man who was a Miami version of his uncle,
the hated Joe Katz.

Singer was a man of civic accomplishment: Miami citizen of the
year, friend of the governor, builder of highways and hospitals; the
Miami newspapers dubbed him Mr. Can Do It. But he was not someone with whom you'd care to share an airplane ride or play golf with if
you could help it. He was always William D. or Mr. Singer, never Bill,
not even to his admirers. He was imposing at six feet tall and 185
pounds and his bald pate and perpetual sneer made him look like a big
snapping turtle. He acted the part, too, seeing no value either in humor or tact. Singer was a pragmatist who dedicated himself to moving
directly from the setting of a goal to its achievement even if it meant,
literally, bulldozing other people's houses. People either revered Singer
or despised him, the notable exception being his only son, Larry, who
wavered between the reverence his father demanded of all three of his
children and resentment of his authoritarian ways. The friction between Larry, who was twenty-two years older than Beck, and William
D. was subterranean but continuous. It eventually led to the ruination
of the Singer family company and the diminution of its fortune.

Like many self-made, self-important men, William D. could not
resist the temptations of self-mythology. Although the innumerable
profiles of Singer published over the years by Miami newspapers in-
variably listed his birthplace as Cleveland, he was actually born in
Russia, in 1900. After moving to Ohio as a boy, he attended Ohio
State University, leaving without a degree to start a lumberyard in
Cleveland. When it went bust, Singer joined the stampede of northerners seeking their fortunes in Florida. He started a little brewing
plant in Hialeah to make birch beer but it, too, went under. In 1938,
William D. finally hit his stride, sinking a thousand dollars into a nine-
stool lunch stand on the outskirts of Miami that offered hamburgers
for a nickel. That first stand did nicely, and it wasn't long before
Singer opened a second joint, then a third. Before long, he was
blanketing Miami with branches and had been crowned "King of the
Hamburger."

On the basis of local newspaper coverage, one could only conclude that it was Singer who'd reinvented the hamburger as fast food. In truth, William D.'s burgers were virtually identical to the tiny, onion-flecked "sliders" sold up North by White Castle. Founded in Kansas in 1921, White Castle had relocated its headquarters to Ohio, Singer's home state, in 1934. Singer not only lifted the Ohio chain's basic recipe but its design concept, albeit with minor modifications. Instead of "White Castle," Singer used the name "Royal Castle." His stands, too, were designed to look like miniature white castles except with orange trim. In 1940 and 1958 White Castle sent cease-and-desist letters to Singer, who apparently ignored them. For some reason—perhaps a failure to envision the burger business going national—White Castle never sued Royal Castle, which expanded with alacrity. By the time Singer took his company public in 1965, Royal Castle had $4 million in annual revenues, 1,200 employees, and 144 restaurants in Florida, Louisiana, and Georgia.

In a business built on volume sales, penny-pinching was essential to success. Singer could squeeze with the best of them. His strength as a businessman was the meticulous, hard-nosed pragmatism with which he pursued profit. He required his workers to take a daily inventory of every bun, patty, and doughnut in every branch and to drop all large bills (anything over ten dollars) through a slot into a little safe to which no branch employee knew the combination. Inflexibility was a Singer trademark. Royal Castle's rigid policy of racial segregation (blacks could order through a window but not come inside) made the chain a favorite target for demonstrations by civil-rights groups. And not until 1967 would Singer hire his first female employee. Singer believed that a woman's place was at home. In a 1959 newspaper profile, his first wife, Esther, came across as joyously servile: " 'I want him to be the king,' says the charming woman whose major interest in life is keeping her husband happy. 'This is only logical. Because when he gets things done and is a success, I go right along with him in the same wagon.' . . . In her spare time, when she's not traveling with Bill ('I have one cosmetic case packed at all times') or entertaining his business associates, Mrs. Singer can be found in her sewing room."

These were times when a man could own a company that was overtly racist and sexist and yet still be named Miami's Outstanding Citizen, as Singer was in 1959. Like Katz in Pittsburgh, he began his rise to social prominence by supporting specifically Jewish causes. But as Royal Castle grew larger and Singer's net worth reached seven figures, he moved into the mainstream of civic affairs in Miami, heading the United Way and rotating through positions on the boards of the city's most influential zoning committees and business-development groups. He also became a major contributor to the Democratic party, and in 1958 Governor LeRoy Collins appointed him South Florida's lone representative to the powerful state road board. In his years on the road board, Singer made a name for himself by ramming through to completion stalled highway construction projects in Dade County. "More than most any other fellow in our state these days, Singer has introduced hard business practices in government," noted *The Miami Herald* approvingly.

Through his son-in-law, Richard Stone, the influence of Miami's hamburger king eventually would reach all the way to the U.S. Senate. Stone, a graduate of Harvard College and Columbia Law School and a scion of the family that owned the Blackstone Hotel on Miami Beach, was well connected even before he married into the Singer family. After Stone wed Marlene Singer, William D. began directing most of his legal business to the law firm of which Stone was a partner and appointed him general counsel and a director of Royal Castle. He also spent heavily on his son-in-law's political career, which, beginning with Stone's appointment as city attorney of Miami in 1966, would lead to election as a state senator and later the position of Florida's secretary of state.

In 1965, Singer took Royal Castle public in a transaction that transformed him at sixty-five from a prosperous to a truly wealthy man. While the sale of stock was well timed to capitalize on a hot market, it had to be more than coincidence that Singer decided to sell a big piece of his twenty-seven-year-old company a few months after marrying a woman whose heart's desire was to live in grand nouveau-riche style. In exchange for shares he owned or controlled, Singer received $6.7 million in cash while retaining shares worth $2.8 million. His three children and their children held another $12.7 million worth of Royal Castle shares. Just before taking the hamburger chain public, Singer also cashed in his investment in a sixty-five-store chain of army-navy discount centers that he'd cofounded in 1955, selling it to a grocery-store chain for $5 million in cash. All of this financial maneuvering produced a stunning "wedding present" for Ida: She'd married into a family worth about $25 million. Her joy must have been diluted, though, by Singer's insistence that she sign a postnuptial agreement limiting her claim on his assets. She moved with William D. into a luxury high rise in which they leased five separate apartments and had them combined into one vast residence, opulently outfitted and staffed with a maid and a housekeeper.

Ida's glamorous new life took a turn for the bizarre even before she'd celebrated her first wedding anniversary. One afternoon she was getting into her car after a visit to the doctor when a black-gloved hand came from behind and covered her mouth, according to an account of the incident given the newspapers by the police. She felt a sharp object pressed into her back, and a man said: "Do as I say and you won't get hurt." He ordered Ida to slide over to the passenger side and duck out of sight. The kidnaper drove her car to a Coral Gables sewer-pumping station, where he made her strip off her stockings, which he used to bind her hands and feet. He tied her hands to the handle of the car door. Rifling her purse, he found $800 in cash and also took from her fingers two rings, one valued at $27,000, the other at $8,000. A few minutes after he'd made his getaway, in what the police presumed was a car driven by an accomplice, two city employees checking the sewer pump came along and freed Mrs. Singer. Later, Ida was said to be "in seclusion" and too upset to talk to reporters. "He threatened to return to our apartment and kill her if she said anything," William D. told the press. "He didn't hurt her physically but he scared her."

The police never recovered the jewels or arrested anyone in connection with the robbery, leaving more questions than answers. According to Jeff, Ida concluded that the crime was an inside job. But why would anyone with direct access to Mrs. Singer's unguarded jewels kidnap her to obtain them? And if someone had taken the risk of kidnaping a multimillionaire's wife, why not hold her for ransom in the customary way? One last question: Why would a woman wear a $27,000 diamond ring on a visit to the doctor? William D. had an answer for that one at least. As *The Miami Herald* reported, "Mrs. Singer wore the expensive diamond, her husband said, because she felt it was safer on her finger than in their Brickell Town House apartment . . . which had been burglarized at least once before." At least once? Didn't Singer know how many times he'd been robbed?

At the time of his mother's marriage to Singer, Jeff was nearing the end of a wildly uneven career at Perkiomen Prep. He proved such an enterprising, diligent student that he quickly made up the year he'd lost in transferring, and graduated in two years as he would have had he remained at Coral Gables High. In the 1963 Perkiomen yearbook he was singled out for praise: "In its pursuit of academic excellence, the Junior Class was bolstered by Jeff Beck." Beck also was elected vice president of his class and played junior varsity football on a team that lost all seven of its games and a basketball squad that went 3-11.

While impersonating a typical boy-most-likely-to-succeed, Jeff claimed to have masterminded a black-market operation worthy of Joseph Heller's Milo Minderbinder. He began his nefarious activities by landing the strategic job of headwaiter in the school dining room. For a fee, Beck would forge the signatures of kids who wanted to spend the weekend off campus. By giving a few of the school's more bruising football players a slender slice of the action, Beck managed to intimidate would-be squealers into silence. With his roommate, he set up a birthday-cake concession in the dining room, charging parents $10 to deliver cakes purchased from a local bakery for $2.50. Beck and his cohort plowed their profits into liquor and cigarettes. Beck, who looked a few years older than sixteen, just walked into local stores and bought the stuff, marking it up 500 percent for resale to his classmates and underage townies. By the time he was nabbed, Beck had put away a few thousand dollars. The headmaster threatened to expel him, but his mother flew up and negotiated a compromise that obligated Jeff to spend most of his free time painting school buildings. "Basically, I was the lowest-paid janitor in the world," Beck said.

After graduating from Perkiomen, Beck returned to Coral Gables and moved into a roomy apartment his mother and stepfather provided for him on the floor just below their own palatial quarters. Initially, Singer tried to put his relationship with Jeff on a business footing, offering him a munificent allowance of $1,500 a month if he behaved himself. Having just left high school without a clue as to what to do with the rest of his life, Jeff desperately needed direction, and Singer was nothing if not commanding. Jeff accepted the money. However, the pomp and glitter of life chez Singer instantly grated on Jeff, who was especially annoyed by his mother's insistence on summoning her servants with a little silver bell. It seemed that no matter where their dinner conversation began it ended up on the subject of money: money as status, money as power, money as panacea. Worse, his mother deferred to William D. as if he were royalty and expected Jeff to do the same. With a sinking feeling, Jeff realized that in exchange for his $1,500 a month his stepfather expected to control every facet of his life. When William D. ordered him to stop associating with high-school friends who'd grown up on the poor side of town, Jeff told him he didn't want his money. From then on, he and his stepfather feuded constantly. Their conflict took a perilous turn one Saturday when William D. locked Jeff out on one of the many balcony terraces that ringed the Singers' penthouse apartment. Ida was not scheduled to return from shopping for a few hours.

When his stepfather refused to unlock the door and began taunting him, Jeff leaped across several feet of open space to an adjacent balcony, grabbing its railing with both hands and then hoisting himself up and over to safety. The door was locked, so Jeff jumped to the next balcony as William D. moved along with him inside, mocking his exertions. This door was locked, too. Beck had to jump halfway around the building before he finally found an unlocked terrace door. As Singer rushed to lock it, Beck slammed it open and shouted at the top of his lungs, "If I were you, I'd get out of this apartment right now, because if you stay here I'm going to kill you." Singer backed out of the room and left the apartment. Jeff was at Jenny's house a few hours later when his mother called in a rage, insisting that he apologize to William D. Jeff refused, though as it turned out, Singer considered the whole incident so comical that he recounted it repeatedly for years to come, telling the tale as late as 1983 to Margo Beck the very first time he met her.

Defying his mother, who had wanted him to go to an Ivy League school, in the fall of 1964 Beck enrolled at Florida State University in Tallahassee. Jeff's grades and test scores probably were good enough to get him into Brown if not Harvard. But after his years at Perkiomen, Jeff was set on going to college in his home state. Beck lasted all of one quarter at FSU, time enough to realize that Singer was as big a man in Tallahassee, the capital of Florida, as he was in Miami. Singer's ally Governor Collins was at the height of his popularity, and Royal Castles were everywhere. Loath to be known mainly as Singer's stepson, Beck transferred to the College of William and Mary, a first-rate, genteelly Southern school in Williamsburg, Virginia. In choosing it, Jeff made a double concession to his mother, who since her remarriage had been trying to promote closer relations between Jeff and his sister. By this time, Judy was twenty-five and living with her second husband in Newport News, just down the road from Williamsburg. In retrospect, Beck attributed Ida's resurgent family feeling to her competitive instincts: "My guess is that she wanted to show all the Singers that we were as close as she mistakenly thought they were. I went along, I

guess, because despite all that had happened I still wanted a family—
desperately." However, Judy soon left her husband and moved back to
Coral Gables. After finishing his freshman year, Jeff transferred back
to Florida State.

Beck returned from Virginia with a new physique that startled old
Coral Gables buddies who hadn't seen him in a while. Tired of being
razzed about his underdeveloped body, he'd begun lifting weights the
summer after he'd graduated from Perkiomen but didn't really apply
himself until he hit William and Mary. By his sophomore year, Beck
had added thirty pounds of muscle, transforming himself from painfully skinny to a muscular 170 pounds. Even with his added bulk,
though, Beck lacked the size and speed to play ball for a big-time
school like FSU, where football was king. He didn't even bother trying
out. This disappointment seemingly left scars, for years later when
Beck got around to fabricating the personas of Vietnam Hero and
Billionaire, he would also concoct Football Man. Beck's Football Man
was not a star but a gritty, 168-pound safety who compensated for his
lack of size with kamikaze courage. As a result of his penchant for
tackling much bigger players head-on, Football Man broke each of his
ribs at least once and spent most of his career on the bench nursing
injuries. As Beck told it, though, he did start about ten games at free
safety and played in the Orange Bowl against Nebraska.

It was in attempting to verify his gridiron career that I first caught
Beck in a lie, though even this seemingly straightforward matter was
complicated by the power of money to compel belief. It was easy
enough to determine that Beck's name did not appear on any football
roster in his four years at FSU. Just to be sure, I called Bill Peterson,
who was the football coach at the time. At first, Peterson couldn't
remember anybody named Jeff Beck, though his interest was piqued
when I told him that Beck was a Wall Street investment banker who'd
made a $4.5 million fee on one deal alone. Peterson said he'd check
with his assistant coaches and by the time I called him back had
succeeded in glimpsing through the haze of distant memory the faint
outlines of an often injured second-string safety named Jeff Beck. "He
didn't play much but he was a fine person," Peterson said. Then he
asked for Beck's phone number. When I told Beck that his old football coach was in bad health and planning to call, presumably to ask
for money, he acted as if he'd just been informed that he'd been
scheduled for root-canal surgery. Beck ducked Peterson until he
stopped calling. When I confronted Beck with the fact that there was

no record of him having played football at FSU, he simply nodded in acknowledgment and never again mentioned double sessions, broken ribs, or the Orange Bowl.

Beck had adapted his football legend, modest as it was, from the experiences of his fraternity brothers, two of whom actually were starting safeties. Beck was one of the first Jews accepted into Phi Delta Theta, a frat that was a favorite among jocks while boasting the highest academic ranking of all the frats on campus. While Beck's rebelliousness made him an isolate at Perkiomen, at Florida State his urge to insubordination was channeled into the sociable form of frat-house pranksterism; Holden Caulfield was reborn as John Belushi's Bluto. Beck was not merely active in frat activities but made them the cornerstone of his identity. He worked at being a colorful, outrageous character. He was Phi Delt's representative in the annual campus "Ugly Man" contest and once was taken in a moaning heap to the emergency room to get his stomach pumped after celebrating his victory in an oyster-eating contest by drinking most of a case of beer.

Despite the notoriety he gained through such antics, Beck wasn't seen as a leader by other Phi Delts, who called him Steve Junior because of his almost slavish emulation of his Phi Delta "big brother," Steve Schultz, a star swimmer with a sardonic sense of humor. "Steve could cut people down and get away with it, but with Jeff it just didn't fly," said Lon Fellenz, Beck's old junior-high-school buddy, who'd become a Phi Delt, too. "If he was around someone he was trying to impress, he could get into the sort of heavy, heavy kidding that could really hurt people. When he was like that you were better off just walking away." Beck dove so deep into his Frat Man identity that it even began to strain his relationship with Jenny McGlannan, who was 120 miles away in Gainesville at the University of Florida. By the time Jenny left on a European vacation in the summer of 1966 she held little hope of ever working things out with Jeff. Jenny and a girlfriend were in Copenhagen when they bumped into Jeff striking a brooding pose in Hamlet's Castle. Although a bit nonplussed by Jeff's insistence that their meeting was a coincidence, Jenny was not unhappy to see him. However, they had a fight in a restaurant that night and Jeff disappeared, resurfacing in Jenny's path a few days later in Brussels. Once again they fought; Jeff headed back to the States alone, to the summer job awaiting him in Miami.

Although Lou Beck had left his son a little money, Jeff basically put himself through school by working odd jobs year-round. While refusing to take an allowance from Singer, he did ask his stepfather to arrange a job for him at Royal Castle. Singer obliged, though certainly not with cushy positions. One year, Beck worked the night shift in one of the chain's butcher warehouses, slinging sides of beef around on hooks. He also took a midnight-to-nine A.M. shift in a one-man Royal Castle stand in Miami's Little Cuba section, home to vagrants and hookers. On one alcohol-soaked night off, Beck and some friends stumbled into a brand-new Royal Castle in a nicer part of Miami. Beck and the others dropped their pants and pressed their rears against the window of the shop—a maneuver known as a pressed ham in the fraternity lexicon—just as two cop cars were rolling into the parking lot. Beck and his buddies spent an hour in jail and were released uncharged when Jeff's claimed relationship to Royal Castle's owner proved out. Although the cops found the whole episode pretty comical, William D. and Ida were furious.

In his junior year at FSU, Beck met a woman at a sorority party who would finally carry him beyond Jenny into marriage. Sylvia Beata Pfotenhauer was a sister in Delta Gamma, the sorority most closely affiliated with Beck's frat. Her father, Alexander Pfotenhauer, was a professional yacht captain who had emigrated to the United States from Germany after World War II. Sylvia had attended North Miami High, where she was the all-American girl: near-straight-A student, homecoming-queen finalist, drill-team member, Beta Club sweetheart, Girl's State representative. At Florida State it was more of the same. Blond, gentile, and German, Sylvia represented an irresistible mix of romance and rebellion for Jeff, whose mother had been urging nice Jewish girls upon him ever since high school. Immediately following their junior year, Jeff and Sylvia were married in a court-house ceremony in Tallahassee. Jeff waited for a few days before informing his mother who was none too pleased with the marriage. After their wedding, Jeff and Sylvia moved into an off-campus apartment of their own. While remaining a member of Phi Delta Theta, Beck was no longer very active in it. By coincidence, his new next-door neighbor was Fellenz. While still friendly with Beck, Fellenz saw little of him as he withdrew generally from the society of his old beer-drinking buddies into private preoccupation with his future.

In July 1967, only a few weeks after Beck's wedding, Congress threw the college world into upheaval by terminating graduate-school deferments. Overnight, the entire graduating class of 1968—Beck's class—had lost its most reliable avenue of escape from the military draft at a time when the Vietnam War was escalating alarmingly. Beck was already in the army in a sense. At the time he enrolled at Florida State, Reserve Officer Training Corps was mandatory for all male students. In fact, FSU was a veritable ROTC factory, second among all universities in the number of officers commissioned annually into the U.S. Air Force. The prospect of a military career had never appealed to Beck, who had looked forward to stowing his uniform for good when the time came to leave FSU and move on to graduate school. Beck finally had begun hitting the books hard in his junior year, but with the sudden elimination of graduate-school deferments, he changed tactics. By switching majors (from English to history), Beck delayed his graduation by nearly six months, to mid-December 1968. "He felt like everyone else," Sylvia later told *The Wall Street Journal.* "He didn't want to be drafted."

At the same time, Beck repeatedly petitioned to have his ROTC branch assignment shifted from infantry to less hazardous duty. Failing to arrange such a transfer, Beck apparently availed himself of one of the most exclusive draft havens: the National Guard. Getting into the National Guard at the peak of the Vietnam War was no mean feat, as the controversy over Dan Quayle during the 1988 presidential election reminded the nation. As draft calls mounted, applications to the Guard soared, until by the end of 1968 the Army National Guard alone had a waiting list of 100,000. Many of the applicants who managed to gain entry leapfrogged waiting lists by getting some influential person to recommend them. This seems to have been what Beck did, though it is unclear who pulled strings on his behalf. According to National Guard records, Beck first enlisted in New York in October 1968—six weeks before his graduation from FSU—and in a matter of days arranged a transfer to Florida, where he was assigned to the First Battalion of the 124th Infantry.

Curiously, even after Beck admitted to me that he hadn't fought in Vietnam, he denied that he'd ever joined the National Guard, insisting instead that he'd been commissioned into a local army reserve unit in Tallahassee. Sylvia seemed to support her husband on this point, telling the *Journal* that Jeff joined the army reserves and left home for several weeks of training exercises. However, there are no records affirming Beck's membership in the army reserves on file at the national army personnel data center in St. Louis or in the county court house in Tallahassee, and Beck failed to produce so much as a scrap of documentation on his own, though he once claimed to have thirty cartons of material pertaining to his military service stored in a Manhattan warehouse.

Aside from an occasional military training exercise, Jeff remained in Tallahassee while Sylvia attended graduate school in German at Florida State. By the time Sylvia was awarded her master's degree in August 1969, Beck had decided, for lack of a better alternative, to attend business school. Actually, he found the idea of teaching history at the collegiate level more appealing than a business career, but where was the money in that? Jeff was accepted into Columbia University's business school, then viewed as a mediocre program, and in the fall of 1969 he and Sylvia left Tallahassee for New York City. Shortly after he began classes, Beck transferred to the New York State National Guard as a private second class. Columbia borders Harlem on Manhattan's Upper West Side, in what at the time was a decrepit and déclassé neighborhood. Opting for respectability over convenience, the Becks rented a one-bedroom apartment across town on East 83rd Street. Coincidentally, Sylvia's parents moved into an apartment nearby on Park Avenue. Her father had landed a job as captain of Malcolm Forbes's famous yacht, which was berthed in Manhattan.

In leaving Florida State for Columbia, the Becks moved from the distant periphery of campus revolt to its symbolic center. In the spring of 1968, the nationwide protest movement had escalated to a new stage of violent confrontation when hundreds of students took over the administration building and others on the Columbia campus in protest over the university's sponsorship of war-related research and its neglect of the surrounding black community. After an eight-day stand-off, the police cleared the demonstrators out and carted hundreds of them off to jail. Outrage over the billy-club brutality of the cops inspired a student strike that effectively shut down the university for weeks. Although Columbia had returned to a normal operating schedule by the time Jeff and Sylvia arrived, the campus still simmered with protest.

Columbia University apparently had a swiftly radicalizing effect on Sylvia, who had been admitted to the Ph.D. program in German. All evident traces of her prom-queen, sorority-sister past were eradicated as she ditched her designer dresses in favor of blue jeans and bandannas and began delving into leftist politics and Eastern mysticism. As the edge of her interest in academics was dulled, she floundered in her position as a teaching assistant. Ellen Feld, the professor in charge of supervising the German-department TAs, remembered Sylvia as "a very difficult person. Any attempt to teach her was futile." Sylvia taught an undergraduate class in German for which she was required to contribute part of an exam—specifically, to write an essay in German and a series of questions. Sylvia chose as her subject Frank Zappa and the Mothers of Invention, the most audacious of the American avant-garde rock bands of the 1960s. Feld urged Sylvia to reconsider her choice of topics, since Frank Zappa was "not a German subject and so obscure that it was unfair." Sylvia refused to heed Feld's advice and completed her essay on Zappa even though she'd been told it would not be used.

Meanwhile, Jeff was having his own troubles fitting in. At a time when beards and patched blue jeans were the standard-issue campus uniform, Beck was unusual even among business-school students in showing up for classes in a jacket and tie as well as a Burberrys-style overcoat. By his second semester, though, Beck had stowed the Young Republican gear in favor of jeans (carefully creased, to be sure) and the olive-drab army jacket he wore on his National Guard maneuvers. Like his wife, Jeff floundered in the classroom during his first year, as he found it increasingly difficult to focus on academics. He was distracted not by the heady late-sixties brew of politics and music that beguiled Sylvia but by Sylvia herself, or rather his growing estrangement from her. As a business student, Beck inhabited one of the campus's staunchest bastions of conservatism. The natural antipathy between the left and the B-school was amplified as Uris Hall became a favorite target of protest groups, stirring resentment among the B-school students, many of whom were military veterans.

It was in this fractious, emotionally charged environment that Beck began experimenting with a Vietnam identity. Beck's closest friend at Columbia was Ron Peters, who'd done a stint with the U.S. Army in West Germany. Peters, in turn, had a friend, Julien "Jeff" De Pree, who had come directly from Vietnam to Columbia. De Pree had spent eighteen months in Vietnam, ending as a first lieutenant in the intelligence branch of the army. Peters and Beck had several classes together and decided late one afternoon to grab a beer with De Pree. Beck casually mentioned that he had been in Vietnam but that he wasn't at liberty to say much more than that. Peters and De Pree thought nothing of it. The war was not a topic they were eager to discuss, anyway. With De Pree, Beck never again brought up the subject of Vietnam. However, as he and Peters grew closer, Beck mentioned several times that in Vietnam he'd been in the LRPs, or long-range patrols, which included top-secret forays into Cambodia and Laos. At this stage, Beck's war stories were brief, cryptic, and contextless—little snippets about jungle sleuthing, helicopter drops, and the like, though once he told Peters that he'd been called down to Washington to testify in a closed-door congressional hearing.

By the end of their first year in New York, Jeff and Sylvia had drifted so far apart that their marriage was over in all but name. According to the *Journal*, Sylvia was infuriated after it got back to her that Jeff not only was claiming to have fought in Vietnam but that he had been involved in secret intelligence work. "That was the big coverup," Sylvia said. "He would tell people there were secrets he just couldn't talk about . . . I gave him an ultimatum: This has to be cleared up or else. For me, it all of a sudden got too weird. I literally said I want out of this as soon as possible. I wanted a very simple clean divorce."

For his part, Beck denied that his wife ever confronted him over his Vietnam tale-telling and insisted that Sylvia had precipitated their separation by leaving him for another man, one of her classmates in the German program at Columbia. Late one night in early 1971, Beck called Peters to ask if he could spend the night at his apartment on the West Side. After letting Beck in, Peters went back to sleep. By the time Peters awoke the next morning, Beck had been admitted to a hospital. Desperate to see Sylvia, he'd decided in the middle of the night to go back to the East Side. On the way, his cab had collided with another cab. Thrown through the back door onto the street, Beck ruptured a disc and tore ligaments in his lower back. Beck spent the next few months living with Peters and his fiancée, Susan, in their apartment near the campus. He slept on a couch in the living room. His daily routine began with a cigarette, a Coke, a Snickers bar (occasionally eaten in the shower) and a couple of prescription pain pills. "He pretty much spent those months spaced out," said Peters, who helped Beck through his final courses. "Basically, Ron Peters got me through business school," Beck said.

Jeff and Sylvia never reconciled. While their breakup was not particularly acrimonious, it was so deeply hurtful to Beck that later he edited Sylvia out of the story of his life. "My life with Sylvia was such a catastrophe that I wanted to block it from my mind," Beck told me. This admission was a long time coming. I didn't learn of Sylvia until

1987, when Beck's lawyer inadvertently mentioned her in my prescence. Even then, Beck refused to tell me anything about her, even her last name. "I don't know you well enough yet," he said.

As Beck began seriously contemplating a career during his last semesters of business school, all that he knew for sure was that he wanted to get rich—really, really rich. While this was an ambition common to American dreamers, in Beck's case it came heavily freighted with psychological baggage. Only through net worth could Beck establish self-worth, for in what remained of his family, money was nothing less than identity. Only by amassing a fortune of his own could he ever convince his mother that his very existence was not in fact a mistake to be forever lamented. Only by amassing a fortune larger than his stepfather's and larger than his Uncle Joe's could he beat the arrogant bastards at their own game and avenge their high-handed treatment of him *and* his father. David Zenoff, Beck's faculty adviser at Columbia, remembered Beck clearly almost twenty years later. "Of all the students I've ever taught"—some three thousand—"Jeff was the most driven to make a lot of money and really be something in the world," Zenoff said. On the other hand, he was also one of Zenoff's most confused students. "He had a tremendous need for mentoring," the professor added. "We must have talked fifty times about what he should do."

Located at the opposite end of Manhattan Island from Columbia University was the Wall Street district, the world's preeminent hub of securities dealing. In deciding to seek his fortune on Wall Street, Beck defied the conventional business-school wisdom of his day. By the mid-1980s 30 percent to 35 percent of the graduating class of Harvard Business School would be flocking to Wall Street every year, but in 1971 the figure was merely 8 percent. Dozens of brokerages had collapsed over the preceding few years and a seat on the New York Stock Exchange could be had for less than the price of a McDonald's franchise. Who wanted to join an industry seemingly heading the way of the dinosaur? It was no wonder that the vast majority of Beck's B-school generation saw their brightest opportunity in signing on with a *Fortune* 500 corporation or management-consulting firm. For many of Beck's peers, this proved a fateful miscalculation, for it wasn't Wall Street that was dying but rather the elitist establishment that had stifled the district for decades and ruled it for nearly a century. Having stagnated for generations, the securities industry was in the early stages of transformation along vastly expanded, democratized lines. In the 1980s, as in the 1890s, Wall Street again would command center stage in the great American drama of fortune making.

The vast majority of the great American fortunes of this century have been derived from ownership of a single corporation. In the classic pattern, the future mogul founds a company that gains early dominance in an important new growth industry and grows huge as it matures. However, a company's size does not determine the size of the personal fortune accruing to its owner. The X factor in the wealth equation is financial leverage—the power to use other people's money —and that's where Wall Street comes in. The public corporation affords two main types of leverage to those who control it. Through the artful use of debt—borrowing neither too little nor too much—a would-be mogul can increase his budding fortune geometrically. This is because a company's debtors do not share in the profits produced by investing the funds borrowed from them; they are entitled only to their money back with interest. The second type of leverage comes into play when a company converts from private to public ownership by issuing new shares of stock for public trading. As a rule, these new shares debut at a multiple of their intrinsic value, thus creating wealth literally overnight.

Few companies make it to Wall Street; indeed 85 percent of all new companies fail within six years of their founding, while most that do manage to survive remain modest, local businesses. Even so, it wasn't the manifest risks of entrepreneurship that dissuaded Beck from trying to follow in the footsteps of Singer and Katz, as much as the prospect of devoting himself to something intrinsically dull—gift wrap or hamburgers—and patiently enduring twenty or thirty years of hard slogging for a payoff that might never come. Nor did Beck like the idea of putting in time at some big, established corporation. Like his father, who'd been unsatisfied in Pittsburgh with his legitimate vocation of paper selling, Beck was drawn to constant action and the prospect of quick, outsized reward. At the time he was casting about for a career, Beck's knowledge of the theoretical underpinnings of the financial markets was virtually nonexistent, but he understood intuitively that Wall Street offered him his best shot of getting rich fast anyplace east of Las Vegas. To work in investment banking was to position oneself within the only industry in America that was itself in a position to cream off a piece of the fortunes made in every other industry.

3

Just because Jeff Beck was ready for Wall Street didn't mean Wall Street was ready for him. As he neared graduation, Beck applied to a dozen premier investment banks and brokerages. The response was underwhelming, consisting of one job interview and no job offers. While a Wall Street career may have been unfashionable in 1971, Beck's credentials—mediocre grades from a second-tier business school—still put him at a disadvantage in competing for what few vacancies existed at the best firms. As the job-hunting season drew to a close, Beck sank into depression: after six years of higher education, he seemed to be unemployable in his chosen field. What was he supposed to do now? Go on bended knee to William D.? Every time he imagined returning to Miami, there popped into his mind a nightmare vision of his stepfather's turtle-face sneering in triumph.

Beck was scraping emotional bottom when someone from First Union National Bank of Charlotte, North Carolina, called and offered him $14,000 a year to join the bank's fledgling international department. First Union was not even the largest bank in Charlotte—but working there sure beat unemployment. After picking up his MBA in mid-1971, Beck headed back south to Charlotte, which was closer to Tallahassee than to Wall Street. He was twenty-five now, separated from Sylvia, and almost broke. At First Union, Beck applied himself to the routine work of analyzing loan applications and issuing letters of credit while angling for special projects. Beck took on the job of preliminary planning for the office First Union was opening in London, hoping that he'd be chosen to run it. When the bank dispatched a more experienced banker to London instead, he was disappointed but not crushed. Charlotte wasn't London, but it had its consolations—mainly a plentiful supply of unattached women. In November 1971, Jeff's divorce from Sylvia was finalized, ending a four-year marriage.

Beck met Rosemary Hall Hicks, a twenty-nine-year-old secretary, at the bank. Born in Augusta, Hicks grew up in small towns throughout Georgia and the Carolinas and attended junior college for two years. She had married young, and divorced in 1965. She was unassuming, athletic, and levelheaded, a woman of strong, simple preferences who felt not the slightest attraction to the complexities of academia or big-city life. Although Rosemary was soft-spoken, she was extraordinarily direct in expressing her opinions and, though basically sweet-tempered, had a streak of defiant contrariness. Beck clove to her with a speed that suggested he saw her as not only Sylvia's opposite but her antidote. A few months after they met, Jeff moved in with Rosemary.

In mid-1972, Beck returned from lunch to find a message on his desk: "Call Marty Siegel, DLJ." He didn't recognize Siegel's name (this, by the way, was not the Marty Siegel who would be one of the 1980s' most infamous inside traders), but the initials "DLJ" were excitingly familiar. To business-school students of Beck's generation, the success of Donaldson, Lufkin & Jenrette was a definitive example of the American entrepreneurial dream—an inspiring tale of three smart MBAs from Harvard who'd founded a brokerage house of their own and then forced the New York Stock Exchange to change its long-standing rule prohibiting public ownership of member firms. DLJ's founders were innovators who'd changed the world for the better and had been rewarded with multimillion-dollar fortunes. Wasn't that the way capitalism was supposed to work? Beck admired DLJ's rebel spirit and while attending Columbia had read everything he could find about the firm. His interest hadn't been reciprocated, though; DLJ hadn't even bothered to send him a form rejection letter.

Returning the call, Beck learned that Siegel was an international arbitrageur at DLJ and was looking for an assistant. Beck's Columbia mentor, David Zenoff, had recommended him. "It's not the greatest job, but it's a foot in the door," Siegel said.

Beck had no idea what international arbitrage even was. "I'll be there tomorrow," he told Siegel.

The next morning he caught the first flight to New York City. During his interview with Siegel, Beck was dismayed to learn that the position paid a thousand dollars less than he was making at First Union. Beck knew that he should have said something like "Sounds interesting. Let me sleep on it." But after eleven months of biding his time as a North Carolina apprentice banker, he was incapable of such guile.

"I'll do whatever you need done," Beck blurted out. "I'll get coffee, open mail, anything."

Siegel decided to take a chance on Beck, who struck him as bright and eager to learn. Beck accepted his job offer instantly. The prospect of moving to New York City forced Beck to resolve the ambivalence he felt about getting married again. In the end, he proposed, Rosemary accepted, and they were married in Charlotte, by a rabbi. Only family members attended the ceremony. Ida and William D. flew up from Miami and signed the marriage license as witnesses. After their honeymoon, the newlyweds headed straight to New York City.

Susan Peters, by now Ron's wife, helped Jeff and Rosemary find a one-bedroom apartment at 159 West Seventy-fourth Street. Across the street was a drug rehabilitation facility. Down the block was a triangular patch of grass and asphalt known as Needle Park. It was crawling with junkies and assorted species of weirdos seldom seen in Charlotte. From the distance of North Carolina, Rosemary had found the idea of living in New York exciting, a feeling that lasted until she pulled up in a taxicab before her new home. Oh God, Rosemary thought to herself. This can't be happening to me.

Early one morning in October 1972, Jeff Beck walked into a skyscraper, a few blocks from the New York Stock Exchange, that housed Donaldson, Lufkin & Jenrette. Upstairs, he walked into a large, windowless room reverberating with the tumult of money in motion. Men in suits (sans jackets) and ties sat side by side at big desks democratically arrayed in rows and clusters. All the desks were the same size; there were no visible signs of rank. No one seemed to be in charge. A riot of electronic cables sprouted from the ground and snaked across the floor to banks of computer screens and telephone consoles piled on the desks. The place looked like a cross between a newspaper city room and the control room of a power plant, but it was noisier than both combined. There was a constant buzz of urgent conversation frequently punctuated by ear-splitting bursts of noise as a trader stood up at his desk like a jack-in-the-box and yelled what sounded like code at another trader across the room. Clerks bustled about bearing cups of coffee and assorted pieces of paper. Beck felt his pulse quicken as he stood at the doorway, absorbing the scene. Spotting Marty Siegel across the room, Beck picked his way through the tangle to his new boss's desk.

"I'm Beck, Jeff Beck. The new guy."

Siegel took a quick peek at Beck and swiveled his head back to his computer screen. "Oh, yeah," he said. "We're kind of low on chairs. Take a look in the room down the hall." He pointed to the door through which Beck had just entered.

Beck retraced his steps, walked down the hall, and found a room filled with all sorts of stuff, none of which resembled a chair. He selected a wooden packing carton and dragged it back down the hall-way. As he reentered the trading room, Beck sensed a decline in its noise level. While maneuvering the carton through an obstacle course of desks and chairs, he thought he heard someone snicker. Beck re-sisted the impulse to look up as he positioned the carton near Siegel's desk. As embarrassed as he was annoyed, he sat down hard on his makeshift chair and stared at the back of Siegel's head.

"At last," he muttered to himself. "The big time."

Arbitrage is the simultaneous trading of securities that are related in some way but traded in separate markets. The brand of arbitrage prac-ticed by Siegel involved stocks listed both in New York and on foreign exchanges. If, for example, IBM was momentarily trading at a higher price in New York than in London, a clever arbitrageur would buy IBM shares in London, contract to sell an equal amount of IBM stock in New York, and thus lock in a quick profit. Speed was of the essence in arbitrage since price discrepancies between electronically linked markets tend to be fleeting. Every sort of arbitrage has its own prob-lematic nuances; international arbitrage was complicated by foreign currency exchange rates. Because one paid for stocks in dollars in New York and in pounds sterling in London, an international arb had to watch the fluctuations in currency prices as closely as he did stock prices. The tiny discrepancy between the price of IBM stock in the two cities might disappear, or even be reversed, when adjusted for currency values, which were extraordinarily volatile in the early 1970s. Beck found himself apprenticed to chaos as much as to Marty Siegel.

Beck did his homework, poring through securities manuals and text-books, and made a point of getting to work so early that he'd finished *The Wall Street Journal* and *The Financial Times* before Siegel had even arrived. Soon, Siegel was letting Beck handle the occasional trade. Unlike many traders, Beck was not at heart a gambler. What he found exhilarating was not the inherent risk taking but the process itself. Into the trader's brain pours an unending flow of information via electronic screen, telephone, and news wire, each new bit of data and opinion forcing a recalculation of perception and strategy, however slight. A trader is expected to absorb the implications of an unexpected event, extrapolate from it a price, and act on it *now*. The intense introspection required by trading came naturally to Beck, who found life on the desk completely absorbing. To him, trading was more than a living. It was almost better than sex. It was survival.

Even so, Beck didn't last long as Siegel's assistant. A self-described "brash Jewish boy from Brooklyn," Siegel quickly got on Beck's nerves. After a few months under Siegel's blustery tutelage, Beck jumped to the convertible-arbitrage desk, which was run by Randall Smith. Smith was Siegel's stylistic opposite, cerebral and soft-spoken. Like the "straight" bond, the convertible entitles the holder to receive periodic interest payments. In addition, an investor can convert his bonds into shares of the issuing company's common stock if that stock climbs above a predetermined price. Like Siegel, Smith bought theoretically undervalued securities, sold overvalued ones, and locked in a profit that was realized when prices moved into proper alignment. This was classic arbitrage. Smith also generated commissions by persuading institutional investors who owned an overvalued stock to swap into the related convertible issue or vice versa—through DLJ, which would earn a commission on both sides of the trade. Like all novel investment strategies, convertible swapping proved a tough sell at first, and selling wasn't something Smith was very good at. Indeed, Smith's existing clientele of institutional bond buyers wasn't adequate to support his operating costs. Needing someone to bring in new clients, he offered a position to Beck, who had come to the Street with no sales experience and no great eagerness to obtain it, especially after he'd immersed himself in the isolation of trading. Still, Smith was offering him an opportunity to advance. Beck took the job, bent on willing himself into becoming a salesman as he'd willed himself into becoming the most popular kid in school. In no time at all, the "polite, soft-spoken Southern boy" that Siegel recalled having hired would transform himself into Mad Dog, supersalesman.

The morning huddle was over and now it was time again for Beck to do what he did best—smile and dial. Today's first priority was finding buyers for a $1 million position in National Industries that one of DLJ's institutional clients wanted to unload. As Beck walked back to his desk he scanned the data sheet on National Industries, a down-at-the-mouth conglomerate. "What a piece of shit," he said. "I love it."

Beck returned to his seat on the convertible desk and made several quick calls to portfolio managers around the country. "No guts," said Beck, slamming down the telephone receiver after another rejection. Through the grapevine Beck had heard of a money manager in Houston who wasn't afraid of high risk as long as the potential rewards were commensurately high. Roger Jenswold was his name and he ran the American General Securities Fund, a mutual fund listed on the New York Stock Exchange. Out of frustration and admiration, convertible traders on the Street had nicknamed the wily Jenswold Roger the Dodger. His good-ol'-boy drawl and disarmingly casual manner disguised a razor-sharp mind. No one knew the convertible market better than Jenswold, who danced around the typical broker's sales pitch as easily as if he were Muhammad Ali sparring with a one-legged man.

Beck had never met Jenswold and was unable to find anyone at DLJ to provide an introduction to him. He looked up Roger the Dodger in his bond-buyers directory and dialed his number. There was nobody Beck wouldn't call, and call cold if necessary.

Jenswold's secretary answered.

"My name is Jeff Beck," he said. "How are you today?"

She ignored the pleasantry. "How can I help you, Mr. Beck?"

"I'm with the New York Stock Exchange firm of Donaldson, Lufkin and Jenrette. I have an idea that I believe might interest Mr. Jenswold."

"Please hold," she replied with the perfunctory cordiality of someone accustomed to repelling a half-dozen cold-calling brokers a day. She returned. "I'm sorry. Mr. Jenswold is very busy."

"I must tell you that this involves an urgent market-related transaction," replied Beck, suddenly all business. "You should also know that I will keep calling until I get your boss on the phone. Good-bye."

A few minutes later Beck called back. Jenswold's secretary stiff-armed him again, less politely this time. Beck called again a few minutes later. And again. And again. Again. Again. Again. And still no Roger the Dodger. Beck called again and got a busy signal. Did she really think that taking the phone off the hook would stop him? Resistance was futile. Beck prided himself on his ability to get anybody to come to the phone. Usually, sometime before the twentieth call, the secretarial stonewall crumbled and the boss finally picked up the phone, as Jenswold finally did. Like most of Beck's telephone quarry, Jenswold was more amused than angry when he came on the line.

Jenswold accepted Beck's offer to come to Houston. Beck flew down the next day and took Roger the Dodger out to dinner. It was the beginning of a productive relationship for both. Jenswold didn't bite on the National Industries bonds, but in time he did direct some orders to Beck, who flew to Houston every few months to meet with Jenswold and other buyers in the area. Fifteen years later, Jenswold remembered Beck vividly. "Unlike a lot of salesmen, he wasn't just looking for some mullet to milk." Beck smiled and dialed, and he dialed and smiled. Gradually, he managed to build a clientele of about thirty major institutional buyers and even stole a few trades away from the dread Johnny Bigel, the head convertible-bond trader at mighty Salomon Brothers.

Pleased by Beck's progress, Smith hired a second assistant, Bing Sung, a twenty-five-year-old whiz kid from Harvard. Sung's father was a wealthy businessman and real-estate mogul who had owned the Coca-Cola franchise for all of China before the Communists seized power on the mainland. The Sungs fled to Hong Kong and then to New York City, where Bing was born and schooled. He enrolled at Harvard at age sixteen and had earned a master's degree in applied statistics before he reached twenty. Sung picked up a doctorate in the same field and accepted a teaching position at Harvard Business School. But Sung was too much his father's son to be content for long with the academic life. In 1973, he resigned from Harvard and headed south to Wall Street.

Despite his academic credentials, Sung was an amiable, unpretentious New Yorker whose speech was flavored more by the streetwise slang of the city than by the abstruse lingo of higher mathematics. A half-dozen times a year Sung flew off to match wits with the baccarat and craps dealers of Las Vegas and Paradise Island, where he wagered modestly and won steadily. Beck was frankly dazzled by Sung's intellect and, to his colleague's embarrassment, told him frequently that he was the smartest person he'd ever met. Sung was equally taken with Beck, whom he recalled as "a whirling dervish of activity," and quickly became his best friend at DLJ. Sung, too, was married and living in New Jersey, not far from where Jeff and Rosemary relocated after leaving the Upper West Side in 1973. The two couples saw each other frequently on weekends.

On the convertible-bond desk, Sung and Beck generally worked as a team, with Beck taking the lead in the selling and Sung in the analysis. One day after they'd teamed up to execute a particularly lucrative

trade, Beck grabbed Sung and danced him around the trading floor.
"We're in the money," they sang. "We're in the money."

From then on, every big trade Beck and Sung engineered moved
them to musical celebration. Beck's antics likely would have gone un-
noticed at a rough and ready house like Salomon Brothers, which had a
long and glorious history of trader lunacy. Ralph "Crackpot" Martin,
for example, would throw violent temper tantrums on the desk every
time the market went against him. And when he was on a roll, Martin
would leap up on top of his desk and gleefully bellow orders at anyone
in sight—even his boss. Compared to the likes of Crackpot, Beck was
almost staid at this stage of his career. Not until he shifted to DLJ's
investment-banking division would he develop the manic persona of
Mad Dog Beck. Still, at a firm dominated not by traders but by sober-
miened, Harvard-educated analysts even something as innocuous as an
occasional high-spirited jig was generally considered offensive.

A senior stock trader once walked over to the convertible desk after
one of Beck's and Sung's ballets and complained, "Please, let's have
some decorum here. This is a professional trading operation." Beck
stared at him until he walked away, and proceeded to dance his next
dance with exaggerated glee.

Beck's rebellious instincts were moderated by self-interest. The
amount of business that Beck generated depended in part on his ability to get DLJ's institutional-equity salesmen to work with him. Most
of the ideas he and Smith and Sung thought up hinged on whether
they could convince a money manager to swap a block of stock for
convertible bonds issued by the same company. Since DLJ's historic
forte was stock brokerage, almost all of the major money managers
already had a relationship with the firm's equity department. To reach
them, Beck was required by firm protocol to work through the stockbroker assigned to each account. Many equity salesmen were not excited by the prospect of sharing their clients with a Florida State grad
who danced in the trading room, even though they would receive part
of the commission generated by any swap the convertible department
masterminded. One notable exception was Irv Cross, who had become
a DLJ broker after a distinguished professional football career with the
Philadelphia Eagles. (Cross, an All-Pro cornerback, later became a pro-
football announcer for CBS Sports.) Cross liked Beck and Sung and
brought them with him several times when he made his rounds in
Philadelphia. With Cross's help, Beck developed a bulging book of
business in the Philadelphia area.

By the end of 1973, his first full year under Smith's tutelage, Beck emerged as one of DLJ's most promising young broker-traders. Although he was knocking in commissions at the rate of nearly $400,000 a year, he still wasn't taking much money home. The effect of Beck's initial success was to make him feel cheated as his compensation lagged behind his production. Unlike most Wall Street houses, which allowed their brokers to keep as much as 40 percent of the commissions they generated, DLJ paid a straight salary and a bonus. Beck lobbied almost continually for raises, and with some success. He took home $14,279 in 1972, $20,946 in 1973 and $31,250 in 1974. Beck believed that he deserved a lot more money, but by the end of 1974 he was thankful just to have a job.

Walking through DLJ's trading room one day in the spring of 1974, Beck overheard a bit of gossip that hit him like a punch to the solar plexus: "Did you hear? Tiedemann's gone to Bermuda."

Beck immediately called Carl Tiedemann, whose secretary said that her boss was indeed on his way to Bermuda "to relax." The industrialized world was collapsing, the financial markets had gone into shock, and DLJ's president had decided to go sit on a beach somewhere? Beck didn't buy it. And he knew that if Tiedemann was in trouble, then he was in trouble, too. As one of DLJ's most senior executives, Tiedemann had been the chief proponent of the trading expansion that had created both the jobs Beck had held at DLJ. If Tiedemann had been removed, retrenchment was sure to follow. With less than two years' experience, Beck had to consider himself a prime candidate for unemployment.

In October 1973 war had broken out in the Middle East; almost simultaneously, the Organization of Petroleum Exporting Countries swiftly imposed an embargo on oil shipments to America. The posted price of OPEC crude quadrupled to $12 a barrel and at times went as high as $22. As the higher costs of energy rippled through the industrial system in the United States, inflation soared and took interest rates along for the ride. The sharply higher cost of borrowing put a damper on industrial production and eventually induced the worst recession since World War II. Usually, recession suppresses inflation, but not this time. Inflation and unemployment climbed together, causing havoc in the financial markets.

All over Wall Street, traders took it in the teeth. Victimized by its inexperience in the trading game, DLJ was hit especially hard. The firm would lose \$11.5 million over the full course of the year, which was more than DLJ had earned in all its 15 years. Although DLJ's executives kept up a brave public face, they realized that the firm might fail if hit by another round of big trading losses. DLJ had to cut its risk taking. Tiedemann was supplanted by George Gould, who began restructuring the firm's bond-trading operations. Every week someone Beck knew was fired or seemed to have been fired. There were few official announcements and little gossip. A discreet silence was maintained—not out of sympathy for the departed so much as fear of jinxing oneself by publicly speculating over the fate of a co-worker. The departures were unceremonious to the point of surrealism. Beck would come into work in the morning and another chair would be vacant, while the people sitting nearby all looked like they had a mild case of indigestion. Miss two consecutive days of work and even your boss might assume the worst. By the end of 1974, DLJ had fired a hundred people, reducing total employment by 15 percent.

Lack of seniority was not the only reason that Beck feared for his neck. Stock prices had fallen so low that the conversion price for many convertible-bond issues could be presumed forever out of reach. This meant that Randy Smith's whole swap strategy was out the window. Smith resigned to take a better job elsewhere; Sung, deciding that he'd had enough of the convertible game, transferred to the stock-option desk, leaving his buddy to dance alone. Although sorry to see Sung go, Beck leaped at the opportunity his departure created, pointing out to all concerned that he was the likeliest candidate to succeed Smith as head of convertible arbitrage. The decision over Smith's successor was hanging in the balance when Tiedemann caught that plane to Bermuda. To Beck's suprise, he got the job anyway, though it came with a catch that only became evident later: He had been put in charge of a trading desk that no longer had access to anything more than a token amount of capital. A trader without capital is like a computer without software: costly, useless, and expendable. Beck eventually realized that what he'd thought was a promotion was really the kiss of death.

By the time Gould shut down the convertible desk, Beck had already abandoned it and, like a refugee in a war zone, had gone in desperate search of a way to survive. He found it in the securities equivalent of a pile of rubble. Beck was aware that big banks like Bank of America and Chase Manhattan had been stuck holding loans to corporations that had been nailed by the recession and were at least temporarily unable to repay their debts. He also knew that many of his old convertible-bond buyers were always looking for a bargain; he suspected some might buy these bad loans from the banks if offered them at a substantial discount from their face value. Beck bounced his idea off a few of his associates, who looked at him as if he'd just tracked dog shit all over the floor. Needing no further confirmation, Beck set up meetings with loan officers at a half-dozen banks, which, as he'd anticipated, were more than eager to deal. Working twelve to fourteen hours a day, Beck built a decent book of business—nothing spectacular, to be sure, but over six months or so he managed to bring in $175,000 in revenues, aiding the cause in the hour of DLJ's greatest need.

Beck breathed a bit easier but kept scrambling. Seeking to parlay his improvised franchise into the security of an official job, Beck drew up a business plan proposing, in effect, that DLJ set up a trading desk to deal in distressed paper of all kinds—discounted loans, busted convertibles, straight bonds of troubled companies. Beck pointed out that dealing in this cut-rate merchandise could be very lucrative, with spreads (a spread is the gap between the price the seller got and the price the buyer paid) of 5 percent, compared with 1 percent or less for blue-chip bonds. About the same time, he wrote up a more detailed proposal suggesting that DLJ create a mutual fund to invest in busted convertibles. Beck analyzed 578 convertible issues according to various criteria he'd devised to minimize the risk that the issuer would default and came up with 160 preliminary candidates for inclusion in the fund. Beck asked for a part-time assistant and a few months to complete a more detailed analysis. If the right bonds were selected and if interest rates declined from currently high levels, he wrote, "investments of this nature can realize incredible long-term capital gains." Beck, in short, was urging DLJ to make a business out of what would come to be known as junk bonds—one of the most lucrative Wall Street specialties of the mid-1980s. To Beck's annoyance, though, his proposals never made it past the middle-management level.

When Dan Lufkin called him to his office one day in 1975, Beck assumed that he'd finally been marked for execution. But Lufkin had recognized in Beck a spark of talent not unlike his own. "It was evident to me that Jeff was an imaginative guy who was thinking creatively about solutions to problems," Lufkin recalled. "And he was willing to take risks, calculated risks—he did his homework." Lufkin complimented Beck on his resourcefulness in making a business out of private placements of bank loans and invited him to begin applying his salesmanship to the deal-making side of DLJ's business. Beck fairly leaped from his chair in his eagerness to accept. He couldn't believe it! He'd been singled out by the great Lufkin!

Although Lufkin was best known on Wall Street as the cofounder of DLJ, he was also one of the 1960s' and early 1970s' most creative promoters of merger and acquisition deals. He'd done his first deal in partnership with a wealthy boyhood buddy, Louis Marx, Jr. In 1962 Marx, who had put up some of the money with which DLJ was founded, invited DLJ to invest alongside him in an oil-drilling program in Kansas. Lufkin was all for the plan but was outvoted by Donaldson and Jenrette. So Lufkin put up $37,500 of his own money—and made it back ten times over when the drilling program brought in a gusher on its first well. Next, Lufkin and Marx bought a controlling block of stock in a big Western cattle-ranching company. While continuing to do deals with Marx on the side, Lufkin also put together, within DLJ, a freewheeling little band of deal makers who ranged far and wide in search of opportunity.

In 1968, Lufkin charmed his way into one of the first billion-dollar M & A deals, advising E. R. Squibb & Son, which was spun off from Olin Mathieson Chemical and merged with Beech-Nut LifeSavers to form a giant new company, Squibb Beech-Nut. At the same time, DLJ moved beyond merely providing M & A advice to investing its own money in deals. Over the 1960s, DLJ organized a couple of dozen small deals, many of them quite lucrative. If Lufkin had had his druthers, DLJ would have sunk most of its capital into deal making. However, Donaldson and Jenrette were more comfortable with the modest risks and rewards of the brokerage business and were loath to wager DLJ's future on merchant banking. As a result, DLJ missed out on Lufkin's greatest deal. With Marx and two other partners, Lufkin invested $235,000 in 1968 to start Pan Ocean Oil, an oil exploration company. When Pan Ocean went public a year later, the value of the founders' stake soared to $16.8 million. After making a massive oil strike in the North Sea, Pan Ocean sold out to Marathon Oil for $268 million. In the lexicon of M & A, Pan Ocean was a grand slam—one that confirmed Lufkin's place in the first rank of 1970s deal men.

Under Lufkin's direction, Beck functioned as a sort of roving apprentice, shuffling among deals shepherded by more senior bankers, all the while scrambling to gain the secure foothold of an official position. For a time the best he could do was to invent for himself, in his pitch letters to prospective clients, the role of DLJ's specialist in "nontraditional" financing—whatever that meant. (Beck wasn't sure himself.) He gathered the prospectuses for Pan Ocean and other Lufkin deals and studied them as if they were instructional manuals. Every few days, he'd stop by his mentor's office and pepper him with questions. While Beck had much to learn about the technical aspects of dealing, he was far more interested in absorbing what he could of Lufkin's style. "In my opinion Dan Lufkin was the best salesman in America," Beck said. "He could have sold manure to cows. He was good-looking, very charming, smart, and full of energy. He had all the right instincts and made all the right moves. He could size up people instantly and figure out just what levers to pull. He made himself fortune after fortune. I watched Lufkin operate and I decided I would be a deal man, too."

4

In the time-honored manner of the blue-blooded investment banker, Beck launched his M & A career by milking his family connections. The fact that Beck was able to suppress his filial rage and assume the role of dutiful son, thoughtful stepbrother, and respectful nephew was the most telling measure of the intensity of ambition he brought to deal making. "I was willing to use anything to get myself positioned for a better life than the one I had," Beck said. This resurgence of family feeling did not emerge solely from commercial calculation. Beneath the tough-guy façade Beck cultivated was an optimist who couldn't help hoping that somehow he would find a way to make everything right between his mother and himself. The combination of professional advancement and domestic stability had softened the bristly edge of Beck's personality. In Rosemary, Jeff had found a solid counterweight to his own instability.

Reluctant to venture forth from the Seventy-fourth Street apartment and dissuaded by her husband from looking for a job of her own, Rosemary had begun her life in New York in quasi-solitary confinement. Jeff left for DLJ before sunup and returned long after sundown, and he was so utterly taken with his work that he hardly noticed the grimness of the neighborhood. After a year on the Upper West Side, the Becks moved out of the big city that so oppressed Rosemary's every sensibility into a cottage on the grounds of an old estate near Gladstone, New Jersey. This was the serious country, with deer and wild turkey in the yard, an hour and forty-five minutes removed from Wall Street by train. Beck rode the old Erie-Lackawanna line, which still featured wicker seats and white-jacketed waiters in the bar car and was packed each day with men of his own age headed to Wall Street. Beck rather enjoyed the bleary-eyed camaraderie of commuting; most of the friendships he made at DLJ were forged riding the Erie-

Lackawanna. Beck began catching the same train a couple of stops closer to New York beginning in 1975, when he and Rosemary abandoned the cottage and bought a house of their own in New Vernon, paying $125,000 for a colonial with three bedrooms, a swimming pool, and a trout stream running through the property. Beck, a city dweller his entire life, was so smitten by the romance of rural living that some of his colleagues at DLJ teasingly called him the country squire. He bought a riding mower and began to cart wheelbarrows full of dirt and manure in the interest of growing better corn and tomatoes. In their new Mercedes 280 SE, the Becks tooled about the countryside on weekends, shopping for antiques. Jeff began to collect handmade wooden duck decoys; soon the collection burst the confines of his study and spilled throughout the house.

Beck financed his improved standard of living with a bank loan guaranteed by his stepfather. While Rosemary was appreciative of the helping hand, she did not care much for Jeff's moneyed relations, whom she found mean-spirited and tiresome. On one of Ida's rare visits to New Jersey, Rosemary became so exasperated with her mother-in-law's provocations that she asked her to leave the house. Rosemary was not to be trifled with. She pointedly stayed home in the spring of 1975 when Jeff and Judy accompanied their mother and stepfather on a trip to the West Coast in celebration of the hamburger king's seventy-fifth birthday. After a brief stay in San Francisco, the four of them flew to Anchorage, Alaska. Judy and the Singers departed on a cruise down the Alaskan coast while Jeff relieved his pent-up frustration with a few days of big-game hunting. Jeff even began spending the odd weekend in Coral Gables, usually in connection with a business trip. Leon Pomerance, a senior trader in DLJ's Miami office, was invited to dinner at the Singers' and saw no hint of disagreement between Beck and his mother or stepfather.

However calculating Beck's placidity might have been, no one could accuse him of angling for Royal Castle's investment-banking business. South Florida's most celebrated hamburger chain was defunct; intrafamily squabbling and deceit having played no small part in its demise. The trouble revolved around the unhappy relationship of William D. and Larry. Over the years, the elder Singer gradually had shifted responsibility for daily management to Larry, who was given the title of president while his father remained chairman. Making its debut right at a frothy peak in the market for fast-food shares, Royal Castle fetched nineteen times current earnings—a rich multiple that allowed no margin of disappointment. Sure enough, when Royal Castle's earnings declined slightly in 1966, its stock collapsed, falling to $5 a share from a peak of $19. The Singer family, which still owned 70 percent of the stock, watched the major portion of its wealth vanish in a few weeks. However, Royal Castle's earnings were only off by 7 percent; Larry was certain he could turn the trend around and restore value to the stock. His father, though, apparently didn't share Larry's confidence. In the fall of 1966—only a year after the initial public offering—William D. went behind his son's back and reached preliminary agreement to sell Royal Castle for $6 a share to a New York company. When Larry found out about his father's treachery, he was outraged and, with an assist from some shareholders who filed suit over the low price, managed to kill the deal.

Over the next few years, Royal Castle shares climbed back above $10, seemingly vindicating Larry in his opposition to selling the company. On the other hand, he was unable to reverse the decline in earnings, and when profits spurted ahead again briefly at the start of 1969, the Singer family once again conspired to sell Royal Castle out from under Larry. His sisters, Marlene Stone and Dorothy Jacobs, granted an option on their shares at $12 a share to Performance Systems, a Tennessee company that operated Minnie Pearl fried-chicken and roast-beef stands. William D. decided to sell his shares to Performance Systems, too. In time, Larry surrendered to the inevitable, selling his shares to Performance Systems as well. He was replaced as president by LeRoy Collins, the former governor of Florida; adding insult to injury, William D. came out of retirement and rejoined the Royal Castle board to lend his old political ally a hand. This sorry spectacle, which Beck observed from the safe distance of Tallahassee, confirmed his youthful view of his stepfather as a domineering tyrant.

In selling to Performance Systems, the Singers salvaged $9 million of their fortune but doomed the family company to oblivion: The new owners eventually liquidated it for its real estate. Although his flagship had sunk without a trace, old man Singer's business connections remained usefully intact as his stepson began prospecting for M & A business. Singer was, for example, the second-largest shareholder in Atlanta's small but profitable Fulton National Bank. With an introduction from his stepfather, Beck called on Fulton National, but was cordially told that the bank wasn't planning any acquisitions or financings and didn't require the services of an investment banker. Beck followed up with a polite letter in which he reminded the bank's president that "my family considers itself a longterm investor in your bank. . . . Perhaps a situation might arise in which a company in your loan portfolio may seek an infusion of equity capital."

With an assist from his stepfather, Jeff did persuade two small banks in Miami to retain him to look for buyers. These were contingent-fee arrangements, which meant that Beck would get paid only if a deal were done. DLJ, in turn, agreed to pass on 5 percent of any such payments to Singer as a finder's fee. A group of Venezuelan investors looking for a bank to buy hired Beck on the same basis. As it turned out, though, nothing much came of this opportunity, nor of the others unearthed by Beck during his swings through Florida in 1975 and 1976.

Meanwhile, Beck also devoted considerable energy to cultivating his brother-in-law, Richard Stone, who was elected to the U.S. Senate in 1974, becoming the first Jewish senator from the South elected by popular vote—a historic achievement that was as much a result of Singer's money and influence as of Stone's political skills. Singer called in all his political chits in support of Stone, who won with only 43 percent of the vote in a bitter three-way race after having narrowly defeated the Democratic incumbent in the primary. Beck, who'd helped out a bit with fund-raising, stayed in touch by sending his brother-in-law DLJ research reports on matters pertaining to Stone's political interests. In mid-1975, the Stones invited Jeff and Rosemary to Washington for dinner at the Florida house with a group of senators that included Harry Byrd, Russell Long, Abraham Ribicoff, Lawton Chiles, Walter Huddleston, Bennett Johnston, and Dale Bumpers. Through Stone, Beck also arranged for DLJ's chief economist to have lunch with Senator Bumpers and got the firm's director of research considered for a job at the Department of Energy. An early supporter of Jimmy Carter, Stone saw his influence in Washington grow after the Georgian was elected president. He was, for example, one of a few senators asked to put together a list of candidates for the coveted posts of White House fellows. Stone sought the input of Beck, who succeeded in getting a few DLJ names onto the list submitted by the senator.

As he was launching his M & A career, Beck even flew to Pittsburgh several times to meet with his father's nemesis: Joe Katz. While Beck did indeed covet Papercraft's business, he had an ulterior motive in calling on his uncle. During each of his flights to Pittsburgh, Jeff worked himself into a lather as he debated whether to demand from his uncle an explanation of what had really happened between him and his father all those years ago. As it turned out, though, Jeff was never able to broach the subject of his father and Katz never volunteered a word about Lou Beck.

At the time Beck came calling on his uncle, Papercraft had reached a critical juncture in its history. Like Royal Castle, Papercraft had come to grief—not, however, through Singer-style intrafamily strife but through Joe Katz's stubbornness. In 1967 Papercraft had acquired one of its biggest rivals, Chicago Paper & String. A year later, though, the Federal Trade Commission informed Papercraft that it intended to force the divestiture of CPS on antitrust grounds. After tying up the FTC in court for five years and refusing to comply with the order after his appeals were exhausted, Katz finally unloaded CPS at a fire-sale price in 1975 and paid the FTC $1.8 million in fines.

Katz's pride may have been deeply dented by the CPS fiasco but his net worth was mostly intact. With 23 percent of Papercraft's stock, the Katz family fortune amounted to at least $3.3 million at the time Cousin Jeff came calling. Beck's timing was perfect. Papercraft had built up $30 million in cash even before the sale of CPS and was looking to acquire a consumer-products businesses. Beck met with Joe Katz and his thirty-seven-year-old son, Marshall, eight years Beck's senior. Beck didn't trust his Uncle Joe and had more disdain than affection for Marshall, whom he considered a Pittsburgh version of Larry Singer—that is, the weak son of a bullying mogul. But Beck was all smiles as he made his pitch, and was received with cordial neutrality. However, Katz was not about to shift from his longtime Wall Street investment bank (the venerable Blyth Eastman Dillon) to DLJ simply because DLJ employed his nephew. Beck persisted, returning three or four times to Pittsburgh, usually in the company of a more senior DLJ colleague. In mid-1977 Katz briefly relented, authorizing DLJ to search for companies for Papercraft to acquire. Despite protracted negotiations with one company brought to Katz by DLJ, Beck never did do a deal with Papercraft.

Still, Beck didn't come away empty-handed. His cousin Marshall introduced him to Scottish & Universal Investments Limited, or SUITs, as it was known, a company formed from the diverse holdings of the Fraser family, one of Scotland's wealthiest. Thrilled by the prospect of representing a European dynasty, Beck flew off to Edinburgh with DLJ's Mike Rosenthal, M & A chief, returning with a $10,000-a-month retainer to hunt acquisition candidates. Within

DLJ's existing stable of clients, Beck quickly found a gift-wrap company to dangle before the Scots. Bill Donaldson was a director of Cole National, a company that owned a hodgepodge of businesses including the Susan Crane Company, which made custom gift wrap for department stores. SUITs took a look but decided against making a bid, disregarding Beck's advice. Convinced that Susan Crane was a great buy, Beck urged DLJ to acquire the company itself. When DLJ passed, Beck obtained permission to buy Susan Crane himself, and convinced his stepfather to help him finance the deal as co-owner.

Returning to New York, Beck invited Rosenthal to participate in the deal with the Singers. Rosenthal accepted, and took the lead in negotiating a purchase price of $4.2 million and the terms of the bank loan with which it was financed. The deal closed in November 1976, not quite a year and a half into Beck's M & A career, and was structured as a leveraged buyout—that is, most of the money used to buy the company was borrowed. Larry and William D. Singer joined with Beck and Rosenthal to form a partnership that invested $800,000, almost all of it contributed by the hamburger king. Beck's equity investment amounted to $30, 000, which he borrowed from a bank through a note guaranteed by his stepfather. The partnership borrowed the remaining $3.4 million needed to swing the deal—$1.4 million in the form of a note to Cole National and $2 million from Citicorp. After the deal closed, the new owners fired Susan Crane's top two managers and replaced them with Robert Macht, a veteran retailing executive whom Singer had known for years.

Susan Crane gave a big boost to Beck's ego. He'd yet to turn thirty-one but already he'd achieved something that had eluded his father: He was an owner now, not just an employee. And like Dan Lufkin he was an honest-to-God merchant banker, not just an adviser. Beck's enthusiasm fired visions of using Susan Crane as a vehicle through which he and his stepfather could make other acquisitions and build a diversified company—a company bigger and better than Papercraft. Just a few weeks after the deal closed, Beck began peppering his stepfather with acquisition ideas. His business letters to Singer now were downright chummy. "Dear Dad," he wrote just before Christmas, "I feel that our investing group would probably want to acquire a company to leverage Susan Crane."

The names William Singer, Joe Katz, and Richard Stone might as well have been printed on the flip side of Beck's business card, so assiduously did he promote them to coworkers and prospective clients alike. A banker who often worked with Beck recalled, "You'd think Stone was God the way Jeff talked about him." While Beck spoke incessantly *of* his relatives, he never talked of his relationships *with* them. Although by this time the clandestine quality of Beck's emotional life was as much a reflex as a tactic, his evasions were critical to his image making. After all, he couldn't very well hold out his relatives as aces in the hole if it were known that he'd been almost continually at odds with them throughout his adult life. The impression that Beck strove to create was not simply that he came from money and one day would come into money, but that he was an heir to an entrepreneurial tradition, that money-making was in his blood. To this end, Beck tried to wreathe himself in an aura of great expectations, adopting a knowing manner that insinuated, "Take me seriously now or one day you may regret it."

Aside from the Susan Crane deal, none of Beck's family-related maneuverings ever advanced his cause meaningfully. To the extent that Beck was able to convince his colleagues at DLJ that he had powerful allies—and most people took his claims at only a slight discount from face value—this bit of added esteem may have buoyed his professional confidence. But he was unable to use his relatives to generate income for DLJ's M & A department, and in retrospect Beck would conclude that the family-connections aspect of his promoting was worse than a waste of time. "The time I spent on it would have been better spent elsewhere," he said. "There was just too much bullshit in it."

All this fussing around with the people who knew him best might have been more understandable had not Beck been so adept at striking up relationships with total strangers. In late 1975, Beck, Rosenthal, and a DLJ stock analyst flew down to Greenville, South Carolina, to meet with Ronald Craigmyle, the son of the founder of Giant Portland Cement. A gracious, earnest man of forty-three, Craigmyle drove his visitors to Harleyville to take a look at Giant Portland's cement factory. They arrived about noon and spent the afternoon nosing around the plant in hard hats and business suits. Late in the afternoon, Craigmyle led the visitors up a metal ladder and out onto the roof of the main building, a good hundred feet in the air. Craigmyle pointed out the factory of a rival cement maker, Gifford Hill, a mile and a half due east, and then swung his arm 180 degrees to the left to where Keystone Cement's plant was faintly visible in the distance.

Beck clambered a few feet past his companions onto the roof and faced the cement-belt panorama. He raised his arms like a preacher importuning the heavens. "Industry," he roared above the noise of the plant clanking away beneath him. "I love it."

Craigmyle and the others burst out laughing. "I often think of that moment," Craigmyle said more than a decade later. "It was uplifting. Jeff liked to kid around a little but, you know, I think he had the same feeling about that old Harleyville plant that I did."

In time, Beck would come to see rainmaking as a kind of high-wire routine in which the promoter "walks the line between fact and fiction" and "shades reality" in his attempts to overcome his two great adversaries—inertia and skepticism. At the start, though, Beck's method was quite straightforward. He was not so cynical that he could bring himself to attempt to convince somebody of something he disbelieved himself. To the contrary, the foundation of his rainmaking talent was an extraordinary ability to empathize with strangers and personalize business relationships. He couldn't help it. When Beck cold-called corporate executives it wasn't just their business he wanted, but their curiosity, their sympathy. He wanted to be liked, *needed* to be liked, and pursued prospective clients with an ardor usually reserved for romance or warfare. For Beck "the engagement agreement was the jugular," said Patrick Bromley, one of his closest associates at DLJ. "Clients would actually go away feeling bad if for some reason they couldn't use him."

Although overlaid with sales techniques that were beyond his ken as a teenaged mogul of popularity, the basis of Beck's method was the same on Wall Street as in Coral Gables. He began the process of establishing a connection with strangers by assuming the burden of amusing them, as he did with Craigmyle in Harleyville. Beck was capable of entering a get-acquainted meeting with a corporate executive with all the bravado of a stand-up comedian taking the stage for the late show. He was fearless that way. Typically, Beck would begin his pitch by touting DLJ with such extravagant hyperbole that his host couldn't help but at least smile—a reaction that Beck's own evident amusement invited. The essence of Beck's appeal wasn't that he was funny or irreverent or unpredictable, though he was all of that. He had a rare capacity for romanticizing the routine drudgery of business into adventure, making deals more fun than they had any right to be.

In staging a business meeting as entertainment, Beck took the risk of quick rejection, of instant humiliation. No one fails quite as abjectly

as the comedian who can't get a laugh. Inevitably, the Jeff Beck Show
played most effectively to his contemporaries, to other members of the
baby-boom generation, but Beck was able to strike up relationships
with executives of all ages, backgrounds, and even nationalities. His act
was saved from shtick by his ability to take the measure of people
quickly and adjust his presentation to maximize his appeal. Despite his
calculation, Beck was not insincere. His personality was so diverse that
there was a facet of himself that could, if properly highlighted, appeal
to almost anybody he met. That many of his facets were contradictory
made them no less real.

Beck's best client at DLJ, George Hromadko, was a Catholic born
and raised in Czechoslovakia. Shortly after the Soviets lowered the
Iron Curtain across Eastern Europe, Hromadko and his wife escaped
to the West, arriving in Germany with nothing but a suitcase full of
clothes. After a few years of abject poverty, the Hromadkos made their
way to New York City. Hromadko earned an MBA at New York University and went to work at the headquarters of Warner-Lambert
Company. He had a brilliant financial mind and eventually was promoted to chief financial officer and then to vice chairman. A stern,
humorless man who spoke four languages with a heavy German accent, Hromadko was famed within the company as a wily, indomitable
negotiator. Once, during a protracted negotiating session, his opposite
numbers had tried to fluster and intimidate Hromadko by mimicking
his accent. Hromadko simply ignored them, persisting as if he'd not
even heard their insults. "All that matters," he told his assistant afterward, "is that we prevailed."

Beck was inspired to call Hromadko by a DLJ analyst's report on
Warner-Lambert, a major pharmaceutical and consumer-products
company that had been put together through a string of mergers and
acquisitions in the 1960s and early 1970s. It seemed obvious to Beck
from his quick examination of news reports and analysts' studies that
Warner-Lambert was pregnant with possible deals—not only acquisitions but also divestitures of some of the businesses it had accumulated
so hastily. The fact that Warner-Lambert long had split its M & A
business between Morgan Stanley and Lazard Frères gave him only
momentary pause. What did he have to lose? Beck extracted a few
names of likely acquisition candidates from the reports and put in a
cold call to Hromadko.

Hromadko had inherited the relationship with Morgan Stanley from
his predecessor and had no intention of being confined by it. If an

investment banker he'd never met from a firm that he'd never heard of asked for a meeting, chances were Hromadko would grant him an audience and listen—impassively, imposingly—to whatever he had to say. By the time Beck called, Hromadko was noddingly familiar with DLJ but had never done business with the firm. He invited Beck to come and see him. Beck was in his office the next day. No doubt it took the Czech just a few minutes to realize that his young visitor knew next to nothing about Warner-Lambert's business—not that Beck pretended to such knowledge. He spent the better part of an hour discoursing on arbitrage and behind-the-scenes machinations of Wall Street deal making, a subject that endlessly intrigued Hromadko. The Czech found himself taking a liking to Beck that he would have been hard pressed to justify objectively. He decided to take a chance on young Beck.

Hromadko called one of his assistants, Steve McGrath, and said: "I've got someone in my office that I'd like you to meet."

Hromadko pointed Beck down the hallway to the office of McGrath, who'd been given the assignment of finding buyers for a couple of ailing subsidiaries that no longer fit into Warner-Lambert's plans. Although McGrath no longer could be properly described as a whiz kid, his career had yet to level off after more than a decade's rise. An accountant by training, McGrath had a quick, analytical mind and a facility for intramural corporate politics that more than compensated for lack of physical presence and unimpressive academic credentials. Unable to afford business school, McGrath took night-school accounting classes to become a CPA. After a few years at Price Waterhouse, McGrath started climbing the corporate ladder. By the age of thirty-four, he had become vice president for planning and development at Warner-Lambert. McGrath's quiet amiability masked driving ambition and a self-confidence bordering on arrogance. While McGrath felt that he had a good shot at running Warner-Lambert one day, he wisely kept that thought to himself.

McGrath's first impression was that Beck was his elder by at least five years and must be one of DLJ's most senior investment bankers. He found Beck to be a refreshing break from the third- and fourth-level junior bankers from Morgan, First Boston, and the other major houses who paraded regularly through his office, delivering a perfunctory spiel about what a perfectly marvelous firm it was they worked for and ending with this less-than-rousing pitch: "Well, Mr. McGrath, what can we do for you?" McGrath usually responded with a curt

"You tell me," which, after a suitable amount of hemming and hawing, brought the interview to a close. Beck, though, had a ready answer for McGrath's most important question:

"Do you know who'd buy Medical Data Systems?"

Beck had recently called for the first time on Medtronic, the manufacturer of pacemakers, to sound out the company on its M & A plans. Beck was prepared to make an educated guess and make it with a flourish. "I know one company that will buy it. Medtronic."

McGrath laughed, a bit startled by the swiftness and finality of Beck's reply. He gave Beck the assignment of peddling Medical Data Systems and, after protracted negotiations headed by McGrath, Medtronic did indeed buy the unwanted subsidiary for $6.9 million. DLJ earned a fee of $172,155 (excluding expenses) and Beck parlayed the transaction into a continuing relationship not only with Warner-Lambert but with Medtronic, too. Steve Mahle, Medtronic's vice president for corporate development, put Beck on a six-month, $50,000 retainer to search for additional companies Medtronic might acquire. To Beck's delight, Mahle chose DLJ over Smith Barney, Harris Upham & Company, the old-line investment bank that had taken Medtronic public and managed its underwritings. Beck got on so well with Mahle, a soft-spoken, unassuming University of Minnesota graduate about his own age, that he was an overnight guest in Mahle's home during his trips to Minneapolis and reciprocated when the Minnesotan came to New York. With Mahle, Beck featured his regular-guy Coral Gables side. There were none of the tales of backroom Wall Street intrigue with which he'd entranced Hromadko. "Unlike some investment bankers I'd dealt with, Jeff didn't seem overly taken with himself or what was going on on Wall Street," Mahle said. "He was down-to-earth and able to see things in broad context, not just through Wall Street eyes."

Another of Beck's most prized early clients was SUITs, the Scottish company he'd approached through his cousin Marshall. As the principal holding of SUITs, House of Fraser operated dozens of department stores—including London's most famous, Harrod's. In addition to SUITs, Beck signed up House of Fraser, which faced a hostile-takeover threat. Through Sir Hugh Fraser, the executives of SUITs, and several of its well-connected board members Beck obtained introductions to other companies in the United Kingdom. The investment-banking business in London remained far less competitive than in the United States, largely because few of the old-line Wall Street houses had yet to make a concerted effort to prospect for clients in Europe. Perversely, London's principal attraction to Beck was the sheer difficulty of operating there as an American under a rigorous but unwritten code of etiquette. To Beck, the chilly, closed upper reaches of the English class system presented an irresistible challenge that would occupy him for years.

Working quickly, Beck mounted on the wall of his new office the four posters that he'd bought at the British Museum, and then sat down behind his desk, put his feet up, and admired his handiwork. Beck was no art expert, but he felt that these reproductions—mythological scenes, by anonymous artists, of ancient battlefield butchery—set just the right tone for a young deal man's digs. Just look at the bright rivers of blood spouting from all those limbless torsos! Such gore, such butchery! Even the horses were getting sliced to ribbons!

Beck taped a caption beneath each of his rustic masterpieces— "CLOSING THE DEAL," "GOOD EXECUTION," and the like.

Beck smiled with pleasure at the thought of how the male debutantes would react to his display of monumentally tasteless art. "Male debutantes" was Beck's sneering nickname for the polite, well-bred Ivy Leaguers who surrounded him in such numbers at DLJ and who, he was certain, were conspiring to kill him softly with their nice manners and nose-in-the air respectability. As Beck envisioned it, one of the debutantes would be sitting in the chair across from him, rattling on pompously about some utterly insignificant matter as if the security of the free world hung in the balance, when he would stop in mid-sentence and swivel his head slowly to the wall. The deb might stifle a gasp but would refrain from intelligible expressions of surprise or disgust. After a second or two, the deb would return his gaze front and center and resume the conversation without mentioning the posters. But Beck was certain that he'd be able to read a reaction in those debutante eyes, that he would see what he'd come to think of as "The Look"—a look of condescension mixed with bewilderment and a hint of fear, a look that plaintively asked, "Who *are* you, anyway, and what are you doing here, at a firm like this, with someone like *me*?"

Although this was a good question, perhaps even a fair question, Beck recognized no obligation to answer it. He was a nobody from nowhere and he hadn't come to DLJ to fill the gaps in his social calendar. To most of DLJ's other investment bankers, Beck was an enigma wrapped in pandemonium. Great clouds of smoke billowing through a doorway into the hallway announced to one and all that Beck was in his office. Chances were that he had a cigarette in his mouth, tapping his foot to some insistent internal rhythm, growling something like "Yeah, man, yeah—right!" into a telephone receiver. To punctuate moments of triumph, Beck would switch to cigars—big, expensive cigars—and come bounding out of his office to stand in the hallway and howl like a dog baying at the moon: "Aooooooooh! Aooooooooh!"

Beck's darker moods also found canine expression. After passing a debutante in the hallway, Beck would growl menacingly and then stop and look back over his shoulder, baring his teeth. In his less demure moments, Beck would put his nose right in a debutante's face, like a Doberman with an attitude.

"Grrrrrrrr," Beck would growl. "How much business have you brought in today? Huh? How much? Grrrrrrrr."

Inevitably, the others called him Mad Dog. Beck promoted the nickname, preferring it to his alternate moniker, "Spike," which evoked the kind of slobbering family pet that scarfs up scraps under the table and is always rolling over, begging to be petted. But a mad dog was pure menace, frothing and unfathomable. A mad dog was something to fear, and Beck preferred being feared to being belittled, since he assumed those were his only choices. Shifting from trading to investment banking had so aggravated his class anxieties that he was jumping all over the most effete of his new colleagues before they'd even had a chance to snub him. When one of the debutantes fell asleep in a meeting, Beck was so outraged by the man's seeming indifference to the business at hand that he shook him awake. Even after he learned that this fellow was suffering from narcolepsy, Beck was unchastened. To the contrary, sensing fatal weakness, he escalated his growling hallway attacks.

Beck's insecurities were aggravated by the departure of his mentor and protector, Dan Lufkin. A few months after he'd taken Beck under his wing as a junior deal man, Lufkin made a fatal misstep. Believing that he'd lined up sufficient support to dislodge Dick Jenrette from the position of co-CEO, Lufkin readied plans to force a shift in DLJ's emphasis from brokerage to deal making. However, a reporter at *The Wall Street Journal* whom Lufkin had tipped to the changes in store at DLJ ran his story prematurely—on the very day that Lufkin had scheduled a management meeting at which he planned to force a final showdown. Jenrette got off a red-eye flight to Denver that morning to read that he had been deposed. He immediately got on a plane to New York. Back at the office, Jenrette found that even Lufkin's supporters were angry over the leak. The possibility that DLJ would devote itself to deal making died as Lufkin resigned in defeat, leaving Jenrette alone at the top of a firm that would uneasily continue to straddle brokerage and investment banking, to Beck's detriment. "Jeff would have been on the cutting edge of DLJ the deal firm," Lufkin said. "He was the right guy at the right time but he was in the wrong place."

Beck would have left DLJ in a second had Lufkin asked him to join in starting a new firm devoted exclusively to deals. But after seventeen years at DLJ, Lufkin had had his fill of managing and retreated from Wall Street, leaving Beck no alternative. Luckily, Beck immediately attracted another high-ranking mentor, John Castle, who was himself a former Lufkin protégé. Although Castle had a degree from Harvard, he was no debutante. Castle was brilliant and strange and looked the part, with an enormous bald dome of a head and a nose that was Pinocchio-esque in its length and pointiness. Castle was a bit hunched over even when he stood as straight as he could, and he smiled in a way that suggested he was suffering from mild nausea. He looked like someone who should be tending a linear accelerator in the desert somewhere or conducting secret experiments on small animals for the CIA. Born and raised in a small Iowa town, Castle had been a superb physics student at MIT and a Baker Scholar at Harvard Business School, ranking in the top 2.5 percent of the class of 1965. After joining DLJ as an analyst, Castle ascended rapidly into senior management and by the time Lufkin resigned had responsibility for the firm's whole investment-banking operation. A perfectionist, Castle drove himself relentlessly and expected maximum effort from his subordinates. Every now and then frustration would melt Castle's innate reserve and he'd snap a pencil in two or rip a telephone cord out of the wall. Behind his back, he was called the Doberman pinscher, in recognition of both his repressed ferocity and his fearsome snout.

While Beck generally didn't react well to authority, he admired Castle's intellect and deal savvy and submitted willingly to his direction. For his part, Castle let Beck be Beck, tolerating his temperamental flamboyance despite frequent complaints from the Mad Dog's colleagues. One day Castle was walking down the hallway when he came across a young female investment banker slumped against the wall. She stopped Castle and looked wearily into his eyes. "He's crazy," she said to Castle. "He really *is* crazy, you know." Castle didn't have to ask to whom she was referring. Nor did he disagree. "At that point in his career," Castle recalled, "Jeff probably could not have retained a job at any other investment-banking firm. I lived with the howling and growling because he had an unusual facility for getting to people running corporations and bringing them through the door."

Although Castle occasionally found it necessary to rein Beck in, the Mad Dog never lost control of his temper to the point of taking a swing at someone. He barked but was careful never to bite. Most of his temper tantrums were staged to intimidate his rivals. Pat Bromley, a young banker with whom Beck was friendly, was standing in the hallway one day when the Mad Dog stormed past him into a nearby office. Through the closed door, the sound of Beck's raised voice could be heard all down the corridor as he railed at the occupant about some error involving one of Beck's deals. Beck's quarry made the mistake of yelling back. "If you tried to contest Jeff's energy, he'd just escalate his intensity and blow you away," Bromley said. Afterward, as was his habit, Beck came into Bromley's office, shut the door, and laughingly dissected his latest confrontation like an actor analyzing a scene.

After his promotion to vice president in mid-1976, Beck was in a position to shift much of the number crunching and drudge work associated with his deals to younger M & A bankers. He came to rely particularly heavily on Bromley and on Fred Lane. At DLJ, associates were not subject to a formal assignment system; both Bromley and Lane basically volunteered for duty with the Mad Dog. Like Mike Rosenthal, Lane was a CPA. After graduating from Harvard Business School, he had spent three years at an accounting firm before boredom brought him to Wall Street and DLJ. In contrast to Bromley, a born numbers jockey, Lane considered himself as good a salesman as he was a technician. While Beck and Lane worked well together, their relationship was more one of rivalry than friendship. Beck was closer to Bromley, who was more self-effacing. The son of an English toolmaker, he'd been educated at Cambridge and Harvard Business School. Naturally, Bromley was especially useful on Beck's frequent prospecting trips to the United Kingdom.

Bromley and his wife lived only a mile or two from the Becks' house in New Jersey. Returning from a business trip late one Friday night, Beck dropped Bromley off at his house and went home. Bromley entered an empty house. After ten months of marriage, his wife had cleared out and taken every stick of furniture with her. Disconsolate, Bromley immediately called Beck, who insisted that he come over and stay with him and Rosemary as long as he liked. The two deal men spent the whole weekend together, talking, fishing, and cutting wood on Beck's property. "He was really hurting," Beck said, "so I tried to work him till he dropped." After a few days, Bromley returned to his empty house, still miserable but with a deepened appreciation of Beck's friendship.

Beck, who at times operated on such little sleep that he had trouble walking, drove Bromley and Lane as hard as he drove himself. On one swing through England, Bromley, who prided himself on his iron constitution, collapsed from exhaustion after several nights spent preparing presentations and several days of nonstop meetings. Excusing himself from a lunch with Beck and Sir Hugh Fraser, he returned to his hotel and was virtually comatose for the rest of the day.

Bromley and Lane considered Beck very demanding but equitable. Unlike many other bankers, he let associates work directly with his clients. Beck lobbied as relentlessly for raises for Lane, Bromley, and his secretary-assistant as for himself, and made certain that senior management was informed of their contributions, no matter how minor. Beck once formally objected to Castle when the firm's in-house newsletter failed to credit Lane and a more senior banker for their work putting together a new corporate finance brochure. "I was somewhat disappointed," Beck wrote, that his two colleagues "did not receive credit . . . for their invaluable roles."

Landing a corporation as a client was only the first step in the art of rainmaking. While the retainer fees that Beck collected in $20,000 and $25,000 increments added up nicely, they paled beside the fees pocketed for actually completing a transaction. And for all of Beck's success in signing up companies, he completed very few deals, less than half a dozen in his three full years as a DLJ banker. Beck's problem, according to the consensus among the firm's traditionalists, was that he was deficient technically—his deals didn't get done because he didn't know *how* to get them done. Such criticisms, almost always delivered behind his back, infuriated Beck, who saw himself as a deal promoter by choice, not by necessity. "I knew more about the numbers than 90 percent of the guys at DLJ," he insisted. While Beck was prone to overstate his technical knowledge, his failures could not fairly be attributed to a lack of attention to detail. If anything, he was obsessed with nuance. Before important meetings or phone calls, Beck usually organized his tactical thoughts on paper. In postmortem sessions with colleagues, Beck was capable of recreating a meeting from memory, line by line. And while handing off as much of the grunt work as possible, he scrutinized every piece of work done for one of his clients with a diligent, critical eye.

The most apt criticism of Beck was that his pursuit of business was indiscriminate—in commercial though not moral terms. Unable to distinguish persistence from stubbornness or optimism from wishful thinking, Beck pursued each opportunity with unwavering intensity. In fact, the more daunting or exotic the challenge, the greater his devotion to meeting it. For example, after Sir Hugh Fraser resigned as managing director of SUITs, in the wake of a gambling scandal, the company fell into chaos, and Beck's chances of doing a deal for it were practically nil. Instead of resigning the account, though, Beck flew to Scotland to repitch SUITs executives and to meet with Sir Hugh. Even after SUITs was threatened with takeover by Roland "Tiny" Rowland, a notorious industrialist-adventurer, Beck continued to try to turn the situation to his advantage. In nearly three years of representing SUITs, Beck made six trips to Scotland and approached dozens upon dozens of U.S. companies, but never did a single deal. The fault seemed to lie not with him but with SUITs, which was never quite ready to make a decisive move.

To his credit, Beck also lost some deals because of his own refusal to compromise his professional ethics. For example, though Giant Portland Cement had hired DLJ in hopes of making an acquisition, Beck concluded that the company would be better off modernizing everything from its logo and computer systems to the creaking Harleyville plant before it started making acquisitions. Beck presented DLJ's recommendations to Giant Portland's board, which authorized an overhaul of the company's operations. Beck, in effect, had talked himself out of a big payday. DLJ did earn a $23,000 fee, but that was a pittance compared to what it would have been due had Beck negotiated an acquisition. "Jeff's advice was, 'Get your own house in order first,' and he was right," Craigmyle said.

In his dealings with Amicor, an Atlanta-based manufacturer of industrial parts, Beck was so outraged by the unethical behavior of its CEO that he helped prod the company's board into firing the man. Amicor was desperately in need of additional capital and Beck was commissioned to find a large investor to provide it. A month after Beck began his search, though, Amicor's Italian subsidiary started losing gobs of money. Charles Tennesson, Jr., Amicor's CEO, told Beck that he would sell the company if the price was right. In a two-birds-with-one-stone gambit, Beck urged Tennesson to merge with Giant Portland Cement. But after preliminary talks, Giant Portland backed away, as did a half-dozen other potential buyers DLJ approached. Six months into his relationship with DLJ, Tennesson complained that "nothing productive" had come from it and refused to pay a $23,200 bill Beck submitted. Beck responded with a revised invoice for $9,500 and a sharply worded letter: "I have steadfastly advised you that Amicor is not in the best position to sell and would be in a much stronger position if it could enhance its financial situation and bring its business operations under control." Beck went on to summarize in considerable detail his negotiations with prospective buyers and point-edly reminded Tennesson that he had told him his asking price was too high for a company posting such "dismal results."

Having succeeded in getting DLJ to cut its fee, and with Amicor's condition worsening each day, Tennesson patched things up with Beck and urged him to continue the search for a buyer. Beck persisted and managed to find another suitor. Tennesson told Beck that he would not negotiate the sale of the company unless the prospective acquirer first agreed to buy out his employment contract and stock options at a premium over book value. Outraged by Tennesson's behavior, Beck resigned and met privately with Grinnell Morris, Amicor's chairman. "Jeff was mad as anything," Morris recalled. After the board voted to fire Tennesson, Beck got so many harassing hang-up phone calls late at night that he switched to an unlisted number.

Even as his professional disappointments mounted, though, Beck was able to resist the old temptation to seek refuge in macho myth—at least in his professional dealings. None of Beck's colleagues at DLJ recall him ever claiming that he'd fought in Vietnam, much less re-galing them with tales of derring-do. Indeed, on one occasion during his DLJ days Beck was forced to *listen* at excruciating length to tales of 'Nam. One weekend, Jeff and Rosemary threw a dinner party at-tended by Bing Sung, Sung's wife, and Beck's secretary and her hus-band, who was a former Green Beret. He started telling Vietnam stories at dinner and continued late into the night, oblivious to the others' lack of interest. "Jeff and I were rolling our eyes at each other," Sung said. "We couldn't figure out a way to get the guy to stop that wouldn't offend him." About one A.M. Sung sneaked off to bed. Beck stayed up until about four o'clock, when the ex–Green Beret finally nodded off in his chair.

Yet, in initially discussing his DLJ days with me, Beck explained his Mad Dog persona as an outgrowth of his imaginary career in Vietnam. "I'd just come from the worst kind of combat and I had nothing to lose. I said to myself that if I could do ambushes, I could survive anything. I told myself that if I just treated Wall Street like the jungle, I'd be fine. If guys keep sniping at you, I said, just roll over and keep firing back at them." Beck usually made such comments in the context of embarrassment over the manic extremes of his behavior at DLJ, which he feared would make him appear not bold but buffoonish. More often than not, though, Beck seemed quite comfortable in the role of angry iconoclast—and at times even embroidered his macho image with imaginary adventures. One of his favorites was lifted from a 1977 French movie, *Pardon Mon Affaire* (later remade in the U.S. as *The Woman in Red*), and it went like this:

When one of the few chums he had at DLJ was feeling blue, Beck would, like John Belushi chanting "Toga" in *Animal House*, declaim a call to action: "Blind man, blind man!"

That evening, Beck and his buddies would gather at one of Manhattan's finest restaurants. Usually, Beck would don the dark glasses and take the role of the blind man. In the standard staging of the blind-man ruse, a companion advises the bartender that poor, blind "Mr. Smith" is jittery when out in public.

The solicitous bartender says, "What can I get you, Mr. Smith?"

The blind man is startled. "How did you know my name?" he replies, and begins swinging his cane in a spasm of paranoia, laying waste to every bottle of liquor within reach. He then careens through the restaurant, trashing tables and sending diners fleeing for cover. In pretending to try to halt the blind man's rampage, his companions add to the devastation. The art of "doing a blind man," as Beck called it, lies not in the extent of the damage done but in the timing of one's escape. The ultimate achievement is for the blind man to stumble out to a car parked at the curb, get in on the driver's side, remove the dark glasses, wave at the pursuing maître d', and lay rubber just as the wail of police sirens becomes audible in the distance.

Beck's recountings of his blind-man escapades were as hilarious as the scene in the movie he borrowed the idea from. He claimed to have trashed a half-dozen restaurants, though he refused to name them or his companions in these capers. I spoke with most of Beck's friends at

DLJ and none of them admitted knowing anything about the blind-man routine.

Beck also "confessed" to one imaginary act of violence at the office. Late one afternoon, Beck came charging into Lane's office to remind him that he had an assignment due the next day. When Lane responded with an indifferent shrug, Beck issued a more forceful reminder, bumping his chest up against the younger banker like a baseball manager challenging an umpire. At six foot three and 190 pounds, Lane was a former championship rower who'd kept in shape by running marathons. But when Lane shoved back, Beck claimed to have dropped him to his knees with a punch to the solar plexus. "Do that again," Beck growled, "and I'll kill you."

This was Beck's version. Lane's account was no less suspect. As Lane told it, he lifted Beck up by the armpits, deposited him in the hallway, and shut the door to his office. Beck came back in with tears in his eyes. "We can't have this," he said. "We have to be friends."

At DLJ, Beck had been approached every now and then by headhunters but wasn't tempted to leave until he came across an opening at Lehman Brothers, one of the great Our Crowd bastions. On the morning train from New Jersey, Beck had gotten friendly with a Lehman partner who mentioned one day in the spring of 1978 that Lehman had formed an M & A department, which was looking for experienced help. The prospect of working at Lehman crystallized Beck's latent dissatisfactions with DLJ. Although the firm had snapped back from the debacle of 1973–1974 and was nicely profitable, it was still torn between brokerage and investment banking, emphasizing the former while excelling at neither. It seemed to Beck not only that the investment-banking group was perpetually starved for capital but that Jenrette was using it as a dumping ground for failed analysts and salesmen from the brokerage side of the business. Beck felt surrounded by mediocrity and was increasingly inclined to take the inadequacies of his colleagues as a personal affront. He would not hesitate to chew out a peer who did something Beck considered stupid, even if it had no direct connection to one of his own deals. And if it did, look out.

As a professional courtesy, Beck once invited the head of DLJ's London sales office to a dinner at Le Gavroche with Lord Nicholas Redmayne, a distinguished board member of SUITs. Beck was angling for introductions from Redmayne to other highly placed London businessmen. The DLJ sales manager, an American with a put-on English accent, tried to impress Redmayne by dropping the names of people he pretended to know. Redmayne, who actually knew those people, toyed with this pompous fellow, leading him into traps that the sales manager wasn't even aware had ensnared him. Beck managed to restrain his temper at dinner but first thing the next morning stormed into DLJ's offices and emptied both barrels of his anger and frustration into the sales manager, lambasting him for a good half hour before storming out in a rage.

Beck's annoyance over such incidents was exacerbated by dissatisfaction over his pay. His income had bounded upward from $34,923 in 1975 to $54,633 in 1976 and $69,884 in 1977. Along the way, in recognition of his accomplishments (and in response to his threats to leave), Beck was promoted to senior vice president. The promotion and the raises placated Beck without satisfying him. He kept a running tally of his fees and was offended by the knowledge that his compensation in 1977 amounted to only about 13 percent of the $530,000 in revenues (all of it in retainer fees) that he'd generated that year. Lehman Brothers Kuhn Loeb dangled before Beck a lure that a publicly owned company like DLJ couldn't match: the prospect of becoming a partner. In mid-1978, after a few weeks of agonized indecision, Beck accepted Lehman's job offer.

The end of Beck's six-year stint at DLJ was not marked by any farewell parties. Although more perplexed than offended by the Mad Dog's behavior, Jenrette didn't consider him much of a loss. Perhaps only Castle was unambivalently sorry to see him go. While Lane and especially Bromley remained on friendly terms with Beck, they'd reached the stage in their own careers at which they wanted to devote most of their time to their own deals, not Beck's. Beck's M & A colleagues also had tired of his unremitting Mad Dog act. "Jeff saw the world as a series of conquests," Lane recalled. "He was always saying, 'It's war out there.' To an extent, even clients existed to be conquered. Every transaction was a mission. With him, everything was combat. If a meeting went well, it was a great victory. If it went poorly, it was the end of the world."

5

In joining Lehman Brothers Kuhn Loeb in June 1978, Beck was certain that he was taking a giant step toward the fulfillment of the ambitions that had brought him to Wall Street in the first place. He was now a vice president at a storied old line investment bank rich in deal-making tradition and multimillionaire partners, a firm that was a charter member of the Wall Street establishment—and one that had refused even to interview him coming out of business school. It was no wonder that, at first anyway, he felt as if he were being initiated into the deeper mysteries of investment banking, that he was nudging closer to the heart of the matter. More practically, Beck was also happily aware that Lehman Brothers had a list of prime corporate clients as long as its history. After six wearying years of scrambling to create a book of business at DLJ, Beck keenly anticipated the prospect of operating within an investment bank whose very name was a magnet for corporations. His timing, too, seemed auspicious. M & A activity had lifted out of its mid-1970s doldrums and was building steadily to what would become the fourth great merger wave in U.S. history. With Lehman's backing, there was no telling what he could do. It was good-bye DLJ, hello Big Time.

Lehman Brothers was no less an elite Ivy League bastion than DLJ had been, and Beck remained as self-conscious an outsider as ever, though he did make an effort to tone down the histrionics. He disowned his old nickname, Mad Dog, left his gory posters with Pat Bromley (who never put them up) and limited himself to only the occasional howl and growl. It didn't much matter. Compared to the typical Lehman Brothers banker, Beck was as dignified as fireworks. He just didn't fit. Asked about Beck a decade later, one Lehman partner struggled to express his disdain adequately: "He was . . . ummm . . . he, he was . . . a maniac. . . . He wasn't," the partner added, having finally found the clincher, "classically trained, you know."

So potent was Beck's aura of irreverence that he managed to antagonize the majority of his fellow Lehman bankers even as they carefully maintained their distance from him—a distance that was as much a function of the firm's tradition of excessive individualism as of Beck's violations of decorum. Very few people outside of the M & A department ever worked closely or extensively enough with Beck to have a clue as to whether he was competent or not. In terms of professional performance, nothing Beck did or didn't do was egregious enough in its substance to explain his ostracism. What really rankled was his style; his offense lay in lacking the dignity that his peers believed befitting of his—and their—position. It was undeniable: Beck wasn't classically trained. But then M & A was hardly classic banking, was it? In part, the generalist bankers' contempt for Beck reflected their fear and loathing of the department to which he belonged. At every old-line house, the mid-1970s rise of M & A as a top-dollar specialty threatened the preeminence of the old-style generalist. Tellingly, at first Beck was as popular inside Lehman's M & A department as he was unpopular without. "Jeff has a very animated style, which for someone at my level was a lot of fun," recalled Conrad Meyer, a young analyst who worked closely with him. "I'd been thrust into an environment that was grander than I expected and he was a breath of fresh air. He was a cheerleader—Wild Man Jeff. He'd get excited and he'd take you with him into the excitement of his deals."

Beck continued to be more proficient at initiating transactions than completing them, and that left him vulnerable at a firm where large, lucrative deals were almost routine. But what hurt Beck the most at Lehman, the most politically treacherous of investment banks, was his utter, almost willful lack of political finesse. Despite its exalted image, Lehman Brothers was a nasty place, seething with subterranean feuds and rivalries so intense that when they finally exploded to the surface in the early 1980s the firm would be ripped asunder and nearly capsized. Beck was fortunate to get out when he could—though he sure didn't feel lucky at the time. While Beck's stay at Lehman was short, it was traumatic enough to disabuse him of the notion that he would ever be able to fit into an Establishment house.

Lehman Brothers was one of the few Wall Street firms to occupy an entire building of its own—One William Street. The building's extreme narrowness and triangular shape made it look more like a columnar monument than an office building. Its façade, weathered white marble fashioned in the baroque style of the late Italian Renaissance, added to the refined effect. On the third floor was the partners' lounge, with its luxuriant Oriental rugs and dark wood paneling. On the eighth floor was an equally elegant dining room, which contained a huge oval walnut table that, until the mid-1970s, could accommodate all the firm's partners at once. On the top floor was a gymnasium staffed by a full-time masseur. Throughout the building, which Lehman had occupied since 1928, paintings by Goya, Botticelli, Matisse, and other masters graced the walls. Beck moved into a tiny wedge-shaped office on the seventh floor, sharing the space with another young M & A banker, Stephen Waters, with whom he got on well, which was fortunate since the rabbit-warren oddities of One William's architecture forced them to sit practically on top of each other.

Founded in 1850, Lehman had reached its greatest glory under Robert "Bobbie" Lehman, a grandson of one of the founding brothers, who presided as senior partner from the 1920s until his death in 1969. Under his lead, Lehman Brothers became a driving force behind the emergence of commercial aviation, the motion-picture industry, television broadcasting, and department-store retailing. Like other old-line houses, though, Lehman Brothers was ill prepared for the advent of the trader's world. Amid the bear-market chaos of 1973, the firm took crippling trading losses. Fearing that the firm would be bankrupted, a quarter of its partners pulled out, taking their capital with them. As the shadow of impending liquidation lengthened across One William Street, the remaining partners chose as their new leader a man who'd joined the firm just a few weeks before. With Peter G. Peterson, who'd been secretary of commerce under Nixon, as its new chairman, Lehman managed to avoid collapse. Peterson, a former corporate whiz kid, saved Lehman by restructuring it into a corporation equipped with all the modern conveniences: cost accounting, annual budgets, long-range planning, and the like. Bolstered by a market rally, Lehman Brothers was profitable again by 1975, when Peterson appeared on the cover of *Business Week*, looking grimly confident under the headline "BACK FROM THE BRINK COMES LEHMAN BROTHERS." As a former CEO (of Bell & Howell) and former cabinet member, Peterson found himself in great demand as a corporate director and also was welcomed onto the boards of such Establishment bastions as the Council on Foreign Relations. Working diligently to parlay his connections into investment-banking business, Peterson emerged as a rainmaker of the first rank.

Peterson reorganized the firm without altering its peculiarly fractious personality, its "culture of the virtuoso." Bobbie Lehman had gathered around him a stable of talented prima-donna bankers and deliberately pitted them against one another in hopes of extracting maximum performance from them all. The firm's rich lore of intramural conflict included tales of fistfights in the Polo Lounge in Beverly Hills and of the two partners who did not speak for nineteen years, though their desks were five feet apart. Despite incessant squabbling, the system worked because Bobbie Lehman commanded the universal respect of his partners and thus was able to function as peacemaker as well as provocateur. Peterson had no hope of equaling the authority that was his predecessor's birthright, and his self-absorbed, patronizing manner incited rather than soothed disagreements. In Pete Peterson, Lehman had gained not only its savior but its supreme prima donna.

Under Peterson, Lehman Brothers became the last of the major investment banks to set up a full-fledged M & A department. The impetus, however, came not from Peterson or any of the firm's other senior bankers but from Eric Gleacher, an ambitious junior partner who felt certain that Lehman would lose clients to Morgan Stanley and other rivals if it didn't match them with an M & A department of its own. In mid-1977, Gleacher sought an audience with Peterson, who reacted skeptically. "I'm not sure a statistical department makes sense," the chairman said. To Gleacher's amazement, Peterson apparently thought that an M & A department would merely provide statistics and analysis to the generalist bankers. Gleacher explained that the department would not subordinate itself to the corporate-finance partners but would assist them in their M & A transactions while also doing deals of its own. Peterson still didn't seem to quite get it, but he told Gleacher to go ahead if that was what he really wanted. Despite Peterson's lack of enthusiasm, the young banker was satisfied. "I just wanted Peterson to stay out of my way," recalled Gleacher, who immediately invited Waters, one of the firm's most promising junior bankers, to join him. Waters accepted, though the partner in charge of investment banking had advised him that the opposition of the corporate-finance partners would doom the new M & A department to failure.

Gleacher and Waters were indeed cold-shouldered by the generalist banking partners, most of whom had no intention of cooperating with

the new department. But by early 1978, through signing on corporations that were not already Lehman clients, Gleacher and Waters had
generated more business than they and the few assistants who'd joined
them could handle. After interviewing a dozen or so candidates,
Gleacher hired Beck as a vice president. "He had reasonable credentials as a new-business getter and I kind of liked him in the interview,"
Gleacher recalled. Gleacher's opinion of Beck would soar over the next
few months, as he and his new recruit quickly became the best of
friends. Waters, too, got a big charge out of Beck's promotional intensity. "Sometimes Jeff produced and sometimes he didn't produce, but
he always talked a terrific line," Waters recalled. "When he was
bullshitting me, I'd call him on it and we'd both get a good laugh
out of it."

At Lehman, Beck didn't have to devote himself to cold-calling to
the extent he had at DLJ. While assisting Gleacher with his deals,
Beck focused at first on persuading his clients at DLJ to come with
him to Lehman and was primarily occupied thereafter by attending to
the half-dozen companies that stuck loyally with him. Ignoring Lehman's tradition of bristling individualism, Beck also tried to bring
DLJ's team approach with him. In contrast to Gleacher and Waters,
for example, Beck made a point of involving Conrad Meyer, the
twenty-two-year-old analyst, in every aspect of his dealing. In encour-
aging Meyer's eagerness to learn, Beck was indulging his own desire
for an audience as well as a genuine pedagogical instinct.

Before many of his most important meetings with clients, Beck
would sit with Meyer and go over in great detail what he intended to
do and say. Beck then would bring the analyst into the meeting as an
observer who spoke only if spoken to, which wasn't often. During the
many hours he spent watching Beck in action, Meyer came to appreci-
ate the subtlety of his method. "His sessions could go on for hours,"
Meyer recalled. "But he'd carefully orchestrate things so he'd negotiate right to the point where his client was getting restless, and then
he'd call a fifteen-minute break. He seemed to know just when to pull
back and when to push, all based on his understanding of his clients.
He had an uncanny ability to have clients take him on almost as part
of a family. One almost had the feeling that a lot of CEOs looked on
him as a long-lost son."

At Lehman, as at DLJ, the company to which he was principally
devoted was Warner-Lambert. George Hromadko got Beck off to a
good start by departing from his standard procedure in agreeing to put

Lehman on a retainer, graciously pointing out in the contract that he'd decided to do so only because Beck was handling the account. Shortly thereafter, Beck scored another coup, completing the sale of Warner-Lambert's Allercreme and Dubarry lotions business for $12.5 million. Hromadko, who'd expected to get no more than a few million dollars, rewarded Beck with an exceptionally generous fee of $300,000. At Gleacher's urging, Lehman Brothers spent $7,425 to run an ad heralding the transaction in *The Wall Street Journal* and elsewhere. Gleacher sent a copy of the ad, along with a memo lauding his new recruit, to Peterson and a half-dozen other senior partners. "This business and ongoing relationship is the direct result of Jeff Beck's work with the Warner-Lambert Co.," wrote Gleacher. "As you may know, Warner-Lambert is a longstanding Morgan Stanley client." In response, Peterson and other partners dropped brief congratulatory notes to Beck, in whose head danced visions of the Lehman partnership he was certain would soon be his.

While Gleacher was delighted to have hired someone who so quickly seemed to justify his personnel judgment, he also found Beck hugely entertaining. Among the firm's associates, Gleacher was known not for a sense of humor but for marinelike implacability. He had, in fact, spent four years in the marines at bases throughout Europe and the Caribbean and had risen to the rank of lieutenant by the time of his discharge in 1966. Beck was able to bring out the prankster submerged beneath Gleacher's taskmasterly hard shell. While Beck was not above currying favor with his new boss, he genuinely liked Gleacher. He quickly came to share Gleacher's dislike of Peterson, and the two deal men frequently entertained each other with impersonations of the chairman at his name-dropping best. During lulls in the deal action, Gleacher and Beck would make the rounds of the firm's eccentrics in quest of amusement. They periodically inspected the smelly, garbage-strewn office of one aged partner in hopes (never realized) of capturing a rodent. Down the hallway was another elderly partner who seemed to do nothing but telephone his wife in between naps at his desk. Beck and Gleacher liked to stand in his doorway and run through their full repertoire of birdcalls and other barnyard sounds, none of which seemed to disturb his slumbers.

The delight that Beck and Gleacher took in each other was so obvious that when they made their first business trip together to Europe one partner snidely referred to it as a "honeymoon." On that trip, they traveled to the French Riviera to negotiate the sale of Dunbee,

Combex and Marx (DCM), one of the clients Beck had brought from DLJ. CBS Incorporated had just entered the toy business, and Beck had managed to interest the broadcasting giant in acquiring DCM. The negotiations were to take place near Cavalière, where DCM's chairman, Richard Beechum, owned a villa and a large yacht. Beck arrived in France almost giddy with excitement. He'd only been at Lehman just a few weeks and yet here he was, accompanied by his new boss, blowing into the south of France to do a deal while sailing the Mediterranean. Everything was perfect—except that Beechum got cold feet and hemmed and hawed over the smallest points. The CBS people, meanwhile, had a weakness for pompous declarations that frustrated Beck's every attempt to defrost his client's toes. After a few hours of desultory conversation in the cabin of Beechum's yacht, Beck was literally driven off the edge. He looked at Gleacher, raised his eyebrows, and then stood up. He was wearing a swim suit.

"Excuse me," he said. "I'm gonna get a drink."

"I'll join you," said Gleacher, pushing away from the table.

Beck led the way out of the cabin to the aft deck, where he took off his glasses and his watch and set them on a chair. He tilted his head back, let loose with his best Mad Dog howl, and jumped into the sea. Gleacher was right behind him.

Back in the cabin, Beechum and the DCM executives turned and gazed inquisitively at Elizabeth Eveillard, a Lehman vice president who'd come down from the firm's Paris office to help with the negotiations. Fighting back a smile, Eveillard made no attempt at explanation. "Perhaps," she said, "we should take a break." The talks resumed but went nowhere. Eventually, DCM would file for bankruptcy.

The friendship of Gleacher and Beck was sealed by scandal—an insider-trading investigation that would stand as the biggest until the epic scandals of the late 1980s. One of Gleacher's deal makers was a handsome young Romanian immigrant by the name of Adrian Antoniu, who'd begun his M & A career at Morgan Stanley. Almost as soon as he joined Morgan, Antoniu began feeding confidential information about pending deals to a stockbroker whom he'd met at college. The broker bought shares in acquisition targets, sold after the stock had run up on the announcement of the offer, and split the profits with Antoniu. Eight days before Warner-Lambert made a $38-a-share bid for Deseret Pharmaceutical—an M & A assignment Beck would have killed for but didn't get—Antoniu and his confederate bought twelve thousand shares at $27. The two brought others into their scheme, including another young Morgan banker named Jacques Courtois. When Antoniu left Morgan Stanley in 1975, Courtois assumed the role of mole. Antoniu, meanwhile, moved on to Kuhn Loeb and began expropriating inside information on its deals. When Kuhn Loeb was acquired by Lehman, Antoniu became Gleacher's responsibility.

By the time government investigators caught up with Antoniu, he was engaged to be married to Francesca Stanfill, whose father, Dennis Stanfill, was head of Twentieth Century Fox, one of Lehman's oldest clients. The wedding was set for July 1, 1978, and was to be a global high-society extravaganza. Hundreds of guests from all over the world were invited to Venice, where the ceremony would take place in the landmark church of San Pietro di Costello. A few weeks before the wedding, federal officials informed Gleacher that Antoniu was under investigation for insider trading. Gleacher was furious that Antoniu hadn't told him of the investigation, as required by the firm's policy. He immediately called Antoniu on the carpet and insisted that he inform Dennis Stanfill before the wedding. Antoniu promised to do so but didn't. Two days after the ceremony, Beck was working in his office when federal marshals came in and impounded the contents of Antoniu's desk. Gleacher immediately fired Antoniu, whose marriage was annulled after his honeymoon. Later, Antoniu pleaded guilty and received a suspended sentence. Although Antoniu wasn't accused of leaking information about Lehman deals, the publicity was embarrassing to the firm and especially to its M & A men. Beck and Gleacher took it personally indeed, working themselves into a proper rage over what they viewed as Antoniu's betrayal. "It was a bizarre situation that I still associate with Beck," Gleacher said a decade later. "He was my only release and source of humor throughout it."

Although Beck played his family connections a bit less aggressively at Lehman than he had at DLJ, he was so convincing in this role that, ironically, he came to be resented among the firm's younger bankers as an exemplar of the privileged heir who'd risen through string pulling rather than merit. Senator Stone had breakfast with many of the firm's senior partners during a brief Arab-nation blacklist of U.S. investment-banking firms with ties to Israel, Lehman included. For the first time, Beck began making frequent trips to New Orleans to see his other brother-in-law, Marvin Jacobs, husband of William D.'s daughter Dorothy. A native of New Orleans, Jacobs had gone to work for his father-in-law and was put in charge of Royal Castle's expansion into his hometown. In his two decades of managing Royal Castle's fortunes in Louisiana, Jacobs had forged many connections in the New Orleans business community. Not long after Beck joined Lehman Brothers he got a call from Jacobs, who said he had a skiing buddy who was looking for financing to buy a little oil-drilling company.

Jacobs' ski pal, Patrick Taylor, was an associate of John W. Mecom, one of the Southwest's legendary wildcat oil drillers. One of his properties was Circle Bar Drilling Company, which owned and operated a dozen rigs on the Gulf Coast. When Mecom ran short of cash, Taylor and his wife, who also worked for Mecom, negotiated an agreement to buy a controlling interest in Circle Bar on what seemed to Beck to be remarkably advantageous terms. After failing to interest Lehman in investing with Taylor in Circle Bar, Beck decided to take a piece of the buyout himself. The deal was set to close when Beck pulled out, acting on what he later claimed were concerns over the conflict of interest inherent in the Taylors' dual role as employees of Mecom and buyers of his company. (Within a few years, the Taylors sold Circle Bar at a profit huge enough to make them millionaires many times over. Beck was so disappointed that he'd withdrawn from the deal that in time he would claim not only that he had gone ahead and made the investment but that he owned a bigger piece of Circle Bar than the Taylors did.)

While dickering with the Taylors, Beck was also lobbying Jacobs on behalf of Lehman's municipal-bond department. Jacobs was on the board of directors of the New Orleans Home Mortgage Authority, which was planning an $85 million underwriting. While Lehman was virtually certain to be selected as a comanager of the offering, the firm hoped to convince the authority to name it the lead underwriter instead of the New Orleans investment bank to which the assignment customarily went. The competition for the spot was far advanced when Robert Brown, the Lehman banker on the account, heard that Beck was related to Jacobs. Brown called Beck and asked if he could help out. Beck began calling Jacobs almost every day and as a final decision neared put the arm on his brother-in-law in person, spending an entire weekend in New Orleans. Lehman got the assignment, which produced a $250,000 fee.

But at Lehman Beck began bumping up against the limits of his patience in seeking to exploit his relatives. He'd had his fill of prostrating himself before Joe Katz in hopes of getting business out of Papercraft. At Beck's suggestion, Gleacher had included Katz on the mailing list of form letters that he'd sent out announcing Beck's hiring. Katz promptly wrote back with an enthusiasm that he'd never shown over DLJ's approaches. "I remember Bobby [sic] Lehman well years ago, as well as a number of partners," Katz declared. Katz mentioned that Papercraft had "a very active acquisition program afoot" and invited Gleacher "and Jeff Beck, as well," to come to Pittsburgh.

Gleacher sent the Katz letter to Beck with a note scrawled in the margin: "Jeff, What should we do?"

"Impossible to work with," Beck wrote back. "He busted Gabriel deal [an acquisition that Beck had nearly completed for Papercraft while at DLJ]. More of a target."

Meanwhile, in Beck's dealings with his stepfather, the harmony of the DLJ years gradually was supplanted by animosity, with Susan Crane Company as the focus of contention. The gift-wrap company was thriving under its new owners, with cash flow proving more than adequate to repay the money borrowed to finance the acquisition; by 1979 operating earnings had more than tripled since the 1976 buyout, to $1.7 million. Envisioning Susan Crane as the foundation of a diversified corporation not unlike Papercraft, Beck wanted to use the excess cash flow to finance other acquisitions. However, William D. and Larry Singer saw Susan Crane's success as an end in itself and in any event were loath to jeopardize the company's future by releveraging it right away to satisfy Beck's dreams of corporate empire. While pressing particular acquisition prospects on his partners at every opportunity by phone and letter, Beck also made periodic visits to the company's offices in Dallas, where he mystified Robert Macht, its president, and other managers with his operating advice, which varied from month to month and as a rule was tactlessly delivered. To Macht's horror, Beck at one point even talked of resigning from DLJ to join the management of Susan Crane.

As it became apparent that his stepfather was not even tempted by the companies he dangled before him as acquisition bait, Beck abruptly reversed tack and urged the sale of Susan Crane, the value of which had appreciated nicely. However, the Singers saw the company as a long-term investment and were no more compelled to take a quick profit by selling than to incur additional debt in buying. And as majority owners, the Singers had the power to do as they pleased. The frustration Beck felt at being locked into his investment in Susan Crane would persist long after his stepfather and stepbrother had bought him out (at no better than book value) in the early 1980s and apparently inspired him to insist, however implausibly, that the Singers had double-crossed him. As Beck told it, Singer had reneged on a promise to cede control as soon as the transaction closed. Given Beck's deep mistrust of Singer, it seems unlikely that he would have taken his stepfather's word on so important a matter. Yet Beck was unable to produce any documents to support his claim.

Early one morning in 1979, Jenny McGlannan was making preparations to leave a little hotel in Camden, Maine, packing up her car for a drive to the airport in Portland. With her was her fiancé, who'd just proposed the night before. As Jenny was packing her car, she saw a vaguely familiar figure walking up the road toward the hotel. When he was about twenty yards away, his features came into sharp focus. She almost fainted with surprise: It was Jeff Beck, her old beau. She hadn't seen him in years.

"What are you doing here?" McGlannan croaked as he approached.

"Hi, Jenny," he said, cheerfully ignoring her question. He walked up to her friend and stuck out his hand.

"Hello," he said. "I'm Jeff Beck. I'd like to congratulate you. You're marrying a wonderful lady."

McGlannan had no more idea how Beck had found her in Camden than she had in the summer of 1966 when they were college sophomores and she'd bumped into him brooding in Hamlet's Castle in Copenhagen. And how could he possibly have known that she'd gotten engaged the night before? McGlannan was too stunned to ask for an explanation and Beck didn't offer one. After a few minutes of small talk, Beck said good-bye and walked back down the road, disappearing into the morning fog.

Despite a bounty of clients and a profusion of ideas, Beck would complete only about a half-dozen small deals in his time at Lehman. Beck's low productivity was partly a function of his rather old-fashioned approach to investment banking. Like the gentleman bankers and in conspicuous contrast to Gleacher and most other M & A men, Beck's overriding interest was in cultivating close, long-term relationships with corporate clients, trusting that someday they would redound to his and his firm's financial benefit. One virtue of this approach was that Beck could draw on ever-expanding knowledge of his companies and their industries. While Beck was moving beyond the typical trader's superficiality of knowledge, and though he was admirably constant in his motives, he remained self-defeatingly unsystematic in his day-to-day dealings, ricocheting around the world like a human pinball, bouncing excitedly from one idea to another in pursuit of the Big Deal. At DLJ, Beck had been able to count on Mike Rosenthal or Fred Lane or Pat Bromley to keep his deals on track while he went chasing new opportunities. Under Lehman's individualistic system, each banker was responsible for seeing his own transactions through from beginning to end. Too often, Beck's deals died somewhere in the middle.

Beck did come heartbreakingly close to brokering one deal so huge that it would have eclipsed the sum total of his failures. It involved Brascan Limited, an idiosyncratic Canadian company that owned large interests in mining, brewing, utilities, and real estate. Beck met senior executives of Brascan, a Lehman client of long standing, at a lunch at the firm and came away with the feeling that here was a company amenable to selling out. The CEO and the president were getting on in years and, it seemed to Beck, were unwilling to retire only because they had so little faith in the executives positioned to succeed them. Something had to be done, if only because Brascan soon would have to figure out how to reinvest a huge cash payment it was due from selling an interest in one of its properties.

After spending a week or so nosing around Brascan, Beck called Byron Radaker, the CEO of Congoleum, one of the companies he'd worked with at DLJ. Beck knew that Radaker was flush with cash and eager to make a large acquisition. "I've got the craziest deal for you," he said. "But I have the feeling that it might just be a perfect fit."

It was indeed. As Radaker looked over the Brascan documents Beck sent him, he could hardly keep from drooling over its vast portfolio of undervalued assets. Radaker and Brascan's top brass hit it off immediately and the negotiations rapidly moved toward climax. Agreement was reached on a price of $1.5 billion. Radaker expected his acquisition of Brascan to propel Congoleum's stock from $20 to the neighborhood of $80 a share while doubling the company's revenues and tripling its profits. One final dinner was scheduled at the Links Club in New York City, at which Radaker was joined by William Kyle, who still held the title of chairman though Radaker had supplanted him in running Congoleum. "I figured that we'd come out of the dinner and tell the lawyers to start drawing up the papers," Radaker said. "But Kyle made a total ass of himself."

Kyle had been kept posted on the progress of the talks with Brascan and had said he favored the deal. But he had had too much to drink at the Links Club and became quite truculent, insisting in slurred words that Brascan should lower its price. Radaker kicked Kyle under the table but to no avail. Merely appalled at first at Kyle's behavior, the Brascan executives grew angry as he persisted. Beck did his best to smooth things over, but Kyle would not be stilled and Beck could do little more than fight back nausea as the billion-dollar deal that he'd thought was in the bag was sabotaged by a man who was in the bag. As Beck had feared, Brascan immediately ended its talks with Congoleum (and later was scooped up by the billionaire Bronfman family).

Shortly thereafter, a Lehman stock analyst wrote a bullish report on Congoleum, arguing that its stock was undervalued in the market by at least 50 percent. George Heyman, a senior Lehman partner, passed the report along to Gleacher with a note suggesting that Congoleum be shopped as a candidate for acquisition. "It is our view that the present management will not encourage friendly discussions," he advised Gleacher. "We would be inclined to the view that a hostile tender will be required."

Beck was horrified when Gleacher showed him the memo, and hoped to hell that Radaker wouldn't get wind of it. Here he was trying to work with Congoleum at the same time another Lehman banker was marking the company for a raid. Beck wrote a tactful memo in response to Heyman, pointing out that Congolcum was likely to make a major acquisition in 1979 and that Lehman had a good shot at representing the company. He also took issue with the senior partner's contention that Radaker was likely to oppose any attempt to acquire Congoleum, arguing that he and Eddy Nicholson, the company's president, "could be approached on a friendly basis since they have completed the turnaround at Congoleum."

Almost on the very day that Congoleum retained Lehman to do a comprehensive analysis of all its M & A options, Radaker began confidential talks with investment bankers from a rival house, First Boston, about a leveraged buyout. When he learned of the talks, Beck accused Radaker of double-crossing him, as a leveraged buyout had been high on his own list of recommendations to Congoleum. However, Beck didn't learn of Radaker's alliance with First Boston until they had virtually completed the deal, by which time it was too late for him to do anything but curse and moan. The announcement of the $461 million leveraged buyout of Congoleum—at the time the largest LBO ever—left Beck almost catatonic with disappointment. Adding injury to insult, Radaker infuriated Beck by refusing to pay him for the work that he'd done for Congoleum before the LBO.

While Beck struggled, the M & A department as a whole was progressing nicely—so nicely, in fact, that Peterson's initial indifference to its existence gave way, in Gleacher's view, to a desire to horn in on its success. "Peterson became our biggest competitor," Gleacher said. "He started thinking he was Felix Rohatyn or something." One day, after finishing a particularly newsworthy transaction, Gleacher got a call from Peterson, who suggested that in the future he be alerted in advance when the department had a large deal to announce. Gleacher made no attempt to mask his suspicion of Peterson's motives. "Well, we all want to help the firm, don't we, Pete?" he snapped, and hung up.

Peterson retaliated against Gleacher's refusal to alert him as requested by directing the M & A deals that came his way by virtue of his far-flung contacts to partners outside Gleacher's group, particularly to Stephen Schwarzman, a brash Harvard graduate in his early thirties. In 1978, for example, Peterson handed Schwarzman the plum assignment of developing an acquisition program for RCA Corporation, one of Lehman's most important clients. Peterson, who himself was a director of RCA, also skewed the firm's deal publicity away from Gleacher to Schwarzman, who in January 1980 was featured in a *New York Times* profile entitled "Stephen Schwarzman, Lehman's Merger Maker." Not until the night before it appeared was Gleacher informed of the piece, which made nary a mention of the M & A department. There were, however, laudatory quotes from Peterson and—to Schwarzman's retrospective embarrassment—one from the future felon Ivan Boesky, who said that Schwarzman was "the most imaginative and creative of the new investment bankers on Wall Street."

While Beck abhorred Peterson—and Schwarzman, as well—his high opinion of Gleacher deteriorated as he came to realize the extent to which the M & A chief, too, was absorbed by political gamesmanship. "Eric would spend countless hours plotting about who he was going to have lunch with that day or who he was going to try to cut out of a meeting with a client," said Beck, who nonetheless was often a willing participant in these schemes. Protecting the M & A department's interests was one thing, but Beck couldn't abide the way Gleacher drove Meyer and the other young bankers even when there was no real deadline pressure to justify it. Meyer practically lived at One William Street. One Saturday night, he and another analyst were working on a report when their office filled with smoke. The two of them ran down the stairs as pieces of flaming scaffolding clattered down the elevator shaft, which had caught fire. They returned two hours later to find One William plastered with warning signs: "DO NOT ENTER BY ORDER OF THE NEW YORK CITY FIRE DEPARTMENT." Meyer and his colleague hesitated. "We calculated which was the greater danger: not having the books ready for Eric or explaining to a fireman why I was crawling around on the floor collecting charred pieces of paper," Meyer recalled. "We went back to work."

Never one to keep his opinions to himself, Beck repeatedly confronted Gleacher. Caught up in a bitter internecine struggle in which his own professional survival was at stake, Gleacher grew increasingly annoyed not only with Beck's insubordinate attitude but his inability to rack up major transactions. As the novelty of Beck's presence wore off, Gleacher no longer cared to hear about his bad breaks, near misses, and great expectations. "You've got to become much more transactional," Gleacher would tell Beck over and over.

To which Beck would repeatedly respond, "What does that mean, Eric? What the hell does that really mean?"

One thing it meant to Gleacher was not devoting so much time to projects unlikely to provide swift reward. "Overkill was not a word in Jeff's vocabulary at the time," Gleacher recalled. "He'd absolutely smother a situation with attention whether it was real or not. If left to his own devices, he would have spent ninety percent of his time on Warner-Lambert alone. In this business you have to strategize the fees, and Jeff wasn't far enough along to do that on his own. He came to me for that. In fact, he was taking up so much of my time that he was driving me crazy."

Another aspect of Gleacher's definition of "transactional" was the preemptively generous bid—that is, he would urge his clients to make an offer high enough to scare off other prospective bidders. Beck, on the other hand, was equally emphatic in his belief that it was better for a client to lose a bidding contest than to overpay for a company. "Almost every day we had this same disagreement," Beck recalled. "It was like Eric was always saying, 'Look, the sun is out,' and I was saying, 'No, you're wrong. It's the middle of the night.'" Aside from an occasional volley of shouting from Gleacher's office, only through the subtlest signs were the M & A department's other members alerted to

the widening rift between Beck and his boss. Smiles segued quickly
into frowns, doors were left closed instead of open, trips were made
alone or endured in silence. Eventually, push came to shove over the
quintessential Lehman issue: Who gets the credit?

Shortly before Beck started at Lehman, a stock analyst at the firm
had written a report on National Nederlanden, the largest insurer in
Holland, highlighting its desire to make an acquisition in the U.S.
After reading the report, Gleacher decided to fly to Amsterdam and
make a pitch for National Nederlanden's business. He and the company's president hit it off, and Gleacher was hired to help plan a bid
for the Life Insurance Company of Georgia. In the fall of 1978, Life
of Georgia's board formally rebuffed National Nederlanden, refusing
even to discuss a preliminary offer that amounted to twice its current
market value. To Gleacher, the board's opposition seemed to end the
matter, since the family that had founded Life of Georgia held enough
shares to doom a hostile tender offer. He told National Nederlanden to
look elsewhere. But Beck, whose interest had been aroused in working
with Gleacher on the proposal, spent a few more weeks nosing around
Life of Georgia and uncovered discord within the family. He kept
after Gleacher until he resumed working with National Nederlanden.
In early 1979, four months after the first bid, the Dutch company
made a second offer, which Life of Georgia's board also summarily
rejected. However, with the assistance of a well-placed Atlanta banker
they'd secretly hired as a consultant, Gleacher and Beck orchestrated a
series of behind-the-scenes meetings through which they eventually
managed to win the support of a dissident wing of the family. Through
key family members, Lehman Brothers was able to exert enough pressure on Life of Georgia to cause the board to capitulate. In mid-1979,
National Nederlanden acquired Life of Georgia for $361 million and
paid Lehman a hefty $2.6 million.

In looking back at the National Nederlanden deal a decade later,
Gleacher graciously acknowledged Beck's contribution. "If not for
Jeff's pushing me, I would never have spent the time needed to get
that deal done," he said. At the time, though, he was not inclined to
share the credit—in part because Peterson was trying to claim the deal
as his own. When Beck was informed in the fall of 1979 that he would
be receiving an annual bonus far smaller than he believed he deserved,
he went to Gleacher and angrily demanded a deal-by-deal itemization.
He was no happier after Gleacher finished reading through the list of
his credits.

"What about National Nederlanden?" Beck demanded.

"What do you mean, National Nederlanden?" Gleacher responded sharply. "That was *my* deal."

Beck saw red. "Oh, yeah," he yelled. "Why do you think I took all those trips to Atlanta? The fucking fun of it? I can't believe this, man. Every deal is your deal, isn't it?"

Gleacher didn't say anything. He didn't need to, for Beck could read the fury in his eyes plainly enough. As Beck walked down the hallway from Gleacher's office to his own, he heard a door slam behind him.

As his conflicts with Gleacher intensified, Beck's second marriage was coming unraveled. Moving from the Upper West Side to the New Jersey countryside had placated Rosemary, but at the cost of exacerbating her basic complaint: that she'd been widowed by Wall Street. She saw even less of her husband than before as his commuting time lengthened from forty-five minutes round-trip on the subway to nearly four hours by train. Meanwhile, Rosemary liked less and less of what she saw in Jeff as his obsession with Wall Street deepened. "Since I'd met him, he'd become a lot less carefree and more driven than was necessary," recalled Rosemary, who repeatedly urged her husband to shift careers. "I could see him getting caught up in the material part of it. I never wanted a mansion, but Jeff did."

With each year, too, there were more unexplained absences from home, more phone calls at odd hours, more assorted weirdness. Rosemary was not one to pry and accepted the only explanation Jeff offered —that he was enmeshed in sensitive government-related work that he was not permitted to discuss. "There was just a sort of air of mystery around him that I never put my nose in," Rosemary said. "I never questioned too much. It was hinted that he couldn't tell me right then, but if I wanted, one day I'd find out what was going on."

"Just give me a few more years," he'd tell Rosemary—and himself, as well. Just a few more years and he'd start making big money doing big deals. Just a few more years, he promised, and then he'd retire from deal making and leave Wall Street for good. In the meantime, though, Jeff lobbied Rosemary to move back into Manhattan with him —this time to the Upper East Side, where most of the big Wall Streeters lived and played. But Rosemary would have none of it. To her, the idea of abandoning a peaceful, reclusive life in the country for the whirl of moneyed Manhattan was unthinkable. To her, even a night out in the city was an ordeal. She stubbornly refused to consider returning to New York.

This impasse was inflated into full-blown crisis when Jeff told Rosemary in the fall of 1979 that he thought he was falling in love with a woman who worked for the advertising agency that handled the Lehman Brothers account. She was blond and beautiful—"a modest bimbo," in the description of one of Beck's colleagues. Jeff moved out of the house in New Jersey into an apartment in New York City. After his blowout with Gleacher over his year-end bonus, Beck was invited by his new paramour on a trip to Taos, New Mexico. Two weeks away was enough to convince Beck that the time had come to leave Lehman —a realization speeded along by a fortuitously timed telephone call from a recruiter, who asked if he was interested in founding an M & A department at Oppenheimer & Company. Beck promised to think about it and he did—endlessly.

Shortly after Beck returned to Lehman from New Mexico, Gleacher summoned him to his office. "Well, I hate to tell you this, but I'm going to have to let you go."

Beck had gone into Gleacher's office prepared to resign, but getting fired was another matter. "You can't, asshole. You don't have the authority," he yelled. "And anyway I *quit!*"

In discussing the Lehman stint with me, Beck at first sought solace inside a lie or two—chief among them, the claim that he had been a partner in the firm. Later, he amended this assertion to the claim that Sheldon Gordon, the head of investment banking, had guaranteed him that he'd be made a partner in a year while assuring him that Gleacher did not have the power to fire him. As Beck told it, this guarantee was kept secret from Gleacher. Unhappily for Beck, neither Gordon nor anyone else that I spoke with at Lehman could recall such a guarantee. It doesn't much matter either way. The overriding fact was that Beck had failed at Lehman Brothers—his second Wall Street firm—even as he was failing at his second marriage. As the 1970s ended and the era of the Big Deal was dawning, Beck had nowhere to go but up.

6

On October 8, 1979, Beck was thrilled to see his name in *The New York Times* for the first time. The story was only a few paragraphs long, but he was its sole subject. "Oppenheimer & Co., the securities firm, has established its first mergers and acquisitions department and has named Jeffrey P. Beck as its head," it read. "The 33-year-old Mr. Beck has spent nine and a half years in this field with Donaldson, Lufkin & Jenrette and, most recently, with Lehman Brothers Kuhn Loeb." Beck marveled gratefully at the *Times*'s restraint. How dignified it all sounded—*Mister* Beck, indeed. No mention of Mad Dog antics or screaming matches with Gleacher. Beck had no idea where the bit about nine and a half years had come from. Even if you threw in his bond-brokering stint at DLJ, Beck's Wall Street experience still added up to no more than seven years. He sure liked the sound of it, though; only thirty-three years old and already he had nearly a decade of deal making to his credit—or so said the *Times*, which even allowed him space for a little sales pitch: "I have over a $1 million budget to hire the best people we can possibly get. Companies coming to us will want help in strategic planning, as opposed to our being just mechanics on a transaction."

Although Beck's contract negotiations with Oppenheimer had dragged on long past the point where the flow of paychecks from Lehman ceased, Beck hung tough and succeeded in cutting a handsome deal for himself: a base salary of $150,000 a year, about one third more than he was making at Lehman. Moreover, the M & A department would be allowed to keep 25 percent of the profits it generated, to be distributed as bonuses at Beck's discretion. In effect, M & A would act as a partnership within a partnership. To Beck's delight, he would be able to function as his own boss to a far greater extent than either Mike Rosenthal at DLJ or Eric Gleacher at Lehman had. His abrupt rise in status from M & A Indian to chief went a long way toward salving his wounded pride.

Beck wasn't Oppenheimer's first choice. The job had been dangled before bankers at every one of the top M & A houses—Morgan Stanley; First Boston; Goldman, Sachs; Kidder, Peabody; and Smith Barney among them. The first Lehman banker approached was Gleacher, not Beck. "I don't think that even most people in M & A knew who Jeff was at the time," said Hobson Brown, a Russell Reynolds & Company headhunter hired by Oppenheimer. In the end, none of the established deal men would foresake the shelter of hundred-year-old franchises and step out into the void, though Oppenheimer certainly got their attention by offering a profit cut—an arrangement unheard-of at the old-line houses. On the other hand, 25 percent of nothing is still nothing. Opco had no M & A clients and its existing list of corporate-finance clients was both brief and studded with infamous names, most notably DeLorean Motors, which used Opco to help finance the development of its ill-fated platinum sports car.

Hob Brown had first heard Beck's name from an investment banker at Goldman Sachs who remembered the Mad Dog favorably from his days at DLJ. In checking around the Street, Brown found a sharp divergence of opinion on Beck. His supporters described him as creative, energetic, even charismatic. But in the majority view, he was exasperating—temperamental, wacky, overbearing at times—though even his most acerbic critics had to admit that he had a talent for bringing in business. In his interviews, Beck tried to come across as confidently nonchalant, staking out the position that he'd always wanted to try his hand at building a business from scratch but had no intention of sticking around once it was successfully established— which should take no more than four or five years. In the end, Oppenheimer's choice of Beck was based on the conviction that, for better or worse, he would make things happen.

By this time, Beck had moved into an apartment in a cooperative building at 163 East Eighty-first Street, paying $100,000—a pittance by Upper East Side standards—for three rooms on the basement floor. The undersized windows in the oversized closet that passed for a living room were fitted with wooden slats and admitted little light even on the sunniest days. Beck's only view was of pairs of legs striding down Eighty-first Street. He furnished the apartment with a bare minimum of furniture and a profusion of antique wooden duck decoys. By the time of his separation from Rosemary, Jeff had amassed a flock of a few hundred of these birds, about a hundred of which he brought to his new apartment. This worked out to one duck per five square feet, a population density approximating that of a wild-game reserve. The surreal effect could be quite unnerving to first-time visitors, especially those who arrived after sundown and were confronted by a hundred pairs of beady duck eyes glowing in the dark. Beck would do his best to set his guest at ease.

"Welcome," he'd whisper, "to the Bates Motel."

Beck could have afforded a much grander place, having listed a net worth of $1.6 million on his application for a mortgage loan to buy the Eighty-first Street apartment. To be sure, his wealth, like that of many a new eighties millionaire, was as much a product of accounting technique as cash in the bank. Beck's principal asset was his thirty thousand shares of Susan Crane. As the company's operating earnings had risen smartly, the book value of Beck's shares had jumped to $600,000 from $75,000. However, the market value of Susan Crane stock was not so reliably determined since, the company being privately held, its shares were not traded on any exchange. On the basis of comparisons to the company's competitors, Susan Crane's auditors assigned a market value of about twice book—or $1.25 million for Beck's shares, for which he'd paid $1 each. While not an unreasonable estimate, it was a price not easily obtained in cash. Indeed, when Beck finally convinced his stepfather to buy his shares he was paid a price exactly equal to book value.

Solely on the basis of his Oppenheimer salary, Beck could have financed the purchase of a residence three times as expensive as the place on Eighty-first Street. But to what end? Beck loved his dark little cave of an apartment, which he nicknamed the Bunker. With the help of a cleaning woman who came once a week, he kept the place immaculate. Beck had always lived with a wife or a roommate, but the Bunker was his own place and he could not have been more absurdly proud of it had he been a nineteen-year-old college kid moving into his first off-campus apartment. Beck luxuriated in the contrast between the humbleness of his quarters and his burgeoning net worth, and used the Bunker as a Rorschach test of the women he dated after his separation from Rosemary. "I was trying to find out if they liked me for who I was instead of what I did," Beck said.

In response to the inevitable question, "What do you do?" Beck had a stock answer: "I'm a comptroller for the Acme Cleaning Company."

If there was a second or third date, Beck would admit to being the head of mergers and acquisitions at Oppenheimer. It hardly mattered. "They didn't believe me anyway," Beck said.

Although the Bunker was only a few blocks from Elaine's, the trendy nightspot famed as a celebrity hangout, Beck never once went there. He wasn't keen on bars in general, much preferring to invite women to the Bunker for a dinner delivered from Pinocchio, the Italian restaurant directly across the street. Beck was so regular a customer that the staff of Pinocchio treated his living room as if it were an adjunct of the restaurant. About seven-thirty a waiter would come by to set the table and open a bottle of wine. Then came the first of three separate courses that Beck had specially ordered in advance from his buddy Al the chef. Beck had a similar arrangement with Parma, which was just around the corner on Third Avenue. "I was a sort of neighborhood king," Beck recalled.

In some respects, Oppenheimer and Donaldson, Lufkin & Jenrette were upstart twins. The only firms among Wall Street's twenty-five largest that had been founded after World War II, both Oppenheimer and DLJ had risen by the same basic strategy, using sophisticated investment research to build an institutional-brokerage business. And like Dan Lufkin at DLJ, Jack Nash and his alter ego, Leon Levy, had begun dabbling in deal investing long before it was fashionable, making millions of dollars for themselves and their partners through dozens of leveraged-buyout and venture-capital transactions. In some ways, though, DLJ and Opco were opposites. Oppenheimer's roots were as emphatically Jewish as DLJ's were WASPish. And while the principals of DLJ were rebel reformers who took their firm public in high-profile defiance of the Wall Street Establishment, Nash and Levy were secretive, almost paranoid, inside operators.

Officially, Nash was responsible for Oppenheimer's brokerage and trading operations while Levy ran Oppenheimer's mutual funds and its small corporate-finance department. In practice, though, Nash and Levy collaborated in everything. Levy was the stranger-looking and more affable of the two. Like Nash, he was stubby, no more than five foot five, with a thick shock of jet-black hair. He wore thick glasses with heavy black rims and constantly smoked a pipe. A stroke had left Levy a bit goggle-eyed and unable to direct his left eye straight ahead. He could have played the mad scientist in a horror film without benefit of makeup. Levy was indeed a dreamer and a schemer, who once was described by a colleague as "the partner in charge of outer space." Almost everyone at Opco had a Leon Levy story. John Sanzo, who left First Boston to join Beck's M & A department, had his Levy moment his first day at Opco. Seeing Levy alone at a table in the dining room, Sanzo walked up and introduced himself.

"Mr. Levy, I'm John Sanzo," he said.

Levy gave him a look of what seemed to be deep mistrust. "How do you know that I don't already know who you are?" he said.

Steve Robert, who eventually succeeded Nash as CEO of the firm, once went with Levy to a black-tie reception at a mutual-fund sales conference at a New York hotel. They rented a room and hung their tuxedos in the bathroom. While Robert was out on an errand, Levy got dressed and went down to the reception. Robert, who is a good six inches taller than Levy, returned and put on his pants. They fit like Bermuda shorts. He called down to the ballroom and had Levy paged.

"Leon," Robert said, "is everything all right?"

"I'd say it's a pretty good party," Levy said.

"Look at your pants, Leon."

He looked. "Oh, my God," he moaned, and hung up.

Levy had a mind that continually spewed forth money-making schemes, some of which were ingenious and others simply berserk. For all his otherworldliness, Levy was a relentless champion of his ideas, no matter how half-baked—a man, it was said around the firm, with "a whim of iron." He would hammer away at skeptical subordinates until they did whatever was necessary to *prove* his latest hunch right or wrong. Robert, who started out as a mutual-fund manager, was more or less required to ride to the office each morning from the Upper East Side with Levy in his chauffeured sedan. "A couple mornings I said I'd rather take the subway and Leon just laughed," Robert said. "He saw it as an opportunity to give me the benefit of forty more minutes of his views on stocks."

Levy mesmerized almost everyone but Nash. No one mesmerized Nash. His entire being was focused on determining the shortest and surest route between today's investment and tomorrow's killing. If Nash couldn't see a profit in it, he wasn't interested and he wouldn't waste time explaining himself. If something could be said in three words, he'd use two and a half and leave his meaning hanging a bit. He managed through intimidation. At times, Nash's intensity had the same disconcerting effect as Levy's distractedness. A slight arch of his alarmingly bushy black eyebrows or a cryptic comment underscored by a Cheshire-cat smile usually sufficed, though every now and then Nash would bark out an order or hurl an ashtray someone's way.

Perfectly matched misfit-savants, Nash and Levy fashioned Oppenheimer from humble clay into a first-rate brokerage in the 1960s and then reinvented the firm amid the market turbulence of the 1970s. While DLJ equivocated and many lesser houses disappeared after commission rates on stock trades were deregulated, Oppenheimer decisively shifted its focus from institutional investors to the wealthiest and most sophisticated retail clientele—the "high-net-worth individual," in Wall Street lingo. Opco hired traders and investment bankers by the dozen to supply its expanded force of brokers with such exotica as managed commodity accounts and limited partnerships in venture capital, oil and gas, real estate, and equipment leases. Prestige without profit held no appeal for Nash and Levy, who were comfortable inhabiting the shadowy fringes of respectability. Oppenheimer was forever pushing the limits of the acceptable, doing regular battle with government regulators and private lawyers. Oppenheimer's distinctive blend of visionary savvy and blunt avarice was tellingly evident in the firm's mid-1970s pioneering of its version of the leveraged buyout.

Ira J. Hechler, the principal architect of Oppenheimer's LBO strategy, devised an ingenious technique for acquiring small family-controlled companies that had been pummeled by the stock-market debacle of 1973–1974, the effect of which was to triple or even quadruple the income of the present owners while enabling the buyers to pay book value or less. One night at dinner, Hechler explained his plan to Levy and Nash, who quickly tumbled to its beauty and cut a deal: Hechler would find companies and negotiate their purchase while Oppenheimer handled the financing and legal work. Hechler would get a one-third interest in the new company that would be created to take possession of the acquired corporate assets while the remaining two thirds would go to Oppenheimer and its clients. And so it was that Hechler became Opco's "director for special acquisitions."

Hechler hit the jackpot on his first deal, acquiring an Ohio supermarket chain called Big Bear Stores for $42 million (it was later resold for $350 million). Hechler completed two more buyouts in 1976—each valued at less than $10 million—and then went deal crazy. In 1977 alone Oppenheimer announced agreements to acquire eleven companies for a total of $215 million. Naturally, this barrage attracted the attention not only of other Wall Street deal promoters, who began imitating Hechler's method, but also of the Securities and Exchange

Commission, which blocked Opco's acquisition of Spartek Incorporated, charging Spartek's top officers with trying to cut a sweetheart deal.

Refusing to take the hint, Hechler immediately went back to doing buyouts at a frenetic pace until mid-1979, when the SEC came down on him with full force, accusing him of trading in the stocks of twenty-seven companies at the time he was negotiating with them and thus privy to information not available to other investors. By the standards of the time, this was a whopper insider-trading scandal. But because the judicial precedents against Hechler were fuzzy, the SEC offered an out-of-court settlement. Hechler signed the usual consent decree, promising never again to do what he'd done without admitting that he'd done it. He also had to surrender $145,263 in trading profits. The government found no evidence that Oppenheimer was party to Hechler's scheme, though the firm was reprimanded for failing to supervise him. Hechler had done his trading through secret accounts at another brokerage house. "I was very upset," Levy said. "I had to wonder if Ira really was a black hat after all." Wonder though he might, Levy did not sever Opco's ties to Hechler until the IRS persuaded Congress a few months later to outlaw the conversion of a business corporation into an investment company—invalidating a critical component of Hechler's technique. The jig was finally up. Hechler resigned as acquisitions director of Opco, but within six months he had thought up a completely different but equally novel LBO technique and went on to make more money at his own firm, Ira Hechler & Associates, than he ever did with Oppenheimer. Hechler never worked with Opco again. However, in the spirit of forgive and accrue, Nash and Levy invested as individuals in several of Hechler's deals, including an astoundingly lucrative buyout of Leslie Fay in 1983. Whatever his hat color, Hechler was a money-maker, and in the end that was what really seemed to count with Nash and Levy.

Nash and Levy had made their decision to start an M & A department just as the government was putting the screws to Hechler. As the scandal garnered newsprint, it would have been futile to try to reposition as an M & A adviser anyone who'd had any connection to Hechler's LBO program. Nash and Levy needed someone who'd worked at a respectable mainline investment bank, someone untainted by scandal—someone like Beck, who insisted that he would not join Opco if it meant working with Hechler. Although Nash assured him that he need not have any involvement with Hechler, Beck joined the firm harboring doubts about its reputation. In the first news story about his M & A department, Beck was quoted as saying that Oppenheimer was seen as "creative, shrewd—but of course ethical and moral." Beck made this statement more in hope than belief.

However, his immediate problem upon joining Oppenheimer was the firm's corps of 350 stockbrokers, many of whom had clients who owned substantial companies and needed advice on an M & A transaction. If a broker could generate a fee by providing deal counsel, Nash and Levy were not about to stand in his way. By the late 1970s, many an Opco broker had managed to make a lucrative sideline out of M & A advisory work. This surge in deal activity among Opco's brokerage clients was instrumental in convincing Nash and Levy to set up a full-fledged M & A department, the original purpose of which was not to supplant the brokers but to augment their efforts. Beck had other ideas. Every Monday morning, Nash and Levy convened a breakfast meeting known informally as the merger committee, which consisted of about a dozen brokers, analysts, and bankers interested in brainstorming deal ideas. Beck began his first week on the job by attending the merger committee meeting and was appalled by what he heard. "They had General Motors acquiring Ford, Eli Lilly buying Merck, fantasyland stuff," Beck recalled. "These guys were stockbrokers who thought they were big deal guys."

At the end of the meeting, Beck stood up. "Gentlemen," he said. "I've been hired to start a professional merger group. This will be the last meeting of the committee. Can I have your files, please."

A howl of protest went up as Beck walked out of the room. Within minutes, he was summoned to Nash's office. According to Beck's recollection, Nash was furious. It was the first of many showdowns with his M & A chief. When Nash stopped yelling, Beck pointed out that allowing each broker to sign clients to merger-fee agreements created an enormous open-ended legal liability for Opco that could cripple the firm if something went wrong—as was inevitable, Beck argued, when deals were being done by amateurs. Beck also said that he'd quit on the spot if he wasn't given authority over all the firm's M & A advisory work. Apparently, the merger committee never met again. Score one for Beck, who, while keeping an eye peeled for vengeful brokers, turned his attention to hiring some help.

Beck began with a temporary secretary, some file cabinets, and two dingy rooms in the back alleys of Oppenheimer's headquarters at 1 New York Plaza. Working with Hob Brown, he began scouting the

available talent. He knew that he didn't have the money or the reputation to attract big-name bankers, and he was unable to persuade any of
his former colleagues from Lehman or DLJ to join him. Deciding to
launch a more systematic search, he required all applicants to submit
to a battery of psychological tests administered by a Princeton, New
Jersey, bureau that Oppenheimer had used in the past. Beck got the
idea from Nash, who'd had him take the same test before hiring him
as M & A chief. Beck enjoyed taking the test and was perversely proud
at having conformed to the psychological profile of the driven overachiever motivated by anger. "Normal is overrated," Beck said.
"Wackos make the best deal men."

However, Beck's first hire, a young lawyer with the epic name of
Byron Hero, didn't seem to conform to his criteria at all. The son of an
eminent New York City surgeon and a Ph.D. historian, Hero came
complete with a law degree from Columbia and all the trimmings:
square-jawed good looks, social graces, a great tennis game, and fluency
in French. He'd developed an interest in M & A deals as an associate
at Winthrop, Stimson, Putnam & Roberts, one of the stodgiest of the
white-shoe Wall Street law firms. Unbeknownst to Beck, the Russell
Reynolds agency had first tempted Hero with jobs at two more prestigious investment banks, Morgan Stanley and Kidder, Peabody. But
Hero had had his fill of of stuffy institutions. He dreamed of setting up
his own M & A firm and thought Oppenheimer would be a good place
to learn the financial side of deal making. Nash especially was keen on
Hero, whom he saw as the kind of person who could help Opco cultivate a more benign image. A senior partner at Winthrop, Stimson
gave Hero a glowing recommendation, leaving Beck with no defensible
reason not to hire him. He was not prepared to look Hero in the eye
and say, "I'm sorry, Byron, but you flunked the wacko test."

In Beck's opinion, his next two recruits aced the test. At thirty,
John Sanzo had a gilt-edged résumé. Sanzo had graduated from
Brown, picked up an MBA at Harvard, and gone on to First Boston,
where, after spending five years in corporate finance and M & A, he
was bored shitless.

"What do you want to do?" Beck asked Sanzo during his job
interview.

"I want to go out and find some deals of my own, out of the mainstream," Sanzo replied. "What do you want to do?"

"John," said Beck, launching into one of his favorite recruiting spiels, "what I want to do is make you rich. You and I are going to do some big deals together."

A few minutes into the interview, Beck offered Sanzo a job. Sanzo accepted, on one condition: that he not start until after the first of the year (in about six months). That way, he wouldn't have to inform First Boston of his decision to leave until his year-end bonus check was safely in hand. (Even after he received the check, Sanzo was still so worried that the firm would retaliate for his defection that he ran to the issuing bank and had it certified. He joined Opco the next day.)

During Sanzo's last week at First Boston, a Lehman Brothers banker named Philip Ean Cohen moved his belongings into the empty office next door. Sanzo knew Cohen slightly and asked him what he was doing at First Boston. "Waiting to go to Oppenheimer," Cohen said. Sure enough, a month after Sanzo joined the Jeff Beck Group, Cohen again moved his stuff into the office next to Sanzo's.

With his tailored Savile Row suits, Oxford accent, and patronizing manner, Cohen seemed the quintessential Wall Street sophisticate— very polished, very international. In actuality, though, he was Australian, not English, and his diffidence masked extreme aggressiveness. He'd arrived at Harvard Business School missing many teeth, which he'd lost as an undersized but indomitable rugby player. Cohen went from Harvard to the investment bank of Kuhn Loeb, where he'd survived a purge following Lehman's acquisition of the firm in 1977, only to be pushed out two years later amid vague rumors of improprieties. He then went to First Boston but called Beck, whom he'd known a bit at Lehman, as soon as he heard that Oppenheimer was hiring. Beck hired Cohen over the mild objections of Nash. Still smarting from his own ouster from Lehman Brothers, Beck argued that Cohen's rumored transgression was more likely political than ethical. After all, would a classy firm like First Boston have hired Cohen if he hadn't checked out?

About a year after forming the department, Beck hired his old Columbia Business School friend and savior, Ron Peters, who was going nowhere as a loan officer at Citibank. Peters was a methodical numbers man and Beck thought his addition would not only strengthen the group's analytical abilities but would add a conservative counterweight to the trio of flamboyant personalities already in the group. Peters, whose undergraduate degree was in engineering, was the group's administrator and senior number cruncher. Tall, bald, and bony, with sharply etched features, Peters had the ascetic look of a medieval monk. Beck gave Peters, who was cautious to a fault, two unwanted nicknames: Dr. No and Eraserhead.

Peters more than filled the void left by the departure of Hero, who lasted all of nine months. In a larger department, Hero might have been allowed to absorb the fundamentals of corporate finance at his own pace. But a four-man group could tolerate only a fast learner—which Hero was not—or perhaps a slow learner who put in long hours, which Hero did not, at least by M & A standards. He shared an office with Sanzo, a perfectionist who drove himself mercilessly and expected no less of his colleagues. Beck often heard Sanzo pounding his fist on the wall that separated their offices. Sanzo also took out his frustrations on Hero, whom he called "Zero." Unable to handle the stress, Hero regularly broke out in hives. When he passed on an assignment to his former law firm rather than take care of it himself as had been intended, Beck's patience was exhausted and he sent Hero packing.

David Aaron joined the Jeff Beck Group in 1981 directly from the White House, where he'd spent four years as President Jimmy Carter's deputy assistant for national security affairs. Aaron and his famously assertive boss, Zbigniew Brzezinski, had wielded so much power over the nation's covert intelligence-gathering agencies—including the Central Intelligence Agency—that at one point legislation was introduced requiring that future appointees to the posts they held be subject to Senate approval. As Brzezinski's top deputy, Aaron managed the staff of the National Security Council, the agency through which U.S. response to crises in foreign policy is coordinated. Although Aaron was little known outside Washington, Capitol cognoscenti considered him to be among the half-dozen most influential foreign-policy officials of the Carter years. "Indeed," noted *The New York Times* in 1979, "some White House aides suggest that Mr. Aaron's bureaucratic skills and political ties to Vice President Walter Mondale have, on occasion, given him greater power than Mr. Brzezinski. In the process, Mr. Aaron has also become as controversial in high Administration circles as his boss, with many officials complaining that his strong views, his quick temper and what one called his 'roughhouse tactics' in internal debates have worsened strains between the council and other agencies."

Although for the most part Aaron operated behind the scenes, every now and then special assignments thrust him into the spotlight. Carter sent him as his personal envoy to Ethiopia, with which the U.S. earlier had severed diplomatic relations, in hopes of forestalling an invasion of

Somalia. Aaron also headed a delegation sent to Europe to build
NATO support for an administration plan to station hundreds of new
medium-range missiles in Germany, and was the administration's
choice to make its case for the MX missile system in a nationally
televised debate carried live on the Public Broadcasting System. There
was no shortage of foreign-affairs controversy during the Carter years,
and Aaron was right in the middle of the one that most damaged the
president: the ill-fated attempt to rescue the American hostages held
by Iranian revolutionaries in Tehran. Aaron was one of eight key advisers summoned by Carter for the first in a series of high-level meetings
that led to the decision to send a commando force in after the hostages.

With the Carter administration embattled on every front and facing an election in the fall, Aaron decided in the spring of 1980 that it
was time for him to get out of government and make some money. In
deciding at age forty-one to go to Wall Street, Aaron was attracted by
an image of investment banking that he came to realize was hopelessly
old-fashioned and idealized. "There was a common belief within the
foreign-policy establishment that investment banking was a dignified
way to make a living, and I fell for it," he said. Having been introduced to Leon Levy by a mutual friend, Aaron was brought into Oppenheimer & Company for interviews with the heads of corporate
finance, trading, arbitrage, and M & A. For Beck, Aaron was something approximating the ultimate hire. Here was a man as expert in
subjects that fascinated Beck—international diplomacy and espionage
—as he was ignorant of Wall Street. In his initial dealings with Aaron,
Beck could be quite sincerely inquisitive and deferential on one hand
and swaggeringly self-confident on the other. Partly because Beck impressed him as being "a unique character," Aaron opted for M & A.
The Mad Dog was delighted to have him.

Although the other members of the department were dubious about
cutting in for a share of the profits someone with no business experience whatsoever, it was soon apparent that no one at Oppenheimer
could come close to matching the breadth or quality of Aaron's international contacts. He'd brought with him from the inner councils of
government a Rolodex stuffed with the names and numbers of power
brokers the world over. There was nothing particularly original in
Opco's attempt to parlay Aaron's contacts into investment-banking
business; almost every Wall Street house periodically imported from
Washington retired statesmen or out-of-power politicians to act as

glad-handers and door-openers. In Beck's opinion, though, Aaron had the potential to develop into a bona fide M & A rainmaker. Beck suggested that he begin by focusing his search for new business on European companies and on defense and aerospace contractors in the United States.

Aaron was game but very green. "I came home after my first week on Wall Street and said, sort of amazedly, 'It's only about money. It's nothing else.' " Next, though, Aaron realized that what was simple in motive was quite complex in execution. "I'd come out of a situation where my phone was ringing off the hook and my job was to spend most of my time saying no," he said. "Now, psychologically, it was reversed. As an investment banker, nothing happened unless you made it happen. It was incredibly frustrating. I'd always had some disdain for commerce, for selling. Once I got to Oppenheimer, I learned humility."

In a sense, Aaron was as much mentor as trainee to Beck. Beck quickly made the newcomer his favorite sounding board, soliciting his opinions on every aspect of the department's deals, on personnel matters, and especially on client relationships. "Talking to me made him feel more confident as he began dealing with more high-powered CEOs," said Aaron, who often traveled with Beck on his prospecting trips and studied his technique closely. "Jeff was a bit intimidated by some of them, and he could be very supplicating. With other CEOs, though, he'd be very open and aggressive and even contemptuous at times, if he thought they were stick-in-the-muds. Jeff was a chess player—not a technical one, an incredibly instinctual one. He used to tell me that the key to his success was the manipulation of marginal personalities."

Aaron became so intrigued with Beck that he would use him as the model for the protagonist of *Agent of Influence*, a spy thriller published in 1989. It tells the story of Jayson Lyman, an M & A banker who is chosen to advise Marcel Bresson, a shadowy French industrialist bent on acquiring America's largest media company, News/ Worldweek. Lyman frets over the suspicious gaps in Bresson's life story but is unable to fill them in until he meets up with Heidi Bruce, deputy director of the Senate Intelligence Committee. With the help of a maverick CIA agent, Lyman and Bruce race around Europe and discover that Bresson is a top Soviet agent. Heroically foregoing a $20 million fee (this is fiction, remember), Lyman thwarts Bresson even though he has to queer the deal of a lifetime to do it. Lyman does get the girl, though, and a measure of hard-won wisdom. At his wedding reception, Lyman learns that a Japanese company is preparing to go after News/Worldweek. Instead of jumping right back into the fray by accepting the assignment to defend News/Worldweek, Lyman suggests referring the business to a colleague and bids M & A adieu. In the love of a woman, the manic deal man has, at last, found emotional balance. "But you can't just leave!" News/Worldweek's president protests.

"Relax," Lyman says. "It's only business."

Although Beck never would attain such serenity himself, it is obvious from the moment of Lyman's first appearance in the book—yelling "Money, money, money!" down the hallway of his firm—that he was derived from Aaron's close observation of the Mad Dog. "Lacking the established corporate connections of a Goldman, Sachs or a First Boston," Aaron wrote, "Jay Lyman had driven Gould, Axeworth to the top ranks of the deal makers by being aggressive to the point of shamelessness, and attentive to the point of obsession. He worried each deal as if it were a fetus threatened with miscarriage, and when he gave birth, he sank into a slough of depression." Although Beck was flattered that Aaron had immortalized him in fictional form as Jay Lyman, emotional warts and all, his initial reaction after reading *Agent of Influence* was a half-serious complaint. "I can't believe this," he said. "Aaron stole all my best lines."

It was during his years at Oppenheimer that Beck grew into his Vietnam identity, though he did so gradually and gingerly—at least at the office. Thinking back later on his four years at the firm, Aaron was unable to recall ever once hearing Beck claim to have fought in Vietnam. Nor could Sanzo remember him so much as mentioning Vietnam. While Peters had witnessed Beck's earliest Vietnam experimentations at Columbia Business School, they didn't much interest him then and interested him less now, his former classmate's military background having no apparent bearing on the business of the department. At Oppenheimer, Beck's first tentative Vietnam fabrications were put into general circulation through the department's handful of junior analysts, its youngest and most impressionable members. By the time that Steve McGrath joined in 1983, an embryonic version of the Vietnam legend was already part of the "folklore" of the department. "Someone would mention something every now and then," McGrath recalled. "It wasn't a big deal. I don't think anyone believed he'd been there. But no one really cared either."

Outside of work, though, Beck began putting his imagination to much more intensive use, fashioning a burgeoning repertoire of combat allusions and anecdotes into a fledgling persona. The Legend of the Mad Dog originally took the form of pillow talk inspired by Sarah Lawson, whom Beck first met at a dinner party on a business trip to London in 1980. The following day Lawson telephoned him at his hotel with an unusual request. "May I pick your brain?" she said. Suspicious and flattered in equal measure, Beck invited Lawson to dinner.

Lawson was a bona fide member of the English aristocracy that had fascinated and repelled Beck ever since his first trip to London for DLJ. She was the youngest daughter of William Edward Harry Lawson, the fifth Baron Burnham. A career military officer who retired in 1968, Lord Burnham was descended from Joseph Moses Levy, who founded the *Daily Telegraph* newspaper in the mid-nineteenth century. The Burnham family crest depicts Clio (the muse of history) and Hermes and carries the motto "OF OLD I HOLD." Hall Barn, the family's estate in Buckinghamshire, was featured in the film *Chariots of Fire*. Sarah had just earned a law degree and was, by her own admission, on the naïve side of twenty-five when she met Jeff. Bored with the law, she was looking for a way into the film business and thought Beck might be able to help. Lawson had never before come across an American businessman and presumed that Beck was typical of the breed. "I guess you could say that I had led something of a sheltered life," Lawson later conceded.

To their mutual surprise, Beck and Lawson hit it off famously. They talked late into the night, and she invited him to spend the weekend at the family estate and meet Lord and Lady Burnham. While Jeff found himself strongly attracted to Sarah, he'd never before felt so thoroughly patronized as by her and her parents. By Sunday evening he was no longer able to placate himself by deliberately referring to Hall Barn as Barn Hall. "Well, Sarah," he said in a voice heavy with sarcasm, "it was so nice to meet your family and be treated like a fucking moron for a whole weekend. I really don't see any point in seeing each other again. In fact, I think I'll go now. So have a nice life."

Lawson was stunned—and chastened. "I had badly underestimated him," she recalled. "I'd thought that here was a guy who was quite fun to play with but didn't need much attention." Lawson apologized profusely and, to make a long story short, she and Beck soon were conducting a transatlantic romance. Sarah came to New York for the first time and was impressed with the city but had expected a dwelling grander than the Bunker, which, in the sort of casually rendered judgment that so inflamed Beck's class sensitivities, she laughingly pronounced "terribly poky."

The Honorable Sarah was a powerful stimulus to Beck's fantasy life, which his second marriage had constrained. Rosemary was regular folks, and Jeff was secure in her affection. While he'd told Rosemary that he'd gone to Vietnam, Jeff rarely mentioned his army experiences and never in detail. Rosemary didn't think anything of her husband's seeming aversion to talking about the war. He never talked about his father, either. "There was a lot about Jeff's past that I knew nothing about," she said. With Sarah, though, Jeff made Vietnam the cornerstone of his identity. Lawson bought Beck's Mad Dog act totally. "Jeff came across as knowing very much more than the average investment banker," Lawson observed years later, still convinced of Beck's veracity. "Part of it is his background. When you've been to hell and back —when you've lived through *Platoon* in real life—everything else must seem a bit dull and trivial by comparison. It gives you a different view. When one of us would get banged up a bit in the course of our daily lives, Jeff would say, 'Well, no one died.' "

On a visit to Hall Barn, Lady Burnham took Beck aside and asked him what his intentions were regarding her daughter. Beck replied that they were pretty serious, but later claimed that he took care not to utter the word "marriage." On his next trip, Lord Burnham asked the same question and Beck gave the same guardedly positive answer. At a black-tie party at Hall Barn shortly thereafter, Beck was at first amused and then alarmed as people kept shaking his hand and making knowing comments, all but congratulating him on his impending marriage to the baron's daughter. Jeff took Sarah aside. "I remember saying to Sarah, 'I love you, but we're from two different worlds and this is just not going to work.' "

That's not the way Sarah remembers it, though. As she recalls it, about a year into their romance Jeff asked her to marry him—that is, as soon as he was divorced from Rosemary. Lawson accepted and suggested that he go to her father and ask for her hand in the traditional way. When Beck dutifully did so, though, he "didn't meet with a fantastically good response," Sarah recalled. However, the absence of active opposition from her father was good enough for Sarah. Several months later, though, Lady Burnham confronted her daughter: "This man is already married."

"I know that," she replied. "But how do you know?"

It turned out that Lord Burnham had asked a friend of his to check Beck out. "I was totally shocked," Lawson said. So was Beck, especially when he heard that the baron's friend was affiliated with British intelligence. "It's over," he told Sarah, and beat a hasty retreat back to New York, panicked by the prospect of being exposed as an impostor. "You know what I was really afraid of, don't you?" Beck told me. "That after they got done with the military stuff the next thing would be Louis Victor Beck." Beck's secrets were safe, from Sarah anyway, whose image of him as heroic survivor remained intact. Amid all the emotional fireworks, though, love fizzled and died. "Jeff and I didn't throw insults at one another but there were a number of them lying around," Lawson said. They agreed to a cooling-off period. After nearly a year of silence, Jeff and Sarah resumed their friendship but not their romance. A decade later, Beck still retained fond memories of Sarah—and of her pedigree. "You know," he joked, "I could have been Lord Jeff."

In their first hard-slogging months on the road in pursuit of clients—any clients—for the new M & A department, Beck and Sanzo thought up a group slogan that was unsuitable for advertising: "We Do Shit." The motto was crude but accurate—literally so, in the case of Avco New Idea, a subsidiary of Avco Corporation, which manufactured an implement that was indeed a new idea when the company was organized in 1890: the manure spreader. New Idea's motto: "We *never* stand behind our product." Actually, the manure spreader was quite an invention. Almost ninety years later, it had yet to be superseded by new technology. However, the declining buying power of the American farmer was hurting sales, so Avco wanted to unload New Idea and reinvest the proceeds in its defense-contracting businesses. The Oppenheimer team came calling one day and was rewarded with the assignment, which Beck handed to Sanzo.

In managing an exclusive sale, most big investment banks used what might be called the Claude Rains method: They rounded up the usual suspects. In the case of Avco New Idea, Sanzo mailed out offering circulars to the big agricultural-equipment companies but wasn't optimistic. Other manufacturers were looking to unload their own floundering divisions, not to buy another company's castoffs. Sanzo's best

bet was to find an independent willing to roll the dice. The difficulty
with this approach was not merely that more effort was required to
ferret out individual buyers but that once found, they tended to be
more tenacious bargainers than the big corporations were. One prospective buyer walked with Sanzo through the forty-acre lot behind
New Idea's factory and pointed out all the rust on the spreaders waiting to be shipped to dealers. He said that they would have to be
sanded and repainted and that it was only fair that the cost be de-
ducted from the sale price. That sounded reasonable to Sanzo until he
wandered into a farm-implement dealership one Saturday afternoon
and noticed that a lot of the equipment was rusted. "Farmers don't
give a damn how this stuff looks," a salesman told him. "Pretty don't
matter when you're spreading manure."

Sanzo persevered through many such practical lessons and, after
hawking New Idea for more than a year, finally found a buyer in Allied
Products. The deal was cleverly structured as an off-balance-sheet
leveraged buyout, which enabled Oppenheimer to earn a fee from
both parties to the sale. From Allied Products, Opco received two-year
notes with a market value of about $500,000. Avco, meanwhile, sent
Sanzo a check for $450,000 and a glowing letter from its treasurer.
"Your hard work is truly appreciated," it read, "and your service was
way 'beyond the call.' This was a difficult, complex transaction that
anyone else would have given up on a long time ago."

Tough as the New Idea sale was, at least Avco was a major corporation, which was definitely not the case with Drag Specialties. A tip
from a seemingly friendly Oppenheimer broker brought Beck and
Sanzo to the suburban Minneapolis offices of what had been described
to them as a "nice little catalogue company." The broker failed to
mention that it was run by a scowling, three-hundred-pound, bearded
giant who was dressed in full cycle-gang regalia and made no attempt
to hide his displeasure at making the acquaintance of a couple of pin-
striped Wall Streeters. They sat down and batted a few numbers
around. Sanzo didn't like the feel of the situation and called Beck
outside to confer. They never returned to the giant, instead beating a
hasty retreat to the parking lot. Once safely back in their rented car,
Beck and Sanzo looked at each other and cracked up. Sanzo was laughing partly to keep from crying. "I couldn't fucking believe it," he
recalled. "I'd left First Boston for this?"

As at DLJ and Lehman Brothers, Beck's first noteworthy deal at
Oppenheimer stemmed from his relationship with Warner-Lambert,

which by now was desperate to rid itself of its American Optical subsidiary. American Optical was an old-line company that began as a manufacturer of microscopes and then diversified into eyeglasses and contact lenses while doing pioneering work in heart pacemakers, fiber optics, and lasers. Like many technology-focused companies, though, American Optical was much better at creating products than at selling them. After acquiring American Optical in 1967 for $200 million, Warner-Lambert failed to upgrade the company's marketing to its own expectations while burdening its new subsidiary with all the usual problems of conglomerate ownership. After years of gradual decline, American Optical collapsed in 1980, losing $11 million. Faced with the prospect of additional losses and mounting shareholder backlash, Warner-Lambert's CEO decided to sell American Optical and gave the assignment to Steve McGrath, the Warner-Lambert executive to whom Beck was closest.

Beck was disappointed when McGrath at first turned for help to Morgan Stanley. But after six fruitless months, McGrath fired Morgan and gave the job to Oppenheimer. McGrath concluded that no investment bank was likely to find a corporate buyer for all of American Optical, whose annual revenues of $500 million made it a big company in its own right. McGrath began reorganizing the wreckage while Opco scoured the hinterlands for individual buyers. None of the hundred people it approached was interested at a price that made sense to Warner-Lambert. After a year spent traipsing all over the country, Sanzo finally found a buyer comically close to home. Maurice Cuniffe lived down the street from Sanzo in Greenwich, and his son had dated McGrath's daughter in high school. Cuniffe, a low-profile buyout investor, had passed on the first go-round. As Warner-Lambert's asking price dropped, Cuniffe worked out an arrangement for no-money-down financing and bought what remained of American Optical for $45 million. All parties to the deal walked away happy: Cuniffe ended up making a fortune (later selling American Optical's contact-lens division for $92 million while retaining ownership of three fourths of the company), Warner-Lambert had rid itself of one of its biggest headaches, and the Jeff Beck Group got a fee of about $250,000.

Delighted to have prevailed where mighty Morgan Stanley had failed, Beck let pass no opportunity to point out his department's triumph to prospective clients and reporters alike. The world paid little attention, though. *The Wall Street Journal* noted the transaction in exactly two sentences—neither of which so much as mentioned Oppenheimer—and buried them on page 45: "Warner-Lambert Co. said it sold certain businesses of its American Optical Corp. unit to a new concern controlled by closely held M & R Industries [Cuniffe's company]. Terms were not disclosed."

7

While the Jeff Beck Group was out flogging American Optical, the billion-dollar transaction had become the new standard of measurement in M & A land. The very first billion-dollar deal—the multisided merger by which J. P. Morgan created U.S. Steel in 1902—had been a bounding leap into the future, inspired by the greed and visionary optimism of its promoters. In their eagerness to exploit the enthusiasm of bond-buying investors, U.S. Steel's architects loaded the company with twice as much capital as it needed, gambling that the steelmaker would grow into its oversized balance sheet, as indeed it did. Despite the subsequent growth of the U.S. economy and the dramatic inflation of the 1960s and 1970s, the billion-dollar deal remained a rarity until 1981, when nine of them were completed. What put the M & A over the top was a paroxysm of fear and greed that could be summed up by the letters O, P, E, C, as in Organization of Petroleum Exporting Countries. After the shah was toppled in 1979, Iran's oil output was temporarily reduced to zero and panic spread through the energy markets, carried by predictions of massive shortages of petroleum. As oil consumers began hoarding supplies, some of America's largest corporations began loading up on oil companies. In history's largest acquisition, E. I. Du Pont de Nemours & Company acquired Conoco for $7.8 billion. All told, some $81 billion worth of deals was completed in 1981, more than double the previous year's total.

Oppenheimer's timing in starting an M & A department had been fortunate indeed. From 1979 through 1982, no less than twenty-one of the twenty-five largest mergers and acquisitions of all time were completed. While Beck's strategy of focusing his fledgling department on the small, problematic transaction was proving out on its own terms, the advent of the megadeal made Oppenheimer's M & A achievements seem insignificant. For brokering the Du Pont–Conoco merger alone Morgan Stanley and First Boston split $30 million in fees. Thirty million dollars for two weeks of work! For Beck, it was enough to make his hard-won initial success at Oppenheimer feel suspiciously like failure. Indeed, it sometimes seemed to Beck that he'd been shunted off into a parallel M & A universe that was just like Big Deal Land in every respect except that deals and the reputations of deal makers were shrunken in scale by an order of 100 or perhaps 1,000—to virtual invisibility, at any rate. Beck was an M & A professional, wasn't he? He lived in New York City and put in eighty to a hundred hours a week every week, didn't he? And yet not once had he crossed paths with Felix Rohatyn, Bob Greenhill, Joe Flom, Bruce Wasserstein, or any of the other star deal men whose exploits he read about with growing envy.

By the time Beck joined Oppenheimer, Wall Street deal making was ruled by an oligopoly—or, more precisely, by an oligopoly of investment banks reinforced by a joint monopoly of law firms. Almost all of that $81 billion M & A bonanza was funneled through a relative handful of firms, which constituted a close-knit fraternity as insidious in its own way as the clubby system through which the old gentleman-banker élite had ruled securities underwriting for decades. The inner circle of the Wall Street Deal Club included the old-line investment banks Morgan Stanley; Goldman, Sachs; and First Boston. Rounding out a second tier were Lazard Frères; Lehman Brothers; Kidder, Peabody; Salomon Brothers; Merrill Lynch; and Smith Barney. By the end of 1981, these firms collectively employed maybe six hundred M & A specialists. An additional two hundred M & A bankers toiled on the periphery at upstart firms, many of them smaller and more obscure than Oppenheimer. The flow of deal business was even more concentrated in the simultaneously burgeoning field of M & A law. Of the few hundred lawyers who specialized in M & A, the majority worked for two New York firms: Skadden, Arps, Slate, Meagher & Flom—Joe Flom's firm—and Wachtell, Lipton, Rosen & Katz—Marty Lipton's firm.

Despite their extravagantly combative rhetoric, the leading M & A men tended to collaborate as much as they competed—or, more accurately, they collaborated as competitors. Although deal men did go to great lengths to steal away one another's clients, once a takeover battle actually began it was in the overriding economic interest of both the defensive and the offensive advisers to complete a transaction. It was a simple matter of money: Defense didn't pay. Under the prevailing fee system, *all* the advisers involved in a takeover fight received fees three or four times greater when a deal was consummated than when it was not. In the private code of the Deal Club, it wasn't whether you won or lost or even how you played the game. What mattered was getting the deal done—preferably at the highest price possible. For another fundamental principle of the deal was this: The greater the value of a deal, the bigger the fee. The Deal Club liked nothing better than a spirited contest among rival bidders, and the more the merrier—as long as, in the end, one of the combatants carried off the prize (and doled out the advisory fees).

On a personal level, the definitive Deal Club relationship was that between Flom and Lipton, whose careers were spectacular testaments to the old legal aphorism, One lawyer in a town struggles; two get rich beyond dreams of avarice. The 1976 magazine article that cemented the myth of Flom's and Lipton's archrivalry—"Two Tough Lawyers in the Tender-Offer Game"—contains an anecdote meant to illustrate their fiercely competitive relationship. Both lawyers had been invited to a dinner party thrown by Loews Corporation, which was run by Bob and Larry Tisch. The party, *New York* magazine observed,

> turned into an embarrassing one-upmanship match between Flom and Lipton. "It was terrible," recalls one guest. "Every time there was a toast Joe would butt in with some crack. And then if Joe said something, Marty felt obliged to top him and vice versa. These guys are hysterically competitive. It ruined [the] party. Not only that, they kept jockeying with each other to get Bob or Larry's ear about a deal." Flom seemed more guilty than Lipton, just as he did at a recent *Law Journal* seminar on tender offers when he alone among the participants seemed reluctant to share his methods with the audience, except when an opportunity came to contradict Lipton.

"Hysterically competitive" was close to the mark; "theatrically competitive" would have hit it dead on. For Flom and Lipton were indulging in a subtler version of the promotional posturing that precedes professional wrestling matches. You know the ritual: In the prematch interview, Hulk Hogan and Rowdy Roddy threaten to rip each other's eyeballs out. Then they go and throw each other around a ring in a carefully orchestrated, harmless series of falls and pratfalls. If Flom and Lipton in fact had been professional wrestlers instead of takeover lawyers, Flom no doubt would have been the fan favorite. Runtish, with an avuncular smile and soft-spoken manner, he looked like a classic underdog. In this corner, Gentle Joe Flom. Lipton was tall (for a person, if not for a pro wrestler) at six foot one, loud, and alarmingly pear-shaped—a Wall Street version of Mayor Ed Koch. He always wore a black suit with a silver tie and a white shirt. The lenses on his eyeglasses were Coke-bottle thick. Hide the women and children, it's Mean Marty Lipton!

In a nation cursed with a surplus of lawyers—thousands upon thousands of them—Flom and Lipton created the impression that they alone were capable of safely guiding the nation's major corporations through the deal wars. In the annals of M & A rainmaking, their monopolizing of the business of takeover law was the preeminent achievement, ranking far above what any investment banker had accomplished, for Flom and Lipton created their M & A practices from scratch, in defiance of the old Wall Street legal establishment, which well into the 1970s WASPily persisted in dismissing M & A law as an unworthy fad. While their success was predicated on the blindness of the Establishment, Flom and Lipton immensely aided their cause with an inspired job of mutual promotion. The names Flom and Lipton were so frequently and flatteringly linked in the press that after a time they no longer found it necessary to continue recommending one another to the corporations they opposed. If one side had Gentle Joe, the other got Mean Marty, and vice versa. It was as if Flom and Lipton were listed in the legal equivalent of the *Physicians' Desk Reference* as the only known antidotes to each other's brand of poison.

Flom made his name first. He grew up poor, smart, and Jewish in Brooklyn. After graduating from City College of New York and spending a few years in the army, he attended Harvard Law School on the GI Bill. At Harvard, Flom was one of the most accomplished members of his class, and yet when he graduated in 1948 did not receive a single offer from an old-line Wall Street firm. He took a job at Skadden, Arps & Slate, a midtown firm just formed by a trio of young lawyers who'd grown disenchanted with the downtown legal scene. It's safe to say that Flom—Skadden, Arps's first associate—was not hired because of the dashing figure he cut. He was stoop-shouldered and his head looked a good two hat sizes too big for his body. His suits were rumpled, his socks bagged at the ankle, his ties looked like second prize in the ring toss at the county fair. He smiled often and talked hardly at all. All in all, he was a man easily underestimated. Despite his unprepossessing appearance, Flom was not only a brilliant lawyer but a hustling, creative promoter.

Skadden, Arps's preeminence in the emerging field of M & A law was forged in the 1960s by its repeated service as special counsel to Davis Polk & Wardwell, the so-called Tiffany of law firms. With roots dating back to the 1850s, Davis Polk had handled the House of Morgan's legal business for the better part of a century and boasted a higher proportion of partners in the Social Register than any other law firm. It was the sort of firm that never would have made Joe Flom a partner. But as its special counsel Flom was able to exploit his ties to Davis Polk to cultivate personal relationships with key Morgan partners, including Bob Greenhill. In 1972, Morgan Stanley became the first major investment bank to set up a department dedicated to M & A work. It was headed by Greenhill, who by this time looked upon Flom not merely as a lawyer but as an ally. "I wanted to build an M & A business here, and I knew he could help me do it," said Greenhill, who broke with Morgan tradition and made Skadden, Arps his department's chief outside counsel.

Flom's association with the House of Morgan put him over the top in his campaign to sell Skadden, Arps's services to the other leading investment banks. There was no more telling evidence of Flom's promotional genius than the widespread belief among M & A bankers that the surest way to counter Greenhill or Rohatyn was to hire Skadden before they did. As Marty Lipton, graciously subordinating himself to Flom's promotional ends, noted in an oft-quoted 1973 article in the *Michigan Law Review:* "One member of the New York bar has become so renowned for his specialized defense against takeovers that the first question on Wall Street is 'which side has him.' " Even as he curried favor with Flom, Mean Marty was emerging as the leading alternative to Gentle Joe. His big break came in representing Loews Corporation in its tenacious and triumphant pursuit of CNA Corporation—the most heavily publicized deal of 1974. Lipton got the assignment through a personal connection; he'd been a classmate of Loews's general counsel at New York University Law School.

Flom and Lipton became the most inseparable of foes. Most Saturdays, they could be found having lunch together at a midtown landmark, the "21" Club. Flom and Lipton also frequently shared breakfast at another of Manhattan's business-meal showcases, the dining room of the Regency Hotel. While Flom's and Lipton's basic promotional strategy was that of constant association, they refined their pitch through differentiation. Flom became known as counsel to the raider and Lipton wrapped himself in the mantle of defender, though neither lawyer constrained themselves or their firms by specializing exclusively. In fact, one of Flom's most lucrative marketing stratagems emphasized defense: the signing of corporations to annual retainers. Left unspoken was the prime selling point—that a retainer payment now would ensure that if an attack came, Skadden would not be working for the raider. In deal circles, signing a Skadden retainer was known as "sterilizing Joe." As part of defining itself in opposition to Skadden, Arps, Wachtell, Lipton made a point of not soliciting retainer payments. "Marty used to brag about not charging retainers," said Robert Pirie, a Skadden partner who was a close friend of Lipton's. "I'd tell him, 'Marty, you know that if we hadn't asked for retainers, you would have.'"

Although the top deal banks had been instrumental in the rise of Flom and Lipton, once established the two lawyers wielded far greater influence within the Deal Club than any bankers did. Their power was rooted in sheer ubiquity; it was estimated that between them Skadden, Arps and Wachtell, Lipton were involved in 90 percent of all contested takeovers. On the investment-banking side of the Street, meanwhile, the same flow of deals was divided among nine or ten houses. As a result, Flom and Lipton were far more often in a position to refer business to one of the established deal banks than those investment banks were to recommend a law firm to a corporate client. There were few investment bankers to whom Flom or Lipton couldn't say, "You owe me one."

For aspiring investment bankers and lawyers, the overriding criterion for admission into the Deal Club was a demonstrated ability to get big deals done—to bring something to the party. To meet this requirement, a deal man had to not only be in a position to represent large corporations but possess the correct attitude. He had to be willing to go along to get along, to accept his place in the larger scheme of things. This meant paying proper homage to the senior eminences of the Deal Club—especially Flom and Lipton—and, most important, not let personal ambitions or rivalries with other deal men impede the burgeoning flow of multibillion-dollar transactions initiated and completed.

With the emergence of the billion-dollar deal in the early 1980s, a second generation of star M & A bankers came to the fore within the Deal Club. Without exception, they'd risen within one of the traditionally dominant houses. There was Gleacher at Lehman Brothers, Geoff Boisi at Goldman, Marty Siegel at Kidder, Peabody. As fellow defensive specialists, Siegel and Lipton developed such a close personal relationship that in deal circles they were referred to, a bit snidely, as "the two Martys." All the new M & A stars were overshadowed by Bruce Wasserstein, who, with Joe Perella, ran the M & A department at First Boston. Variously known as "Bruce the Moose," "Juicy Brucey" and "Bid 'em up Bruce," Wasserstein had a mixture of guile, audacity, and media savvy that made him the definitive deal personality of the first half of the 1980s.

Of average height, Wasserstein was a bit tubby and unkempt. The Wasserstein shirttails spent considerable time liberated from the confines of the Wasserstein pants. His shoes apparently preferred scuff to shine. If he owned a comb, he didn't often use it. Yet his presence conveyed solemnity, even dignity. Wasserstein's fleshy, slightly saturnine features seemed to have set permanently in an expression suggesting reserve and mild boredom. He almost never smiled and he never lost his temper. Pressure seemed to have no effect on him at all. He was imperturbable. An angry Wasserstein once walked into the office of a colleague and said calmly: "Rant. Rant. Rant." Pause. "It's out of my system now." Other than his mind, the chief instrument of Wasserstein's aggression was his voice, a basso profundo of such room-rattling resonance that it used to prompt complaints from his upstairs dormmates at Harvard. Secure in his ability to drown out others with a slight boost in voice-box volume, Wasserstein declaimed his counsel unhurriedly in long and cleverly structured paragraphs of assertion that betrayed not a whit of self-doubt and brooked no disagreement. He sounded a lot like Henry Kissinger without the accent, but with the arrogance.

With First Boston's masterful handling of Du Pont's huge bid for Conoco, Wasserstein could justifiably lay claim—and did, repeatedly—to being Wall Street's supreme M & A strategist, eclipsing both Rohatyn, who'd advised Seagram's in its losing cause, and Greenhill, who had failed to preserve Conoco's independence. While there was no doubting Wasserstein's intelligence, his wizardly reputation was as much a product of his skill at self-promotion as of his brilliance as a deal strategist. While the old gentleman banker had shied away from journalists as members of an alien and perhaps dangerous species, Wasserstein initiated contact with the press. Like Rohatyn, his only peer as a press handler, Wasserstein did his own public relations. A former

college journalist, he understood the difference between "not for attribution," "background," and "off the record." He knew that *The Wall
Street Journal* and *The New York Times* had deadlines hours apart, and
how the slant of a *Business Week* story likely would differ from that of
a piece in *Fortune* or *Forbes*. Wasserstein went so far as to publicly
profess his respect for reporters. "A lot of these MBA types [on Wall
Street] think people in the press are fools," he said. "The fact is, a lot
of these guys are smarter than the guys at investment-banking firms
who lunch well."

While tossing an occasional bouquet of flattery didn't hurt, Wasserstein's good press was mainly a function of the generous access he
provided. He understood that what drives a reporter above all else is
the need to know what is going on and he made himself continuously
available to reporters from major business publications. Wasserstein
and Perella were the first heads of a major M & A department to sit
down with Tim Metz of *The Wall Street Journal* and provide a step-
by-step postmortem of a big deal. The truest measure of Wasserstein's
flair for publicity wasn't merely that his name had an uncanny way of
appearing in stories recounting the deals on which he worked or that
he was usually cast in a flattering light or widely credited with daring
innovations that in fact were slight variations on established techniques. Thanks in large part to Wasserstein, the advent of the billion-
dollar deal was presented to the nation as the triumph of the M & A
strategist. Relegated to the periphery of 1960s takeover battles, the
Wall Street deal man by the early 1980s was the glamorous pivot
around which deals seemed to turn.

Beck's own cultivation of Tim Metz finally paid off with a feature
story in *The Wall Street Journal* early in 1982. Metz had met Beck a
few years earlier and taken an immediate liking to him but said that
the Jeff Beck Group would have to do some deals before it warranted
the *Journal*'s attention. Metz threw the Mad Dog a bone in 1980 by
quoting him in a little story on the effect of rising interest rates on
takeover activity. The quote was classic boilerplate: " 'We're seeing the
interest level very high for deals in the range of $15 million to $100
million,' said Jeff Beck, director of Oppenheimer's mergers and acquisitions department. 'Corporate liquidity is still relatively high and
many major companies can handle deals in this range without external
financing.' " It wasn't much but it was a start. Beck began calling

Metz virtually every week to swap gossip and to keep him apprised of the progress of his M & A group.

By March 1982, Metz had heard enough. He wrote a piece head-lined "OPPENHEIMER FINDS A NICHE IN MERGER FIELD BY ARRANGING LOTS OF SMALLER TRANSACTIONS. " Drawings of Beck and Nash ac-companied the story, which was fairly prominently placed on the front page of the second section.

> By Wall Street standards [Metz began] Oppenheimer & Co.'s merger and acquisition advisory business is a dwarf in a land of giants.
>
> Its revenue last year was about $5 million, a fraction of the amount taken in by the merger and acquisitions businesses of First Boston Corp., Lehman Brothers Kuhn Loeb Inc. and other investment-banking giants. Without a doubt, Oppenheimer's eight-member "M & A" staff would be ill-advised to enter hand-to-hand combat with, say, Morgan Stanley & Co., which has 100 merger professionals.
>
> But then Oppenheimer hasn't tried. Instead, it advises participants in transactions that involve as little as $15 million. Its specialty is "boutique" activities, like private company sales, corporate divestitures and the pur-chase or sale of "strategic blocks," which can influence, but not necessarily determine, corporate control.

Metz's story implied that Beck was being considered for membership in the Deal Club: "Even some of the merger industry's giants are taking note. Skadden, Arps, Slate, Meagher & Flom, a huge Wall Street law firm, has been courting Oppenheimer to get legal work associated with the M & A transactions. 'We think Oppenheimer has built a very competent group in a short period of time,' says Skadden, Arps partner Robert S. Pirie."

The *Journal* piece paid a quick dividend, in the form of a telephone call from the CEO of Varian Associates, a California high-tech-instrument maker and defense contractor. As an adviser to Varian, Beck for the first time managed to insinuate himself into a high-profile takeover battle—and on the winning side, yet. In successfully fighting off a takeover threat by the Madison Fund, Varian Associates tri-umphed over such long odds that Metz would feature its saga in a front-page *Journal* story on takeover defenses. In effect, the Varian-Madison battle was Beck's audition for membership in the Deal Club —an audition he failed in spectacular fashion, managing in the course of a single deal to embarrass Goldman, Sachs, annoy Skadden, Arps, and antagonize not only Rohatyn but a future under secretary of the treasury.

Beck had joined Oppenheimer without having established even the flimsiest of ties to the Deal Club. He was, in fact, only dimly aware of its existence. Like any avid reader of the business press, Beck was well acquainted with the names Flom, Lipton, Rohatyn, and the rest but he couldn't yet perceive the threads of mutual self-interest that united the leading deal men and helped sustain them in their dominance. Even at Lehman Brothers, the deals that he'd done were too small to bring him into direct contact with the inner circle of the M & A fraternity, much less qualify him for membership. It was like watching football from a stadium's third deck: The outcome of each play was apparent but the subtleties of player interaction were lost.

Beck's understanding of the symbiotic inner workings of the big-deal action was further obscured by the blinders of his own competitive ferocity. For Beck, deal making was not a career or even a business so much as it was a daily test of manhood in which ordinary notions of professional success and failure were metamorphosed into Complete Victory and Utter Defeat. Winning was everything, and Beck allowed his ego no escape in ambiguity of definition. To him, winning meant landing the client and completing the assignment, whether it were making an acquisition or preventing one. Period. Beck's concept of successful takeover defense did not include finding a friendlier company willing to pay a higher price than the assailant. He'd cut a deal with such a "white knight" if so instructed by his client, but he would feel as if he'd lost, despite the higher fee. Beck was no fool. Given a choice, he'd take a larger fee over a smaller one every time, but no fee was large enough to enable him, emotionally or intellectually, to transform loss into victory.

Beck's need to win was a product not only of his competitiveness but of a deep and contradictory desire for moral clarity in his professional life. Beck himself later would explain his almost self-righteous abhorrence of ethical gray zones as a reaction to his father's transgressions. As the son of a criminal, it was important to him to earn a livelihood that would put him above reproach, above suspicion. However, while he wanted to do right, he also desperately wanted to get rich. It was his pursuit of this latter desire that landed him amid the moral murk of Wall Street. Beck's compulsion to clarity was frustrated not only by Wall Street's nature but by his own inclination toward deception—a trait that no doubt attracted him to the gamesmanship of M & A dealing in the first place. Not realizing initially that the game he was playing was more like professional wrestling than professional football, Beck naïvely assumed that he not only could win his way to stardom but that winning would bring him the respect and acceptance of the M & A elite. He still had a lot to learn about the way Wall Street worked, and for him the Varian-Madison Fund deal would be a graduate seminar in the politics of deals.

In its mid-1960s glamour days, Varian Associates had been admiringly known as the Polaroid of the West in tribute to its soaring stock price. The 1970s were not kind to Varian, though, as a variety of management and technical problems slowed its growth and sabotaged its stock market performance. Varian was operating in the red by 1981 and, with its stock trading below book value, was vulnerable to takeover. Varian's president was pressed into early retirement and succeeded by Tom Sege, a Hungarian-born scientist. Sege was barely a month into his new job when he received a cheeky letter from a new stockholder, the Madison Fund, which said it was contemplating acquiring as much as 30 percent of Varian's shares in the hope that Varian could be persuaded to restructure. A few weeks later, Sege's concern escalated to alarm when it was revealed that Madison Fund had bought a 10.9 percent stake in Varian.

The chief executive officer of the Madison Fund was none other than George Gould, the pipe-smoking patrician whom Beck had seen as his nemesis during DLJ's restructuring in 1973–1974. Gould had left DLJ to serve under Felix Rohatyn as finance chairman of the Municipal Assistance Corporation and had also been chairman of the New York State Housing Authority. (In Reagan's second term, Gould would win appointment to high position in the Treasury Department.) For all his enviable political connections, though, Gould was still a stock picker at heart, and in 1976 he jumped at the opportunity to resurrect the moribund Madison Fund, which was one of the oldest publicly traded investment funds on Wall Street.

Although Madison's results had improved under Gould, the fund's own stock continued to sell at a discount from net asset value. In other words, Madison was worth more dead than alive. In 1980, Gould was approached by Derald Ruttenberg, who was well known on the Street as one of the most successful practitioners of the art of corporate restructuring. For two decades, Ruttenberg had been buying undervalued companies and reselling them, usually at a handsome profit. He and Gould first met in the 1960s, when Ruttenberg had hired DLJ to help on several deals. Anxious to correct Madison's chronic undervaluation in the market before a raider did it for him, Gould decided to join forces with Ruttenberg, who bought 1 percent of the Madison Fund's shares and was named its chairman. Gould remained as chief executive officer.

Together, Gould and Ruttenberg decided on a bold move: attempting to convert Madison from a closed-end fund to an industrial operating company. As an investment company Madison was subject to the stringent requirements of the Investment Act of 1940. To get out from under the terms of the act, the Madison Fund had to redeploy most of its assets into "controlling" positions in other companies. This meant amassing at least 25 percent of a company's stock *and* getting a seat on its board. Making a big acquisition would have put Gould and his cronies out of a job since they were money managers, not corporate managers. Instead, Madison spread its $700 million in assets among as many as a dozen companies. While buying blocks of stock in the open market was easy enough, Madison couldn't ensure itself a spot on a board without a proxy fight, which would be difficult to win. Gould and Ruttenberg decided that their best bet would be to offer the Madison Fund as a protector to companies vulnerable to takeover. Their basic pitch to such companies would be something like this: "With 25 percent of your stock in our hands, you'll have the time you need to restructure the company and get the stock price up. Once your company is out of danger, we'll sell our shares and move on." The rub would come in trying to convince people that Madison wouldn't use its position to actually take control and force restructuring upon the company involved. Perhaps Gould thought that his Establishment credentials would inspire trust enough to carry the day. If so, he was sadly mistaken.

By the time Madison set its sights on Varian Associates, it had already bought positions in four companies. However, only in the case of Interlake Steel had Gould and Ruttenberg succeeded in working out a friendly arrangement. This one modest success had been more than offset by Madison's blunder with AM International, which had promptly collapsed after the fund bought in, leaving Madison with a $25 million loss on a $28 million investment. Thus it was with an unpleasant sensation of déjà vu that Gould watched Varian's stock drop from $28 to $24 a share even as the fund was accumulating its 10.9 percent block.

Madison and Varian had one thing in common: Both were clients of Goldman, Sachs. In fact, the Madison Fund was one of the earliest customers of Goldman's block-trading desk and remained a large-commission-paying client. Ruttenberg, too, had a long relationship with Goldman, which had been investment banker to Studebaker-Worthington, his principal corporation. By contrast, Varian's relationship with Goldman, Sachs was of recent vintage and only modestly remunerative. Still, after the Madison Fund surfaced as Varian's largest stockholder, CEO Sege had turned to Goldman for help in trying to persuade Gould and Ruttenberg to back off. Instead, though, Madison kept buying Varian shares, reaching the 25 percent level by late 1982. Varian sued, accusing the Madison Fund of having violated federal securities laws by filing inadequate and misleading disclosure forms while amassing its position.

While such a lawsuit was a common legal tactic in a takeover fight, Sege was fortunate in having hired an uncommon lawyer—Edmund Kelly, one of the few experienced M & A lawyers aligned against the Deal Club. As an associate at the old-line Wall Street firm of White & Case, Kelly had lucked into his first assignment in 1967 and followed it up by coauthoring with a White & Case partner a long scholarly article, for a legal publication, on takeover defenses—perhaps the first such piece published anywhere. Two years later, Kelly was involved in the first $1 billion hostile tender offer on the side of B. F. Goodrich, which fought off Northwest Industries by getting Congress to pass a law disallowing the interest deduction for the kind of junk bonds Northwest hoped to use to finance the deal. Winning the first epic takeover battle of Wall Street's modern era had put White & Case in a position to establish itself as the preeminent firm in takeover defense at a time when Marty Lipton was still struggling to make a reputation. In fact, Goldman, Sachs offered its M & A business to Kelly in 1971, several years before the firm turned to Lipton. Kelly turned Goldman, Sachs down. "We didn't want to humor clients into believing there was much that could be done against an all-cash tender offer," Kelly recalled. "We didn't want to make a reputation for doing something that couldn't be done."

Kelly had represented the attacker in the most celebrated hostile deal of the 1970s—J. Ray McDermott & Company's acquisition of Babcock & Wilcox in 1977. And the next year he was hired by the fledgling M & A department at Lehman Brothers on the Cutler-Hammer deal, which deteriorated into an orgy of intercorporate hostility. After these assignments, Kelly decided that he'd had his fill of representing raiders. When Gleacher called after the Cutler-Hammer battle with the offer of more work, Kelly turned him down flat. "Don't even bother calling," he said.

By 1981, when Varian came knocking on his door, Kelly had scaled his M & A practice back to friendly deals, though he still took an occasional defensive assignment if he thought the client had a good shot at winning. Kelly liked Varian's chances, since the Madison Fund was still subject to the demanding requirements of the 1940 act. Kelly accepted the job and advised Sege to hang tough. Varian's CEO got diametrically opposed advice from his advisers at Goldman, Sachs, who, as Sege recalled, "told us our lawsuit wasn't worth a damn. Goldman said the probabilities were against our survival and we ought to seek shelter"—that is, authorize a search for a white knight to buy out the Madison Fund, no doubt at a premium. The Deal Club had spoken, rendering its favorite verdict. Sege, however, refused to follow the script. His natural inclination, to fight, was reinforced when he was made aware of the Madison Fund's long-standing relationship with Goldman. How could Goldman, Sachs possibly serve the best interests of two clients when they were at cross-purposes?

In his search for a second opinion, Sege turned to Beck, who jumped at the chance to join the defense of Varian against Gould, though his eagerness was muted a bit by the fact that Dan Lukfin, his old mentor, had just joined Madison's board. Not long after Sege hired Oppenheimer, Goldman, Sachs resigned as an adviser to Varian. With Kelly and Beck waiting in his corner, Sege took the initiative in trying to work out a compromise with the Madison Fund, going so far as to invite Gould and Ruttenberg out to Palo Alto to tour Varian's main manufacturing plant. Neither side brought lawyers or bankers. Gould said he was willing to sign a standstill agreement, under which Madison wouldn't buy more than 27.5 percent of Varian's stock for five years and wouldn't seek more than two directorships. "We spent a happy day," Gould recalled. "I came back thinking we really had a deal."

The proposal became the basis for formal negotiations, with Kelly generally taking the lead and Beck in close support. Despite the vehemence of his professional opinions, Kelly came across as rather unassuming and even sweet-tempered. He didn't seem the kind of lawyer who made a practice of upstaging co-advisers, and so Beck was quite willing to defer to his greater experience. At times, though, Beck

stepped to the fore to inject his own trademark brand of theatrics into
the deal. During a meeting following the Palo Alto peace talks, it
seemed to Beck that Ruttenberg was trying to stampede Sege by pur-
posely taking the Varian CEO's general amiability for final assent.
After the meeting broke up, Beck left and then returned alone to bait
Ruttenberg. Beck couldn't prove it but suspected that Madison Fund
was getting back-channel advice from Goldman's risk arbitrageurs—
traders specializing in takeover speculation.

Beck claimed to have told Ruttenberg that he thought the meeting
had not gone well at all. "There isn't going to be any five-year standstill," Beck said. "I think what's going on here is rape and pillage."

"But Sege said—"

Beck cut Ruttenberg off. "I don't care what he said. You're running
an investment fund that is turning into an adjunct of Goldman,
Sachs's arbitrage desk. We're not going to let you get away with it."

According to Beck, Ruttenberg called Jack Nash and Leon Levy to
complain. Over the years, Ruttenberg had sent a fair amount of brokerage business Oppenheimer's way, and the Madison Fund had a
trading account at Oppenheimer. To their credit, though, Nash and
Levy chose not to intervene. "I guess you didn't make a good impression with Derald," Nash told Beck, and left it at that.

The talks continued less cordially, with Varian insisting that Madison agree to a permanent standstill at 27.5 percent. At a meeting at
the private Brook Club, to which Gould belonged, Madison's CEO
was accompanied for the first time by a top partner of the blue-blood
Boston law firm of Gaston, Snow, Beekman & Bogue. Off the top of
his head, Kelly proposed an addendum to the standstill agreement, by
which Madison would be obligated to sell its shares to Varian or a
white knight of its choosing at a price 25 percent above the market in
the event of a hostile tender offer. This was a clever bit of trickery on
Kelly's part that might have made Varian invulnerable to takeover and
denied the Madison Fund the opportunity to exit with a quick profit.
No raider was likely to take a run at Varian knowing that the company
could deliver a 25 percent block at a mere 25 percent premium. According to Kelly and Beck, the two sides shook hands on a permanent
standstill agreement with the new feature.

Kelly drew up an agreement that night and sent it over to Madison
the next morning. In mid-afternoon, Sege, Kelly, and Beck reconvened
at the Madison Fund's offices to sign the final agreement. As he
walked into Gould's office, Kelly noticed what looked like the framed

original of his favorite *New Yorker* cartoon hanging on the wall. It shows a man at a desk; he is surrounded by caption balloons, each of which contains a flowery alternative to the simple declaration "No," rendered in a variety of elaborate typescripts. Later, Kelly realized that the poster had been an omen. It was his suspicion and Beck's that Gould had talked with Ruttenberg and with Goldman's risk-arbitrage desk overnight and had realized that Madison would in effect be immunizing Varian against takeover. In any event, Gould insisted that there'd never been a handshake agreement on any sort of permanent standstill. In Gould's office there was protracted quibbling over the terms of the agreement Kelly had drawn up. After going around in circles for an hour or so, Gould and his lawyer left the office to consult privately. Sege, who'd been grappling with Madison for nearly a year, was quietly seething at its stalling tactics. He turned to Kelly. "What do you recommend?"

"Sign it and let's leave," Kelly replied.

Sege signed and the group left in a huff. Beck sent a copy of the *New Yorker* poster to Gould, with a sneering note attached. A few days later, Kelly took off the legal gloves and amended Varian's lawsuit against Madison to name Gould and Ruttenberg personally as defendants. Now, if Varian won, Madison's two top executives could, under the 1940 act, be banned for life from associating with all investment companies. "Once they'd pulled that stunt [backing off from the handshake agreement] on us," Kelly said, "we decided, 'All right, then, we're going to beat them.'"

A few weeks after Varian amended its suit, Madison publicly announced that it had hired Lazard Frères to find a buyer for its 25 percent block of Varian. While this unusual move suggested that Madison was losing its resolve and had been unable to find a buyer by more private means, there was no celebration in the Varian camp. If Madison did manage to sell its entire block, Varian would remain in play; indeed, Madison's publicizing of its retreat emphasized Varian's vulnerability. Varian responded in kind, putting out a press release warning prospective buyers that Madison's block was "tainted" because it had been "unlawfully amassed." With Lazard's entry, Beck was up against Rohatyn for the first time. "He'd walk into negotiating sessions with an entourage and people would whisper, 'Felix is here. Felix is here,'" Beck said. "I guess we were supposed to be intimidated. The only trouble was Felix didn't know a thing about Varian." Beck, offended by what he described as the "flourishing condescension"

Rohatyn showed him, devoted much of his working day to finding out who Rohatyn was calling on in his efforts to shop the Varian block. When Beck succeeded in his intelligence work, he'd have Sege call up the prospective buyer. Though Sege wavered at times, with Beck's and Kelly's support he resisted the temptation to find a white knight before Lazard found a black one.

As Varian's shares rose into the high thirties, the company tabled its talks with Madison and, with Oppenheimer's help, began cleaning up its balance sheet. The company issued 1.25 million new shares at $40 and called in its convertible debentures. These moves solidified Varian's finances while diluting Madison's stake to 20 percent.

By this time, Madison had involved itself in two more messy takeover battles and its stock was trading at an even bigger discount from net asset value than when Gould and Ruttenberg had launched the fund in its new direction. Gould's resolve was further undermined when his wife and then Ruttenberg were stricken with cancer. Ruttenberg resigned as chairman and a month later the Madison Fund agreed to be acquired by Warner Communications, which announced plans to liquidate Madison's stock holdings. Gould offered to sell the 25 percent block of Varian stock to the company at market price if Sege would drop his lawsuit. Sege accepted.

One morning at three, Beck went with Kelly to Skadden, Arps's offices to put the finishing touches on the stock repurchase agreement. Michael Goldberg, the Skadden partner present, made no secret of his lack of enthusiasm, keeping his hat on throughout the meeting. Beck had no interest in the legal document under discussion. He was there to keep an eye on the normally mild-mannered Kelly, who'd confided in Beck his fury over the tactics of the Madison Fund and its representatives. "We'd been up for days and I sensed that Ed was carrying a lot of anger," Beck said. "I didn't want the deal to fall apart right at the end."

As Kelly dickered with Goldberg, Beck interrupted every time Kelly showed the slightest sign of annoyance.

"Ed, don't get mad," Beck would say. "Is everything okay?"

When Kelly excused himself to go to the bathroom, Beck went with him to make sure he didn't use the pay phone in the lobby.

"I'd never felt so intensely monitored in my life," Kelly said. "Jeff was on tenterhooks the entire time."

Kelly and Beck managed to complete their business at Skadden, and by the spring of 1983, nearly two years after Madison's first purchases of Varian stock, the California company had succeeded in taking itself out of play. Seldom in takeover history had a shareholder with a position as large as 25 percent been frustrated by its target, absent an antitrust problem. And perhaps never before had a takeover battle ended with that shareholder arranging its own liquidation. Beck relished this against-the-odds victory, not to mention the $2 million fee from Varian, the largest his group had received to date. For the first time he'd worked on a deal whose every twist and turn was chronicled in the press, and to Opco's publicity advantage, for it had outmaneuvered Lazard Frères and proven Goldman wrong in advising Varian to seek a white knight.

As he was fighting to save Varian from being processed by the Deal Club, Beck became aware of the insidious influence of risk arbitrage within Oppenheimer and even within his own department. Oppenheimer's risk-arbitrage activities became a growing annoyance to Beck after Nash and Levy, in mid-1982, cashed out their investment by selling the firm for $162.5 million to Mercantile House, a British company. While retaining a nominal association with Oppenheimer, Nash and Levy then set up Odyssey Partners, which was dedicated to playing the takeover game in various ways, including risk arbitrage. Odyssey was also a limited partner in a closely related firm called Junction Partners, which was wholly dedicated to risk arbitrage. Although Oppenheimer, Odyssey, and Junction were separate entities legally, the same man, Jeffrey Tarr, was head arbitrageur for all three firms. In addition, Steve Robert, Nate Gantcher, and many other top partners in Oppenheimer & Company were also partners in both Odyssey and Junction.

Beck, too, had been invited to invest in Odyssey and Junction. He not only had declined but claimed later to have written a series of memos objecting to the whole three-sided arrangement. The very idea appalled him, since it was likely that both of these firms would be taking arbitrage positions in deals involving his M & A department. If Oppenheimer's own arbitrage desk was precluded by regulation and custom from buying into deals involving its own M & A group, he saw no reason why firms with conveniently different legal identities but widely overlapping ownership should be allowed to do so. The opportunities to trade illicitly on the basis of inside information were just too great to be tolerated. He wasn't sure what exactly was going on behind the scenes, but he got enough dubious phone calls from strategically placed Oppenheimer colleagues to convince him that not everyone in the firm was resisting the temptations posed by all those organizational overlaps.

In addition, Oppenheimer numbered among its brokerage clients a host of independent risk-arbitrage firms that flourished on the shadowy fringes of Wall Street, including Ivan F. Boesky & Company. In rainmaking terms Boesky was to risk arbitrage what Henry Kravis was to leveraged buyouts and Mike Milken was to junk bonds: a master promoter with a gift for luring massive sums of other people's money into risky investments under his sponsorship. Even before he had a bona fide performance record to promote, Boesky violated the canon of self-effacement by which arbitrageurs long had lived, hiring a PR man and trumpeting the attractions of risk arbitrage through advertisements. Other arbs were even more disgusted when scores of investors entrusted many millions of dollars to Boesky & Company on absurdly skewed terms. If Boesky made money, 55 percent of the profits were his; if he lost, his investors would bear 95 percent of the loss.

With this arrangement, Boesky had every incentive to take outsized risks, and he did. While other arbs sensibly spread their bets among twenty or thirty different deals, Boesky habitually wagered his whole pile on a single pending transaction, quite successfully at first. A dollar invested with Boesky in 1975 would have grown to $7.54 at the end of 1980. The money kept pouring in, and by 1980 the $700,000 stake with which he'd started had grown to $90 million, making Boesky's firm one of the most heavily capitalized houses on the Street. With this war chest, Boesky was able to insinuate himself into almost every major takeover contest of the early 1980s. Often, he ended up holding the largest single block of stock, and he was not shy about using his influence to shape the outcome of a battle, for where Boesky's money went, his mouth was soon to follow. The man was constantly on the telephone and thought nothing of calling at almost any hour to cajole or bully information out of corporate executives, lawyers, bankers, analysts, or anyone else in the know. Boesky traded through a wide variety of brokerages and thus strategically spread large sums of commission dollars around the Street.

Almost from the moment he'd entered the deal game, Beck had heard rumors that Boesky was crooked. The Securities and Exchange Commission had fanned such rumors by investigating Boesky several times but had never filed charges against him. An arbitrageur whom Beck had befriended told him that traders on the floor of the New

York Stock Exchange had taken to copying trades made by certain
accounts in Switzerland that seemed always to be buying into stocks
just before a takeover bid sent them soaring. The theory was that these
Swiss accounts were fronts for Boesky and a confederate, thought to be
a well-placed M & A lawyer or banker in the United States. Marty
Siegel of Kidder, Peabody was rumored to be the leading suspect.

To Beck's dismay, he unwittingly attracted Boesky as a prospective
client of his M & A department with an idea he'd thought up in his
efforts to differentiate the group from its rivals—a "strategic-block
service." The idea was that the Jeff Beck Group should pitch its services not just to corporations but also to large individual shareholders
looking to sell their stock. In mid-1981, Opco represented the William
Zale family in selling 1.3 million shares of Zale Corporation, a big
Canadian jewelry firm, back to the company. It was a tidy, profitable
transaction, producing a six-figure fee for Oppenheimer. Beck assigned
Phil Cohen, who'd worked with him on the Zale transaction, the task
of making a business out of strategic-block brokering. The assignment
perfectly suited Cohen's hyperaggressive, resourceful nature. He completed two more transactions in 1982 while insinuating himself into a
tussle that held the promise of producing his biggest fee yet.

Rorer Group was in the midst of an attempt to reduce its dependence on Maalox antacid, its best-known product, by acquiring other
medical-products companies. Meanwhile, Rorer Group itself had repeatedly attracted the attentions of larger acquisition-minded companies, but had spurned all suitors. Management's refusal to consider
selling out angered some of the company's largest shareholders, who
had tired of waiting for diversification to boost the company's flagging
share price. Cohen inflamed matters by persuading more than sixty
disaffected shareholders organized into two groups to hire Oppenheimer as financial adviser for the purpose of selling their stock back to
Rorer. Between them, the two dissident groups advised by Cohen
owned 13.5 percent of the stock, more than the Rorer family did. In
such circumstances, a block of 13.5 percent was sufficient to crystallize
a hostile takeover bid. Rorer Group was now in play and the stock
surged as arbitrageurs began placing their bets. Inspired by the prospect of a maximum fee of $1.5 million, Cohen began making the Wall
Street rounds of big-time stock buyers, arbs included.

Among Cohen's likeliest prospects was Boesky, who already had a
position in Rorer. By this time, Boesky had begun moving beyond
arbitrage into corporate raiding, which he tried to ennoble by mis-

describing his activities as "merchant banking." Instead of waiting like
a good arb for someone to make an offer for a company before buying
into it, Boesky was forcing the issue by amassing a large block and then
disclosing his holding through the required 13D filing. As a rule, other
arbitrageurs then began buying the stock, too. The accumulation of
shares by the arbitrageurs tended to weaken a company's defense
against takeover since arbs as a rule were unmoved by management
appeals to stockholder "loyalty" and the like. Interested only in maximizing their profits and minimizing their risk, the arbs sold to the
highest bidder and moved on. While Boesky was usually content to sell
stock back to a company at a hefty profit—a type of payment dubbed
greenmail—on occasion he bought enough stock to give him control.
As it turned out, Boesky didn't want the Rorer block that Cohen
offered, but the mere prospect that he might become a shareholder so
alarmed Rorer's management that the company filed suit in federal
court against Oppenheimer, alleging violation of various disclosure requirements. Cohen didn't care; such lawsuits were de rigueur on the
hostile side of the M & A game. But to Beck, who took inordinate
pride in never having been sued, Rorer's action—and the news coverage it generated—were a jolt.

Rorer's suit faded into irrelevance as the company's management
was able to placate its dissident shareholders, thus preventing the
placement of a large block into unfriendly hands. The $400,000 fee
that Cohen came away with was largely consumed by legal expenses.
Although he hadn't bitten on Rorer, Boesky wanted to work out an
arrangement by which Oppenheimer would give him first look at strategic blocks that it happened upon. While there would have been
nothing illegal about such an arrangement, Beck didn't want to do
business with someone he suspected of being crooked. Nor did he like
the idea of his group systematically teeing up companies for hostile
bids by Boesky or anybody else, for that matter. To Beck, this seemed
an inherently odious practice that, in addition, was bad business because it would tend to alienate the very corporations whose M & A
business Opco craved. As Cohen began scouting for other targets,
Beck began agonizing over the question of whether the fat fees that
strategic-block brokering produced in the short run were worth the ill
will his group would incur over the long run.

Eventually, this issue was rendered moot by an overriding ethical
altercation between Beck and Cohen. In the Jeff Beck Group's first
year, Cohen's contribution was critical to its very survival. Of the

group's first eleven transactions, four involved a single client, for which
Cohen was responsible: Telecom Equipment Corporation, which paid
Oppenheimer a total of $1.4 million in fees during this period.
Telecom Equipment was a fast-growing company that installed and
serviced private phone systems for business clients in New York, New
Jersey, and a half-dozen other states. During Beck's first months at
Oppenheimer, a senior partner of the firm introduced him to Steven
R. Cohen, the CEO of Telecom (and no relation to Phil). Shortly after
Telecom decided to hire Oppenheimer, Beck shifted responsibility for
the account to Phil Cohen, mainly because he considered Steve Cohen pushy and didn't enjoy working with him. At this point, Beck had
yet to learn that Cohen was a former Wall Street stockbroker who as a
result of federal fraud charges had been barred from the brokerage
business for a five-year period by the Securities and Exchange Commission. Cohen neither admitted nor denied the charge, a not uncommon resolution to SEC actions.

Phil Cohen got on so well with Telecom's CEO that he was invited
to join the company's board in 1983. He worked out an unusually
lucrative personal arrangement with Telecom, under which he was
entitled to cash payments of $50,000 a year, free use of a company-
owned car, and options to buy 100,000 shares of stock at a cut-rate
price. This was just the beginning. Not long after the Opco banker was
named a director of Telecom, the company acquired Triboro Communications, a nearly bankrupt little company that was one of Telecom's
local rivals in the New York market. Telecom agreed to buy 81 percent
of Triboro for about $1 million, or 12 cents a share. At the same time,
the two Cohens and other Telecom executives bought 6.25 percent of
Triboro's stock for themselves for $125,000, or 20 cents a share. Four
months after the acquisition, Telecom arranged to have all its new
contracts in the New York City area fulfilled by Triboro, and in late
1983 assigned to Triboro the rights to a major equipment-distribution
contract. This pushed up the value of Triboro stock sharply. When
Tele-Plus, another company controlled by Telecom, purchased the remaining 19 percent of Triboro, the Cohen group cashed out at a profit
of $2.4 million. In a similarly convoluted series of transactions involv-
ing the acquisition of Maxcell, the two Cohens again were part of an
insider group that reaped a paper profit of $2.5 million.

Eventually, these transactions would prompt shareholder lawsuits
charging Steve Cohen and his cronies with self-dealing and misappro-
priation of company assets. Even before the suits were filed, though,

Phil Cohen was in trouble at Oppenheimer. While there was nothing wrong with Cohen accepting appointment as a director of a client company, New York Stock Exchange regulations required that representatives of member firms disclose to their employers all compensation received in such a capacity. According to Beck and another well-placed source at Oppenheimer, Cohen failed to inform the firm of the options he'd gotten from Telecom, though Telecom itself disclosed this information in various SEC filings. After getting a call from someone who'd come across Cohen's name in a Telecom filing, Beck said that he called the banker into his office and demanded to know whether he had in fact received options from Telecom. When Cohen admitted that he had, Beck claimed to have fired him on the spot. Beck showed me internal Oppenheimer documents stating that Cohen owed the firm $683,000 for stock options that rightfully belonged to the firm and another $83,000 for director's fees he should have passed on.

After leaving Oppenheimer, Cohen kept his seat on the Telecom board and set up his own investment-banking firm, which he named Morgan, Schiff & Company—appropriating for his commercial use the family names of the two greatest gentleman bankers in Wall Street history. "It was my belief that investment banks should go back to advising clients in a closer format, as in the days of Morgan and [Jacob] Schiff," Cohen explained. Over the course of 1984 and 1985 alone, Telecom paid Morgan, Schiff $2.8 million in fees.

In finally settling with his aggrieved shareholders, CEO Steve Cohen agreed to reimburse Telecom for the $4 million Trump Tower apartment he'd bought with corporate funds. The CEO and four of his fellow executives also "voluntarily" transferred to Telecom their options on Maxcell. Phil Cohen alone refused to compromise, holding on to his Maxcell options despite the company's dismal performance. Over the period of his association with Telecom, Cohen personally made more money in fees and capital gains than the company generated in operating earnings. Indeed, from 1979 through 1988, Telecom Equipment posted losses of $45 million. If this was what Cohen—who like Boesky delighted in calling himself a merchant banker—meant by a return to old-fashioned values, then Beck wanted no part of it. To him, a few million dollars in lost revenues was a small price to pay to rid himself of the likes of Phil Cohen.

8

After the Varian–Madison Fund battle, Beck realized that if he was going to graduate to big deals, he was going to have to do it on his own. There would be no client referrals from Flom, no helpful hints from Rohatyn, no flattering quotes courtesy of Wasserstein. In the wake of the Varian-Madison deal, the word on Beck circulated through the Deal Club: He was a most "difficult" personality, a loose cannon. Luckily for Beck, exclusion from the Deal Club was not without its advantages. For one thing, his deal-man's imagination remained unfettered by conventional wisdom and the consensus view—notably the assumption that the only client worth having was a *Fortune* 500 corporation or, for that matter, a corporation per se. Beck thought of himself not merely as an investment banker building a franchise but as a player in the deal game. At first this was largely wishful thinking, but of a constructive sort, for it led Beck into attempting to cultivate anyone whom he perceived capable of initiating or closing a deal— even including other rainmakers.

Beck was one of the first M & A chiefs to see in Henry Kravis not a minor competitive annoyance but someone very much worth his while to get to know. This proved a crucial insight, for it was largely through his relationship with Kravis that Beck would finally bluster and connive his way into the highest level of the deal game. By the end of the 1980s, Kravis would have established himself not only as the most celebrated of all Wall Street deal men—the lead barbarian in *Barbarians at the Gate*—but as the epitome of the nouveau mogul in an era of moneyed grandiosity unequaled since the Gilded Age. Kravis and his pencil-thin celebrity designer wife, Carolyne Roehm, attended so many high-society galas that it seemed they must sleep in black tie and ball gown. Kravis relished spending money in attention-getting ways: $2 million for a gray stone manor and the lake and waterfall that he added; $5 million for a vast Park Avenue residence in a building once occupied by John D. Rockefeller, Jr.; untold millions for an instant collection of fine art that included works by Renoir, Monet, Tissot, and Sargent; $10 million to endow a Kravis wing of the Metropolitan Museum of Art, and another $10 million to attach a Kravis wing to Mt. Sinai Medical Center. By 1990, Kravis would be living a life so far removed in every sense from his native Tulsa that he was capable, with a straight face, of complaining to a reporter (quite inaccurately, by the way) that "even J. P. Morgan was allowed to live in the splendor he wanted without complaints from the press."

To Beck, Kravis was an overwhelmingly provocative figure. Not only was he what Beck most wanted to be professionally—an owner of companies, not merely an adviser to them—but Kravis also was the sort of extravagantly social, graciously rich son whom Ida Beck no doubt would have loved to have. When Beck first met Kravis, though, he was just a short, dapper guy from Oklahoma, who, like thousands of other anonymous Wall Street aspirants—Beck included—was still looking for his big chance. Kravis would find his jackpot in the leveraged buyout, which, depending on one's point of view could be seen as "an idea created in Hell by the Devil himself," as one establishment-corporation executive put it, or, as Kravis himself proclaimed, as the hope and salvation of the U.S. economy. By the end of the decade, the layers of political and ideological rhetoric that collected around the LBO had all but obscured its real significance: It was the greatest technique for getting rich quick in the hallowed American way since the advent of the modern corporation a century before. Kravis's firm, Kohlberg, Kravis, Roberts & Co., would evolve into the hub of a new division of the Deal Club through which Wall Street would promote the takeover game to new heights of profitability and economic irresponsibility.

Like Beck, Kravis grew up in a family obsessed by big money and domineered by a self-made millionaire. "I was always in a hurry—you know, I was born premature," said Kravis by way of explaining his driving ambition. "If you run fast enough, you don't have time to worry about failing." Henry's father, Raymond Kravis, was born in England and emigrated to the United States with his parents—his father was a tailor—when he was only five years old. Ray Kravis grew up in Atlantic City and attended Lehigh University, graduating in 1924 with a degree in geology. He headed down to Tulsa, where he worked in the engineering department of an accounting firm and developed a taste for stock-market speculation on margin. Wiped out in the great crash of 1929, Kravis mollified his creditors and within five years had repaid all his borrowings. He was thirty-four in 1935 when, in the depths of the Depression, he started his own consulting firm, Raymond F. Kravis & Associates.

As a free-lance petroleum engineer, Kravis typically would be hired to validate oil companies' estimates of the size of their petroleum reserves. Kravis was unusual among engineers in that he was as clever at finance as at geology; indeed, the foundation of his fortune was his discovery of a tax loophole that enabled oil producers to sharply reduce their income-tax exposure. Incredibly, it took the government a decade to close the lucrative loophole Kravis had opened, time enough for Kravis to market the hell out of it and establish a network of friends and clients that circled the oil patch and stretched all the way back to Wall Street. Hired by such giants as Sunray, Monsanto, and Texas Gulf to make appraisals connected with mergers and acquisitions, Kravis recycled his bounteous stream of fee income into investments in oil and gas properties. When Joseph P. Kennedy called one day looking for a way into the oil and gas business, Kravis sold him an interest in a company he controlled and became Kennedy's partner. Kravis was a unique combination of petroleum engineer and crafty deal broker; by the time he retired in his mid-eighties he had parlayed his web of connections into a personal fortune thought to exceed $100 million, perhaps by a lot.

Whatever the magnitude of his fortune, though, Ray Kravis luxuriated in his wealth and the things it could buy in the classic fashion of a man who'd started with little and rehabilitated himself from financial ruin. While he and his wife, Bessie, never moved out of Tulsa, they spent a great deal of time in the elite Florida enclave of Palm Beach, where they lived lavishly. It was in Palm Beach, not Tulsa, that Kravis lent his name to a fund-raising drive to build the $51 million Raymond F. Kravis Center for the Performing Arts. The importance of net worth to Kravis's identity was evident in a story he liked to tell about George Bush, whose father, Prescott, was a prominent investment banker close to Kravis. Prescott, Kravis said, "called me one day to tell me his son was graduating from college and was looking for a job in the oil business; could I give him a job? Well, of course. But two days before he was supposed to go to work, George calls and says all of his friends were working in Texas. Would I mind if he doesn't come to

Tulsa? But here's the funny thing. I was in the receiving line at the White House one day, waiting to shake hands with President Reagan. George sees me, takes me aside, and introduces me to his friends. He says, 'I almost went to work for Ray Kravis. If I had, I'd almost be as rich as he is!' I told him, 'Don't kid me, George, you're loaded!' "

Born in 1944, Henry was the second of Ray's and Bessie's two sons. Henry was a runty kid whose early years, as he told it himself, were defined by an almost obstinate self-reliance. He claims to have refused to let his mother teach him how to tie his shoes, experimenting on his own until he got it right. School didn't come easily to him, though he got by with hard work. While still in grade school, though, he distinguished himself at selling, regularly winning the annual contest to sell magazine subscriptions. The prize was something a rich man's son could relate to: Henry was given a shovel and led to a barrelful of pennies. He managed to extract about 3,400—$34. At thirteen, Henry was shipped off to Eaglebrook, a boarding school in Massachusetts, where his scrawniness didn't keep him from playing football. He also won the Neat Award for personal tidiness. One of his teammates and closest friends was a bandy-legged linebacker named Michael Douglas, son of the tough-guy actor Kirk Douglas. After Eaglebrook, Kravis moved on to Loomis Chaffee, an elite prep school near Hartford, Connecticut, where he was captain of the wrestling team, vice president of the student council, and popular to boot. He was generally known by the regular-guy nickname of Hank, though his buddies called him the Lover. "I had a few girlfriends," Kravis recalled.

After graduating, Henry applied to Lehigh University, which had named its auditorium after Ray Kravis in appreciation of his donations over the years. "He just wanted to show me he could get into the same school as I did," Ray Kravis said. Deciding against his father's alma mater, Henry enrolled at Claremont Men's College, near Los Angeles. There, he played on the golf team and majored in economics, though, like Beck, he didn't get serious about his studies until his last year. Even so, he didn't have to sweat a job, since he'd already spent three summers working at Goldman, Sachs. His father was a close friend of the firm's senior partner, Gus Levy. The fact that Ray also was friendly with Levy's great rival, Cy Lewis of Bear, Stearns, was testament to both his charm and the breadth of his Wall Street relationships. "I didn't realize how well-known my father was until I came to New York," said Henry, who was both impressed and dismayed by the discovery. He'd decided to pursue a career in securities rather than submit to paternal pressure to join the family business largely because he "didn't want to just be known as Ray Kravis's son." As Ray's son he could at least insist on the consolation of starting at the bottom once in the door. And so it was that the future king of the leveraged buyout made his Wall Street debut as a messenger boy before shifting into research and then into institutional brokerage and corporate finance. Levy once told Ray that Henry was the best intern that Goldman, Sachs had ever had.

After graduating from Claremont in 1967, Kravis enrolled at Columbia University School of Business. He also landed a part-time job at the Madison Fund, which at the time was headed by Ed Merkle, a veteran stock picker who was yet another crony of Ray Kravis. Like Beck, Kravis wore suits to class and lived across town from campus in an Upper East Side apartment, which, in Henry's case, was decorated with the art collection that he'd precociously begun building with thousand-dollar purchases here and there. With a trio of French Canadian classmates, he made the rounds of Manhattan's fancy French restaurants. He was well-liked and capable of poking fun at his own rich-kid patina. "I'm just an Okie," he liked to say with a smile that politely invited disagreement. By registering his car in Oklahoma, Kravis was able to get license plates featuring the letters "DPL," which, as he'd intended, the meter maids of New York mistook for diplomatic plates, enabling him to park with impunity. Kravis, who was exempted from the draft for medical reasons, had even less curiosity about than sympathy for the student radicals who shut down Columbia in the spring of 1968. "I had some idea about what was going on in Vietnam but to go out and march and carry on about it was not of interest to me." Kravis's sole interest was his career. He scheduled all his classes from Monday through Wednesday so he could devote all day Thursday and Friday to his work as a junior stock picker at the Madison Fund. He pulled B's and C's at school but accomplished his overriding goal—to graduate in the minimum of four semesters—and immediately joined Madison full-time.

In roundabout fashion, the Madison Fund had acquired a controlling interest in Katy Industries, which was the new name adopted by an old railroad as it emerged from court-protected reorganization. In its travails, Katy had accumulated huge tax breaks, which it could fully exploit only by acquiring companies with income to shelter. Merkle, whose approach to management could be charitably described as freewheeling, assigned Kravis the job of finding companies for Katy to buy.

Kravis was twenty-three years old and as green as a golf course. "I don't know anything about buying companies," he told Merkle.

"Kid," said Merkle, "you buy companies just like you buy stocks. And if it turns out you don't like 'em, you sell 'em."

Kravis had just begun searching when Merkle had a heart attack. In addition to running the Madison Fund, Merkle had overseen the administration of Katy, assisted only by a lawyer. Kravis went to his bedridden boss and suggested that Katy needed a full-time president. "Kid," said Merkle, who never called Kravis by his name, "the job is yours."

Kravis had ambition but wasn't crazed with it. He helped Merkle recruit an experienced corporate executive to run Katy—Jacob Saliba, whose son had been a classmate of Henry's at Columbia. Katy Industries set up its executive offices in a two-room suite at the old Delmonico Hotel on the Upper East Side. Kravis and a secretary occupied the living room; Saliba took the bedroom. In shopping for companies, Saliba and Kravis were constrained by severe shortages of cash and prospects. Basically, they had to find companies obscure enough to have been overlooked in the conglomerate feeding frenzy of the 1960s, and convince them to take Katy stock, which wasn't exactly gilt-edged. In New Orleans, Kravis ate crawfish in the bayou kitchen of a tugboat-manufacturing concern run by a grade-school dropout and also romanced a couple of brothers who owned a local dredging company. Katy ended up buying both the tugboat and dredging firms. "Henry could get along with a blue-collar guy as well as a white-collar one," Saliba said. "He didn't put on airs and he never gave up." During Kravis's eighteen-month stint, Katy acquired a dozen small companies. While many of the acquisitions didn't pan out in the long run, they served an expedient purpose, generating cash flow without which the railroad would have failed again.

Kravis left Katy Industries after control of the company passed from the Madison Fund to a wealthy Chicago industrialist. He took a job as a merger banker for a new investment bank called Faherty & Swartwood, which Kravis chose because he thought he'd be able to advance more quickly at a small, unstructured firm. Kravis was indeed unencumbered—not only by bureaucracy but by business to transact. After nine months of underemployment, Kravis was getting a bit frantic with the fear that the Wall Street parade might be passing him by. His next job came through his cousin, George Roberts, who'd grown up in Houston. Henry and George were the same age and had always been close. They'd attended Claremont College together and, thanks to his Uncle Ray, George had spent his summers at Bear, Stearns while Henry was toiling a few blocks away at Goldman, Sachs. After college, Roberts joined Bear, Stearns's corporate-finance department and in 1969 wangled a transfer to the San Francisco office. His departure created a vacancy that Kravis eagerly filled.

Founded in 1923, Bear, Stearns & Company Incorporated was a thriving, predominantly Jewish trading house struggling to carve out a franchise for itself in corporate finance. At the time Kravis joined the Bear, as the firm was known, it wasn't ranked among Wall Street's twenty-five largest underwriters. However, the firm was beginning to make a specialty out of a special acquisition technique called bootstrapping, which traditionally was a transaction of last resort. A bootstrapper put himself in a financial hole by taking on heavy debt to buy a company and then striving to pull himself up by his financial bootstraps by using cash generated by his business to pay off the debt that encumbered it, until he owned it free and clear. Bootstrap deals tended to be born of desperation on one hand—an owner dying to unload—and luck on the other—a person of modest means who managed to borrow immodestly against the assets of the very company that he proposed to acquire. The bootstrap was the deal-making equivalent of a lightning strike: a random, infrequent, and startling event.

Bear, Stearns's resident bootstrapper was Jerome Kohlberg, the firm's corporate-finance chief. A graduate of both Columbia Business School and Harvard Law School, Kohlberg joined Bear, Stearns in 1955 and had quietly developed a reputation for utter reliability. Every aspect of Kohlberg's demeanor advertised him as a man of integrity. His suits were drab and his ties unfashionably narrow; his blue eyes peered out unblinkingly from behind rimless glasses. Given to neither the small talk nor the easy confidences of the salesman, Kohlberg went efficiently about his business with what one reporter described as "a reserve as impenetrable as a two-foot-thick vault door." His idea of night life was reading a book at home with his wife. On drizzly work-day mornings he was known to venture forth carrying an umbrella and wearing galoshes, a trench coat, a scarf, and a big floppy hat. "I thought I'd be prepared," he once explained to a quizzical colleague. Kohlberg was a paradox: a deeply conservative man with an affinity for the risky deal.

Kohlberg had put together his first bootstrap in 1965. H. James

Stern, a wealthy neighbor of Kohlberg's, had come to him with a problem. Stern, seventy-two, was the sole owner of I. Stern & Company, a manufacturer of dental products and precious-metals alloys, and was looking for a way to shift control to other family members without incurring a tax liability so large it would force the sale of the company. Kohlberg had an idea: If Bear, Stearns bought the company in partnership with the Stern heirs, the old man could cash out and yet keep the company under family management. The trick was coming up with the $9.5 million needed to swing the deal. The next generation of Sterns didn't have that kind of cash lying around and the traders who ran Bear, Stearns blanched at tying up the firm's own capital in some little company. Kohlberg was able to persuade the firm and some of its partners to kick in a couple of hundred thousand dollars, and with his own contribution and that of the Sterns, the equity totaled $500,000. Kohlberg then went to work on lenders with whom he'd dealt on other sorts of financings, assuring them that Stern & Company was a solid business with bright prospects and that he personally would ensure that it was properly managed and paid its debts. "Trust me," Kohlberg said—and a few insurance companies eventually did just that, lending $9 million, most of it unsecured.

Stern & Company, renamed Sterndent, thrived as predicted. The buyout debt was quickly pared down through a public stock sale, and when the original investors sold out two years later, they pocketed a profit of $3.5 million on the original $500,000 investment. Impressive as these results were, there was no magic involved. Superb timing was largely responsible; Kohlberg and company bought the business at a modest multiple of its earnings at a time of general softness in the economy and resold it at a richer multiple in a hot stock market. The resulting capital gain was multiplied eighteen times over by the leverage employed in the purchase. This was the beauty of the LBO: When a deal worked, profits accumulated at a geometric rate.

In 1966, Kohlberg did three more bootstraps—which he preferred to describe simply as "purchases"—and another in 1969, the first on which he was assisted by Kravis. Each of these early buyouts was leveraged with about $10 of debt to every $1 of equity and was custom crafted around an elderly owner with an estate problem. Kohlberg was selective in applying the technique, preferring solidly profitable, simple companies in industries that weren't subject to wide seasonal fluctuations in revenue. He also had to be convinced of the competence and integrity of the company's management and was capable of spending months methodically getting to know the principals. For every deal done, three or four died a-borning, usually for lack of financing. Some bankers simply hung up the phone when they heard the outline of the deal. Kohlberg, Kravis, and Roberts, who split his time between San Francisco and New York, each spent countless hours flying anywhere and everywhere to make earnest, crisply authoritative presentations to the money men whom they'd convinced not to hang up on them. Even for small deals, the financial structures they invented resembled layer cakes of various securities designed to meet each investor's partic-ular needs—a five-year senior convertible note, say, or a subordinated debenture with warrants. The art of the design lay in satisfying each individual lender without overburdening the company.

From 1965 to 1975, a total of fourteen buyouts were completed under Kohlberg's aegis. Despite his caution, several turned out poorly, and one was a disaster so complete that its failure seemed divinely ordained—the $27 million buyout of Cobblers, a shoe company. Sev-eral months after the deal was completed, the company's founder walked up to the roof and jumped to his death. Eventually the com-pany was liquidated and the Kohlberg group lost its entire $400,000 investment. Despite such setbacks, the Kohlberg-Kravis-Roberts team gained a reputation for doing its damnedest to solve any post-buyout problem. By thus reassuring lenders they were able to finance ever larger deals, which, in turn, had the effect of overshadowing the other promoters struggling to make a business out of buyouts. Even as Cob-bler was coming unstuck in 1972, the team completed its largest deal to date—the $36.5 million buyout of Vapor Corporation. It was an unqualified triumph, not only because it returned nearly $12 for every $1 invested but because its backers included two top-drawer institu-tions participating in a Kohlberg deal for the first time: Prudential Insurance Company of America and First National Bank of Chicago. After Vapor, the Pru and First Chicago effectively sponsored the move of the Kohlberg team into the mainstream by repeatedly recommend-ing them to other major lenders. They stuck by the trio of LBO specialists even after they came to a bitter parting of the ways with Bear, Stearns.

The methodical Kohlberg had always been an anomaly at Bear, Stearns, which was notorious even in trading circles for its restless, hard-nosed opportunism. The traders who ruled the firm were accus-tomed to turning over the firm's capital in a matter of minutes, not years. That Cy Lewis, the senior partner, had allowed Kohlberg to do buyouts in the first place was telling evidence of his respect for the banker. Eventually, though, Lewis, a man of volcanic temperament, lost patience with Kohlberg and his youthful charges as they shifted their focus from drumming up underwriting and other traditional financing business to promoting leveraged buyouts. The deal makers, on the other hand, grew increasingly frustrated at not being able to concentrate full-time on LBOs. Matters came to a head after Lewis twice refused Kohlberg's proposal to create a freestanding LBO group within Bear, Stearns. In 1976, Kohlberg, Kravis, and Roberts resigned. Kohlberg considered retiring but instead joined with the cousins to found their own firm—Kohlberg, Kravis, Roberts & Company—which set up shop in an office on Fifth Avenue at Fifty-fourth Street. Kravis would later admit to trepidation in striking out on his own. "We didn't know if it was because of us or Bear, Stearns that we'd been able to do these deals," he said.

KKR was founded with $120,000—most of it contributed by Kohlberg—which was about all the cash the three principals could muster from their own pockets. Most of the money they'd made over the years was invested in the stock of the companies they'd taken private while at Bear, Stearns. To cover overhead costs, KKR assembled a group of eight limited partners—Ray Kravis among them—who, in exchange for $50,000 apiece, got the right to invest in any buyout the firm put together. To the deal makers' dismay, the group included only one institution, First Chicago, and even getting that one had been a struggle. Lewis had called Robert Abboud, the CEO of First Chicago, to bad-mouth his ex-employees. Abboud was similarly inclined to view people who'd left his employ as disloyal; he initially opposed backing KKR. But Stan Golder, the First Chicago banker who'd worked most closely with the LBO trio, took up their case. Golder brought KKR's principals in to meet the bank's senior officers and had a series of frank conversations with Abboud that included the comment "You know, Bob, Lincoln freed the slaves." Lewis also called officers of Prudential, who politely told him to get lost. Although the Prudential continued to finance KKR deals on an ad hoc basis, as a matter of policy the insurer did not invest in outside investment-banking firms.

KKR closed a half-dozen deals in its first two years, but struggled with the financing on a couple of them. On the $57 million purchase of L. B. Foster Company in 1977, KKR signed an agreement to buy the company and then came up $5 million short of the financing it needed. Kravis had to go to the firm's chairman and admit failure. "I was scared to death," Kravis recalled. "I said, 'We've done everything we can and we just can't get there.' " Kravis persuaded him to take a $5 million note back from the KKR investors and the deal was closed.

In hopes of avoiding this sort of frustration and humiliation, KKR decided in 1978 to raise a "blind pool" of equity money—that is, line up financing commitments in advance so that the funds would be on hand when the opportunity to do a deal happened along. KKR had tried to put together such a pool upon the firm's formation but gave up when institutional investors insisted on having veto power over each deal. KKR won the debate on this issue the second time around, raising $30 million from a dozen institutions including First Chicago, Penn Mutual Life, and Mutual Benefit Life to invest as its principals saw fit. KKR also prevailed on the issue of fees: The firm would take an annual investment-management fee amounting to 1 percent of the money in the pool and a transaction fee for every deal done equal to 1 percent of its total value. In addition, KKR would get a 20 percent "carry" on each transaction, meaning that when an LBO investment was cashed out, KKR would get 20 percent of the profits. KKR's ability to negotiate this package of extremely advantageous terms was a sign that it was coming of age as a deal promoter. Having $30 million already in hand added greatly to KKR's credibility in its negotiations with companies on the block. KKR ran through that $30 million in no time and in 1979 raised $100 million more.

By this time, Kravis and Roberts were thirty-five years old and seasoned deal men in their own right. In fact, the cousins for some time had been handling most of the nitty-gritty work pertaining to the doing of deals—from scouting for companies to negotiating with corporate executives and romancing lenders. "Jerry was still a lot better known but Henry and George were generally the leaders in getting deals done," recalled Milan Risanovich, the Prudential executive in charge of the KKR account for much of the 1970s. While Kohlberg was still the dominant partner, increasingly his role was to brake his younger and more aggressive partners. Each LBO required the approval of all three partners, and it was Kohlberg who said no most often. Yet KKR kept doing more and bigger deals. By the late 1970s, the high-octane ambition of Kravis and Roberts was propelling KKR. "Other people doing LBOs tended to do again and again what they were already doing; they milked a formula," said Garnett Keith, who succeeded Risanovich at the Pru as the KKR liaison in the late 1970s. "KKR's secret was that it kept pushing back the boundaries for doing bigger and more daring deals—and that was mainly because of the competitiveness of Henry and George."

In 1979, KKR completed a leveraged buyout larger by several orders of magnitude than even they would have believed possible a few years before. The $360 million purchase of Houdaille Industries was a tour de force of financial engineering, with two classes of common stock and two of preferred, one layer of revolving bank credit, two types of senior notes, and a junior subordinated note—all spread among thirty-five institutions. "I knew it was creative," a rival banker conceded, "because I couldn't figure it out." Although the principals of KKR had devoted fourteen years to the pioneering of the LBO, not until the Houdaille deal did they begin to attract the attention of the Wall Street Establishment or the financial press. KKR was deluged with requests for Houdaille prospectuses as reporters and Deal Club bankers alike began trying to figure out just what this funny little fringe firm was doing anyway.

It was right after the Houdaille deal that Oppenheimer president Steve Robert introduced Beck to Kravis. Robert had met Kravis while vacationing in Palm Beach in the late 1960s and had remained friendly with him ever since. Beck and Kravis hit it off immediately, having in common not only similar family histories and professional ambitions but also the recent pain of marital separation. Over dinner at semi-chic Upper East Side restaurants, the two deal men commiserated and talked deals, deals, deals late into many an evening. Although "sweet" and "nice" were the adjectives women most often used to describe Kravis, Beck glimpsed steel often enough beneath the Oklahoman's gracious exterior to convince him that here was a tough and tenacious deal man—"a real killer," as Beck admiringly put it. In furtherance of his research into Kravis's soul, Beck occasionally introduced the subject of Ray Kravis just to set the steel flashing in Henry's eyes. Beck had no doubt that Kravis was hell-bent on making a mark on Wall Street that would eclipse his father's legend once and for all. The question was how to exploit Kravis's ambition for his own ends.

In 1980, Kravis mentioned to Beck that KKR wanted to sell Incom International, a maker of industrial parts, which had been spun out of Rockwell International in 1975, just before Kravis and his partners left Bear, Stearns. At $92 million, the Incom buyout, like that of Vapor, was a milestone: the largest LBO done by Bear, Stearns or anyone else to that point. If all went according to plan, KKR looked to resell the companies it had bought three to five years after the original buyout. Beck was unable to convince Kravis to sign him to a retainer but decided to shop Incom on spec, giving John Sanzo the assignment of identifying a likely buyer. After a few days of running computer screens and perusing Moody's manuals, Sanzo came up with Amstar, an old-line corporation that was the biggest U.S. producer of sweeteners, notably Domino sugar. Based in New York, Amstar was a billion-dollar company that had begun branching into industrial tools in the mid-1960s through small acquisitions, the last of which was completed in 1971. Amstar's diversification had been successful but half-assed; nearly 80 percent of the company's income still came from the sugar side of the business. Perhaps it was time for another deal?

The fact that Amstar long had used Dillon, Read and Goldman, Sachs as its investment banks only sharpened Beck's desire to win its business. Beck dangled Incom International by telephone before Amstar's president, Robert Quittmeyer. Quittmeyer bit—hard. A few days after cold-calling Amstar, Beck and Sanzo were representing the company in negotiations with Kravis. They raced through the preliminaries and quickly reached agreement on price. The deal seemed to be speeding along to its conclusion when, on the very day Kravis traveled to Pittsburgh to inform Incom's employees of the impending sale to Amstar, Quittmeyer suddenly balked over what seemed to Beck to be a minor point. Kravis had already agreed to accept from Amstar a convertible debenture in partial payment for Incom. Quittmeyer now insisted that the price at which the debenture would be convertible into Amstar shares not be determined until after the transaction was announced. If Amstar stock rose on the announcement of the Incom deal, then the conversion price would be adjusted upward accordingly. This wouldn't lower the cost of acquiring Incom but it would diminish KKR's ability to profit from Amstar's future success.

To Beck, Quittmeyer's stubbornness on this issue seemed worse than pointless; it was spiteful. As he pondered the matter, Beck concluded that his client's desire to own Incom hadn't diminished but that he was letting envy intrude on what should have been, in one of the Mad Dog's most often used adjectives, a "clinical" transaction. Quittmeyer, sixty, was a white-shoe corporate lawyer turned executive who'd spent his career methodically climbing the corporate ladder. From the Incom transaction alone, Kravis stood to make more money than Quittmeyer had made in his entire career. Quittmeyer never referred to Kravis as a "Wall Street fast-buck artist" but Beck could read these words in his face and hear them in the tone of his voice. In his attempts to induce Quittmeyer to proceed, Beck succeeded only in putting his client's nose even further out of joint. Quittmeyer would later describe Beck as "a pusher and a shover who wanted to be a doer. He was more than aggressive." Beck, on the other hand, was exasperated by Quittmeyer's petulant passivity. *This* guy was no killer. Late in the afternoon of the Friday that Quittmeyer had scrambled the Incom deal, Beck put in a call to his client and was stunned to find he'd left for the weekend. Around the dinner hour, Beck called the CEO at home and got a frosty reception. "You're interrupting my scotch," he said. Beck could no longer deny his suspicion that the deal was slipping away.

Kravis was adept at disarming executives who had every reason to be leery on first meeting. "Henry had one of the greatest humble-pie routines I'd ever seen," Beck said. With Amstar, though, the negotiations had moved so swiftly that there seemed no need for Kravis to turn on the charm. And after Quittmeyer raised his eleventh-hour objection, Kravis was in no mood to try to charm a man who'd put him in the embarrassing position of announcing a sale to Incom's employees even as it was falling apart. Without telling Beck, Kravis began negotiating with another prospective buyer—IFI, the family investment company of Giovanni Agnelli, the billionaire who controlled the Italian auto giant, Fiat. Kravis and representatives of IFI began negotiating on Saturday and reached agreement on Tuesday afternoon. On Tuesday morning, Sanzo called Kravis and suggested a compromise on the conversion-rate issue. Kravis seemed receptive. "I'll get back to you," Kravis said.

Sanzo went out to lunch with Beck assuming the deal was in the bag. After returning from lunch, Beck asked his secretary if Kravis had called. No, he hadn't. "We're in trouble, John," he said.

Sanzo scoffed. "What are you talking about?" he said. "This is a done deal."

Beck immediately called Kravis, who came on the line only long enough to say, "I'll call you back."

When Kravis called later that afternoon, it was to tell Beck that KKR had signed an agreement to sell Incom to IFI for a bit more than Amstar had offered and all cash. Beck was furious. "Goddammit, Henry," he shouted, "I wish you would have told me you had another offer. That would have got Quittmeyer's ass in gear."

Kravis shrugged off Beck's complaints. He had gotten the deal he wanted. "Jeff's an emotional guy," Kravis said. "He calmed down."

After Quittmeyer retired, Beck suggested to his successor, Howard Wentz, that he consider taking the company private through a leveraged buyout. It seemed to Beck that Wentz was curiously evasive on the subject, and about six weeks later he figured out why: Kravis had beaten him to the punch again. KKR announced a $465 million LBO of Amstar. Although hardly a week went by during which he didn't speak with Kravis, Beck hadn't heard a word of the Amstar deal until he read about it in the newspaper. (Amstar proved one of KKR's best deals; in 1987, KKR sold the sugar concern at a profit of $232 million, producing a compounded annual rate of return of 81.5 percent.) Beck was bitterly disappointed that he wasn't included in the buyout of a company that he'd introduced to Kravis.

"I felt like a piece of used meat for the second time on the same company," Beck said. "But so what? If you're an investment banker you're going to get used." To Beck, it made no sense to stand on ceremony when there were deals by the dozen waiting to be done, killer to killer. Sure enough, before the year was out, Beck would be working with Kravis, his friend and foe, on a buyout five times the size of Amstar.

9

Jeff Beck was in love with the idea of Margaret Atwater Preston McCormick long before he met the flesh and blood of her, which, as it happened, was some weeks after he first heard the cultured, flirtatious purr of her well-modulated voice. For Beck, it was love at first telephone call. He spent more than an hour talking with Margo when, at the suggestion of a mutual acquaintance, he finally got up the nerve to call her one night in March of 1982. There would be hours more of telephone conversation before the two met face-to-face for an official date. Beck was in no hurry. He didn't need to see her to *know*, though Margo proved a most pleasant sight indeed—a trim, leggy, brunette beauty. "Margo," he said later, "was something about the Establishment."

Born in 1949, Margo Preston had grown up in Lake Forest, Illinois, an upper-middle-class enclave on Chicago's North Shore. Both of her grandfathers had had distinguished careers as corporate lawyers and her father, Charles Preston, had started out in law before switching to investment banking. Margo attended Lake Forest Country Day School through ninth grade and at eighteen had two coming-out parties: an afternoon tea at her home and a more formal cotillion in Chicago. At the start of her sophomore year in high school, Margo had gone away to Massachusetts to attend Concord Academy, which was perhaps the finest girls' preparatory school in America. Margo was a bright girl who did well enough in her classes but eased through school without distinguishing herself in any particular way. She had none of the rough edge of ambition—no rough edges at all, in fact. After graduating from Concord, she attended Boston University, concentrating on film studies and art history with no particular vocation in mind. After three years in Boston, Margo dropped out and returned home to Chicago in 1971 to marry a man whom she'd met a few years before at a friend's coming-out party. Margo was twenty-one. Mark Bisbee McCormick was twenty-five.

Margo's wedding was a triumph of debutante promise fulfilled, for she had married into one of Chicago's great families, a dynasty sired by a man known to generations of schoolchildren as the inventor of the mechanical reaper: Cyrus McCormick. From the company he founded in 1848 grew the farm-equipment colossus International Harvester Company. As late as 1937, the McCormicks still held 32 percent of the common stock of International Harvester and were not only Chicago's wealthiest family but one of the dozen richest in America, with a fortune of at least $120 million. In classic Establishment fashion, Harold Fowler McCormick, the son of the reaper king, married Edith Rockefeller, the daughter of the founder of Standard Oil, who reigned over Chicago society in the 1920s in formal splendor from her huge gray stone mansion at 1000 Lake Shore Drive. Her children, when they were grown, could see her only by appointment. Even as the family gradually dwindled in number and fortune, it continued to produce more than its share of grandes dames. When a society columnist decided in 1953 that what Chicago really needed was an officially designated doyenne, the two thousand socialites she polled chose Marion McCormick, Mark's grandmother.

Mark's father, Brooks McCormick, was the last of a long line of McCormicks to run International Harvester. He ascended to the job of chief executive officer in 1971, not long after Mark and Margo married. At the time, McCormick was a student at the University of Chicago Business School. After he got his MBA, McCormick and his new bride moved to New York and bought a spacious co-op on East Sixty-second Street between Park and Madison. Mark had landed a job as an associate in corporate finance at Kuhn Loeb & Company, the doddering Our Crowd bastion later acquired by Lehman Brothers.

According to Margo's accounts, her marriage began blissfully. "Mark and I were truly soul mates," she said. "After parties, we liked to stay up all night in bed talking." Despite an occasional black-tie event, the couple kept a low social profile, associating mostly with mutual friends of long standing and Mark's investment-banking colleagues. "People on Wall Street really liked working together in those days," Margo said. "There didn't seem to be the resentments of later years as the money got bigger." As the years passed, though, Margo grew a bit restive in the life of a young Upper East Side society wife. She enrolled at Hunter College, intending to complete her undergraduate degree and perhaps make a career of art history. While she did work one summer at Sotheby's, the society auction house, nothing much came of Margo's return to school; she left Hunter before accumulating enough credits for her BA. On the home front, meanwhile, fun gradually gave way to discontent.

As breakups go, Mark's and Margo's was extremely traumatic, yet amicable. The irreconcilable difference was Mark's sexuality. That he and Margo remained together for a few years even after Mark acknowledged that he was gay was testament not only to his continued desire for the cover of marriage but to the affection they continued to feel for one another. By all accounts, Mark and Margo never really fell out of love, which only made parting harder, of course. After a final year of mounting unhappiness, Margo moved into an apartment of her own in a brownstone on Seventieth Street. In the interest of expedience, Mark sued for divorce on the grounds of abandonment while agreeing to make equitable alimony payments to Margo. A divorce was granted in February 1980.

At thirty-one, Margo Preston became a working woman. She networked her way into film-production work, ending up as a freelance line producer, working mostly on documentaries, industrial and military training films, and the like. Even combined with her alimony, though, Preston's income from film work apparently was not sufficient to cover her living costs, for she also began dipping into the principal of the trust fund that had been created for her in 1971, just before her father's death. If Preston were going to live in the style to which she'd become accustomed, her best bet was to remarry. Although the odds of her finding a second husband with McCormick's gilt-edged social credentials were slim, there was a plentiful supply of moneyed men, single and otherwise, on the Upper East Side of the early 1980s.

The growth of securities dealing in all its forms during the 1970s had given rise to a whole generation of Wall Streeters who'd shed old wives as they came into new fortunes. By the early 1980s, Manhattan had become the gold-digging capital of America, if not the world. "The men making money in New York in the 1980s attracted a special breed of women," observed John Taylor in *Circus of Ambition*. "These women tended to be in their thirties and had origins that were obscure or exotic, but rarely patrician. . . . They had lived fast and wild in their earlier years, and they usually had one marriage or more already behind them, often to some dubious or rakish character. . . . They had already had their kicks, and when they arrived in the city they were focused on one goal with an unswerving intensity that was, in its own way, ruthless." Gayfryd Johnson, Saul Steinberg's second wife, at age twenty had married a South African businessman, only to divorce him and marry a New Orleans oil tycoon, who committed suicide after being convicted of tax evasion. Patricia Rose, the second wife of billionare John Kluge, was a belly dancer who'd written a lewd advice column and posed nude for an English skin magazine published by her first husband.

Compared with women such as these, Margo Preston McCormick was literally a class act, with a social standing that was a product of pedigree, not audacity. Margo also had the competitive advantage of operating on her home turf, having for a decade inhabited an Upper East Side social milieu thick with Wall Streeters. One of Margo's best friends was the wife of Jeff Tarr, Opco's risk arbitrageur. But Beck and Preston were introduced by Phil Cohen, who'd worked with Mark McCormick at Kuhn Loeb before joining Oppenheimer.

By all accounts, Jeff and Margo fell in love fast and hard. Three months after they'd met, Beck brought her along with him on a business trip to London to which he appended romantic Scottish interludes at the Isle of Eriskay and Inverlochy Castle. Upon their return, Margo all but moved into the Bunker. While Beck continued to log long hours at Oppenheimer, now his workday was punctuated by the pleasant diversion of frequent telephone conversations with Margo, who, when he was out of the office, left messages like this one: "Margo just called to kiss you on your nose." Part of what Preston found so appealing about Beck was that he was nothing like Mark McCormick —that is, he was not only emphatically heterosexual but ambitious and unsettled. Beck *aspired* with an intensity that Margo had rarely encountered in her travels through WASPdom, and which she found both energizing and flattering—for he left no doubt from the very beginning that his highest aspirations included her.

This intelligent, beautiful, cultured, and socially proficient woman, who usually referred to him as "Jeffrey," rarely as just "Jeff," was the WASP princess of Beck's adolescent fantasies. Preston's many enticements were sharpened by propitious timing. About the time he met Margo, his divorce had at long last been finalized. Over the nearly three years of his separation from Rosemary, Beck had made repeated attempts at reconciliation that included moving back into the house in New Jersey for stretches of a month or two, only to feel suffocated again by the cloistered tranquillity of rural life and then succumb all over again to the pull of the big city. As he lurched between city and country, from promiscuity to domesticity, Beck became so depressed that he began seeing a psychiatrist, who was recommended to him by Preston. Beck's desire for Preston would resolve—for a time, anyway—his chronic ambivalence over wealth and its pursuit as he plunged into the social whirl of mid-1980s Manhattan with his very own blue blood at his side.

The romance was helped along by certain strategic omissions and deceptions, the most egregious of them Beck's. "She bought into an illusion and so did I," Beck said. Margo was, for example, less than forthcoming about the peculiar circumstances that caused the unraveling of her marriage. And as a self-proclaimed product of a "small-town, Midwestern environment," she disclaimed any aspiration to a life of moneyed ease in Manhattan—and indeed went so far later as to theorize that Beck was attracted to her in part because of "a lack of concern for money," which, of course, was an attribute of good breeding. While Margo was trusting, even naïve in some ways, she had her own agenda and could be quite manipulative in pursuit of it.

Margo activated Jeff's insecurities and desires more fully than had any other woman, including Sarah Lawson. As with Sarah and several other girlfriends that followed her, Jeff laid a heavy dose of anguished Vietnam fantasy on Margo almost from the moment they met. He went so far as to accompany Margo to several sessions with her psychiatrist and a few with his during which he spoke movingly and at length about his post-combat traumas. Margo believed him and it seemed to her that both psychiatrists did as well. Despite Margo's cultivation of an air of material indifference, Jeff knew better, intuitively at first, and conspired to create the impression that he was a rich man, richer in fact than her first husband had ever been. Jeff's frequent, vague references to his "substantial private interests" were sufficient to convince Margo that he was worth a few hundred million dollars. With Margo, Jeff for the first time would use the name "Rosebud" to describe his secret holdings. Jeff urged Margo to see *Citizen Kane* again and she complied, though she never inferred from her husband's choice of corporate names an invitation to do some digging. If she ever had doubts about Rosebud's existence, she kept them to herself. Jeff would marry Margo under one additional false pretense, failing to so much as mention Sylvia Pfotenhauer. Not until after she gave birth to their daughter, Katherine, in 1984 did Margo learn to her shock that she was not the second but the third Mrs. Beck.

As smitten as Jeff was with Margo, he wasn't quite able to bring himself to commit to her, much as she pressured for clarification of their relationship. For one thing, the prospect of a third marriage filled him with dread. What if it didn't work out—again? For another, he had second and third and fourth thoughts about finally severing his ties to Rosemary, and the country simplicity she represented, for a woman of complex motives and fancy tastes. As the issue of marriage pressed in on him, Beck spent his days in a fog of fatigue and indecision, collecting the same bits of advice from the same friends and colleagues like a weary junkman on his daily route, becoming, in the words of Henry Kravis, "an absolute basket case." One afternoon, Beck went up to Kravis's office for a business meeting. Kravis was busy and kept Beck waiting. After ten minutes Beck got up and started pacing. After fifteen minutes he told the receptionist, "He can't treat me like this," and stormed out.

Even before Jeff met Margo, the snug simplicity of the Bunker had begun to seem confining where it once was comforting. With the press of business at Oppenheimer, Beck hadn't much time to devote to apartment hunting. He quickly assented when Margo offered to take charge of the search, in hopes no doubt that in the end the new apartment would be hers as well as his. Soon Beck found himself in the awkward position of having to choose between admitting that his claims of wealth were fraudulent and looking like a cheapskate in the eyes of a woman he was anxious to impress. Beck played for time, hoping to exhaust Margo's patience. He provided what little encouragement she required to tour multimillion-dollar apartments in Manhattan's grandest co-op buildings and gave protracted consideration to several of them, but in the end always found one reason or another to pass.

On a trip to the French Riviera in the fall of 1982, Jeff took what he later described as "a romantic flier" and finally proposed. Margo accepted. A date had been set and a site selected when Jeff, claiming the press of deal business, requested a postponement. He got it, on one condition. "Either we get married or we don't," Margo told him. "But I'm not going through another postponement." The wedding was rescheduled for March 1983. When it came time to mail out the invitations, Margo insisted that they go together and drop them in the mailbox.

The ceremony was held in their new apartment, into which they'd yet to move. Margo had finally ended their real-estate psychodrama by finding an apartment going for the comparatively reasonable (for Manhattan) sum of $540,000 in a fine old building on the corner of Seventy-ninth Street and Madison Avenue. Beck wanted a rabbi, Margo a minister. In the spirit of compromise, they considered a New York State Supreme Court judge until they went to interview him and found the man sporting a holstered .38 pistol and a loose-leaf binder of wedding plans for every budget. In the aftermath of this fiasco, Beck agreed to a nonsectarian ceremony performed by the rector of St. Thomas's Church on Fifth Avenue. The sixty guests included Jeff's mother and sister as well as Joe and Agnes Katz. The Singer family went unrepresented, to Jeff's relief and annoyance. Virtually the entire merger group from Oppenheimer attended. Kravis was invited but was out of town. The reception was held in L'Orangerie, a private room at Le Cirque, the tony society restaurant on Sixty-fifth Street. After returning from a three-week honeymoon with stops in London, Paris, Venice, and Positano, a romantic Italian seaside village just south of Naples, Mr. and Mrs. Beck got down to the serious business of going to all the right parties with all the right people.

The tie between Wall Street and Fifth Avenue—between high finance and high society—was more than intimate; it was congenital. As Wall Street emerged as the nation's business center with the advent of the capital-hungry modern corporation in the decades after the Civil War, so, too, New York City was established as the center of upper-class social life in America. From Boston, Chicago, New Orleans, Denver, San Francisco, and the other provincial capitals of the capitalist frontier, the newly wealthy flocked to New York City, the money capital, which itself had been transformed by the new fortunes made on Wall Street into what Henry Clewes, a Wall Street financier of the era, described as a city of "imperial wealth" and "Parisian, indeed almost sybaritic luxury and social splendor." On newly fashionable Fifth Avenue, nouveaux riches moguls and their wives entertained with pharaonic lavishness and otherwise aspired (and conspired) to buy themselves a position in upper-class society befitting their wealth. This, the Gilded Age, featured the most intensive period of social climbing since the founding of the Republic.

In the 1980s, the sudden explosion of riches and the social ambition those riches stoked would again force a rapid reworking of the established order. Once again, the drama of upper-class assimilation was centered in New York City, which was revived from its near bankruptcy in the 1970s as swiftly and surely as if money were smelling salts. By the mid-1980s, no fewer than twenty-five members of the *Forbes* 400 had made their multimillions in New York real estate, having loaded up on temporarily depressed properties during the dark years of the mid-1970s. All told, twice as many members of the *Forbes* elect resided in New York City as in any other city, though many of them had relocated to the city from elsewhere. In the 1980s, as in the 1890s, the largest fortunes were amassed by entrepreneurs. Sam Walton, who was America's richest man for much of the decade, was a classic of the breed, having built a fortune of $7 billion by building Wal-Mart Stores into one of the nation's largest discount merchandisers. Men who made their money as Wall Street financiers didn't move onto the *Forbes* list until late in the decade and even then, with the infamous exception of billionaire Michael Milken, were confined to its lower reaches.

However, Wall Streeters were far more prominent in the highest circle of moneyed society in the 1980s—or "Nouvelle Society," as it was dubbed—than the size of their fortunes alone warranted. This had been true, too, of the first Gilded Age; Wall Street financiers and speculators composed nearly a third of Ward McAllister's famous list of the social élite, the Four Hundred. Rare is the great American fortune, then or now, that wasn't created through the ownership of corporate stock and thus inextricably tied in one way or another to Wall Street, the principal conduit through which major corporations are supplied with long-term capital in the form of investments by stock- and bondholders. The Wall Street dealer's access to the fortune-creating machinery of the securities markets has long made him uniquely alluring to anyone who aspires to accumulating wealth. The attraction works both ways, of course. While the industry doesn't exist in which social relationships can't be turned to commercial advantage, to the Wall Street dealer *anyone* with money or corporate position is of potential value professionally.

Never had Wall Street played a more prominent role in the big-money game than it did in the 1980s, a decade in which the very notion of enterprise largely shifted from the building of factories to the reshuffling of existing assets—or "paper entrepreneurism," in the phrase popularized by political economist Robert Reich. Among the most telling signals of this fundamental shift was that the securities industry itself became by many measures the nation's fastest-growing industry, as hundred-year-old investment banks sported the kind of revenue and employment growth rates usually associated with companies newly emerged from Silicon Valley garages. At the same time, Wall Street's influence was aggrandized by the rise of a new breed of corporate entrepreneur. These entrepreneurs were so utterly devoted to high-stakes financial maneuvering that in effect they were nothing but securities dealers in businessmen's clothing. In this regard, Sam Walton was unrepresentative; he made his fortune the old-fashioned way, by running a business. Perhaps the definitive 1980s executive was Revlon Incorporated CEO Ronald Perelman, who through a rapid-fire series of mergers, acquisitions, buyouts, divestitures, and stock and bond underwritings—all engineered through investment banks—over a decade parlayed $1.9 million borrowed in 1978 into a fortune estimated in 1988 at $2.8 billion.

While Wall Street's role remained pivotal, in the interim between the first and second Gilded Ages upper-class society had changed in important respects. It had, for example, broadened beyond the moneyed WASP industrialists and bankers to include people who were famous but not particularly rich—celebrities—as well as those who'd never set foot inside an Episcopalian church. While there remained a separate and distinct Jewish upper class (in which the Russian-dominated "New Crowd" had supplanted the German-dominated "Our Crowd"), Jewishness was no longer cause for automatic disqualification from the social mainstream. In the 1980s, socially ambitious Jews and Catholics were free to join with Protestant climbers in the time-honored American tradition of aping the English aristocracy, the prototypical WASPs.

Nouvelle Society's pioneering couple were John and Susan Gutfreund, or "Solemn John" and "Social Susie." She was a former stewardess who'd married an heir to a Texas real-estate fortune after meeting him on a Pan Am flight. Divorced after five years, the former Susan Kaposta left Fort Worth behind in 1975 and flew north to the happier husband-hunting grounds of the Upper East Side. She met Gutfreund in 1980 and was out apartment-shopping faster than one could say "gold digger" or "love at first sight," both of which actually seemed appropriate. Gutfreund was Jewish, the son of a meat wholesaler, and a career bond trader—historically, social disqualifications all. But he was also the chief executive officer of Salomon Brothers, which by virtue of its rather ruthless mastery of the age of inflation's perpetually turbulent bond markets had by the early 1980s evolved into the world's most powerful investment bank. And so Gutfreund and his

fiancée were able to smoothly begin their assault on the social pinnacle
by buying a million-dollar duplex in the River House, one of old Manhattan's most exclusive WASP strongholds. Not long after his remarriage, Gutfreund engineered the sale of Salomon Brothers; this tripled
his net worth—to at least $32 million—while converting most of it
to cash, which his new wife dedicated herself to spending in great,
gaudy gobs.

If the Gutfreunds' social career proved that there were no connections like Wall Street connections, it also demonstrated that in Nouvelle Society how one spent one's millions was more important than
how many millions one had to spend. Social Susie used her luxurious
River House apartment as a stage set for parties that created an approving stir in society circles by creatively setting new standards for
opulence. At one Gutfreund soirée, every chair was entwined in roses,
complete with thorns that made sitting a peril. As the pièce de résistance at a birthday party for Henry Kissinger, the Gutfreunds' own
chef spun sugar into iridescent green apples by adapting a technique
used by the famous glassblowers of Murano, Italy. The Gutfreunds
entertained so frequently that the man of the house was once heard to
quip: "When I come home, I have to ask Susan, 'Who's coming for
dinner?' It doesn't matter if I ask her because I don't know most of
them." In the summer of 1983, Manhattan's most-talked-about host
and hostess topped themselves by mailing out engraved invitations
whose message would have astounded McAllister no less than J. P.
Morgan: "Mr. and Mrs. John Gutfreund. At Home, Blenheim." In
truth, the Gutfreunds hadn't purchased Blenheim Palace, the ances-
tral home of the Churchill family, but rented it out for a gala party. It
really didn't matter. By way of proclaiming the social position that
money could buy, renting Blenheim was as evocative as buying it.

At the time of their marriage, Jeff and Margo Beck occupied a spot
somewhere on the periphery of the periphery of Nouvelle Society. In
truth, Beck was worth at most a couple of million dollars, peanuts by
the standards of the social set to which he aspired. Nor was the position of M & A chief of Oppenheimer & Company of any great social
utility. As the Becks launched their social career, their principal asset
was Margo's pedigree, which, for starters, caused the doors of 31 East
Seventy-ninth Street to open to them.

In the minds of carriage-trade realtors and their clients, the great
buildings of New York are arrayed in a hierarchy of prestige derived
from many factors other than quality of design and construction—

notably, who *doesn't* live there. Virtually all of New York's grandest dwellings are cooperatively owned by their residents, who, through boards of directors, are free to accept or reject apartment buyers based on their own infamously discriminatory criteria. As a rule, it is harder to buy into a good cooperative building than to gain admittance to one of the city's most exclusive private social clubs. In the opinion of Edward Lee Cave, the doyen of the city's upscale realtors, the Becks had bought into a co-op that was "the best small building to live well in" on the entire Upper East Side. It contained only fourteen apartments, most of which were occupied by longtime residents whose incomes derived chiefly from stock and bond portfolios or the practice of medicine—"nice, fuddy-duddy WASPs," in the words of one ex-resident. To Beck, though, its most notable resident was the Deal Club eminence Joe Flom, who'd lived there for years with his wife, Claire, a member of the board.

In applying to 31 East Seventy-ninth, the Becks had sought admittance to a quiet, family building run by a board determined to keep it that way. Big party-givers and anyone connected with the entertainment business were "the wrong kind of people." Margo found herself having to explain her involvement in the film business very precisely in her interview with the board. Jeff, meanwhile, caused a bit of a flap by objecting to the board's policy of requiring applicants to present audited statements of net worth. Beck argued that it was absurd for him to spend a few thousand dollars to hire an auditor when his accountant and his banker were perfectly able to attest to his net worth. Beck prevailed, and provided letters attesting to a net worth in the low seven figures. The figures given the board were accurate and complete, but Jeff told Margo that to preserve their privacy he had omitted all mention of his Rosebud wealth.

Jeff and Margo continued to live in the Bunker for months while their new apartment was totally overhauled. Instead of the haute glitz of newer society designers, Margo opted, with Jeff's assent, for the Establishment elegance of Parish-Hadley Associates. Dorothy "Sister" Parish, the aristocratic head of the firm, was notoriously blasé about costs. "I am a complete believer in luxury and comfort," she proclaimed. In hiring Parish-Hadley, Jeffrey and Margo Beck joined a distinguished client list that included such social eminences as Brooke Astor, Annette Reed, Anne and Gordon Getty, Amanda and Carter Burden, Sharon Rockefeller, Babe and Bill Paley, Henry Kissinger, and Oscar de la Renta. Jacqueline Kennedy had hired Parish-Hadley to decorate the White House state rooms and presidential quarters and when the job was done fired Sister Parish for telling little Caroline to keep her feet off the upholstery. More than two decades later Parish-Hadley was again at the center of high-level controversy, this time in England. The Duchess of Kent chose the American firm to redo her house only to be overruled by the queen of England, who thought Parish-Hadley's $2 million estimate a trifle much. By the time the last painting was hung and centered, the Becks had spent $400,000 to decorate an apartment that had cost not much more than that.

Nouvelle Society differed from preceding élites in its insistence on adapting many of the city's greatest cultural institutions to double duty as party palaces. While the moguls of the Gilded Age had supported, if not founded, many of these same institutions, for the most part they'd confined their entertaining to private homes and private clubs. Of course, many of the robber barons kept Fifth Avenue homes that were the size of major museums. (Some even became major museums after their owners' deaths.) If the ambitious hosts of the 1980s were to accommodate the expanded ranks of the socially elect and entertain them in a fashion befitting their sense of their own grandeur, then only the great vaulted halls of high culture would do. It was Nouvelle Society's dubious achievement to turn the ritual drama of upper-class selection into the most public of spectacles. Nouvelle Society's favorite party palace was the city's preeminent cultural institution, the Metropolitan Museum of Art, which served as the setting for so much deluxe entertaining that one gossip columnist dubbed it "Club Met." A notch below the Met in the hierarchy of Nouvelle Society were clustered a half-dozen other institutions, among them the New York Public Library, Mount Sinai Hospital, the Metropolitan Opera, the American Ballet Theatre, and the New York City Ballet, which the Becks made their social fulcrum.

While Jeff's involvement in the City Ballet slightly predated Margo, his participation in it as both contributor and partygoer increased greatly after his marriage. Margo had an appreciation of the ballet that was a natural outgrowth of her upbringing, but no one—least of all himself—would have described Jeff as an aficionado of the dance. Beck's relationship to the New York City Ballet was an extension of his affection for Elaine Felt, its director of development. An elderly single woman with a naggy, slightly abrasive manner and a great big heart, Felt was very solicitous of Beck, who spent many hours with her discussing his feeling that the ballet was elitist. As a result of these talks, the Becks focused their financial support on the ballet's education department, which, among other things, sponsored an annual performance for underprivileged school kids bused in from the outer boroughs.

The Becks' discrimination in giving distinguished them from the ballet's more purely social-climbing patrons, who gave to get—a table at the black-tie balls that opened and closed the season; ultimately, a seat on the board. While Jeff and Margo kept clear of the board's fractious politics, they bought a table (at $5,000 a pop) for many a ball. To Beck's delight, Kravis, too, began involving himself in the ballet in the early 1980s. Jeff and Margo filled the seats at their table by inviting friends and business acquaintances who, in turn, invited them to affairs for the Film Society of Lincoln Center, the New York Philharmonic, Mount Sinai Hospital, the Boys Club of New York, the Central Park Conservancy, and on and on.

Even at his most upwardly mobile, though, Beck never was fully comfortable doing what he later termed "the black-tie flashdance." As a rainmaker, Beck could highlight particular facets of his personality with the self-control of a veteran actor. Try as he might, though, he could never quite lose himself in the identity of swank cosmopolitan benefactor. In black tie, Beck always felt like an impostor, a poseur— or worse, like an aspiring William D. Singer or Joe Katz. Unable to take himself seriously as social aspirant, Beck was unable as well to take his fellow climbers as seriously as they took themselves; thus, he entered Nouvelle Society dangerously poised between feelings of inadequacy on one hand and disdain for his fellow climbers on the other. The danger lay in high society's and high finance's intimate overlap, which, of course, was partly what had fueled Beck's social ambition in the first place. Beck would learn the hard way that the social-climbing game worked both ways; if a deal man could enhance his franchise through the right connections, he could also imperil that franchise by antagonizing the wrong people at the right parties. In attempting to infiltrate the highest circle of moneyed society, Beck, in short, was getting in over his head—and he sensed it, which only compounded the awkwardness he felt in self-important society.

As in his Wall Street dealings, Beck dealt with his feelings of social inferiority by grabbing the offensive. Beck's Mad Dog persona, which he'd managed to short-leash in his professional life, now returned as black-tie party animal. Beck would be making polite conversation at a banquet table at one grand Nouvelle Society gathering or another when suddenly he'd slam the edge of his hand down on the tines of a fork and send it somersaulting through the air to the next table. When the old Animal House mood came over Beck, he might put someone in a playful headlock or do pratfalls on the dance floor, leaving a red-faced Margo holding nothing but air. In Beck's opinion, his high jinks initially enhanced his social career by making him, however briefly, the center of attention. Beck's court-jester act didn't wear well, though, either with him or his audience. After his exit/expulsion from polite society, Beck took such perverse pride in his disregard of decorum at stodgy events that, as with his adventures at DLJ, he was inspired to embroider his rambunctiousness in the retelling. Several times he told me of his "mushroom-soup trick," which, like the imaginary "Blind Man" routine of his DLJ days, he'd lifted from a movie, in this case *The Great Santini.* Beck said that on occasion during fancy dinners he would pretend to vomit, spilling mushroom soup from a plastic bag secreted inside his tuxedo jacket. Then, as his dining companions looked on in horror, he'd say, "I feel much better now," and begin spooning up the faux vomit and eating it with conspicuous contentment.

When Beck told the mushroom-soup story, the hosts of his imaginary dinner were often Henry Kravis and Carolyne Roehm, who would in time supplant the Gutfreunds as the First Couple of Nouvelle Society. The more prominent Kravis became, the more Beck luxuriated in his access to him, bragging to his colleagues at Oppenheimer of his ability to get Mr. LBO on the phone any time of day or night—which, in fact, wasn't at all far from the truth. Not that Beck's relationship with Kravis was limited to business. In his premarital misery, hadn't he turned to Henry for advice, bachelor to bachelor, and received wise counsel? —After, that is, he got over his anger at being kept waiting in KKR's anteroom. All in all, Beck was proud to number Kravis among his very best friends.

Unfortunately for Beck, that's not exactly how Kravis saw him, at least in retrospect. "I always liked Jeff," Kravis told me in 1989. "He was funny and entertaining and Margo was a good wife. But I never thought of them as being part of our crowd. Carolyne and I would see them at parties but we never traveled with them. They were around for a while but were never close friends. Yet," he added pointedly, "it seems that Jeff considers me one of his very, very good friends." Kravis insisted that it was apparent to him from the moment he first met

Beck that he "led a fictional life in his own mind. You had to decipher what was real and what wasn't. But you take him for what he is, and Jeff is a guy with a damn good idea from time to time."

While Beck gradually would come to resent the LBO promoter, he disliked Roehm quickly and overtly, undermining his relationship with Kravis. Beck would call me on occasion to read disgustedly from the latest Roehm profile in *Vogue, Mademoiselle, W,* or *Town and Country.* As the women's and society magazines ran out of new things to say about Roehm, they dressed up the same old puffery in ever more precious and overblown language, until, by 1990, *Vogue* offered these verbal snapshots of the lady, presumably with a straight face:

> Carolyne Roehm, calling goodbye to Henry while playing a Chopin nocturne on the 1851 Erard piano, trying to concentrate on piano teacher Rosi Grunschlag's pencil note—Don't rush!—aware of the Bentley running, poised to deliver her to Seventh Avenue by 8:30 a.m. And Carolyne Roehm, totally pooped, lunching in her Park Avenue apartment under paintings by Sargent, Gainsborough, Reynolds, and Joseph Wright of Derby, suddenly laying down her soufflé fork on the vermeil plate, head bent, cornflower eyes welling, a tear dropping onto the Venetian crystal. "Ignore it!" she says immediately. "I'm always like this after the show."

Carolyne Roehm, socialite fashion designer, was every bit as willful and fanciful an invention as Jeff Beck, M & A Mad Dog. Carolyne Jane Smith, nicknamed Janey, was the only child of a high-school principal and a speech pathologist. She grew up in the small town of Kirksville, Missouri. Little Janey was very shy and spent so much time talking to imaginary friends that her grandparents worried about her future. She twinkled around the house in a tutu, wearing a rhinestone necklace that was the first thing she ever bought herself. At thirteen, she saw Susan Hayward in the 1961 remake of *Back Street* and decided to become a designer. She did indeed major in fashion design at Washington University and after getting her degree moved to New York City to make a career in clothes. She lasted only a few days at her first job, quitting when asked to clean the bathroom. Persevering, Smith caught on with a company that made polyester sportswear for Sears, and then talked her way into a girl Friday job with Oscar de la Renta, who eventually promoted her to showroom fit model and then to assistant designer. In an orgy of self-improvement, she took instruction in cooking, riding, and French. She kept her cramped apartment stocked with fresh flowers and bubble bath. "Beauty and glamour," she declared, "are a state of mind."

Smith took to calling herself Carolyne at the suggestion of Axel Roehm, whom she met and married in 1978. Smith was engaged at the time she met Roehm but broke it off to be with a man who, she said, fulfilled her every romantic fantasy. Roehm was tall, dark, handsome, European, and an heir to a German chemical fortune. He and his bride moved to West Germany. Within a year, Carolyne had returned to New York, with teary stories of a chauvinist who'd prevented the continuation of her career in fashion. However, her vehemence on the subject wasn't sufficient to still the rumors that, in truth, she'd so antagonized her husband's relatives with her pretensions to grandeur that the family had frozen her out. In any event, Carolyne kept her new old-money last name and got her job back with de la Renta. Having returned alimony-less to the workaday world, she rented another dinky apartment and decorated it entirely in blue and white de la Renta sheets.

Roehm was still on the mend when she met Kravis at a smart-set party in Manhattan in 1981. Roehm was slow to warm up to a man who was three inches shorter than she, worked in finance (boring), had a bachelor pad with white walls (tacky), and last but probably not least, had yet to come into the big money. Although taken with the beanpole designer, Kravis still had hopes of reconciling with his wife, Hedi, and seesawed back and forth between the two women for a few years. After Hedi publicly embarassed him with an ill-concealed affair, though, Kravis dedicated himself with a vengeance to the dual pursuit of Roehm and Nouvelle Society. What better way to get back at Hedi than to attain, in the company of another woman, the social pinnacle to which she'd always aspired? Roehm, meanwhile, was warming to the man she called her "little Jewish cowboy." As Carolyne told the tale, omitting the traditional once-upon-a-time beginning, the geometric increase in Kravis's net worth over the period of their protracted courtship had nothing to do with her eventual softening of heart. "I remember saying to everybody, 'This man is so kind, and so nice,' " Roehm recalled. "It was like someone putting salve on a terribly cut or burned body. I finally discovered what the essence of him was, that made him so special, and why everyone loved him so much—I realized that he made me feel good about *me*."

However, Kravis apparently had second and third thoughts. Even after his divorce from Hedi was finalized in 1984, Kravis seemed in no hurry to actually propose to Roehm. Instead of marriage, he first proposed a business partnership. Roehm quickly accepted his offer to invest a million or two to set her up in a fashion-design business of her own. She rented half a floor in a building on Seventh Avenue and got down to designing a collection that would be described by her publicist as perfect for "the young couture-minded woman who wants pretty but simple, unfussy clothes for day and who reserves her fantasy for evening. It is basically the way Carolyne Roehm herself dresses." While the financial performance of Carolyne Roehm Incorporated remained a closely guarded secret, most Wall Streeters assumed that the business generated more headlines than profits. Which was the point, after all. In terms of public relations, the fashion business was a brilliant stroke, serving a dual purpose. On one hand, it gave Kravis the business rationale he seemed to need to justify his incessant party-prowling and frequent appearance in society gossip columns. Carolyne, meanwhile, could present herself not as a silly social butterfly but as a hardworking entrepreneur in her own right. Society writers ate it up. In almost every profile of Roehm appears the following quote, uttered by a woman who was a whiter shade of pale and pampered during an era of mounting misery in the black underclass: "I work like a slave."

Any resemblance between Carolyne Roehm, Nouvelle celebrity designer, and Janey Smith, aspirant, was purely unintentional. "She's a different person now," said a friend who'd known her when she first came to New York. "Total transformation . . . It's Eliza Doolittle, honey. A different voice, everything." All traces of the flat Midwestern nasality of her youth were indeed gone, replaced by a burbly, faux-English accent. Although Roehm was no classic American beauty, she was pretty in a pixieish way, with her retroussé nose and her frail, elongated, and very socially correct physique. Skinny to the point of androgyny, Roehm was, in Tom Wolfe's phrase, definitively a "Social X-Ray." Although she'd perfected her look, Roehm was as compulsive as ever about acquiring culture. She studied cooking and French in France and opera in Salzburg; she learned to ride English-style and took up the piano, proclaiming her joy in her new hobby with characteristic fatuousness. "Oh, Mozart," she once exclaimed in an interview. "What he must have gone through!" And elsewhere: "I believe in my former life I was Brahms."

To Beck, Roehm was a creature at once alien and frighteningly familiar. As a self-invented fashion princess, Roehm's domain was distantly removed from his own fantasy milieu of macho intrigue and combat. Yet she reminded him of nothing so much as a 1980s New York version of his mother, whose lifelong pursuit of deluxe accommodations continued unabated in Miami. Beck first met Roehm in 1983 at one of the black-tie galas thrown by the New York City Ballet. Shortly thereafter, Beck bumped into Richard Beattie, a lawyer and Kravis confidant with whom he was friendly. Beattie was struck by Beck's anxiety over Roehm's first impressions of him. "Do you think she likes me, Dick?" he asked. Several weeks later, Beattie got a telephone call from Beck, who had come to the realization that he and Roehm were not destined to become soul mates. "We've got to stop her, Dick," Beck said. "Henry should not marry this woman." Beck claimed that he'd cornered Roehm at some swanky affair and asked her point-blank what she wanted out of life. "I'll never forget it," he recalled. "She looked right at me and said, 'Oh, Jeffrey. I want to be rich and I want to be famous.' "

Beattie saw no percentage in criticizing Kravis, his best client, over his taste in women and suggested that Beck mind his own business, too. As Beck told it, though, he later went to Kravis alone and warned him against marrying someone with values as "twisted" as Roehm's— not realizing that Kravis shared those values. "I went from the 'A' list to the shit list," Beck recalled, overstating on both counts. The fact was that Roehm put a premium on social graces that Beck knew he didn't possess and wasn't particularly anxious to acquire. The more awkward Beck felt in Roehm's presence, the more provocative his behavior became. And the more the fashion designer took offense at the Mad Dog's "barf and fart jokes," as Margo put it, the more animated he became. At a dinner at The Four Seasons also attended by Henry, Margo, and Dick Beattie and his wife, Carolyne took such offense to Jeff's baiting that she called him a "laughing hyena." Beck responded with a child's taunt: "Sticks and stones, Carolyne. Sticks and stones."

Aside from an equally awkward if more sedate dinner at "21," the Becks spent time alone with Henry and Carolyne on only one other occasion, accepting their invitation to spend a Saturday at Weatherstone, Kravis's Connecticut estate. Beck was on his best behavior and the day proved easily the most pleasant of their interludes. In his relief, Beck composed a thank-you note so unctuous that it embarrassed him to reread it years later: "You and Caroline [*sic*] are both well reflected in Weatherstone, one of the most unique homes I have ever had the fortune of visiting. Most importantly the home reflects the happiness that both of you richly deserve. . . . I told Margo after lunch at Weatherstone that it felt good to have a friend like Henry and how nice it was to see a friend so happy with such an attractive and warm person like Caroline." Behind Kravis's back, though, Beck took to calling Weatherstone "Weatherdick," in accordance with his theory that the ostentatious possessions of rich men were basically penis extensions.

Having won Roehm, Kravis had second thoughts about marrying her. Beck was delighted to hear at one point that Kravis had moved the fashion designer out of his apartment and had begun seeing other women. As Beck told the story, which may well be apocryphal but is revealing of their odd relationship nonetheless, he went to have lunch with Kravis one day at The Four Seasons assuming that Henry and Roehm were quits.

"What do you really think of Carolyne?" Kravis supposedly asked.

"Well, Henry," Beck replied. "I think Carolyne Roehm may be the best-looking guy in America."

Kravis was not amused. "I'm thinking of marrying her, Jeff," he said stonily, as Beck almost blew his soup through his nostrils in surprise. "I was coldcocked," he said later. "I was sure they were through."

In another possibly apocryphal account, Beck recalled visiting Kravis shortly after his wedding. Kravis had mentioned to Beck that he'd hired a new Italian chef. When Beck kiddingly said that he liked pasta so much that he had it for breakfast, Kravis called his bluff. Early one morning at Kravis's, Beck breakfasted on salmon fettucine while his host had eggs. Carolyne was in her boudoir, having had her customary breakfast of a single Oreo cookie. After the meal, Kravis took Beck into his study for a bit of deal talk. As Kravis settled back into a massively overstuffed sofa, Beck noticed that the LBO king's shoes were dangling an inch or two off the floor.

"Nice furniture, Henry," he said, gazing at Kravis's feet while trying not to laugh out loud.

Kravis tried to move forward on the couch but couldn't quite get over the hump. As he thrashed about a bit trying to gain traction, Beck couldn't help but laugh. "Need some help?" he asked. Kravis said nothing. But the look in his eyes told Beck that he'd overstepped yet again.

10

J eff Beck stood at the window in his office high atop One New York Plaza and gazed out at the Statue of Liberty in the distance. Lady Liberty looked a little fuzzy around the edges today, as if she were on the verge of dematerializing in the heat. Beck could feel hot air leaking in through the window, infiltrating the outer defenses of his air-conditioning system through gaps too tiny to see.

He wiped the sweat off his brow with the back of his hand and retreated back into the cool zone of his office. He shed his suit coat, revealing a smart pair of suspenders and a dark half-moon around each armpit of his blue shirt. "Damn," he muttered, slipping the jacket onto a hanger behind the door to his office. It wasn't even ten in the morning and already he was in serious need of a shower.

Beck walked over to his desk and took a pad of yellow legal-sized paper out of a drawer. He sat down behind the desk, picked up a pen, and wrote a single word: "partners." Beck underlined the word twice and stared at it hard for a few seconds. He put pen to paper again. "Your partner, not your investment banker." He underlined "not" and paused briefly before continuing. "Somerset—Distillers relationship secure?" he wrote, adding "Avis—off-balance sheet liabilities!!"

Beck went through the exercise of organizing his thoughts on paper before almost every important phone call he made. Since he'd started on Wall Street, he'd rung hundreds, maybe even thousands, of people whom he'd never met and who had no apparent desire to make his acquaintance. "Cold" seemed entirely too mild an adjective to de-scribe these calls; "frigid," "frozen," "icy," "subarctic," "ultrapolar" were more like it. He got tired just thinking of all the hustling he'd done in his dozen years of Wall Street dealing. All the cold calls, the red-eye flights, the room-service meals, the seven A.M. meetings in windowless conference rooms, the midnight sessions in lawyers' offices

—all of it, by June 1983, had at last brought him, unwittingly, to the threshold of a billion-dollar deal that would be the turning point of his Wall Street career.

Beck's telephone rang. "Sandy," he bellowed in the general direction of his secretary, who sat just outside the door to his office. "Unless it's God, I'm not here."

Sandy picked up the receiver and after a few quick words pushed her hold button. "Is Steve Robert God, Jeffrey?" she said.

Beck made a loud exclamation somewhere between a laugh and a snort. "Right, Sandy," he said. "Steve Robert is God and I'm the fuckin' pope."

Sandy took a message.

Beck sat up straight and picked up his pen. Near the bottom of the sheet of paper he wrote:

> face to face
> tomorrow?

Robert was Beck's new boss, having succeeded Jack Nash as the CEO of Oppenheimer after the firm was sold to Mercantile House. Although Beck had repeatedly clashed with Nash, usually over Beck's attempts to increase his group's profit cut, he was sorry to see him go. Nash had lived up to his end of their agreement, holding steady in his support of the M & A department. And why not? While Nash had been prepared to drop as much as $5 million during the department's first three years, Beck and crew eked out a tiny profit in 1980, the department's first full year, and in 1982 generated revenues of a few million dollars, much of it profit. With the $2 million fee from the defense of Varian Associates already in hand, 1983 was shaping up as the Jeff Beck Group's breakthrough year.

Beck had met several times with Mercantile's top executives, who assured him that there would be no diminution of commitment to building his M & A department nor any change in its arrangement with Opco, which would be operated as a discrete subsidiary of Mercantile. To Beck's relief, the Mercantile people proved as good as their word. He wasn't so sure about Robert and about Nate Gantcher, who'd moved up to president as Robert ascended to CEO. Monosyllabic and venal though he was, Nash at least was tough-minded and deal-savvy. Robert, on the other hand, had never done a deal in his life. He was a reserved, handsome Ivy League graduate who'd started as an analyst and money manager and had risen, in Beck's estimation, by subordinating his own ego to Nash and Leon Levy. In joining Opco, Beck had tactlessly complained about Nash's original suggestion that he report to Robert, who'd taken Beck's refusal in the spirit in which it was intended: as a defiant insult. With the sale to Mercantile, though, Robert became his boss, like it or not—and Beck most em phatically didn't.

As yet, though, Robert hadn't given Beck any cause for complaint. To the contrary, Robert had just okayed Beck's plan to set up a new subsidiary to do leveraged buyouts and hire his old buddy from Warner-Lambert, Steve McGrath, to run it. In recognition of a job well done, Beck's original three-year contract had recently been extended. To his title of senior vice president had been appended the additional title of chairman of the new LBO unit, Oppenheimer Strategic Services. Beck also had been given a seat on Oppenheimer's executive committee.

With the addition of McGrath, the Jeff Beck Group was twelve strong. Beck liked to think of his department as the Wall Street equivalent of the Dirty Dozen, a collection of misfits and underdogs that had coalesced into a superb if unconventional fighting force. The Dirty Dozen of Deal Making. Beck liked the sound of that. If Morgan Stanley was white-shoe, then Oppenheimer would be combat-boot. And why not? In finding a buyer for American Optical, hadn't they succeeded where Morgan had failed? And in defending Varian Associates, hadn't the group outsmarted Lazard and accomplished what Goldman, Sachs had advised could not be done? For all his cheerleader's bravado, though, Beck realized that the burden of obscurity that increasingly oppressed him would not be lifted unless the Jeff Beck Group did a billion-dollar deal. And on this hot June day, Beck was working what seemed to be a very likely prospect.

He swiveled around to the Quotron machine behind his desk. He punched a few buttons. A set of numbers flashed onto the screen. No news out of Norton Simon this morning, but the stock was up another point or so on heavy volume. The game was definitely on.

"Sandy," Beck bellowed in the general direction of his office door. "Get Steve in here. Let's make that call to Chicago."

For the first time since Beck had started on the Street, the moon of his ambitions and the stars of macroeconomic conditions had come into perfect alignment. The last missing ingredient had been added in mid-

1982, when the stock market suddenly roared to life after more than a decade of inflation-induced feebleness. The rate of inflation had begun slowing months before as a result of harsh measures imposed by the Federal Reserve Board under its new chairman, Paul Volcker. Ever since inflation had begun worrying the financial markets in the late 1960s, presidents and Fed chairmen had been grimly vowing to halt the chronic debasement of the dollar. Only Volcker, though, had the political fortitude to impose measures harsh enough for long enough to wring inflation out of the economic system. As the Volcker Fed clamped down hard on the nation's money-supply growth, interest rates soared to record levels—the prime tickled 21 percent for a time —and the economy tumbled into the worst recession since World War II, dragging the stock market down with it into the depths. But Volcker's strong medicine slowly took effect. Inflation dropped to 9.4 percent in 1981 from 10.7 percent in 1980 and had fallen to about 7.2 percent by August 1982, when Volcker decided it was time for the Fed to pump more money into the system. As if on cue, interest rates fell and a stock-price surge inaugurated the roaringest bull market of the twentieth century. In June, as Beck sat sweltering in his Oppenheimer office, the Dow Jones industrial average already had climbed to 1140 from a bear-market bottom of 776 on its way to a record 2722 in 1987.

Without exception, the peaks of every one of three previous merger waves—1898–1902, 1925–1929, and 1965–1969—had coincided with epic bull markets. While the historical correlation between stock prices and M & A activity is strong, it seems to offend the basic laws of supply and demand. Why should more corporations change hands when the cost of acquiring them peaks? For the same reasons that sales of houses tend to boom along with home prices. Markets move in cycles of optimism and pessimism, and human nature seems to dictate that buyers outnumber sellers in good times, not hard times. While major corporations almost always have compelling business reasons to make acquisitions, the vast majority are more inclined to accept the extraordinary risk inherent in any big undertaking when the general economy is strong than when it is weak. And when the economy is strong, naturally the financial markets are buoyant and financing for the acquisition of almost any costly thing—from corporations to lawn mowers—tends to be most plentiful. Too plentiful, in fact. History shows that as financial markets build to speculative climax, more and more deals are done simply to capitalize on the sheer availability of financing—especially when the federal government allows antitrust restrictions to lapse into disuse, as the Reagan administration did in the 1980s.

Viewed in retrospect, the rising tide of M & A activity during the 1970s would seem a mere premonitory swelling to the fourth great wave of deals. That the 1980s M & A wave towered above its three predecessors was largely because it was formed atop an abnormally large base—that is, M & A volume during the 1970s was much higher than stock-market conditions alone would have warranted. Of the countervailing factors at work during the decade, the most important were the rise of inflation and of the Wall Street M & A man. Chronic inflation profoundly disordered the vast nexus of commercial relationships that underlay the economy, forcing whole industries to adapt quickly if they were to continue to prosper or, in some cases, survive. For many corporations, the natural bear-market inclination to just sit tight and await better times was a prescription for suicide. At the same time, the stock-market values of so many corporations fell so far below the cost of replacing their assets that not even the combination of long-standing Establishment proscription against intercorporate hostility with fears of impending economic collapse could keep buyer greed under wraps. Then, too, for the first time, there had emerged on Wall Street a takeover industry—hundreds of M & A bankers and lawyers whose prodigious energies were wholly channeled into getting deals done. All of these factors had coalesced in spectacular fashion in the billion-dollar-deal explosion of 1981. But even the $82.6 billion in M & A transactions announced that year would seem small beer in comparison to 1988's total of $246.9 billion.

Like most of his M & A rivals, Beck kept tabs on macroeconomic and political conditions the way fishermen monitor the weather—constantly and with overriding commercial calculation. The future rate of inflation didn't interest Beck in the slightest as an abstract proposition. He was a deal man, not an economist.

McGrath walked into Beck's office with Norm Brown, who'd come from E. F. Hutton to join the group as its eleventh member a few months before. "You guys all set?" Beck said. "Anything new?"

"Not really, Jeff," McGrath said. "Thomas says to go ahead and call Kelly direct."

Kelly was Donald Kelly, the chief executive officer of Esmark, Incorporated, and Philip Thomas was that company's vice president for investor relations. Beck had never met Kelly, but he knew of him. What deal man didn't? From what Beck had heard, Kelly was fa-

mously easy to get to—he was even known to answer his own phone—
but a tough guy to bullshit. That was a risk Beck would just have to
take. What choice did he have? The franchise firms would be swarm-
ing over Kelly today more than ever.

Donald Philip Kelly arrived at the corporate pinnacle bearing the
truculent imprint of his humble origins as indelibly as if the words
"South Side Irish Catholic. Fuck you, too" had been tattooed across
his smiling, rosy face. Even after he'd reinvented in his own image a
corporation that was one of the stoutest pillars of Chicago's old WASP
Establishment, he went right on thumbing his nose at respectable
convention. As chief executive officer of Esmark, Kelly spurned countless black-tie champagne receptions on behalf of the opera, the symphony, and the ballet for the simple pleasure of hoisting a few tall ones
at the local tavern with old buddies from the neighborhood. He went
right on loving the White Sox and hating the Cubs, the team of
choice on the North Side. Other than his wife and his kids, only Notre
Dame University—the educational cathedral of Irish-American aspiration—seemed to inspire Kelly's complete devotion, even though he'd
never attended a class there. Although indeed Kelly had never graduated from any college, late in his career he was honored with an invitation to impart his hard-earned wisdom to MBA candidates during a
seminar at Harvard Business School. In discussing the economics of
the meat-packing business, Kelly got off one of the more infamous of
the one-liners for which he was known. "I never met a pig I really
liked," he told the future leaders of American business, "at least not
before ten P.M." As women in his audience booed and hissed, Kelly
beamed, a provocateur happily in his element.

Kelly was a hundred percent Irish and third-generation American.
Born in 1923, he was raised on the South Side of Chicago in an Irish-
American enclave known as St. Killian's Parish. While Kelly, unlike
Beck, never strayed far from the facts in his self-mythologizing, the
greater his acclaim, the more his recounting of his early years sounded
like excerpts from the Studs Lonigan novels. As a lad of twelve, Kelly
started working in a gas station. "Summers, I would work all night,"
Kelly told *Fortune* magazine. "Mr. Jones, who ran the numbers racket,
used to stop in every night with his three Cadillacs and bodyguards.
He had a little vase on the side of his car with roses in it, and every
night he would give me a rose for my mother. One night I was robbed.
He came in and said, 'What did you lose?' I told him I lost my coin

changer, and some money. 'And the man,' he said. 'Can you describe the man?' I told him about the man. The next night he drove in, handed me the changer, handed me the money, and said, 'You will not be bothered by him again.' I said, 'Thank you, Mr. Jones.' " Although Kelly steered clear of the rackets that flourished in Depression-era Chicago no less than in Lou Beck's Pittsburgh, he had his scrapes with the law. "I spent my time at the police station with the rest of the guys, but never got in any serious trouble. A number of the people I was raised with ended up not turning out very well. Some were killed; some were put in jail. It was not a Boy Scout neighborhood."

However, South Side contemporaries of Kelly's remember St. Killian's as a solid middle-class neighborhood best known not for rough stuff but for its popular Saturday-night dances at the local Catholic church. Don's father was a white-collar professional—an accountant who worked for a local steel company and finished his career as a high-level administrator at the U.S. Navy's Cost Inspection Service. Except for a brief stretch after the steel company went down, the Kellys lived comfortably. Don took the job at the gas station to earn spending money of his own, not to put bread on his mother's table. His early years, however, were a prophecy of downward mobility. Constantly in trouble at school, he graduated twelfth from the bottom of a large high-school class and immediately left home to bum around the country for two years, working construction or clerking in stores when his money ran out. Kelly enlisted in the navy in 1942 and saw combat in the Pacific as a torpedoman on destroyers and destroyer escorts. He went in as a seaman and left as a seaman first class, having been promoted to higher rank several times only to be busted back down for one minor infraction or another. At a base in Manila, Kelly played navy football as a 185-pound linebacker and offensive guard, and boxed as a light heavyweight. "They called me Canvasback Kelly," he said. "I'd get the crap kicked out of me and then get up and go back at it again. I was a tough kid."

Kelly's rebel-without-a-cause bellicosity is not easily explained. Certainly, his implication that he was the rough product of a bad neighborhood doesn't cut it. Don was the second of three sons, and both his brothers were accomplished students who graduated from good colleges—Northwestern and Loyola—and got good jobs at major Chicago-based corporations. When I asked Kelly why he seemed so different from his brothers, he quickly dismissed the question. "That's too deep psychologically," he said. "People are different and react differently to the same circumstances. People say I'm like my mother in my drive. My father was a super guy but very laid-back." The psychological roots of Kelly's anger appear to have something to do with his relationship to his father, a chain-smoker who died of lung cancer in 1949, when he was only in his fifties. Even some of Kelly's closest confidants at Esmark could not recall him ever once mentioning his father in twenty-five to thirty years of association, even though much of his humor was rooted in family reminiscence. Kelly, like Beck, was a man who would much prefer to discuss deals than family history.

The one focused ambition of Kelly's early years brought him only grief. He returned from the navy dying to play football for Notre Dame but was unable to talk his way into a scholarship. Kelly's Notre Dame dream died hard. He carried steel rail and worked out all summer long "hoping they would suddenly see the light, that God would become just." After taking a few classes at a junior college, Kelly drifted into a career in data processing in the dawn of the computer age. He spent the better part of a decade working at an insurance company (where he met and married a Catholic girl from the South Side) and at a soap maker before joining the meat-packing concern of Swift & Company as a low-level employee in its controller's office. Kelly began work at Swift aspiring to nothing more than a raise and a windowed office. Hard as he was willing to work, Kelly was unable to imagine a career for himself at the stodgy WASP stronghold that was Swift, where a Catholic was a curiosity, where failure to wear one's suit coat might bring a reprimand, and where a man could work for fifteen years and still be referred to as "the new boy." Kelly put in his time at the office, paid his bills, drank his beers, honed his arsenal of one-liners, and kept a gimlet eye on the bastards—waiting for unimagined opportunity to activate ambition.

Founded in 1875 by a transplanted Cape Cod Yankee whose forebears really had sailed on the *Mayflower,* Swift & Company was one of the great archetypes of the American industrial corporation. In developing a refrigerated railcar that made possible the long-distance shipment of freshly slaughtered meat, Gustavus Franklin Swift created a vast new industry from one of mankind's oldest activities. To supply the big cities of the East with fresh beef and pork, Swift and his archrival, Philip Armour, built gargantuan packing plants in Chicago and other Midwestern cattle centers. The plants were technological marvels. Two decades before Henry Ford's assembly lines began churning out Model Ts, the Chicago packers perfected "disassembly"

lines to make more efficient the slaughtering and dismembering of
livestock, and also devised ingenious methods of turning animal parts
formerly discarded as waste into brushes, fertilizer, soap, and dozens of
other products. By the 1890s, Swift & Company had begun exporting
beef in its own refrigerator ships to Europe and later broadened its
reach to include much of Latin America and Asia. At the same time, it
branched into the distribution of butter, eggs, cheese, poultry, and
other perishable products as well as canned meats, vegetables, and
evaporated milk—all produced under its own brand names in its own
factories. By the time G. F. Swift died in 1903, Swift & Company had
18,000 employees, outlets in 400 cities and $200 million in annual
revenues—more than any other corporation in the United States.

As great a visionary as he was, G. F. Swift never figured on the
truck. The advent of the refrigerated truck after World War I altered
the economics of packing for the better by liberating the packers from
their dependence on the railroad system, making possible the decentralization of the industry. No longer was it necessary to incur the costs
of shipping livestock from the countryside to railway hubs or of operating vast stockyards and packing plants in these cities. Animals could be
slaughtered and dismembered a few miles from where they'd been
raised. Starting in the 1920s, new packing companies built hundreds of
down-sized plants in the country and began chipping away at the
commanding 60 percent share of the national market held by Swift,
Armour, and the other Big Five packers. Instead of adapting to the
new realities of the marketplace, the Big Five condemned themselves
to creeping obsolescence by using their wealth and market power to
obstruct the new technology. From 1927 to 1947, the Big Five acquired sixty-five independent packing companies—in effect, repurchas-
ing the market share lost to more innovative companies. But as long as
the Chicago packers obtained the bulk of their production from the
increasingly inefficient big-city plants built by their founders, the country entrepreneur would have a decisive cost advantage.

With an arrogance born of decades of utter domination and generations of management inbreeding, the Chicago packers were unable
even to recognize the need for basic change until it was imposed on
them from the outside. It was fitting that meat packing, as one of the
spawning grounds of the modern corporation, should be one of the
first industries to undergo the forcible restructuring that in time would
be visited upon them all. Of the Big Five, only Swift & Company
survived the conglomerate merger wave of the 1960s as an indepen-

dent company, renaming itself Esmark in 1973. Sheer size protected the company from takeover while Kelly and his mentor, Robert Reneker, set in motion one of the most radical transformations in corporate history.

By the time Kelly joined Swift & Company in 1953, not many jobs at the meat-packing company were on the right side of history. But Kelly had one of them, overseeing the installation of automated data-processing systems at Swift facilities around the world. He spent at least part of 99 of his first 104 weeks at Swift on the road. The first two of Kelly's three kids were fortuitously born on Sundays, allowing the expectant father to fly into Chicago on a Saturday and hit the road again on Monday. By the late 1950s, Kelly had probably seen the inside of more Swift plants than anyone since G. F. Swift himself, who was fanatically attentive to operating detail. Moreover, unlike the typical visitor from Chicago, Kelly got on well with the blue-collar locals at every whistle-stop. He had a joke for every occasion and could drink you under the table after beating you at arm wrestling. Kelly worked the Swift labor force like a Chicago ward heeler on his neighborhood rounds. "The guys who wanted to talk about baseball, I'd talk baseball," he said. "The guys who wanted to talk sex, I'd talk sex. Whatever turned them on. The key was to establish some sort of camaraderie, so that I was not the son of a bitch from the home office, the person who, if someone said, 'I think the chairman is a jerk,' was going to run back to Chicago and tell everyone. Then, when I needed to know, 'Does what we're doing make any sense?' I could call up Pete, or Mike, or whoever, and be able to count on him giving me his unvarnished opinion."

As a roving data-processing expert and junior controller, Kelly's job was essentially to understand the information needs of every manager at every plant. No one at Swift had a better worm's-eye view of the company's massive, pervasive inefficiencies than did Don Kelly. And no one at the home office was less inclined to blind reverence for company tradition than Kelly, whose many recommendations for improvements fell, as a rule, on deaf ears. Kelly took it personally, but he wasn't the only one ignored. A management consultant hired by Porter Jarvis, who was president in the 1950s and early 1960s, made the mistake of suggesting that certain of Swift's accounting procedures were substandard. "How can that be?" replied Jarvis. "We're the world's largest meat packer, aren't we?"

That the men who ran Swift were not interested in what he had to say became a source of enormous frustration to Kelly, who might well have resigned had it not been for Bob Reneker, Jarvis's successor. On paper, Reneker was indistinguishable from all the other well-meaning executives who'd run Swift & Company into the ground over the years. He'd spent his whole career at the company, as had his father, who'd risen to chief hog buyer. The younger Reneker pursued a more genteel career path that led through purchasing, transportation, industrial relations, and planning. It was impossible to imagine Bob Reneker slitting a pig's throat. With his silver temples and gracious manner, Reneker was the very picture of the WASP Establishment executive. At the peak of his career, Reneker served as a director of a dozen corporations and civic organizations. He was the only two-time president of the Boy Scouts of America in its history. Yet, miraculously, Reneker was not pompous or distant. *Everybody* liked Bob Reneker. Present an idea to Reneker and he'd look you in the eye, ask a hundred questions, and actually listen to the answers. Although uncommonly open-minded, Reneker was no pushover. During a management meeting years after Jarvis had departed, Reneker and Kelly had become embroiled in protracted disagreement. Roger Briggs, the company's chief financial officer, tried to intervene as peacemaker but Reneker fixed him with a cold stare. "Roger," he said quietly, "please shut the fuck up." Briggs *and* Kelly were shocked into silence.

Even before he succeeded Jarvis as president, Reneker took under his wing Kelly and a few other talented Young Turks disaffected by the glacial pace of reform. The restructuring of Swift didn't begin in earnest until 1967, when Jarvis severed his last tie to the company by stepping down as chairman and Reneker was given the added title of chief executive officer. In the interim, Kelly was chosen to attend an advanced management seminar at Harvard Business School, where one of his instructors was so impressed that he offered Kelly a job at the accounting firm of which he was a partner. Reneker helped convinced Kelly to stay by tripling his salary and assuring him that when the controller retired the job would be his. As soon as Reneker consolidated his power by adding the CEO title, Kelly seized the initiative by submitting a long memo arguing that the moment of truth had arrived for Swift—that the company had to reinvent itself to survive, and fast. This blunt warning inspired Reneker to form the Corporate Analysis Group, which was headed by Kelly and consisted of five middle managers chosen by him.

CAG gathered for the first time in 1968 in a conference room at

Swift headquarters. "Before we get started," Kelly told the group, "let's go over the voting principles."

Kelly went to the blackboard and with a piece of chalk drew five equal-sized boxes in a row. Inside each box he wrote the name of one man in the room: Elson, Huskisson, O'Bryant, Imhoff, Caruso.

"Each of you has one vote," he said, pointing to each of the smaller boxes in turn. "If I agree with you, I have one vote, too."

Kelly then drew a bigger square, a giant of a box above the five smaller boxes. Inside it, he wrote three letters: "G O D." His five colleagues started to laugh and fidget. Kelly had a big smile on his face as he turned to face the group.

"But if I disagree with you," he said, pointing at the "GOD" box, "then I have six votes."

Despite its bland name, the Corporate Analysis Group was nothing less than a tribunal of corporate revolution, with the authority to recommend the elimination of any job, the closing of any plant or warehouse, the sale of any division. To the many senior vice presidents and executive vice presidents who outranked Kelly, CAG's very existence was an affront. But that Kelly, a mere vice president, should run it was intolerable. Secure in his relationships with Reneker and with the company's major shareholders, Kelly was ready for a showdown with Swift's old guard. "Nothing and nobody is sacred," he told his fellow CAG members as the group began its work. "Do not be intimidated."

CAG's recommendations were massively radical—and almost wholly approved by Reneker and the board. Kelly's group recommended changes that would result in the closing of dozens of plants, the elimination of thousands of jobs, and a complete overhaul of the entire administrative structure. Howls of outrage went up from the old guard and Kelly worried that his proposals would be ignored to death at the middle-management level. In a startling departure for a company that as a matter of policy had stonewalled the press for nearly a century, Reneker used reporters to lob warning shots at his own employees: "We have given deadlines to certain complete groups, saying: 'In twenty-four months if you're not here [at the target level], you're gone.' If this sounds threatening, it is. This procrastinating, saying 'all we need are a few more hogs' or 'the gals are going to start buying our wieners instead of Oscar Mayer's'—this is what I'm trying to avoid."

By 1972, Swift & Company had closed down 330 of its 700 plants, representing nearly half of its sales volume, and phased out a third of its work force—thirteen thousand jobs—exceeding even CAG's rec-

ommendations. Meanwhile, Kelly prodded Reneker into using the capital freed by these long-overdue cutbacks to diversify into businesses
more lucrative than meat packing and unrelated to it. The boldest of
its eight acquisitions (totaling $175 million) from 1968 to 1972 put
Swift into offshore oil exploration, which in many respects was packing's opposite. While meat packing was an exercise in squcczing out
eighth-of-a-cent-per-pound profits on massive volume, exploring for oil
was a matter of laying down massive wagers in hopes of winning larger
jackpots. It was a business of pure risk. Or as an incredulous Reneker
said to Kelly not long after he first suggested moving into oil: "How
are we going to go before the board and say, 'We are going to spend a
hundred million dollars to buy a piece of ocean?' " Kelly spent a lot of
time hanging out with the executives of the oil companies Swift acquired. "They were a different breed of cat," Kelly said. "These guys
thought nothing of playing golf from Monday through Wednesday
and then staying up until two in the morning for the next four days to
get a deal done."

In 1973, another of Kelly's initiatives was implemented as Swift &
Company completed its reorganization into an intricately constructed
holding company called Esmark. When Reneker had become CEO
seven years earlier, nineteen vice presidents reported to him. "I was
involved in everything," he said, "because there was no one with the
authority to make decisions." Kelly designed Esmark so that only the
presidents of four subholding companies—food, energy, chemicals,
and financial services—reported directly to Reneker. These four units
in turn were divided into twenty operating companies, which were
further broken down into a thousand distinct profit centers, each of
which was required to come up with its own performance targets and
was held accountable for meeting them. Salaries were pegged to profit
performance for the first time. Decentralization made most of the
home-office employees superfluous; in converting Swift to Esmark, the
corporate staff was shrunk from 2,500 to 125. The survivors moved
into new quarters. "This was the real break with the past," Kelly said.
"We had to physically separate the holding-company people or the
operating people never would have believed that they really were responsible." While operating control was more broadly distributed, the
new system pulled financial control to the top under Kelly, who was
rewarded for his resolve with a promotion to president.

While the dramatic changes wrought by Reneker and Kelly doubled
the company's return on equity—the crucial measure of profitability

—its stock went nowhere. At the end of 1973, Esmark shares were trading at an anemic price-to-earnings ratio of 8.2, compared with 13.4 for the Standard & Poor's 400 and 13.3 for the typical food company. Kelly found Wall Street's indifference enormously frustrating since he'd come to think of stock-market value as the ultimate measure of his and the company's progress. With Esmark's stock price increasingly in mind, Kelly restructured continuously. By the time Reneker retired in 1977, the company had closed another hundred of the old Swift plants and shelled out $575 million to buy seventeen more companies—including, most improbably, International Playtex, the mass-market maker of bras and girdles, which provided Kelly and the boys with a rich new source of Rabelaisian humor. Even Reneker could not resist. "What do you know about *that* business?" a skeptic inquired of Reneker in a Q & A session following a speech in Los Angeles. "Well, we've always been meat packers," Reneker replied in Kelly-esque fashion.

When it came time for Reneker to step down, he wholeheartedly endorsed Kelly as his successor. The board gave its approval, but not before some heated discussion touched off by Brooks McCormick, the CEO of International Harvester and, at the time, Margo Preston's father-in-law. McCormick was a quintessential Brahmin—tall, tweedy, and Yale to the nines—and a great admirer of Reneker, who was his neighbor on Lake Shore Drive. Obliquely, McCormick raised the issue of whether a man of Kelly's "background" had the "breadth of experience" to succeed Reneker. McCormick's reservations were seconded by Dr. Allan Wallis, the chancellor of the University of Rochester.

As McCormick prattled elliptically on about his concerns, Samuel B. Casey lost his temper. Casey, Esmark's newest director, was the chief executive officer of Pullman, Incorporated, the old-line Chicago corporation best known for its railcars. A shrewd and salty second-generation Irish Catholic, Casey had started out as an engineer and industrial contractor. As it happened, he knew Brooks McCormick even better than he did Reneker. Casey lived at 1500 Lake Shore Drive, just down the street from McCormick's mansion; he had done a fair amount of business with the International Harvester CEO and had traveled with him in the Soviet Union and Eastern Europe. Casey liked McCormick and considered him a pretty decent guy, if somewhat stuffy. But this was too much.

"Brooks," growled Casey, "why don't you shove it up your ass?"

"All you Irish stick together, don't you?" McCormick retorted.

"It has nothing to do with being Irish," Casey said. "Reneker made this guy president three years ago and there's no one else—with the possible exception of Joe Sullivan—who's remotely qualified."

McCormick did a slow burn. "Joe Sullivan?" he said. "Is that all we have left at this company—Irishmen?"

Between them, McCormick and Wallis owned less than a thousand shares of Esmark stock. Reneker and all the major stockholders were squarely in Kelly's corner. In the end, the vote was unanimous in Kelly's favor. McCormick resigned as a director a few years later. Casey stayed.

By 1980, Kelly had spent thirteen years restructuring Swift-Esmark and still its stock price languished disrespectfully. Determined to shake off the Rodney Dangerfield role Wall Street had assigned him and his company, Kelly unveiled a reorganization plan as drastic in its own way as the one that had launched his career as an asset-shuffler. Having already shrunk the fresh-meat operation by half, Kelly announced that he would write off another $300 million in outmoded packing plants and then put what remained of the foundation of G. F. Swift's old empire up for sale. The company that invented meat packing would kiss it good-bye. To cover the costs of restructuring, the company would sell its oil subsidiary, the most profitable of all its businesses, and a grab bag of other stuff. Esmark would shrink by half. When a reporter asked how he felt about the prospect of heading a company with $3 billion instead of $6.7 billion in revenues, Kelly laughed and said, "I don't care if I'm head of a $200,000 company as long as we make a good profit."

Esmark's disposal of its oil operation was perfectly timed to capitalize on the first OPEC oil shock. And Kelly maximized Esmark's take by holding an auction and selling off its oil properties in pieces for a total of $1.2 billion, three times book value. Esmark left the oil business with an eye-popping capital gain of $562 million. However, the slaughtering operation proved far harder to divest. Kelly went through all sorts of contortions before succeeding in spinning off Swift Independent Corporation to investors through a public stock offering. By 1982, Kelly had finally earned the respect of Wall Street. Esmark's stock soared from about $22 in 1980 to more than $50 a share even before the great bull market got rolling in mid-1982.

But no stock-price comparison—nor any set of numbers, for that matter—could fully measure the distance Swift & Company had come. A century after its founding, the company was once again a prototype. Kelly had salvaged what remained of the economic value created by G. F. Swift by disembodying the company he'd founded and distilling its essence down into fungible assets. Swift & Company was a vast assemblage of things—400 plants, 250 cold-storage warehouses, 6,000 railcars—and people; at its peak after World War I, the company had more than 70,000 employees. Esmark, by comparison, was little more than a concept, a postindustrial abstraction of economic activity. It made nothing itself, though it owned companies that did. It directly employed only 125 people, almost all of whom manipulated information for a living—accountants, treasurers, analysts, planners, a few lawyers. Esmark was designed to do three things: monitor the performance of the diverse array of operating businesses that it owned; scout for undervalued businesses in which to invest; and arrange the buying and selling of these businesses. In structure a holding company, in practice an industrial conglomerate, in spirit Esmark was a deal company as obsessively devoted to the takeover game as any house on Wall Street. What began as an expedient means to an end— that end being the salvage of Swift & Company—had become an end in itself.

During his early years at Swift, Kelly had immersed himself in the realities of the empire of meat. He knew hundreds of people at dozens of plants. As CEO of Esmark, though, Kelly never visited a plant if there was any way he could avoid it, and involved himself as little as possible in actually running the companies Esmark owned. He didn't even like to discuss the running of them, for that matter. "If you talked operations to Don for more than ten minutes, he'd lose interest," said Joseph Sullivan, who as head of the Swift foods subsidiary was generally seen within Esmark as Kelly's heir apparent. Even before he took over from Reneker, Kelly had begun using Esmark funds to trade in and out of positions in companies he and Roger Briggs, his chief financial officer, perceived as undervalued. In effect, Esmark moved into Ivan Boesky's specialty—risk arbitrage—and in a big way. At any given time, Esmark had $100 million to $200 million invested in as many as two dozen companies that Kelly and Briggs considered likely candidates for future acquisition. This way, if Esmark decided to make an offer to acquire one of these companies and was rebuffed or outbid, it would at least come away with a trading profit. By the late 1970s, if not earlier, Don Kelly was a deal man masquerading, perhaps unwittingly, as corporate executive.

By late 1982, with the fresh-meats business disposed of and Esmark's remaining businesses chugging smoothly along, Kelly told his board that he was considering early retirement. Had all his wheeling and dealing left Kelly burnt out at age sixty? To the contrary, he was bored. "I told the board that I was unwilling to be CEO on a caretaker basis," Kelly said. "I said, 'Unless you're willing to make a major acquisition, sayonara. You've got the wrong horse.' I guess some of them thought that anyway." When the directors, who'd heard such grousing before, failed to move fast enough to satisfy the CEO's yen for deal action, Kelly put out a press release announcing his intention to retire before he reached sixty-five. He even went so far as to designate three prospective successors. Kelly admitted that he hadn't any specific plans but that he saw "a lot of opportunities" outside Esmark. "People have asked me to work on a lot of things." They probably had. But what Kelly was working on seven months later was the biggest acquisition in Esmark's hyperactive history.

In his quest for ways to differentiate his M & A group from its rivals, Beck had been toying with a concept he called "corporate venturing." The gist of it was that Oppenheimer was not really an investment bank at all but a group of businessmen who happened to be on Wall Street. Because the Jeff Beck Group brought a businessman's point of view to transactions, so the spiel went, it was uniquely capable of going beyond the role of mere adviser and entering into partnership with client companies. In Beck's opportunistic definition, partnership could take a mushy and basically spiritual form—i.e., "We really *feel* for you, man"—or one as tangible as dollar bills. That is, Oppenheimer was willing to risk its own capital to buy businesses in partnership with clients on a highly leveraged basis—to do leveraged buyouts, which in 1983 were still a novelty even in sophisticated financial circles. It was an intriguing pitch and Beck could deliver it with something approximating credibility after Steve McGrath joined his group from Warner-Lambert.

McGrath's new business card presented him as president of Oppenheimer Strategic Investments, an impressive-sounding title that allowed him the privilege of sitting at a desk in a room next to some other department's rattling Xerox machine in the bowels of One New York Plaza and dream up leveraged-buyout ideas. McGrath was the only member of the group who had worked in the corporate mainstream and who would have been described as a businessman by a businessman. He looked the part, too—to Beck's ceaseless amusement.

Beck was willing to bet that McGrath had never set foot in Paul Stuart, Hermès, Turnbull & Asser, or any of the other high-toned haberdashers favored by the pace-setting M & A men. McGrath wore polyester suits off the rack and round-toed, zip-up ankle boots that Beck delighted in describing as "disco boots"—as in, "Enough about me, what do you think of my friend Steve's disco boots?"

McGrath was just a few weeks into his new job when he came across a headline in *The Wall Street Journal* that grabbed his attention: "NORTON SIMON'S CHAIRMAN LEADS BID TO GO PRIVATE." McGrath was noddingly familiar with Norton Simon, which, though it didn't compete directly with Warner-Lambert, was essentially a marketing company, too, with a stable of well-known consumer brands in food (Hunt-Wesson), car rental (Avis), cosmetics (Max Factor) and liquor (Johnnie Walker and Tanqueray). As McGrath read the story, his pulse quickened. David Mahoney, Norton Simon's chairman and CEO, had offered to buy the company in a leveraged buyout. The Wall Street analysts quoted in the story were incredulous, not so much at Mahoney's audacity in bidding to buy the very company he was running but at the price he'd offered—$29.50 a share, only 50 cents above book value. "How does Mahoney figure they're going to let him get away with this?" said one. Already the stock had risen above $30 a share, suggesting that a higher offer was expected. McGrath read further and was delighted to learn that Mahoney had yet to arrange the $1.65 billion in financing he'd need to swing his leveraged buyout.

McGrath thought immediately of Esmark. As an acquisitive conglomerate with its own stable of consumer businesses, Esmark was a logical buyer. And McGrath had an in at Esmark. He and Briggs had worked together at Price Waterhouse and Sterling Drug, and had remained friendly ever since. After consulting with Beck, who had also been pondering a way into the impending battle for Norton Simon, McGrath put in a call to Briggs, whose secretary said he was out recovering from an operation for cancer of the larynx. McGrath, feeling a bit guilty that he hadn't kept in closer touch with Briggs, was transferred to Phil Thomas, Kelly's liaison with Wall Street. Did Esmark have any interest in acquiring Norton Simon? Perhaps, replied Thomas, who advised McGrath to have Beck call Kelly directly.

Beck checked around and found that neither of the investment banks Kelly had used most frequently in the past—Salomon Brothers and Goldman, Sachs—would be able to aid him in a bid for Norton Simon. The directors of Norton Simon had already hired Salomon and

Lazard Frères to advise the company. Mahoney had signed up
Goldman, Sachs and Drexel Burnham Lambert. That still left Morgan
Stanley; First Boston; Lehman; Kidder, Peabody; Merrill Lynch; and a
half-dozen other investment banks that might make a play for Esmark,
which, unfortunately, was if anything too obvious a prospect. On the
very morning after McGrath had called Thomas, *The Wall Street
Journal* ran a story that singled out three companies as the likeliest
suitors for Norton Simon: Brascan, Esmark, and Seagram.

Beck needed a promotable angle, a gimmick. Perhaps Oppenheimer
should buy Norton Simon in partnership with Esmark, offering to take
subsidiaries that might not fit into Kelly's plans? In Beck's opinion,
most consumer-products companies—Norton Simon included—were
grossly undervalued in the stock market. Beck saw only two possible
problems with the joint-venture approach: Kelly might reject Oppenheimer on the suspicion that it couldn't really come up with the
money to buy the remainder of Norton Simon or—perhaps worse—
Kelly might take the firm at its word, and then Beck would somehow
have to come up with, say, $500 million. The third, vastly preferable
possibility was that Kelly would decide that he didn't need a partner
but would be so enthralled with Oppenheimer's dash and daring that
he'd choose the group as his adviser in a play for Norton Simon, and
after they'd won would present Beck with a check for a couple of
million dollars. After several hours of staring out his window, at his
ceiling, and at his yellow pad of paper, Beck decided to risk offering a
joint venture. He'd find a way to come up with the cash if need be. He
hoped.

"Sandy!" Beck shouted from his desk. "Get Don Kelly on the
phone." McGrath and Brown were standing at the window, looking
his way with the fidgety expectancy of a couple of kids early on Christmas morning.

"Okay, Jeff," said Sandy. "He's on."

"Mr. Kelly," said Beck in a booming, demonically cheerful voice.
"My name is Jeff Beck. I'm the head of mergers and acquisitions at
Oppenheimer & Company and I have an unusual idea for you."

"Well, what is it?" said Kelly, with what sounded to Beck encourag-
ingly like cordiality.

"We think Hunt-Wesson would fit beautifully into Esmark, which
I'm sure is not news to you. The thing is, though, we're not really
interested in being your investment banker on this one. We'd like to

be your partner. We're prepared, Mr. Kelly, to buy any pieces of Norton Simon that you don't want."

"Oh, really? Which pieces did you have in mind?" Kelly replied, sounding faintly amused.

"That's something I'd really prefer to discuss in person."

"How soon could you be here?"

"I could have my team in Chicago tomorrow."

After a momentary silence, Kelly said, "See you tomorrow afternoon then, Mr. Beck."

Beck put down the receiver. "Well, boys," he said, smiling slyly and sweating profusely, "we've got some work to do."

When investment bankers go deal pitching, they typically arm themselves with volumes of data and analysis bound in hardcover and dressed up with color graphics. These "blue books," as they are generically known because of the color of choice in binders, are used by bankers both to overwhelm clients with their thorough preparation and to try to control discussion. With Esmark, Oppenheimer was starting from zero and had to whip something up in less than twenty-four hours, not enough time for full-fledged blue-book treatment. Working late into the night and beginning early the next morning, a half-dozen members of the group worked up a range of valuations for each Norton Simon business based on its past performance, its financial condition, the likely course of the U.S. economy—all the usual variables. Also included was an analysis of the tactical options open to Kelly should he decide to make a play for Norton Simon.

Just before heading for the airport, Beck, McGrath, Peters, Sanzo, and Brown gathered in a conference room to review the presentation to Kelly. While not the slickest package the group had ever put together, it was presentable enough and persuasive in a direct, elemental way. The basic economics of the deal appeared so compelling that it wasn't necessary to attempt any analytical razzle-dazzle anyway. A quick scan reassured Beck that the values McGrath and Peters had assigned to each Norton Simon division were reasonable enough as a starting point for negotiations with Esmark. Sanzo, who was busy on his own deals, had declined to participate in the pursuit of Esmark, arguing that the group would be better off sticking to the small, unglamorous deals that were its forte than trying to infiltrate the billion-dollar club. But even Sanzo had no problem with the numbers in the blue book, and so it was off to Chicago, with Beck, McGrath, Peters, and Brown sitting four abreast in the first-class cabin of a United Airlines flight to O'Hare.

Mastering the nuances of air travel is an essential part of a deal man's training. A deal man who can't sleep on airplanes finds himself at a mounting competitive disadvantage over the course of a marathon deal and runs a definite risk of bouncing his chin off the table during the climactic negotiating session. Although first class made sleeping easier, it also exposed the unwary to the menace of gluttony. Beck's Air Travel Rule Number One: On all-night flights, to Europe especially, take it easy on the food and drink. Rule Number Two: *Always* sit on the aisle. During his Lehman days, Beck once flew to London with a rotund young associate making his first overseas business trip. He lapped up Pan Am's luxurious menu offerings as if he were a condemned man eating his last meal. About dawn, Beck was awakened by the sound of moaning. He glanced at his companion, whose face seemed oddly green in the early-morning light. As his colleague swiveled to meet his gaze, Beck rolled over his armrest and onto the floor just in time. A man sitting in the next row reached for his motion discomfort bag and missed. As Beck lay laughing in the aisle, the sound of vomiting rolled forward through the cabin like a peristaltic wave.

Beck's Air Travel Rule Number Three, a helpful hint for civilians: When sitting next to two or more investment bankers, always take the window seat. Investment bankers in the throes of a deal tend to leave their seats as often as little kids insist on going to the bathroom. Deal men occasionally use airplane bathrooms, too, of course, but mostly they can be spotted in the service alcoves, safely removed from the prying ears of other passengers, any one of whom might be an inside trader or, worse, a minion of a rival house.

After landing at O'Hare, Beck and his colleagues made their first tactical error of the day, hailing a taxicab without a working air conditioner. Peters took the front seat and Beck, McGrath, and Brown squeezed into the back. Almost instantly, Beck felt perspiration beading up all over his body. The temperature had to be in the nineties and it was humid, too. Traffic was slow. They'd be lucky to make it to Esmark's offices downtown in an hour. There was only one thing to do: jive. Beck slipped into the thundering evangelical twang of a character he called the Reverend Billy Joe Bubba of Del Rio, Texas.

"Ah now undahstand why there are no signs of human life on the streets of your city in the spring, the summah, the fall, or the wintah," declared the Reverend Bubba. "You either freeze to death or die of the heat heah. How can you live heah?" Beck asked the cabdriver, a black man about his own age. "Ah just don't undahstand. But let us pray, let us pray for coolness, the coolness of the rain that is God's muhcy."

Beck went on in this vein at length, to much general merriment. Suddenly, though, the Reverend Billy Joe vanished. "Stop the car!" Beck shouted. "Stop the car right now."

The cabdriver pulled off on the shoulder and stopped. Beck opened his door and got out. "I'm going to look for a breeze," he said. "Be right back." Beck frolicked around for a few seconds on the side of the road and then jumped back into his seat and slammed the door. "What are you waiting for, man?" he yelled. "Let's go."

Beck had assumed his gangster character. "Oh, so you think that's funny. Is that it?" he muttered to the cabdriver. "I'd like you to tell me exactly what is so funny. I don't think I'm so funny. You know where we're from, don't you? New York." Beck said the city's name as if it were a fatal disease. "We're businessmen from New York and we've come to Chicago to meet with some very important guys in the same line of work, if you know what I mean." Beck's eyelid began twitching maniacally as he leaned forward and rested his elbows on the top of the front seat. "So I ask you, my friend, what's so fuckin' funny? Huh, what? What!"

And so it went all the way to Esmark's offices. The cab pulled up at 1400 Michigan Avenue a good ten minutes before the appointment with Kelly. Beck gave the driver a thirty-dollar tip and exchanged high-fives and a "brother" handshake with him. He also offered some free advice: "Hey, man, why don't you fix this piece of shit."

As the group ascended in the elevator, Beck fell oddly silent. His expression went blank, his eyes narrowed to slits and seemed to focus inward. He breathed through his nose in rapid little snorts. Someone who didn't know Beck would have assumed he was having an anxiety attack. Brown asked him a question as they left the elevator on the fortieth floor but he didn't respond to it. He didn't even seem to hear Brown. But by the time Phil Thomas came to greet his visitors in the reception area, Beck had fully reanimated. He leaped from a chair to his feet at Thomas's approach and could not quite manage to stand still during the obligatory introductory chitchat. His whole body seemed to be grooving along to some insistent up-tempo internal rhythm. He was absolutely wired for action. Brown, who'd never before gone deal pitching with Beck, was startled by the transformation. It was as if Beck had come equipped with a secret on/off switch.

Thomas brought the four deal men to Esmark's "war room," a large conference room sandwiched between Kelly's and Briggs's offices and packed with computer gear and state-of-the-art telecommunications equipment. Four Esmark executives rose from their chairs. Thomas handled the introductions. In walked Kelly, heralding his entrance with a flourish of one-liners. Kelly laughed, his lieutenants laughed, Beck laughed, everybody laughed. When Kelly stopped laughing, everyone else stopped, too.

Beck did most of the talking as he walked the group through the Oppenheimer deal book, mixing a joke or two in with the numbers. Kelly listened—impassively but carefully—as he doodled on a pad of paper. For all Kelly's informality, an undercurrent of urgency ran through the meeting. It was obvious to his visitors that Kelly already knew a great deal about Norton Simon—much more about the company, in fact, than they ever would. Very few food companies had escaped Kelly's scrutiny as he scouted for acquisitions over the years. Norton Simon interested him more than most because he believed its brands were stronger than Mahoney's poor management had allowed them to be. Ever since Mahoney's announcement put his company in play three days ago, Esmark's war-room computers had been crunching out Norton Simon numbers.

Kelly's initial inclination had been to bid for Norton Simon unassisted by Wall Street. But Briggs and Thomas had convinced the boss that it made sense to use an investment bank, if only as an insurance policy against lawsuits by shareholders should something go awry. The first call Thomas got after Mahoney made his bid was from A. G. Becker, a midsized New York investment bank with deep Chicago roots. Kelly had also heard from Greenhill at Morgan Stanley. Kelly had met Greenhill and taken an instant, visceral dislike to him—too Ivy League, too upper-crusty. Thomas was surprised not to hear from Wasserstein of First Boston, which, it turned out, was working another angle on the Norton Simon deal that would end up costing Esmark about $160 million.

The Oppenheimer contingent left Esmark that afternoon not knowing where they stood; Kelly had been cordial but cryptic. As Beck and McGrath had surmised, the only part of Norton Simon that Kelly really coveted was Hunt-Wesson. As a veteran deal maker, though, Kelly was intimidated neither by the cost of acquiring all of Norton

Simon nor by the task of carving Hunt-Wesson out of it afterward. Although Kelly didn't need a partner, he had been impressed by the pluck and originality of Beck's offer to buy Norton Simon in tandem with Esmark.

The next day Kelly called Beck. The other members of the group had gathered in Beck's office for a meeting. Beck put Kelly on the speakerphone. Kelly, as usual, got right to the point. "How would you like to represent us, along with A. G. Becker?" he asked.

Beck was ecstatic. His gambit had worked! He'd landed Esmark without having to go out and raise a few hundred million dollars in financing. He felt like singing a few choruses of his old DLJ theme song—"We're in the money." Instead, Beck deliberately laid the humble enthusiasm on a bit thick. "Really?" he said. "Oh, that would be just great, Don."

"I want you to call Barry Friedberg at A. G. Becker," Kelly said. "He's expecting your call."

Kelly hung up and pandemonium erupted in Beck's office as he and his cohorts began dancing around the room in single file like some demented tribe of Wall Street Indians about to hit the warpath.

11

The approving words "regular guy" immediately popped into Beck's head as he shook Barry Friedberg's hand at LaGuardia Airport, shortly before the scheduled departure of their flight to Chicago. Friedberg, the M & A chief for A. G. Becker, Incorporated, was short, curly-haired, and bespectacled, with a sweet, almost shy smile. Friedberg may have looked a bit cute for an M & A warrior, but in fact he was one of the most astute and respected deal men of his generation—technically proficient and quite decisive for all his unpretentiousness. A few years older than Beck, Friedberg brought a good deal more experience to the Norton Simon deal, having started at A. G. Becker in 1964 after graduating from Princeton University. After fifteen years as a corporate-finance generalist, in 1980 Friedberg was put in charge of the firm's M & A department.

Like Beck, Friedberg spent much of his time scrambling to find a way to insert his firm into big deals. As soon as he'd read of David Mahoney's bid for Norton Simon, Friedberg alerted A. G. Becker's Chicago office and a banker there immediately telephoned Esmark, seeking an audience with Kelly. A. G. Becker was the first investment bank to call Esmark in the wake of the Norton Simon news, beating Oppenheimer to the punch by about twenty-four hours. Kelly invited the firm to make a presentation, and Friedberg flew out from New York to lead it. When Kelly called to offer A. G. Becker the assignment, Friedberg was pleasantly surprised. When Kelly called back to say that he wanted A. G. Becker to work alongside Oppenheimer, Friedberg was more surprised. Oppenheimer? Friedberg didn't even know it had an M & A department.

"How do you guys know Kelly, anyway?" Friedberg asked Beck while they waited for their plane. Friedberg might as well have asked a new father for a peek at the pictures. Complete with comic flourishes,

Beck told Friedberg the story of how Oppenheimer had its way into the deal by offering to buy Norton Simon in partnership with Esmark.

Friedberg chuckled good-naturedly. This was starting to look like it might be a fun deal. A few days earlier, he and Beck had worked out over the telephone their first joint decision: hiring a lawyer. Friedberg had suggested Jack MacAtee of Davis Polk & Wardwell and Beck, who'd met the lawyer on a deal during his DLJ days, happily concurred. MacAtee would be accompanying them on today's trip to Chicago for their first strategy session with Kelly. Friedberg and MacAtee sat together in coach. "I guess you guys are riding the subway," teased Beck from his seat in first class as MacAtee and Friedberg filed past him to their seats in the rear.

The meeting with Kelly was brief and productive. The first item on the agenda was investment-banker fees. Kelly took the initiative, offering Beck and Friedberg a pretty standard arrangement: expenses plus $150,000 apiece at the start of the tender offer. If Esmark gained control of Norton Simon each investment banker would get $600,000 more. And if Esmark were to acquire 100 percent of Norton Simon, Oppenheimer and Beck each would get another $750,000. This worked out to a total fee of $1.5 million per investment bank. Kelly laid out the terms, then smiled, "Take it or leave it" written across his features.

"Excuse us a minute," Friedberg said.

He and Beck went into an adjoining office. "Let's take it," each man immediately blurted out. They stood around for a few minutes to give the appearance of deliberation and returned to accept Kelly's offer.

The matter of fees settled, Kelly moved on to the subject of Norton Simon. Kelly had been eycing the company for some time, intrigued by the idea of combining Swift's food businesses with Hunt-Wesson. As for the rest of Norton Simon, Kelly was willing to take a deal man's gamble: If Esmark decided it didn't want to stay in the car-rental, liquor-importing, or cosmetics businesses, Kelly was confident he could sell them—and probably at a profit. Esmark started buying Norton Simon shares in the open market the day after Mahoney had announced his bid to buy the company. By the time Beck and Friedberg entered the picture, Esmark had shelled out $5 million to buy 161,000 shares—less than 1 percent—and Kelly had pretty much decided to go ahead and make a play for Norton Simon. The questions at hand were,

How much should Esmark bid for it and how should its offer be structured?

These issues were complicated a bit by the presence of a second bidder. Not long after Mahoney had put his $29.50-a-share bid on the table, Kohlberg, Kravis & Roberts offered $33 a share, or $27 million, which was almost double the amount of its largest leveraged buyout to date. As usual, KKR's offer was made subject to financing—meaning that the firm wanted Norton Simon but didn't yet have the money in hand to actually pay for it.

In the view of Kelly's trio of Wall Street advisers, Esmark probably would be the only corporate bidder for Norton Simon. Although many other corporations would be keenly interested in parts of Mahoney's company, few if any would be willing to assume the risk inherent in acquiring the whole thing. While KKR's bid had effectively established a floor price of $33 a share, Kelly believed that Norton Simon was worth more, and Beck and Friedberg concurred. The beauty of the situation, though, was that Esmark could best KKR merely by matching its $33 offer. While KKR would have to spend weeks lining up the bank loans it needed, Esmark could borrow huge sums in a matter of hours; indeed, it had an untapped $1 billion line of credit with a consortium of large banks. The advantage of cash in hand was that it would allow Esmark to cast its bid in the form of a tender offer, which could be announced and completed in twenty days, far less time than KKR was likely to need to round up bank financing for an LBO. Mahoney, too, had put himself at the disadvantage of announcing an unfinanced buyout bid. Beck returned to New York from his first meeting with Kelly in a state of high excitement, certain that Norton Simon would soon be Esmark's.

When Esmark went ahead and announced a $33-a-share tender offer for Norton Simon, both KKR and Mahoney immediately terminated their offers. The battle would have ended right there had Kelly been less determined to minimize the expense of the acquisition. Esmark's tender offer provided for a cash purchase of only 51 percent of Norton Simon's shares, and a new issue of convertible preferred stock for the remaining 49 percent. The pricing of the preferred issue was the trickiest part of the deal from an investment-banking standpoint, and Beck was only too happy to defer to Friedberg on the matter. "It's all right with me if you run the deal," Beck told him, confident that Friedberg wouldn't try to upstage him. (In fact, by deal's end, Beck thought so highly of Friedberg that when A. G. Becker ran into serious financial problems, he urged Friedberg to join Oppenheimer and offered to step aside as M & A chief to accommodate him. Instead, Friedberg went to Merrill Lynch, where he was soon running the entire investment-banking operation.)

Citing the indeterminate value of the preferred stock Esmark was offering, Norton Simon's board immediately rejected its bid, giving every M & A man on Wall Street more time to find a white knight. And so it was that Beck for the first time found himself matching wits with Wasserstein. The competing tender offer for Norton Simon that First Boston crafted on behalf of Anderson Clayton & Company, a Houston-based food company best known for Chiffon margarine, was unusually convoluted even by Wassersteinian standards. On the face of it, Anderson Clayton had outbid Esmark by offering $35 a share for 51 percent of Norton Simon's stock. There was a catch, though, and it was a big one. Anderson Clayton said that it might not actually keep and pay for the shares tendered to it unless it could persuade Norton Simon to sell it Hunt-Wesson and Hunt-Wesson only. On the other hand, Anderson Clayton reserved the right to amend its offer to buy 100 percent of Norton Simon's shares if it found a partner willing to take Avis, Max Factor, and Somerset. Beck disdainfully dismissed Anderson Clayton's offer as "a Bruce Wasserstein two-step no-step." Wasserstein's client did indeed back out, but not before inducing Kelly to boost his bid to $35.50 a share, pushing the value of the deal over $1 billion.

Kelly was pleased with Oppenheimer's and A. G. Becker's performance as his investment-banking advisers, though later he was hard-pressed to specify their contribution. "What contribution did they make? We won," he said. "If you have bright people in a meeting, something good will come from it, and Beck and Friedberg are both bright. They established a rapport between themselves and didn't try that one-upmanship shit you see a lot of from investment bankers. Also, they didn't try to explain how deals work. I get so tired of bankers giving me the ABCs of deals when I've forgotten more deals than they'll ever make." For what Beck and Friedberg didn't do as much as for what they did do, Kelly paid Oppenheimer and A. G. Becker each a $1.5 million fee.

In the middle of the Norton Simon deal, Beck had been sitting in his office one day when Sandy, his secretary, shouted in to him from her desk just outside his door: "Ivan Boesky for you."

Holy shit, Beck thought, Boesky.

Like squaring off against Felix Rohatyn or Bruce Wasserstein, a call from Boesky was a rite of passage into the M & A big time. Beck picked up the telephone and identified himself.

"This *is* Ivan Boesky," said Boesky, as if it were in doubt. He began by pouring a little flattery in Beck's ear, saying that he'd heard he was one of the coming stars in M & A. "We should get together for dinner sometime," Boesky said.

Beck let the invitation pass. "What can I do for you?" he said.

Boesky said he owned shares in Norton Simon and was wondering what Esmark might do next.

"Don't you read the papers?" Beck said.

Boesky, as always, was in a hurry. He grew testy. "You don't understand," he said. "I am a major shareholder of Norton Simon. I want to know what Esmark's options are."

"You are going to experience a dial tone very shortly," Beck said.

"What?"

Beck hung up on Boesky, who called back repeatedly and berated Sandy when she refused to put him through.

For Beck, the phone call was confirmation enough of the persistent rumors that Boesky was trading illegally on inside information. His first conversation with the king of arbitrage left him feeling angry and disoriented, almost as if he'd returned to his apartment to find that he'd been robbed. Beck became so obsessed with Boesky and what he believed was the pernicious influence of risk arbitrage that he was even distracted from his efforts to convince *The Wall Street Journal*'s Metz to write another story about his group. "Jeff was really convinced that Boesky would end up ruining the takeover business," said Metz, who'd heard the rumors, too. "After a while it was all we talked about." A few months after Esmark's acquisition of Norton Simon, Beck invited Metz to dinner at his apartment with two arbitrageurs: Jeff Tarr of Oppenheimer and Martin Gruss of Gruss & Company, which ran one of the biggest risk-arb desks on the Street. The talk, naturally, turned to Boesky and insider trading. As Beck had hoped, the dinner inspired Metz to try to put together a story. Metz did some digging and ended up bouncing the Swiss-connection rumors off Boesky and Marty Siegel —each of whom issued indignant denials—and the enforcement chief of the SEC. In the end, though, Metz didn't have enough to hang a story on. Beck urged Metz to hire a private investigator to tail Boesky, but the reporter was not willing to go that far. Beck kept hammering away at Metz: "There's a Pulitzer in it for you," he said.

The Esmark–Norton Simon deal was also noteworthy as Beck's second confrontation with the Deal Club in general, and with Rohatyn of Lazard and Geoff Boisi of Goldman, Sachs in particular. Rohatyn was friendly with Mahoney as well as with Richard Shinn, the chief executive officer of Metropolitan Life Insurance and the most influential of Norton Simon's outside directors. After Mahoney made his LBO proposal, the outside directors hired Lazard Frères and Salomon Brothers to advise them. While it was Rohatyn who'd landed the Norton Simon assignment, Lazard was represented at most meetings by Peter Jacquith, who had come up as a spear-carrier to Rohatyn and hadn't been able to extricate himself from the role. After having missed some important early meetings, Rohatyn called Jacquith from his summer house at Southampton and asked him to set up a private meeting with Kelly. Jacquith called Beck and relayed Rohatyn's request. Kelly saw no point in a solo session with Rohatyn and indeed was annoyed by the arrogance of the request, quickly assenting to Beck's suggestion that he and Friedberg go in his stead. Beck called Jacquith.

"No problem, Peter," Beck said. "See you at ten."

Beck and Friedberg left Esmark's suit at the Helmsley Palace Hotel at about nine fifty-five. It was only a few blocks to the Lazard Frères offices in Rockefeller Center, but Beck was determined to be late and dallied before the windows of the luxury shops on Fifth Avenue. At ten fifteen, Friedberg reminded Beck that they'd been due at Lazard at ten. "You look like you could use a beer," said Beck. It was about ten thirty when they finally arrived at Lazard Frères. Rohatyn was waiting in a conference room with Jacquith and a half-dozen other people. Rohatyn was wearing an open-necked shirt and moccasins. He was freshly tanned—and moderately steamed. "Where's Kelly?" he demanded.

"I have a message from Don," Beck said. "He specifically said that he wants you to deal with me and Barry."

Rohatyn did a slow burn. "Well, what do you have to say, then?"

"We're here to hear what you have to say," Beck retorted. "You called the meeting."

"I don't think we have anything to talk about then," Rohatyn said.

"I guess not," Beck said. "We'll own it at thirty-three."

Later, Beck called Jacquith to apologize for misleading him. Jacquith was not immediately inclined toward forgiveness. "Don't take it personally," Beck said. "This is war."

As for Boisi, Beck came away from the Norton Simon deal with an even lower opinion of Goldman, Sachs than had been left by the Varian defense. When Mahoney decided to put together a leveraged-buyout proposal, he turned first to Goldman, Sachs, the firm's long-time banker, and later added Drexel Burnham Lambert for its junk-bond expertise. While many much larger LBO attempts would be made over the course of the decade, Mahoney's bid for Norton Simon was perhaps unequaled in terms of sheer venality. In the classic lever-aged buyout, ownership is widely distributed throughout the com-pany's senior management, which ends up with 10 percent to 15 percent of the equity. But Mahoney's LBO investor "group" consisted of himself and three members of the company's finance staff, who put the buyout proposal together in strictest secrecy and who never were publicly identified even after the plan was announced. If their LBO had been consummated, this quartet of insiders would have owned 60 percent of a company with $2 billion in assets and 35,000 employees. Nearly all of this 60 percent stake would have been held by Mahoney himself.

Mahoney's other grievous error was trying to buy the company on the cheap—a mere 50 cents a share above its book value. In his out-landishly self-congratulatory memoirs, *Confessions of a Street-Smart Manager*, published in 1988, Mahoney warned his readers against let-ting themselves be "trapped" by outside experts into making wrong decisions. "I can bring in three different consultants and get them to give me three different opinions on the same subject," Mahoney wrote. "Never fail to trust your own knowledge and instincts. When something sounds fishy, ask: 'Says who? Where is it written?'" In readying his LBO bid, Mahoney's reverence for his own street-fighting instincts led him into the worst misstep of his career. Both Boisi and Leon Black of Drexel Burnham advised Mahoney to offer more than $29.50 a share, and they compiled a list of sixteen companies—includ-ing Esmark—that were likely to intervene unless he did. Mahoney went through the list, debunking each prospective bidder one by one. He was nonchalant. Who would dare to make a play for *his* company? Where was it written?

After he terminated his LBO bid, Mahoney insisted that Goldman, Sachs be restored to its traditional position as Norton Simon's lead investment banker, even though the board already had retained Lazard and Salomon Brothers. As usual, though, Mahoney got his way and the other two investment banks were grumblingly relegated to subordinate status. This little maneuver saved Mahoney a pretty penny in invest- ment-banking fees. At deal's end, Goldman, Sachs billed Norton Si- mon for all its work—including its efforts on behalf of Mahoney personally. (Mahoney stiffed Drexel, except for the tennis racket he gave to one banker.) Publicly anyway, Mahoney played the role of statesman after he dropped his bid, issuing a press release that said Esmark's proposal was "under very serious review and would be dis- cussed at a board of directors meeting." Privately, though, he appar- ently was panicked at the prospect of losing control of a company that he'd run as a satrapy for nearly fifteen years. Jay Higgins of Salomon Brothers returned home late one night to find an urgent message from Mahoney. Higgins returned the call and listened sleepily to the out- pourings of a distraught man. "Jay," he said, "they're trying to steal my company."

Boisi raised many an eyebrow within the Norton Simon camp by making an impassioned plea to the board to liquidate the company rather than accept Esmark's $33 a share—this from a banker whose client had offered $29.50 for the same company. Even after Esmark had boosted its bid and both Lazard Frères and Salomon Brothers were prepared to formally certify that $35.50 was a fair price, Boisi equivocated. "No one could believe that at the eleventh hour, there would have to be a fight with Goldman, Sachs over a fairness opinion," said one insider. "I can't prove that Boisi was trying to help Mahoney kill the deal for his own selfish purposes, regardless of the interests of the shareholders. But I had the feeling that all the board members and the company's other advisers went directly from this affair to the shower to cleanse themselves."

On July 21, 1983, nearly a month after Mahoney had put his com- pany in play, Esmark's sweetened offer triggered a barrage of tendering by arbitrageurs and other big shareholders, giving Esmark control. The battle was over. From London, Mahoney announced his immediate resignation. Although he'd lost his company, he had the considerable consolation of getting $35 million in cash from Esmark, which bought out the CEO's employment contract and his stock options. Back in New York, Mahoney's minions issued a farewell statement that had been on file for weeks. In it, Mahoney vowed to "remain active in the business community" and continue to work for "better health care, helping disadvantaged youth, good government and promoting equal opportunity for all men and women."

Beck hadn't read anything funnier in weeks.

After the Norton Simon transaction closed, Beck made a point of staying in close contact with Kelly. He and Margo flew to Chicago with Steve and Jean McGrath to have dinner with Kelly and his wife, Byrd Mary, and to attend Esmark's Christmas party. Kelly was charming but relentless in tweaking Margo about her Lake Forest heritage, apparently unaware that she'd once been married to the son of his former nemesis on the Swift board. At the party, Jay Higgins and Ira Harris of Salomon Brothers were not pleased to run into Beck and McGrath. The relationship between Salomon Brothers and Esmark dated back to 1935, when the old Swift & Company became the bond-trading house's very first corporate-finance client. Ever since, Salomon had jealously guarded its relationship with Esmark. The relations had been cemented by a personal friendship of long standing between Kelly and Harris, who was Salomon's top M & A man, operating out of Chicago.

"What are you guys doing here?" Harris hissed at Beck and Mc-Grath.

"Just making sure you get enough to eat, Ira," said Beck, who'd taken an instant dislike to the hefty Harris during the Norton Simon deal. Upon first meeting, Beck had deliberately tried to irk Harris by referring to him by someone else's name. (Although Beck didn't know it, Harris had in fact changed his name, from Ike Horowitz.) Beck liked to tell the story, perhaps apocryphal, of how Harris, whom he called Fat Ira, disrupted one meeting by just coming in and sitting down. "There was a loud noise and everyone started looking around," Beck said. "Ira had ripped his pants at the seam." Harris responded to Beck's baiting with scorn; he disdained Beck as a smart-ass who was more of an irritant than a serious rival. By a cruel twist of fate, both Beck and Harris were devotees of the Hôtel du Cap d'Antibes and indeed often took their vacations there at the same time.

With Salomon and A. G. Becker, Oppenheimer was comanager of a $300 million stock offering by Esmark, which used the proceeds to pay down the bank loans it had taken on to finance the acquisition of Norton Simon. This was the largest underwriting that Opco had ever comanaged and produced another $1.2 million in fees, as Beck proudly pointed out to Robert and anyone else who doubted that his M & A department wasn't the best thing that had ever happened to Oppen-heimer.

As Esmark's profits rose smartly after the Norton Simon acquisition, Kelly and crew were hailed as masters of the increasingly fashionable art of extracting higher stock-market value from languishing corporate assets. Wall Street eagerly awaited Kelly's next move. Even before the acquisition had closed, Kelly was deluged by people interested in buy-ing parts of Norton Simon. Avis, which had been rumored to be on the block under Mahoney, alone drew a dozen inquiries. Although the car-rental operation had lost $35 million the previous year, Kelly was not about to be stampeded into a deal. "It would be ridiculous for us to even entertain discussions at this point," Kelly told a reporter. "We don't know what these companies are worth separately." As for Avis, "I've taken down the 'for sale' sign and put up a 'for rent' sign," he said. "Avis is not for sale." Not yet, anyway.

Virtually all of the 155 employees in Norton Simon's home office were dismissed and its lavish Park Avenue quarters—Esmark staffers dubbed Mahoney's old office the Taj Mahal—were sublet. Kelly put Joel Smilow, the head of International Playtex, in charge of Norton Simon's fashion businesses—Max Factor, Halston, McCall patterns—though they weren't intermingled with Playtex. The key to the eco-nomics of the merger lay in the point of operational overlap between Esmark and Norton Simon—the food business. Although the slaugh-terhouse business had been spun off, Esmark's Swift & Company divi-sion had retained a pantryful of processed-food brands that included Butterball poultry, Brown & Serve sausages, and Peter Pan peanut butter. Heavily concentrated in refrigerated foods, the Swift division beautifully complemented Norton Simon's Hunt-Wesson subsidiary, which, with its top-selling lines of canned tomato products and edible oils, was predominantly a "dry" grocery business. Equally important, Hunt-Wesson had its own sales force, while Swift had to work through brokers to get its stuff into grocery stores. There were enormous effi-ciencies to be gained by carefully fitting Swift into the larger and more thoroughly integrated Hunt-Wesson, and Kelly unsentimentally as-signed the task not to one of his own loyalists but to Fred Rentschler, Hunt-Wesson's chief.

The complicated process of melding Esmark and Norton Simon had barely begun when Beck decided to put his new relationship with Kelly at risk. As Beck watched Esmark's stock rise, he thought back to a night in the midst of the Norton Simon deal. He and McGrath had been in Esmark's suite at the Helmsley Palace Hotel when a member of Kelly's entourage asked him if he wasn't afraid that Mahoney might try to "Pac-Man" him—that is, have Norton Simon tender for Esmark even while Esmark was tendering for it. "If the price is right," Kelly had instantly answered, "it's his. Everything is always for sale." At its post-deal price of $44 a share, Esmark was valued at a price-earnings multiple of 12, exceeding the food industry average by a healthy margin. While seemingly wagering that Kelly would not only wring synergies out of Hunt-Wesson but get top dollar for Avis and other assets likely to be auctioned off, the market was overlooking two large question marks: the outcome of product-liability lawsuits filed against Playtex by victims of toxic-shock syndrome and a pending IRS decision on the tax-reduction techniques used in accounting for profits made in selling Esmark's oil operations.

As much as Beck respected Kelly, it seemed to him that Esmark, after years of undervaluation, was now overvalued in the stock market. As surely as a leg twitches from a well-placed blow at the knee, so the phrase "time to sell" forms in the mind of a deal man entranced by the prospect of an overvalued client company. On the other hand, the typical CEO just as reflexively tends to see his stock as perpetually undervalued. For an investment banker to suggest otherwise, however tactfully, is to risk disfavor and even dismissal. In the brief time that he'd known Kelly, though, Beck had come to understand that Kelly was a CEO by title but a deal man by inclination. It seemed to Beck that Kelly allowed neither sentimental attachments nor his own considerable ego to interfere with appraising and maximizing corporate value. The question was whether Kelly would follow the ruthless logic underlying his success to its ultimate conclusion and make Esmark's next deal not its latest acquisition but its last: its own sale.

Operating on the premise that Kelly had meant what he said, Beck had McGrath supervise a staff study of likely buyers of Esmark. The study highlighted two European food giants: Unilever and Nestlé, both of which were loaded with cash and eager to expand their presence in the vast U.S. market. However, McGrath argued against risking the group's new relationship with Kelly by urging him to sell out so soon after his Norton Simon triumph. But in mid-November of 1983, only five months after Esmark had launched its Norton Simon bid, Beck invited Kelly to lunch at The Four Seasons and insisted that McGrath come, too.

"What's up?" Kelly said almost as soon as they'd sat down.

"You know and I know that Esmark is overvalued," Beck said, "and you're the guy who said that he'd sell when the time is right."

Kelly stared at Beck. "You're right," he said.

"Good," Beck replied. "Let's sell Esmark."

"Who do you have in mind?" Kelly asked.

"Nestlé, Unilever, maybe someone else. What's the price?"

"What do you think?"

"I guess in the fifties."

Kelly smiled. "Fifty-five dollars a share, all cash," he said.

And that was that. When he returned to Oppenheimer, Beck walked down the hallway shouting his glee. "We're going to sell Esmark!" he boomed. "We're going to sell Esmark! Let's rock and rooooooll!"

In getting the go-ahead to shop Esmark, Beck consolidated his group's relationship with Kelly, getting the drop on A. G. Becker. In his enthusiasm over the new assignment, though, it would take Beck a while to realize that selling out was only one of the alternatives Kelly was juggling—that the CEO's willingness to sell was but one facet of his deal-making compulsion. In any organization devoted to deal making, the exultation produced by a triumphant transaction was quickly reformulated into an expectation of greater things to come. "The preoccupation after Norton Simon was, What are we going to do for an encore?" said Chance Bahadour, Esmark's treasurer. "We felt we had to do something big, if only because it seemed like we could have done anything we wanted." Although he'd authorized Beck to pursue the sale of Esmark, Kelly's innate preference was to make another big acquisition. "If a team is doing well," Kelly said later, "they want the game to go on."

While success was a powerful spur to action, even a crushing disappointment visited upon Kelly following the Norton Simon acquisition sharpened his desire to make another deal. In 1982, Kelly had designated three prospective successors: Roger Briggs, Esmark's chief financial officer; Joel Smilow, head of International Playtex; and Joe Sullivan, who was running the Swift food businesses. Kelly later denied that he had any preference, but within Esmark his favorite was presumed to be Sullivan, a hardworking former Golden Gloves champion who'd joined the old Swift & Company in 1959 and had been Kelly's friend and confidant ever since. Kelly had included his old friend in his trio of heirs apparent even though Sullivan had told him that he in-

tended to take early retirement when his contract expired at the end of
1983. Originally, Sullivan had intended to leave in 1981, telling Kelly
he wanted to devote more time to his wife, who was ill, and to charity
work. Kelly persuaded Sullivan to stay by attaching so-called golden
handcuffs to his contract; they stipulated that if he stayed on another
two years, he'd receive his full $560,000 annual salary for the first
three years after he retired. Sullivan agreed to the arrangement,
though he was dismayed that Kelly seemed to think his avowed desire
to leave a mere negotiating ploy.

As Esmark prepared to launch its bid for Norton Simon, Sullivan
reminded Kelly that he intended to leave when his renewed contract
expired at year's end. Kelly was nonchalant. After the transaction was
completed, Kelly initially gave his old friend responsibility for running
the combined food companies. Sullivan reluctantly accepted, reminding his boss of his desire to retire. A month later, Sullivan told
Kelly that after much soul-searching he had decided to leave at the
end of 1983.

Finally, Kelly heard the message. His ruddy complexion deepened to
vermilion. "Okay, then," he snapped. "That's it."

Kelly and Sullivan nodded at each other in passing in the hallway
but never spoke again. No farewell party commemorated Sullivan's
twenty-four years with the company, and other Esmark executives
dared to take him to lunch only when Kelly was out of town. "Underneath all the quips, Don is like an old tribal chieftain," Sullivan said.
"Loyalty is all. If you weren't with Don, you became a nonperson."

While Sullivan's resignation ostensibly left Briggs and Smilow as
rival heirs apparent, other Esmark executives suspected that Kelly considered neither man a worthy successor, much as he appreciated their
value in their current positions. With mandatory retirement looming,
Kelly had backed himself into a corner. If he stalled, the board would
impose a successor. If he hired someone more to his liking from outside the company, Briggs and Smilow were likely to resign, leaving
Esmark bereft of two talented executives. There was one way out, and
fortunately for Kelly it was the same door through which he'd entered:
deal making. By selling the company for a rich price, Kelly could
eliminate the need for a successor, while exiting a hero to his shareholders. Alternatively, he could make his last hurrah the acquisition of
a major company run by an executive more to his liking as a successor.

Enter Ira Harris, who well understood Kelly's personal dilemma and
was anxious to reassert himself with Esmark after having represented

the other side on the Norton Simon deal. As it happened, Harris was also friendly with Ross Johnson, the head of Nabisco Brands, the old-line cookie and cracker giant. Aside from his nouveau-riche social adventuring, Johnson basically was a younger, Canadian version of Don Kelly: a shrewd, glib, and ferociously ambitious executive with a flair for deal making. Starting as a salesman, Johnson had risen through the ranks at Standard Brands, gaining the top job through a palace coup. After a few years as CEO, he negotiated a lucrative sale of the company to the much larger Nabisco and became the combined companies' second-ranking executive. Johnson was still looking to deal—and with good reason. With each megamerger, control of the food industry was consolidating in the hands of a shrinking number of giant companies. No corporation was big enough to stand pat. At the urging of Harris, Johnson came to Chicago in 1984 and proposed a merger between Esmark and Nabisco Brands.

Kelly was noddingly familiar with Nabisco, as indeed he was with every major food company, having at one time or another at least considered buying stock in most of them. "On the surface, it's a great idea," responded Kelly, who'd never bought Nabisco stock. "We'd have to push some numbers on it. One thing, though," he hastened to add. "There would be only one CEO and his name would be Kelly."

While the prospect of a friendly deal with Nabisco intrigued Kelly, he hedged his bets by siccing his numbers men on two other likely prospects that he felt certain would rather fight than sell. One was Beatrice Company, a huge Chicago food concern suffering the effects of chronic management turmoil. After accumulating a 3 percent to 4 percent stake in Beatrice, Kelly made his move in early 1984. He gave Bahadour forty-eight hours to line up $3 billion in bank loans to finance a tender offer for Beatrice. When Bahadour got to $2.5 billion, Kelly told him to stop. Through a leak at a law firm it had in common with Esmark, Beatrice had discovered that it was in Kelly's sights. James Dutt, Beatrice's imperious CEO, conveyed threatening messages to Kelly through every private channel to which he had access. Although Kelly later claimed to have laughed at the threats, he backed away from a tender offer for Beatrice, insisting quite implausibly that he'd suddenly decided that Sterling Drug was a better takeover target, even though he'd had an eye on Sterling for years. Through its investment banker, the ubiquitous Harris, Beatrice bought Esmark's block of shares, giving Kelly a tidy trading profit and planting the suspicion in some circles that the Esmark chief had never really been serious about bidding for Beatrice but was just out make a quick buck by rattling Dutt's cage.

While Beck, who was not informed of Kelly's dalliances with Beatrice and Nabisco, pressed the search for a buyer for Esmark, he was also working his first deal for A. Alfred Taubman, a billionaire who was one of the major moguls of Nouvelle Society and looked the part to a T, which happened to be a letter much in evidence throughout the Taubman manse in Bloomfield Hills, Michigan. There was even a big "T" on the punching bag in his gymnasium. At six foot four and 250 pounds, Taubman was a big bear of a man who could dominate a crowded room merely by entering it. He was a mogul to his toenails. Beck was once in Taubman's office in the Steuben Glass Building when a woman came in carrying a tub full of water, which she placed on a wooden stand. Taubman took off his shoe and sock, submerged one massive foot in the tub, and let it soak while talking business with Beck and a colleague. When Taubman's pedicurist removed the great foot from its bath and began clipping away, Beck could restrain himself no longer. "Look, Al," he said, "if you're going to continue, could you pass out the safety goggles?"

Born in Detroit, Taubman started his own contracting company with a borrowed $5,000 and built it into one of the nation's largest developers of enclosed shopping malls. Having accumulated some eighteen megamalls, Taubman branched out a bit in 1977 by leading a group of investors who paid $337 million for the Irvine Ranch, the choicest undeveloped tract in southern California. Six years later, the group sold out at $1 billion; Taubman personally cleared $150 million. Taubman was well known nationally in the retailing business and had developed an international reputation in art circles as a serious, knowledgeable collector of paintings and as a trustee of the Whitney Museum of American Art in New York. But he abhorred personal publicity and for years even refused to divulge his first name, which was often misreported as Alfred (the "A," in fact was for Adolph). Miraculously, he even managed to keep his name out of *Who's Who in America.* As he neared sixty, though, Taubman began to indulge in the sort of mogulish behavior that inevitably, if not intentionally, thrust him into the limelight. He divorced his first wife, married a former Miss Israel, and began high-stepping his way around the black-tie party circuit in New York. Like Donald Trump, Taubman bought a franchise in the short-lived United States Football League: the Michigan Panthers. And in 1983 Taubman jumped into the deal game with a big splash, paying $150 million for Sotheby Parke Bernet, the prestigious Anglo-American auction house better known simply as Sotheby's.

The manner in which Taubman came to own Sotheby's was as important to him as the acquisition itself. In 1979, Sotheby's earnings went into a three-year swoon that put the venerable old company into the red by 1982. The company's depressed stock attracted the notice of Marshall Cogan and Stephen Swid, two New York financiers who began buying Sotheby's shares on the open market through their General Felt Industries, a maker of padding for rugs. Appalled at the prospect of working for two American "rug merchants," Sotheby's management succeeded in persuading a government commission to block further purchases by General Felt while it searched for a white knight through Lazard Brothers, Lazard Frères' English cousin. Lazard found Taubman, a longtime customer of Sotheby's who indeed had just paid top dollar for a Picasso crayon drawing. With General Felt frozen at 29.9 percent, Taubman bought a 15 percent stake and made a tender offer for the rest, with the blessing of Sotheby's management. "The chemistry didn't exist in the case of the previous bid," sniffed Sotheby's CEO. "It exists very strongly in this particular case." General Felt conceded defeat, selling its stake to Taubman, whose takeover later received the official stamp of approval from Britain's Monopolies and Mergers Commission. And so it was that a shopping-center magnate from Detroit was welcomed as savior into one of the treasure houses of Old World art.

Sotheby's was Taubman's dream deal. For one thing, he'd demonstrated that he could afford to pay more than anyone else and still get what he considered a good price—a judgement that was controversial at the time of the transaction but was quickly proven correct. But there was nothing quite so rewarding to Taubman as acting in the role of white knight. He'd never made a hostile takeover and swore that he never would. Although Taubman had nothing against straightforward, friendly acquisitions, they just didn't satisfy the soul like riding to the rescue of a raider-besieged company. At the start of the Sotheby's battle, one of Taubman's newest lieutenants asked him what he hoped to accomplish in bidding for the auction house. "Look," Taubman replied, "I have a desire to continue to make money. And I have a desire to be sure that I have fun doing it. I enjoy transactions in which I make money, but I want to be sure I enjoy it per se."

Beck wasn't even aware of Taubman until the Sotheby's deal, which he followed closely, and didn't meet him until after it had closed. But everything that he'd read and heard about the Detroit billionaire convinced Beck of one thing: Al Taubman was his kind of guy.

Not long afterward, Beck was in London trying to insinuate himself into the next big English takeover battle by involving a client from his DLJ days—Sir Hugh Fraser and his family investment company, Scottish & Universal Investments Limited. SUITs had failed to fend off a takeover by Lonhro, which in the process had gained title to a 23 percent interest in the House of Fraser, the other major Fraser family holding. Now, Lonhro was maneuvering to take control of the House of Fraser, which owned the grand London department store Harrod's, among other retailing properties. With Sir Hugh out of the picture, Beck no longer knew any of the people at the House of Fraser. However, through Michael Stoddardt of Electra House, an important investor in the firm that owned Oppenheimer & Company, Beck arranged an introduction to Rowland Smith, who was CEO of the House of Fraser. Beck told Smith that he knew of two substantial investors who might be interested in leading a leveraged buyout of the House of Fraser: Henry Kravis and Al Taubman.

Smith was impressed. "The same Alfred Taubman of Sotheby's?" he said. "Do you know Mr. Taubman?"

"Of course," said Beck, who in fact knew Taubman only slightly, having met him once.

Beck did have a personal connection to Taubman, tenuous though it was, through Jack MacAtee, the legal counsel on the Esmark–Norton Simon deal. MacAtee was friendly with the headmistress of the Connecticut prep school that Taubman's daughter attended; he had spent time with the Detroit mogul on several occasions. MacAtee got Beck in to see Taubman, who, as Beck had supposed, was intrigued by the idea of acquiring the House of Fraser. Harrod's was as distinguished, in its own way, as Sotheby's, and was equally in need of a white knight. As landlord to every major retail chain in America, Taubman was intimately familiar with the department-store business and, in fact, had been thinking of acquiring a retail chain for some time. In a matter of days, Beck's bluff had become reality: Now he not only knew Taubman but was pursuing a $2 billion transaction on his behalf. The negotiations moved rapidly along but foundered when Taubman, who was meticulous to a fault, insisted on seeing confiden-

tial information that would enable his staff to analyze the lease of
every one of the House of Fraser's several hundred stores. Smith was
perfectly willing to give Taubman a look. His problem was that under
English law the House of Fraser then would be required to make the
information available to anyone else who sought it—namely Lonrho.
Beck urged Taubman to back away from the deal, even though he
stood to make millions if a transaction had been consummated.

Taubman came away favorably impressed not only by the objectivity
of Beck's advice but by the madcap intensity he brought to deal making. No M & A man was better than Beck at delivering fun out of
failure. For his part, Beck found Taubman to be more teddy bear than
tyrant. Beck liked to describe Taubman as one of the few wealthy
people he knew who seemed content and squared away. Beck dubbed
Taubman the "happy billionaire" and usually gave him a quick hug in
greeting, which seemed to please and exasperate Taubman in equal
measure. Beck's relationship with Taubman deepened when William
"Billy" Taubman, the mogul's youngest son, joined the Oppenheimer
M & A department as an analyst after graduating from Oxford University. Billy chose Oppenheimer over Salomon Brothers because he suspected that he would be able to learn faster at a smaller, more
freewheeling firm. About the same time that Taubman joined, Beck
also hired John Atwater, the son of Brewster Atwater, who was chief
executive officer of General Mills. That two of the nation's most es-
teemed businessmen were willing to entrust their heirs to his supervi-
sion was a great source of pride and satisfaction to Beck, who made a
point of telling both fathers that he would not give their sons special
treatment, and proved true to his word.

When Taubman again was approached by a company in search of a
white knight, he immediately hired Oppenheimer as his investment
banker. Woodward & Lothrop, affectionately known as Woodie's, an
old-line department-store chain in Washington, D.C., owned seventeen stores, two of which were in Taubman malls. Woodie's had been
spooked into Taubman's arms by a Wall Street money manager who
said he and his clients owned 17 percent of its shares and offered $60 a
share for the rest in a leveraged buyout. Beck and Norm Brown helped
Taubman negotiate an agreement to acquire the venerable company at
$59 a share. As part of the deal, Taubman was granted an option to
buy 33 percent of the Woodie's shares. This gave him the power to
block other would-be acquirers, since under District of Columbia law

any change in control had to be approved by a two-thirds majority of shareholders. Members of one of Woodward & Lothrop's founding families helped organize a dissident group of shareholders who opposed Taubman on the grounds that the company was worth as much as $5 or $6 more a share than he'd agreed to pay. Wall Street arbitrageurs began buying the stock on the expectation that someone would in fact top $59 a share.

For months, rival groups of Woodie's shareholders maneuvered for advantage in the courts and in the stock market in anticipation of the shareholder vote scheduled for September 1984. The night before the climactic meeting Beck was up until three A.M. negotiating with large Wall Street holders including Martin Gruss, an independent arbitrageur with whom he'd gotten friendly. As the voting began, Beck's tally had Taubman falling 2 percent to 3 percent short of the votes he needed. Working through Gruss, Beck finally succeeded in getting the dissidents and Taubman to sit down together for the first time about an hour before the voting was to end at six P.M. Many large stockholders had yet to be heard from. With the outcome hanging in the balance, Beck helped convince Taubman to boost his bid to $60.50 a share. The dissident group then agreed to vote their 10 percent for Taubman. The battle was over; for $220 million, Woodie's was Taubman's. In appreciation Big Al paid Oppenheimer & Company $2 million.

At a post-closing banquet at the Sherry-Netherland hotel, Taubman awarded Beck a Michigan Panthers cheerleading outfit, complete with pom-poms, for enthusiasm above and beyond the call of duty. The gesture moved Beck as much as it surprised him. He walked up to the dais and shook Taubman's hand. He did not give a speech. Instead, he turned to the microphone and shouted:

"Give me a 'T.' "

"T," came the answering cry.

"Give me an 'A.' "

"A."

"Give me a 'U.' "

"U."

"Give me a 'B.' "

"B."

"Give me a 'MAN.' "

"MAN."

"What's that spell?"

"Taubman."

"I CAN'T HEAR YOU!"

"Taubman!"

"Ladies and gentlemen," Beck said. "Al Taubman."

12

ike everyone else on Wall Street, Beck devoured *The Bonfire of the
Vanities* when Tom Wolfe's novel was published in 1987. After
Beck's life—like that of Sherman McCoy, Wolfe's bond trader—had
come disastrously unraveled, he read the book again and offered this
self-deprecating reaction: "Sherman Beck." In *Bonfire*, McCoy's own
magnificence is revealed to him in a flash: "One fine day, in a fit of
euphoria, after he had picked up the telephone and taken an order for
zero-coupon bonds that had brought him a $50,000 commission, *just
like that*, this very phrase had bubbled up into his brain. On Wall
Street he and a few others—how many?—three hundred, four hundred, five hundred?—had become precisely that . . . Masters of the
Universe. There was . . . no limit whatsoever!" Wolfe really should
have made McCoy a deal man. On real-life Wall Street in the 1980s,
the M & A man, who measured success in million-dollar increments,
sat alone atop the hierarchy of hubris. In Beck's case, hallucinations of
grandeur took over his consciousness not all at once but gradually and
inexorably, as if being fed into his bloodstream drop by drop with each
big deal and black-tie ball. By 1984, if not earlier, Beck's transformation from M & A aspirant to Master of the Universe was complete.

The proof lay not in his purchase of a new $35,000 Mercedes sedan
but in deciding that he wanted—no, *needed*— his own driver to trans-
port him around town in a style befitting his flowering importance in
the deal game. On the wall of his office, Beck put up a framed, poster-
sized photograph of his other Mercedes sedan parked (by computer
simulation) in the courtyard of the Louvre Museum in Paris. The
photo was a gift from Rosemary, with whom he remained friendly.
Beck's youthful days of barking in hallways were a hazy memory from
another life. "Jeff started moving about almost like an ambassador,"
said David Aaron, the former deputy national security adviser turned

M & A man. "For the first time, he took on a dignity about himself. It's a syndrome you see: Someone makes vice president and suddenly his suits fit him better." And no wonder. Beck had begun buying thousand-dollar suits by the score at the Paul Stuart store on Madison Avenue and getting his hair cut at the Vidal Sassoon salon near the Plaza Hotel. He marked his Norton Simon triumph by spending $12,000 on a big Dutch warmblood that he named Cyrus, inaugurating a celebratory ritual of buying a new horse after each big deal. (He eventually accumulated five animals, collectively worth close to $100,000). Less than a year after having moved into 31 East Seventy-ninth, Jeff and Margo began scouting the choicest sections of Westchester County for an estate to serve as a weekend retreat during the winter and a full-time residence during the warm months.

In the parlance of the M & A trade, Beck was "big-dealing it," albeit with his own trademark playfulness. Asked by a *New York Times* reporter how Wall Street could justify the high fees charged for M & A advice, Beck replied, tongue firmly in cheek, "Well, we're not just riding around in the limos talking to our cigars, you know"—a quote that perfectly evoked the jubilant swagger of the Big Deal Man at mid-decade.

When Carolyne Roehm introduced her first eighty-piece collection of fashion wear at the old Latin Quarter nightclub, the Becks were in attendance as guests of Henry Kravis. In an accompanying press release, the designer divulged the philosophy behind the fashion. "Roehm believes in the important blouse—the key element for every suit look for day and evening." "Like most women, Roehm is 'crazy about diamonds, so I've embroidered them on everything.' . . . Some of the most exquisite embroideries, executed by LeSage, are inspired by 18th century jewels and are lavished on bodices of black velvet gowns that are beautiful enough to make any woman feel like a queen." And finally: "Roehm, who loves parties, literally blossoms for evening. . . . As she puts it, 'sometimes a woman feels sexy and flirty; sometimes she wants to be swan-like in a sleek evening dress, or like Cinderella in a big ball gown.'"

Roehm's debut won enthusiastic notices in the press and a standing ovation at the close of the show. That skinny little girl from Missouri had real talent after all, it seemed. As Roehm strolled out on stage to bask in her Cinderella moment, she gave a teary little wave to Kravis, who was crying, too. Next to him was Oscar de la Renta, the proud mentor. In the chairs right behind Kravis were the Becks, who were on

their feet applauding with everyone else. Despite himself, Jeff was
genuinely impressed with Roehm's work and even accompanied
Margo on a buying expedition to her showroom, where he wrote a very
large check for a dozen dresses. By now, Jeff was taking a keen interest
in his wife's wardrobe with the aim of ensuring that she featured a
wide variety of outfits within a certain basic style, which Margo
termed "a conservative, Le Cirque look." For the moguls of Nouvelle
Society, "bedecking and bejeweling" women, as Beck put it, was
an important aspect of their competition—as indeed it was for
the women themselves—and in this regard the Becks at last held
their own.

Several times a week Beck could be seen decked out in his own deal
man's finery, dining at his favorite restaurant, The Four Seasons. Ensconced in the bottom two floors of the Seagram Building on Park
Avenue, The Four Seasons was beloved by deal makers of publishing
and entertainment no less than investment banking. While the food
and service were first-rate, The Four Seasons' outstanding claim to
fame was architectural. The place was enormous, with twenty-foot
ceilings and eight thousand square feet of floor space divided into two
rooms—a clubby Grill Room, with dark rosewood walls and rippling
copper-chain curtains, and the romantic, airy Pool Room, in which
graciously appointed tables were organized around an illuminated marble pool set off by lofty foliage. The monumentality of the setting and
the sleek sophistication of The Four Seasons' decor brilliantly evoked
Manhattan itself, or at least the Manhattan the city's movers and
shakers preferred to envision themselves inhabiting; The Four Seasons
was unquestionably the most spectacular restaurant stage-set in the
nation's most theatrical city.

Beck loved the restaurant and used it with increasing frequency as
success came to his M & A group. He spread around enough charm
(and generous tips) to ensure that his every arrival was celebrated by
the staff like a prodigal son's return. Like those in such other New York
power-dining spots as the "21" Club and the Russian Tea Room, the
tables at The Four Seasons were arrayed in a hierarchy of prestige that
made every seating a status ritual as elaborate as kabuki theater. The
most favored patrons were allowed the privilege of always sitting at the
same table—*their* table. Although Beck had yet to scale this Olympian
pinnacle of status, more often than not he and his guests were ushered
to one of the choicest tables in the Pool Room, which he much preferred to the stuffier private-club milieu of the Grill Room.

Beck made full use of the theatrical possibilities offered by The Four Seasons, which indulged its favored patrons by making it a point of honor to satisfy their special requests. Beck brought one of his favorite clients, Arnout Loudon, the aristocratic chairman of the Dutch chemical giant Akzo, Incorporated, to The Four Seasons shortly after Loudon had received his country's highest honor, the Order of the Netherlands Lion. For dessert, the waiter brought a chocolate cake decorated with a marzipan lion that had been rendered with painstaking accuracy from a drawing obtained by The Four Seasons from the Dutch consulate. To Beck's delight, The Four Seasons was also the kind of place that would bring a telephone—on a tray, of course—to a guest who wanted to make or receive a phone call from his table, which was equipped with a jack. When Fred Bleakley, a *New York Times* reporter, and his wife arrived one night for dinner with Beck, they found their host already seated and in the midst of a telephone conversation so arch that they both assumed he was speaking to a dial tone, though in fact he was talking to Margo.

Steve McGrath arrived in Geneva wishing he were dead. The chicken he'd eaten on the airplane had given him the worst case of food poisoning he'd ever had. In their search for a buyer for Esmark, Beck and McGrath had flown to Switzerland to meet with Nestlé & Company. Beck had worked with Nestlé's treasurer during his stint at Lehman Brothers and McGrath was acquainted with the company's chief financial officer from his days at Warner-Lambert. These personal connections got them in the door, but not to the top floor of Nestlé's headquarters. Beck and McGrath were informed by their contacts that Nestlé was interested in U.S. food companies but in "purer plays" than Esmark, which owned car-rental, cosmetics, fertilizer, and dozens of other businesses with inedible product lines. Beck left Switzerland frustrated not so much by his failure to strike a deal—the odds were always against that—but by his inability even to gain an audience with Nestlé's CEO. (His rainmaker's pride was salved a few months later when Nestlé laid out $4 billion to buy the Carnation Company of condensed-milk fame. Carnation was indeed more purely a food company than Esmark, and Beck was convinced that the deal had been in the works at the time of his visit.)

From Geneva, Beck and McGrath flew to London to meet with Unilever. Opco's approach to Unilever was made through Sir John Buckley, the retired chairman of a large English construction company and one of more than a half-dozen prominent businessmen whom Beck had persuaded to join the board of Oppenheimer International, which the firm created to drum up M & A business in England. Buckley was an acquaintance of A.W.P. "Cob" Stenham, who was the chief financial officer of Unilever and one of those belligerently stuffy British gents who could exhaust Beck's patience merely by saying hello. Although Beck's first meeting with Stenham couldn't have been more unproductive had they spoken different languages, he persisted and finally arranged to have Kelly at least meet with Unilever's co-chairmen in London. To Beck's annoyance, Stenham had sprinkled their conversations with frequent mentions of Felix Rohatyn, affirming and reaffirming his intention to run the notion of an Esmark deal by the Lazard Frères banker. Stenham's Rohatyn fixation seemed less odd to Beck after he learned that the Unilever executive was married to a daughter of the former senior partner of Lazard Brothers.

Immediately upon his return to the United States, Beck flew to Chicago to brief Kelly, who was intrigued by Stenham's connection to Rohatyn. By the mid-1980s, Rohatyn had developed a reputation in deal circles for urging on well-heeled corporate acquirers the strategy of making an initial bid so high that it preempted rival offers. While it was Bruce Wasserstein who would be tarred with the moniker "Bid 'em up Bruce," Rohatyn was no less deserving. Ever the gamesman, Kelly apparently decided that if Felix was going to get a peek at Esmark's inside numbers, he might as well try to turn the situation to advantage. Kelly knew that another of Lazard Frères' clients was his crosstown rival, Beatrice, with which he'd been jousting for months. While the blue books sent to Unilever were scrupulously accurate in terms of the basic financial data presented, derived from the operating numbers were highly optimistic estimates of the value of Esmark's businesses. According to Beck, Esmark's breakup value was inflated by at least $800 million.

Kelly was planning to go to London anyway in his efforts to sell Norton Simon's liquor business. He took Beck and McGrath with him on Esmark's new G-3 jet, which had come with Norton Simon. While Kelly was a man of modest material indulgence in general, he loved private planes and had insisted on being provided with one even before he moved up to CEO of Esmark. (After Reneker retired, Esmark built a fleet of a half-dozen jets and began buying and selling positions on the waiting lists of airplane makers like so many baseball cards, usually booking a nice trading profit.) For Beck, the trip's highlight was the

The Beck family, circa 1951. *Left to right:* Ida, Jeff, Judy, Louis.
COURTESY OF JEFFREY P. BECK

Jeff's high school graduation photograph, Perkiomen School, 1964.
COURTESY OF JEFFREY P. BECK

Right: Jeff's aunt and uncle, Agnes and Joseph Katz, Pittsburgh's first couple of giftwrap, arrive for the opening of the Hilton Hotel in 1959.
THE PITTSBURGH PRESS

The "black tie flashdance," first generation. *Top left:* William D. Singer, founder of Royal Castle, Inc., and Jeff's mother, the second Mrs. Singer, on the town in Miami, 1965.
THE MIAMI HERALD

Right: Singer's son-in-law, Richard Stone, campaigning in Miami in the 1970s. At left is his wife, Marlene Singer Stone.
THE MIAMI HERALD

From burgers to ballots. *Left:* William D. Singer and his son Larry outside a Royal Castle restaurant in the late 1950s.
THE MIAMI HERALD

Dan Lufkin, the investment banker who first inspired Beck to become a dealman.
AP/WIDE WORLD

Eric Gleacher, Lehman Brothers' mergers and acquisitions chief, who hired Beck in 1978 and showed him the door the following year.
AP/WIDE WORLD

Finally his own boss: The senior members of Oppenheimer & Co.'s M & A group flanking their leader. Behind Beck, from *left* to *right*, are John Sanzo, Ron Peters, Norm Brown, Steve McGrath, and Clarke Bailey.
ROB KINMONTH

Margo and Katherine, 1986.
SALMIERI/COURTESY OF MARGO BECK

Beck and his wife Margo on vacation in Europe, 1983.
COURTESY OF MARGO BECK

The Wall Street couple of the decade: Henry Kravis and Carolyne Roehm at the Police Athletic League's 1989 Superstar Dinner honoring Donald Trump, for which Kravis served as chairman.
ANTHONY SAVIGNANO/GALELLA, LTD.

Richard Rainwater, the rainmaker behind the Bass brothers and Beck's mid-1980s deal buddy.
PETER POULIDES

CEO as dealman: Esmark's Don Kelly, basking in the afterglow of the Norton Simon acquisition, Beck's first billion-dollar deal.
J. ROSS BAUGHMAN/VISIONS

A. Alfred Taubman, "the happy billionaire," outside Sotheby's, his most celebrated acquisition.
AP/WIDE WORLD

J. Peter Grace in his company's Manhattan headquarters. It is unclear from the photograph whether or not he is packing heat.
ANDY FREEBERG

A legend is born: Beck with the author on
the terrace outside the owner's villa at the
Hotel du Cap d'Antibes. It was during this
conversation that Beck first detailed his
imaginary Vietnam adventures.
COURTESY OF JEFFREY P. BECK

Beck with Michael Douglas at
the Hotel du Cap, 1987.
JEAN PIGOZZI

On the set of *Wall Street. Left* to *right:* Ken
Lipper, Oliver Stone, Jeff Beck, Charlie
Sheen.
ANDY SCHWARTZ

As his career on Wall Street was collapsing in 1989, Beck sought solace in a rigorous training program involving swimming, bicycling, and long-distance running. His great ambition became to enter the "Iron Man" triathlon competition in Hawaii.
SHONNA VALESKA

Beck on the balcony of his Upper East Side apartment, fall 1990.
SHONNA VALESKA

plane ride over, which gave him a chance to study Kelly at close quarters. The uniformed steward served a meal that Beck dubbed the "Don Kelly special": a big plank of rare steak, baked potatoes, and a few Michelobs. Kelly, in the full flush of his Norton Simon triumph, was in an expansive mood, regaling the investment bankers with tales of his ragged youth, which seemed to have been largely spent in bars and in fights, often simultaneously. "Kelly," concluded Beck, "was the kind of guy you wanted to watch a football game with." But a movie? No way. Somewhere over the Atlantic, Kelly put *Gandhi* on the VCR and punctuated the screening with a monologue of enthusiastic commentary as McGrath dropped off to sleep.

"Will you look at that?" Kelly would say. "Isn't that great?"

Finally, Beck could take no more. "Yeah, Don," he said sarcastically, "that's really great. Now let me get some sleep, okay?"

At lunchtime, Beck found himself in a large executive dining room done up in sleek Euro-modern style. Unilever's two chairmen—one English, the other Dutch—were both present, as were Stenham and the chairmen's heirs apparent. The powwow began cordially, with a long stretch of big-picture palaver—or "great-man talk," as Beck called it—between Kelly and Unilever's two gracious, cosmopolitan executives.

As the large small talk petered out, Stenham struck a discordant note. "Mr. Kelly," he said, "tell us why you are here."

While Oppenheimer had indeed requested an audience, Beck was offended by Stenham's condescension. "We are here at your invitation and that's how this meeting should be conducted," he said.

One of the cochairmen interceded; the powwow proceeded without incident and with little further commentary from Beck. "Jeff is smart enough to know when to be quiet," said Kelly, who needed neither help nor notes in outlining the business advantages he saw in folding Esmark into the European consumer-products giant. Although, to Beck's mind, Kelly's performance was impressively authoritative, he was not able to talk the Unilever chairmen out of their reluctance to acquire Esmark in its entirety. Like Nestlé, Unilever was interested only in acquiring those parts of the U.S. company that dovetailed into its existing operations—basically, the food business. For his part, Kelly refused to consider selling Esmark in pieces and that was that.

Back in Kelly's room at Inn on the Park, Beck sprung on the CEO an idea that he'd been mulling over for weeks.

"You know, Don," he said. "I think Esmark would work as a leveraged buyout."

Kelly was unconvinced. Although Kelly was a maverick in many ways, he was quite conventionally averse to debt. He considered it one of his and Briggs's greatest achievements that the sweeping restructuring of Swift into Esmark had been accomplished without more than briefly exceeding the traditionally acceptable ratios of debt to equity. True to form, Esmark had just finished issuing a raft of stock in order to pay down the $1 billion in short-term debt incurred in buying Norton Simon, and now along came Beck suggesting that three times as much in long-term debt be loaded onto the company. Kelly didn't want to run a company with eight times more debt than equity and he doubted, moreover, whether any buyer could justify meeting his asking price of $55 a share except by merging Esmark into another food company, thus taking advantage of the economies of scale like those created by Esmark's own absorption of Norton Simon. McGrath, too, was immediately dubious and remained so after he ran Esmark through the LBO model on his computer back at Oppenheimer. "Frankly, the numbers just didn't work," he recalled.

Beck emphatically disagreed, arguing that Esmark could carry considerably more debt and still cover its interest payments comfortably. Meanwhile, if, as Beck expected, the market value of food businesses continued rising sharply for a few more years, Kelly would have the option of selling pieces of the company at a handsome profit. As a rainmaker, Beck operated on the principle that, as beauty existed in the eye of the beholder, so the ultimate validity of deal numbers existed in the mind of the buyer. If Kelly didn't want to buy Esmark himself at $55 a share, well then, all that was needed to make the numbers "work" was someone else willing to meet the price. Beck believed he knew just the person. Leaving McGrath with Kelly, Beck returned to his own hotel, Claridges, intending to call Henry Kravis from his room. Beck was cognizant of the risk he was taking, pitching the idea of an LBO of Esmark without authorization—indeed, over Kelly's explicit opposition to the notion of buyout. But Beck had been taking calculated risks based on his reading of Kelly's personality from the moment he first met the man, and he was ready to take another leap into the unknown.

As for Kravis, it had quickly become obvious to Beck that losing out on Norton Simon grievously offended the buyout mogul's increasingly exalted sense of self. Kravis had recently bought Weatherstone, his

Sharon, Connecticut, manor which was regarded as one of the most splendid prerevolutionary houses in all of New England. Kravis, however, found Weatherstone inadequately equipped and so made improvements, including a lake complete with an island, a waterfall, and a fleet of gondolas; he also installed a ventilation system by which the smells of coffee and croissants could be made to waft up from the kitchen and into the bedrooms of his and Carolyne's guests of a morning. The grand style of living that Kravis had adopted was out of synch with his professional life in a sense. This wasn't a matter of money; by 1983, Kravis's net worth probably exceeded $100 million and was climbing rapidly. Rather, the businesses that KKR owned were deficient in the panache one might expect of a man compelled to replicate Venice in his backyard. Marly Company, Fred Meyer, Incorporated, PT Components, Lily Tulip—the mention of none of these fine KKR-controlled businesses would have elicited the tiniest flicker of recognition in the Fifth Avenue circles in which Henry and Carolyne were beginning to move.

As Beck was striding through the lobby of Claridges, lost in thought, the gods of rainmaking blessed him with a most auspicious deal omen: He ran right into Henry Kravis, who, unbeknownst to Beck, had also checked into Claridges on a business trip. As Kravis recalled, he responded skeptically to Beck's enthusiastic urging to consider a buyout of Esmark. "Jeff was just prospecting," Kravis said. "I reminded him that I'd seen Kelly two years before and he wasn't interested then. In looking back now, the fact that Jeff didn't tell me that Kelly was still opposed doesn't surprise me. That's the way he was."

Beck's version of his chance meeting with Kravis was quite different —and more overtly nasty. "I had been carefully feeding Esmark and Kelly to Kravis's megalomaniacal mind ever since he could not figure out how to buy Norton Simon," Beck said. "Not only did Henry jump at the idea but his entire little body began to quiver, nostrils flaring and diminutive feet stamping at the very thought of Esmark under his control. Why? Small men always seem to want big things. For example, I have never met a small man who smoked a small cigar."

In Kravis's view, KKR had lost out on Norton Simon because "it was too big in relation to our financing capacity." KKR had graduated from its first blind pool of $50 million in 1978 to a $350 million fund, which in its entirety would have been more than sufficient to finance a bid for Norton Simon exceeding the sum bid by Esmark. However, under the terms of its agreement with its investors, no more than 25 percent of KKR's pool could be invested in a single deal. In theory, even if this $87.5 million foundation of equity were leveraged at a slightly higher-than-usual 10-to-1 ratio with borrowed money, KKR would have fallen short of the $1 billion needed merely to match Esmark. In practice, Kravis had had to struggle to get any money out of KKR's banks, which, unnerved by Avis's frightfully complex financial structure, insisted that KKR find a third party to guarantee the repayment of any loan made for the purpose of acquiring Norton Simon. To be told, after fifteen years of doing deals, that he'd have to find someone to countersign a loan got Kravis right where he lived. Still, he had set aside his pride and tried to work out an alliance with Anderson Clayton, which had had the money but not, as it turned out, the will to use it. Kravis could do nothing but watch as Kelly completed his acquisition. "After all the hours I'd spent on it night and day, losing Norton Simon was very disappointing to me," Kravis recalled.

If KKR was going to really make a mark, it was apparent to Kravis and George Roberts that the firm would have to gird itself for takeover battle. Norton Simon was only his biggest disappointment. Time and time again, companies that KKR had pursued through quiet, protracted negotiation were snatched away at the last minute by rival bidders making fully financed tender offers. That KKR would join the ranks of the raiders was unthinkable—at least as long as Jerry Kohlberg had a say. Although Kravis's own deal morality was much more flexible, corporate raiding remained déclassé in the Establishment circles to which he aspired. The natural role for KKR was that of white knight. To play it, though, KKR had to ride a bigger horse. In the wake of the Norton Simon humbling, KKR set about raising its fourth pool of LBO equity, with the goal of raising $1 billion.

KKR's timing was fortuitous. The same robust bull market that had sent Esmark's stock soaring was both emboldening institutional investors to take greater risks and bringing new funds flowing into their coffers in ever-rising amounts. Kravis and Roberts could dangle a dazzling performance record before prospective investors: thirty-two buyouts with a compounded rate of return advertised at 60 percent a year. Such numbers—not to mention the restrained but tenacious salesmanship of Kravis and Roberts—were not easily resisted, and

KKR at last opened wide a vast new funding source by bringing into its fold a host of state employee-pension funds. The state retirement funds of Washington and Oregon put $100 million apiece into KKR's billion-dollar fund, which was just about to close at the time Beck and Kelly lunched with Unilever.

This sudden leap in KKR's financial capacity coincided with a stimulating shift of power away from Kohlberg to his younger, brasher partners. In early 1984, surgeons removed a tumor from Kohlberg's brain. He was in bed beginning a long convalescence when Kravis and Roberts took a gargantuan flier by bidding for Gulf Oil, the century-old Pittsburgh giant that was the cornerstone of the Mellon fortune. To Kravis's delight, KKR's involvement had been solicited by the management of Gulf, which was under assault by T. Boone Pickens, the maverick oilman and corporate raider. In February 1984, KKR made an offer for Gulf Oil that it valued at $15.6 billion—larger by a factor of 15 than any previous LBO. On four days' notice, KKR rounded up $500 million in equity and $6 billion in bank loans; most of the remainder of its offer consisted of a package of junk bonds and preferred stock of uncertain value. Although KKR claimed that its offer was worth $87.50 a share, Gulf's board instead accepted $80 a share in cash—or $13.2 billion, a record high—from Standard Oil of California. At the climactic board meeting, Jay Higgins of Salomon Brothers, advisers to Gulf, made a speech urging the directors to choose Standard Oil's all-cash bid that included a recitation of Standard & Poor's definition of a non-investment-grade security.

In bidding for Gulf, Kravis's ambitions seemingly had vaulted so far ahead of KKR's finances that his bid really wasn't taken all that seriously on Wall Street. Coming as it did at the last minute of a protracted takeover battle, the Gulf LBO proposal seemed nothing more than a colossal fluke, like some massive new airplane that had been designed to impress but couldn't get off the ground. Had KKR been given a little more time, though, Kravis was positive that the firm could have offered more cash and less junk. As it was, raising $6.5 billion in four days was a mind-boggling feat for a firm that recently had failed to finance a $1 billion bid. While even Beck was astounded at the sheer ballsiness of KKR's play for Gulf, he saw in the bid not a fluke but the future. Who now could doubt that the higher mathematics of deals—the subjective art of Wall Street numbers—was changing faster than any numbers jockey could hope to reprogram his computer?

*   *   *

Beck didn't know it, but Kelly and Kravis had met for the first time in 1982. While vacationing in Palm Beach, Kravis had met the chairman of Sara Lee Corporation, who was a longtime shareholder in Esmark. At the chairman's suggestion, Kravis flew to Chicago for a get-acquainted session with Kelly and Briggs, who shortly thereafter called to say that Esmark was not interested in pursuing an LBO. It had taken little more than running into Beck at Claridges to induce Kravis to take another look at the company's numbers. On the basis of a preliminary analysis of cash flow and asset values, it looked like a deal might fly, though, as usual, Kravis needed inside numbers to be sure. Kelly, on the other hand, remained leery not only of the leveraged buyout in general but of KKR, which always structured its deals to give it ultimate control of the companies it acquired. Kravis made a point of calling KKR's deals "management" buyouts because corporate managers got a big piece of the action. But beneath KKR's participatory rhetoric, the unappealing reality that Kelly glimpsed was that he would be working *for* a couple of wealthy cousins young enough to be his sons.

Beck made it his business to bridge the chasm of age and social class separating Kelly and Kravis. Through sheer attentiveness, Beck made himself the principal conduit of communication between the two, and thus was in a position to edit any message that might have inadvertently given offense as they gingerly explored the possibility of a deal. On the very day after Gulf had rejected KKR's bid, Kelly, Kravis, and Beck had lunch together at the Chicago Club. A month later, Kravis invited Kelly to dinner at his Manhattan apartment. George Roberts, as well as a couple of KKR analysts, attended. McGrath came with Beck. The session got off to a shaky start during the cocktail hour when Roberts opined that it must be difficult to get along with people like the Crowns, the wealthy Jewish family that was Esmark's largest shareholder. While Roberts's meaning wasn't clear, the remark visibly annoyed Kelly, who defended the Crowns. Beck took Kravis aside. "Tell George to cool it on the Crowns," he whispered. The evening proceeded without further incident and ended well, with Kelly saying explicitly for the first time that he would consider an LBO.

Basically, Kelly had signaled his willingness to cede power for money. As CEO of Esmark Kelly was making $525,000 a year plus various incentives that pushed his annual income close to $1 million, which Kelly described as "a hell of a lot more money than I ever thought I'd make in my life." Through stock-option programs, he'd accumulated 220,000 shares of Esmark stock, a mere .5 percent of the total outstanding. By the standards of St. Killian's Parish, certainly, Kelly was a very wealthy man. But Kelly scanned the *Forbes* 400 like everybody else. He understood that it was a list not of people who ran companies but of people who owned them—people like Lester Crown and Henry Kravis. Through an LBO at $55 a share, Kelly could cash out his Esmark stock at $12 million and reinvest a small portion of the proceeds to buy a larger stake in the privatized Esmark than he'd ever owned in the public company. Kelly wasn't David Mahoney, which is to say he wasn't so blind with greed that he believed he could acquire majority control of Esmark at book value. In KKR's deals, the management group as a rule came away with 10 percent to 15 percent, a third of which went to the CEO. Kelly could live with that. If he could get a good price for his shareholders—and $55 a share was generous by almost any standard—while giving himself a shot at the big money, why not do it?

Kelly's next meeting with Kravis took place in central Florida, at a residential resort owned by Esmark. Kelly dispatched two of Esmark's jets to New York to pick up Kravis and a half-dozen advisers, including Beck. In Florida, Beck for the first time raised the subject of fees with Kelly, who agreed to pay Oppenheimer $20 million if the buyout were consummated. The Florida junket ended happily, as Kelly said that he was prepared to recommend the LBO to his board. However, he refused to grant KKR a "lockup"—an ironclad option allowing KKR to buy Hunt-Wesson or some other part of Esmark no matter what fate befell the LBO proposal. Obtaining a lockup would have greatly enhanced KKR's chances of success, since Esmark minus its best business would have been far less attractive to other potential bidders. Beck was mildly disappointed but couldn't complain, since, as Kelly pointed out, a lockup was indeed not in the best interests of Esmark's shareholders.

In late April, Kravis, Roberts, Beck, and McGrath flew to Chicago and stood by in a hotel suite at the Ritz-Carlton as Esmark's board of directors met in special session. Dispensing with the routine agenda, Kelly presented three "opportunities" in no particular order of priority or recommendation: a hostile takeover of Sterling Drug; merger with Nabisco; a leveraged buyout with KKR. The board discussion dragged on, and over at the Ritz anticipation gave way to puzzlement, concern, and irritation as the hours ticked by with no word from Kelly. Beck kept calling Esmark and leaving messages for him. When the telephone finally rang at about one P.M., Beck fairly pounced on it.

"I just want Henry to know that the probabilities look low at this point," Kelly said.

Beck was annoyed. "We've been sitting here for four hours," he said. "Henry and George are only here because you wanted them to address the board."

"I know that," said Kelly, a bit annoyed himself.

As the afternoon dragged, Beck told stories, cracked jokes, suggested card games—anything to keep Kravis and Roberts from bolting from the Ritz. Finally, Kelly called Kravis and told him, "The board has decided to go in another direction right now." Kelly was not at liberty to disclose what the directors had decided: After rejecting a bid for Sterling, the board had tabled the leveraged-buyout proposal and set up a special committee to begin immediate negotiations with Nabisco. Kravis, who'd also been kept waiting in a hotel room by Gulf's board, was seething with frustration and indignation by the time he and Roberts finally headed for the airport in the late afternoon.

Beck redoubled his efforts at shuttle diplomacy. About a week after the Ritz-Carlton fiasco, Kelly invited Kravis to breakfast at Esmark's suite in the Helmsley Palace. The tone was polite but tense. Kelly apologized, sort of.

"It's not that we don't like you guys, but we're working on something else," Kelly told Kravis. "I'll get back to you."

"When?" Kravis said.

"Probably about ten days."

That very afternoon, though, Kelly terminated his negotiations with Nabisco. A few hours later, Kravis got a call from a Mad Dog in ecstasy. "We did it, man," Beck said. "Kelly wants you to come to Chicago. He's ready to do the deal."

Kravis was dubious. "You were at the meeting this morning, Jeff," Kravis said. "You heard what he said."

"Yeah, but he's changed his mind," Beck said. "Really."

"I want to hear *him* say it," Kravis said.

Kelly called a few minutes later and confirmed his change of heart. When Kravis said he had to attend a board meeting in California the next day, Kelly offered the use of an Esmark plane. Kravis flew out with Beck, quickly worked things out with Kelly, and flew on alone to Los Angeles. Kelly called the next day, saying he would have a merger

agreement ready soon. Word of the impending deal leaked, forcing Esmark to ask the NYSE to halt trading in its stock on May third. The next day KKR signed a definitive agreement to acquire Esmark for $55 a share in cash—$2.4 billion—or more than twice as much as the previous record for an LBO. Having spurted by $1 1/4 before the announcement, Esmark's shares soared $12 a share to close at $57 3/5 —a clear indication that Ivan Boesky and the other Wall Street arbitrageurs who'd loaded up on the stock expected someone to top KKR's bid. Beck told a *New York Times* reporter for the record that a higher offer was unlikely, and Kravis was so unconcerned that he went to the Dominican Republic with Roehm to celebrate his first blue-chip acquisition.

Esmark's stock had drifted back down to the $52 range when, on May twentieth, Beatrice jumped in with a $56-a-share tender offer for Esmark. "I don't lose," Dutt snarled to reporters, apparently still inflamed by Kelly's greenmailing of Beatrice. Kravis cut short his vacation and dashed to Chicago while a thoroughly agitated Beck flew in with McGrath from New York. On the same plane was Higgins of Salomon Brothers, the firm Kelly had hired to represent Esmark in dealing with Beatrice, which was represented by Lazard Frères. This time Higgins was delighted to bump into his rivals from Oppenheimer. "I guess Beatrice did a number on your twenty-million-dollar fee," he said.

Beck liked Higgins but not his comment. "Jay, you and the large one [Ira Harris] know perfectly well who catalyzed this deal," he snapped.

With Kelly's concurrence, Kravis decided against raising KKR's bid. Both men thought KKR was already paying full price at $55. However, Kelly told Kravis that he thought he could bluff Dutt into raising his bid because, as Kelly put it, "he wants to beat me so bad." Kelly announced that Esmark would not oppose Beatrice's bid but did not rule out the possibility that KKR would boost its offer. Through Harris, who was representing Esmark this time, Kelly told Dutt he would give him a lockup on Hunt-Wesson for $1.8 billion if Beatrice raised its bid to $60 a share. Dutt's initial reaction was, "What's a lockup?" Louis Perlmutter, the Lazard partner on the deal, explained the concept to Dutt and recommended that he accept, though it meant topping his own bid. Dutt got the approval of his board and at Harris's condominium shook hands with Kelly on $60 a share, or $2.8 billion—

a rich twenty-three times earning. The Esmark saga was over and Don Kelly seemed headed for retirement. Few CEOs of the post-war era had done better by their shareholders than this "fat, red-faced Irishman," as Kelly called himself. In his dozen years of running Esmark, its stock rose by an average of 28 percent per annum.

Instead of the $20 million Oppenheimer would have gotten had the KKR deal gone through, Kelly paid the firm $7.5 million in addition to a $500,000 retainer payment already received. While Beck believed Opco deserved more, it was by far the largest the firm had ever gotten —and, nearly as satisfying, Opco's paycheck was larger than Salomon Brothers', which was $7.5 million. KKR got a hefty breakup fee but that provided no consolation to Kravis, who said hardly a word on the plane back to New York with Beck and McGrath. "This was really disappointing," Kravis said later. "Unlike Norton Simon, this deal was very financeable."

In June 1984, Esmark held a farewell bash at the Sky Club in New York for its friends on Wall Street. Beck was in the audience as Kelly kicked things off with a slide show. One slide showed his new business card. "Retired," it read. "No business, no worries, no plans, no problems, no money, no prospects." He flashed a picture of a castle on the screen. "That's my new home," he said to a roar of appreciative laughter. "I call it On Golden Parachute." The last slide featured a deal man's interpretation of the important dates in the history of Esmark. There were two: "1885—Gus Swift buys cows" and "1984—Beatrice buys Esmark."

In November, only four months after Beatrice had wrapped up its acquisition of Esmark, Beck and McGrath met Kelly and Fred Rentschler for dinner at Billy's on the Upper East Side. Rentschler had grown up in an apartment two blocks from the restaurant, which remained his favorite Manhattan watering hole. Billy's was loud and raucous and both Kelly and Beck were in rare form that night, cracking up each other and half the restaurant. In the midst of the fun, Beck suddenly got serious.

"I'll tell you what I think's going to happen to you, Kelly," he said. "Within one year, you'll be CEO of Beatrice."

Kelly laughed with everyone else. "Bullshit," he said. "There's a fellow named Dutt who'd rather die first."

Beck waited poker-faced for the laughter to subside. "Here's the

bet: two hundred fifty thousand dollars and the winner gets his choice of a meal at any restaurant in Rio de Janeiro or Paris."

"You're on," Kelly roared, and they shook hands.

One year to the day later, Beatrice would agree to an $8.2 billion leveraged buyout by KKR and its CEO-designate: Don Kelly.

13

A few weeks after the Esmark-Beatrice deal was completed, Jeff Beck and Richard Rainwater spent a sunny Saturday in the deal-resplendent summer of 1984 talking takeovers on the porch of a weather-beaten beach house on Nantucket. In the photo taken to commemorate the occasion, Rainwater looks the taller of the two by several inches, a lean, handsome man with a full head of thick, dark-brown hair and a hint of swarthiness suggestive of his Lebanese ancestry. He is wearing a blue denim workshirt and has an arm draped around the shoulder of his more muscular companion, who looks a bit owlish in round, horn-rimmed glasses and a tight T-shirt. Beck and Rainwater look like members of alien nations, except for one thing: they have the exact same smile—a huge, joyous smile unconstrained, it seemed, by doubt or inhibition, a smile that loved the camera completely and forever. There is a boyish mischievousness about them that belies the years beginning to show around their eyes and waists. They could be a couple of high-school buddies who'd just been named co-captains of the football team or stopped for a souvenir photo after their first visit to a Mexican border-town brothel—"Richie" and "Jeffy," as they called one another, compadres in deals.

A few weeks after returning to New York from his weekend stay on Nantucket, Beck opened a letter from Rainwater. Out fell a copy of the photo. "We're cool," Rainwater had written on the back.

In Rainwater, Beck for the first time encountered another deal man who was fully his match in the exuberant audacity he brought to deal making. Rainwater was a hypercharged deal romantic, a funmeister of deals who, like Beck, recognized no dividing line between the professional and the personal. If you made an appointment to see Rainwater in his glass-walled office high atop an office tower in Fort Worth, you could be certain only that he would in fact be there—eventually, though perhaps not as scheduled. You might have to make your pitch to him while he worked a telephone console with as many blinking lights as a Christmas tree. If he was in the midst of a deal with hostile overtones, chances were he'd be wearing his shark cap. "Want to talk to T. Boone Pickens [or David Geffen or Ross Perot]?" he might ask, and then put whoever it was on the speakerphone while he went off to use the bathroom or write something in Magic Marker on the white erasable wall of his office. Or he might put you in a conference room and return every fifteen minutes for five minutes of conversation. Or you might find yourself refereeing a Little League soccer game or racing go-carts or heading out to his ranch outside town to take a look at his springboks and oryxes. If you wanted to see him in the summertime, you'd have to go to Nantucket, where Rainwater might pick you up at the airport in his Mustang. Otherwise, you could find him in his "office"—a chair stationed oceanside at the Cliffside Beach Club. Just look for the guy surrounded by cellular-telephone equipment.

By the time Beck made his first visit to Nantucket in 1984, Rainwater had been working for the Bass family for fourteen years. Although he had grown up in Fort Worth, on the right side of the tracks, in a middle-class neighborhood not far from the family wholesale business, Rainwater had had to leave town to meet a scion of the city's first family, the Basses. At Stanford University Business School, he was a classmate of Sid Bass, the eldest of Perry Bass's four sons. After Sid picked up his MBA in 1968, he succeeded his father as the head of Bass Brothers Enterprises, the family's lucrative oil and gas business. Having returned to Fort Worth determined to diversify the family holdings, Sid had realized that he needed help. Rainwater, meanwhile, had joined the Dallas office of Goldman, Sachs, where he quickly distinguished himself as an institutional broker. He was surprised when Bass called him in 1970 with a job offer. At Stanford they'd been classmates but hardly friends and, anyway, the Bass family already had a large retinue of financial advisers. But Sid wanted a fresher, more creative approach. He turned to Rainwater.

The two Fort Worth boys began with certain advantages, not the least of which was the energy-industry expertise of the management of Bass Brothers Enterprises. And, although the Basses were not as wealthy as the Hunts—not yet, anyway—they were more respectable: genteel, self-effacing, philanthropic, cultured. Starting with perhaps $50 million in assets and an annual cash flow of a few million dollars from the oil business, Bass and Rainwater made a series of quasi-experimental outlays while struggling toward a comprehensive philoso-phy of investing. Like Warren Buffet and the other great investors whose methods they studied, Bass and Rainwater came under the intellectual sway of Benjamin Graham and David Dodd, two profes-sors whose pioneering 1930s tome, *Security Analysis,* was the bible of "value investing." Ignoring Wall Street convention, Graham and Dodd focused not on a company's earnings prospects but rather on its current condition in their search for businesses whose intrinsic value (as measured by liquidation value among other things) was not re-flected in the market price of its securities.

Bass and Rainwater started as classic "bottom-fishers," systemati-cally trawling the lower depths of the stock and bond markets in search of bargains. Bass Brothers Enterprises set up its own trading desk, which gathered market intelligence from the unlikely locale of Fort Worth while orchestrating elaborate arbitrage plays in a wide variety of securities. Bass and Rainwater brought the hard-nosed sense of value honed in contrarian market players to another more original and personal mode of investing that led them into deal making. The idea was to identify businessmen who'd demonstrated an ability to make money at something very specific—"world-class niche players," Rainwater called them—and become their partners. This was harder than it sounded, since smart, proven operators usually are precisely those least in need of capital. However, the Bass family possessed two traits rarely found together in wealthy backers—generosity and passiv-ity—and Rainwater proved a cheerfully relentless talent scout. Unlike KKR, Bass and Rainwater did not start with a particular type of trans-action and go in search of opportunities to apply it. Rather, the struc-ture of their deals followed from the particularities of the opportunity. Whether the deal involved refinancing an existing business, acquiring a company, or starting a new one, Bass, Rainwater, and a small staff of financial specialists handled it all themselves. What the two Stanford classmates had done, in effect, was to attach a self-contained merchant bank to the oil company that was Bass Brothers Enterprises.

From the beginning, Rainwater was as much partner as employee. He invested his own money with the Basses' in many of the deals he crafted with Gentleman Sid. For years, Rainwater and Bass shared the same secretary and the wall between their adjoining offices was made of glass. "Sid and I were together breath to breath, heartbeat to heart-beat," Rainwater said after he'd finally split from Sid. "He couldn't have done it on his own and I couldn't have done it on my own. We complemented each other." Rainwater, like Beck, was incapable of embarrassment in the pursuit of a deal. For the greater glory of Bassland (as Beck called it) he would go call on anyone, anywhere, anytime, using his enthusiasm as a battering ram. Bass, meanwhile, functioned as the methodical behind-the-scenes presence who weighed opportunities Rainwater the rainmaker plucked from the chaos of the marketplace. By the time Beck met Rainwater in 1980, he had become the human switchboard on a formidable and very private deal-making network. Bass Brothers Enterprises had partners in dozens of businesses with no connection to oil, virtually all of which were closely held, like BBE itself. Through its securities-trading operation, Bassland was plugged into every major house on Wall Street as well as the Beverly Hills junk-bond outpost of Drexel Burnham. Socially speaking, as third-generation heirs, Sid and his three Yale-educated brothers were nearly as well connected within the old-money establishments of the East as within the Texas elite.

In 1980, not long after Oppenheimer had established its M & A department, Rainwater stopped by the firm for a get-acquainted meeting he'd arranged with Jack Nash, who called his new deal chief in to meet the Texan. Nash left after ten minutes, but Beck spent the next hour and a half with Rainwater. Although Beck barely knew who the Basses were, he was always glad for an opportunity to observe another deal promoter at work, and by meeting's end he was willing to concede that Rainwater's folksy brand of Texan deal evangelism was pretty potent stuff. He also pegged Rainwater as a most likely prospect, even though he knew that Bass Brothers Enterprises, like KKR, didn't hire investment bankers in the conventional way. In Beck's estimation, Rainwater, no less than Kravis, was a budding major-league player in a deal game that was rapidly broadening beyond the megacorporations of the *Fortune* 500 and their Establishment investment banks. Only two weeks after he'd met Rainwater for the first time, Beck caught a plane to Fort Worth to pitch a deal his way.

Beck had learned through the grapevine that Wickes Company was amenable to selling its ailing subsidiary Gamble-Skogmo, which ran a chain of retail stores. Although Bear, Stearns & Company was already acting as investment banker to Wickes, Beck hoped he'd at least get a finder's fee if he could interest the Basses in buying Gamble-Skogmo, which, he reasoned, was troubled enough to intrigue the bargain hunter in Rainwater. Gamble-Skogmo was indeed the sort of opportunity that appealed to Rainwater, who took a close look before concluding that Wickes was asking too much for the business. Beck failed in his quest for a fee but succeeded in striking up friendly relationships with both Rainwater and Sid Bass. Beck began flying down to Fort Worth every so often to lay a piece of distressed corporate merchandise before Bass and Rainwater, all to no avail—though they came close to buying American Optical, the ailing Warner-Lambert subsidiary. During the negotiations, Beck made the mistake of bringing along Steve McGrath, who at this point was still an officer of Warner-Lambert. Rainwater as a rule made no effort to hide the disdain he felt for most big-company executives, whom he considered little more than glorified bureaucrats. Annoyed by McGrath's inflexibility on the matter of price, Rainwater said, "I guess you'll have to be bleeding out of your ears and mouth before we can take this piece of junk off your hands."

Beck took Rainwater aside and told him he was acting like a jerk and should apologize to McGrath. Contrite, Rainwater walked over to McGrath. "Let me show you something, Steve," he said. He took him to the window and put his arm around the Warner-Lambert executive.

"I don't think you understand who you're dealing with," Rainwater said. "Look out there. Everything is owned by the Basses."

Beck groaned. This was an apology?

Although Rainwater possessed in spades the essential trait of the rainmaker—the ability to impart enthusiasm—there was no psychological subtlety to his method. Unlike Beck, he made no attempt to adjust his pitch to conform to his audience. Beck heard a dozen versions of Rainwater's basic Homage to Bassland, and they varied only in the intensity with which they were delivered—ranging from fervid to perfervid. When Rainwater really got cranked up, Fort Worth was a new Florence shining on the Texas plain and the Basses were a latter-day American version of the Medicis—a great commercial dynasty whose enlightenment was equal to their wealth, which was, of course, colossal. It was as if every time Luciano Pavarotti opened his mouth, *donna e mobile* came cascading out; Rainwater's aria was impassioned, and could be inspiring and even poetic, but it just wasn't appropriate to every deal occasion.

Although Rainwater understood the importance of guile in theory, he just couldn't help himself in practice. There was something emotionally overwrought about him. It was terribly important to him that he still lived in the city where he'd grown up, that his pursuit of wealth not come between him and home. He'd married his high-school sweetheart and when the money started rolling in bought for her the big house in Westover Hills that they had long fantasized about living in. I was sitting in the kitchen of Rainwater's house one evening in 1988 when he went to get the pie that his mother had brought him that morning, displaying it for my inspection with all the tender delight of a father bearing a newborn child. At the office, I saw Rainwater deliver a congratulatory muffin to a blushing secretary who'd just decided to join the office exercise group. He gathered a few other people around and led them in singing a few choruses of "Happy Workout to You," to the tune of "Happy Birthday." Later that same day, in a business meeting, I watched Rainwater mash some hapless executive to an egoless pulp with his cheerful, tactless incisiveness. There was no malice in Rainwater. He just seemed oblivious to his effect.

Before bringing someone to meet Rainwater, Beck spent hours on the telephone coaching the Texan on how his client was best approached, at times even engaging him in role playing, with Beck taking the role of the unsuspecting visitor to Bassland. Beck called this "programming Richard to be nice." While Rainwater seemed eager to heed Beck's advice, he often failed to follow it as, in the excitement of the moment, he surrendered to his promoter's enthusiasm. Afterward, Beck would call with a blunt, unflattering critique of Rainwater's performance. Rainwater didn't mind. To the contrary, he was impressed, both with Beck's psychological astuteness and with his directness. "He was one of the very few investment bankers who told me: 'Rainwater, you fucked up.' I thought that was great," Rainwater recalled. "I don't think I ever left a meeting where Jeff didn't give me his analysis of where it went into overdrive or reverse. He remembered everything. He was incredibly gifted in his ability to read people in the midst of chaos."

Sid Bass, meanwhile, thought enough of Beck that he invited him to his gala fortieth birthday party. On his way to the party site from the airport, Beck's progress was halted by a parade downtown. "What's going on?" he asked his driver. "Bass Day," the driver replied. Perhaps this Medici stuff wasn't so farfetched after all, Beck thought. Sid's wife, Anne, made a point of matching Beck with her recently divorced sister at the party. They hit it off, began seeing each other, mainly in New York, and even made plans to take a trip with Sid and Anne Bass, but then along came Margo Preston and his fling ended before it had really begun. Although brief, Beck's Texas romance added considerably to his store of knowledge about Bassland.

He began to glimpse the method in Rainwater's promotional madness, though it would take several years more before he came to full realization. "Richard was very good," Beck recalled. "I totally bought into his bullshit that the Basses had limitless money."

For years, it was virtually impossible for outsiders to gauge the size of the Bass fortune, since most of the companies in which Bass and Rainwater had invested were privately held. In buying into public companies, meanwhile, they rarely crossed the 5 percent threshold at which a stockholder was required to disclose his ownership to the SEC. The Basses worked harder even than most aristocratic clans at keeping their names out of the newspapers—as did Rainwater, who wasn't the subject of an article in the national press until *Business Week* put him on its cover in 1986. (Because there was not a single photograph of Rainwater in the public domain at the time, his cover likeness was a painting based on the "We're cool" photo, which I borrowed from Beck.) By promoting the Basses as unremittingly in smart-money deal circles as Donald Trump later would tout himself to the tabloid press, Rainwater helped shroud the family in a self-fulfilling mystique of super-wealth; the pervasive impression that the Basses were far richer than they actually were helped them become that rich in fact. Mystique was skillfully converted into wealth through the take-over game. It was the ultimate achievement of Bass and Rainwater as investors to reap grander profits than anyone else during the formative years of the 1980s hostile-takeover wave without once resorting to actually making a hostile tender offer. Sid and Richard were more subtle in their menace.

As they became increasingly aggressive in their pursuit of stock-market bargains, Bass and Rainwater perfected a technique of creeping accumulation of shares that unnerved CEOs into paying them an enormous premium to go away. In early 1980, for example, it was revealed by the SEC that a Bass investor group held 9.1 percent of Blue Bell, the company that makes Wrangler jeans. Rainwater told its management that the Basses were friendly folk who, though they could afford to buy the rest of the stock out of petty cash, had no intention of seeking control. Rainwater repeatedly offered the same assurance as the Basses methodically made six more SEC filings and boosted their stake to 22.4 percent. Finally, Blue Bell bought the shares back for $116 million, giving the Bass group a $51 million profit. At the same time, Bass and Rainwater were exploiting the massive undervaluation of oil-company shares. A week after the Basses disclosed a 5.1 percent stake in Marathon Oil in 1981, the oil giant was hit with a bid from Mobil Oil, inaugurating the first of the oil megadeals that put the hostile-takeover movement over the top. On Marathon, the Basses made $160 million on an investment of $165 million. But Sid's and Richard's most lucrative greenmail play came in 1984, just before Beck came up to Nantucket, when they sold a 10 percent block back to Texaco for $1.2 billion. Apparently, neither Texaco nor Wall Street realized at the time that the Basses had strained their financial resources nearly to the limit in building the 10 percent position and had no intention of burying themselves in debt to acquire the rest.

With the quick $450 million profit handed them by Texaco added to their net worth, the Basses now could in fact afford to buy something nearly as big as Texaco and a whole lot more glamorous. They chose the Walt Disney Company, which was appealing not only because it was famous and undervalued but because it was under attack by a ratpack of raiders—Saul Steinberg, Ivan Boesky, and Irwin Jacobs. By coming to the rescue of Mickey Mouse, Donald Duck, and Snow White, the Bass family succeeded in obliterating the blot on its reputation left by its adventures in greenmail. Although Bass and Rainwater accumulated their 25 percent position in Disney at what were thought to be high prices, within eighteen months the Bass group was sitting on a capital gain of $850 million. While Rainwater and other members of the investor group sold their stock, Sid added to his holdings and vowed that his stake in Walt Disney would be passed on to his heirs. At about the same time, he and Anne moved to New York City and into the black-tie swirl of Nouvelle Society; Rainwater and his wife stayed in Fort Worth. As it turned out, the saving of the Mouse would be Sid's and Richard's last hurrah together. When Bass Brothers Enterprises was liquidated in the spring of 1985, the Bass family would walk away with assets worth at least $4 billion in a nicely diversified array of businesses. Rainwater, who'd started with next to nothing, was now a mogul in his own right, worth about $175 million.

Shortly after Esmark accepted Beatrice's acquisition offer, Beck took Don Kelly down to Fort Worth to meet Rainwater. Roger Briggs and Steve McGrath came along, too, flying down from Chicago in Esmark's G-3, which would cease being available to Kelly when the sale to Beatrice closed in a few weeks. Although Kelly was a bit nostalgic about the impending loss of his beloved Esmark air force, he was not one to dwell in the past. As always, Kelly was absorbed in contemplating his next deal. With Briggs, he intended to set up a partnership and get back in the deal game. With the kudos for Esmark's lucrative sale to Beatrice resounding through Wall Street, Kelly's standing as a deal man had never been higher. Reputation, though, was not money in the bank—a lesson that Kelly would learn the hard way. Gone with Esmark was the ability to summon $2.5 billion in forty-eight hours with a phone call to his treasurer. After Esmark's sale, Marty Siegel of Kidder, Peabody had teased Kelly by saying, "Don, you've still got the big hat but all the cattle are gone." Although Kelly laughed at Siegel's witticism, he was not at all amused at the prospect of having to go hat in hand to lending institutions every time he wanted to do a deal. As Beck well knew, Kelly could use a well-heeled partner or two, and that was where Rainwater and the Basses came in.

Kelly was no stranger to the Bass family. Perry Bass had been a large stockholder in Swift & Company, accumulating the position through his broker, who'd been invited to join the board as Bass's representative. Operating behind the scenes, Bass had been one of Kelly's staunchest champions in those critical early years of Swift's restructuring into Esmark. Although Kelly had never met Rainwater, he'd spoken to him during the final hours of Esmark's negotiations with Beatrice. In his frantic efforts to save his Esmark-KKR buyout, Beck had come up with the idea of having Esmark set up a new subsidiary in partnership with KKR that would tender for 51 percent of Beatrice's stock. While McGrath was seeking Lester Crown's help in financing this transaction, Beck (with Kravis listening in) was on the phone to Rainwater, trying to convince him to put up a few hundred million dollars to the same end. Although it was all pretty farfetched, Beck at least succeeded in getting Rainwater and Kelly on the telephone together. As always, Beck was optimistic, though he suspected that pairing Kelly with Rainwater would be even tougher than matching him with Kravis, who possessed tact in proportion to his ambition. Beck called from Chicago the day before he was to arrive with Kelly to beg Rainwater to be on his best behavior. Beck also prepped Kelly, reminding him he was there "to listen and to sell."

"I'm not selling anything," Kelly snapped.

Oh, no, Beck thought. We're not even there yet and already Kelly's having a great-man attack.

A limousine dropped Kelly, Briggs, Beck, and McGrath in front of Bass Tower I, a gleaming skyscraper sprouting incongruously out of a low-rise section of downtown Fort Worth. A high-speed elevator whisked them to the top floor. The glass doors to Bass Brothers Enterprises opened by remote control as they approached. Inside stood two uniformed security guards with walkie-talkies at the ready. A secretary ushered the visitors through the office. On every door was a nameplate and behind every desk a smiling secretary. Modernist paintings based on oil and gas imagery filled the walls, which were trimmed in blond wood. Bassland was quiet, very white, and meticulously ordered, like a Swiss clinic. On the erasable wall of a conference room someone had left a Magic Marker schematic diagram of the Basses' real-estate holdings, which Beck studied as he nervously awaited the arrival of Rainwater, who was a good fifteen minutes late. By this time, he and Sid were deep in their Walt Disney gambit.

Beck's nervousness proved prophetic. What began as a two-way conversation mediated by Beck soon careened into an epic Rainwater monologue. Beck tried several times to steer the meeting to safety but it was like trying to stop a runaway truck with an outstretched arm. As Rainwater went on and on about all the money made by the Basses and their partners, Beck sneaked a look at Kelly, who was uncharacteristically silent and redder than usual. A vision of a side of beef on a hook flashed into Beck's mind. "Basically, Richard was positioning Kelly as a subordinate in a fairly crass way," Beck recalled. "His message to Kelly was, 'Well, you've done some interesting things, but now you are hung meat—a CEO without a corporation. What can we do for you?' " In truth, Rainwater didn't think enough of Kelly to try to position him any particular way, not being especially interested in going into partnership with someone who was over sixty and still hadn't managed to amass a nine-figure net worth. To Rainwater, the $15 million or so that Kelly made in selling Esmark to Beatrice was spare change. "I was still learning about life," Rainwater said later. "I hadn't realized yet that an executive could work really hard and still never make any real money."

Rainwater's assault was interrupted when Sid Bass strolled in to shake Kelly's hand. Sir Sid was his usual gracious self but stayed only a few minutes, which only served to underscore Kelly's unimportance. "Kelly," Beck said, "went from hung meat to butchered meat." As noon drew near, Rainwater halted his harangue and suggested they all go to lunch. Kelly said that he didn't want anything to eat.

"Why don't we go into my office, then, and you can watch me make deal calls and see how I work," Rainwater said.

In all of his dealings with Rainwater, Beck had never heard him utter anything quite as insulting as this. In the sheer awfulness of the moment, time seemed to stop as Beck turned to gauge the reaction of his companions and was reminded of the colors of the seasons: Kelly was bright red with heat, Briggs as pale as winter, and McGrath as mottled as the leaves of autumn. Trying to lighten things up, Beck laughed. "Oh, sure, Richard," he said teasingly, "we'd all *love* to come in and watch you make phone calls." Rainwater persisted. "No, really," he said. "I have this technique for getting people on the phone and . . ."

Beck led Kelly and Briggs out of Bassland to the safety of the sidewalk, where he looked Kelly in the eye and said, "This is just a bad day, Don. If they've got the money, who gives a shit how they act." Kelly was not mollified. Six years later, his annoyance was still evident. "I went down there to see if there was an opportunity for us to work together and I was updated on the wonder that was Mr. Rainwater," Kelly recalled. "He could have just sent me a tape."

Beck took his leave of Kelly and Briggs and went back into Bassland in search of Rainwater. He found him in his office. "How did I do?" Rainwater said, in a tone that suggested to Beck he was expecting praise. Beck was incredulous. "How did you *do*?" he said exasperatedly. "Are you out of your fucking mind, Richard?"

"Well, they've got to like me, too," Rainwater said.

"*Like* you!" Beck roared. "These guys left thinking you are one of the largest assholes they've ever met."

"What do you mean?" said Rainwater suspiciously. When Beck finally succeeded in impressing upon Rainwater how self-defeating his performance had been, the Texan was contrite and then dejected. Rainwater asked Beck to stay, and over dinner they tried to figure out a way to make a fresh approach to Kelly. Rainwater, who was preparing to make his annual summer migration to Nantucket, suggested inviting Kelly to spend a weekend on the island. Although Beck was unable to get Kelly to go anywhere near Rainwater, he succeeded in getting his permission to go to Nantucket himself to attempt to broach the subject of an alliance with the Basses once again. A month after the fiasco in Fort Worth, Jeff and Margo, who was seven months pregnant, went to Nantucket to spend the weekend with Richard and his wife, Karen. As it turned out, Rainwater was no keener than before on the idea of joining forces with Kelly and Briggs. Beck was at once appalled and flattered when it dawned on him that Rainwater had lured him to Nantucket with the hope of persuading him to affiliate with Bassland. "Jeff was a guy with deal magic but he was working in the wrong forum," Rainwater recalled. "His capital base should have been a group of smart investors instead of a Wall Street firm."

On Saturday night, Jeff and Margo piled into the back of a Blazer pickup cluttered with toys—Richard's toys—and drove off with the Rainwaters to have dinner at a local greasy spoon. Rainwater insisted on ordering for the table a supply of food that could have fed eight. Soon, Beck's view of Rainwater was partially obscured by double and triple orders of nachos and fried clams piling up between them. Even before the waitress took their orders, Richard had begun one of his monologues. While Beck had heard many a Rainwater ode to Bassland, never had he heard a version to match the stem-winding, steamrolling gospel of wealth he heard that night in Nantucket. Apparently taking the numbed speechlessness of his listeners as rapt interest, Rainwater held forth for three hours, ringing endless rhetorical changes on this basic theme: I made the Basses rich, I made myself rich, and I can do the same for you. Today Fort Worth, tomorrow New York City and the world!

Rainwater and his guests rode home in exhausted silence. The next day Beck confronted Rainwater. "Richard, your performance last night was unbelievable," he said. "I'm offended, Margo's offended. Things aren't getting better between us, they're getting worse."

Rainwater was contrite. Tears came to his eyes as he put his arm around Beck and asked him to please stay the day as planned. Beck did, and the mood changed totally. Rainwater was a different person— gracious, attentive, relaxed, fun. Although he and Rainwater would part friends, Beck would never make a serious attempt to follow up on the Texan's offer to back him, even though capital was the commodity that had always been in shortest supply in the Mad Dog's pursuit of fortune through deal making. Later, Beck said that he never pursued an alliance with Bassland because, despite Rainwater's assurances to the contrary, he suspected that he would end up not as a partner of the Basses but their employee. "You could not be associated with the Bass organization without being a family retainer, and that was just not me." Rainwater's own theory probably was a lot closer to the mark: "I think I thought more of Jeff than he thought of himself."

14

In *The Bonfire of the Vanities*, a wrong turn in the Bronx sets in motion a chain of mishaps that exposes the deceptions and false assumptions on which Sherman McCoy's life is based. He is a Master of the Universe no more as he loses wife, mistress, home, job, and self-respect. In a matter of months in 1985, Beck was similarly reduced from a Big Deal Man at full strut to an embittered, bewildered exile from Wall Street. The initial catalyst of Beck's unraveling was nothing as mundane as McCoy's errant driving but a profound and joyous event: the birth of his first child, Katherine Louisa Beck, on September 24, 1984. Katherine's birth coincided with the announcement of a deal that Beck assumed would be the triumphant culmination of his relationship with Don Kelly: the $1 billion buyout of Northwest Industries by the newly formed partnership of Kelly Briggs Oppenheimer. However, the Northwest transaction soon degenerated into a highly publicized fiasco, dealing Beck the second blow of a one-two combination so psychologically debilitating that for a time he was virtually incapacitated as a deal man.

As Margo's due date approached, Beck's behavior at home grew increasingly odd. For one thing, his sleep was haunted by dreams so disturbing that a few times each night he'd awaken himself and Margo with his thrashing and shouting. After Katherine's birth, the nightmares worsened and began invading Beck's waking hours. Unpredictably and at the slightest provocation—the sound of Katherine crying, the sight of a television commercial, the smell of burnt toast—Beck would turn pale and break into a cold sweat as there came over him a feeling of disorientation that at times was so extreme he could barely talk. At home anyway, Beck blamed the war, telling his wife that Katherine's birth had exacerbated the post-traumatic stress disorder from which he suffered. He said he was especially afflicted by the sound of Katherine's crying, since the memory of combat that haunted him most was the sound of Vietnamese babies crying in massacred villages. While Beck had claimed to suffer 'Nam nightmares from the outset of his romance with Margo, these supposedly were more intense and featured long-forgotten memories freshly dredged up from his subconscious by the emotional trauma of first fatherhood. Margo had no reason to doubt Beck's story and didn't. "Sometimes he'd be playing with Katherine and—boiinngg!—he was back in Vietnam," she said. "It was like he could see, smell, and taste it."

Margo had never seen her husband in worse shape. He interrupted his chain-smoking only to eat, which he did voraciously, causing his weight to balloon to about two hundred pounds. "I was so fat," he said later, "that I looked like my glasses had been surgically implanted." At the time, though, he was not inclined to find humor in his condition. He was short-tempered and perpetually on edge. At a black-tie reception at the Whitney Museum one evening, Bill Green, a member of the U.S. House of Representatives, approached Beck and was talking about the Reagan administration's backing of the Nicaraguan Contras when all the color drained out of Jeff's face and he was struck dumb. Margo, who had never before seen her husband incapable of speech, intervened and led Jeff out into the hallway, where he sucked on a cigarette as if it were an oxygen tube and he was a drowning man. The whole front of his shirt was soaked through with sweat. After about fifteen minutes in the hallway, Beck was able to pull himself together. He told Margo that Green had triggered his post-traumatic stress condition because he recalled that during his stint in the U.S. Special Forces he'd met Congressman Green, who was passing through Vietnam on an inspection tour.

At the office, meanwhile, Beck made no attempt at first to invoke Vietnam to justify his behavior, which in any event wasn't yet so erratic as to require a heavy-duty psychological explanation anyway. While Beck looked like he could use a couple of weeks' sleep and was more frequently absent, his colleagues at Oppenheimer had no reason to doubt the explanation Beck offered: that his wife was suffering a bad case of postpartum depression. The Mad Dog was still capable of bedazzling corporate execs with promotional razzmatazz. Shortly after the Northwest Industries acquisition was announced, Don Kelly persuaded Fred Rentschler, who'd run Esmark's food businesses, to join the buyout group as president-designate of Northwest. Rentschler met Beck for the first time one afternoon in Kelly's offices in Chicago.

Over the years Rentschler had become accustomed to watching Kelly effortlessly intimidate his visitors, but he noticed that this guy Beck was pacing around the office like it was his own, puffing a big cigar and gesticulating dramatically as he held forth on deal-related issues with a boom box of a voice. Kelly didn't seem to mind; in fact, he gave every indication of enjoying Beck's histrionics as much as Beck enjoyed Kelly's egging him on. While Beck and Kelly entertained one another, Rentschler was transfixed, marveling to himself, Who is this guy?

It was during this period that I first began spending a lot of time with Beck in researching a profile of him that appeared in *Business Week* in December of 1984. Beck was exceptionally cooperative, even going to the trouble of presenting me at the outset with a long list of "selected contacts." He insisted that I meet with every member of the group, including its most junior analysts. In discussing his transactions, Beck played it quite straight, keeping in check his Master of the Universe tendencies and often downplaying his own role to give credit to his clients. All of his deal stories checked out. In fact, the executives and lawyers that he'd worked with most closely not only were highly complimentary of Beck but seemed quite fond of him. "In the case of Beck and me, by laughing at ourselves and others it relieved some of the tension in what is a very intense business," Kelly said. "You had better get relaxation or you go ape." Consistent with the low business-press profile he maintained until the late 1980s, Kravis wouldn't be interviewed. But Dick Beattie, who as a partner of Simpson Thacher & Bartlett acted as lawyer on many a KKR deal, fairly gushed: "Jeff has established himself as a very major player. People get a kick out of him but they take him very seriously. He just lacks that sense of self-importance that so many people have in this business." Jack MacAtee, the Davis Polk lawyer who'd helped Beck land Taubman, was even more effusive: "If he stays at it, he could become one of the really senior gurus on Wall Street; he could be the next André Meyer [the late senior partner of Lazard Frères], though with a different style."

In time, I would learn of strategic omissions in Beck's account of his career to me—no mention, for example, of his falling-out with Gleacher. This was neither surprising nor culpable; almost everyone tends to edit his own life story to his advantage, especially with a reporter. At this stage, Beck told me none of the falsehoods with which he'd been sprinkling his conversation with colleagues ever since he started at DLJ: that he'd played football at Florida State and captained his college tennis team. Nor did he tell me that he'd been a partner of Lehman Brothers, as he'd told John Sanzo during his job interview.

However, Beck did give me my first fleeting glimpse of his imaginary self, beginning by claiming that while at DLJ and Lehman Brothers he'd "leveraged himself to the eyeballs" to buy a series of small companies. He made no mention yet of Rosebud, and in fact volunteered no company names at all, not even Susan Crane. When I pressed Beck on the subject of his outside interests, he cryptically implied that patriotic duty prevented him from discussing them in detail. While I wasn't sure that I believed in the implied connection to undercover activities, Beck succeeded in making the issue in my mind not the existence of his outside interests but rather their size and nature. Unfortunately, I included these two sentences in my story: "Never content with a mere advisory role, Beck borrowed heavily to invest his own money in buyout deals turned down by his employer and client companies. Much of that debt has been paid down since, leaving Beck with a little empire of privately held consumer products and insurance companies."

Beck broached the subject of Vietnam only when we were alone, and never in detail. He said that he'd been in the U.S. Special Forces —that he'd gone to jungle training in the Canal Zone and jump training at Fort Bragg before shipping out to 'Nam. That was about it. He told no nightmare tales of combat. With me, Beck introduced the subject of Vietnam to establish his credentials not as a suffering antihero but as a business manager, especially of the younger members of the Jeff Beck Group. "There's no greater pressure than combat, and I suspect that the merger business is very combative," he said. "If the young guys don't get good disciplined training, how are they ever going to be assertive, somewhat aggressive team players? If we can't rely on each other, we're not going to win. So I put them through boot camp. They have to feel as if they are always being watched and that it's me who's watching them. All I can tell is if I hadn't done my time in boot camp before I was shipped out to 'Nam, this would be an empty chair." I made no mention of the military angle in my story, omitting it because it seemed, not suspect, but self-serving and irrelevant.

To me, Beck didn't seem anguished at all. The impression I came away with was of someone reveling in success with an unabashed exuberance of a sort I'd rarely encountered. He put on quite a show for me. After taking a phone call, he interrupted one of our conversations to go careening through the hallways, bellowing, "Sanzo just secured a seven-hundred-million-dollar bid! Hey, guys, Sanzo just secured a seven-hundred-million-dollar bid!" (I forget for what.) While Beck's behavior was eccentric—appealingly so—he didn't come across as deranged. To the contrary, it was even more evident to me in retrospect that he'd been quite purposeful and disciplined in touting the group's achievements and had even found a way to turn his private pain to humorous advantage. "We're working seven days a week here," he said. "People say, 'But you just had a daughter, Jeff.' 'Yeah,' I say, 'I saw her when she was born.' "

In truth, Beck was a very devoted father. Throughout all the craziness ahead, the one constant in Beck's behavior was his concern and affection for his daughter. Just the same, first fatherhood is inherently stressful in ways that Beck's unusual psychohistory had rendered him incapable of coping with at first. In a sense, the effect of assuming the responsibilities of parenthood is akin to that of a lifetime of New Year's Eves rolled into one; that is, it is an impetus to introspection, to measuring the discrepancy between one's ideals and one's actual circumstances. The implacable innocence of baby Katherine forced upon Beck the realization that he'd layered his life with lies and evasions. For starters, he'd never told anyone the truth about his own father, who indeed had never told his son or daughter the whole truth about himself. Would he make the same mistake? Would Katherine, too, grow up having staked her own identity to a false version of her father's life? Would he ever be able to bring himself to tell his daughter the truth? Of course, first he'd somehow have to strip the falsehoods from his marriage and admit to Margo that his net worth wasn't inflated by ownership of vast hidden interests and that his psychological problems had nothing to do with Vietnam combat.

Beyond these deceptions, Beck was haunted by the thought that one day he would have to explain to his daughter exactly what it was that he did for a living. Suddenly, his habit of describing his forte as "the manipulation of marginal personalities" no longer sounded so clever, though it seemed no less accurate. Beck didn't know himself what the words "investment banker" really meant sans the promotional rhetoric. To him, the phrase had begun to sound almost like a contradiction in terms. The relentless hit-and-run fee-grubbing of many of the Wall Street bankers he'd come across bore no connection to notions of investment described in economics texts. Would he one day find the words to explain to Katherine why her daddy's income was fifty times that of her teacher or a hundred times that of her nanny? Or why they lived in a fancy apartment when people were sleeping in cardboard cartons on Madison Avenue?

After the Esmark-Beatrice deal Beck talked incessantly of leaving Oppenheimer. But he had no idea how he would fill his days if not with deals. He knew nothing else. And he couldn't afford just to go sit on a beach somewhere. He was supporting a deluxe wife, a million-dollar residence, a car and driver, assorted charities and institutions, and now, in addition, a daughter, whose mother no doubt expected to raise her in the pricey style in which she herself had grown up. It seemed that the more money he made, the more he needed to make. But to what end, finally? He'd done two billion-dollar deals and had another in the works, he was making more than a million a year and had accumulated all the gilt-edged trappings of the 1980s "life-style," and yet deep down he felt not contentment or pride but the first dark flutterings of despair. It had begun to dawn on Beck that the notions of success that had driven him all these years were not of his own devising but had been planted inside him like little Trojan horses stuffed with hallucinogens. The more money he amassed and the higher he climbed in society, the more he conformed to his mother's values—the very values that he'd spent much of his youth rebelling against and that the regular guy in him still considered base if not despicable. When Beck looked out at the world he no longer saw possibility but an indecipherable void, and when he looked in the mirror, he saw someone he no longer recognized as himself.

At first, though, the increase in Beck's pyschic pain only served to exaggerate his swagger. It was as if he'd concluded that the cause of his mounting unhappiness was not excess but timidity. Instead of relocating to more modest quarters, for example, Beck hung on to the apartment at 31 East Seventy-ninth and continued looking for a place in the country, using Katherine's arrival as his rationale: We simply must have more room. More to the point, everyone who was anyone in the world of deals had at least two residences.

Even as Beck was contemplating a major outlay for a country house, he began dabbling in the world of big-ticket art. In keeping with his elevated social aspirations, Beck had stopped accumulating duck decoys and begun collecting paintings, initially favoring the same sort of English sporting canvases of horses and birds for which Kravis had particular affection. Befriending Taubman, who was not only the owner of Sotheby's—the leading supplier of collectible merchandise to

Nouvelle Society—but a noted collector in his own right, inflamed Beck's artistic pretensions. He began frequenting Sotheby's to consult its various experts and attend auctions. At one session, Beck made a bid of $4 million on a Modigliani—but only after having been informed by a member of Sotheby's staff that the painting should fetch much more, as indeed it did. When I interviewed Taubman in the fall of 1984, he seemed tickled by the idea of Beck as art collector. He laughed when I asked him how much Beck knew about painting. "If I may offer a criticism, he has a long way to go to be an art fancier," Taubman said. "From what I can tell, he's doing more looking than collecting." Within a few months, though, Beck had given Taubman reason enough to stop chuckling.

Through a London gallery owner, Beck had met William Acquavella, a leading Manhattan art dealer and Nouvelle Society figure. Conveniently, Acquavella's gallery, on Seventy-ninth Street, was just across the street from Beck's apartment. In response to Beck's strong expressions of interest, Acquavella agreed to hang a half-dozen paintings in his apartment, including a Renoir that recently had been deaccessioned from the Norton Simon Museum and two paintings by Degas—one of dancers and the other of horses. Jeff and Margo took their time in deciding that their favorite was Degas's horse canvas. Beck agreed to buy it for about $2.5 million—double his current annual income and roughly equal to the sum total of his cash savings. The transaction had proceeded nearly to closing when Beck reneged, saying the price was too high. When Taubman called later to say that Acquavella was still so keen on selling him the painting that he was willing to trim his price to $2.1 million, Beck could not say no. Beck later claimed that he never told Acquavella that he'd decided to buy the painting the second time around but did imply the intention to do so in talking to Taubman, who told Acquavella that his lower price had been accepted. Once again, Beck backed out.

"I am sorry for busting the deal," Beck wrote to Acquavella, "but hopefully you understand that other pressing financial commitments which I had no control over got in the way. I do believe that you are entitled to a busted deal fee and would like to know after your consideration what a fair fee would be." Even in the act of apologizing, though, Beck couldn't quite bring himself to let the Degas horses go. "Perhaps in the next few months I will be in a better position to entertain a transaction of this magnitude and hope that any busted deal fee would be applied to the ultimate purchase price." Beck added a hopeful postscript. "As you said, 'there will be others.'" Beck sent a copy of the letter to Taubman, along with a separate note of regret that read, "I want to thank you for assisting me in this transaction and hope that this has not caused you any personal embarrassment. If it has, I sincerely apologize." Once again, Beck appended a postscript: "As promised, I will be sending a check for $25,000 to the Whitney Museum."

The pressing financial commitments to which Beck referred involved his purchase of a house in Pound Ridge, not far from the stable where he and Margo boarded their horses and took riding lessons. Pound Ridge is an élite township in a part of Westchester Country where the houses are grand enough to have their own names and identities, distinct from those of their current owners. Pound Ridge, Bedford, and the adjoining townships were dotted with grand old estates, many of which had recently passed into the hands of Wall Street deal men. Boesky had lived in the area since 1976, in a Georgian mansion on a hundred wooded acres. (Not long after Boesky was packed off to prison on insider-trading charges, Mrs. Boesky stirred up a local ruckus by applying to the zoning board for a variance to add a ten-foot-high Jeffersonian dome to their mansion. The board said no, apparently fearing that if the Boeskys were permitted to add a touch of Monticello to their abode, their neighbors might be inspired to replicate Notre Dame cathedral or Windsor Castle or the Taj Mahal. It was that kind of neighborhood.)

Beck again was a country squire, though on a much grander scale than during his New Jersey incarnation. The Becks paid $825,000 for Barrett Farm, which was indeed a working farm—in George Washington's day, that is. Almost anywhere else in America, Barrett Farm would have been called an estate, not a farm—though, by the standards of the neighborhood, it was rather modest and certainly more comfortable than grand. Remnants of animal husbandry were visible. A small red barn and a few sheds were arranged in a tidy compound not far from the swimming pool. The original white-clapboard farmhouse, built in 1785, had been retained, too, and formed the nucleus of an extensive and somewhat rambling series of additions. Inside the fourteen-room house, every effort had been made to retain the antique country charm of the place. The oaken floorboards in the living room were worn and warped, and a man of average height had to duck a little to pass through one or two of the doorways. The house sat atop a gentle hill overlooking a vast expanse of lawn and rolling meadow fringed by forest. Next to the house was a manmade pond stocked with bass. Almost as soon as the Becks moved in, they began planning a remodeling that would push their total investment in Barrett Farm above $1.3 million.

As the Northwest Industries deal came unraveled, Beck's increasingly bizarre behavior began to mar his professional life as well. In the true and steady light of retrospect, the Northwest deal would seem doomed from the beginning by a host of obstacles, not the least of which was the blithe arrogance of its promoters. After the unexpectedly lucrative sale of Esmark, Kelly and Beck had formed Kelly Briggs Oppenheimer and piled into the Northwest deal with more enthusiasm than thought, banking on their ability to improvise as they went along. "There was a feeling of 'When you're hot, you're hot. Take advantage of it,' " admitted Roger Briggs, Kelly's longtime Esmark colleague.

Kelly was familiar with Northwest Industries, which had played an important cameo role in his early career. Beginning in the early 1960s, a Chicago lawyer named Ben Heineman had erected Northwest Industries from the corporate ruins of the old Chicago and North Western Railroad through shrewdly opportunistic deal making. At one point, Heineman had sent out merger feelers to Swift & Company, which assigned the task of analyzing a combination with Northwest to an up-and-coming vice president by the name of Kelly, who strongly recommended against a deal. Later, as president and CEO of Esmark, Kelly had become friendly with Heineman, maverick to maverick. After a long run, Northwest hit the skids in 1982 as several of the largest markets for its products began contracting sharply. A proud and contentious man, Heineman put off retiring and set about trying to salvage his reputation and the company he'd built. By mid-1984, the company had improved marginally and he was again looking to retire, if only he could find a worthy successor. Ira Harris, who was friendly with Heineman, suggested that Kelly lead a buyout of Northwest. Heineman and Kelly quickly established their mutual interest in a transaction at a price of $50 a share. So far, so good.

With Salomon Brothers already representing Northwest, Kelly turned to Oppenheimer for help in analyzing the deal. As Beck looked over the numbers, he repeated the same pitch that had gotten him in Kelly's door in the first place: Make us your partner, not just your investment banker. This time, Kelly took Beck up on his offer. With Esmark's corporate treasury no longer at his disposal, Kelly figured he needed all the financing help he could get. The result was Kelly Briggs Oppenheimer, a partnership created for the sole purpose of acquiring Northwest Industries. Kelly Briggs got a 60 percent interest and Oppenheimer 40 percent—but Beck didn't mind. "At the time, getting a 40 percent carry on Don Kelly's next deal seemed like finding money in the street," Beck said.

In jumping into partnership with Kelly, Beck essentially steamrolled Steve Robert, Oppenheimer's CEO. For years now, Beck had been trying to push Oppenheimer back into LBO investing almost single-handedly. Beck had made slow headway, winning authorization in 1983 to bring in Steve McGrath to set up a new buyout entity. By the time the Northwest deal happened along, McGrath had spent many months on the paperwork for an LBO partnership called Value Investors, the goal of which was raising $100 million to $250 million from institutional investors. Robert told Beck that the LBO fund would have to take a backseat to another acquisition fund that Oppenheimer was promoting in conjunction with a leading corporate rejuvenator. Robert might be able to sandbag an LBO fund with bureaucratic obstacles but he didn't dare let a $1 billion deal languish in his in-box, Beck correctly reasoned.

While the Jeff Beck Group had advised on two billion-dollar deals, it had never attempted to raise financing for a large leveraged buyout à la KKR. As they made the rounds of institutional investors, Beck and his colleagues gained new appreciation of the value of the credibility that KKR had accumulated over the years of small deals reliably and profitably completed. While many money men routinely gave KKR the benefit of the doubt, the principals of Kelly Briggs Oppenheimer had to prove in a hundred different ways that they really knew what they were doing, though in fact they were learning by doing. Beck's increasingly erratic attention span certainly didn't help. Even Kelly proved a liability. In his days as CEO of a *Fortune* 500 company, Kelly had been able to raise a fortune in financing with a single phone call to his own treasurer. Now he found himself having to go hat in hand to a dozen fund managers, each of whom had particular concerns to be addressed and demands to be accommodated. And accommodating did not come naturally to Kelly, who at Esmark had enjoyed great latitude as a deal maker. Even after the Northwest Industries buyout collapsed, he was unpenitent, telling a reporter that he was "not going to spend my life every other day picking up the phone and having some lender or investor saying, 'By June 1, 1986, you were to have paid down $1.14 million [in debt] and you're only at $1.12 million.'"

By mid-December 1985, three months after the agreement to buy Northwest had been announced, Kelly Briggs Oppenheimer had yet to obtain commitments from equity investors sufficient to finance the deal. With the December 31 deadline looming, it had become apparent to all the principals that they'd rush to judgment in buying a company that was far more complex and problematic than anticipated. The rudest surprise involved Northwest's Velsicol subsidiary, which in the late 1970s had sold contaminated feed that killed millions of farm animals. If the cash reserves that Velsicol had set aside to cover damages proved inadequate, Northwest Industries itself could be hit with big legal judgments. While investors were fretting over this potential liability, a leak of methyl isocyanate gas from a Union Carbide plant in Bhopal, India, killed two thousand people. In the uproar that followed, Velsicol admitted holding a small amount of methyl isocyanate in inventory. An unnamed member of the Kelly Briggs Oppenheimer group was quoted in *The Wall Street Journal* bemoaning Bhopal's effect on the Northwest buyout: "We have a major problem . . . You couldn't have dreamt of a scenario for this deal that was more nightmarish.'"

Beck recognized his own words. As was the case with his earlier transactions involving Kelly, Beck had taken it upon himself to keep reporters from key publications informed as the deal progressed, though strictly on a background basis. Many of the M & A men of Beck's generation—following the lead of Bruce Wasserstein—had grown increasingly assertive in their public relations over the course of the decade, and massaging the press had become an essential ingredient of the tactical maneuvering involved in large deals. While Beck enjoyed this aspect of deal making, Kelly preferred to avoid all contact with reporters until a deal was safely completed. It had become evident to Kelly midway through the Northwest deal that one or more of his advisers was operating a back channel to the press. He didn't much care, though, until Ben Heineman read Beck's "nightmarish scenario" quote and called to complain quite forcefully. In hopes of solving the group's financing difficulties, Kelly had been trying to persuade Heineman to cut his price by $100 million or so. Beck's quote made it appear that Kelly Briggs Oppenheimer was trying to exploit Bhopal to pressure Northwest into a price reduction and Heineman didn't like that one bit.

Heineman's M & A adviser, Ira Harris, decided to go right to the source. He called Beck and berated him for negotiating in bad faith. "Give me a break, Ira," said Beck, refusing to confirm or deny that he had talked with the *Journal* reporter. Beck was not nearly as cavalier with Kelly, who called shortly afterward and angrily demanded to know whether someone from Oppenheimer was denigrating Velsicol to the press. Beck denied that he was the source. "I'll find out who was," Beck promised. Kelly never got an answer. While Kelly never confronted Beck, other group members (including McGrath and Peters) reproached their chief for lying to Kelly. In our interviews, Beck at first scoffed at the naïveté of his colleagues. "All of a sudden it was Boy Scoutsville," he sneered. "When you're trying to get a price reduction of $100 million, you're in a junglelike environment and you do what you have to do." Not only did Beck persist in denying that he was the *Journal*'s source, but he later devised a convoluted story in an attempt to shift the blame to another member of the group.

In any event, after Kelly managed to placate Heineman, the focus of attention shifted back to the urgent need to find a lead equity investor. General Electric Pension Fund initially had indicated it might invest as much as $100 million but opted out after weeks of talks. The other likely prospect as a lead investor, Prudential Insurance Company, offered to finance the entire deal—but only if the price dropped into the range of $40 to $43 a share. Kelly stormed out of the Pru's office in anger. Meanwhile, other institutions insisted on the quid pro quo of a debt repayment schedule, which would bind Kelly Briggs Oppenheimer to a series of deadlines for the divestiture of certain of Northwest's subsidiaries. While such restrictions were not uncommon in LBOs, Kelly had become accustomed to almost complete freedom to improvise in his deal making and was loath to alter the approach that had proven so successful when he was head of Esmark.

In their increasingly desperate search, Kelly and Beck shifted their emphasis from institutions to private investors. Beck struck out with Rainwater and with Kravis, who made a cursory inspection of the numbers and declined to participate. Finally, Lester Crown made a preliminary commitment to invest as much as $60 million and the Belzberg brothers, who were notoriously rapacious raider-greenmailers out of Canada, decided to take a look. Although the prospect of intimate association with the Belzbergs was repellent to both Kelly and Beck, it was preferable to the public humiliation of a busted deal. Briggs and Beck pitched the deal to Sam Belzberg over lunch at the

Regency Hotel in New York. Belzberg was forty-five minutes late, but Beck found such indignity a bit easier to endure after the Canadian tentatively agreed to put in $50 million or so.

The post-Bhopal salvaging of the buyout was proceeding apace when disaster struck again. On December twenty-seventh, the First National Bank of Chicago pulled out, leaving the Kelly-Beck group in the lurch only four days before the financing deadline. As the lead bank on the deal, First Chicago had agreed to lend $150 million and to manage a syndicate of a dozen other banks that were to lend the remainder. First Chicago had serious financial problems unconnected to the Northwest buyout and might well have withdrawn even if the deal hadn't been as problematic as it was. No matter. First Chicago's sudden exit obliterated KBO's credibility—all the more so because it had been Northwest Industries' main bank for years; Ben Heineman was on its board of directors. At Kelly's request, Heineman extended the deadline to January 31, 1985. While KBO scrambled to replace First Chicago, Belzberg got cold feet. He called Kelly. "This is a forty-four-dollar deal," he said. "Count us out."

Beck was devastated. Distraught over the latest in a series of setbacks on the Northwest LBO and beleaguered as never before by his private emotional agonies, Beck for the first time injected his fantasies into the heart of a deal. He told McGrath and Peters that he was prepared to invest as much as $50 million of his own money to save the Northwest transaction. While McGrath over the years had heard Beck make vague references to his family's wealth, he doubted that he had $50 million to invest. And as a Citibank banker involved with the financing of the Susan Crane buyout, Peters knew that the Singer family's net worth had fallen far short of $50 million a decade earlier and, moreover, that Beck had had to borrow all of the money that he'd invested in the buyout. Suspecting that Beck's fortune was mostly imaginary, McGrath and Peters urged him not to imperil his and Oppenheimer's credibility by taking his proposal to Kelly.

Beck later insisted that he had never claimed that all $50 million was to have come from him personally. He said that he had gone to Citibank and offered to pledge the sum total of his liquid assets—about $4 million—as collateral for a personal loan. Citibank said that it might be able to lend him as much as $15 million if William D. Singer would guarantee the loan. Setting aside his pride and resentment, Beck called his stepfather and asked for his help as he had done a decade before when the opportunity to acquire Susan Crane arose.

This time, though, Singer wanted no part of anything his stepson was selling. "You're on your own," he said. After Singer's rebuff, Beck began frantically calling wealthy people with whom he'd dealt over the years. While Beck's story has the ring of authenticity to this point, what follows seems suspect. Beck claimed that after a few days of dialing for dollars, he obtained tentative commitments of $45 million from Al Taubman and other investors, all of whom presumably had already been approached during the many months that Oppenheimer had spent unsuccessfully arranging financing for the Northwest buyout. Why would these investors suddenly want a piece of a deal verging on collapse?

Ignoring McGrath's and Peters's advice, Beck told Kelly that he was willing to invest $50 million but in so casual and sheepish a manner that Kelly didn't take the offer all that seriously. "Jeff, I don't know what you're worth," Kelly said, "but I do know that I don't want to get involved in a situation where my investment banker is a major share-holder. That's not the way I want to run a company."

"Yeah, I guess you're right," Beck said.

"We've dragged this on long enough," Kelly replied. "It's just not fair to Ben. I'm going to pull the plug."

And so he did.

Beck had always looked on his M & A group as a second family. He was, in fact, godfather to Ron Peters's eldest son and had been de-lighted to recruit Steve McGrath, Jr., as well as his father into the group. He'd even made Peters and McGrath the executors of his will. If some corporations are aptly described as cults of personality, then the Oppenheimer M & A department at its height was a cult of friendship. Beck's personal approach had proved indispensable in unit-ing and inspiring the group in its difficult early years; it's doubtful whether the department would have survived under more conven-tional management. However, there's an obvious risk in making per-sonal relationships the basis of professional association and Beck's compulsion to intimacy backfired on him badly as he became the focus of disappointment following the failure to acquire Northwest. Al-though the blame Beck got probably exceeded his culpability, he brought it on himself by having promoted the Northwest deal to his colleagues as their best shot at making big money, since the group would for the first time have been investing in a transaction. As failure unraveled the fabric of friendship that had held the group together, resentment and greed would combine to destroy the Jeff Beck Group, which had been weakened by intensifying internal strife for some time.

Before Northwest, the principal cause of discord had been Beck's self-aggrandizement—the chauffeur, the ten-thousand-dollar tables at the ballet, the Hôtel du Cap competitive-vacationing scene, the Henry-Kravis-is-a-close-personal-friend-of-mine name-dropping. Or, as Sanzo put it later, "Jeff had started to see himself in a different light. He became a different guy. Suddenly, he was the major mogul and the rest of us were nothing." The more Beck swaggered, the less he bothered to attend to mundane detail, thereby forcing his colleagues to continually clean up after him. While Beck's behavior may have been overbearing, the annoyance of the other senior group members was laced with envy. The fact was that they wouldn't have been reduced to acting as deal valets to Beck had the department not been almost completely dependent on him to generate new clients and assignments. None of the other members of the group had proven capable of acting as a rainmaker in his own right.

The resentments within the group over the division of labor were inseparable from the even more explosive issue of the distribution of reward. Within every firm on Wall Street in the 1980s, conflict over annual bonuses was the intramural blood sport of choice. Under Beck's original agreement with Nash and Levy, 20 percent of the M & A department's revenues after expenses were to go into a bonus pool for individual payouts as determined almost wholly by Beck. In 1984, the Jeff Beck Group had a banner year, generating $15 million in income —$8 million of which was from one deal, Esmark-Beatrice. In the fall, just before the Northwest deal ran into trouble, Beck decided on bonus payouts that would put his own total compensation (including base salary) for the year in the neighborhood of $1.7 million while McGrath would get $900,000 and Sanzo, Peters, and Brown about $400,000 apiece.

Sanzo was outraged that McGrath's pay should be twice his own, and complained vehemently to Beck. Meanwhile, McGrath, too, complained that he'd been shortchanged—that Beck had claimed for himself a portion of the credit for the Esmark business that was rightfully his. The rivalry between McGrath and Sanzo ran much deeper than pay. Sanzo had been second in stature to Beck before McGrath supplanted him; he never reconciled himself to being subordinate to someone with no previous experience in investment banking. Mc-

Grath, on the other hand, was confident in having more extensive business experience than anyone else in the group. While Beck at times deliberately played McGrath and Sanzo against each other, he unwittingly sharpened their rivalry by constantly proclaiming his intention to leave and set up his own firm. McGrath made use of the political skills he'd developed in years of corporate infighting to fashion a working alliance with Peters and Clark Bailey, who'd joined in early 1984 as the department's sixth senior member.

In the wake of the Northwest fiasco, Beck exacerbated the tensions within the group with his oddly aggressive inconsolability. Although Beck had always been an unusually democratic boss, now when he asked, "How am I doing?" he was seeking reassurance, not criticism, no matter how constructive. And he sought it relentlessly, calling members of the group in to discuss over and over again the same details of the same pending transactions. The other bankers came to dread being called to Beck's office, which once had functioned as a sort of clubhouse. Increasingly, they began ignoring the boss's summonses —but to no avail, for then Beck would come to their offices and camp out for ten or fifteen minutes. He just couldn't stand to be alone.

On the other hand, when someone needed Beck's advice, often he was nowhere to be found. In the first half of 1985, he took two separate vacations totaling seven weeks, from which he returned all charged up. After an initial flurry of inspired let's-get-back-to-basics sermons to the group, Beck's reborn intensity quickly vanished. He came in to work later and later in the morning and left earlier and earlier in the afternoon. His moods swung more violently than ever before, and he was often forgetful and fuzzy-headed. As McGrath, Peters, Sanzo, and the rest began broaching the delicate topic of his condition, Beck for the first time at work sought to justify his behavior by resorting to the Vietnam identity he'd used so effectively with Margo and with Sarah Lawson. Apropos of nothing much at all, he'd begin talking about his combat experience in Vietnam and then pull an article on post-traumatic stress disorder out of his briefcase. "This is my problem," he'd say.

Even after Beck admitted having lied about Vietnam, he insisted that *The Wall Street Journal* had erred in reporting that he had claimed that he was being blackmailed over some lurid photos of Margo. According to the *Journal*, Beck told McGrath and others that he'd already sent $250,000 to a secret Swiss bank account, but that his blackmailers were persisting in demanding cash. When McGrath accused him of lying, Beck looked him dead in the eye. "Want to see the pictures?" he said.

As a practical matter, the fortunes of the Jeff Beck Group depended not a whit on whether its founder had actually survived a Vietnam ambush or was in truth coming into a family fortune that he variously estimated at anywhere from a few hundred million to $1.5 billion dollars. But as the conflicting claims and stories piled up over Beck like an skyful of airplanes waiting for landing slots, he lost his credibility, a loss that in turn destroyed the very basis of his authority as M & A chief. It wasn't just the big lies he told, but the fact that he'd become pettily, pointlessly conspiratorial. When Beck had a juicy bit of gossip to pass along, he'd separately tell several members of the group that he was confiding in them alone and under strictest secrecy. Oppenheimer was far too small a place to get away with such games for long. "On every level, it became difficult to figure out what was real and not real with this guy," recalled Peters, who was Beck's friend of longest standing in the group. "You wanted to believe him on one hand, but on the other you didn't want to get suckered again."

By the spring of 1985, conditions within the department had become intolerable for all concerned, including Beck, who went to Robert and asked for a leave of absence. Meanwhile, McGrath and Sanzo each went separately to Robert and threatened to resign if Beck remained as M & A chief. While Peters decided against complaining to Robert, he began looking for work elsewhere, as did most of his colleagues.

Late one afternoon, Beck tried the handle on the door to McGrath's office. It was locked.

"Steve, open up, it's Jeff," Beck said.

"I'm busy, Jeff," McGrath replied. "Go away."

"Come on, man, it's me," Beck said.

"I know. Go away."

Beck turned in surprise to McGrath's secretary. "I guess he doesn't want to talk to me," he said quietly and wandered away.

15

Even as Beck was losing his grip at Oppenheimer, he continued to operate effectively as a rainmaker. Indeed, during the nightmarish months of early 1985 he planted the seeds of a transaction that would flower into one of the largest and most celebrated deals of the decade: the $8.2 billion buyout of Beatrice Companies by KKR in partnership with Don Kelly. Beck had begun contemplating the possibility of a Beatrice LBO only a few months after the Chicago food giant completed its $2.8 billion acquisition of Esmark in mid-1984. From the beginning, the stock market had not reacted well to the acquisition, largely because Beatrice was judged to have overpaid. Nor was Wall Street encouraged by the clumsy initial attempts of James Dutt, Beatrice's CEO, to blend the operations of the two huge companies. In the months after the deal, Beatrice's shares were marked down even as the stocks of other food producers continued their bull-market rise, opening a valuation gap that heightened the company's vulnerability to takeover.

Meanwhile, it had become clear to Beck—and to almost everyone who knew Kelly—that he was suffering a bad case of withdrawal from the perks and power of CEO-hood. It was evident, too, that Kelly harbored vindictive feelings about Beatrice, which, after all, had spoiled his carefully orchestrated deal with KKR. While Kelly had never let personal feelings distract him from his fiduciary duties to Esmark shareholders, over the years he'd usually found a way to get back at almost anyone who'd menaced his company or messed up one of his M & A deals. As for Kravis, Beck judged his desire to own a company as well known on Fifth Avenue as on Wall Street to be undiminished, even though KKR had completed some $7 billion worth of deals after losing Esmark to Beatrice.

Nonetheless, when Beck first floated the notion of a buyout of Beatrice he got nothing but grief and for months remained the idea's lone champion. To Steve McGrath, Sr., and Ron Peters, Beck's stubborn insistence on the inevitability of a Beatrice deal seemed no more plausible than his tales of Vietnam and family fortunes. McGrath was so vocal in opposing Beck's pursuit of a Beatrice LBO that he all but refused to work on it and wrote complaining memos to Steve Robert. Kelly, too, thought it "an outlandish idea," though he had no doubt that he could outmanage Dutt. "I took the idea seriously on the basis of unrealized values in the business, but I thought Dutt was secure in his position and that KKR never would have gone after him in any event," Kelly said. "Had we made an unfriendly offer with Dutt in there it would have been World Wars Three, Four, Five, *and* Six incorporated into one." In fact, it seemed to Beck, who was as perceptive in recognizing the symptoms of self-destruction in others as he was blind to them in himself, that Dutt had gone a bit wacko in his intensity. As Beck studied the situation, he concluded that eventually Beatrice's board would fire Dutt and turn to the man who knew Esmark best. Hence his $250,000 bet that Kelly would be Beatrice's next CEO.

Then, too, while the collapse of the Northwest Industries deal had left Kelly free to answer a distress call from the Beatrice board, he was peeved at Kravis—and none too happy with Beck, either. Relations among all members of the Kelly Briggs Oppenheimer contingent had been strained by postmortem finger pointing among all its members. However, in public anyway, Kelly magnanimously accepted the lion's share of blame. "If we'd done the deal, I'd have taken the credit," Kelly explained later. After the final round of Northwest articles appeared, Beck called Kelly to thank him for not criticizing Oppenheimer. For his part, Kelly continued to take Beck's phone calls—even after that infuriating meeting with Rainwater in Fort Worth. And why not? The Northwest transaction might have failed, but Kelly was still looking for deals to do and Beck remained a fertile source of deal opportunity. Relieved that his relationship with Kelly had survived, Beck set about repairing the Kelly-Kravis rift, which had opened wider than ever during the attempted buyout.

As Kelly Briggs Oppenheimer was struggling to arrange financing, Beck had tried to entice Kravis into the deal, bringing Kelly into KKR's offices. In Kelly's lengthy meeting with Kravis, almost every aspect of a prospective transaction was hashed over, including the percentage of the equity ownership that would go to Kelly, who left mightily encouraged. A few days later, though, Kravis decided that he didn't want any part of Northwest Industries and chose to break the news to Beck. Unlike Kelly, Beck really hadn't expected KKR to join the deal and was only mildly disappointed by Kravis's official verdict.

"Should I call Don?" Kravis asked.

"No," replied Beck. "Better let me." As Beck had expected, Kelly was miffed, feeling that Kravis had strung him along. Kravis later conceded that, by allowing what was intended as a theoretical discussion to proceed into such detail, he might have inadvertently led Kelly to believe that KKR had committed itself to backing the deal.

About a month after the Northwest deal collapsed, Beck met separately with Kelly and Kravis in hopes of effecting a rapprochement. Immediately after meeting with Beck, Kravis wrote Kelly a belated letter of condolence. "Even though KKR declined to participate in this particular transaction, our decision was based totally on the numbers," Kravis declared. "It was nothing personal." Kelly never wrote back. Instead, Kravis could read his response in the announcement that McGraw-Edison, a big Chicago industrial-equipment manufacturer, planned a leveraged buyout with Forstmann Little & Company, KKR's archrival. Kravis was doubly disappointed because he knew that Kelly was a director of McGraw-Edison. After nosing around a bit, Kravis learned that Kelly not only had favored Forstmann Little's bid but had paved its way to the extent that he was in line for a finder's fee.

Kravis called Beck. "Why didn't you guys come to us instead of Forstmann Little?" he demanded.

"Kelly went to them on his own," Beck said. "And anyway he's upset with you because, one, he feels you misled him with all this talk of equity participations on Northwest and, two, because you didn't call and tell him yourself that you were out on Northwest."

"You said not to," said Kravis, his temper rising. "You were the one who should have clarified the situation for him."

"Right, Henry," Beck said sarcastically. "My relationship with Kelly isn't so great anymore either."

Kravis immediately called Kelly and apologized for any "miscommunication" between them. "I feel terrible," Kravis said. "I didn't know anything about how you felt." His message delivered, Kelly was conciliatory. "Forget it," he said. "It's over now."

Beck served as intermediary in arranging a bury-the-hatchet lunch, also attended by George Roberts, at KKR's offices and on subsequent negotiations of a formal alliance between Kelly and KKR. The lunch went well, though there remained many details to work out. "You know," Kelly said to Beck afterward, "not getting Northwest might turn out to be the best thing that could have happened."

Like Kelly, Jim Dutt had inherited a company imprisoned by a glorious past. Founded in 1898 in the small Nebraska town from which it took its name, Beatrice was an old-line dairy company that in the 1950s and 1960s was transformed by a genial, gimlet-eyed ex-lawyer named William Karnes into one of the great American growth companies. On Wall Street, Beatrice was classed with IBM as a paragon of corporate dynamism and solidity, though, in contrast to IBM, the vehicle of Beatrice's preeminence was the acquisition. During its heyday, Beatrice made more acquisitions than any company in America—more than three hundred—as it put together a string of quarterly earnings increases that stretched unbroken through twenty-nine years. While its acquisitiveness suggests profligacy, Karnes actually was an extraordinarily disciplined deal man who engineered a huge return to Beatrice shareholders over the years. He bought only small, healthy companies with narrow product lines and higher profit margins than Beatrice itself. Practicing what was once described as "religious devotion to decentralization," Karnes encouraged the founders of acquired companies to remain and operate as they had previously, providing them with capital and as much help from headquarters as requested. Many did stay, and their companies continued to thrive.

Karnes's formula worked beautifully until the early 1970s, when Wall Street became less enamored of growth and more conscious of profitability, particularly as measured by return on equity. Beatrice's return on equity was respectable but seemingly immutable. Because the company was able to post only tiny improvements in its rate of profitability, its stock went nowhere throughout the 1970s. Many of the little companies Karnes had acquired over the years had reached the limits of growth, sapped of vibrancy by the retirement of their founders and the consolidation of the industries in which they competed. The regional brands that Beatrice owned by the hundreds were getting squeezed off supermarket shelves as consolidation put more marketing and advertising muscle behind national brands. The company had become unmanageable, a vast mixed bag of quasi-autonomous businesses loosely organized into 430 separate profit centers. By the time Karnes retired in 1976, the very concept of Beatrice was outmoded.

Dutt, a former dairyman who'd joined Beatrice from college, was a product of the cult of Karnes; after he was named CEO in 1979, Dutt installed a bronze bust of Karnes at headquarters, and on the cover of his first annual report proclaimed his fealty to "a growth formula that has proven itself for the past 28 years, and one we're going to stick with"—though Dutt did acknowledge the need to get the company's stock moving again by boosting profits. However, the Street was not impressed with Dutt's modest initial efforts to rationalize Beatrice by divesting businesses that didn't meet his new profitability criteria, and was overtly skeptical when he shifted focus from streamlining back to expanding the company through its largest acquisition ever. Foreshadowing his excessive bid for Esmark, Dutt in 1981 paid an enormous premium—22 times earnings—for the soft drink division of Northwest Industries. By mid-1982 Beatrice's market value had fallen to $1.8 billion from $3.7 billion at Karnes's retirement.

The opprobrium Wall Street heaped on Dutt's head after the beverage acquisition seemed to affect him constructively at first. In 1983, Dutt announced a two-year plan of drastic reorganization. For the first time, he began promoting his own "vision" of Beatrice as the next Procter & Gamble—meaning a centralized, marketing-driven company that put big bucks behind a stable of national brands. Dutt finally got a bit of provisional respect from Wall Street as he began consolidating businesses, eliminating hundreds of superfluous jobs in the process.

Somewhere along the line, though, Dutt crossed the line separating conviction from megalomania. Once an affable and rather low-key manager, he was transformed into a fiery-tempered autocrat who pounded tables and harangued underlings relentlessly with his vision—and his image. In every Beatrice plant throughout the world was installed a large photograph of Dutt. The CEO began reviewing every press release, sometimes ordering five or more rewrites, and decided to try to write his own corporate slogan after rejecting all eleven thousand suggestions generated though an employee contest. The authorship of the slogan adopted—"We're Beatrice"—was never publicly established. Dutt was so intent on increasing Beatrice's profile that only the unified opposition of other key executives stopped him from putting the company's name on every one of the thousands of products it manufactured. Dutt committed $30 million to sponsor Grand Prix racing teams and another $30 million for corporate-image ads during the 1984 Olympics. When asked how all the money spent pounding the name Beatrice into consumer brains was going to sell more Stiffel lamps, Waterloo toolboxes, or Martha White cake mix, Dutt sounded like the profligate owner of a major-league team: "We're willing to spend the money to be a winner."

Wall Street's old doubts about Dutt gained new currency, punishing the company's stock. As takeover rumors began buffeting Beatrice, Dutt gave a speech at a food-industry conference in Florida. Asked an innocuous question about the prospect of a deal, Dutt slammed the podium with his fist. "I've spent my whole life working at Beatrice," he said angrily. "Our people have worked very hard. We're street fighters. No one is going to move in and harvest the results."

And especially not Don Kelly, who'd earned Dutt's enmity by greenmailing Beatrice. Dutt got revenge of sorts by topping KKR's buyout bid for Esmark, though in the process he made a mockery of his avowed strategy of consolidation. To foreclose the possibility of a rival offer, Dutt had topped his own bid, adding nearly $200 million to the cost of the $2.8 billion deal, which was financed wholly through borrowing. Dutt, who'd recently separated from his wife (she would soon sue him for divorce on grounds of mental cruelty) held hands with his thirty-two-year-old assistant, Kathleen Kallman, all through the formal meeting at which the final papers were signed on the Esmark deal. After the big acquisition, Dutt threw his much-ballyhooed restructuring plan into reverse. Deciding that the company was now too big to be run directly from headquarters, Dutt began decentralizing the only-recently-centralized company. Many Wall Streeters simply gave up on Beatrice, which, as one disgusted observer put it, "has left skid marks in three directions."

Only two days after Dutt was officially elected chairman of Esmark, he purged the widely respected chief of its food operations, Fred Rentschler. Initially, Dutt had told Rentschler that he'd be put in charge of combining the food businesses of the merged companies. As Dutt and Rentschler got to talking after the deal, though, they found themselves in disagreement over basic issues—including Dutt's pet "We're Beatrice" campaign, which Rentschler criticized as a senseless diversion of funds from promoting product lines.

"How are you going to work with my people?" Dutt asked.

"If I do my job, my principal effort will be never to surprise you," said Rentschler, a forthright, independent sort who'd thrived under Kelly's hands-off management. "I'll be in touch as often as suits your style. But I would hope that our relationship would be close enough where it wouldn't be necessary to have excessive contact."

Dutt moved forward to the edge of his chair and thrust his face a few inches from Rentschler's. "I can't do that," he said excitedly and began fluttering the fingers of both hands next to his ears, "because I've been burned before."

Shortly thereafter, Dutt sent two underlings out to California to fire Rentschler, who was told that he had five minutes to vacate the premises. His replacement was hanging out at a local coffee shop, awaiting word of Rentschler's exit. Dutt put out the word to the press that Rentschler hadn't been offered a job at the new Beatrice. "We need team players and teamwork," said his PR mouthpiece.

News of Rentschler's ouster in August 1984, piqued Beck's interest. He was following the turmoil at Beatrice from afar much as a reporter would, making phone calls, searching company documents, collecting articles—many of which announced a high-level firing or resignation. The other top executive from Esmark, Joel Smilow, resigned in disgust, lasting only a few months longer than had Rentchsler. Beck waited until April 1985 to pitch Kravis on a Beatrice deal. By this time, the stock-market valuation gap between Beatrice and other food producers yawned most invitingly and Beck was convinced that the basic economics of a buyout made more sense than ever, even though Beatrice was weighed down with debt from its acquisition of Esmark. On paper anyway, the two companys' food businesses fit together quite nicely, though Dutt had just begun the complex process of realizing the enormous potential economic benefits by actually merging them. Strategically, Dutt's big mistake lay in trying at the same time to hang onto all sorts of nonfood businesses, including Avis and Playtex, that could be easily detached and sold separately for a higher value than the stock market was placing on them as part of Beatrice.

Kravis was immediately intrigued with the idea of busting up Beatrice through an LBO. Like Kelly, though, he believed that a deal was impossible as long as Dutt was CEO. After first broaching the subject of Beatrice with Kravis, Beck flew out to San Francisco to pitch the idea of a Beatrice buyout to Roberts, who was regarded as more analytically astute than his cousin. Roberts was interested but busy. Three days after Beck's visit, KKR announced a bid that would lead to the largest of its pre-Beatrice buyouts: a $2.5 billion deal for Storer Communications, the fifth-largest cable TV operator.

Beck hired his lawyer buddy Jack MacAtee to begin analyzing the legal aspects of a Beatrice buyout and shifted his promoting focus to the Kelly side of the equation. Kelly was becoming interested in spite of himself as he worked through preliminary cash-value and asset-value numbers with Beck and members of his staff. The project gained considerable momentum when Kelly recruited Rentschler and Smilow to the cause. Among them, Kelly, Rentschler, and Smilow probably knew more about Beatrice's operations than any trio of executives still in Dutt's employ. Rentschler and Smilow were not only indignant at Dutt's high-handed treatment but frustrated at having been interrupted in their work. The two operating executives were convinced, in addition, that Dutt had made a grievous, fundamental mistake in trying to force all the Esmark operations into the existing Beatrice structure, since Hunt-Wesson and Swift had far stronger and more efficient marketing and distribution systems. "I will go to my grave believing that if someone hadn't come along and reversed course at Beatrice, it was headed for disaster," Rentschler said.

While Beck was agonizing through his final months at Oppenheimer, things were getting curiouser and curiouser at Beatrice as Dutt impersonated Howard Hughes. The company's other top operating executives had no idea of Dutt's whereabouts for days at a time. He'd taken to spending much of his time flying around in his Gulfstream III inspecting Beatrice's far-flung international operations, instructing his secretary to inform no one of his itinerary. Dutt was not much more accessible when he was in Chicago. Any executive who wished to meet with him had to submit a written request to Kallman, to whom Dutt had delegated the power to approve or deny such requests. Near the end, Dutt ordered the offices next to his vacated and began to suspect former Esmark employees and even directors of plotting against him. According to Sam Casey, the former CEO of the Pullman Company and a longtime director of Esmark, Dutt went so far as to put a tail on him. Casey, who was working in Chicago as a consultant to an accounting firm, had come across a prospective buyer for an Esmark subsidiary that Dutt had put on the block. He immediately called Dutt, whom he'd known since his days as an ice-cream salesman in Pittsburgh.

"I'm sorry, Mr. Casey," said Dutt's secretary. "Mr. Dutt is not here at the moment."

"Can I reach him this afternoon?" Casey asked.

"No, he's out of town," he replied.

"Well, is there somewhere else I can reach him?"

"Now, I know you know Mr. Dutt, but I'm not allowed to tell you where he is," she said. "I'm sorry."

The next day Dutt returned and called Casey, "You are no longer welcome in any Beatrice office and I don't want you to talk to anyone here who used to work at Esmark," said Dutt, who threatened to turn the matter of Casey's "security violation" over to the FBI. "I know what you're doing. You're trying to break our security."

The hot-tempered Casey flipped. "Fuck you, Dutt!" he shouted. "I've forgotten more about security than you'll ever know. If I wanted to break your security, I would. And another thing, Dutt, take my fucking name out of your Rolodex, you ice-cream salesman."

While using every bit of his rainmaker's guile to goose a Beatrice buyout along, Beck was unable to halt the continuing degeneration of his merger group into near paralysis. Ideally, Beck would have been relieved of his administrative duties as head of the M & A department, given a figurehead title like vice chairman, and been encouraged to devote himself wholly to managing his own client relationships and bringing in new business. However, Beck's rehabilitation into a free-lance senior rainmaker would have required a significant change in attitude on the part not only of his M & A colleagues but of Steve Robert, who was not secure enough in his authority as CEO to let anyone float free of the firm's official power structure—especially the founder of the firm's single most profitable department. Given Beck's unparalleled ability to bring in the bucks, though, Robert might well have taken the risk of unchaining the Mad Dog had not Beck over the years made himself such a politically subversive force within Oppenheimer.

The disputes in which Beck was almost continually embroiled ranged from serious matters of policy to petty bureaucratic bullshit. Most notably—and justifiably—Beck made himself a nuisance in objecting to the conflicts of interest inherent in the overlapping ownership of Odyssey Partners, Junction Partners, and Oppenheimer. At the same time, he was a forceful, at times belligerent advocate of the economic interests of his group, successfully lobbying for an increase in the M & A group's profit-sharing cut from 25 percent to 45 percent of its income after expenses. But Beck also would go to the mat on something as trivial as office remodeling. "We will not contribute one dime to the payment of service until everything is rectified to our standards," Beck wrote in a memo to Opco's chief operating officer. "The incompetence on this job is overwhelming, as I am sure many of my colleagues will support. The list of mistakes goes from wall papering to improper furniture and coordination of the office furniture to the dimensions of each individual office. . . . It is my opinion that these people should be terminated immediately and that for once we hire competent advisors."

The Jeff Beck Group feuded most bitterly with the department with which its activities overlapped most closely: corporate finance. The basic issue, as always on the Street, was money. An impressive number of the corporate clients brought in by the M & A group decided to also use Oppenheimer to manage the underwriting of new securities issues. While a portion of the underwriting fees was credited to M & A, the department's cut was never large enough to satisfy Beck. As the M & A group blossomed into one of Oppenheimer's most profitable divisions, Beck dispensed with any semblance of tact, becoming openly contemptuous of his corporate-finance colleagues' abilities and increasingly shrill in his complaints—especially when it came to protecting his turf, no matter how petty the incursion. When he discovered that the corporate-finance department had run a magazine ad offering for sale a steel mill in Alabama, Beck immediately dashed off a memo to Gantcher, the president of Opco. "The ad appeared right next to a Goldman Sachs tombstone and needless to say this has caused us some grief in the marketplace."

At the same time, Beck went out of his way to personally antagonize Robert. It was Beck's contention, which he often made to his M & A colleagues and which doubtless got back to Robert, that Nash had picked Robert as his successor because he wanted someone he could bully from afar even after he'd severed his official ties with Oppenheimer. Robert was indeed more thoughtful than decisive, and he was afflicted with an unfortunate nervous tic; in moments of tension, he had a habit of opening his eyes and his mouth wide in seeming astonishment. Beck called Robert "the silent screamer." As his M & A group started bringing in big bucks, Beck let his disdain for Robert show in pointlessly provocative behavior. For example, in mid-1984, Robert had appeared on a cable-television show in New York to offer advice on managing an investment portfolio. Beck watched and later sent his boss a letter and a dollar bill.

Dear Mr. Robert,
   Because of your most sincere demeanor and your obvious knowledge, I was wondering whether you could adopt me as one of the following:

- an older son
- a younger uncle
- a middle-aged brother

After seeing the program, I would even settle for a distant cousin.
   In any event could you please consider managing my portfolio. All you have to do is double the enclosed dollar each day and after one year you and I could retire for the rest of our lives.
   Let me put it another way—I could retire for the rest of my life.

After receiving the letter, Robert immediately called Beck into his office and demanded to know what he meant by it. It's a joke, Beck explained unconvincingly. Robert screamed silently.

In retrospect, Beck would accuse Robert of having deliberately inflamed the resentments of his M & A colleagues in surreptitiously organizing his ouster. For his part, Robert insisted that he and Gantcher tried to intervene as little as possible in the M & A department's mounting strife. "We delayed and agonized over it, hoping some Solomon-like solution would come forth," said Robert.

It was with a feeling of foreboding that Beck left on June first for a month's vacation in the south of France at the Hôtel du Cap d'Antibes. In Beck's absence, the department ground to a halt. While Beck later accused his colleagues of "plotting a palace revolution," McGrath, Sanzo, Peters, and the rest were spending most of their time sitting together disconsolately in someone's office, wondering out loud what to do. By this time, almost every member of the group had been interviewing at other firms. Some had job offers. All were worried about maintaining their standard of living, which, in each case, had vastly improved since joining Opco. Could the old spirit be revived in time to prevent a precipitous decline in their annual incomes? Hell, the way it was going they couldn't be sure there would even *be* an M & A department in six months.

David Aaron had been the first to resign. He'd taken a leave of absence to work on Walter Mondale's failed presidential campaign and

had returned to find an M & A department that had markedly
changed in the interim. "There were deep tensions within the group
that I didn't understand and that weren't being directly addressed,"
Aaron recalled. The malaise contributed to Aaron's realization that he
wasn't cut out for a career on Wall Street. He'd already begun work on
his first novel and in March 1985, left Opco to devote himself fully to
writing—as Beck had urged him to do. Beck was not so understanding,
though, when Norm Brown called him in France to say that he was
taking a job at Beck's old firm, DLJ. Although Brown's productivity
had never quite measured up to expectations and Beck had encouraged
him to begin looking for work elsewhere, he'd expected Brown to let
him know when he started job hunting.

When Beck returned to the office on July second, everyone seemed
tense, guarded. At an executive-committee meeting, someone made a
crack about Beck's "fifty-thousand-dollar tan." The mood was no
friendlier at an M & A staff meeting later in the day, though Beck had
good news: The CEO of Akzo, Arnout Loudon, who'd been Beck's
guest at the Hôtel du Cap, had retained the group for a major transaction, as had Varian Associates. He also brought them up to date on the
progress of the Beatrice LBO. On this July afternoon, though, none of
Beck's colleagues seemed to give a damn about Beatrice or, for that
matter, anything else Beck had to say. After the meeting, Beck took
McGrath and Peters aside for a private word. Beck had barely got a
few words out before McGrath said he had better things to do. As
McGrath walked away, he waved a scornful good-bye. Beck turned to
Peters for an explanation. Peters was looking at the ground.

Later in the day, Beck went to see Robert to discuss his future with
the firm. Robert proposed that Beck be kicked upstairs to a position as
vice chairman of Oppenheimer and that McGrath move up to head
of the corporate-finance department, while Sanzo took the post of
M & A chief. Although Beck himself had proposed such an arrangement earlier, he told Robert that he needed some time to think it over.
Five days later, he met again with Robert and Gantcher.

"We're not going to be able to make you vice chairman after all,"
Robert said. "People are just too hot."

Beck was too tired to remonstrate. He just stared.

"I'd like to propose an indefinite-leave-of-absence scenario," Robert
said. "That way we can minimize client drainage."

Beck's anger flared. "Forget it," he said. "I'll stick around for thirty
days but no longer."

"I'm sorry it had to come to this, Jeff," Robert continued.

Beck cut him off. "No, you're not. You fed it."

Feeling more defeated than angry, Beck wrote a memo to the executive committee explaining his decision to leave and listened without comment as Robert read over the telephone a press release that would go out the next morning. Beck met briefly with McGrath and Sanzo to mediate a discussion of revenue-splitting arrangements between the M & A and corporate-finance departments and then headed home in a deep funk. As humiliating as it was to have lost his job for the second time in his career, what really hurt was the feeling of having been betrayed. At Lehman Brothers, it only had been Eric Gleacher who'd turned against him. In leaving Oppenheimer, Beck felt universally double-crossed; even Peters, his oldest friend, had in the end knifed him. At home, he held baby Katherine on his lap and said nothing. Margo had never seen him lower.

Beck returned to Oppenheimer the next morning determined to "act with dignity." He put on his most ebullient face, kidding around with his colleagues just like in the old days. "That," Beck recalled, "was the hardest acting job of all." About eleven o'clock, Robert, Gantcher, and the twelve members of the Jeff Beck Group gathered in a conference room. As Beck entered he noticed that most of his colleagues were looking at their shoes. Sanzo spoke first. Eyes welling with tears, Sanzo lauded Beck for the unique accomplishment of having built an M & A department at a firm without a corporate-finance franchise. Beck was touched in spite of himself. McGrath spoke next, mainly about his plans for the future. Then Robert and Gantcher rose and spoke a few words in tribute to Beck, who wasn't buying any of it. Then it was Beck's turn. He began to speak in a voice husky with emotion.

"I guess everybody knew about the third act but me, and now here it is," he said. "But I guess all of us can be proud of the first act." He paused, struggling to keep his composure. "If there's anything I can be helpful with in terms of the transition, I'd like to do that. I will always be proud of having founded this group. I hope everybody has a lot of fun and makes a lot of money."

At about two o'clock that afternoon, Beck was sitting morosely in his office when he got a call from a *Wall Street Journal* reporter, who, alerted by Robert's press release, was writing a little piece on the realignment of duties at Oppenheimer & Company. The reporter said that she'd already spoken to Robert and that he had implied that Beck had actually been fired. Beck stifled his annoyance over this parting double-cross and played the interview according to the script, even mustering a dash of humor that made it into the story, which ran on July eleventh. It read:

> Jeffrey Beck, who had headed mergers and acquisitions, will take a leave of absence from the firm. Mr. Beck, who started the firm's merger unit, said he had recommended reshaping the firm's investment-banking management. "I think of myself as an entrepreneur-builder," more than a manager, he added. Mr. Beck said he wanted a chance to pay attention to his outside investments and interests, which included his first child, born last September.
>
> "Superman," he said, "only exists in the movies."

16

Halfway between Nice and Cannes on the Côte d'Azur, a tiny
finger of land juts into the Mediterranean. At the tip of this
peninsula is one of the great hotels of the world, the Hôtel du Cap
d'Antibes. Although the Hôtel du Cap is not a small establishment, it
has managed to shield itself almost completely from detection by the
ordinary tourist. Only one very discreet sign on the the twisting two-
lane coastal road connecting Nice and Cannes announces the hotel,
which is largely obscured from view by a hedgerow. While the main
building is visible through the opening created by the driveway, a
motorist can peer in only at risk of serious accident, since the entryway
to the hotel coincides with a treacherous bend in the road. After a
week at the manicured oasis of luxury that is the Hôtel du Cap, it
seemed to me plausible, even likely, that the placement of the driveway was the result not of happenstance but design. For the Hôtel du
Cap d'Antibes exemplified an aristocratic aesthetic of *private* luxury
that was more than just an ocean removed from the tabloid peacockery
of that epitome of the 1980s American tycoon, Donald Trump. Naturally, the Hôtel du Cap's aura of Old World exclusivity made it irresistible to the new-money moguls of the takeover game.

Beck came fairly early in the parade, making his first visit to the
Hôtel du Cap in 1982. He'd returned at least once every year, usually
during June, and since marrying Margo had taken to spending September at the hotel as well. After his ouster from Oppenheimer, Beck
returned as planned to the south of France in September of 1985, and
I went with him. During those last stormy weeks at Oppenheimer,
Beck had proposed that we write a book based on his experiences on
the Street. Over the next few months, we got together fairly often to
talk over the idea. Depending on his mood, the working title swung
from *Adventures of a Wall Street Deal Man* to *Confessions of a Wall*

Street Deal Man, though once we got down to it, I realized that "accusations" was really the operative word. We shook hands on the project in New York and flew to France intending to start the interviews on which the book would be based.

A limousine sent by the Hôtel du Cap awaited us at the Nice airport. It was a twenty-minute ride to the hotel, where the assistant manager and concierge were on hand to greet M. Beck with most efficient effusion. Only after we'd walked through the lobby and out the rear double doors onto the terrace did the magnificence of the setting become apparent. The main building, a palatial villa, sits atop a gentle hill two hundred yards from the sea, amid fragrant stands of olive, pine, and cedar. Aside from its wooden shutters and filigreed iron balconies, which are painted light blue, the villa is the color of cream and on sunny days—and almost every day is sunny here—it takes on so rich a glow that it appears lit from within. A wide boulevard connects the main building to Eden Roc Pavillon, a restaurant and adjoining swimming pool, built into cliffs of dark basalt. Eden Roc's terrace opens onto a broad vista that stretches from the low-lying island of Sainte-Marguerite across the iridescent blue expanse of the Golfe de Juan to the pastels of the city of Cannes and the green foothills of the Esterel rising behind it.

This spectacular panorama has a long history of bedazzling wealthy Americans, the first of whom arrived in the 1920s following a trail blazed by the ultrafashionable Gerald and Sarah Murphy, the wealthy American expatriates memorialized in *Living Well Is the Best Revenge.* At the time of the Murphys' first visit to Antibes, in 1922, the American smart set wouldn't have dreamed of summering anywhere but Newport, Palm Beach, or Deauville. The Murphys had come down from Paris to visit Cole Porter, who'd rented a château for the summer. The songwriter didn't care for Antibes, but the Murphys returned the next spring, taking a room at the Hôtel du Cap. Although the hotel (which dates from the 1870s) normally closed in May for the summer, the Murphys convinced the owner to stay open throughout the summers of 1923 and 1924 and invited their friends to visit. Among those who dropped by were Pablo Picasso, Ernest Hemingway, Rudolph Valentino, and Scott and Zelda Fitzgerald, who liked to top off their nightly revels by diving into the sea from the thirty-five-foot bluffs into which Eden Roc later was built. "One could get away with more on the summer Riviera, and whatever happened seemed to have something to do with art," Fitzgerald wrote, explaining his preference for Antibes over Palm Beach. "Pretty much of anything went at Antibes—by 1929, at the most gorgeous paradise for swimmers on the Mediterranean no one swam any more, save for a short hangover dip at noon."

The summer Riviera survived the great Wall Street crash of October 1929 and a local event of more cataclysmic impact: the departure of the Murphys, who in 1933 closed their private villa and returned to New York. By this time the hotel had been renamed the Grand Hôtel du Cap d'Antibes and its brand new Eden Roc swimming pool was becoming a summer adjunct to the American film colony at Cannes. At the Hôtel du Cap the likes of Clark Gable, Gary Cooper, and Darryl Zanuck rubbed shoulders with European royalty and industrialists from all over the world. When Edward VIII of England abdicated in 1936 to marry an American divorcée, the world's most famous honeymooners spent a week at the Hôtel du Cap as the Duke and Duchess of Windsor. The self-made Argentine meat mogul, Alfredo Fortibra, would arrive every summer with two Rolls-Royces—one for himself and one for the chauffeur whom he never used. For years, Joseph P. Kennedy spent his summers in Antibes, conducting his various machinations from a cabana at the hotel. While still a U.S. senator from Massachusetts, John F. Kennedy stayed at the hotel with his new bride, Jacqueline Bouvier. To the amusement of other guests, Jack and Jackie foreshadowed their domestic difficulties in the White House by staying at opposite ends of the hotel. Television's rise brought a new breed of Hollywood tycoon, including Johnny Carson and Bill Cosby.

I would have had little chance on my own of getting a room at the Hôtel du Cap, which was as much a private club as a commercial hostelry. To be sure, the cashier was perfectly happy to accept your money (cash only, *s'il vous plaît*) and lots of it. But money alone won't buy a room at the Hôtel du Cap. When it opens in April, the hotel is pretty much booked through to its mid-October close. Minions of the Sheik of Qatar once tried to book five rooms on short notice for the entire month of August and had to be told repeatedly that there was simply no room at any price. Most guests are repeat visitors; many arrive on the same date, stay in the same room, occupy the same seaside cabana, sit at the same table in Eden Roc and pass out gratuities to the same concierges, waiters, bartenders, and attendants year after year. The few vacancies created by last-minute cancellations are filled by referrals from guests. But any newcomer who bullies the staff, undertips, complains about prices, or otherwise acts the boor will find that the hotel has no room next summer or ever again. As Jean-Claude Irondelle, the hotel's suavely imperious managing director, was fond of saying: "You can have a bad guest once, but twice? *Mais non!*"

Over the years, Beck had cultivated Irondelle and other important members of the hotel staff as assiduously as he'd ever courted any CEO, dispensing magnanimous tips and good humor in equal measure. Beck incorporated the Hôtel du Cap into his rainmaker's routine with great purposefulness. He got a good deal of social mileage merely out of helping people get into the hotel. Ray and Bessie Kravis, Henry's parents, who'd left just before we arrived, were the most recent in a lengthy list of first-time guests Beck had sponsored. Richard Rainwater was another. Beck's own stays at the hotel were working vacations to the extent that he always invited a CEO or two to join him there for a week at a time. If all the world was a deal-making stage to Beck, the Hôtel du Cap was his Great White Way. He was ensconced in the hotel's best lodgings, a three-bedroom villa conspicuously situated about twenty yards off the boulevard connecting the main building to Eden Roc. Informally known as the owner's villa, it was the only stand-alone residence on the grounds. In the driveway were two Mercedes sedans that Beck had rented, one of which was for Margo, who in a few days would be joining him.

Beck had come to the hotel determined to exercise himself into shape; within a half hour of our arrival, we were on the tennis courts, taking on the hotel's two teaching pros in a doubles match. As a teenager in the 1960s I'd spent my summers playing tennis tournaments throughout the upper Midwest. By the time I stepped on the Hôtel du Cap's superb clay courts, though, there was more rust on my game than game left. It was quickly apparent that we were badly overmatched against Antoine and his son, Patrick. However, Beck seemed too intent on winning to notice that we didn't stand a chance. Though he carried an extra twenty pounds, he was fairly quick afoot and strong enough to pound the ball pretty hard despite badly flawed technique—all arm, no leg. After five minutes of play in moderate heat, his shirt was soaked through with sweat. Beck made a lot of noise, grunting and groaning on every shot. A couple of his line calls were awfully close. After muffing an easy volley, he thrashed the net with his racquet, shouting "No, no, no, no." The outburst stopped play four courts down. We lost, 6–2, 6–1, in the first of a dozen ritual thrashings over the next week.

The other staple of Beck's daily workout was swimming. Ignoring the chic and crowded poolside scene at Eden Roc, Beck swam in the ocean and sunbathed in one of the private cabanas scattered about on a broad swath of rocky seascape adjoining Eden Roc. These were green-and-white thatched-hut affairs about the size of a Manhattan studio apartment but more sturdily constructed. Renting one of these seaside bungalows was one of the truest measures of status at the hotel, which had only twenty-five cabanas to accommodate its 170 guests. Beck occupied one of the largest and best-situated of the cabanas and rarely left it during the sunlight hours except to swim or to swat tennis balls. He spent endless hours on the telephone, calling all around the world. Christian, the hotel's sausage-fingered 225-pound masseur, made daily calls with his portable table. Beck got on as well with Christian as with Antoine. They swapped hotel gossip and off-color jokes and laughed their way through the language barrier. To Christian's boundless amusement, Beck would occasionally thump his chest and let loose with an earsplitting Tarzan yell. He'd keep up the caterwauling until a frowning head or two popped out of the neighboring cabanas. Then, apparently satisfied, he'd stop.

Beck's deliberate rowdiness didn't seem to have hurt him with the hotel's management. Irondelle himself stopped by several times to pay his respects. Beck introduced me as a reporter for *Business Week* and lavished praise upon Irondelle, who swelled with pride under the verbal caress like some giant Gallic puffer fish. Beck liked to call him *le roi* —the king—though never to his face.

In the evenings, when Beck's preternatural supplies of energy ran low, he and I sat on the terrace of the villa and talked. Usually, I took notes. He looked a bit frazzled but seemed in pretty good spirits, except when the subject was Oppenheimer. While Beck was vowing revenge against Robert, McGrath, and the others, he stared at me with such laser-beam fury that I was occasionally unnerved into feeling that he'd mistaken me for one of his betrayers. Although by his own admission Beck had "the attention span of a butterfly," once he began unburdening himself he could hold forth for hours. One evening we began talking at twilight, as the other guests were strolling down to Eden Roc for dinner, and didn't stop until the sky was beginning to lighten over the Mediterranean and preparations for breakfast were under way on the terrace of the hotel.

Left to his own devices, Beck would spend the entire day at the villa, on the tennis court, or in his private cabana. It wasn't that Beck wasn't

interested in the goings-on at the hotel. Indeed, he'd assembled an
intelligence network made up of members of the staff who kept him
supplied with up-to-the-minute gossip about famous hotel guests and
their antics. But he seemed to have absolutely no interest in seeing
these people in action and indeed did what he could to avert chance
meetings. Instead of traversing the main boulevard, we'd move between the tennis courts and the cabana by a less-traveled back path.
He preferred swimming alone in the ocean to the crowded Eden Roc
pool and he had his breakfast delivered to the villa every morning and
his lunch to the cabana almost every afternoon. Some nights, we even
had room-service dinner in the villa. Having at great expense and by
dint of great effort occupied the most visible of lodgings at one of the
world's most social resort hotels, Beck was curiously reclusive.

One afternoon after our daily tennis humiliation, I suggested that
we do some sunbathing at the Eden Roc pool, which is the social
center of the Hôtel du Cap. It was the first and only time in my week
at the hotel that we hung out at the pool. A few dozen sunbathers
were scattered around us on foam mats. Diamonds, gold, and exposed
breasts were everywhere. Waiters in sneakers and blue-and-white-
striped French sailor jerseys padded soundlessly by with trays of drinks
and little dishes of green olives and potato chips. Behind us, three
potbellied Americans smoked cigars and talked California real estate.
Below, a woman of about thirty was swimming alone, traversing the
entire length of the pool with a few smoothly powerful breaststrokes,
waist-length blond hair trailing behind her in perfect fantail symmetry.
The effect was surreal. Beck and I noticed her simultaneously and were
transfixed.

"Look," said Beck quietly. "It's a mermaid."

After completing her swim, the mermaid returned to the terrace
and lay down on a mat next to a dark-haired woman.

"Do you want to meet her?" he asked.

"Do you know her?" I said.

"It doesn't matter," he replied. "I know what to do."

We withdrew to the cabana to plot strategy. Beck summoned the
head cabana attendant, an amiable middle-aged woman named Mag-
gie who'd worked at the Hôtel du Cap for many years and seemed
overjoyed daily at the mere sight of M. Beck. From her, we learned
that the mermaid was a local—an Antibes resident who swam almost
daily but didn't stay at the hotel. She was unmarried and was fluent in
English. Beck arranged to have a bottle of Roederer Cristal cham-

pagne delivered to the mermaid and her companion at poolside with a
card inviting them to come to the villa for dinner that night. Twenty
minutes later, we received a handwritten and rather formal note of
acceptance on personal stationery. When our guests arrived that evening, a spread of Beluga caviar and two more bottles of Cristal
awaited. We went to dinner at Le Bacon, a three-star restaurant a few
miles from the hotel on the road to Nice. The maitre d' recognized
Beck and led us to one of the best tables. The Cristal continued to
flow freely as a great time was had by all.

I saw this woman frequently over the next few days, though my
interest abruptly vanished after she showed me her National Front
card in a restaurant at Mougins and made this outrageous statement:
"Better that one million Chinese die than to have my cat suffer for
one day." I don't think she was kidding. At least, she took great offense when I defended the Chinese. Beck would constantly grill me
for details about my wooing of the mermaid and offered minutely
detailed advice on where to take her and even what to say to her. He
stopped just short of writing me a script. The vicarious pleasure Beck
derived from this seemed to have little to do with sex or romance. For
him, matchmaking was a tactical challenge, a sort of leisure-time sub-
stitute for corporate-merger making.

Beck's obsessiveness was not always so benignly directed, as I discovered one night when I walked into an ambush of sorts at the villa. One
moment he was making small talk and the next he was in my face,
angrily accusing me of double-crossing him. I gathered that he'd been
on the phone with someone in New York who'd told him that the
word at *Business Week* was that I was writing a book other than the
one we'd been discussing. I denied it and for fifteen minutes we stood
face-to-face yelling at each other, until he realized that I was telling
the truth. The next day, he apologized profusely and I accepted,
though I remained shaken by his paranoia and resentful of his tactics.
Beck's fury was all the more unfathomable because of the seeming
tenuousness of his own commitment to our project. For a man who'd
sworn off the deal game forever, Beck sure seemed to spend an awful
lot of his time on urgent transatlantic telephone calls—even during
our tennis matches. The phone at courtside had a habit of ringing at
inopportune moments, summoning Beck for a few minutes of cryptic
conversation at set point.

* * *

One afternoon, Beck surprised me by suggesting that we have lunch at Eden Roc. The maître d' led us to what seemed to be the best table in the place, right on the rail of a balcony that jutted out into the sea. It was a spectacular day, hot and dazzlingly clear. The outline of an ocean liner was visible on the horizon, which today seemed to reach halfway to Corsica. Beck ordered a bottle of Cristal. He rarely drank at lunch, but today, apparently, was a special occasion of some sort. After a half hour of deal chitchat, Beck asked me what I thought of the Hôtel du Cap. I enthused appropriately.

Beck turned his head and gazed off at the ocean liner. "I'm glad you like it," he said with a cryptic little smile. "Because I own it."

This startling claim served as a prelude to the even more fantastic tale of Rosebud, which Beck unfurled during my remaining days at the Hôtel du Cap. The story began in 1974, when he was beginning his deal-making apprenticeship at DLJ. Two small-time insurance executives from Omaha had come to DLJ looking for growth capital and were referred to Beck because, as he put it, "all the dog-shit stuff was shuffled to me." It was a time of great turmoil in the insurance business. Interest rates had shot up throughout 1973 and 1974, sharply reducing the value of the bond portfolios held by insurance companies, some of which had been reduced nearly to insolvency. The men from Omaha believed they could expand their small but solidly profitable company (the name of which Beck claimed he was unable to remember) by approaching their floundering competitors and offering to take charge of managing their assets and liabilities in exchange for a cut of their premium income. In short, the pair would assume the burden of all the calculations critical to designing insurance policies but would remain in the background as very private consultants. The companies that were their clients would continue to sell policies under their own names, but would be in a position to offer more generous investment returns.

Beck thought it was such a great idea that he urged his visitors to begin by buying from its current owners the company they were running. And he suggested to his superiors that DLJ acquire the firm in partnership with the pair. But DLJ wasn't interested and the two executives were reluctant to risk their own money, so Beck agreed to finance the deal himself, taking 95 percent of the equity in the company. (The remaining 5 percent went to the two executives.) The little insurer that Beck had acquired quickly became a gold mine, as his partners proved themselves to be absolute financial geniuses. Beck capitalized on the success of the venture by setting up a holding company called Rosebud through which he began acquiring and rehabilitating dozens of small insurance companies in the United States and Europe. All of the acquired companies kept their own names and corporate identities.

Beck described to me in great detail how Rosebud had masked its very existence through an intricately constructed network of dummy partnerships and paper corporations that snaked through Switzerland, Panama, Grand Cayman, and other havens of corporate secrecy. The cash thrown off by all the insurance companies was used by Rosebud as capital for securities-trading desks that it operated around the world under the brilliantly eccentric direction of its senior trader, whom Beck described as a cross between Mike Milken and Howard Hughes. Since our arrival at the hotel, this trading whiz supposedly had made a one-day $120 million profit in the foreign currency markets by correctly anticipating the outcome of the recent economic summit conference among the so-called Group of Seven nations. Beck told me that Rosebud's real-estate holdings alone were valued at $1.5 billion and that, though there were obvious difficulties in converting Rosebud's assets into cash, his personal net worth was nearing $5 billion, which included his 49 percent interest in the Hôtel du Cap. Beck said that his partner was a German industrialist who had traded him a minority interest in the hotel in exchange for a maritime-insurance company owned by Rosebud.

As Beck told it, Rosebud not only was an instrument of great wealth but one of far-reaching influence. Over the previous year, Beck had begun dropping vague hints of CIA affiliation into our conversations, usually to bolster the credibility of one assertion or another about the state of Wall Street or the world. Increasingly, too, he had begun referring to his rainmaking maneuvers as "intelligence gathering" while boasting of his "predictive capabilities." Through Rosebud, which he hinted was a CIA front company, Beck gave shape and form to the identity of covert operative that he had been experimenting with since business school. Although he never spelled out the undercover role Rosebud supposedly played, there were evocative references to monitoring cross-border capital flows and combatting narco-terrorism—both subjects he seemed to know a lot about. I asked Beck why he was telling me about a company the very existence of which supposedly was secret. He said that the operation soon would end—

assuming that he could find buyers for Rosebud's legitimate businesses
—and let it go at that.

My initial belief in the reality of Rosebud was a product not only of
the extreme detail of his explanation and the quality of his acting but
his artful use of the Hôtel du Cap as a stage. Even now I can't imagine
how the hotel staff could been more attentive or deferential to anyone
—including the actual owner. And, as Beck no doubt expected, the
Hôtel du Cap's many charms had an effect on me as altogether intoxi-
cating as the Roederer Cristal that seemed to flow everywhere we
went. In this oasis of fairy-tale luxury, almost anything seemed possible.

On the same afternoon on which Beck had first told me about his
secret life, he and I were playing tennis, when a tall elderly man
wearing glasses and staidly overdressed in a dark business suit suddenly
appeared outside the fence at the far end of the court. He stood there
expressionless and watched us play a few points. I thought I saw him
nod slightly in Beck's direction but I couldn't be sure.

"That's him," Beck whispered. "That's my partner."

When I turned to take a closer look, the man was gone.

If Beck's choice of the name Rosebud for his secret empire implied a
desire to be unmasked, he didn't make it easy for me. Without a
highly placed source within the CIA, it proved virtually impossible to
verify Rosebud's existence. Meanwhile, Beck offered me not a single
clue that would lead me to Pittsburgh and his father's criminal record.

Although in retrospect Beck emphasized his Rosebud fabrication as
a plea for help, there is an alternative psychological explanation to
which Beck himself hinted at in his frequent, approving references to
Karen Horney, the late psychiatrist best known for her work on the
causes and treatment of neuroses. In *Self-Analysis,* Horney wrote: "Instead of moving away from others, the neurotic moved away from
himself. His whole actual self became somewhat unreal to him and he
created in its place an idealized image of himself in which the conflicting parts were so transfigured that they no longer appeared as conflicts
but as various aspects of a rich personality. . . . The craving for admiration could be seen as the patient's need to have outside affirmation
that he really was his idealized image. And the farther the image was
removed from reality the more insatiable this latter need would be."

Having gotten away with telling me fledgling versions of his Vietnam and Rosebud fantasies in our interviews in 1984 for the *Business*

Week article, perhaps Beck really saw me not as his "confessor" but as a willing conduit for getting a much grander version of his legend into circulation in book form. Certainly, Beck's propensity for self-aggrandizement was never more pronounced than in the months after his ouster from Oppenheimer. In our conversations at the Hôtel du Cap, Beck inflated his aptitude for deal making into a persona that I dubbed the Deal Svengali. Through his profound understanding of psychology and superior showmanship, the Deal Svengali bent lesser mortals to his will. "I've led a lot of people into major ambushes," Beck boasted. "I'm a good poker player. I can create chaos and reformulate it into substance. I can be completely circular. I also felt at all times that I was invincible." Eventually, Beck extended his philosophy of promotion as manipulation to encompass the exercise of power in all its forms. "What people have to realize," he said, "is that the whole world is run by promoters. Some great promoters were leaders of sovereign nations. Winston Churchill was a promoter in a way. So was Genghis Khan. War is the ultimate consequence of the promoter's action. What happens on Wall Street is just a subset of a larger game in which men driven by power and ego jockey for position to create the reality that is most rewarding for them."

By thus aggrandizing deal making, Beck gained a rationale for the moral corner-cutting to which he occasionally resorted in pursuit of success on Wall Street—like saying that he knew Al Taubman when he really didn't or claiming that he hadn't leaked something to a reporter when he had. While this sort of self-serving misrepresentation was common in deal making and business in general, Beck could not easily square it with the ethical sensitivities instilled in him by his reaction to his father's wrongdoing. By apotheosizing the conniving deal maker in him into the Deal Svengali, Beck awarded himself the moral exemption of genius. What application could ordinary morality have to a brilliant daredevil of a deal man who traversed the lines between fiction and reality, between right and wrong, with the artistry of a high-wire dancer?

But if the Deal Svengali was the smartest player in the deal game, why wasn't he the richest? Beck's annual income was approaching $2 million by the time he left Oppenheimer but that was peanuts compared with the money being made by the owners of the corporations that the M & A men advised. To Beck, the charm of the leveraged buyout was that it enabled the deal man to have it both ways: to take

big advisory fees on the front end of the transaction and hefty capital
gains on the back end. Despite his early success with the Susan Crane
deal, Beck had failed to make headway as an LBO investor, seemingly
not so much because for lack of capital as lack of nerve. Unable to rival
Kravis in real life, Beck outdid him in his imagination, creating Rosebud. "I don't know anybody who was more leveraged than I was in the
mid-1970s," Beck told me. "I love starting businesses or straightening
them out, but I'm not a good detail guy when it comes to managing so
I brought in professionals to do that. For years, I didn't take one dime
out of Rosebud—no salary, no dividends, no fees, no free airplane
rides. But 10 percent of the profits went to charity—anonymously, of
course." And so on and so on. Beck had some success promoting
himself to clients as an adviser-investor, as this 1984 comment from
Taubman suggested: "It's easier to be a salesman than an investor, but
Jeff's always willing to put his own money into a deal."

Beck's Super Kravis identity overlapped with another of his personas
—the Heir, which he created by exaggerating his stepfather's wealth
and inserting himself by imaginative fiat into his will. The Heir
lurched to the fore as the Northwest Industries deal was collapsing and
hung around afterward, making sure that everyone in the group—
secretaries included —understood that he would be inheriting serious
money when he turned forty in March 1986. The size of Beck's
claimed inheritance grew with every passing month, beginning with a
few hundred million and ending at $1.5 billion. In Beck's final weeks
at Oppenheimer, he asked McGrath and Peters to leave the firm with
him to help manage the fortune. He extended the same invitation to
Dick Beattie, with whom he'd gotten quite friendly during his attempt
to promote an LBO of Esmark. Startled by the size of Beck's supposed
$400 million fortune, Beattie mentioned the figure to Kravis, who
replied that Beck had confided in him that he was coming into $4
billion. By the time that Beck got around to dazzling me with his
wealth, he'd abandoned the role of heir in favor of secret empire-
builder. After all, it was far more impressive to have built one's fortune
than to have inherited it.

However, no amount of money—real or imaginary—would have
been sufficient to satisfy Beck's craving for heroism. Unlike many of
the best-known moguls of the 1980s, Beck never believed in wealth
either as an end in itself or even as a reward for commercial valor. To
the contrary, to accumulate money and social position was to succeed

on his mother's terms, which repelled Beck nearly as much as it compelled him. Enter Beck's first heroic persona, the Green Beret. By the early 1980s, the Vietnam vet had moved out from the deep recesses of the national consciousness and into the limelight as novelists and film directors belatedly adopted the war as a subject. Tellingly, one of the first Vietnam films to gain wide commercial release was not a combat film in the classic sense but a poignant tale of a soldier's difficult readjustment to life in America, *Coming Home.* As the societal perception of the Vietnam veteran was altered by new awareness of post-traumatic stress syndrome, Beck's idealized identity evolved, too, from crazed macho warrior to sensitive, suffering antihero.

In our conversations at the Hôtel du Cap, Beck used his Vietnam legend to add moral weight to his pronouncements, both professional and personal. Let these other bankers make glib comparisons between deal making and combat, what did they know? He'd lived it, man. At this stage, Vietnam was not something Beck talked about off-handedly, which made his accounts seem all the more credible. Although the imagery and pacing of Beck's tales were cinematically vivid, his voice was devoid of emotion, adding a cool chill of authenticity. Although I had to prod Beck into a detailed recounting of his Vietnam adventures, he would draw parallels between combat and Wall Street at the drop of a rival M & A man's name. Beck also used Vietnam to add rhetorical vehemence to his strongest expressions of emotions, which was like seasoning a jalapeño pepper with cayenne powder. Late one night as we were talking on the terrace of the villa, he reached for a metaphor to express the perfidy of his colleagues at Oppenheimer: "I felt like I'd been shot in the back by my own men for my weapon, the ten dollars in my pocket, and my canteen."

Through the persona of Secret Agent Man, Beck was able to extend his military identity into the present by repackaging it. The secret missions in which he'd specialized in Vietnam as a member of the Special Forces dovetailed seamlessly into his Rosebud secret service. As founder and CEO of Rosebud, Secret Agent Man represented a melding of Green Beret and Super Kravis, and was the alternate identity Beck would increasingly inhabit as the 1980s built to a speculative climax. Not only was this the most broadly encompassing of all his personas but the most safely self-contained. Whenever Beck's recounting of his imaginary adventures put him crossways to reality, along came Secret Agent Man to save the day with the ultimate cover: Sorry, classified top secret.

I believe that even at his most self-deluded Beck never lost the ability to distinguish his falsehoods from reality. Because deep down he knew that he was lying and because he knew as well that real heroes don't lie, Beck was left with yet another layer of psychic conflict to idealize away. Enter the Whistleblower. Unlike the Green Beret, Beck's other heroic construct, the Whistleblower was more fact than fiction. It was the Whistleblower in Beck who during his DLJ days had gotten the CEO of Amicor fired, had pushed Phil Cohen out of Oppenheimer, and had put the *Journal*'s Tim Metz on Boesky's trail. However, fantasy intruded into even this most admirable of Beck's personas. After Fred Bleakley started covering Wall Street for *The New York Times* in mid-1984, Beck urged him to investigate Boesky. Like Metz, though, Bleakley was unable to collect enough evidence to expose the arbitrageur. Beck prolonged Bleakley's interest by telling the *Times* reporter that he was prepared to help federal authorities make a case against Boesky by wearing a wire. At one point, he claimed to actually have done so, though later he backed off from this assertion. Beck told Bleakley that plans to include him in a government surveillance operation were dropped because Boesky had grown leery of him. Beck suspected that Boesky was on to him because one night he saw a couple of baseball bat–wielding goons outside the front door of his apartment building. Assuming that the two were emissaries from Boesky, Beck returned to his apartment. When he left for work the next morning, they were gone.

Midway through my stay at the Hôtel du Cap, Margo and Katherine arrived from New York with Jeff's sister, Judy. Beck seemed delighted to see them all. On the night they arrived, in fact, Beck got so carried away entertaining Katherine with a mock ballet in the living room of the villa that he leaped atop a glass coffee table, which shattered as he crashed through to the floor. He looked every bit as startled as did his daughter, who burst into tears. Miraculously, Beck wasn't cut. He sheepishly called the front desk, which had the broken table carted away in about three minutes.

My last day at the Hôtel du Cap was Katherine's second birthday. Her father and I celebrated by finally taking a match from Antoine and Patrick, winning the third set 6–2. Antoine was a bit surly in defeat, which was enough to convince me that they hadn't let us win. I

don't think Jeff even considered the possibility. We returned to the
villa for an afternoon birthday party. The Becks had invited no guests
other than hotel employees and their families. Irondelle arrived with
his daughter and baby granddaughter. She and Katherine sat side by
side in baby chairs on the terrace, like tiny princesses on makeshift
thrones, blinking in the bright sunshine at the baby-talking courtiers
who surrounded them. Beck fiddled with an uncooperative video camera, alternately cursing the machine and shouting endearments to his
daughter.

It was a stupefyingly hot day and Wall Street seemed as distant and
alien as Antarctica. That morning's *International Herald Tribune* had
carried a story about Hurricane Gloria, which was howling up the east
coast toward New York City. I went into the villa and called a friend of
mine back home. She said that the storm was closing in fast and
thousands of Long Island residents were fleeing inland. I called my
secretary at *Business Week,* who said the office was closing and she
was on her way home. She'd heard on the radio that most of the
midtown skyscrapers had shut down and that the New York Stock
Exchange, in a rare admission of the existence of a superior force, had
halted trading. I hung up and went to tell Beck that the wrath of God
was descending on Wall Street. He handed me the video camera,
leaned his head back, and paid earsplitting homage to the King of the
Jungle.

A month later, I was sitting with Beck in the living room of his apartment when he handed me a sheet of Drexel Burnham Lambert stationery. "What do you think?" he said. It was an employment agreement
guaranteeing a first-year bonus of $1 million. My opinion was irrele-
vant, for Beck already had made up his mind. Only three months after
he'd left Oppenheimer & Company, vowing never again to set foot on
Wall Street, Beck was returning to the deal game. The book would
have to wait. I was disappointed but not surprised. It had been evident
at the Hôtel du Cap that unresolved emotions were ricocheting around
inside Beck like pebbles in a high-speed blender. The collapse of the
Northwest Industries deal and his ouster from Oppenheimer had revived Beck's need to prove himself and added revenge to the complex
of motives that drove him. Instead of abating with time, Beck's anger
had been exacerbated by a protracted dispute with Robert and Sanzo
over the fees that he believed were due him on deals in progress at the
time he'd left Oppenheimer. It was surely no coincidence that in

accepting a job offer from Drexel, Beck had signed on with the firm that successfully financed the leveraged buyout of Northwest Industries after Kelly Briggs Oppenheimer pulled out. "If you can't beat 'em, join 'em," Beck told *The Wall Street Journal,* which in late October 1985 briefly noted his return to action.

17

The pairing of Beck and Drexel Burnham had a certain fatefulness. For one thing, Beck needed a job at a time when Drexel was short of experienced deal men. Beyond that, Beck and Drexel were kin —self-styled Wall Street outsiders looking to parlay a maverick rain-making talent into money, influence, and acceptance on their own terms. While Beck had spent nearly fifteen years thrashing about on the periphery of power, Drexel by 1985 had established itself as the only truly revolutionary investment bank of the twentieth century. Over the decades, there had been other upstart houses that had prospered by virtue of their creative audacity, but they had defined success in terms of Establishment acceptance; their goal was to climb to the top of the underwriting pyramid. Drexel, on the other hand, opted out of the syndicate system and defiantly created its own parallel universe —the junk-bond market—where the most basic traditional notions of creditworthiness and corporate respectability were inverted to spectacularly lucrative purpose. Within Drexel World, indebtedness was not a badge of inadequacy but the means to power and wealth beyond the wildest middle-class dreams of avarice.

The means by which Drexel and its resident genius, Michael Milken, had worked their revolution would remain a subject of great confusion and debate long after the U.S. government's investigation of the firm had ended with several hard-won felony convictions in 1989 and 1990. In establishing a virtually proprietary $200 billion market and entwining it with hundreds of private partnerships, Milken and his Drexel cohorts created a structure of such staggering complexity that it may never be fully fathomed. Moreover, the criminal charges to which the firm and Milken pleaded guilty were so trivial compared to the accusations lodged against them, and the whole process by which Milken in particular was brought to justice so politicized, that one could only conclude that the real story had yet to be told. Was Mike Milken the most venal financier of the century, the most self-deluded, the most misunderstood, or some bizarre combination thereof? Did Drexel create a real market or the illusion of a market? These questions will be years in the answering.

Without doubt, though, Milken was the greatest Wall Street rainmaker of the takeover era, eclipsing Henry Kravis, who as the commercializer of the leveraged buyout ranked a distant second. Milken and Kravis were financial missionaries belonging to the same order and preaching the same basic gospel: that the system by which credit had been supplied to business ever since the Great Depression was grievously flawed by excessive conservatism and élitism. But while Kravis dedicated himself to drawing funds from the margins of the credit system into one arcane species of M & A deal, Milken was creating a securities market adaptable to almost all genres of financial transactions, including the LBO. It was only after Milken put his junk-bond muscle behind the leveraged buyout that KKR was lifted into the realm of the multibillion-dollar deal in the mid-1980s. While the Wall Street Establishment had been slow to recognize the opportunity for profit opened by Kravis's pioneering, it was even slower in responding to the competitive implications of Milken's innovations. Drexel's development of the junk-bond weapon threatened to topple the whole towering, precarious system of cross-subsidy on which modern Wall Street was built.

Private and almost willfully tiny for three-quarters of a century, the leading investment banks had transformed themselves by the mid-1980s into public corporations that were coining vast profits while doubling in size every few years with the rapid proliferation of new markets. There was a frenetic, almost desperate edge to their innovation that reflected not only the pace of change but the disproportionate profit in novelty. With the notable exception of M & A, on Wall Street in the 1980s the big money was made on the frontier—by inventing a new trading strategy or financial instrument and milking it before the other houses caught on and came piling in with me-too versions. The men who ran the big houses believed that they had no choice but to turn every new market into a battleground and to keep on fighting for market share even if doing so meant losing money. They came to see the investment bank as a tower built of hundreds of interlocking pieces, which they called products. If just one piece was missing, the whole tower could come tumbling down as clients were lured to rival firms by the promise of "full service." The full-service imperative added urgency to the quest for novelty. Firms couldn't afford to keep paying the outlandish bonuses to which their employees in each specialty had become accustomed during their pioneering days without continually tapping into fresh sources of outsized profit on the new-product frontier.

Like M & A, junk-bond dealing as practiced by Drexel defied the standard pattern of declining profitability. In fact, it was a sort of magic wand that could bestow superior profit margins at Milken's touch. Milken began in the early 1970s as a trader, earning 100 percent returns on a few million dollars of capital by buying up existing low-rated bond issues and selling them to a tightly interwoven circle of investors persuaded by his radical critique of traditional credit analysis —not to mention the huge returns they earned when the bonds they bought from him soared in value. In the late 1970s, Milken touched his junk-bond wand to corporate finance and soon Drexel was earning underwriting commissions of 3 percent to 4 percent marketing new issues of low-rated bonds at a time when rival houses were lucky to make 7/8 of a percentage point on blue-chip bond financings. In contradiction of the usual dynamics of free markets, Drexel succeeded in monopolizing junk-bond finance with a market share that actually increased as the market grew, eventually topping out at about 70 percent. To Milken, one of the most driven monopolists in business history, this remarkable figure was evidence not of success but of failure. "Mike Milken believes in one hundred percent market share," one of his awestruck Drexel colleagues once told me. "I seriously believe that he wants every trade."

In the early 1980s, Milken was persuaded by his Drexel colleagues in New York to wave his wand over the M & A business. All hell broke loose as obscure pipsqueaks were transformed into fearsome raiders capable of menacing the largest corporations in the land. While Beck was struggling to raise money for the Northwest Industries deal in early 1985, Carl Icahn, a Wall Street arbitrageur turned raider, made an $8 billion tender offer for Phillips Petroleum without a nickel of financing in place. Drexel said it was "highly confident" of raising the money, and that was sufficient to panic Phillips's management into paying greenmail, as it bought back Icahn's stock at a $75 million premium. There ensued a rapid-fire series of enormously lucrative Drexel-backed greenmailings of Gulf Oil, Unocal, and Walt Disney Company.

Any lingering doubts that Milken could in fact have tapped his network of junk-bond buyers for sums large enough to acquire companies of this size were laid to rest in mid-1985 by the successful siege of Revlon Incorporated, a prime glamour company run by a sultanlike CEO, Michel Bergerac, and defended by those Deal Club eminences Felix Rohatyn and Marty Lipton. Ron Perelman, whose original credential was marrying into money, was Milken's proxy in an exceptionally bitter battle freighted with class overtones. The sight of Perelman and his advisers arriving at Revlon headquarters filled Bergerac with scorn. "I'll never forget those twenty or thirty guys coming off the elevators," Bergerac sneered. "All short, bald, with big cigars! If Central Casting had to produce thirty guys like that, they couldn't do it. They looked like they were in a grade-D movie that took place in Mississippi or Louisiana, about guys fixing elections in a backroom." Drexel, though, laughed last when Bergerac and Revlon capitulated to a $1.8 billion takeover. "All the brainpower, clout and class connections that Revlon summoned were no match for the raw financial might of Drexel," wrote Connie Bruck in *The Predators' Ball.* "Michael Milken had become the great equalizer." Who was next on Drexel's hit list—IBM, General Motors, General Electric?

The advent of the junk-bond takeover lifted M & A dealing to a fabulous new peak of profitability. On the Revlon deal, for example, Lazard Frères received $11 million and Wachtell, Lipton and Paul Weiss, Rifkind, Wharton and Garrison split $10 million for advising on Revlon's unsuccessful defense—very handsome recompense by traditional Deal Club standards. On the winning side, Morgan Stanley collected $25 million while Drexel pocketed $66 million, mainly in junk-bond financing fees. Drexel's rise to power in the deal game transfixed rival deal men, inciting in them a volatile mix of envy, dread, and bewilderment. While Rohatyn and Lipton elevated their public blather about the menace of takeovers to new heights of high-minded hypocrisy, the question that preoccupied most deal men in their heart of hearts was simply, How much money are Drexel and Milken making? In time, all estimates would be proven shockingly low. When finally revealed by the government, Milken's W-2 forms read like the earnings statement of an exceptionally robust *Fortune* 500 company. Milken made $46 million in 1983, $124 million in 1984, $135 million in 1985, and $295 million in 1986. In 1987, his peak year, Milken pocketed $550 million—more than Boeing, Procter & Gamble, USX, or Kraft. And Milken's gargantuan salary represented just a fraction of

Drexel's total earnings. By long-standing arrangement with Drexel, Milken's junk-bond department, which totaled two hundred people by the mid-1980s, kept 35 percent of the profits it generated to be distributed as bonuses at Milken's discretion.

Income from the issuance and trading of junk bonds alone was sufficient to make Drexel's junk-bond group the single most lucrative business unit on Wall Street in the 1980s, if not of all time. Yet Milken and an élite coterie of other Drexelites also reaped huge gains through a byzantine network of private investment partnerships. According to federal authorities, partnerships controlled by Milken and his brother, Lowell, paid out at least $2 billion to Drexel staffers, families, and friends—including Beck, who had interests in at least three partnerships. This sum was generated by only the twenty-five largest of the more than six hundred Drexel partnerships that investigators had been able to identify by 1990. Their search hadn't ended. "We don't know whether this is the tip of the iceberg or half the iceberg or . . . one third or what," admitted one person involved in the inquiry. Most of these partnerships owned securities issued by Drexel's corporate clients. While there was nothing inherently illegal about such partnerships, their very existence was a gross affront to traditional notions of conflict of interest in investment banking. The partnerships not only swapped securities back and forth among themselves but traded with dozens of Drexel trading accounts also controlled by Milken. The activities of the partnerships would figure prominently in the market manipulation charges eventually brought by federal authorities against Milken and Drexel Burnham.

In one of Drexel's few concessions to securities-industry orthodoxy, the firm used its share of the great junk-bond bonanza to finance its expansion in virtually every other area of securities dealing. The architect of this traditional diversification strategy was not Milken, to whom junk was a universe, but his friend and colleague, Fred Joseph, the firm's longtime corporate-finance chief and, beginning in 1985, its CEO. The son of a cabdriver, Joseph had grown up poor and Jewish in the Roxbury section of Boston and put himself through Boston College, where he excelled as a boxer, and Harvard Business School. A self-styled outsider, Joseph lived with his wife and daughters on a farm in what he liked to describe as "a part of New Jersey where they don't hunt foxes" and derided the politics of underwriting as "Wall Street's old comedy of manners." Yet Joseph framed his ambitions for Drexel in Establishment terms, aspiring to nothing less than reinventing

Goldman, Sachs on a junk-bond base. Goldman, Sachs was respected
by its peers as much for its low-key but shrewd conservatism and old-
fashioned collegiality as for its large, steady profits. While Goldman's
unusual culture was the product of many decades of disciplined effort,
Joseph was in a hurry. By dangling hooks baited with great chunks of
junk-bond profit, Joseph succeeded in luring traders, brokers, analysts,
and bankers by the score away from the old-line houses, thus eating
away at the very foundation of the Street's mightiest investment-
banking towers—Goldman, Sachs included.

Even while the Establishment houses responded to Drexel's incur-
sions by bringing heavy political pressure to bear against Drexel in
Washington, they were justifying their own radical departures from
tradition by the need to combat the junk-bond upstart. Unable to
inspire fear and loathing merely by uttering the words "highly confident," First Boston, Merrill Lynch, and other major M & A houses
ventured out well beyond Drexel on the risk-reward continuum to
make "bridge" loans—unsecured short-term loans to raiders who otherwise would have taken their business to Drexel. Some members of
the Deal Club even broke ranks and collaborated with the evil empire
of junk—notably Eric Gleacher, who by this time had left Lehman to
run the M & A department at Morgan Stanley. In fact, it was
Gleacher who'd first laid before Perelman the idea of taking a run at
Revlon, which was a longtime Lehman client. Gleacher overcame the
opposition of many of his partners and convinced the firm's senior
leaders that Morgan Stanley should represent Perelman in his play for
Revlon, even though it meant aligning with Drexel—and in an officially subordinate position to it.

Of all the investment bankers I spoke with as I made the rounds in
1984 and 1985 for a series of articles on Drexel for *Business Week,*
Beck was the most emphatic—and, as it would turn out, uncannily
prophetic—in his criticisms. "You have to distinguish between deals
that are being done just for the up-front fees and those that are good
economic deals," he told me. "In limited amounts, junk financing is
okay. But in these big deals everything has to go right. There is very
little margin for error. In fact, I've never seen risk this astounding.
Sure, you can recapitalize a company and run it on cash flow instead of
earnings but it just can't work when you reach this level of leverage
and of gouging—all the fees and warrants these people take. It's a very
dangerous game they're playing. . . . Drexel understands how to use
other people's money better than anyone I've ever seen. But when you

get to the bottom of it, I think you'll find a malicious intent to control the market. Mike Milken is out of control. He's like Hugh Hefner in the Playboy mansion, staying up all night, hanging around in his pajamas all day. Hefner couldn't help himself and neither can Milken when it comes to deals. Milken's brilliant, Joseph has done an incredible job, and I think they may be out of business in two years. One way or another, they won't be able to buck the Establishment forever. It will kill them."

While I have no doubt even in hindsight that Beck was sincere in his criticisms of Drexel, the disconnection between belief and action that haunted Beck in so many aspects of his life was plain with respect to Drexel and high-leverage finance. During the early stages of the Northwest Industries deal, Beck had sent a memo to Steve Robert along with a copy of an article by Lipton blasting junk-bond takeovers. "The junk bond bust-up has become a major financing opportunity which we are continually missing," Beck declared. "There is no question that we have the bust-ups but do not have the capability of financing them. It is my opinion that this trend will continue regardless of what Mr. Lipton says and that we should be discussing ways of establishing a financing capability that will allow us not only to collect significant merger fees but to underwrite disaggregations." The proposal fell on deaf ears. A few months later the Northwest deal unraveled precisely because of the financing deficiency Beck had pointed out. Along came Drexel, which smoothly placed $500 million more in junk bonds, enabling William Farley, an obscure, egomaniacal investment banker turned industrialist, to acquire Northwest Industries in a $1.4 billion deal.

"There's no comparison between Oppenheimer raising mezzanine money [the highest-risk portion of a debt financing] and Drexel raising mezzanine money," Farley told *The New York Times*, adding, "I don't think there's another investment bank in America that can do what [Drexel] can do." Ironically, the same *Times* story, which was a profile of Fred Joseph, contained a quote from Beck, who was on his last legs at Oppenheimer. "Fred and Drexel have done a terrific job of developing that market," Beck said. "But the jury is still out on junk bonds. With all the questions everybody is asking about defaults in the next recession, you have to wonder if they'll be around in the next three to five years." By this time, Drexel's fate was of considerable personal interest to Beck, who had already held a couple of secret meetings with Joseph to discuss the possibility of his joining the firm. Although, as the quote in the *Times* suggested, Beck remained skeptical, his doubts were beginning to soften under Joseph's charm offensive. With his breezily articulate manner, his Kennedy haircut, and his easy amiability, Joseph seemed more like a new-age congressman than a Wall Streeter. In those days, Joseph charmed almost every outsider he dealt with—myself and other reporters included. All in all, he was a most beguiling front man for Milken, Drexel's self-proclaimed "Dr. Feelgood."

Drexel's progress in building an M & A department had been slowed by the desire of Joseph and David Kay, Drexel's M & A chief, to hire a superstar. In 1982, they'd drawn up a short list of prospects and gone in pursuit of Felix Rohatyn, Bruce Wasserstein, Eric Gleacher, and Marty Siegel, among others. Siegel alone was interested, though in no hurry to make up his mind. While waiting on Siegel, Kay brought in scores of junior bankers and in January 1985 hired Dennis Levine, a hustling thirty-two-year-old from Lehman Brothers, who became the M & A department's fifth managing director. Drexel doubled Levine's base salary, to $140,000, and guaranteed him a bonus of at least $750,000.

At about the same time that Levine was hired, Joe Flom brought up Beck's name in a meeting with Joseph, who approached the Mad Dog through a headhunter. By the time they met, Beck's emotional unraveling was well advanced, but Joseph didn't notice, or didn't care. "I thought the guy had good presence and knew how to sell," Joseph recalled. "There was a heavy appearance element with him. He made a big deal of having lunch in secret—at a hotel, in his apartment. But he was bright, he knew the business, and I thought he was the kind of guy who could persuade clients to do things." For his part, Beck was pleasantly surprised. "I thought Fred was very impressive, sincere, humble, well presented," Beck said. "I wanted him to adopt me." Beck also met Kay several times over breakfast in Drexel's dining room. Kay found Beck to be very self-confident, forthcoming, and as focused as "a heat-seeking missile."

As Joseph checked around the Street on Beck he was struck by the sharp divergence of opinion: He got raves or pans and little in between. After many months of slow-motion courtship, Joseph finally asked Kay for a verdict. "I'm on the fence, Fred," Kay said, "but my gut feel is we shouldn't hire him. I don't think he'd fit. He gave no indication to me of being a team player." Leon Black, who was about to be promoted to cochief of M & A with Kay and who'd crossed paths with Beck on one recent deal, mildly disagreed. "It's a risk, but I don't think I'd come down on the same side as David," Black said. "He's a business-getter."

Beck kept to himself his uncertainty about whether to accept Joseph's job offer, presenting his decision to join Drexel as a fait accompli to Margo, who was surprised to hear her husband explain why he was joining the very firm that he'd been criticizing so vehemently. At Beck's request, he was attached not to the M & A department but to a fledgling new business group affiliated with Drexel's corporate-finance department. Beck thought he'd have more latitude to free-lance this way, though Drexel was so loosely organized that it hardly mattered. In the fall of 1985, Beck moved what remained of his deal files (certain documents had mysteriously disappeared during his last weeks at Oppenheimer) into a window office on the eleventh floor of 55 Broad Street, where Drexel's corporate-finance group was quartered. Joseph and the rest of the firm's headquarters staff was directly across the street, at 60 Broad. In keeping with its maverick sensibility, Drexel did not lavish money on interior decorating or other perquisites. As long as his office was no smaller or plainer than any other managing director's —and it wasn't—Beck didn't give his surroundings a second thought, since he didn't intend to spend much time in the office anyway.

In joining Drexel, Beck succumbed not only to the desire for vindication but to the momentum of his latest deal. Just a few days after Beck had delivered his emotional farewell at Oppenheimer, *Fortune* had published a profile—"The Controversial Boss of Beatrice"—that raised the issue of Dutt's erratic behavior in print for the first time. The article dealt a damaging blow to Beatrice's credibility and roused some members of its board to behind-the-scenes action. When Dutt abruptly fired his senior corporate strategist and another of the company's top executives resigned, the board finally reached the limits of its tolerance and demanded Dutt's resignation. Dutt complied with little fuss and was replaced by Bill Granger, a sixty-six-year-old retired vice chairman who received a standing ovation at the start of his first meeting with employees. This was the best news Beck had heard in months; not only had Dutt been booted but the board had replaced him with a man widely seen on Wall Street as a mere caretaker. Take-over speculation continued to mount. The rumor mill's favorite candidate to replace Granger was none other than Don Kelly, who told a reporter: "I am not going to make a leveraged buyout offer for

Beatrice, don't own a single share of Beatrice, haven't talked to any-body at Beatrice and have no immediate plans to do so." (While misleading, Kelly's statement was technically correct, since the LBO offer would be made not by him but KKR.)

Thanks in part to Beck's persistent prodding, KKR was ready to move. Just a few weeks before Dutt fell, a young KKR analyst named Kevin Bousquette had been assigned to do a detailed analysis of the feasibility of a Beatrice LBO. Since KKR wasn't working with manage-ment, Bousquette could not get the inside numbers but did have ac-cess to the next best thing: the informed judgment of Kelly, Rentschler, and Smilow. Bousquette's basic task was to extrapolate Beatrice's performance into the future based on a series of assumptions about the prospects of each of its operating units. Food companies were attractive to LBO promoters because they tend to grow at steady rates, unaffected by modest fluctuations in the economy. Bousquette took a conservative approach, projecting revenue growth of less than 10 percent a year for every Beatrice division while searching at the same time for ways to boost cash flow by reducing operating costs. He concluded that the company's $220 million in annual corporate over-head costs could be cut in half by eliminating redundant layers of headquarters management and by terminating Dutt's schemes for pro-moting the Beatrice name. After a few weeks, Bousquette had reached preliminary conclusions sufficiently encouraging to cause KKR to hire an investment bank. For a buyout of this size, there was one choice: Drexel.

As part of Drexel's push to develop its M & A business, Milken and Peter Ackerman, his top deputy, had begun calling on Kravis and Roberts in 1983. "At first we couldn't figure out their hocus-pocus," Kravis said. "With Milken, you thought you were talking about one thing and it turned out he was talking about another." Shortly after its unsuccessful offer for Esmark in 1984, KKR ran into problems com-pleting the financing for a buyout of Cole National. Kravis called Drexel and, with Roberts, was ushered out to Beverly Hills for a ses-sion with Milken and some of his biggest bond buyers. Milken im-pressed Kravis by raising the $100 million needed to swing the $450 million Cole deal in forty-eight hours. "I thought, 'Wow, this is ter-rific,'" Kravis said. "I used to work for weeks with the Prudential to raise that kind of money." After the Cole buyout, KKR hired Drexel to help finance its two biggest deals ever: the $1.6 billion purchase of a controlling stake in Union Texas Petroleum and the Storer Communications LBO, for which Drexel raised $1.5 billion.

Drexel had struggled to complete the Storer financing. Beatrice promised to be even tougher, since it already carried a fairly heavy debt load—$2.2 billion, a fair hunk of it taken on in acquiring Esmark. KKR would have to assume this existing debt in addition to buying out Beatrice's stockholders. Judging by Bousquette's projections, Beatrice could safely carry $3.5 billion more in long-term debt, assuming that KKR invested an additional $500 million in equity. However, a total financing amounting to $4 billion would enable KKR to pay only about $37 a share, which wasn't much of a premium over Beatrice's current trading price. Kravis and Roberts concluded that it would take at least $45 a share or about $5 billion to gain control of Beatrice. KKR had its choice of two basic ways by which it could close this billion-dollar gap. One was to substitute equity for debt, which would solidify the company's balance sheet at the expense of lowering the prospective returns to KKR. Or KKR could sell off pieces of Beatrice after it gained control and use the proceeds to pay down debt. KKR chose the latter approach; Beatrice would be its first big "bust-up" deal.

According to Bousquette's numbers, if KKR could raise $1.2 billion through asset sales, it could earn handsome returns by operating the remainder of the company for three to five years. In estimating the value of Beatrice's parts, Bousquette came up with best-case projections and then cut them all by 25 percent. "We decided to be conservative," Bousquette said. "But we knew in our guts that we could get more for selling these businesses than we'd projected we could."

Beck, who'd left Oppenheimer but had yet to join Drexel, was not invited to involve himself in KKR's financing decisions. But he did play a tactical role, urging Kravis to approach the board of Beatrice and offer to make a friendly investment in its stock even before Dutt resigned. KKR decided to bide its time, in hopes that Dutt would soon depart. While Beck was off entertaining me at the Hôtel du Cap, Kravis hired Marty Siegel of Kidder, Peabody as KKR's second investment-banking adviser. Beck pressed Kravis for assurance that if a buyout of Beatrice was done he'd be compensated as the "originator" of the deal. Kravis agreed in principle, though he refused to go so far as to accede to Beck's demand that, whatever his fee, it exceed that paid to Oppenheimer.

On October 17, 1985, KKR finally made its move, delivering a letter to the Beatrice board offering $45 a share. While the offer was unfriendly in the sense that it wasn't solicited, KKR stopped short of outright hostility in not threatening to take the offer directly to the firm's stockholders. Using a tactic known as a bear hug, KKR hoped to pressure the Beatrice board to submit to negotiations. KKR said that a major bank—later revealed to be Bankers Trust—had committed itself to arranging $3.5 billion in bank loans and that Drexel Burnham was "highly confident" of its ability to raise additional funds. As Boesky, Icahn, and other arbitrageurs began snapping up Beatrice shares, its stock rose above the price offered by KKR, giving the company's board ample justification to reject the bid as inadequate—especially since Beatrice's investment bankers, Salomon Brothers and Lazard Frères, had come in with studies that estimated the company's breakup value at $46 to $56.50 a share.

At a critical KKR strategy session of a dozen people, Roberts threw out for discussion the idea of making a hostile tender for Beatrice. Kohlberg was vehemently opposed, as indeed were most of the attendees, and that was the end of it, though KKR applied pressure on the Beatrice board by letting drop dark hints in the press that it was considering a hostile offer. On October 29, KKR upped its bid to $47 and Beatrice agreed to open discussions with the buyout firm.

Bankers from Salomon and Lazard hit the phones, contacting some seventy-five corporations to solicit their interest in topping KKR. Although many companies were interested in acquiring parts of the firm, only one was willing to bid for Beatrice in its entirety. Dart Group, which owned auto-parts stores and discount bookstores, made a bid of $48 in partnership with E. F. Hutton Group, which was particularly aggressive in its attempts to rival Drexel as a deal financier. Although none of the financing for the Dart-Hutton bid was in hand, KKR decided to seize the initiative by sweetening its bid to $50 a share. While adding to their holdings, certain arbitrageurs began calling Beatrice directors, urging acceptance of KKR's offer. After a protracted bargaining session, Granger and the board finally capitulated on November thirteenth. At about eleven o'clock that night, Kravis telephoned Beck from Chicago with the good news. Amazingly, it was a year to the day since Beck made his bet with Kelly, who, to Beck's irritation, claimed that he had won the bet because the Beatrice transaction wouldn't officially close until the financing was completed (in April 1986). In the end, neither man would admit defeat and the bet was left unsettled.

In upping its bid from the initial $45 a share to $50 a share, KKR added $1.3 billion to the cost of the buyout. Drexel Burnham was able to cover the full amount of the difference by increasing the junk-bond component of the financing to $2.5 billion; Milken and company raised so much money, in fact, that KKR was able to shave its equity investment from the $500 million originally planned to $417 million. According to Drexel, though, it hadn't been easy. Financing Beatrice was "an enormous task," Milken said later. "There were a lot of non-believers." To complete the financing, Milken had to buy $235 million of the Beatrice bonds, mainly through private partnerships he controlled.

In his speeches from this period, Milken held out Beatrice as a shining example of one of his central tenets, which soon would be applied on an even larger scale with the buyout of RJR Nabisco. "Different industries demand different capital structures," Milken said. "Brand-name consumer companies were among those that came into the 1980s capable of operating with more debt than they had carried historically." To the old-fashioned investor, though, Beatrice's balance sheet was as alien as a spaceship. Had Beatrice been carrying the debt incurred in the buyout during its last fiscal year, it would have reported a net loss of $253 million instead of a profit of $479 million —mainly because of a crushing annual interest expense of $800 million. The prospectus warned that Beatrice's cash flow would be inadequate to cover the first two installments on its bank loans. If Beatrice dodged this hazard, other dangers loomed, the prospectus warned—that is, "operating cash flow will not be sufficient to make all of the principal payments under the Bank Credit Agreement which will become due in 1990, or to make required sinking fund payments on the Debt Securities which commence in 1994." In essence, buying Beatrice bonds was a bet that Kelly and KKR (presumably with Milken's sponsorship) would be able to improvise as fruitfully in the future as they had in the past.

In the immediate aftermath of the buyout, Kravis—apparently attempting to disarm his critics both within Beatrice and in Washington —repeatedly and publicly insisted that the economics of the deal did not hinge on busting up Beatrice for resale. KKR's agreement with its lenders and investors "isn't contingent on our selling anything off," said Kravis, whose statement was disingenuous at least. Within weeks after KKR's offer was accepted, Beatrice disclosed in an official government filing that it would not be able to meet its first big debt repayment in mid-1987 without selling at least $1.45 billion in assets.

While cementing the alliance between Drexel and KKR, the Beatrice deal set an exalted new standard of deal-maker self-enrichment, generating $250 million in middleman's fees. KKR paid itself an investment-banking fee of $45 million while Drexel pocketed $86 million in up-front fees, making Beatrice the single most lucrative deal the firm had ever done. Kidder, Peabody got $15 million and Lazard Frères and Salomon Brothers $8 million apiece. Kravis fulfilled his pledge to pay Beck a personal fee. The Mad Dog was exultant that the $4.5 million he received exceeded Oppenheimer's take by a comfortable margin—and that when it came time to celebrate the closing of the deal with a sumptuous banquet at the New-York Historical Society he was asked to sit at the head table with Kravis and Kelly while Steve Robert and the rest of the Oppenheimer contingent were stuck somewhere in the back.

Kravis was no less exultant than Beck. For starters, the Beatrice deal washed away the residue of frustration and embarrassment left by KKR's loss of Norton Simon to Esmark and its loss of Esmark to Beatrice. Kravis and his partners now controlled all three companies, which constituted a treasure trove of famous brands. Meanwhile, thanks to the Beatrice deal, KKR was as widely known in business circles as Avis, Hunt, Wesson, Swift, Playtex, and Tropicana were in the consumer marketplace. At a total value of $8.2 billion, Beatrice ranked not only as the largest LBO ever but as the largest takeover ever outside the oil industry. "Kohlberg," "Kravis," and "Roberts" may not have been household names, but you can bet that every CEO in the *Fortune* 500 was now aware of KKR's existence, if uncertain about the implications of the firm's rise to preeminence.

On Wall Street, meanwhile, Kravis and KKR had become a very big deal indeed. All traces of the investment-banking Establishment's lingering skepticism about KKR and the leveraged buyout were obliterated as the major houses began falling over one another in their eagerness to cultivate good relations with the firm synonomous with the LBO. From an M & A man's point of view, the beauty of Beatrice was not just that it generated outsized advisory fees but that it was a transaction predicated on future transactions. To pay off the debt incurred to finance the LBO, Beatrice had to sell billions of dollars of assets, subsidiary by subsidiary, M & A fee by M & A fee. To the extent that these sales were themselves accomplished through LBOs, then the new owners would also have to sell assets, creating a whole new round of transactions and so on and so on as the old Beatrice was atomized. In this sense, Beatrice wasn't just a deal but a deal industry in embryo. So eager were Morgan Stanley, Salomon Brothers, Merrill Lynch, and the rest to get in on the mega-LBO action that they set about raising funds to do their own buyouts in direct competition with KKR. Much as Kravis gloried in the expanded influence that was one result of the Beatrice deal, the intensifying competition it also produced would increasingly bring out the worst in him.

Kravis's professional apotheosis through Beatrice neatly coincided with his social apotheosis through marriage to Carolyne Roehm. Engaged at long last in the spring of 1985, Kravis and Roehm were married in November, only a few days after the Beatrice board accepted KKR's offer. Jeff was honored that he and Margo were among the 101 guests (or the "101 Dalmations," as they were nicknamed by one wag) invited to what *Gentleman's Quarterly* confusingly described as one of the "twenty weddings of the century since 1980." Kravis and Roehm were married in their new $5.5 million apartment in 740 Park Avenue. They'd bought the sixteen-room duplex in July and Roehm immediately began to direct its makeover, finishing just days before the wedding. "Make me a beautiful cocoon," she had instructed designer Vincent Fourcade, and embarked on a shopping tour of Europe. Back by the truckload came English and French antique furniture and paintings from the eighteenth and nineteenth centuries. On the celadon-green walls of the living room, a Renoir was hung across from a Monet landscape and a Tissot portrait. A drawing room held a second Renoir and a Sisley. Coral damask lined the walls and silk festoon shades adorned the windows. On one wall of the dining room, which was done up in apricot-and-yellow damask, was a massive Sargent portrait of the sixth marquess of London. Even for Ray Kravis, no stranger to the joys of conspicuous consumption, it was all a bit much. Looking at the Sargent portrait, he gently chided his son: "Which one of our relatives is this?"

At the dinner that followed the wedding ceremony, the elder Kravis, fairly bursting with paternal pride, preceded his toast to his son with a folksy reminiscence that had to rank as *the* most embarrassing anecdote delivered at any wedding of the century before or after 1980. "You wouldn't know it to look at him now," Ray said. "But when Henry came out of Bessie he looked like a skinned rat." Beck, who had to bite his tongue to keep from laughing out loud, added the story of

Ray's toast to his repertoire of favorite tales from the deal trade, though he wisely avoided telling it in Henry's presence.

Standing on ceremony, Beck waited until the very day that the Beatrice transaction officially closed in the spring of 1986 to send out a round of thank-you letters. In his letter to Don Kelly, Beck wrote:

> Well, they said it couldn't be done and you and Henry have done it. I guess this beats re-arranging the "refrigerator" and my particular congratulations to Byrd Mary [Kelly's wife]. I want to thank you for giving me several opportunities starting with Norton Simon followed by Esmark/KKR, followed by Esmark/Beatrice and then followed by the acquisition of Beatrice. I guess from both of our points of view the deal that we did not do was the best thing that ever happened to us. Speaking for myself, I learned a lot and want to thank you for being supportive during a very difficult period.

To Dick Beattie, who'd acted as lawyer to KKR and who'd endorsed Beck's request to Kravis for a personal fee:

> I want to thank you for speaking up for me during a very difficult period of my life. I guess all's well that ends well and in the case of Beatrice that ending was obviously very gratifying for me. I know that this transaction could not have been done without you and for my own personal point of view I also know that your help in doing what was right and fair was invaluable to me. Your statement that you and Henry have been and will continue to be people that I can count on are not only words but facts.

And to Kravis himself:

> Congratulations and thank you for being such a great friend. It is hard for me to believe that the Beatrice transaction has been executed and that I was fortunate enough to participate in a transaction of this size and complexity. I want to thank you for your fairness and understanding during a very difficult period in my life and as I said before, I will never forget it.

A few weeks after sending the letters, Beck said thank you in a different way by writing out large checks to three organizations that had seen fit to name Kravis to their boards in recognition of his generosity. Specifying in each case that his gift was in honor of Kravis, Beck gave $25,000 to Mount Sinai Hospital, $25,000 to Channel Thirteen, and $60,000 to the New York City Ballet. Kravis had solicited the contributions after the Beatrice deal closed, and Beck didn't have to be reminded that he'd recently deposited a multimillion-dollar check from KKR. This was the way the game was played. Kravis knew it and so did he.

18

No, it couldn't be! . . . Could it? . . . Yes, it could. It moved!
. . . Or had it? Beck took a peek at the guy sitting to his left and
then the guy to his right. Not the slightest flicker of amusement was
evident on either man's face as, rapt with attention, they listened to
the words of Mike Milken. Beck wasn't uninterested in what Milken
had to say. But as the junk-bond king held forth on his favorite subject,
Beck couldn't help but tune out his words and concentrate instead on
his hairline. There was no doubt about it: Milken's toupee had slid
down an inch or so onto his forehead. The thing was crooked, too.
You'd think a guy with his own capital market could afford a decent
hairpiece. Uh-oh. Beck could feel an uncontrollable urge welling up
inside. He got up from his chair, excused himself, and bolted for the
bathroom. A few minutes later he returned to the conference room,
safely purged of laughter.

Although Beck had spoken briefly by phone with Milken before
joining Drexel, he waited until his third week at the firm to make his
first visit to Beverly Hills. Beatrice had accepted KKR's bid a few days
before, and Beck was basking in postdeal acclaim. He'd made certain
that his new colleagues in Drexel's New York offices were aware of the
role that he'd played in catalyzing history's largest leveraged buyout
and was confident that word had penetrated the innermost recesses of
Milken's lair. Fresh from the crowning triumph of his career, Beck had
flown out to Beverly Hills brimming with restored enthusiasm and self-
confidence, ready to expose his rainmaker's aura to Milken's greater
glow. They'd met the first time more than a decade before, while Beck
was in convertible bonds at DLJ. Milken, who traded converts, too,
had come in for a job interview and a tour of the trading room. They'd
shaken hands, talked a little shop, and that was that. Beck had often
wondered what would have become of DLJ and his own career had

Milken joined that firm instead of staying at Drexel. Beck decided, though, not to make any mention of their earlier meeting, mainly to spare himself embarrassment if, as seemed likely, Milken failed to remember. And anyway, this was a business trip, not a social call.

Beck had brokered a meeting between Milken and John Childs, who, as head of the capital-markets group at Prudential Insurance Company of America, oversaw a bulging investment portfolio of some $80 billion. No financial institution in the country—Drexel included —had a longer history of successful experimentation at the margins of the credit-rating system than did the Pru, which had begun making high-yielding loans to small entrepreneurs while Milken was still in grade school. As the largest lender on the private side of the LBO business, the Pru found it more lucrative to invest directly in deals than to take a secondhand slice of Drexel-engineered transactions. Then, too, Prudential had shied away from investing in hostile take-overs of any kind. While individual managers had come and gone over the years, the Pru had maintained a formidably disciplined approach to investment. Despite Milken's persistent salesmanship, the New Jersey–based insurer had never had done more than a token amount of junk-bond business with Drexel Burnham.

Childs happened to be a distant cousin of Margo Beck, though Jeff wasn't aware of this family connection when he first met the Pru executive during his ill-fated attempt to scare up financing for the Northwest Industries transaction. Childs had offered to provide virtually all the financing—but only if Kelly Briggs Oppenheimer sharply reduced the price it had already agreed to pay for Northwest. A compromise proved elusive, but Childs had gone away impressed by Beck's creativity and tenacity and had stayed in touch with him. In pondering how to convert his existing relationships into new business for Drexel, Beck hit on the idea of inviting Childs on a tour of Milkenland. If the Pru's resistance softened as a result of Childs's visit, Beck would have done Milken a service of the sort he no doubt appreciated most. In the interests of maintaining good relations with Wall Street's fastest-rising investment bank—and out of sheer curiosity—Childs accepted, and brought along to Beverly Hills a half dozen of his top lieutenants.

Beck and his guests didn't see much of Milken during their two-day visit, which began with a five-thirty A.M. breakfast and a tour of the facilities conducted by Harry Horowitz, a boyhood buddy of Milken's who served as his chief aide-de-camp. They spent endless hours in a conference room listening as a parade of analysts and salesmen took turns making the statistical case for junk bonds. Beck thought it all quite impressive. Milken's minions had marshaled an enormous amount of data and custom-tailored it to fit the Prudential's particular concerns. After a few hours of buildup on the first morning, Milken made his entrance, looking deceptively ordinary in a modest blue suit and polka-dot tie. Although Milken had a certain square-jawed, high-cheekboned handsomeness when viewed obliquely, he would have been disqualified from a modeling career by eyes that were a bit closely set and a forehead that protruded over an undersized nose. A few inches taller than Beck, Milken had the solid, broad-shouldered build of an athlete and a winning, almost shy smile. During his many years of junk-bond missionary work, he'd developed the salesman's flair for preliminary small talk, usually sports-related, since Milken was a big Los Angeles Lakers fan.

All frivolity ended, though, the instant Milken began his presentation. While Beck and Childs were impressed with Milken's mastery of his subject, neither found his performance spellbinding. Milken overwhelmed not with artfulness of language or with emotional intensity à la Richard Rainwater, but with sheer volume of data and argument. A barrage of statistics, anecdotes, and opinions came rat-a-tat-tatting out of him like lead out of a machine gun locked on continuous fire. He seemed to know everything. Although Beck at times found it difficult to follow the thread of Milken's argument—his mind tended to leap without transition from one subject to another—there seemed nothing alarmingly odd about him. He came across as a very intense professor of finance. The weirdness was introduced by his assistants, who every now and then interjected paeans to their leader, often speaking in the third person—as in, Mike-believes-this or Mike-did-that. It's like Milken isn't even in the room, Beck thought, suppressing the urge to say something like "The guy is sitting right there. Let *him* tell us what he thinks." During these periodic tributes, Beck kept an eye on Milken, who seemed oblivious to what was being said, lost no doubt in contemplating some new abstraction of the yield curve. Beck was beginning to feel as if he'd wandered by mistake into the command center of some financially futuristic offshoot of the Church of Scientology.

While Milkenism, in keeping with the press-paranoid inclinations of its guru, was a very private cult, many of its followers' most worshipful accolades would find their way into print over the years. John Kissick, who was in charge of Drexel's corporate-finance operation on the West

Coast (and who would succeed Milken after his ouster from Drexel), once told a reporter: "Mike is what we would all like our sons to be." Dort Cameron, who was one of Milken's very first assistants and an exceptionally cagey character (when I called him once at the suggestion of Drexel's PR department, he said nothing for a few seconds after I identified myself and then hissed, "How did you get my name?"), proclaimed that "Michael is the most important individual who has lived in this century." Another even more devout follower amended Cameron's statement to include "the last five hundred years."

Not being by nature a cult follower of anything, Beck flew back to New York thinking that the whole scene in Beverly Hills was creepy. On the other hand, he had to admit that Milken was impressive. He radiated such extraordinary energy, intellectual command, and devotion to his work that Beck's competitive mechanisms were never activated. Who could imagine competing with a guy like that?

Despite the misgivings he'd voiced while at Oppenheimer, Beck soon found himself not only admiring Milken but liking him. Although by no means a "regular guy" as Beck usually defined his highest compliment, Milken seemed completely without pretension, intellectual or material. Although he was rumored to be a billionaire, Milken lived in a modest house on Tara Drive in Encino just a few blocks from where he'd grown up and was still happily married to the same woman—his high-school sweetheart, yet. From what Beck heard, you wouldn't find Mike and Lori Milken out flashdancing every night in celebration of their charitable generosity. They preferred to stay home, even though their walls weren't packed with Renoirs or Tissots and no live-in servants served them dinner in their dining room, which wouldn't come close to holding 101 of their closest friends. Beck and Milken got to know each other by long distance mainly, talking regularly on the telephone, about not only particular transactions but overarching issues of business strategy and philosophy, especially those pertaining to the management of Drexel itself. Although Beck's view of Milken would take on darker shadings as he learned more about how Milken and Drexel operated, Beck would remain basically sympathetic to him, offering his blunt-spoken advice throughout the heavy trouble to come.

For his part, Milken came to respect Beck's talents as a rainmaker. "Jeff had his own unique style," Milken said. "He had a certain way about him that enabled him to have a very good rapport with businessmen who were assertive and had a great deal of self-confidence. Jeff knew how to make people feel comfortable and how to ask a question or state an opinion without beating around the bush like a lot of people. Other people might be thinking the same thing but keep it to themselves. But I can't think of anything that Jeff would be unwilling to say."

Milken's and Beck's affinity was more deeply rooted psychologically than either of them realized, for neither rainmaker knew that the other had come of age idealizing a father who was bent on escaping the reality of a past painful beyond mention. Like Beck and other rainmakers of the era, Milken was an extreme, even bizarre personality who'd been shaped by what outwardly appeared to be most the conventional of American middle-class circumstances. Milken was just a few months younger than Beck and, like him, had come of age in a baby-boom paradise of endless summers, perfect waves, and great expectations—in his case, southern California in the heyday of the Beach Boys.

But when Milken was fourteen, he belatedly realized that his father was not who he appeared to be—at least to his adoring son. One day Mike and his dad, Bernard, were playing touch football on the dead-end street on which the Milkens lived in Encino. As usual, the elder Milken was playing quarterback. One of the neighbor kids came up to Mike and said, "Hey, what's wrong with your dad? He's limping." Mike looked at his father and saw it was true. "What's wrong?" he asked his father, who ignored the question and called the next play. After the game, Milken was surprised to see that his father was still walking funny. But there was nothing wrong with Bernard Milken, at least nothing that hadn't been wrong with him since he'd contracted polio as a little boy. A lifelong limp was his only concession to his handicap. Through sheer force of will, Bernard had even made himself into a good dancer and tennis player, though he wore long pants on the court to hide his bad leg. Bernard's disease was but one aspect of a past that he never talked about, a past so awful that it seemed like something out of Dickens.

Born Bernhard Milkewitz, he'd grown up in Kenosha, Wisconsin, the son of Jewish immigrants from Eastern Europe. His mother died of illness about the time he contracted polio at age two, and a car crash claimed the life of his father seven years later. Bernhard's father left him a small inheritance that was dissipated by the executor of his estate. The boy was packed off to a boarding school that could easily have been mistaken for an orphanage, so penurious were its conditions. Bernhard wrote letters to his cousins pleading for a quarter so that he could buy a sweater. After surviving this ordeal, he returned to Kenosha to attend high school, living with a family that took him in. Bernard (he'd officially changed his name, dropping the "h") studied at the University of Wisconsin, where he majored in accounting and supported himself with odd jobs, including a peanut-machine concession. After graduating he went on to law school at Wisconsin, graduating in 1943. The next year he married Fay Zax, an undergraduate student, and took the bar in Illinois, where her parents lived. Bernard took the test on a Monday and left on Thursday for Los Angeles, never to return and never, for that matter, to practice law. In the Golden State, Milkewitz found work as a CPA and was inspired to change his last name to Milken by the impending arrival of his first child, Michael, born on the Fourth of July, 1946.

Bernard and "Fern" Milken were founts of energy and optimism, who raised Michael and his younger brother and sister with what one magazine writer would describe as "a transcendent belief in their own possibilities, as if they did not want to burden them with the grim reality of Bernard's childhood." From earliest boyhood, Michael was a confident, driven overachiever. By the time he was eight he was handling routine accounting chores for his father, who encouraged his son to ask questions about everything—other than his own past, that is. Mike would buttonhole guests at his parents' bridge-club parties and quiz them. When were they born? Where had they gone to school? What did they do for a living? What's the capital of South Dakota? While down in Coral Gables Beck's adolescence was taking a turn into rebelliousness, young Milken was as happy and wholesome as a glass of milk. He didn't drink or smoke or even consume caffeine in any form. No Cokes for Mike, whose abstinence was more a matter of physiology than ideology. Even then, the Milken brain allowed the Milken body only three or four hours of rest a night. For Milken, drinking a cup of coffee would have been like trying to put another gallon of gas into a full tank.

As Milken became famous and then infamous and was subjected to the mythologizing effects of journalism (compounded in his case by a penchant for secrecy that approached paranoia), nothing infuriated him more than the widely retailed notion that he'd grown up an egghead nerd whose only idea of fun was doing advanced multiplication problems in his head. Yes, it was true that he'd been head cheer-leader at Birmingham High School, but, he'd hasten to add, he was a popular kid who'd been elected to this highly coveted position by his classmates and, though too skinny to play football on one of the state's best teams, he excelled at baseball, basketball, and tennis. "I was one of the two best athletes in my grammar school," he once told me in all seriousness. Yes, he'd married his high-school sweetheart, who was indeed prom queen to his king, but in between the time they met in seventh grade and married after college, he went out with plenty of other women. And he categorically denied the vivid anecdote with which Connie Bruck opened *The Predators' Ball,* the first book on Drexel—that is, never, *ever,* did he strap a miner's headlamp over a leather aviator's cap so that he could read annual reports during his early-morning bus trips from New Jersey to Drexel's Wall Street offices. Yes, he caught the bus at five-thirty A.M. and read the fine print of corporate documents throughout his commute, but the overhead light provided all the illumination he required.

Invited to join the math brigade at the California Institute of Technology, Milken instead chose to go to the University of California at Berkeley, knowing full well that it was a chaotic hub of life-style experimentation and and extremist politics. For someone of Milken's inquisitiveness, Berkeley in the mid-1960s was an intellectual playground. Milken would go down to Telegraph and Bancroft and make the rounds of all the booths run by the Free Love Society, the American Nazi Party, the American Communist Party, the Black Panthers, and many other radical organizations. "I would sit and listen, not take issue. You learn more by asking questions—particularly when you're talking to a zealot," recalled Milken, without irony. (When Milken started his famous annual conference years later, he envisioned it not as a business convention—much less as a "predators' ball"—but as a bazaar of ideas in the Berkeley mold. "It was very hurtful to me the way it was misrepresented.") While Milken did a lot of listening, he confined his activism to helping run his fraternity while he studied math and finance. Outspoken neither in support of nor opposition to the Vietnam war, he received a 4-F draft classification because of a slight heart murmur.

It was at Berkeley that Milken's own incipient zealotry crystallized around corporate finance. While still in college, Milken had taken a summer job with one of his father's clients, a well-heeled investor with a special interest in low-rated convertible bonds. Intrigued by the hefty returns this man was earning investing in bonds shunned as déclassé by most investors, Milken began studying the methods by which the rating agencies analyzed debt issues, and second-guessing many ratings. Backing his analysis with cash, he began investing his money in low-rated bonds. At Berkeley, Milken got very, very excited after reading a 1958 study by a professor named W. Bradford Hickman, who'd studied the performance of every corporate bond issue extant from 1900 to 1943. "The Hickman study validated what seemed to me to be intuitively correct, which was that the risk premium on low-rate debt was greatly exaggerated compared to the spread. And if that was true, then there was in fact something seriously wrong with traditional credit analysis." Although Hickman's and other related treatises were written in the dry prose of academia, it was Milken's nature to read into them a call to the barricades.

After graduating from Berkeley in 1968, Milken headed to the Wharton School of Business, where his critique of convention moved beyond bond ratings to encompass the whole stodgy universe of traditional corporate finance. Contrary to legend, Milken's famous thesis at Wharton dealt not with the rating system per se but with the notion of "optimal capital structure." Simply put, the basic idea that Milken would inflate, with compulsive brilliance, into his life's work was that a company's financial structure should be derived not from a set of universal standards passed on from generation to generation like stone tablets but from the particularities of its business, its prospects, and the abilities of its management. A debt-to-equity ratio of 5 to 1 may have been suicide for a stagnant company of the past but be the means to greatness for a growth company of the future. As Milken saw it, the function of the financier was not to mindlessly follow formulas from the old corporate-finance cookbook—one part debt for every two parts equity and a pinch of preferred—but to achieve a deep understanding of a business and help tailor a capital structure that best suited it, using debt as liberally as necessary. When the idea was stated this way, who could disagree? Wasn't this a nation devoted to life, liberty, and the perfectability of the mousetrap?

In his political naïveté, Milken failed at first to recognize the radical implications of his approach, which would massively divert credit from the corporate haves to the have-nots. What was good for the country was not necessarily good for the men who ran the country. "I was naïve in that I thought I was in a position to solve all problems," Milken told me after pleading guilty in 1990 to six felony counts. "I still believe there is a solution for all problems but that I can't be the one to solve them."

Milken was rudely introduced to Establishment realities at the old-line investment bank of Drexel Harriman Ripley, for which he went to work full-time in 1970, beginning to trade low-rated bonds shortly thereafter. Milken could not have picked a more unlikely place to put his ideas into practice than Drexel, an aristocratic WASP bastion with a lineage traced back to J. P. Morgan himself. From his earliest years all the way through Wharton, Milken had been the golden boy, the California dreamer limited only by his self-definition of destiny. At Drexel, though, they stuck him in a corner and laughed at him behind his back, making fun of his clothes, his ill-fitting toupee, and above all his tacky, tacky merchandise. "The high-grade bond guys considered him a leper," said a colleague. "They said, 'Drexel can't be presenting itself to these high-grade, *Fortune* 500 companies and have Mike out peddling this *crap.*'" Resisting the temptation to return to school, Milken dedicated himself to winning not acceptance but vindication. The more entrenched interests and conventional wisdom conspired against him, the more Milken's self-confidence would harden into self-righteousness; what had begun as a career inflated into a cause. He *knew* he was right, and he intended to prove it. Nothing could stop him. What was a little class prejudice to a man who even as a boy possessed the evangelical power of mind to mentally make a crippled father whole?

A young Drexel banker by the name of Marc Utay was sitting at Beck's desk, talking business over the speakerphone as the Mad Dog paced restlessly nearby, psyching himself up for a full day's deal making. Suddenly, Beck jumped onto the couch, trampolined off it onto a nearby table, and then with a great leap landed atop the desk. As Utay watched wide-eyed, Beck gave a Tarzan yell and threw himself against the Plexiglas that formed part of one wall of the office. Beck's 190 pounds made a mighty thud, quickly followed by a scream as a secretary sitting in the hallway outside ran for cover. The partition held as Beck, recoiling from the impact, barely managed to keep his balance. The secretary came storming in, shaking with anger and dread. She'd thought the whole wall was coming down on top of her. Suddenly sheepish, Beck apologized profusely from atop the desk. When the woman left, he jumped down. "She's not broken in yet," he said to Utay.

Revived by his Beatrice triumph, Beck brought enormous raw energy to his initial rainmaking efforts at Drexel Burnham. Optimism springing eternal was one of Beck's most endearing traits; he began work at his fourth Wall Street firm suffused with feelings of fellowship and giddy good cheer that caused him to consider almost every one of his new colleagues a promising talent and potential good buddy—even as he continued to seethe with bitterness toward his erstwhile chums at Oppenheimer. In the grip of this initial enthusiasm, Beck even went so far as to suggest that Fred Joseph would make a good candidate for president—of the United States. After battling the naysayers of Oppenheimer & Company for so many years, it was liberating for Beck to be representing an investment bank that prized audacity of imagination as much as he did and that seemed capable of financing any project that he was capable of dreaming up.

Beck began, naturally, by trying to convince his clients at Oppenheimer to make the jump with him. Beck didn't bother calling his client of longest standing, Warner-Lambert, which had just changed CEOs and was absorbing a big loss on its most recent acquisition. Nor did he pursue Varian Associates right away, since it was in the midst of a transaction with Oppenheimer. While Al Taubman and Arnout Loudon of Akzo had loyally protested Beck's dismissal by snubbing John Sanzo, Beck's successor, neither mogul was in the position of having to rely on junk-bond financing, and each was leery of Drexel. Affiliating with an investment bank was not a matter of trifling concern to businessmen of position and integrity like Taubman and Loudon, both of whom eventually did sign on with Drexel because of their regard for Beck. The relationship of investment bank and corporation might have been determined relatively more by economics and less by social ties in the 1980s than in the 1890s, but it still contained an implicit element of mutual endorsement. In other words, with *whom* one did business mattered no less on Mike Milken's Wall Street than it had in J. P. Morgan's day.

As for KKR, the buyout firm was already solidly in the Drexel fold before Beck's arrival. Leon Black considered KKR to be one of the most important of *his* clients and as cohead of the M & A department had the authority to enforce his claim, as Beck discovered in trying unsuccessfully to involve himself in the financing of the Beatrice buyout. While it annoyed Beck to be relegated to a subordinate role in Drexel's dealings with Kravis, he didn't make much of a fuss. For one thing, he realized that he was in no position to take on Black. For another, Beck quite liked Black and was eager to cultivate a good working relationship with the younger banker, who was a consummate deal technician of the sort he'd relied on throughout his career. Then, too, with deal-making activity continuing to rise sharply—in no small measure because of Drexel's increasingly assertive use of its power and influence—there was no shortage of new prospects for Beck to pursue. For an M & A rainmaker, 1986 was prime time.

In his job interviews with Joseph, Beck had argued that the best way for Drexel to ensure its prosperity over the long term was to gradually dissociate itself from the corporate-raider fraternity and begin putting its muscle at the service of blue-chip corporations, in effect helping them restructure on their own terms instead of on those imposed by Wall Street. Joseph didn't disagree in concept. To the contrary, Joseph could not hope to realize his aspiration of making Drexel the Goldman, Sachs of the 1990s without moving the firm into the mainstream of corporate finance. In practice, though, Joseph and the rest of Drexel's leadership would prove utterly incapable of resisting the allure of the quick and dirty buck in the interest of securing the firm's future. Even as Joseph encouraged Beck's pursuit of Establishment firms on one hand, Drexel was antagonizing America's self-consciously respectable corporations with its belligerent opportunism on the other. While it was inevitable that Beck and his new firm increasingly would find themselves at cross-purposes, the Mad Dog began his turbulent stay at Drexel with a remarkable burst of rainmaking success. By the end of his first year, Beck had added to his and Drexel's roster of clients some of America's oldest and most eminent corporations: Ralston Purina, RJR Nabisco, and Pillsbury among them. But of all the new relationships Beck initiated at Drexel Burnham, the most personal and gratifying was that with W. R. Grace & Company.

Although W. R. Grace was a giant company by any measure, it could not have been more completely dominated by one man had it been a storefront pizza parlor or shoeshine stand. J. Peter Grace was far and away the longest-reigning CEO of any *Fortune* 500 company and one of the last great blue-blooded eccentrics of American industry. Peter Grace's executive power was a function less of the perquisites of capital—by the time Beck met him in 1986 his family's ownership stake in W. R. Grace's stock had shriveled to less than 2 percent—than of sheer force of personality and the ferocity of the man's commitment, not so much to the family company (founded by his Irish immigrant grandfather, William Russell Grace, in 1854) but to his own control of it. The gun didn't hurt, either; Grace, who was seventy-four when Beck met him, packed a fully loaded Cobra .38 Special pistol in a holster he wore on his belt. After forty years of imperial sovereignty, Grace always said what he thought when he thought it. After a particularly frustrating visit to Washington, Grace remarked to a reporter: "I didn't realize what a bunch of shits congressmen are." He was the one CEO whom Beck considered a more colorful character than he was himself.

One day, Beck, Black, and a W. R. Grace executive were standing around a conference room at the company awaiting Peter Grace's arrival. Grace came in late and, as was his wont, immediately challenged Beck to an arm-wrestling contest. Beck tried just hard enough to lose, though, for his age, Grace was no pushover. Grace got up from the table and sidled right up next to Black, who at six foot three towered over Grace and was noticeably overfed at about 250 pounds. Like Elmer Fudd, Grace pronounced his "l's" and "r's" as "w's."

"My, my, Weon," Grace said to Black. "You're a big, big boy."

As Grace giggled, Black stared at America's longest-reigning CEO in stark amazement. Was this really happening?

"You must eat a wot for bweakfast," Grace said. "Tell me, Weon, what *do* you eat for bweakfast? How about wunch? Heh-heh. Dinner?"

Grace giggled all the way to the door and then left. He didn't return. Today's meeting was over before it had begun.

Beck gave Black his best deadpan look. "There goes another average American just trying to do business in the United States."

This incident inspired Beck to change his nickname for Black from "Pizza the Hut" to "Weon," which was later refined, so to speak, to "Wee-Wee." When he realized that Black found none of these names amusing or even tolerable, Beck used them more often.

Peter Grace has always been evasive on the question of the psychological dynamics of his youthful transformation from a trust-fund playboy who wanted no part of W. R. Grace into an efficiency-obsessed workaholic who outlasted generation after generation of heirs apparent in stubborn refusal to surrender even a pittance of control over the company he'd inherited. Might the death of a dear friend have brought on intimations of his own mortality? Was his strict Catholic upbringing finally kicking in? The latent power of parental example?

Probably.

In any event, the catalyst was the sudden incapacitation of his fa-

ther, who had a stroke in 1945. Peter was thirty-two years old at the
time, an ex-Yalie who'd lettered in hockey as a goalie in the days before
face masks. He'd spent many a summer sailing on his father's 150-foot
yacht with its twenty-man crew, and shooting grouse on a castle estate
in Scotland. He had a sixteen-cylinder Cadillac, a private polo field
with thirty ponies, a hefty income from a trust fund, and girlfriends
galore. What did he want with the burden of corporate management?
But when the call came, Grace answered it. And at a time when Don
Kelly was still kicking around in low-level accounting jobs in Chicago,
Grace came to the conclusion that the family company, despite its
appearance of good health (its profits had quadrupled over the preceding decade), in reality needed a thorough overhaul. In introducing a
speech by Grace at Drexel's annual junk-bond conference, Beck aptly
described him as "the forefather of restructuring." Intent on lessening
W. R. Grace's heavy dependence on its steamship line and its vast
plantations and trading and textile operations in Latin America, Peter
gradually established the company as one of the world's largest manufacturers of specialty chemicals and then ventured into diverse other
pursuits, including auto parts, office supplies, brewing, specialty retailing, and restaurants. Meanwhile, he was disposing of the historic operations, including the twenty-three-ship Grace Line, the most visible
symbol of the old empire. By the 1970s, nary a business that Grace
had inherited in 1945 remained part of the company.

Grace not only dodged looming oblivion but reinvented the family
company on a vastly expanded scale; by 1986 total assets had risen to
$5.4 billion, from $165 million in 1950. Obsessed with securing W. R.
Grace's long-term future in an increasingly insecure world, Grace
adopted deal making as a way of life; under his stewardship, W. R.
Grace made more than 150 major acquisitions and 75 divestitures. For
years, Wall Street searched for evidence of a cohesive master plan in
Grace's churning, but found only the flaky, unabashed opportunism of
J. Peter Grace, proprietor. After a while, Grace just stopped listening
to his critics. Certainly, he held the average Wall Streeter in no higher
esteem than he did the typical congressman. Within the company,
meanwhile, Grace surrounded himself with yes-men whom he kept
hopping through hoops with incessant demands for voluminous statistical information. In support of a $2 million acquisition, executives had
to prepare a spreadsheet that, at one thousand columns, had to be
tacked up along sixty feet of hallway for the CEO's perusal. Grace had
a superior mind for figures and a deep faith in their value: "Numbers

are reality," he liked to say. Numbers also provided a ready means of justifying his habitual browbeating of underlings, who were required to provide so many minutely detailed forecasts of corporate performance that they couldn't help but err frequently. Executive turnover was epidemic. Four of Grace's nine children chose to work at the company, but not even they lasted very long.

Grace was as compulsive in his good works as in his exercise of corporate power. Taking to heart the scriptural admonition "For unto whomsoever much is given, of him shall be much required," Grace lived like a man convinced that he could never do enough to assure his passage through the pearly gates. Long before Beck met him, Grace had established himself as the most prominent lay Catholic in America and the undisputed leader of the fifteen hundred American members of the Sovereign Order of Malta, the oldest chivalric order in Christendom. Every year, Grace raised millions for the church while serving as a benefactor, director, or adviser to more than fifty Catholic charities and institutions. He spent so much time flying around the world on church-related missions—often with ecclesiastics of many ranks in tow—that it was often said that his corporate jet could have been mistaken for the pope's. Grace's most prized possession was a tiny wooden statue of the Virgin Mary given him by Mother Theresa in appreciation of the use of the Grace jet on a speaking tour. Grace carried the statue with him everywhere—just like his gun.

Peter Grace's web of influence extended beyond the corporate and Catholic worlds to encompass the highest level of governmental power. A virulent anticommunist, Grace was rumored to have used his company's influence in South America over the years to support various covert activities of the Central Intelligence Agency, including the military coup against Salvador Allende in Chile. Grace, a lifelong Republican and combative conservative, reached his zenith of political influence during the presidency of Ronald Reagan, who in 1982 appointed him to head a high-level group to study waste in government. Known informally as the Grace Commission, the group recommended 2,478 cost-cutting measures that, it claimed, would save $424 billion over three years. Grace barnstormed the country in support of his commission's findings, generating enormous publicity with bombastic speeches. With Reagan in the White House, the various strands of Grace's influence reinforced one another more powerfully than ever before. For example, the Knights of Malta funneled millions of dollars in "humanitarian" aid to Honduran refugee camps, which supplied the Reagan-backed Contra guerrilla force waging war against the Marxist government of Nicaragua. Meanwhile, Grace intervened to obtain federal financing for a leprosy-vaccination program in Latin America, advancing him another step closer to heaven.

Beneath all of Grace's idiosyncrasies, though, was a classic Establishment power broker: a third-generation heir who presided over a major industrial corporation as a family fiefdom and whose personal network of friendships and alliances encompassed wealth and power in all forms. Grace also was a man of principle, though some of his principles were not easily reconciled with one another. Given the extent of his influence and the ferocity of his belief, Grace definitely was not someone to trifle with. But even Grace, in the end, was accountable to the free-market forces so beloved—at least in the abstract—by him and his fellow conservatives. When the threat of takeover finally brought Grace to his day of reckoning in 1985, he did not, to his credit, go running to his friends in Washington but instead turned to Drexel Burnham.

W. R. Grace was a temptingly obvious target. Four straight years of steeply diminishing earnings had knocked down the price of its stock from low to subterranean. Overhead costs were excessive and cash flow barely adequate to cover the dividend. W. R. Grace would have come under attack earlier had not Grace sold a 26 percent interest to the Flick Group of West Germany in the 1970s. Friedrich Karl Flick, the billionaire owner of the Flick Group, was a bosom buddy of Grace's who'd once worked at W. R. Grace and remained a director. In 1985 Flick sold his entire empire to Deutsche Bank, which decided to liquidate the Grace stock, giving W. R. Grace itself the right of first refusal. Peter Grace decided that he had to buy the Flick block if he were to have any chance of keeping the company independent, even though to buy he would have to borrow the entire $600 million required. The added interest costs, however, would reduce Grace's already inadequate earnings, further aggravating its vulnerability to takeover. Something had to give. After years of resisting suggestions that he consider restructuring, Peter Grace finally relented. A long-time client of Merrill Lynch, W. R. Grace also hired First Boston to help weigh strategic options. To forestall the threat of a junk-bond raid, a senior Grace executive, Terrence Daniels, called Fred Joseph to indicate preliminary interest in retaining Drexel as an adviser. Joseph invited Daniels down to lunch at the firm.

When Daniels arrived for lunch, he was shocked to find an old acquaintance at Joseph's side. Daniels had gotten to know Beck in the mid-1970s while commuting from New Jersey to New York City on the Erie-Lackawanna Railroad. Daniels got a kick out of Beck's manic chutzpah, and still recalled a cocktail party at the Becks' during which Jeff announced that he was making a transatlantic call to the infamous English raider Roland "Tiny" Rowland. Daniels listened as Beck growled in a gangsterish voice: "Hey, Tiny, baby, how are ya? It's Beck." Daniels never knew for sure if Rowland really had been on the line. He'd lost track of Beck for five or six years as they both moved up in the world and left the Erie-Lackawanna behind. In late 1984, Daniels read my profile of Beck in *Business Week* and called him. After briefly renewing their acquaintance, Daniels and Beck again lost touch as the Mad Dog was caught up in the concluding traumas of his Oppenheimer years. As far as Daniels knew, Beck was still at Oppenheimer. When Beck heard through the grapevine that Daniels was coming in for lunch, he invited himself. Afterward, Beck gave the Grace executive a ride back to the office in his chauffeured Mercedes. Beck had always liked Daniels and he was not about to let the opportunity he represented slip away again.

The second time Daniels lunched at Drexel with Joseph he brought Peter Grace with him. For Grace and Beck, the experience was something approximating love at first sight. "Jeff, like Peter, is the kind of guy you talk about," Daniels said. "When he leaves the room, you sit there and say, 'Can you believe that?'" Grace's customary way of getting to know someone was to subject them to inquisition, unleashing a barrage of personal and often offbeat questions in good-natured but relentless fashion—as in: "You seem like a well-adjusted person, Fred. But are you? . . . You seem young to have gray hair. When did your hair start turning gray? . . . Did you grow up in a warm family?" And on and on.

Beck found Grace's routine quite amusing, but thought that Joseph wasn't his usual loquacious and opinionated self. Afterward, Beck asked Joseph why he hadn't put up more resistance to Grace's verbal thrusts. "Didn't you see?" Joseph said. "The fucking guy had a gun." Beck considered this the funniest thing Joseph ever said.

Grace came away "very impressed" with Joseph. "I thought he was extremely controlled and sensible. He seemed to be a very cool cookie and I trusted him." Any lingering doubts Grace might have had about hiring Drexel were jettisoned when GAF Corporation aborted its hostile takeover bid for Union Carbide. GAF was a client of Drexel, which had nearly completed raising $3.5 billion on its behalf when the company decided for its own reasons not to proceed. With Union Carbide in play, Wall Street's takeover spotlight was trained with new intensity on other chemical producers, notably W. R. Grace. Takeover speculators began loading up on W. R. Grace shares as rumors that GAF was preparing a hostile tender made the rounds. Beck lobbied Joseph to side with Grace rather than finance a raid against him, and his argument carried the day. By hiring Drexel, Grace not only immunized itself against junk-bond attack but gained access to sorely needed financing. "Their muscle was confidence-inspiring," Grace said. "You look more powerful with Drexel behind you."

To raise cash to reduce the crushing burden of debt it carried after buying the Flick block, W. R. Grace had no choice but to sell assets. But which ones, and how to dispose of them? Grace and his advisers decided to maintain chemical manufacturing as the company's core and to sell off the half-dozen chains of retail stores that it owned. Daniels split this assignment between Merrill Lynch and First Boston. When it became apparent that still more cash would be needed, Daniels mustered his nerve and urged the sale of Grace's 690 restaurants, which were organized in a dozen chains, including Coco's, Charley Brown's, and Houlihan's. Although the restaurant group had never been more than modestly profitable, Peter Grace had taken a keen personal interest in the business and was attached to it. Daniels overcame the boss's initial objections by proposing a leveraged buyout through which W. R. Grace could sell control of the restaurant group to the Grace executives currently managing it and yet retain an ownership interest. For help with the restaurant LBO, Daniels turned to Beck and Leon Black.

The deal started smoothly. Beck took care to wine and dine Anwar Solimon, a twenty-two-year W. R. Grace veteran who would be heading the buyout group. A native of Egypt, Solimon had come to the United States on a Fulbright scholarship and earned a Ph.D. in business administration from New York University. He was a cosmopolitan smoothie who looked like a pudgy Omar Sharif and whom many of his colleagues considered overly devoted to deal making and neglectful of operations. Solimon, however, was a particular favorite of Grace, who had ignored much criticism of the Egyptian over the years. Within a few months, Beck had helped structure a $776 million transaction by which 53 percent of the restaurant operation would be sold to an investor group headed by Solimon and a half-dozen other managers and renamed the Restaurant Enterprises Group. In deference to Peter Grace's paternal feeling for the restaurants, W. R. Grace would get warrants convertible into the remaining 47 percent of the equity. Drexel would be an equity investor, too, and also provide $275 million of junk-bond financing. The deal was cleverly structured so that W. R. Grace wouldn't have to carry any of the debt incurred in the buyout on its own balance sheet. After a preliminary agreement was signed, Beck and Daniels headed off to Europe on separate vacations.

Late one night in July 1986, Peter Grace was awakened by a telephone call from Solimon, who informed his boss that he was resigning from the company and dropping out of the buyout group in order to negotiate the purchase of Marriott Corporation's Saga restaurant subsidiary. He said that three of his lieutenants were coming with him. Grace was crushed. A few hours later, Daniels picked up the telephone in his hotel in the Black Forest and was verbally assaulted. "Where the hell have you been?" Grace screamed. "The worst thing has happened! Get back here."

As the company's lead negotiator on the LBO, Daniels was not as surprised at Solimon's perfidy as was Grace. It was obvious to Daniels that Solimon had signed the preliminary agreement despite serious misgivings. He seemed to resent the contractual restrictions placed on his ability to make future acquisitions and Grace's insistence on retaining a large stake. It wasn't so much that Solimon wanted one hundred percent control but that he did not want Peter Grace as his partner. Solimon didn't deny that he owed Grace a debt of gratitude for his support over the years. But after twenty-two years of feeling the hot breath of Grace's idiosyncratic demands, he wanted his freedom—and perhaps even a bit of revenge, as well.

In his haste to return to New York to attempt to salvage the deal, Daniels and his wife flew from Zurich to London for passage on the Concorde. While walking through the Concorde lounge, Daniels was startled to bump into Beck, who was returning to New York from the Hôtel du Cap, with Margo, Katherine, and his sister, Judy, in tow. At this point, Daniel couldn't be sure that Drexel hadn't surreptitiously shifted its support to Solimon to finance his other deal. Beck was pleased to run into Daniels, but puzzled by his seeming sheepishness. Just three days before, Beck had called Solimon from the villa at the hotel and had been assured that all was proceeding according to plan. But now Beck felt the first butterfly flutters of alarm tickling his stomach lining.

"How's the deal going?" he asked Daniels.

Daniels studied Beck's face a moment. He really doesn't know, he thought. "Excuse me," Daniels said. "I'll be right back."

Daniels telephoned Grace and explained that he'd just run into Beck, who seemed unaware of the crisis.

"Should I tell him?" Daniels asked.

"I can't believe Jeff is in on this crap," Grace responded. "You've got to tell him. We need all the help we can get."

After Daniels told him what had happened, Beck thought back to something Solimon had said over dinner a few months ago—that after the deal was done, they should team up to acquire Saga and merge it into the Restaurant Enterprises Group. What had once seemed to Beck to be nothing more than "flight-of-fantasy deal talk" now smacked of treachery. He was convinced that Solimon had been double-dealing Grace all along, intending to use the Marriott opportunity to bludgeon better terms out of his old company. The bastard. On the plane, Daniels said that Grace had asked David Yunich, a longtime director, to serve as his intermediary in trying to persuade Solimon to remain within the W. R. Grace fold. Beck was incredulous. "Why do you *want* to keep a piece of shit like this?" he said. "You can't let him get away with this."

At JFK, Daniels and Beck were met by Charles Erhart, who was vice chairman of W. R. Grace and a cousin of Peter Grace. Erhart relayed instructions from Grace that they were not to speak directly with Solimon but rather let Yunich do the talking.

"This is bullshit," Beck replied. "It's not right."

"Well, it's what Peter wants," Erhart said. "I'm certainly not going to countermand his order."

"I don't care," Beck said. "You can tell Peter that it was all my doing. But I'm gonna talk to the guy."

Erhart and Daniels dropped Beck off at the Helmsley Palace Hotel, where Solimon was staying, and drove on to the "21" Club, where Yunich and Solimon were scheduled to meet later. By this time, Beck hadn't slept in twenty-four hours. He needed a shave and was dressed in blue jeans. He called Solimon from the lobby. Solimon met him in the hotel bar. Beck refused to shake his hand and immediately lit into him. "Anwar," he said, "what the fuck do you think you're doing? Are you crazy?"

Solimon recited his grievances against Grace and the terms of the transaction. Beck's basic response to every one of Solimon's points was,

"How can you do this to Peter Grace?" When Solimon suggested that Drexel wasn't losing a client but gaining one—that the firm could find another buyer for the Grace restaurants and also finance his Saga buyout—Beck said that he would do whatever he could to prevent Drexel from taking him on as a client. Beck and Solimon went at it for nearly an hour, their voices rising as their exasperation mounted, until they were almost yelling at each other. Their debate continued during the short ride from the Helmsley to the "21" Club, which refused to bend its dress code for Beck. He raced home, took a shower, put on a suit and returned to "21." Solimon and Yunich were at a banquette in the upstairs dining room. Yunich was not pleased to see him. "This is my meeting," he said. Beck found Grace, Erhart, and Daniels at a table downstairs, nervously awaiting the outcome of the upstairs meeting, which proved inconclusive. Grace decided that he had to proceed on the assumption that Solimon had left for good.

Beck went home but didn't sleep. He was on the phone all night with Daniels and Grace, whose back was really up against the wall now. A few weeks earlier, the leveraged buyout of Grace's retailing group had fallen apart. If the Restaurant Enterprises buyout collapsed, too, the company risked the loss of its last shred of credibility with money men. And without the $500 million in proceeds from the LBO, W. R. Grace would be left so short of cash by the end of the year that it might have to suspend its dividend, which would further depress its stock. As it happens, no deal is harder to salvage than an aborted management buyout. When the executives who know a company best back away from buying it, their backers tend to assume that something has gone wrong with the business itself and pull out, too. And if Citibank, the lead bank on the deal, and Drexel Burnham withdrew, the chances of finding other institutions willing to provide financing were next to nil. After a fitful hour or so of couch sleep, Beck met Daniels at the airport. They were in the Newport Beach, California, offices of the Grace restaurant group before noon. The first order of business was persuading Norman Haberman, the highest-ranking remaining manager, to take Solimon's place and reconstitute an investor group. Only after Haberman had signed on did Beck call Joseph. There was serious talk within Drexel of killing the deal, but Beck's vehement support convinced Joseph that Solimon had left some good managers behind and, moreover, that Peter Grace was exactly the kind of ally the firm needed in Washington.

Beck and Daniels spent three days in Newport Beach in nonstop meetings with Grace, Haberman, and his associates, bankers, lawyers, and accountants. (Late one night, Beck and Daniels fell asleep simultaneously while talking on the telephone from their hotel rooms. Hours later, Beck was awakened by the sound of electronic snoring in his ear.) Weary but relieved, Beck flew back to New York on Grace's 727. While they'd managed to keep the deal together, the terms of the transaction had to be wholly renegotiated as it became apparent that the cash flow was indeed below projections. The buyout didn't close until December 28, 1986, some seven months after agreement had been reached with Solimon. "The Grace restaurant deal was the hardest deal I ever did," recalled Beck. While Drexel earned fees of $14 million, Beck found it nearly as satisfying to be invited to join the board of Restaurant Enterprises Group—the first directorship of his career.

This difficult transaction brought W. R. Grace proceeds that, at $537 million, slightly exceeded expectations and gave Beck the admiration and gratitude of one of American's oddest and most powerful men. "If you were in a street fight, you'd want to have Jeff Beck in there with you," Grace said. "It's the same thing in an intellectual fight. He's almost defeatless. Beck doesn't know what hours are. He'll work all night if he has to. He doesn't give a damn about his health. The guy is just loaded with guts. I've never seen such a gutty guy."

By this time, a month short of the completion of the restaurant buyout, Beck's relationship with Grace was already the closest of his entire career. Daniels couldn't help but smile every time he saw Beck wrap an arm around Grace's shoulders and hug him in greeting. In all his years at the company, Daniels had never seen anyone who dared treat Grace with such familiar affection—or who was able to relate to him with such seemingly effortless consistency. Despite basic differences—Beck's Jewishness and basically liberal political bent, Grace's devout Irish Catholicism and bristling conservatism, not to mention more than thirty years' difference in age—they took great delight and even a measure of comfort in each other's presence. Obsessed as Grace was with the efficient use of time, he spent hours upon hours sitting and talking with Beck about anything and everything. Beck marveled over Grace endlessly, as if he were a mythic figure who'd died long ago and been miraculously restored to life. "He is one of the few people I know with true wisdom," he told me. When Beck contributed $75,000 to help finance a documentary about the life of Mother Theresa, he insisted that he be identified in the credits only as "a friend of Peter Grace."

At Beck's invitation, Grace attended Drexel's junk-bond conference in early 1987—the first of three Predators' Balls to be held under the cloud of impending doom, all of which Grace would attend. In 1987, Grace was a featured speaker, and Beck handled the introduction. Fred Joseph was there, looking ill and suddenly aged. Other Drexelites carried the haggard look of men who knew their darkest secrets were about to be exposed. Milken, though, seemed as resolute and energetic as ever and was buoyed by several standing ovations from the crowd of two thousand guests and true believers. Diana Ross performed at the closing banquet, and Grace had a great good time of it. Beck, who was at Grace's side during much of the conference, flew back to New York with him in the W. R. Grace corporate jet. A few days later, Grace sent Beck a letter of thanks:

> May I thank you for your many, many generous acts of kindness in Beverly Hills. You are the "host with the most" and, definitely a warm and kind individual. Net net, I had a ball everywhere I went.
> All de best, pal.

After a decade and a half on Wall Street, Beck no longer had the slightest interest in transactions modest in size, obscure in origin, or routine in execution—though, if truth be told, the Grace restaurant deal was idiosyncratic even beyond his avowed desire for novelty. From the moment he entered Drexel Burnham as the self-proclaimed instigator of history's largest leveraged buyout, Beck styled himself as a specialist in the megatransaction—"an elephant hunter," as the firm's youthful M & A men described him. Near the end of his stint at Drexel, Beck would tell me, in a voice as plaintive as boastful, that since joining the firm he'd had a hand in some $50 billion worth of deals. This was an accurate sum, give or take a few billion, and was heavily weighted to the food industry, which had increasingly absorbed Beck's attention ever since he first hooked up with Don Kelly and Esmark in 1983.

In retrospect, Esmark's acquisition of Norton Simon was a harbinger of a massive consolidation in the food industry that gathered momentum throughout the mid-1980s, unslowed by the steep rise in stock prices. The M & A business boomed in 1985 as deal volume spurted 47 percent, to nearly $180 billion; the food industry was disproportionately responsible. Including Beatrice, four of the ten largest acquisitions were of food companies: Philip Morris paid $5.6 billion for General Foods, R. J. Reynolds bought Nabisco for $4.9 billion, and Nestlé acquired Carnation in a $2.9 billion deal. Although by the start of 1986, food-company stocks had risen about 140 percent since the bull market began, Beck was convinced that the industry remained undervalued at 16 times earnings. Beck expected this multiple to rise as more and more producers—and LBO promoters—acted on the premise that it was increasingly more cost-effective to buy existing brands than to start new ones from scratch. In Beck's view, this meant that any publicly owned food company that wasn't taking the offensive in building market share and boosting earnings was likely to soon find itself on the defensive, resisting takeover.

Ralston Purina was a classic example. The door into St. Louis's famed "checkerboard square" company was opened for Beck by David Kay, a cochief of Drexel's M & A department. Kay introduced Beck to William Stiritz, who since becoming CEO in 1982 had transformed Ralston from a marginally profitable antiquity into a well-managed company with one of the highest returns on equity in food. A shrewd, stoic plainsman who'd risen through Ralston's animal-feed business, Stiritz eschewed the moneyed suburbs of St. Louis for a farm across the river in Illinois. As the pace of the food industry's consolidation accelerated, Stiritz's obsession with safeguarding Ralston's independence overcame his distaste for Drexel Burnham's sharp-elbowed avarice, and he put the firm on a retainer to help erect obstacles to takeover.

Like Kelly, Stiritz was basically a loner who kept his own counsel as he quietly maneuvered for advantage in the takeover wars. He was shrewd but mercurial, lacking Kelly's brute decisiveness. With characteristic guile, Stiritz insinuated himself into the Beatrice deal at the last minute, indicating that he was primarily interested in certain divisions of Beatrice but that he might bid for the whole company to get them. The question of whether Stiritz could or would finance a bid became a subject of urgent discussion at Drexel involving Beck, Kay, and Leon Black. The consensus was that he was bluffing; Beck surmised that all Stiritz really wanted was a peek at the inside numbers of a rival company, a common tactic in the deal wars. Although Stiritz in the end declined to make an offer for Beatrice, Beck had caught the scent of deal lust in his tactics and resolved to try to shift the focus of Ralston Purina's affiliation with Drexel from defense to offense.

Accompanied by Jack MacAtee, who'd represented Ralston Purina for many years, Beck flew out to St. Louis for a big-picture session with Stiritz. Beck played it straight, attempting to ease Stiritz's mind on two matters that seemed to worry the CEO to the point of paranoia. He assured Stiritz that he personally would see to it that Drexel didn't double-cross him by using its access to Ralston Purina's confidential data to tee it up for one of Milken's raiders. And he told Stiritz that investment bankers from other firms—including Goldman, Sachs, Ralston's longtime banker—were wrong in arguing that his company was vulnerable to takeover. In support of his argument and at his own initiative, Beck worked up a pro forma analysis of the economics of a raid by RJR Nabisco—the acquirer that Stiritz apparently feared most —and a few other food giants. Within a month or two, Beck had succeeded in superseding Kay's uneasy relationship with Ralston Purina and signed the company to a $250,000 retainer for the purpose of negotiating a merger with the Campbell Soup Company.

Campbell Soup had been Beck's idea. To Beck, the union of Ralston and Campbell seemed a match made in deal heaven. Here were two grand old conservative companies still very much under the sway of their founding families and with complementary product lines and organizational strengths—scientific research in the soup company's case, marketing and distribution in Ralston Purina's. Although Stiritz was keenly interested, Campbell was no less emphatic than Ralston in its avowed desire to remain independent. After nosing around the Philadelphia-based soup company for a few weeks, though, Beck detected beneath its placid surface signs of instability that could be manipulated to produce a deal. It appeared that the board and the descendants of founder John Dorrance were beginning to polarize over fundamental issues of corporate strategy and the performance of the company's nonfamily CEO. Talks between Campbell and Ralston were convened several times but foundered over the issue of which management group would control the combined companies. Dorrance's will stipulated that Campbell Soup could merge with another company only if it emerged the dominant entity. The problem, certainly from Stiritz's vantage point, was that Ralston Purina was the better-run company. While Beck agreed wholeheartedly, he urged Stiritz to accept the number two position for the sake of the deal and to bide his time. Apparently the vehemence of his argument offended Stiritz, for Beck found himself increasingly shunted aside. Although impaired, his relationship with Ralston continued, sustained largely by Stiritz's fear of attack by RJR Nabisco. It was only natural that Stiritz would seek reassurance from Beck, who'd fortuitously added RJR Nabisco to his stable of clients.

While Beck consciously repressed his showman's flair in the company of a sober-miened executive like Stiritz, he gave free rein to his flamboyance with Ross Johnson, RJR's chief executive officer, who was eminently capable of responding in kind. Not long after he first met Beck, Johnson presented him with a box of Milk-Bone dog biscuits (a Nabisco product) in good-natured recognition of the aptness of his

Mad Dog nickname. At fifty, Johnson was a shaggy-haired, irreverent, hang-loose kind of guy who ignored most of the fun-inhibiting conventions and proprieties of corporate America. Over the years, he'd gathered around himself a loyal cadre of crackerjack executives who doubled as late-night drinking buddies and who'd dubbed themselves "the Merry Men." Johnson resembled Don Kelly in many ways, both superficial and profound—from his obsession with golf and love of hobnobbing with sports celebrities, to his relentless quipping and mastery of creative profanity, to his utterly unsentimental devotion to maximizing shareholder value.

Like Kelly, Johnson had started out in accounting and had a sophistication with numbers that gave him much greater fluency in the language of deals than the typical big-company CEO had. Like Kelly, too, Johnson had a Machiavellian flair for corporate politics. While Kelly had applied his talents to the rescue and transformation of Swift & Company, Johnson forcibly made over three major old-line corporations—none of which had originally hired him as CEO. After working his way up at Standard Brands, Johnson finally captured the top job by turning the tables on his boss, a crusty autocrat who'd gone to the board to ask for authority to fire Johnson. In 1981, Johnson accepted a $1.9 billion merger offer from Nabisco, maker of Oreo cookies and Ritz crackers, and became the second-ranked executive of the merged company, Nabisco Brands. By 1984, Johnson had maneuvered the CEO into voluntarily ceding him his title. Having grown bored with the mundanities of corporate life and seeing no quick way to rehabilitate Nabisco's aged factories, Johnson dispatched the ubiquitous Ira Harris to dangle Nabisco before Esmark. When Kelly backed away at the last minute from merging with Nabisco, Johnson turned around and in 1985 sold the company for a rich $4.9 billion to R. J. Reynolds Tobacco, of Lucky Strike fame. Once again, Johnson did what Bill Stiritz had refused to do and accepted the number two job at the new company created through a megamerger. And at RJR Nabisco, once again Johnson quickly wrested away the CEO title from his boss.

Johnson's appointment as CEO of RJR Nabisco in July 1986 prompted Beck to swing into action. As a man who prided himself on unconventional thinking, Johnson was exceptionally open to the ideas of investment bankers, and yet he was an extremely tough sell. Johnson regarded the constant flow of unsolicited suggestions from Wall Street as free advice; as he put it, with an intentionally unflattering metaphor, "Why have a dog and bark for yourself?" Although Harris was Johnson's favorite investment banker, he listened to everybody. By the time Johnson was named CEO, Beck had for months been mulling over a complex idea for RJR Nabisco but had seen no point in presenting it to Tylee Wilson, Johnson's predecessor. Before pitching Beatrice to KKR, Beck had tried to interest Wilson in acquiring an equity interest in Beatrice in partnership with Kelly. In Beck's opinion, Wilson didn't have the slightest understanding of this admittedly unconventional proposal and, in any event, wasn't the sort of CEO who would deign to do business with Drexel Burnham. Ross Johnson had never done business with Drexel either, but Johnson was a deal man and thus open to possibility. Not long after Wilson's ouster, Beck's name began appearing frequently on the new CEO's telephone-message board.

Beck set himself apart from the ratpack of bankers in pursuit of Johnson with his favorite promotional prop: the Hôtel du Cap d'Antibes. Although Johnson was quite capable of booking a room at the hotel on his own, Beck insisted on intervening to get him and his wife upgraded to a better suite while arranging for the delivery of a chilled bottle of Roederer Cristal and a bouquet of roses with a card wishing the Johnsons a pleasant vacation. The usual pleasure Beck took in such grandly hospitable gestures was deepened in this case by the knowledge that Harris would be vacationing at the Hôtel du Cap at the same time as the Johnsons. "I knew that Ross would tweak Ira by telling him that I'd sent champagne and roses," Beck said. "This was my way of letting Ira know that once again, as with Esmark, he was about to experience the nightmare of Jeff Beck taking his client."

To Johnson's dismay, the merger of RJR and Nabisco had been an exercise in reverse synergy—that is, the stock-market value of the combined companies didn't come close to equaling the sum of the values investors had assigned to RJR and Nabisco as separate companies. Beck convinced Johnson to meet with a group from Drexel Burnham to discuss the valuation problem and what could be done about it. Johnson suggested dinner in early September at the Links Club. This get-acquainted session went well and was followed by other meetings, including one at which Johnson met Mike Milken.

After extensive consultations with Milken, Beck proposed a novel solution to RJR's valuation blues: reconfiguration by means of a master limited partnership. Although the mathematics were a bit tricky, the concept was nothing more than separation without divorce. In Beck's analysis, RJR's basic valuation problem had to do with the growing expectation that the tobacco industry eventually would be held legally liable for the adverse health effects of smoking. The potential liabilities were so breathtaking that investors were discounting not only RJR's enormous current cash flow from tobacco—$1 billion a year—but the attractive prospects of its vast food operations. Beck proposed segregating the tobacco assets in a limited partnership and replacing most of the company's common stock with partnership units consisting of one piece of paper entitling investors to tax-free dividend income from tobacco and another piece of paper representing equity ownership in the food business. By isolating the food assets in this way, their true value would become apparent. If all went according to plan, the combined value of one partnership unit would be greater than the current value of the common stock.

Johnson was intrigued with the master-limited-partnership idea, and Beck and various junior bankers spent months shuttling between New York and RJR headquarters, fleshing out the proposal with encylopedic detail and finding ways around the obstacles thrown up by Johnson's other advisers. While none of them proved insurmountable, Johnson eventually decided that an accumulation of inconveniences and uncertainties would make converting to a limited partnership more trouble than it was worth. Beck hadn't billed RJR for any of Drexel's work. When Johnson offered to send a check, Beck declined. "I want to do the bigger deal," he said. Although the Street was rife with rumors of RJR's next big acquisition, Beck figured that Johnson was more likely to sell RJR, as he had earlier sold Standard Brands and Nabisco. "You know, Ross," he told Johnson, "everyone thinks you are a buyer, but I think you're a seller." Johnson laughed—but didn't disagree. In late 1988, RJR Nabisco would indeed be sold, in the largest LBO in history. In the meantime, Beck peppered Johnson with ideas, including an unusual alliance with another of the new clients he'd brought to Drexel: the Pillsbury Company.

There's not the slimmest chance that William Spoor, the longtime CEO of Pillsbury, served as the inspiration for the Pillsbury Doughboy, the company's sweet-tempered mascot. One of the legendary autocrats of American industry, Spoor was a man of such abrasive manner and volanic temper that—as company legend had it, anyway—his public-relations man used to cower under his desk when he heard the boss coming down the hallway on a bad-news day. To Beck, though, Spoor was a joy. "There are good guys and then there are great guys," Beck said, "and Spoor goes down in my book as a great guy." Spoor clinched great-guy status during a meeting in a conference room at Pillsbury headquarters also attended by Dean Kehler of Drexel and Jerry Levin, Pillsbury's top in-house deal man. Beck was running through a list of measures that he believed Pillsbury had to take to stay independent when Spoor started screaming at Levin, who said nothing in his defense.

Spoor cut short his diatribe to extend a plate of cookies (made with Pillsbury flour) to Beck and Kehler. "Would you like a cookie?" he said and flashed a smile. Beck and Kehler hurriedly took one apiece.

Spoor set the plate down and resumed his harangue. A few minutes later, Spoor again reached for the plate. "Have you tried one of these?" he purred, pointing to a peanut-butter cookie with M & Ms, his personal favorite. Spoor then pulled a rubber comb from his jacket pocket. "I'm going to go to the bathroom and comb my hair now," he announced to Beck and Kehler. "Want to come with me?"

By this time Beck was laughing so hard that he couldn't stand, much less walk to the bathroom with Spoor, who did indeed leave the room and return in a few minutes with neater-looking hair. Levin, who was one of Spoor's favorites, seemed undisturbed by the verbal pounding administered by his mentor for what Beck assumed to be his and Kehler's amusement. While Spoor was reputed to be tough, irascible, and almost brutally decisive, Beck never saw the mean-spirited tyrant in him—though, of course, he had to admit that he'd never been a Pillsbury employee either. What Beck liked most about the man was his lack of pretension. He was a self-made Midwesterner who never tried to impress anyone—unless scaring the hell out of underlings could be considered impressing.

Beginning in 1973, Spoor engineered a series of acquisitions that transformed Pillsbury, one of the Midwest's oldest corporations, from a sleepy milling concern to the nation's fourth-largest food and restaurant company. Spoor retired at age sixty-two, hoping apparently that he'd be named to a post in the second Reagan administration. No such appointment materialized, and by mid-1986 Spoor was bored with leisure and looking for a business to run. Beck met Spoor through Levin, whom he'd gotten to know slightly while working at Oppenheimer. Beck urged Spoor to follow Don Kelly's lead and help put together a leveraged buyout of a major food company. Spoor was skeptical but agreed to at least meet with Kravis, who gave him his best pitch. Beck was advised by certain colleagues at Drexel to stop wasting his time with an out-to-pasture executive. He ignored them.

Meanwhile, through Levin, Beck began trying to worm his way into Pillsbury. He made several trips to Minneapolis and finally got the attention of James Stafford, Spoor's successor as CEO, with a pro-forma analysis of a combination of Pillsbury and the company that had been its great crosstown rival in flour milling for a century: General Mills. Apparently, this was so obvious an idea—the economies of scale were enormous—that it struck Pillsbury as novel. Although Beck made a presentation to Stafford, nothing came of his proposal. General Mills had not announced that it was for sale, after all, and the antitrust implications were problematic, even in the age of Reagan. But now that he had a foot in Pillsbury's door Beck began sounding a warning: Pillsbury was vulnerable to takeover and needed to recapitalize to en-sure its continued independence. This gloomy message was not well received within Pillsbury, a 113-year-old company steeped in tradition and accustomed to dominance. The fact was, though, that earnings were in steep descent because of the faltering performance of Pills-bury's restaurant business—including Burger King, which was losing market share to McDonald's. Stafford had made a series of clumsy moves that reinforced Wall Street's pervasive impression that he was in over his head. Pillsbury's stock had been marked down to less than twice book value, compared to three or four times book for the average food producer.

As Stafford dithered, Pillsbury's board of directors turned to Spoor, whom Beck had continued to cultivate. At a meeting kept secret from Stafford, the board in the fall of 1987 reinstalled Spoor as chairman of the executive committee and put out to the press the phony story that he'd been invited back by Stafford. Beck knew the truth, though, and told Spoor that he should come back either as Stafford's replacement or not at all. The compromise of having an official CEO and a shadow CEO would be interpreted by outsiders as evidence of indecision on the board's part and would virtually invite a takeover bid. Although Spoor returned to Pillsbury intending to shake things up, he, too, believed that Beck's sense of the company's vulnerability was exagger-ated. Undaunted, Beck kept pitching ideas at Spoor, including an alliance with Ross Johnson. Under this plan, RJR Nabisco would trans-fer to Pillsbury its cupboardful of nonbakery food brands and make a large cash investment in return for 35 percent of Pillsbury's stock. Johnson loved the idea and invited Spoor to his office to discuss it.

During the meeting, Johnson demonstrated the new smokeless cigarette under development at RJR. He lit up, took a few puffs, and tossed the cigarette on the carpeted floor of his office by way of proving its self-extinguishing properties. Spoor tried it, too. Beck was tickled by the absurdity of the situation, thinking, Here are the heads of two of the largest food companies in the world sitting around watching cigarettes die.

In the end, the deal couldn't be worked out, mainly because Spoor and his directors feared that RJR would exploit its foothold to eventually acquire control of Pillsbury. Spoor refused to give up more than a 20 percent interest and he insisted that Johnson sign an open-ended standstill agreement under which RJR would promise never to add to its position in Pillsbury. For Beck, the slow death of the proposed alliance was agonizing, for he saw the idea as a mutually beneficial solution to the basic problems of two major clients. He begged and pleaded with Spoor to reconsider, arguing that since Pillsbury was going to be taken over anyway, the company at least should choose its likely acquirer. Conceding defeat, Beck bet Spoor that within a year Pillsbury would be attacked, probably by a foreign company. To his dismay, this was a bet he would win, as Pillsbury lost its independence in a takeover by Grand Metropolitan, the British food and beverage giant.

As Beck occupied himself with W. R. Grace, Ralston Purina, RJR Nabisco, and Pillsbury, Kelly and Kravis were disassembling Beatrice in record time. In the interest of widening its Wall Street sphere of influence, KKR spread the investment-banking business generated by the bust-up of Beatrice around the Street, though Drexel probably profited to a greater extent than any other firm. Beck halfheartedly tried to end-run Leon Black and insinuate himself into the process, but to little avail. He and Kravis were no longer in synch. Although he continued to telephone both Kravis and Kelly periodically to offer his views, his opinions were solicited sparingly and heeded even less. What Beck hoped to see emerge from the postbuyout restructuring of Beatrice was a financially tidy, operationally strapping food company that could be merged with another American food giant—Nabisco or Pillsbury would do nicely—to create the most powerful and profitable food producer in the world. In this he would be severely disappointed.

Avis was the first Beatrice subsidiary divested, purchased for $250 million by Wesray, a leveraged-buyout firm. Next to go was its Coca-

Cola bottling operation, bought by the Coca-Cola Company for $1 billion. Then, in August 1986, a mere four months after the buyout's close, International Playtex was sold in a billion-dollar leveraged buyout led by Joel Smilow, Playtex's top executive, and financed by Drexel. With the sale of Playtex, the total proceeds from Beatrice's asset sales topped $2.4 billion, comfortably exceeding the requirements of Beatrice's agreements with lenders. But Kelly and Kravis kept right on busting up Beatrice. By the end of 1986 they'd raised another $700 million by selling its Americold cold-storage warehouse operation and Webcraft printing subsidiary through separate leveraged buyouts, and still they showed no sign of slowing the pace of liquidation. Indeed, within eighteen months after the completion of the buyout, all of the company's remaining operations—including the huge food business that was its core—were on the block.

As a rule, companies taken private through leveraged buyouts are bought to be resold, either through sales of assets to other companies or to public investors through stock issues. Usually, though, this process of restructuring for resale takes five years or so. Why such urgency to liquidate Beatrice? Most important, the faster a profit is realized, the higher the annualized return on investment; the 50 to 60 percent annualized returns on equity that KKR boasted going into the Beatrice deal was the very essence of its appeal to institutional investors and hence the foundation of its clout and prosperity. In its devotion to maximizing returns, KKR was well matched with Kelly, for the former Esmark executive had reached a stage in his evolution from manager to deal man where he no longer had a frisson of interest in running a business a moment longer than required to resell it at a satisfactory profit. Intimately familiar with most of Beatrice's businesses on the day he became CEO, Kelly lost little time to deliberation. Almost immediately, he cut $100 million out of Beatrice's annual operating expenses by reducing the headquarters staff built by Jim Dutt and by axing the former CEO's pet "We're Beatrice" ad campaign and promotional extravaganzas involving race cars and marathons.

With this out of the way, Kelly and Kravis were free to turn their attention to dealing. And with every firm on Wall Street seemingly intent on spending itself to prominence as the next KKR, they could indulge their opportunism as never before. In their eagerness to invest the billions of dollars of new capital flowing into their coffers, LBO promoters bid up prices in the private market for businesses at a pace that exceeded even the stock market's rise. As a result, Kelly and KKR could raise cash to pay off bank loans and yet book a profit selling assets they'd owned only a few months. For example, at the time of the buyout, KKR estimated Americold's value for tax purposes at $425 million but sold it for $480 million, a gain of $55 million.

In a sense, selling assets beyond the requirements of debt-repayment schedules was a prudent financial strategy. In contenting itself with taking a small profit today instead of holding out for a larger profit tomorrow, KKR could reduce the risk borne by its investors and the burden of debt borne by Beatrice. However, if in its haste to liquidate, KKR left too much profit on the table, it would have obviated the point of doing an LBO in the first place—to realize an *outsized* profit —while subjecting Beatrice and its 112,000 employees to the outsized risks of radical corporate surgery. As the liquidation of Beatrice gathered momentum, Kelly and Kravis began butting heads. "Don and I used to have knock-down drag-outs over asset sales," Kravis recalled. "The growth wasn't great in the food business—it was okay but not great. So we had the idea to sell off everything but consumer durables" —a collection of miscellaneous businesses including Samsonite luggage, Culligan water softeners, and Stiffel lamps. However, Kelly drew the line at haphazardly splintering the company's huge food operations, which he'd spent the better part of a decade fitting together; he told Kravis that he was not going to preside over a total liquidation. "That was Don's soft side," Kravis recalled. "He was tired of firing people, of running a shrinking company. He wanted to use Beatrice to go after other companies. We didn't."

While KKR was loath to let Kelly turn Beatrice into an Esmark-style takeover vehicle, the firm was hardly opposed to acquisitions per se. Indeed, in the wake of Beatrice, KKR capitalized on its ascending cachet by raising a new $2 billion equity fund and using it to finance a string of megadeals, acquiring Safeway Stores, Owens Illinois, and Jim Walter Corporation for a total of nearly $9 billion. In the process, KKR was able to lift its up-front fee to a new plateau. The $60 million it took both on Safeway and Owens Illinois amounted to about 1.4 percent of each deal's purchase price, nearly twice the percentage of KKR's take on Beatrice. When Forstmann Little, KKR's archrival, announced plans to raise a $2.4 billion fund, Kravis and his partners decided in mid-1987 to begin assembling a $5 billion war chest, though they'd yet to exhaust the $2 billion raised just the year before. "By 1987 everyone had a pot of money," explained a KKR partner. "We wanted to have by far the biggest pot." Four months later, KKR

had outdone itself, collecting $5.6 billion in commitments. If lever-
aged with debt at the standard 8-to-1 ratio, the new fund would give
KKR buying power of $45 billion—sufficient, *Fortune* magazine
pointed out, to buy all ten *Fortune* 500 companies headquartered in
Minneapolis. Remarkably, KKR had mustered all this muscle with
little financial risk to itself. The firm's own contribution to its new
megafund was $56 million, a scant 1 percent of the total.

In the midst of this binge of deal promoting, Kravis worked out a
compromise with Kelly. Under their plan, about 20 percent of Beatrice's assets would be spun off to form a new company, which Kelly
would be free to use to make acquisitions even while continuing as
chairman of Beatrice. The new company's purpose was suggested by
its name—E-II Holdings, with the "E" standing for "Esmark." While
giving Kelly an opportunity to return to the takeover hunt, E-II also
furthered KKR's liquidation strategy. The assets to be spun off and
taken public through E-II were fifteen consumer-durable and food
businesses of no particular distinction. Packaging this grab bag of assets as the second coming of Esmark was an obvious attempt to exploit
Kelly's deal-man aura to unload Beatrice's most unglamorous properties at prices higher than warranted by business fundamentals. At a
proposed 30 times earnings, E-II's stock offering was richly priced
indeed. Kelly did his bit by swaggering through a round of press interviews. "I don't have upper limits any more," he told the *Chicago
Tribune*, "but the marketplace has shown me that a $5 billion or $10
billion deal are all doable—$15 billion or whatever." With *The Wall
Street Journal*, he was comparatively restrained, declaring: "Nine billion dollars doesn't scare me." However, as Kelly began making the
rounds of institutional investors, he encountered skepticism about his
ability to duplicate his successes at Esmark now that the market was
crowded with self-proclaimed takeover geniuses. Kelly's stock answer:
"A lot of dogs chase Cadillacs, but few dogs drive Cadillacs."

The prospectus for E-II's stock offering was eagerly read on Wall
Street and helped prompt a congressional hearing as well. Through the
E-II filing, which was required by law, it was revealed for the first time
that Drexel partnerships held warrants entitling them to 24 percent of
the equity in Beatrice. A warrant is a security entitling the holder to
buy shares of stock in a company at a preset price (usually quite low) at
a future date. Warrants as a rule are the most eagerly sought of LBO
securities because they minimize cash investment while maximizing
potential capital gains. For example, various Drexel partnerships had

paid $5.7 million for Beatrice warrants that only two years later had a value estimated at $500 million. In arranging financing for the buyout, Black apparently had gone to KKR and insisted that Drexel would need warrants to induce reluctant bond buyers to invest. Drexel maintained after its ownership had come to light that it had been entitled to the warrants because it ended up buying bonds that would have gone unsold otherwise. However, many junk bond buyers said they'd never even been offered the warrants, and as Congress began investigating Drexel's sales practices, KKR leaked word through the press that Kravis was furious at having recently learned that Drexel had kept the warrants rather than distributing them to investors as promised. Although the hearings left many unanswered questions about Drexel's and KKR's relationship—Milken invoked Fifth Amendment protections against self-incrimination and said nothing—Drexel's image as the House of Greed was vividly reinforced.

Beck followed these hearings with keen interest, believing that he was among the Drexel employees that owned the Beatrice warrants. When he discovered later that he had no warrants whatsoever, Beck angrily claimed that the firm's senior management had double-crossed him. Indeed, Beck hired a lawyer to prepare a lawsuit alleging that he had decided to join Drexel in part because he'd been assured that he would receive warrants in Beatrice. The suit, which as of this writing remains unfiled, claimed that the firm owed Beck at least $50 million for warrants promised but never awarded.

Despite the warrants controversy the E-II gambit worked pretty well, although the number of shares had to be scaled back and the price trimmed a bit. Through the stock offering managed by Salomon Brothers and a simultaneous junk-bond sale organized by Drexel Burnham, E-II raised enough cash to retire another $800 million in Beatrice debt and still have more than $1 billion for Kelly to play with in the deal game.

Through a distribution of E-II shares, KKR returned to its investors their original equity stake in the Beatrice buyout. From here on, it would all be gravy. In the offering circular for its new $5 billion fund, KKR estimated that what remained of Beatrice after E-II—essentially Tropicana, Hunt-Wesson, Swift-Eckrich, and Beatrice Cheese—had a net worth of $1.3 billion. However, when KKR put the remainder of Beatrice on the auction block shortly after this circular went out, its minimum asking price was said to be three times this figure. Egged on by insiders at KKR and Beatrice, reporters began publishing stories

suggesting that Beatrice was on the verge of being cashed out at a
profit of $3 billion to $4 billion—a figure big enough to excite even the
professional investors that KKR was busily soliciting for its latest fund.
"Others have done transactions like this, but few have turned them
over this fast, and none have churned out such profits," noted a *New
York Times* article, which also contained this Kravis quote: "We knew
it was a good deal, but we didn't anticipate it would turn out quite this
well."

There was one flaw in all this heavily publicized optimism: No one
wanted what was left of Beatrice, despite Bruce Wasserstein's and
First Boston's best efforts to flog it on KKR's behalf. (Kravis had hired
Wasserstein over the objections of Kelly, who considered First Boston's star M & A man something of a blowhard.) Every major food
producer in America, if not the world—some hundred companies all
told—took a look at Beatrice, and though some coveted its parts not
one made an offer for the whole company. In the midst of the twentieth century's greatest bull market in deals, Beatrice was unsalable.
Debt wasn't the deterrent, having been pared from $8.2 billion after
the buyout to a manageable $1.4 billion. And the company had plenty
of strong brands and was nicely if not spectacularly profitable. The
problem was perception among potential buyers that the financial and
legal residue left by a decade of ceaseless deal making had turned
Beatrice into the corporate equivalent of a toxic-waste dump.

Urged on by Beck, Pillsbury was among the legion of companies
that considered Beatrice. Pillsbury's and Beatrice's food businesses
were fairly complementary, and Spoor had once interviewed Fred
Rentschler, Kelly's heir apparent as CEO of Beatrice, coming away
favorably impressed with him. Beck accompanied several Pillsbury executives to a meeting at KKR's offices that started auspiciously with
presentations by Rentschler and top operating executives. Afterward,
however, the visitors were shepherded into a conference room, where a
First Boston representative passed out what appeared to be copies of a
telephone directory for a good-sized city but which in fact was a listing
of Beatrice's miscellaneous and contingent liabilities. Jerry Levin shot
a quizzical look at Beck, who shrugged his shoulders. Contained in the
listing's pages were complex disputes with the IRS over the tax due on
divestitures dating back to 1980 and exposure to product-liability
claims related to subsidiaries long sold. Then there was the matter of
the "goodwill" incurred each time Beatrice and Esmark acquired a
company at a price above book value. Although tax regulations allowed

goodwill to be amortized over forty years, in Beatrice's case the total was so large that it would depress the earnings of any public company that acquired it by a hefty $75 million a year, *every* year until 2026.

While not all of these matters were subject to management cure (as anyone who has battled the IRS can attest), some things could have been done to tidy Beatrice's balance sheet. However, all of them were time-consuming and a good deal duller than was E-II's search for fresh acquisitions, which preoccupied not only Kelly but most of the head-quarters staff of Beatrice as well. Even with the cleanup required, a large, financially robust food producer might have bid for Beatrice had KKR knocked its lofty price down, perhaps by a billion or so. But KKR was not yet willing to accept so great a diminution in the huge profit that was presumed to be just within its reach. In refusing to accept a less than optimal price, Kravis and his partners miscalculated severely. For as everyone who was anyone in the food business was looking through Beatrice's books, Wall Street was teetering on the brink of the worst stock-market collapse since the great Crash of 1929.

20

Despite the promisingly productive beginning to Beck's career at Drexel, he would fit in at the House of Greed no better than he did at Donaldson, Lufkin & Jenrette, Lehman Brothers, or Oppenheimer. He would remain at Drexel Burnham for five tumultuous years, but his honeymoon with his new mates was over almost before it started, and he would finish out his days at the firm in a form of lonely internal exile.

Beck's troubles were partly a matter of style. Although he got rid of his chauffeur not long after joining Drexel, his initial string of rainmaking triumphs had reinforced the Master-of-the-Universe tendencies that had first come to the fore at Oppenheimer. While Beck swaggered from the beginning, he became increasingly abrasive and confrontational as he discovered that Drexel was not what it pretended to be. Despite the firm's zealous entrepreneurial rhetoric, there was in fact little room at Drexel Burnham for a rainmaker of independent ways and means. In fact, at few houses had the rainmaking ethic been as thoroughly subverted as it had in Drexel's investment-banking group in New York. This might seem ironic, since Milken epitomized Wall Street's rainmaking era. It wasn't irony, though, but destiny. As Drexel had used its junk-bond trading muscle to build a junk-bond underwriting business, Milken personally began cultivating executives from all over the country as he'd long courted bond buyers. The only difference was that Milken no longer had to hit the road as often as he did in his early days. By the early 1980s, his aura of wizardry had become so magnetic that executives by the dozen were lining up in Beverly Hills to see him. Demonically energetic though he was, Milken couldn't possibly handle all the corporate-finance business he attracted, and so Joseph's corporate-finance department in New York

developed its identity in processing the business generated in such
abundance by the junk-bond king.

Because of the peculiar circumstances of the department's development, Drexel's corporate-finance staff was long on youthful and relentless technicians—"Hitler Youth," as Beck sometimes called them—
and short on experienced bankers with a flair for bringing in new
clients and tending to existing clients between transactions. Although
Joseph hired Beck to help fill this void, he didn't alter the system that
had made his hiring desirable in the first place. Beck thus became a
stranger in a strange land—a Wall Street rainmaker in a corporate-
finance department inimical to rainmaking. The department's bias was
evident in its bonus system. At most firms, the big money went to the
people who generated and worked the biggest deals; this was emphatically true of Drexel Beverly Hills, as ruthlessly Darwinian a mer-
itocracy as the Street had ever seen. But at Drexel New York the
largest bonuses went to the people with the biggest titles—to the
administrators whose responsibility it was to see to it that the flood
tide of Milken business was smoothly processed. Like Joseph himself,
the men who held the top corporate-finance jobs tended to have precociously administrative personalities, having moved into managerial
slots early in their careers after short stints as working bankers. Some
had never signed up a client. The place was highly politicized, to boot.
So many top investment-banking officials had come over with Joseph
from Shearson that they were known collectively within the firm as the
"Shearson mafia."

As a free-lance deal maker attached to a fledgling new-business
group grandly known as the Investment Banking Group, Beck floated
in the administrative void somewhere between M & A and corporate
finance—unencumbered by managerial responsibility, to be sure, but
powerless because of that. Beck's nominal boss was Chris Anderson,
who had been shunted off to the backwater of new business because he
was thought too mercurial to make a good administrator. The only real
power Beck had was the power of suggestion, and he did at first make
attempts at constructive criticism, urging Joseph to strengthen the
firm's token rainmaking efforts by giving more authority to Anderson
and the IBG. In retrospect, Beck would realize that his strategy was
naïve, since Anderson's power could only be increased by diminishing
Milken's power, and that was out of the question. But Beck went so
far as to commit to paper a plan to set up an élite twenty-five-person
cadre of rainmakers:

A program should be established immediately to spotlight the future "rainmakers" from within Drexel. These people are our best bet in that we have had time to observe their interpersonal skills, their drive, their organizational abilities, their leadership on transactions and most importantly how they relate to authority figures. These are the people who will be the future "rainmakers." If we establish a program to allow a few present rainmakers to educate them on how to direct their potential skills into active new business opportunities, we will be creating a continuity of new business development within the firm. The new people will in turn spread the gospel. . . .

Each senior member of the group individually and collectively has a responsibility to create training programs for the group which, if successful, could be incorporated into the corporate finance department. Training is a function of group structure but should include real time transactional training, new call training, war stories, cheerleading and most important, how to infect minds to ensure fruitful negotiations and executions of transactions.

In urging that the group Anderson headed be reconstructed from scratch, Beck was all but calling him incompetent. There was nothing sneaky about Beck's oddly worded critique; indeed, the memo quoted above was addressed *to* Anderson and also included this matter-of-fact jibe: "Adding to the problem, the internal perception of the group and its leadership is bad." Obviously, Beck was no more politically adept at Drexel than he'd been at Oppenheimer. He was, in fact, past the point of caring enough about getting ahead in the conventional sense to even pretend to play the game any more. As his initially favorable opinion of Anderson declined—as Anderson no longer seemed articulate but glib, not creative but confused, not dedicated but deluded—Beck no longer bothered to keep him informed of his activities except as it suited his own purposes. As usual, Beck wanted it both ways: power and freedom, independence and assistance, money and love. Anderson would have been justified in seeing Beck as insubordinate, as Beck was correct in considering Anderson arrogant beyond his powers of tolerance.

The annals of Wall Street contain little that can match the sheer pretentiousness of the following statement by Anderson, made at the height of Drexel's power and glory: "We are the gentlemen who finance and create change. When I read [Alvin] Toffler's *Future Shock*, and he described this vortex of change that whirls around us, and it happens very fast in New York City, and slower in Des Moines, and even slower in the outback of Australia, the thing that was amazing to me was that, when I looked at the funnel of that maelstrom, the vortex of that sits right in the middle of my desk. I am the fella who determines what the change will be. If I don't finance it, it ain't gonna happen."

The ultimate effect of Beck's critique of the IBG was to spur his own transfer out of it and into the M & A department. As a practical matter, this meant changing offices, leaving his digs on the eleventh floor for equally modest new quarters on the fourth floor. And instead of nominally reporting to Anderson, Beck now nominally reported to the trio of bankers who headed M & A, two of whom he quite liked— David Kay and Leon Black. However, the third cochief was Marty Siegel, who'd left Kidder, Peabody for Drexel just a few months after Beck joined. Although Beck had never come up against Siegel in a deal, he was predisposed to believe the worst of the Kidder, Peabody star—including the well-traveled rumor that he was a confederate of Ivan Boesky. And so, when Beck put Tim Metz of *The Wall Street Journal* on Boesky's trail in 1983, he also fingered Siegel as a leading suspect. A version of the Boesky-Siegel rumor made print in an article published by *Fortune* in 1984. "Boesky's competitors whisper darkly about his omniscient timing," the story stated, "and rumors abound that he looks for deals involving Kidder, Peabody and First Boston."

Beck's resentment of Siegel grew as Henry Kravis kept hiring Siegel for prime offensive assignments, including the billion-dollar buyout of Storer Communications and, most annoyingly, the Beatrice deal. On both of these KKR deals, Siegel worked in tandem with Black and other Drexel bankers. Even before the Beatrice transaction closed, Joseph, Black, and Kay asked Beck what he thought of the idea of hiring Siegel. Beck gave them chapter and verse on his suspicions that Siegel was "a very bad guy." And when Siegel finally joined Drexel in February 1986, Beck was appalled to learn that his new colleague had been guaranteed a minimum income of $3 million a year for three years—triple his own guarantee. In his contract negotiations, Siegel had been represented by Marty Lipton, who promised his old pal that he would continue working with him even after he'd joined the firm that Lipton had been fulminating against in print. From Joseph's vantage point, in hiring Siegel Drexel obtained not only the services of one of the biggest names in M & A but an alliance of sorts with its most vociferous Deal Club critic. Siegel, meanwhile, was assured a larger income than he'd been making at Kidder and, if all went according to plan, would make two or three times the minimum. Who would be able to resist the combination of Siegel's charm and Drexel's menace?

Not long after Siegel joined Drexel, Joseph called Beck into his office to reprimand him for bad-mouthing the new recruit to the young M & A bankers. In the name of improved interdepartmental coordination, Joseph insisted that Beck keep Siegel informed of the progress of all his deals. Suspecting that this was nothing more than Joseph's way of subordinating him to Siegel, Beck refused, in effect daring the CEO to fire him. Joseph instead looked for a way to defuse the conflict between his two new rainmakers. He suggested inviting Siegel to a lunch that Beck had arranged with Al Taubman, whom Siegel claimed to know pretty well. Beck agreed, though he threatened dire consequences if Siegel was informed of the transaction he'd begun exploring on Taubman's behalf.

Taubman had accumulated a small stake in Pearson Longman, a large British company that owned *The Financial Times* among other prestigious properties, and was weighing an offer for the company. Through Beck, Taubman had retained Drexel to help determine whether a friendly acquisition of Pearson could be worked out and financed on a highly leveraged basis with Drexel investing in the deal as an equity partner. This was exactly the kind of top-drawer business that Joseph had hoped Beck could bring to Drexel. For his part, Beck was delighted at Taubman's reaffirmation of confidence in him—especially since he knew that Big Al didn't fully trust Drexel. The situation was made all the more delicate by the mogul's insistence on complete confidentiality; if word of his interest leaked, it would appear that he was stalking Pearson.

To Beck's relief, Joseph breathed not a word of the Pearson deal before, during, or after the lunch, which was held at La Côte Basque in midtown Manhattan. By the end of the meal, it was apparent, to Beck, anyway, that Siegel not only had exaggerated his relationship with Taubman but that the shopping-center magnate really didn't want him around. The three Drexel bankers said their good-byes to Taubman and clambered into a waiting stretch limousine. As they headed back downtown to 55 Broad, Joseph bubbled over with enthusiasm as he talked of his plans for Drexel, and Siegel spoke of the great things he hoped to do in his new position. As Beck told it, he held his

tongue until the conversation turned to Drexel's promising new relationship with Taubman.

"Well, Fred," Beck said with heavy sarcasm, "as you can see, Siegel
has a great relationship with Taubman. This is the last time I fall for
this shit."

"We can't have this, Jeff," Joseph said. "You and Marty should be
working together."

"I'm not working with a guy like this," said Beck, and lapsed into a
stony silence that lasted the remaining twenty minutes of the twenty-
five-minute ride back to the headquarters of the hottest house on Wall
Street.

Beck's only enduring friendship among the other senior bankers at
Drexel was with Don Engel, who technically wasn't even an employee
of the firm and operated at even further remove from official power
than did Beck himself. Yet no Drexel banker was more dependent on
Milken or prouder of it than Engel, who referred to himself as "the
richest maître d' in America." Beck found Engel's brazen hustle en-
dearing and vastly preferable to the intellectual pomposity of a Chris
Anderson. In his view, too, Engel was one of the few Drexel bankers as
fastidious in managing client relationships as he was himself. Like
Beck, in fact, Engel was a self-proclaimed master of the psychology of
selling, of "getting inside a guy's mind," as he put it. Like Beck, too,
Engel devoted most of his vacations to entertaining clients at the
Hôtel du Cap d'Antibes. Engel, who was thirteen years older than
Beck, started going to the Hôtel du Cap when Beck was still in high
school.

One of the few holdovers from the lowly pre-Milken days of Burnham & Company, Donnie Engel was the kind of guy who in college
not only always knew where the parties were but which one would
have the best-looking girls. He was an all-American social facilitator, a
winningly excitable man whose great talent lay in making sure everyone had a good time. As a young stockbroker in Manhattan, he hung
out at watering holes favored by sports celebrities and succeeded in
befriending one of the biggest of them all—Fran Tarkenton, then in
his heyday as the quarterback of the New York Giants. Through
Tarkenton, Engel met other Giants players and team hangers-on and
began networking with a vengeance long before the term came into
use. As his network of contacts expanded, Engel met so many small-
time entrepreneurs that he was able to make a good business out of

helping them finance their companies. Eventually, Engel cut a deal with Fred Joseph by which he got a cut of the gross revenue booked by the firm every time one of his clients did a financing. And he was able to maintain this extraordinary arrangement with the firm even after Mike Milken had started transforming Engel's clients from driven, insecure nonentities into driven, insecure, and very wealthy proprietors of billion-dollar corporations.

"No one would take a client down to 60 Broad Street [Drexel's head office] unless they were stupid," Engel said by way of explaining his modus operandi. "You took them out to Beverly Hills to meet Mike. I sold Mike." In attempting to describe the greatness of Milken, Engel often resorted to the language of sports, which for him was liturgy. "Imagine the five greatest quarterbacks in the history of the game rolled into one. That's Mike," Engel said. "I was a good wide receiver and Mike made me into a great wide receiver. The ball was always there."

In 1984, Joseph forced Engel to resign. Word spread through the firm that Engel had improperly borrowed money from a client. Engel declined to publicly explain exactly what did happen, attributing his firing in a vague way to "politics." Some Drexel bankers wanted the firm to sever all ties with Engel, but Milken came to his aid and as a compromise Engel was named a consultant. As a consultant, Engel probably made more money from 1984 to 1989 than any of Drexel's New York employees save Leon Black, netting more than $10 million in 1986 alone, his best year. After he was ousted, Engel moved into an office in the headquarters of MacAndrews & Forbes, one of his clients, though he could still be reached by dialing his old Drexel phone number.

Engel's client list included Steve Ross of Warner Communications, Minneapolis raider Irwin Jacobs, and Chicago billionaire Jay Pritzker. But his quintessential client and ultimate meal ticket was Ronald Perelman, the CEO of MacAndrew & Forbes. A few years after his Drexel-backed takeover of Revlon in 1985, Perelman was hailed by *Institutional Investor* as the richest man in America. But when Engel first met him in 1978, Perelman didn't own a business. He didn't even have a job, having just quit after a dozen years of working for his father. As Engel saw it, Perelman's only qualifications as an aspiring mogul were a Wharton MBA and a burning desire to make it big. That was good enough for Engel. "My job really was to love these guys," Engel said. "That's the only way you can get to know them.

And the sicker the guy was, the more I loved him." By Engel's criterion, there was much to love in Perelman, who was self-consciously short, loud and pushy, and as taut as spandex. He required handling. When Perelman went on one of the road shows customarily used to promote a securities underwriting, Engel was on hand to critique his every presentation. During the Revlon deal, Engel saw Perelman every day for six months. Engel tried to love clients without toadying to them. His motto: "You must know how to say 'Fuck you' with style."

Among Engel's other clients was Victor Posner, a Miami Beach raider who made Perelman seem positively normal. Engel was appointed to the boards of two Posner companies and flew down to Miami every few weeks to see him on what he began thinking of as "suicide missions." Visiting Posner was like walking into an English-language Fellini film. A short man, Posner sat atop a thronelike platform chair surrounded by bodyguards with guns jammed holsterless into their belts. He was liable to lose his temper at any moment. Among the bodyguards' duties was emptying elevators of old ladies and other menacing characters before Posner entered. They were also quick with a coffee cup. Posner was so insistent on drinking his coffee hot that he would drink a few sips and then snap his fingers. The cup was taken away and replaced by a fresh one, repeatedly. One morning, Engel watched this ritual repeated fifteen times before he stopped counting.

After one too many stylish fuck-you's, Posner banished Engel from his crumbling empire in 1985. And after Posner said "Fuck you" to Drexel by failing to meet an interest payment on a bond issue, his relationship with the firm ended. By 1990, Posner was all but ruined and Drexel was bankrupt, but Engel still had fond memories. "I'm an admirer of Victor's, crazy as it sounds," Engel said. "If he was your friend, he was the most loyal guy around. Outside of business, he was the most enjoyable, funny guy you'll ever meet. I miss my evenings drinking with Victor."

Engel's exceptionally close relationship with Milken was formed in collaborating on the development of Drexel's high-yield-bond conference, better known as the Predators' Ball. This annual gala, which dwarfed in size and notoriety all other sales conferences sponsored by Wall Street houses, was a rainmaking extravaganza sprung from humble seed. In 1979, Milken invited representatives of eight Florida corporations he considered likely prospects to a Florida resort for a two-day "seminar" on the junk-bond market. Engel, who was one of the few New York employees invited, was appalled. "The food was diabolical," he said. "Not even the hors d'oeuvres were any good." Undeterred, Milken decided to broaden the conference to include junk-bond buyers as well as issuers and to hold it in Beverly Hills. The next year about sixty guests attended three days of presentations and wining and dining. Engel had never seen such disorganization. In protest, he pulled his own guests out of the concluding banquet and took them to a restaurant. "I had to do something," he recalled. "Candles were dripping all over the place. Even the hors d'oeuvres were dripping!"

Milken called Engel the next day. "Well," he said sternly. "Why'd you leave like that?"

"Mike, let me tell you something," replied Engel, still too angry to feel intimidated. "We're dealing with guys who go all the time to charity dinners and here we give them hors d'oeuvres that are dripping. Dripping, Mike! This is personally embarrassing to me."

"Okay, then," Milken said. "You take care of it."

And so a star was born: Donnie Engel, convention promoter extraordinaire. Dripless hors d'oeuvres were just the beginning. Working with Milken and Harry Horowitz, Engel helped organize a conference that remained a marvel of logistical precision even as the number of attendees topped three thousand and the cost neared $4 million. The bond conference was a triumph of the same compulsiveness that enabled Milken to fashion his own capital market in the first place. Milken spent hundreds of hours with Engel working up schedules and guest lists and seating assignments in hopes of creating pairings that would minimize conflict and maximize business generated. The most exclusive of all the special events within the event was a cocktail party held in Bungalow 8 of the Beverly Hills Hotel for Drexel's most prized clients—a group of about a hundred that included most of the big-name raiders. Milken himself never came to Bungalow 8. As the legend of the Bungalow 8 party grew, fed by the publication of *The Predators' Ball*, Milken's absence was explained in terms of the presence at the party of legions of beautiful prostitutes procured by Engel. While Milken supposedly had been convinced that hookers were a necessary client perk, as an all-around straight-arrow he didn't want to participate.

Beck attended his first Bungalow 8 party in 1986, which, in Engel's expert opinion, was the greatest Predators' Ball of them all. This was the last gasp of the presubpoena era of junk-bond-dom—before Le-

vine, before Boesky, before the prosecution of Milken himself stripped
the swaggering, celebratory edge off the affair and replaced it with
paranoia. Engel would look back on the 1986 party in Bungalow 8 as
"the most awesome group of guys ever in one place anywhere in America." Beck, though, was not impressed. "There was more action in LA
anywhere but Bungalow 8," he said. "Unless you like seeing a lot of
fat-rich or short-rich guys eating caviar, drinking Cristal and bloviat-
ing. Some guys brought their wives. Some women work for clients of
Drexel. There were women from law firms who were attractive. Some
models. A couple of aspiring actresses who were too blond and too
made-up. Some of these women seemed smart, some pretty stupid.
But they were nothing special and certainly not professional hookers."
Beck's discovery of the discrepancy between the image and the reality
of Bungalow 8 served only to deepen his appreciation of Engel's skills
as a promoter.

Once Joseph made a conference call to Beck and Engel to chide
them for objecting to a potentially lucrative transaction that they believed was not in the best interests of one of Engel's clients.

"You know, you guys should be acting more like investment bankers," Joseph said.

"But, Fred," Beck replied, "we're *not* investment bankers."

Pause. "What are you?" Joseph responded.

"We don't know," Engel said, and Beck added, "What are you?"

In hopes of bolstering the firm's new-business solicitation, Joseph
returned Engel to the Drexel payroll not long after Beck had joined
the firm. Engel was to serve with Anderson and another banker as
cohead of the Investment Banking Group. As Beck had so impoliti-
cally pointed out, the IBG was going nowhere under Anderson. Engel
immediately rechristened it the Relationship Group and began trying
to remake it in his image. But Herb Batchelor, who was head of the
overall corporate-finance department and one of the Shearson mafiosi,
threw bureaucratic obstacles in Engel's way and Joseph let him get
away with it. "It was like I was just coaching the running backs,"
Engel said. A few weeks after his return, Anderson refused to let Engel
enter an IBG meeting. After the meeting, Anderson delivered his
resignation to Joseph. Two other senior bankers also threatened to
resign if Engel's reinstatement wasn't rescinded. Joseph asked for one
week to come up with a solution that would "make everyone happy."
Convinced that Joseph never would give him the authority needed to
succeed in his new position, Engel asked to be made a consultant

again. "It took seven months for Joseph to negotiate my return and two weeks for people to change his mind for him," Engel said. "I went to him and said, 'Fred, you don't even know that you're CEO.' "

Despite his compatibility with Engel, Beck didn't often work with him, which wasn't surprising since they were both senior bankers with clients of their own. In addition, Beck more or less refused to work on hostile deals, of which Engel's clients did many. His aversion to hostile takeovers was a product of moral principle, of identification with his own, eminently respectable corporate clients, and of a deep ambivalence he felt toward the raiders themselves. Men like Ron Perelman and Nelson Peltz were maverick outcasts not unlike Beck. The raiders, though, weren't mere middlemen but principals in the deal game. They took the big risks, got the big headlines, and, at least for a few heady years in the mid-1980s, made the big money—and a part of Beck begrudged them their success, which, to be sure, they owned more to audacity than to talent. The result was that when discussing Drexel's stable of infamous raiders, Beck was usually at his most condescendingly sarcastic. Noting their lack of physical stature, Beck suggested that their deal-making drive was nothing more than misdirected sexual frustration.

Engel once brought Beck to Revlon to meet Perelman. "Jeff was a little overbearing," Engel said. "He came on a bit too strong."

Tellingly, Beck's own version of his meeting with Perelman revolved around his macho Vietnam persona. As Beck told it, he put the raider in his place with a thinly veiled warning.

"So tell me about yourself," Perelman is supposed to have said.

"Well," Beck replied, "I was in Vietnam."

"Oh, that must have been terrible," Perelman replied.

"No, I miss it. I got to kill people sometimes."

"Oh, yeah?" said Perelman, suddenly edgy.

"Yeah," growled Beck. "I hope that I never get so angry at some guy on a deal that I have to kill him. Know what I mean?"

Beck's punch line: "He got the message."

Beck had put his Vietnam identity into circulation as soon as he arrived at Drexel, though he told his tales discriminately. Max Liskin, a younger banker who probably heard as much as anyone at the firm about Beck's imaginary Vietnam adventures, was frankly admiring of his colleague's military derring-do. On the other hand, Marc Utay, who wasn't much interested in war stories, never heard Beck make more than passing, indirect mention of Vietnam—as in comments like

"Compared to combat, this is a snap." Beck wouldn't even go that far in the presence of David Kay, the firm's genial M & A cochief, who nonetheless was vaguely aware of Beck's Vietnam legend. "I learned of it more by osmosis than anything direct," Kay recalled. "You'd hear about it just hanging around the office." Kay said he had no reason to doubt the stories until a secretary came to him and asked a hypothetical question: "What should I do if I suspect that someone in the department is fabricating his military experience?" Although she mentioned no one by name, Kay was certain she meant Beck. Not that he cared. "I told her that I didn't know and that we had more important things to do anyway. I just let it drop."

On December 16, 1986, as his first full year at Drexel was drawing to a close, Beck submitted the first of what would be an annual end-of-the-year resignation letter to Joseph. "I want to thank you for the opportunity you created for me at Drexel," Beck wrote. "1986 was certainly an interesting year." However, Beck continued, "it is no longer economic for me to remain at Drexel. I was extremely sorry that my year-end compensation was inadequate and I must say the derivation and approach to my compensation I still do not understand. . . . Given the sensitive environment, I would like to coordinate any announcements regarding my future with you directly. I suggest that no announcement be made until mid-January so that we can assure an orderly and fruitful transition."

While his $1.2 million in total compensation for 1986 had slightly exceeded the minimum he'd been guaranteed—and while Joseph intended the sum as a signal of his satisfaction with Beck's performance —it was less than the $3 million Jeff expected and believed that he deserved. It galled Beck no end that someone like Anderson was reputed to have made more than $5 million even though he hadn't generated much new business in 1986 and hadn't in his entire career landed a single corporation the equal of W. R. Grace, RJR Nabisco, Akzo, Pillsbury, the Taubman Organization, or Ralston Purina—all of which Beck had introduced to Drexel within the span of a single year. In retrospect, Beck would be a bit abashed at having threatened to resign over the inadequacy of a $1.2 million paycheck. "I made millions of dollars at Drexel, but not tens of millions," he said, "and you know something, I'm glad I didn't." Even so, he remained galled by the firm's grossly inequitable distribution of its profits.

Besides his discontent with his pay and his growing sense of isolation, the miasma of scandal and sleaze that increasingly enveloped Drexel also undermined Beck's morale. The scandals began in May 1986, when Dennis Levine was arrested in connection with the largest insider-trading case in history. The Securities and Exchange Commission charged him with making $12.6 million in illicit trading in the securities of fifty-four companies over a five-and-a-half-year period beginning in 1980. Most of the insider transactions had taken place while Levine was working at Lehman Brothers, though they spanned all the firms for which he'd worked and involved five of Drexel's clients. However, Levine had no direct connection to more than twenty of the companies whose stocks he'd traded, a fact that suggested he had not acted alone. Levine was said to be cooperating with the government's continuing investigation.

On the night of Levine's arrest, Beck took Margo to the annual Crystal Ball thrown at the Waldorf-Astoria Hotel on behalf of Mount Sinai Hospital, one of Kravis's favorite charities. The Becks sat at one of several tables Drexel had purchased at the black-tie soirée, which was crawling with deal men from all the big firms. The conversational din that night was even more deafening than usual, in perverse homage to Levine no doubt. Beck noticed two empty chairs and got up to peek at the names on the placecards set before them: Mr. and Mrs. Dennis Levine. He returned to his own seat and exchanged a pensive glance with Margo. While Levine's arrest was gratifying to Beck in the sense that it confirmed his critique of his profession, he felt more disoriented than delighted. It was all a bit surreal. Levine's fantasy life had stopped on a dime. He'd disappeared from the big-deal, black-tie scene as swiftly and surely as if he'd never entered it. Dennis Levine, M & A ghost. Instead of sitting at the next table with his wife, "the guy was down at the Manhattan detention center having a rectal exam," as Beck put it later. Not until a waiter came and took the placecards away did Beck realize that he'd been staring at them for a good five minutes.

Throughout the summer and fall of 1986, the U.S. Department of Justice began exposing the criminal life of Dennis Levine to public view, chapter by lurid chapter. Every few weeks, another young Wall Streeter appeared in federal court in Manhattan to cop a plea to insider-trading charges brought on the basis of information supplied by Levine. Although Levine's confederates worked at the first firms of M & A—Lazard Frères; Goldman, Sachs; Shearson Lehman; Wachtell, Lipton—as individuals they were all second-tier players in the deal game. None were as prominent as Levine himself. While Wall Street awaited the next round of revelations with fear and loathing, at Drexel the predominant emotion was one of relief: Levine hadn't implicated any of his colleagues. Indeed, the public-relations effect of every new indictment or arrest was to dilute the stain on Drexel's reputation as the scandal spread to encompass other firms. Meanwhile, lucrative business continued to pour into the firm in ever-expanding volume. Drexel was back to full swagger by November fourteenth, when the government dropped a bigger bombshell, announcing that Ivan Boesky had agreed to pay a $100 million penalty—the biggest in SEC history—to settle insider-trading charges.

While federal authorities had investigated Boesky for years, they were unable to make a strong case against him until Levine tangled himself in their net. Having been made to understand that the best way to lessen the severity of his own sentence was to provide the evidence the government needed to land a bigger fish, Levine delivered the Great White Shark. Levine had begun passing inside information to Boesky in February 1985, the month he joined Drexel. He made hundreds of calls to Boesky over the course of the year, sometimes as many as twenty a day. Boesky made at least $50 million from information supplied by Levine, who was arrested before he could receive the $2.4 million owed him by the arbitrageur as his cut of the illegal profits. When confronted with the evidence provided by Levine, Boesky quickly agreed to plead guilty to criminal fraud and to help the authorities nail other crooks of his acquaintance, including Marty Siegel, who, beginning in 1982, had supplied Boesky with inside information relating to at least four takeovers in exchange for cash payments totaling $700,000. On the day Boesky's settlement with the government was announced, Siegel was in Marty Lipton's office. When a federal marshal walked in and slapped him with a subpoena, Siegel began crying. Siegel vehemently protested his innocence but a few months later pleaded guilty to criminal charges and agreed to pay a fine of $9 million.

The satisfaction Beck felt at Boesky's and Siegel's apprehension was laced with resurgent anger as what he once regarded as his own pièce de résistance, the leveraged buyout of Beatrice, was dragged into the scandal. Siegel had supplied with inside information on the Beatrice buyout not only Boesky but Robert Freeman, the head arbitrageur at Goldman, Sachs. While the government accused Freeman of multiple instances of insider trading, the only charge prosecutors made stick involved Beatrice.

After Beatrice had accepted KKR's bid in late 1985, Freeman placed a heavy bet that the buyout would in fact be consummated, investing $66 million in Beatrice securities on Goldman, Sachs's behalf while wagering 40 percent of his personal trading capital to buy 25,000 shares for his own account. Freeman was one of several Goldman partners friendly with Kravis, who'd started as a trainee at the firm. When Beatrice's stock plunged in heavy trading on January 6, 1989, Freeman was so worried that he telephoned Kravis, who accepted the call but said little. "He was very abrupt and appeared anxious to end the conversation quickly," Freeman later recalled. Kravis's tone exacerbated Freeman's fears and the next morning the arb began selling Beatrice shares. Freeman got a call from Bernard "Bunny" Lasker, a well-connected trader on the floor of the New York Exchange, tipping him to a problem on Beatrice. Freeman then called Marty Siegel, who was representing KKR on the deal, and said that he'd heard there were problems with Beatrice. Siegel asked Freeman from whom he'd heard this. Freeman said, Bunny Lasker. Replied Siegel, "Your bunny has a good nose." Freeman quickly sold the rest of his Beatrice stock, barely beating an announcement out of KKR that it was lowering the cash portion of its offer. The revision knocked the stock down from about $47 a share to $44. By selling when he did, Freeman was able to dodge about $930,000 in losses. Freeman pleaded guilty to one felony count and was sentenced to four months in jail. Meanwhile, Siegel was rewarded for incriminating Freeman and other confederates with a lenient sentence of two months, outraging Beck all over again.

With Boesky and Siegel safely netted, the government began leaking incriminating information supplied by them to the press—especially to *The Wall Street Journal.* Within days of Boesky's fall, it was reported that the SEC was investigating not only Drexel's ties to Boesky but the firm's entire junk-bond operation as well. By November eighteenth, Drexel felt compelled to issue a press release denying rumors that Milken had resigned. In public anyway, Joseph was as blithe-spirited as ever. "Our internal investigations give me no cause for concern," he insisted. Joseph was even able to find some humor in the Boesky mess. "I'd like to send Mr. Boesky back as a client," he wisecracked at a press lunch, after being told that a U.S. senator had returned a campaign contribution from the discredited arbitrageur.

As a speculator in stocks rather than bonds, Boesky didn't come into Milken's circle until Drexel moved into the financing of takeovers in the early 1980s. In 1983, Drexel floated a $100 million junk-bond offering for a company controlled by Boesky and later renamed the Northview Corporation. As part of its fee, Drexel took warrants convertible into 7 percent of Northview stock. A few months later, one of the employee partnerships controlled by Milken acquired a small equity stake in Boesky's risk-arbitrage operation, for which Drexel subsequently raised $109 million through a private placement. Upon completion of the offering, Drexel-supplied funds accounted for about half of Boesky's total capital. In late 1984, Drexel raised $67 million for yet another Boesky entity based in London.

A few months after Beck had joined the firm, Drexel committed itself to raising yet another $640 million in junk-bond money for Boesky. Under the terms of the agreement, Drexel would buy an interest in Boesky's new risk-arbitrage partnership, cementing the unholy alliance between Wall Street's largest financier of hostile takeovers and its most active speculator in takeover stocks. The conflicts of interest here were flagrant even by Drexel standards. Plus, it was no secret on Wall Street that Boesky had been repeatedly investigated by the Securities and Exchange Commission; indeed, Dan Dorfman, a widely read financial columnist, had recently disclosed in print that the SEC was investigating whether Boesky had traded on inside information during Carl Icahn's bid for Phillips Petroleum—the first of Drexel's junk-bond raids. Even Drexel's own offering circular for Boesky's new partnership contained a very curious disclosure: Boesky had paid Drexel a $5.3 million "consulting fee" for services left unspecified. This fee was rather hefty to go unexplained, though the SEC raised no objections.

Doing business with Boesky was the biggest mistake of Mike Milken's life. Like Boesky, Milken had been repeatedly investigated over the years by the SEC, which had been unable to penetrate the network of incestuous relationships that bound Milken to his major clients and Drexel helpmates. Through its prosecution of Boesky, the government finally managed to carry its investigation into Milken's inner sanctum. Put on the defensive for the first time, the junk-bond king came out swinging. Although Milken remained inaccessible to the press, he issued a defiant public proclamation of sorts a few days after Boesky Day by reaffirming that he was highly confident of raising $3 billion to finance Revlon's takeover of Gillette. And even as Joseph was lamenting Drexel's ties to Boesky, Milken was pulling out all the stops for another arbitrageur widely known to have a suspiciously close relationship with Boesky. On the basis of his dealings with Boesky, John Mulheren eventually would be convicted of criminal conspiracy and fraud. But four days before Boesky's unmasking, Milken had committed Drexel to raising $100 million for a partnership headed by Mulheren and so raised it—though real buyers were so scarce that Drexel and its employees bought $50 million of the paper. This was exactly the sort of muscle-flexing that had led Drexel to become Boesky's banker in the first place.

Milken's show of force produced the desired effect, at least for a while. In the immediate wake of the Boesky debacle, very few of Drexel's corporate clients took their business elsewhere. After all, neither Milken nor Drexel itself had yet to be officially charged with breaking any law, and in fact the firm's officials were able to exploit the antipress sentiment prevalent in corporate America to win sympathy with complaints about prosecution-by-leak. Beck spent a hectic few days reassuring his own clients of his steadfastness in protecting them in their dealings with Drexel. While none of Beck's clients bolted, his salesmanship wasn't enough to restore the flagging enthusiasm of several blue-chippers. But Peter Grace was emphatically not among them. Joseph's decision to stand by the Restaurant Enterprises deal paid a handsome public-relations dividend as Grace was one of the few CEOs willing to speak out on the record in support of Drexel. "I'm still doing business with Drexel," he told me at *Business Week.* "In America, you're innocent until proven guilty." Beck not only encouraged Grace to stand up for Drexel but acted as his unofficial press agent, promoting his availability to Drexel's PR department and to reporters.

For Beck, his relationship with Grace was a pleasant distraction from an increasingly untenable existence. Switching from Oppenheimer to Drexel had done nothing to alleviate the deep psychological stresses and conflicts that had prompted the transfer in the first place. To the contrary, his internal demons had been aggravated by that old bugaboo, success; in terms of deals done and relationships established, Beck's debut year at Drexel—his comeback year—was his most productive ever. But the adrenaline rush that sustained him through 1986 dissipated in 1987. Over the next few years, Beck would have a hand in some of the biggest deals of all time—including the biggest of all, the $25 billion buyout of RJR Nabisco. Emotionally, though, it would all be downhill as, once again, his psyche and his life would gradually come unwound. While force of habit and fear of change continued to compel Beck's pursuit of the next big deal, it was escape that increasingly preoccupied him—escape from Drexel, from Wall Street, from Margo, from reality.

21

Arriving for the Academy Awards is one of the great status rituals of Hollywood. The limousine pulls up before an expectant throng of reporters and fans clustered around the entryway to the Dorothy Chandler Pavilion. A murmur of anticipation builds as fans maneuver for an unobstructed sightline to celebrity. Who will it be? The car door opens and out steps the magical creature in all his or her finery. Flashbulbs pop, television cameras whir, reporters speak reverentially into microphones. Exclamations of delight erupt from the crowd as the star is recognized and cheered. The star flashes his most dazzling smile and waves to the assembled multitude as he runs a red-carpeted gauntlet to the door and passes inside, to the privileged realm of Star Land. Early one evening in March of 1987, the actor-producer Michael Douglas stepped forth from his limo into the limelight, triggering a chorus of female squeals. Looking every inch the matinee idol, Douglas paused by the open car door as he awaited the exit of his companion. Would it be his wife, the gorgeous Diandra? Perhaps his superstar father, Kirk? Old buddy Jack Nicholson? *Romancing the Stone* costar Kathleen Turner?

From the back door of the limo emerged a chunky, bespectacled man of about forty who stood next to Douglas and smiled a funny little smile. His presence had an effect akin to that of a pail of water on a fire. The anticipatory excitement fizzled out and after a moment of dead silence, an undercurrent of confused muttering swept the crowd. Siskel and Ebert exchanged quizzical glances. Who the hell was this guy? Could this be some hot new foreign director who'd escaped their notice? An impostor with a gun in his tuxedo pocket, holding Douglas hostage to some sick Oscar-night fantasy? No, not exactly. It was Jeff Beck, Wall Street star gone Hollywood. Standing there, Beck took in the scene for a moment and then tilted his head in Douglas's direction.

"I don't think they know who I am," he said and laughed, nervously.

Douglas and Beck walked the press gauntlet up the walkway into the Chandler Pavilion and headed backstage to the room where Douglas and the other award presenters would await their cues to go on. Beck's stomach turned cartwheels as he looked around and saw nothing but stars: Shirley MacLaine, Goldie Hawn, Paul Hogan, Sigourney Weaver, Anthony Quinn, Steven Spielberg, Amy Irving. He felt spectacularly out of place. Douglas plugged in a little portable television and settled down to watch a National Collegiate Athletic Association basketball playoff game. Beck was introducing himself to Hogan when the only person in the room whom he didn't recognize tapped his shoulder and extended his hand.

"Congratulations," he said.

Beck shook his hand. "Thank you very much," said Beck, who had no idea what the guy was talking about.

Beck loosened up after a bit and began trading stories with a few of the friendlier male stars. The one Beck liked best was Hogan, who seemed as unpretentious as the character who'd made him famous, Crocodile Dundee. After several hours of backstage hobnobbing with the stars, Beck headed out with Douglas to make a night of it at the celebrity hangout, Spago's. It was almost dawn before Beck dropped off to sleep in his room at the Bel-Air Hotel, with a head full of stars. The next morning he took the first of a dozen phone calls from amused and envious acquaintances who'd seen him on television arriving with Douglas and wondered what he was doing in Hollywood. Beck decided to play it for a laugh. "Beats the hell out of me," he said.

As his dissatisfaction with Drexel Burnham deepened, Beck envisioned for himself a new career in Hollywood, not as an actor—though his appearance in a cameo role in the film *Wall Street* inevitably would inspire passing fantasies of his name in marquee lights—but as a producer of feature films and all-around mogul. Movie producing certainly was more congruent with his experience, since Hollywood no less than Wall Street revolved around money and its idiosyncratic allocation. Film producers, along with M & A bankers, were the most fabulously overcompensated middlemen in all of legitimate commerce. That said, though, Hollywood was a particular and peculiar world unto itself—

the West Coast capital of a separate (or nearly so) kingdom of the big-money deal, with its own cast of players arrayed in a hierarchy of power that, like investment banking, was purposefully impossible to fathom from the outside. A good deal of Hollywood's appeal to Beck was the professional challenge it posed to him as a rainmaker, as a master infiltrator of the commercial fortress. Could he work his way into the Hollywood system as he'd insinuated himself into major corporations and into the M & A game itself? Could he understand the entertainment game on its own terms and make it work for him, something none of his fellow Wall Street M & A men had attempted?

Hollywood appealed even more irresistibly to the fabulist in Beck. By 1987, if not earlier, Beck had gotten as much ego-gratification mileage out of the Legend of the Mad Dog as he could on Wall Street. In deal circles, he was a certified character, though one more controversial than honored. In proudly appropriating the self-description "promoter," Beck was proclaiming a reality that most of his peers shrank from acknowledging: Hype and self-promotion were as much the coin of the realm in the M & A game as was objective reality as respresented in "the numbers." While fantasy wasn't officially respectable on Wall Street, in Hollywood it was the essence, the stuff from which careers and fortunes were made. Hollywood made its money retailing escapism mixed with a bit of art, and not since the 1930s had its product been in greater demand. Nor had it ever before been available in such volume and multiplicity of forms—cable television, home video, compact discs—as in the 1980s, a decade of triumphant self-enrichment for the moguls of mass-market entertainment no less than for the moguls of high finance. These two aspects of the decade were perfectly embodied in Ronald Reagan, who viewed reality through the clouded rearview mirror of the sentimental, black-and-white movies he'd acted in or seen as a kid and who was compelled to proclaim new "heroes" at the drop of a press conference, briefly ennobling with the spotlight of presidential publicity people who often would have been more fittingly identified as victims or, in the case of Oliver North or Ferdinand Marcos, as criminals.

In the faux-hero-crowded, celebrity-crazed environment of postvideo America, Beck began to suffer from the claustrophobia of anonymity. In search of relief, he had no choice but to heed the old adage and go west. Washington may have been the nation's news capital but Hollywood was Center Stage, U.S.A., the electronic hub of national renown. There were dozens of second-rate actors, two-bit musicians, and game-show hosts who were far better known than the greatest M & A men. If Beck were to project his fabricated personas to an audience larger than his peers and the hardcore readers of the business press, he had to go Hollywood.

To be fair, Beck was also impelled toward Hollywood by an artistic impulse, however naïve that might have been. Producers were in a position to influence the content of films, and the artistic aspect of filmmaking appealed strongly to Beck, who felt that corporate deal making alone no longer provided an adequate outlet for his creativity. He wanted to work in a medium of expression in which not all ideas were ultimately reducible to balance sheets and earnings statements. Last and probably least, as a lifelong movie fan, Beck secretly thrilled to the prospect of associating with great directors, famous actors, and beautiful actresses, whether famous, infamous, or utterly obscure.

Beck's initial, tantalizing contacts with the film world had come through Margo and through Chloe Aaron. Chloe, the wife of David Aaron, his former colleague at Oppenheimer, was an independent producer of documentary films. Working with Chloe, Beck had donated money to help finance *Shoah*, the epic documentary of the Holocaust, and an animated version of Stravinsky's *A Soldier's Tale*. Although Beck had no artistic input into these projects, he took an active interest in their development and found the experience satisfying, albeit vicariously so.

Beck's ticket to the Hollywood big time, though, was Michael Douglas. Since moving to New York from Santa Barbara in 1984, Douglas and his wife had begun circulating in Nouvelle Society. Douglas had gone to prep school with Henry Kravis and attended his wedding to Roehm. While Beck had seen Douglas at several other Manhattan affairs, he didn't make his acquaintance until the fall of 1986 at the Hôtel du Cap d'Antibes. When Beck saw Douglas lounging poolside at Eden Roc one afternoon, he decided to walk up and introduce himself. Douglas was sitting with a lawyer from Los Angeles; the three of them went for a swim in the ocean. Afterward, they climbed onto a raft anchored offshore and got to talking while soaking up the hot Mediterranean sun. Beck was delighted to discover that beneath the soft and polished nice-guy image that Douglas projected to the public was a canny, profane operator with a flair for bawdy anecdote. Hey, thought Beck as he traded stories with Douglas, this is a regular guy.

The next evening Beck invited Douglas over to meet Margo and have a few drinks on the terrace of the owner's villa. As the conversation inevitably turned to business, Beck said that Drexel Burnham had done several underwritings for film-production companies and offered to help Douglas look at the financing alternatives open to him—as a friend, which meant free of charge. After finishing a bottle of Roederer Cristal, the Becks and Douglas went off to dinner at La Bonne Auberge with Johnny Carson's ex-wife, Joanna, who was a friend of the actor's. At dinner, Douglas mentioned that he and Diandra had just rented a cottage near Bedford, which, as it turned out, was only a mile from Barrett Farm, the Becks' place. By the time Douglas and the Becks parted company in the south of France, they'd made plans to spend a weekend together in the country.

Back in New York, Beck's relationship with the actor-producer quickly blossomed into fast friendship. Margo and Diandra grew close, too. Like Margo, Diandra had her own professional interest in film, working for the Office of Film and Television at the Metropolitan Museum of Art and as a model. At Jeff's request, Douglas gave Margo a part-time job as a script reader in the New York office of his production company. While the Becks and the Douglases began seeing each other as couples almost every weekend in Westchester County, rare was the day that Jeff and Michael didn't spend at least a half hour speaking on the telephone. While forming intense instant friendships was a forte of Beck's, it was out of character for Douglas. "My stepfather told me, when I was running around hysterically in junior high school, worrying who my friends were, 'Look, you know, you'll be lucky in your lifetime if you can count your good friends on one hand,'" Douglas told an interviewer in 1988. "I remember being very shocked. And I think he's right. He's absolutely right. So I've got a lot of acquaintances."

Born eighteen months apart, Douglas and Beck both drifted through the 1960s as indifferent, problem students to whom the focus of career came late and rather more through default than any grasping of destiny. Along the way, each man's latent ambition had kicked in ferociously, though now that they'd "made it" neither was comfortable with the idea of seeming to be defined by career or even with letting his intensity of purpose show much of the time. Both Beck and Douglas had wrapped a hard core of shrewdness in hip, hang-loose, hey-what's-happenin'-man blue-jeaned nonchalance. This wasn't disguise or even affectation but a basic facet of complex personalities forged amid traumatic circumstance. It was one of the two main modes in which Beck and Douglas dealt with each other when no one else was around. The other was the Machiavellian sensibility of the deal man, for Douglas was as calculating and obsessive a doer of deals in his world as Beck was in his.

Unlike Beck, though, Douglas had the social polish that enabled him to play it straight and easeful in Establishment settings. Douglas's upbringing was an exceptionally disparate combination of show-biz neurosis and old-money refinement. His father, Kirk, was one of the best-known Americans of the postwar decades and the very prototype of the driven, brutal, self-made Hollywood superstar. Michael's mother, Diana Dill, was an actress, too, but less successful and more refined; she was descended from an old, moneyed English family. When Michael was six, his parents divorced and he went to live with his mother, mainly in the East. Douglas attended two élite prep schools: Eaglebrook and Choate. During his teen years, he and his brother spent the summers in Hollywood with their father. Overawed by the sheer iconographic presence of Kirk, Michael Douglas wanted nothing to do with theater all the way through school. "I saw my father as a gladiator, nailed to a cross, as an artist who cut his ear off— and he would be shown doing these superhuman things," he said. "I'd think, 'How can I possibly be a man? How can I be the man this man was?' "

Accepted at Yale, Michael made what he later called "the first big decision of my life" and opted instead for the University of California at Santa Barbara. He promptly flunked out, unmotivated by the fear that kept many draft-age males in school. (He flunked his draft physical, too, thanks to a bad back.) Douglas worked odd jobs for eighteen months, lived in a commune in the mountains, and then returned to school. As a junior, Douglas chose theater as his major for lack of a better idea, though as a neophyte actor he was afflicted with such severe stage fright that he'd keep a wastebasket in the wings into which he'd throw up before going onstage. Douglas was a long time in finding his confidence. He first gained wide notice in the mid-1970s, playing second banana to Karl Malden on the prime-time cop show *The Streets of San Francisco*. After four years, Douglas quit the hit show to devote himself to his own film-production company, through which he bought from his father the rights to Ken Kesey's novel *One Flew over the Cuckoo's Nest*, and finally managed to scrape together financing. Starring Jack Nicholson, the film was a huge critical and commercial success, winning the five top Oscars. Douglas the producer scored again in 1979 with the antinuclear adventure story *The China Syndrome,* in which he also appeared in a supporting role.

Proclaiming himself "an actor first and a producer second," Douglas then began concentrating on acting, appearing in a series of undistinguished roles in forgettable movies that did his reputation no good at all. His careers as producer and actor came together again to beneficial effect in 1984 with *Romancing the Stone,* a big box-office hit. Although Douglas was forty years old and respected as a film producer, as an actor he had yet to escape his father's massive shadow. As *People* magazine put it: "On his best day Michael Douglas couldn't hold the screen against his old man's chin dimple. Kirk in his heyday had a face like an axe, and he swung it at the public with wicked zest. Michael generated the theatrical impact of a glass of warm milk: nice, white, wholesome, put you right to sleep." Michael would not be considered an actor of the first rank until he played a villain and, in effect, showed the world the Kirk in him. "I just don't believe Michael is as sweet and charming as everyone says he is," Kirk Douglas had said. "Oh, Michael is tough. There is a piece of steel inside him."

Not long after he met Beck, Douglas landed back-to-back bad-guy roles that put his acting career over the top. The first was the philandering husband of *Fatal Attraction.* Beck had spent several days on the set of that film and was much more deeply involved in Douglas's next movie, *Wall Street,* which provided Douglas with the role of Gordon Gekko, unscrupulous corporate raider. From the moment Douglas gave him a peek at the first rough script of *Wall Street,* Beck discussed the project endlessly with the actor and others. Before shooting started, Douglas introduced Beck to Oliver Stone, the director and cowriter of *Wall Street,* over dinner at La Côte Basque. To Beck, Stone was a most intriguing figure who'd begun to figure prominently in the Mad Dog's resurgent fantasies even before he'd met the man. Stone had directed *Platoon,* the harrowing Vietnam combat movie that won four Oscars, including Best Picture and Best Director, in 1986. Beck saw *Platoon* the night it opened in New York and was so deeply moved by it that he returned the next night with Margo to see it again.

Stone based *Platoon* on his own Vietnam experiences. The director, six months older than Beck, was the statistical anomaly Beck only imagined himself to be. The only son of a Wall Street stockbroker, Stone attended fine Eastern prep schools and summered in France. He was an unruly, temperamental kid whose sheltered world exploded

during his junior year in high school when his parents divorced and he
discovered that his father was deep in debt. Acceding to his father's
wishes, Stone enrolled at Yale but dropped out. At wit's end after
failing at the writing of a novel, Stone enlisted in the army in 1967,
specifically requesting assignment to a combat unit in Vietnam. He
was offered Officer Training School but turned it down for fear that
the war would end before he got a chance to fight. Assigned to the
25th Infantry Division, he arrived gung-ho to battle communism. "I
believed in the John Wayne view of the world," he recalled. His views
would change dramatically as he was exposed to the terror and camaraderie of combat. "I was with black guys, poor white guys for the first
time. And these poor people see through that upper-class bullshit,"
Stone said. "They don't buy into the rich man's game. They don't buy
into the Pentagon bullshit. They know the score. The score is, 'We've
been fucked, and we are over here in Vietnam.' "

Two weeks into his fifteen-month tour of duty, Stone was hit in the
neck during a night ambush. After he was wounded a second time, he
was shipped from the front lines to a rear-echelon military-police unit
in Saigon. But he got into a fight with a sergeant and to avoid insubordination charges cut a deal that put him back into the field with a
long-range reconnaissance patrol. "I got this horrible grease-bag lifer
sergeant, one of these guys who were raking off the beer concessions.
He had a waxed mustache; I'll never forget that. He didn't like my
attitude, and I told him to go fuck himself. So they sent me across the
road to a regular combat unit. . . . There were a lot of guys over the
edge in that unit. We had a bunker where we used to smoke a lot of
dope. I was wearing beads, started to talk black dialect. 'Hey, what you
doin', man?' All that shit. 'What's happenin'?' I'd do all the raps." In
addition to a Purple Star with oak-leaf clusters, Stone was awarded the
Bronze Star for valor after he took out a Vietcong machine-gun nest
with a hand grenade. But he didn't feel like a hero when he returned
to the United States after his discharge from the army in 1968. "Vietnam completely deadened me and sickened me," he recalled. "If I
went over to Vietnam right-wing, I came back an anarchist. Radical.
Very much like Travis Bickle in *Taxi Driver.* Alienated. A walking time
bomb."

In both tone and content, Beck's Vietnam legend was uncannily
similar to Stone's real-life experience, at least as related by the director.
It's not likely that Beck had read about Stone's Vietnam career by
September 1985, when at the Hôtel du Cap he gave me a full-length

account of his combat career. *Platoon* wouldn't be released for another fifteen months and until then Stone would remain a rather obscure screenwriter-director. At first, Beck told me that he and Stone had known each other in Vietnam in some vague, secretive way, but later he abandoned this assertion and, without acknowledging his revisionism, contented himself with saying that it seemed both to him and to Stone that they'd known one another before somewhere. Beck also implied to me and to others that he was the model for Barnes, the macho jungle fighter of *Platoon*, though he later dropped this assertion, as well.

Whether or not Beck had lifted details of his own combat saga from Stone's real-life history, it's clear that the Mad Dog had never before encountered someone who embodied so fully his own idealized version of himself—from prep-school rebelliousness all the way through the heroic Vietnam antiheroism to postcombat alienation—as did Oliver Stone. In introducing Beck to Stone, Douglas unwittingly called the Mad Dog's Vietnam bluff. From the outset, Beck had regaled Douglas with his Vietnam tales. How else could he hold his own with a real live Hollywood star (who conveniently hadn't gone anywhere near Vietnam)? But Stone had lived the nightmare Beck only pretended to have survived. If anyone was likely to catch him in a mistake, it was Stone. On the other hand, if Beck were simply to edit Vietnam out of his conversation with Stone, Douglas would think it odd. Beck took the plunge at La Côte Basque and began trading 'Nam stories and opinions with Stone, who heard nothing that called into question Beck's credibility. To the contrary. "I sensed he was a man who was troubled," Stone told a reporter. "He was obviously twisted by what happened over there. It was something very repressed in his character. I sensed that with me, it was OK for him to talk about it."

Naturally, Stone's and Beck's conversations covered the Street as well. In researching his movie, Stone met with many Wall Streeters, including raider-arbitrageurs (Carl Icahn and Asher Edelman), heads of major Wall Street houses (John Gutfreund of Salomon Brothers and Alan Greenberg of Bear, Stearns), a confessed insider trader (David Brown of Goldman, Sachs) and government prosecutors and regulators. Kenneth Lipper, a former partner of Salomon Brothers, spent a great deal of time on the set as chief technical adviser. Beck was one of four other technical advisers listed in the credits to the film. Douglas spent parts of several days at Drexel's New York office with Beck, who also brought the actor and Stone out to Beverly Hills to meet Mike

Milken. Stone was fascinated by Drexel Burnham Lambert, which loosely inspired the name of the fictional brokerage in the movie, Jackson Steinem & Company. Bud Fox, the young Jackson Steinem broker played by Charlie Sheen, touts the firm's junk-bond department to Gekko at first meeting. In Beck's judgment, his most tangible contribution to *Wall Street* lay in helping Stone rework some of Gekko's lines to make him a more manifestly violent, angry charecter.

Gekko's memorable first scene, in which he's shown wheeling and dealing in his enormous gizmo-stuffed office, is loaded with the kind of hyperbolic tough-guy talk Beck was partial to in real life. Lines like, "If it looks good on paper, we're in the kill zone, pal. We can lock and load." And: "Delete the son of a bitch. I want every orifice in his body flowing red." To his head trader, Ollie, Gekko offers this touching tribute: "The Terminator! Blow 'em away, Ollie. Rip their fucking throats out. Stuff them in your garbage compactor." ("The Terminator" was one of Beck's nicknames for Milken.) To Fox, a bit of advice later in the movie: "Wanna friend? Buy a dog, pal." While driving down Park Avenue, Gekko says, "See that building? I bought that building ten years ago. My first real-estate deal. Made an $800,000 profit. It was better than sex."

During the filming, Kravis called Beck to check on a disturbing rumor. He'd heard that Beck had suggested that the license plates on Gekko's limo feature the letters "KKR." Beck assured him that he'd done no such thing, but neglected to mention that Gekko's driver had been christened Mohammed, which was the name of Kravis's driver.

Beck was going over some of his script suggestions one day with Stone in the film's production office on the West Side, when the director gave him some lines and suggested he read them out loud by way of auditioning for a cameo role. Beck thought it was a practical joke until Stone summoned a casting director. The role was that of a hyperkinetic, abrasive Jackson Steinem investment banker who is berating a stodgy commercial banker in an effort to complete the financing arrangements for Gekko's acquisition of Blue Star Airlines. The part could have been written for Beck, and since he basically would be playing himself anyway, he asked if he could improvise his lines. He played through the scene his way and afterward read the scripted lines aloud, too. Stone looked at him and said, "You got the part."

A few weeks later, Beck's scene was filmed in the boardroom of the American Telephone & Telegraph building on Madison Avenue. Beck invited me onto the set as his guest and I watched for several hours as

Stone ran through endless takes. When I left, Beck was still reciting with unflagging energy. The scene I saw filmed appeared in truncated version in the film. Wholly eliminated were lines spoken by Lipper, who delivered them as woodenly as one might expect of a nonactor. The deletion of Lipper's speaking part gladdened Beck, since it underscored his own triumph in avoiding the same fate.

Although Beck had only one scene, his speech is one of the longest in the movie and is the pivot on which the plot turns. The scene opens as the camera follows Fox and a lawyer friend into a meeting in progress. Beck is standing directly across the table from the doorway, facing the camera but too distant to recognize at first. He has his suit coat off and is dressed in full deal-man's regalia, complete with red suspenders, and red-striped power tie (no wardrobe assistance was required). The Manhattan skyline is visible through the huge windows beyond him. Beck begins to speak in a loud, belligerent, and slightly gruff voice while pacing agitatedly. The deal language is surprisingly technical for a mainstream movie and quite true to life.

> BECK: "Look, guys, what's the problem? It's time to kill! Gekko's got twelve percent of the stock and climbing. Plus, he's got the unions in his back pocket and everybody knows that the stock's in play. By next week the Street's going to *own* Blue Star. Is the bank financing in place? [With mounting hostility.] Or are we going to sit around and have more and more of these ridiculous meetings? Our firm committed weeks ago to twenty-five percent of the long-term debt structure and [pointing his finger threateningly] unless you guys sign this piece of paper RIGHT NOW I'm going to pull and go to another bank for the seventy-five percent."
>
> COMMERCIAL LOAN OFFICER: "Listen, we've got thirty banks ready to participate . . .
>
> BECK [with withering sarcasm]: "Thirty banks? Isn't that wonderful."
>
> LOAN OFFICER: ". . . in a four-year revolving credit line. But we must have your assurance that you will pay back most of the loan in the first twelve months, and the only way we can see this happening is liquidating the hangars and the planes. Can you people guarantee the liquidation of Blue Star?"

From now on, the camera focuses on Bud Fox, whose father works for Blue Star. It is Fox who has brought the idea of acquiring Blue Star to Gekko, who not only assured the naïve young broker that he would keep the airline intact as an operating company but that he—Fox—

would be its new president. As Beck answers the banker's question, Fox realizes for the first time that he's been played for a sucker by Gekko.

> Guarantee? No sweat. We've got the Beezburg brothers to build condos where the hangars are. We can lay the airplanes off to the Mexicans, who are dumb enough to buy them. And I got the Texas boys drooling at my kneecaps for the routes and the slots. What's your problem? It's done.
>
> Of course, the beauty of this deal is the overfunded pension. Gekko makes seventy-five million there. Fifty million dollars buys him the minimum annuities for six thousand employees. And he walks away with the rest. I figure he'll make sixty—he'll clear sixty to seventy million. Not bad for a month's work! Your boy really did his homework, Fox, and you'll have the shortest executive career since that pope that got poisoned. Now he'll really start believing he's Gekko the Great.

After his hard day's filming, Beck was so exhausted that he wiggled out of his plans to take Jerry Levin, of Pillsbury, and his wife to the ballet that evening. While Margo accompanied the Levins to the ballet, Jeff caught a few hours of deep, dreamless sleep. If truth be told, the dread he felt at the prospect of stepping before the camera had brought on the almost paralytic shyness that he'd felt as a boy. That morning, it had taken all his resolve just to get out of bed. Although he realized that there was no guarantee that he wouldn't end up on the cutting-room floor, Beck was enormously relieved at having at least proved himself capable of standing under those hot lights and delivering his lines. He revived in time to meet his wife and guests for celebratory champagne at The Four Seasons, where he regaled the Levins with the inside poop on his new buddies, Douglas and Stone.

Just before he'd met Beck, Douglas had wrapped up the biggest business deal of his career as an independent producer. Douglas sold Bigstick Productions, through which he'd produced *Cuckoo's Nest* and *The China Syndrome*, to a publicly held movie-production concern named Mercury Entertainment. Mercury was controlled by Michael S. Phillips, a former Wall Street stock analyst turned producer whose first big picture was *The Sting*. When Phillips and Douglas started as movie producers in the early 1970s, only the big, long-established studios like Universal and MGM had the advantage of Wall Street backing. Even the shares of these major studios were considered rather dicey investments, given the inherent unpredictability of the hit-making business. However, investors' aversion to Hollywood diminished markedly amid the general bullishness of the early 1980s, and in 1984 Phillips became one of the first independents to sell shares in his movie-production company to the public. The offer was oversubscribed, and suddenly the producer was a very rich man, with shares valued at more than $6 million. As shares of independent movie companies continued to soar throughout 1985 and in 1986, a host of other producers began cashing in on investors' Hollywood mania with stock offerings.

After watching many of his rivals enrich themselves through Wall Street, Douglas in 1986 finally opted to sell his Bigstick Productions not to the public but to Mercury Entertainment, and not for cash but for 3.5 million shares of Mercury stock, with a value of nearly $4 million at the time of the deal. Bigstick's chief assets were profit participations in *Cuckoo's Nest* and *The China Syndrome*. At the same time, the two producers formed a joint-venture partnership called Mercury/Douglas Films, which was to develop and distribute feature films. Douglas contributed $50,000 plus his profit participations in *Romancing the Stone* and *The Jewel of the Nile* to the new partnership in exchange for warrants for another 2.5 million shares of Mercury stock. Douglas and Phillips pooled their various uncompleted film projects and also contracted to produce exclusively for Mercury/Douglas for at least four years. The essence of these intertwined transactions was this: Phillips surrendered a large ownership stake to give his company a sorely needed infusion of new blood. Despite the stock market's enthusiasm, Phillips hadn't had a hit since 1977 and since forming Mercury had completed only one film, which did no better than break even. And Douglas? By surrendering the future profits generated by his four biggest past hits he was able to repackage his producing career as a publicly traded stock without the legal obligations incumbent on an officer of a public corporation.

The Phillips-Douglas partnership started swimmingly. News of Mercury's transactions with Douglas quickly pushed the value of its stock up by 25 percent, adding millions to each producer's net worth. It was all downhill from there, though. A third party backed out of an agreement to supply Mercury/Douglas with working capital, leaving the partnership desperately short of the funds needed to finance film development. Worse, Douglas apparently found Phillips impossible to work with. Instead of revitalizing Mercury, the effect of Douglas's joining forces with Phillips was to diminish his own productivity to the level of his new partner's. Then, too, Douglas's timing proved awful. He'd bought into Mercury at the top of the market in independent-producer shares. As mounting losses disillusioned star-struck investors, the stock prices of Mercury and other Hollywood start-ups went into a precipitous decline that would end in liquidation for many, including Mercury. Not long after he'd shaken hands with Phillips, Douglas found himself chained to a sinking company in which he'd not only invested much of his net worth but which held exclusive rights to his producing services for four years.

While Douglas by all accounts was genuinely fond of Beck, the fact is that his friendship with the Mad Dog blossomed at precisely that point in his career when the producer stood to benefit most from the assistance of a high-powered Wall Street house like Drexel Burnham, which, by virtue of its Beverly Hills junk-bond stronghold, was a greater force in Hollywood than any other investment bank. Extricating Douglas from his entanglements with Phillips was a project for a lawyer, but one way or another, Douglas would need money to get films made. Beck dedicated himself to helping him find a new source of financing. As a Hollywood producer, Douglas understood as well as Beck did that the way to maximize the profitability of any venture in middlemanship is to maximize one's use of other people's money. Beck got Marc Utay of Drexel to spend considerable time working up a detailed computer modeling of the economics of setting up a new film studio or acquiring an existing one for Douglas to run. Drexel's numbers affirmed the unavoidable truth—that the movie-production business was damn risky. On the other hand, Douglas's record was a good deal better than the industry average.

Armed with Utay's meticulously rendered documentation, Beck approached Ross Johnson of RJR Nabisco. From his past discussions with Johnson, Beck understood his desire to diversify the company by redeploying the cash thrown off by tobacco to create another major division, which would complement the packaged-foods businesses. It was Beck's considered opinion that entertainment would make an ideal third business for RJR. Johnson was so enamored of celebrities, especially professional athletes, that his nickname around Drexel was Starfucker. Johnson had even hired a couple of dozen jocks—collectively known as Team Nabisco—to the tune of millions every year to promote the company at golf tournaments, banquets, and other events. Aside from Johnson's susceptibility to glitter, Beck believed that owning a piece of a film studio made business sense for RJR, one of the largest consumer advertisers in the world, over and above its cut of the profits from film production. What better way to promote a product to the mass market than by tying it into a hit movie? Coca-Cola had the same idea when it acquired Columbia Pictures, though it eventually sold Columbia when the film company's earnings proved erratic beyond the toleration of a corporation with a large Wall Street constituency that demanded consistent performance. Beck told Johnson that RJR could avoid this same problem by investing in a new studio controlled by Douglas. In this way, RJR could get a piece of the Hollywood action without having to consolidate the studio's earnings on its own balance sheet. On the other hand, there were obvious drawbacks for RJR Nabisco in any arrangement under which it would be putting up most of the money yet not have final say over its use.

As Beck had suspected, though, Johnson was intrigued by the idea of diversifying into the film business and agreed to meet Douglas over dinner at The Four Seasons. The CEO and the star hit it off famously. Beck and his hard-drinking guests sat down about eight o'clock and didn't leave the restaurant until well after two A.M. There followed a series of meetings and a delightful dinner at La Côte Basque, to which each of the three men brought his wife. Beck was starting to smell a deal.

While helping Douglas straighten out his business dealings, Beck so embroidered his Vietnam legend that the actor purportedly was inspired to propose making a movie out of it. Assigned the working title *Mad Dog,* the film was to focus on Beck's difficulties at readjusting to civilian life after returning to America in 1970 from Vietnam. Since Beck had never really fought in Vietnam, *Mad Dog* would have been an unwitting fictionalization of a fiction rather than the based-on-a-true-story film that Douglas apparently envisioned. Acting in his capacity as a principal in Mercury/Douglas, Douglas introduced Beck to the screenwriter David Black. A New York lawyer who represented Douglas in business matters aided Beck in negotiating a contract with Black, who by the end of 1987 ostensibly had begun work on a "treatment" of *Mad Dog.*

While working his various Hollywood angles with Douglas, Beck was continually reassuring me of his desire to collaborate on a book. Because Beck conceived of the book in part as an exposé of the immorality of his deal-making brethren, committing to the project meant accepting the likely end to his career on Wall Street. This he was unable to do, even as he constantly and often bitterly proclaimed his disillusionment with Drexel and Wall Street. As he'd done from the beginning, Beck spoke of the book not as a one-shot project but as a bridge into a new career as a writer-commentator on high finance. Like many people who've never written for a living, Beck found romantic the idea of writing—or at least the idea of being able to call himself a writer. This wasn't completely farfetched. He was, after all, one hell of a storyteller.

By the summer of 1987, I'd persuaded Beck to agree to begin looking for a literary agent. Through Douglas, Beck was introduced to Lynn Nesbit of International Creative Management, which was a major force in both New York publishing circles and the Hollywood film colony. With a stable of writers that included Tom Wolfe, John le Carré, and many other top-drawer names, Nesbit was among the highest-powered literary agents in America. She was immediately intrigued with Beck, who presented himself in his full legend-of-the-Mad-Dog glory, complete with Vietnam flourishes and savage attacks on eminent Wall Streeters that were at once telling and comical. He also gave her a little taste of Rosebud, though not by name, insinuating mysteriously that he was worth hundreds of millions of dollars. Beck was no less taken with Nesbit, who, after all, was more prominent in her rainmaking métier than he was in his own and who radiated the sort of taut intensity that, in Beck's opinion, was a trademark of the killer deal maker. And the fact that Nesbit was a woman gave her the added allure of novelty, since Beck had yet to encounter a woman in the top tier of M & A. From the outset of their relationship, Beck engaged Nesbit—deal person to deal person—in shop talk about transaction technique as well as books.

Beck told Nesbit that what he had in mind was not a kiss-and-tell book—though he assured her that he intended to name names—but a sort of Wall Street travelogue, bawdily irreverent and told in the first person. Nesbit thought it over and concluded that the book idea had merit and commercial potential. The three of us decided that the book was best written in the first person; I wrote a sample opening chapter, in which I tried for the first time to write in Beck's voice. The chapter included a two-paragraph account of Beck's Vietnam exploits, which I had yet to realize had been fabricated. During our meetings with publishing-house representatives, Beck played to the hilt the Mad Dog character presented in the sample chapter. Alternately profane, earnest, comical, reflective, humble, and confrontational, he put on quite a show.

At the time, the book-publishing world was just beginning to recognize the commercial potential of Wall Street as a subject for nonfiction works. While it was true that many publishers and editors mixed socially with the most prominent Wall Streeters, as a rule there was more confusion than knowledge in the book world about what was really going on in the trenches of high finance. To bring Beck—M & A macho man—in for an audience with literary executives in 1987 was a bit like displaying a member of some lost tribe of African warriors before a group of medieval scholars. During one of our interviews, Beck concluded an attack on one well-known Wall Streeter of his acquaintance by describing him as "full of shit" over and over again. Shortly thereafter, a senior member of the publishing-house delegation left without explanation, never to return.

While the book and Beck's Hollywood involvements were premised in large part on a desire to escape Wall Street, he was simultaneously pursuing yet another career alternative that would have removed him from Drexel Burnham but kept him in deal making. Option number three was not a new idea but the latest resuscitation of a fantasy that had preoccupied Beck almost from the time he'd come to Wall Street: founding his own investment-banking firm. As avidly as he'd promoted this idea over the years, though, Beck made no serious attempt to realize it until he hooked up with Alfred Checchi. At thirty-eight, Checchi was a few years Beck's junior. After graduating from Harvard Business School, he had begun his business career at the Marriott Corporation, where he distinguished himself as an exceptionally creative member of the finance staff. At age thirty he was named treasurer of the hotel giant. In 1975, Checchi first crossed paths with Richard Rainwater, who in 1982 finally persuaded the Marriott man to come to work with him in Fort Worth. As the unofficial chief financial officer of Bass Brothers Enterprises, Checchi was instrumental in many of the Basses' biggest deals, including their ultimate coup—the lucrative rescue of the Walt Disney Company. After the Bass family gained control of Disney, Checchi was dispatched to Los Angeles for six months to help guide its transformation under a new CEO, Michael Eisner.

Disney was the last hurrah for the Bass-Rainwater-Checchi team. In early 1986, Rainwater decided that after sixteen years of subordinating his ego to the Bass family, it was time to strike out on his own. Checchi, meanwhile, had concluded that after four years of subordinating his equally robust ego to Rainwater, it was time for him and his $50 million net worth to move on, too. While Rainwater remained in his native Fort Worth, Checchi moved his family to Beverly Hills. He had grown up in Washington, the son of a mid-level civil servant, and, with a tidy fortune already tucked away, could afford to indulge his first love: politics. He was a liberal Democrat with an abundance of closely reasoned, articulately expressed opinions and no political experience whatsoever. As he waded into California politics, Checchi was dismayed to find himself in demand not as a thinker or policy maker but as a money man. Eventually, he recognized that this was not simply a problem but a genuine dilemma, as Ron Brownstein later noted in the *Los Angeles Times*: "If a man of his wealth persistently refused to contribute, he'd be seen as a dilettante and a flake, no matter what else he had to offer, but if he became defined primarily as a fund-raiser, he'd find it difficult to ever crawl out of that hole." Checchi evaded this dilemma by gradually refocusing his attention on deal making, with the intention of setting up a merchant-banking firm. And that's where Beck came in.

Although Beck had shaken Checchi's hand a few times in his swings through Fort Worth, the two didn't sit down together for a long conversation until they bumped into each other at the 1986 Drexel bond conference. As Beck told it, they'd been talking for a while when he asked Checchi "what he wanted to be when he grew up."

"I want to be president," replied Checchi.

"Of what?" Beck said.

Checchi looked suprised. "The United States."

Beck told the story in a way that suggested that it was apocryphal. It was just his way of illustrating what he believed was Checchi's most salient trait: an almost endearing self-importance. While there was no question that Checchi took himself very seriously, he was saved from pomposity by earnestness. As abrasive and overbearing as he could be on occasion, he was eager to do the right thing and to be respected for it—as indeed was Beck. Checchi brought out the high-minded side of Beck, who spent many hours with him critiquing the body politic and its faults in the Age of Reagan. While they had political liberalism in common, their business talents were opposed and highly complementary, as both men recognized. Checchi was, in Rainwater's phrase, a "reality guy" of the highest order—a rigorously disciplined thinker and superb negotiator. By the time of the next Drexel bond conference in the spring of 1987, Beck's and Checchi's mutual courtship had advanced to the engaged-to-be-engaged stage.

As described in a business plan drawn up by Checchi, Checchi/ Beck Limited would function as a merchant bank specializing in "corporate strategic analysis, merger and acquisition negotiation, financial restructuring, and real estate finance and acquisition." Under the plan, Checchi and Beck would invest $30 million apiece in a partnership that would also include an institutional investor, which would be expected to make an equity investment of $240 million, and a commercial bank, which would contribute $25 million in equity. In addition, the institution and the bank would each make available as much as $650 million in debt capital, creating total buying power of close to $2 billion—more than enough to make Checchi/Beck a major player in deals.

Before they began approaching investors, Checchi and Beck exchanged notarized documents attesting to their annual incomes and other measures of financial capacity. Although none of the papers that Beck furnished demonstrated an ability to invest $30 million, he assured his prospective partner that he'd have no trouble coming up with a much larger sum if necessary thanks to Rosebud, which he described as a private holding company for the leveraged-buyout investments he'd made over the years. Checchi didn't much care. In his opinion, Beck's critical contribution to the partnership would not be capital but his rainmaking skills. He was intrigued by Beck's choice of Rosebud as a name, though, and they once had a long conversation about Orson Welles's use of *Rosebud* as metaphor in *Citizen Kane,* which Beck claimed to have seen a dozen times.

As a surprise for Beck, Checchi asked Kenneth Rendell, a collectibles dealer he knew, to check into the availability of the *Rosebud* sled featured in *Citizen Kane.* As it turned out, there were at least five *Rosebud* sleds used in the movie, two of which had survived. One was a balsa-wood duplicate that never actually appeared in the movie; it was purchased by Steven Spielberg at auction in 1982 for $60,000. The other was an antique model made of hardwood and was identical to the sled young Kane was seen using at the beginning of the film. This sled was presented to a boy named Arthur Bauer, who won a contest sponsored by RKO Pictures in 1942. Bauer willed the sled to his son, who showed it to Rendell but refused to put a price on it. It was clear, though, that he wouldn't entertain any offer that wasn't substantially more than the $60,000 Spielberg had paid five years previously for an inferior sled. At Checchi's request, Rendell sent a summary of his research on to Beck and attached a note that read: "Al asked me to send this to you—but what I want to know is this: 1. Does the sled simply remind you of your childhood or, 2. Are you really Citizen Kane reincarnated?"

In forging his new connections to Douglas, Nesbit, and Checchi, Beck as usual was compelled to obliterate any of the typical distinctions between the professional and the personal. The ardent and very active friendships he formed with each of them—but especially with Douglas —quickly came to dominate his social life, which revolved less around Nouvelle Society galas and more around informal dinners and Saturday-night-at-the-movies outings. On my weekend visits to Barrett Farm, I ran into Douglas several times. One Saturday, Beck and I beat Douglas and a partner in doubles on the tennis court that came with the cottage the actor was renting in Pound Ridge. That night, the Becks and I had dinner with Douglas and his brother and sister-in-law, who'd just flown in from France, at a burger place on the main drag in Bedford next door to the local movie theater, where later we saw *Hoosiers* amid much popcorn-chomping rambunctiousness from Beck and Douglas. Except for the absence of Diandra, who often rode horses with Margo on weekend afternoons, this was a pretty typical Beck-Douglas night out. Nesbit also spent a good deal of time with the Becks in Bedford in the company of her paramour, Stan Pottinger, a former trial lawyer turned self-employed investment banker. Douglas had invited Nesbit and Pottinger to use his cottage when he and his wife were away, as was frequently the case.

One Saturday night not long after the filming of *Wall Street* had concluded, all three couples gathered at Barrett Farm for a dinner that turned into an epic, vodka-soaked debate on the politics of sex and marriage. Michael Douglas, who'd been indulging his fondness for Stolichnaya with a vengeance, started it off with a manly joust at the feminine sex to which Diandra responded in kind. By this time, the Douglases' ten-year-old marriage had survived numerous separations and reconciliations, and although the ensuing debate remained on a philosophical plane, it seemed to the other four participants that some fresh and very specific resentments were lurking beneath the surface. Jeff rallied to Michael with a broadside that could be summed up in four words—"Women, they're all impossible"—and eventually everyone was heard from repeatedly amid much shouting, laughing, drinking, and general carrying on. A theatrically good time was had by all and no harm was done, at least none that was visible. (It was ironic, though, that within a year, the Becks and Nesbit and Pottinger would have separated while those battling Douglases would be together still.)

While Beck enjoyed playing host, he also attended his share of openings, screenings, and celebrity-filled parties of one sort or another as he began delving into the bicoastal literary-film scene. As a member of the cast of *Wall Street*, he participated in the series of ritualized entertainments by which a movie's progress is measured. The wrap party was held at Tavern on the Green and packed to the rafters. Beck had more fun—too much fun—at the small private party that followed the first New York screening of the film; this party was held in an Upper East Side restaurant just around the corner from the theater. Stone and Douglas attended, as well as the actor's close friends, Danny DeVito and Jann Wenner, the owner of *Rolling Stone* magazine. Yoko Ono was there, too, and Donald Trump appeared briefly to tell Stone the changes he would have made had he directed the film. (No one took notes.) All in all, it was a pretty raucous affair, with a lot of locker-room humor and some serious drinking, both of which Beck joined in enthusiastically. Beck, who rarely drank, got roaring drunk and on the way home stopped his rented limo and got out and puked on Park Avenue while Margo waited inside.

One evening in early December, Beck had returned home from the office to find a telegram from Los Angeles waiting. It read: "Saw your fine performance in *Wall Street* and would like to fly you to Los Angeles for immediate consultations regarding your future as an actor. Understand you have some background in the area but feel confident we could do you some good. Please advise when you can take the meetings."

The telegram was signed Michael S. Ovitz.

Beck didn't know whether to laugh or shout.

Ovitz, the president of Creative Artists Agency, was widely regarded as the most powerful man in Hollywood. He and his sixty-five agents represented the largest and most eminently bankable collection of talent in Hollywood: some 140 directors (including Oliver Stone, Martin Scorsese, and Barry Levinson); 130 actors (including Michael Douglas, Robert Redford, Paul Newman, Dustin Hoffman, Gene Hackman, Kevin Costner, Bill Murray, Barbra Streisand, Cher, Sean Connery, and Robin Williams); and 280 writers. The agency's rock-music clients included three superstars: Michael Jackson, Madonna, and Prince. Although Mike Ovitz didn't dominate Hollywood to the same extent that his friend Mike Milken ruled the junk-bond market from Beverly Hills, he exercised more personal influence over the film business than had any individual since the old Hollywood studio system broke down in the late 1950s. "In today's Hollywood, if you want your career to thrive, you do not cross Michael Ovitz," concluded one reporter. "It is possible to do business in Hollywood without running into Michael Ovitz. But it is difficult."

Beginning in the late 1970s, Ovitz had altered the economics of moviemaking by applying to film the talent-packaging principles he'd learned in the television business. In a Hollywood where many studios began to behave as if they were merchant banks, financing pictures made by independents but themselves having no direct involvement in the projects, Ovitz used the leverage inherent in his glittering client list to fill the role that traditionally had been filled by the studio. CAA took over the casting, choosing the director, and getting the script written. With so many of Hollywood's biggest talents under contract, CAA was in a position to extract higher salaries for its clients and bigger fees for itself. While Milken was pushing Wall Street compensation to unheard-of levels, Ovitz was doing the same thing in Hollywood. Incredibly, the two Mikes had been classmates at Encino's Birmingham High School, which as a training ground of monopolistic middlemen no doubt is without equal in the history of secondary education. Like Milken, Ovitz was a ferociously driven controlmeister who was secretive to the point of paranoia.

Despite rumors to the contrary, Ovitz did have a sense of humor. For a goof, he liked to sign people outside show business to official CAA contracts. He had, for example, once signed up Checchi, who'd met the super-agent through Eisner, the Walt Disney chief, and who introduced him to Beck. After researching Ovitz thoroughly, Beck called him with a few ideas for his business that seemed to have intrigued the agent. After getting the telegram, Beck called Checchi, who assured him that the message was Ovitz's humorous way of offering his congratulations. Beck gladly played along. The next time he was in Los Angeles he and Checchi had lunch with Ovitz at Morton's, one of the Hollywood set's preferred power-dining spots. Ovitz brought along a contract, which Beck duly signed and mailed to CAA from New York with a letter, a copy of which he sent to Checchi:

I am enclosing the agency contract and look forward to you representing me. I am very confident that the viewing public is ready for a chunky, balding, middle-aged Jew. I want you to know that I am working on a screenplay entitled, "Jew Gone Bad" in which I expect to play the lead.

I was most impressed by Al joining us for dinner and acting as my chaperone. He certainly kept us from coming to blows and for that I am thankful, since my career on the stage cannot afford any more band-aids. Just think, Al gave us 2¹/₂ hours of his most valuable time without looking in the mirror once. By the way, Al told me that you had it all wrong with regard to table positioning at Morton's. What he said is that everyone was looking to find out who you and I were since he was the one that was the real power in Hollywood.

You had to hand it to the Mad Dog. Fifteen months after he'd said hello to Michael Douglas for the first time, he'd become a close friend of the hottest actor and of the leading literary agent in the land, auditioned for and won a speaking role in a major feature film, cut a screenwriting deal for a movie based on his own life, and was on joshing terms with the supreme being of the Hollywood deal. He'd come a long way in a very short time. In the process, though, Beck had suspended himself over a viper's nest by the narrowest of threads. In one sense, Beck was more comfortably himself in his new circles than in Nouvelle Society, which was thickly populated with other Wall Streeters. Douglas and Nesbit and much of the rest of the film-lit crowd tended to defer to him on matters of high finance in a way that, say, Henry Kravis never would. More secure in his authority as M & A star, Beck was less compelled to big-deal it. On the other hand, as he began rubbing shoulders with professional tale-spinners and dream merchants, Beck found his Wall Street identity alone inadequate and trafficked more heavily in his self-created Vietnam legend than he ever had before, frequently recounting his exploits at receptions and dinner parties on both coasts. He was the Mad Dog, soon to be featured in a major motion picture. And if Douglas decided not to play the part, who knows? Maybe he'd play himself.

In the fall of 1987, Pottinger and Nesbit had dinner at Barrett Farm and brought along a present for Beck, who was obviously touched by the thoughtfulness of his new friends. It was an elegant silver cigarette box into which these words had been engraved: "Jeffrey P. Beck. In appreciation for Blood, Fear and Courage in the Vietnam War. There but for him, go I." A few months later, Pottinger and Nesbit threw a small dinner party at which Beck was a prime topic of discussion. The last person to leave was Jean Pigazzi, a European heir who owned a villa close to the Hôtel du Cap and was friendly with both Beck and Douglas.

"That Beck is just too much, isn't he?" Pigazzi said to Pottinger on his way out the door.

Pottinger laughed in agreement.

"I just never know what to believe from the guy," Pigazzi continued. "Take Vietnam," he added, with a smile. "I'll bet he was never there."

Pottinger, thinking of the silver box, was taken aback. "Sure, Jeff exaggerates, but I can't believe he just made it all up."

The smile vanished from Pigazzi's face. "Well, I really don't believe that he was there," he said.

Holy shit, Pottinger thought, what if he's right?

22

While Beck was often bold and even reckless in his speech, his actions as a rule were cautious and methodical to a fault. As much as he talked of his grand possibilities in film, he never for a moment considered leaving Wall Street to devote himself to the pursuit of a Hollywood career. Not only was corporate deal making his livelihood but it was the only thing at which he was certain that he excelled. Crazed and brutal though it may have been, deal making was his professional security blanket, and not even after again reaching the point of physical and emotional incapacitation would he voluntarily release his grip on it. Beck never could bring himself to quit Drexel Burnham to start a deal-making firm of his own, though he talked endlessly about leaving. For all his maverick style, deep down he needed to feel that he belonged somewhere, and thus he preferred the mounting annoyances and miseries of working for Drexel to the lonely uncertainties of self-employment.

And so it was that throughout his Hollywood infatuation, Beck continued to juggle an abundance of deal-making schemes, though he could no longer be bothered to actually go down to Drexel's offices at 55 Broad more than once a week on average. It was just so boring there. While the infrequency of his attendance stirred some behind-the-back grumbling among the least entrepreneurial of his colleagues, no one in a position of authority commanded Beck to sit behind his desk more frequently. Beck would not have heeded such an order anyway. As a rainmaker, he knew that it was his prerogative to improvise freely. All that he really needed to turn his ideas into deals was a telephone, and telephones were everywhere. Intensive first-hand research had convinced him that the telephone in his favorite suite at the Bel-Air Hotel was every bit as good as the one in his office at 55

Broad Street—better, in fact, because a two-digit dial summoned room service.

On October 19, 1987, however, Beck not only deigned to put in an appearance at Drexel but made a point of getting to the office early, well before the nine-thirty A.M. trading start. The Dow Jones industrial average had fallen 108 points the previous Friday on frantic trading, and news reports over the weekend suggested that a wave of sell orders would arrive that morning from Japan. Did it ever. The rout began with the opening bell, and like most of Wall Street's denizens Beck spent the day turning from telephone to Quotron machine as stock prices nosedived into free fall with the spread of flat-out panic throughout the entire investing world. For more than two years, Beck had been contending that a market collapse was an inevitable consequence of the overleveraging of the corporate economy—a prophecy that didn't sit well with most of his colleagues at Drexel, the debt hub of the takeover game. Even in his most pessimistic moods, though, Beck had never imagined as chaotically horrific a day as this Monday in October.

When trading halted at last, the Dow had plunged 508 points, to close at 1738.74. Adding the 235-point drop in the preceding few days, the Dow had dropped 30 percent in less than a week. Almost by acclamation, October nineteenth was immediately nicknamed Black Monday, in grim remembrance of the worst day of the great Crash of 1929, Black Tuesday, during which the Dow had lost a comparatively modest 12.8 percent of its value. In the wake of Black Monday, the news columns and airwaves were filled with gloom as pundits and prognosticators began handicapping the odds that this latest crash, like its famous predecessor, foreshadowed not merely a recession but a depression as severe as that of the 1930s.

As it turned out, the U.S. economy proved surprisingly resilient after the jolt of Black Monday. Not even the threat of recession materialized as the economy continued growing, albeit at a modest clip, into the 1990s. For the investment-banking business, though, October nineteenth did indeed mark the beginning of the end of the era that had begun in the early 1970s, just as the careers of Beck, Milken, Kravis, and their baby-boom compatriots were getting under way. After the recession of 1973–1974, there commenced an unparalleled period of expansion as a vanguard of a few dozen Wall Street houses threw off the stodgy legacy of three decades of stagnation and began adding employees by the thousands in the belief that the financial contract didn't exist that couldn't be converted into a stock, a bond, or, more likely, an exotic new security that could be issued and traded in ever-rising volume. The curbing of inflation in the 1980s pushed the value of almost every new line of securities merchandise spectacularly upward, stimulating ever-increasing investor demand as the rich got richer and the popularity of securities speculation rivaled that of Ronald Reagan. It was morning again in America, and as the men who ran the big investment banks planned for the future, they extrapolated the flukishly steep trend lines of the preceding decade into a more and more glorious future of endless growth and rising profits and bonuses.

However, by 1987 it was hard to keep the faith without a set of jumbo-sized blinders. The national debt was on its way to doubling since Reagan took office, far outstripping the modest gains in national economic productivity. Consequently, the U.S. economic system was riddled with severe structural stresses of a sort most evident in the massive "twin deficits"—federal budget and international trade—and the appalling condition of the savings and loan industry. If America, in Reagan's vision, was a "shining city on a hill," then it had been erected atop the economic equivalent of the San Andreas fault. The stock-market crash of 1987 was a major temblor that went unheeded in Washington. With a presidential election approaching, the administration proclaimed continued faith in its have-a-nice-day simplification of free-market ideals: Whatever happens must be good. On Wall Street, though, the spell was broken. The stock-market crash and its whipsaw aftereffects chased millions of investors to the sidelines and wiped out dozens of small brokerages. All the major houses took gargantuan losses, chastening their leaders into taking to heart the most basic Wall Street maxim: What goes up must come down, usually even faster than it went up. Grievously overextended, Wall Street investment banks cut their MBA recruiting in half, slashed expense accounts and bonuses, and started passing out pink slips. The securities industry promptly shed 24,000 jobs, 10 percent of its total, and would continue shrinking into the 1990s as its through-the-looking-glass economics were wrenched back into line with reality.

Wall Street's humbling was slowed by the unexpected revival of the takeover game, which, like a drunk at a wedding reception, roused itself for one last wild careening ramble around the dance floor before passing out facedown in the frosting. In the first weeks after Black Monday, countless deals fell apart as the economy's uncertain fate caused corporations and lenders to pull back. However, many of the underlying forces that had driven the decade-long deal boom retained their propulsive power. Antitrust enforcement was still a joke and more money than ever had been locked into position for deal investment. If KKR and the legions of other deal promoters didn't use the billions they'd raised from institutional investors, they'd have to give the money back. Meanwhile, the declining fortunes of the securities industry had put a new edge of desperation on the fee-greed of the M & A men. While mounting competition and shrinking markets had squeezed the profit out of almost all of Wall Street's other specialties, the M & A business remained miraculously exempt from the laws of supply and demand. The very survival of some large houses now depended on generating outsized M & A fees.

By the end of the year, it had become apparent that the October stock-market collapse had not heralded a collapse of the economy. Corporate cash flow continued strong and the stock market was on the rise again, though share prices on average remained 25 percent below their highs. In the view of the optimistic majority of the M & A fraternity, the overriding significance of the crash was that it enhanced the economics of the takeover business by sharply reducing the market value of the most tempting targets. Among the first players to jump back in the game was Don Kelly, assisted for the last time by Beck.

Although Kelly had yet to make the big acquisition promised in promoting E-II's stock and bond offering, he and his longtime sidekick, Roger Briggs, had reprised the risk-arbitrage tactics they'd used so lucratively at Esmark, sinking much of their $1 billion war chest into accumulating sizable positions in ten to fifteen putatively undervalued companies, mostly in the food industry. Then along came Black Monday, which saddled E-II with $147 million in losses on its arbitrage portfolio. From a high of 17½, E-II's stock fell to 8 and stayed there. This was cause for lament not only for Kelly and his executives, who collectively owned 6 percent of the company, but for KKR and Drexel, which between them owned 44 percent of E-II. With the crash having made manifest Beatrice's unsalability, estimates of the final take from history's biggest LBO were dwindling from grand to substandard. Faced at age sixty-five with an inglorious end to his deal-making career, Kelly initiated a takeover battle of a dubious sort, in effect recasting himself in the disreputable mold of Drexel-backed raider.

Among the crash-ravaged stocks in E-II's portfolio was American Brands, a large consumer-products conglomerate whose brands included Pall Mall and Lucky Strike cigarettes and Jim Beam bourbon. Long a rumored takeover target, American Brands lent itself to a Beatrice-style bust-up. The company also had a newly elected CEO, William Alley, who'd publicly dedicated himself to preserving its independence. Because E-II owned less than 5 percent of American Brands, it was not required to publicly disclose its holding. But Wall Street found out anyway, sending E-II's shares soaring to $12 on speculation that Kelly was about to bid for American Brands. Kelly let Alley sweat it out for a few weeks before suggesting that he might wage a proxy fight for control or make an offer to buy American Brands outright, though it likely would cost E-II at least $8 billion to buy the company, which was a good five times its size. Although Kelly was already being advised by Steve Waters, now M & A chief at Shearson Lehman, he also hired Merrill Lynch and Drexel Burnham to lend credibility to his takeover threat, which would require $3 billion in high-leverage financing. Drexel issued one of its famous "highly confident" letters and assigned Beck to the deal.

Was Kelly bluffing? E-II insiders would insist in retrospect that they were serious about acquiring American Brands, and indeed $8.5 billion in financing had been lined up. While claiming credit on one hand for planting the idea of bidding for a tobacco company in Kelly's mind, Beck dismissed his avowed designs on American Brands as "nothing but atmospherics" on the other. In any event, Alley wasn't inclined to wait around and see. American Brands began a tender offer for E-II at $13 a share, which was $2 below the company's initial offering price and thus unacceptable to Kelly, who boosted his position in American Brands to 6.4 percent. A "Pac-Man" battle loomed. With Kelly's permission, Beck began canvassing Drexel's raider clientele to solicit a higher bid for E-II. Peter Ackerman, Milken's top assistant, told Beck that Ron Perelman of Revlon was interested, only to call back a few minutes later and say that Perelman might have changed his mind. Rumors that Perelman was interested were bouncing around the Street, and Beck didn't want to disavow them. So he avoided taking Perelman's calls. Meanwhile, Nelson Peltz of Triangle Industries actually met with Kelly and made an "unofficial" offer of $17 a share for E-II. After a great deal of negotiation, Alley offered to match Triangle's tentative bid. By his own account, Kelly still was not quite satisfied. "I told our investment banker [Waters] to go back to the other side and try to get another half dollar or quarter," he said.

American Brands was represented by Joseph Fogg, a Morgan Stanley banker whom Kelly disliked and later described simply as "this smart-ass guy on the other side." According to Kelly, "Fogg said, 'We will insult you and give you a nickel.' So our investment banker came back and said he wouldn't give us anything but a nickel. I said, 'Oops. Do you know how many shares are outstanding? Take that nickel. Go in and shake hands with that man because he just gave us another nickel.' "

This story, which Kelly included in an autobiographical *Fortune* magazine account entitled "My Life as a Dealmaker," apparently was his attempt to extract some small piece of his old heroic role as shareholder's champion from what was a pretty pathetic deal. At $17.05 a share, E-II returned a 14 percent gain to its original shareholders, which was better than the huge loss extant before the American Brands bid, certainly, but hardly the second coming of Esmark. Worse, Kelly, once hailed as the grand master of restructuring, now was seen even by some former admirers as just another of Drexel's opportunistic intimidators—a label that Kelly took great pains to disavow. "The value American Brands put on the company was inflated by the position we had in their stock and, I guess, on that basis they preferred to remain independent," Kelly said. "I don't believe it was greenmail. I've never been involved in greenmail"—a statement that not only Alley but Jim Dutt of Beatrice might have disputed, for in truth Kelly's gradual employment of increasingly hostile tactics was an integral part of his evolution from manager to deal man.

In the wake of E-II's sale, Kelly resigned as chairman of Beatrice, though as one of its largest shareholders he retained a tie to KKR. Kelly set up his own little deal-making firm in Chicago, D. P. Kelly & Associates, which struck up an alliance with Salomon Brothers to do midsized leveraged buyouts. There would be no more talk of doing $9 billion or $15 billion deals from Don Kelly, who returned to the low profile of his earlier years a good $100 million richer. Kelly and Beck made no attempt to stay in touch with one another, each seemingly viewing their relationship as a relic of a bygone age. Beck's retrospective opinion of Kelly tended to veer wildly from admiration to resentment depending on whether he was in a mood to claim greater credit for their mutual deals than he'd been given or of a mind to disavow all responsibility for them, especially the Beatrice LBO. As for Kelly, when I interviewed him early in 1990, the strongest endorsement of Beck he offered was this, "If he were to call me right now, I'd take the call."

A vastly expanded net worth was not the only change in Kelly that some of his old Chicago friends noticed. Don Goss, a consultant who'd begun working with Kelly in 1956 and served as his financial adviser on the Beatrice LBO, said, "The most disappointing change in Don was that he seemed to lose his personal feelings of warmth for people, even though warmth and loyalty had been among his most prominent characteristics. He and I aren't the close friends that we were for twenty-five years."

While Kelly had shown flashes of a mean streak in his early career, his treatment of Briggs at the end seemed almost willfully cruel. He and Briggs had never been friends, in part because of hugely dissimilar personalities; Briggs was an introvert who dreaded public speech making and came to resent the ease with which Kelly the showman overshadowed him and amassed credit for their joint deal adventures. But they had worked quite closely together ever since the early 1970s and Kelly, though he didn't see Briggs as a worthy successor to himself, was publicly appreciative of Briggs's financial skills. "Roger Briggs, who was my CFO for many years . . . was one of those very, very bright guys who made it possible to be successful," Kelly observed in "My Life as a Dealmaker." However, Briggs, who desperately wanted to succeed Kelly as CEO, never got the chance at Esmark and was thoroughly eclipsed by Fred Rentschler at Beatrice. Briggs was one of the few top executives for whom Kelly refused to authorize a golden parachute after Beatrice finally was sold. Briggs was crushed, according to his closest associates. "He came to me and said that he didn't need the money but had never felt so insulted in his life," said one ally. There would be no reconciliation. In 1989, Briggs died of cancer.

As E-II's tiff with American Brands was ending, one of the most disastrously misguided deals of the entire era was beginning. The battle for control of Federated Department Stores, owner of Bloomingdale's and the largest department-store chain in American, pitted Federated's archrival R. H. Macy & Company against Robert Campeau, a Canadian real-estate developer who was a very odd duck indeed. For a time Campeau had led a double life, splitting time between his wife and three children and a back-street mistress, whom he later married. Along the way, Campeau suffered two mental breakdowns, the most recent in 1985. Not long afterward, Campeau decided that he wanted to buy Allied Stores, the sixth-largest U.S. department-store chain. Best known for Brooks Brothers and Ann

Taylor, Allied was thirty times larger than Campeau Corporation as measured by profits and ten times its size in market value. In his eagerness to reassert its M & A primacy in the face of Drexel's spectacular intrusions, Bruce Wasserstein convinced his bosses at First Boston to provide a loan to Campeau to cover the entire cost of purchasing control of Allied Stores—about $1.8 billion (though the firm eventually was able to reduce its so-called bridge loan to $865 million as other lenders joined in). A year after capturing Allied, Campeau decided to bid for Federated, which was three times Allied's size.

With Wasserstein again at his side, Campeau offered $47 a share, or $4.2 billion, for Federated, galvanizing Wall Street's M & A legions into a frenzied search for white knights. Beck rushed over to R. H. Macy & Company to meet with Al Taubman, who was a large shareholder and director of the company that was Bloomingdale's archrival. If Edward Finkelstein, Macy's CEO, was able to lift Federated's profit margins to his company's superior level, a merger might work, though the margin for error would be slim. R. H. Macy was heavily indebted, having gone private in 1986 through a $4.4 million leveraged buyout. With the backing of his board, Finkelstein decided to chance the buy, though, and hired Drexel as his banker. While Beck's ties to Taubman aided Drexel in landing R. H. Macy, the firm also gained entree through lawyer Ira Milstein of Weil, Gotshal & Manges, which represented both Macy's and Drexel. Joseph assigned Black and Dean Kehler to the deal in addition to Beck.

On the very day that Federated had tentatively accepted $68 a share from Campeau, in charged R. H. Macy with a last-minute bid of $73.80 a share for 80 percent of the company. Federated immediately pulled out of its preliminary agreement with Campeau and accepted Macy's offer instead. Urged on by its Wall Street advisers, Campeau Corporation refused to accept defeat and revived the hostile tender through which it had initially forced itself on Federated. By this time, Wasserstein and Joe Perella had resigned from First Boston as push had come to shove in a power struggle with the firm's CEO. Taking a large contingent of First Boston people with them, they set up their own firm, Wasserstein, Perella & Company. While Campeau retained First Boston as his lead bank, he also hired Wasserstein, Perella as his "tactical adviser." As a result of their divorce, both First Boston and its erstwhile M & A cochiefs had a dash of extra incentive to see Campeau prevail.

Back came R. H. Macy with an offer of $77.35 a share for 80 percent and stock for the rest. The arbs reacted coolly to the idea of a partial cash bid, giving Campeau all the opening he needed to up his cash offer for 90 percent of Federated's shares to $73 apiece. Macy's revised its offer in a way that boosted the cash portion of its bid while fixing its total value at $73.88 a share. Campeau topped this by 12 cents, going to $74. The Federated board was set to declare the Canadian the winner when Finkelstein put in a conference call to the directors, invoking the merger agreement Macy's had signed only a few weeks before. "Ladies and gentlemen," pleaded Finkelstein, apparently forgetting that Macy had initially barged its way into the deal after Federated had reached an agreement with Campeau, "is there no decency left in corporate America?" Apparently, he was serious. Macy was allowed to bump its offer to $75.14, which could only be considered decent from the standpoint of Federated's shareholders. Still refusing to accept defeat, Campeau immediately began considering an even higher bid. Would it never end?

By this time, Beck was sorry he'd ever gotten involved in the battle, which had deteriorated into a Wall Street version of the theatre of the absurd, featuring long stretches of inactivity punctuated by ferocious screaming matches and late-night gluttony. For Beck, the deal reached its peak of unreality during the few days that he and the other advisers to Finkelstein spent trying to line up buyers for the Federated divisions that R. H. Macy intended to sell if it prevailed over Campeau, an exercise intended to assure Macy's lenders that the massive debt required to finance the acquisition would be quickly paid down after the deal was completed. Prospective buyers from all over the world were invited to Weil, Gotshal, where they were sequestered in separate conference rooms. Beck and the other bankers rushed from one room to another, negotiating the sale of businesses they knew only as sets of numbers with people they'd never met before on behalf of a client that didn't own these businesses in the first place. To Beck, the whole thing felt like a con. "It used to be that I wanted the deal to end my way," Beck told me later. "After Macy's, I just wanted them to end."

After eight weeks of round-the-clock legal and financial gamesmanship, it was finally left to Joe Flom, who was advising Federated, to belatedly proclaim the need for compromise. "There gets to be a point," he said, "when an auction must close in the interest of everyone." On April Fools' Day, Campeau and Finkelstein met face-to-face for the first time in the Macy chief's Upper East Side apartment.

When they emerged, Macy's had dropped its bid in return for the right to buy two Federated divisions for $1.1 billion. For $6.5 billion, almost all of it borrowed, Campeau finally got his prize. As usual, the Deal Club reaped its reward up front. More than $200 million in fees was spread among the seven investment banks and half-dozen law firms that represented Federated and its two suitors, Campeau and Macy's. First Boston got $49 million while Drexel split $25 million with Kidder, Peabody, Macy's other investment-banking adviser. "We're obviously pleased," crowed Wasserstein, whose new firm was paid $10 million. "It was like playing three-dimensional chess." By the end of 1989, however, Wasserstein and everyone else connected with this deal would be backpedaling away from it as fast as possible. In January 1990, Federated collapsed into Chapter 11 bankruptcy along with Allied Stores in what amounted to the biggest mercantile catastrophe in U.S. history.

On the day after the evening meeting between Finkelstein and Campeau that resolved their struggle for control of Federated, I caught a train north out of Grand Central Station. Beck had invited me to spend Easter with him and his wife at Barrett Farm. I was counting on a working weekend. It was only about ten days earlier that Beck had finally committed himself to cooperating as the subject rather than coauthor of *Rainmaker,* and I was eager to begin our interviews.

The Metro North train pulled into the Bedford Hills station right on time. Beck was waiting for me in the parking lot in his Mercedes with the engine running. I hadn't seen Beck for a few months and the change in his appearance was striking. Incongruously attired in a natty dark-brown felt fedora and an official New York Yankees warmup jacket, Beck looked awful. His face was as pale and lumpy as putty, except for what looked to be bruises below his eyes, which were little more than red-rimmed slits. I'd never seen him heavier. Weil, Gotshal was renowned among deal men for the quality and quantity of the food with which it kept its conference rooms stocked during big transactions—"haute deal cuisine," Beck called it, in confessing that he'd put on twenty-four pounds over the course of the Macy's deal. Beck had spent the previous night at the Pierre Hotel, just down Fifth Avenue from Weil, Gotshal, where he'd hung out until about two A.M., drinking champagne and trading war stories with his fellow deal men as their junior associates finished translating the Campeau-Macy's agreement into documentary form. While Finkelstein went home and slept twenty hours straight, Beck was still too keyed up to catch more than a few hours of shut-eye. He'd been up at six A.M., watching the sun rise.

Beck didn't say much as he drove the six miles from the Bedford station through the rolling, wooded countryside to Barrett Farm. He parked the car next to another Mercedes sedan in his two-car garage and we walked into the kitchen. It was too quiet.

"Where's Margo?" I asked.

"Went to Boston to see her sister," he replied. "Katherine, too."

I was surprised. "On Easter weekend?"

Anger flared in Beck's eyes. He looked away. "Yeah, well, she left a week ago. She pulled me out of a meeting at Skadden to tell me and then she just strapped Katherine to her back and left. Can you believe that shit? Right in the middle of the Macy's deal."

"When is she coming back?" I asked.

"I don't know. I don't know if I want her to come back."

In time, I would realize that Jeff's and Margo's personal conflicts were inseparably tangled with basic issues of principle and class. Beck's plunge into the art-and-lit social scene through Douglas and Nesbit had deepened his disillusionment with Nouvelle Society, which was ascending ever higher peaks of ostentation even as the poverty of New York's underclass became increasingly apparent with the spread of homelessness. Beck had found that the more time he spent in a tuxedo, the more the Dickensian contrasts of New York disturbed and oppressed him. He felt guilty, and he increasingly feared for his family's safety after his Mercedes was stolen at gunpoint. The Becks' governess had just parked the car on Seventy-ninth Street right across from the entrance to their apartment house when someone jumped in the backseat, pressed a gun to her head, and ordered her out. By the time the police arrived, the thief and the car were long gone. While the car was recovered, for Beck its theft was the last straw. Over Margo's protests, he sold their apartment at a large profit and established full-time residence at Barrett Farm in late 1987, with the hope of leading not only a safer but a simpler life. "I look back on the money that was spent and I feel nauseous," Beck said. "We were chewing through ten-thousand-dollar bills like Ritz crackers."

While Margo shared her husband's concern for their daughter's safety, she felt no compulsion to frugality. It was not in her nature and, furthermore, she'd been led to believe that Rosebud had added a billion or two to its net worth over the last few years alone. Jeff's and Margo's continuing conflict over money and its pursuit had crystallized into impasse around the issue of how Katherine, who was three at the time of the move to the country, should be raised. Jeff was adamant in wanting his daughter to grow up as a regular kid, educated in public schools, with friends from all walks of life. Margo, on the other hand, insisted on an upper-class upbringing and a private-school education, beginning with kindergarten at one of those tony Upper East Side girls' schools where the admission standards were primarily a function of the parents' social standing and net worth. In marital terms, the Katherine debate was best classified under the general heading of "irreconcilable differences." By the time she was ready to start school, her parents would again be living in Manhattan, but this time in separate apartments.

At the time of my Easter-weekend visit, Beck still seemed hopeful of working things out with his wife. However, it was immediately evident that he was in no condition to help me reconstruct his early years on Wall Street. His reminiscences, no matter my opening question, segued into bittersweet philosophical ruminations about women in general and Margo in particular. Occasionally, Beck dropped off to sleep in mid-sentence for a few minutes.

After a few hours of this we decided to take in an early movie. Bedford had only one theater and it was showing *Bright Lights, Big City*. About forty-five minutes into it Beck turned to me. "Let's get out of here," he said. "I can't take this."

I laughed. It wasn't much of a movie, but it wasn't torture, either. I assumed he was kidding but the queasy look on his face quickly convinced me otherwise. He looked as if he were about to throw up. I edged away from him in my seat. "What's wrong?" I said.

He didn't answer and turned his attention back to the screen. We stayed, but each time the Michael J. Fox character flashed back to the hospital where his mother lay in agony, dying of cancer, Beck shielded his eyes and squirmed in his seat. As soon as it ended, we headed for the exit. "God," he groaned. "Wasn't that terrible?"

First thing next morning, we drove to a little grocery store to buy *The New York Times*. Beck paid for the paper and then stood right at the cash register and read half of the long front-page article on the denouement of the Federated deal. He roused himself from his reverie and returned to the car. But after turning on the engine, he let it idle as he read the rest of the *Times*'s coverage. I bought my own copy of the *Times* and, resisting the temptation to check out the baseball spring-training scores, scanned the Federated postmortem. Most take-overs are covered as if they were sporting contests: There is a winner—by definition, the guy who got the company—and a loser—the guy who didn't. But in the deal game, unlike baseball, it's possible to prevail in today's contest and still end up a loser. Overpaying for an acquisition can cripple a company and force it into bankruptcy (Campeau's eventual fate) or make it vulnerable to takeover, as had been the case with Beatrice. The *Times* played the Federated deal as a victory for Campeau, though the question of whether he had overpaid ran through the coverage like an ominous minor theme in a symphony. In fact, the supposed loser, Finkelstein of Macy, seemed downright jubilant. "I feel terrific," Finkelstein was quoted as saying. "We got a great deal."

"Shit," said Beck, looking up from his paper with a queasy grin. "I guess we didn't do so good, did we?"

"I don't know," I replied. "Did you see what Finkelstein said? He's your client and he's happy. Isn't that what counts?"

Beck seemed to mull this over on the ride back to his house. Back at Barrett Farm, he studied the paper again and his mood brightened visibly. "You know," he said. "Finkelstein really is a good guy."

We spent all Saturday afternoon poring through a dozen file boxes filled with letters, memos, and deal documents from Beck's early years at Donaldson, Lufkin & Jenrette and Lehman Brothers. It looked as if Beck had kept everything. There was even a copy of a letter to a New Jersey neighborhood newspaper offering a reward for the return of his two missing Scottie dogs, believed stolen. Beck was alternately excited and faintly embarrassed by what we unearthed. Twice we were inter-rupted by phone calls. The first was from a local real-estate broker. To my surprise, Beck told him to list Barrett Farm for sale. The other was long distance, from his mother. Beck immediately told her that he didn't want to talk to her. When she persisted, he got angry. He warned her that he was going to hang up on her. And he did.

Down in Miami, William D. Singer lay dying in the Jewish Home and Hospital for the Aged. The erstwhile hamburger king was eighty-seven years old now and suffering from a variety of ailments, though it would be heart disease that finally killed him. Beck hadn't spoken a civil word to Singer in years, but it was only natural that the impend-ing death of the man who'd been his stepfather for a quarter century should release a surge of conflicting emotions—not the least of which was a heightened sense of his own mortality. (As Singer's condition took a turn for the worse in a few months, Beck would be paralyzed with indecision about whether to return to Miami and try to make some sort of peace with his stepfather. But he just couldn't do it, and Singer's death on July 13, 1988, relieved Beck of this decision while substituting another: Should he attend the funeral? In agonizing over it, Beck sought my advice a dozen times in the space of a few days. I urged him to go and he finally did, flying down with his sister, Judy.)

That evening we drove the dozen miles to Greenwich, Connecticut, to have dinner at the home of Jack MacAtee, who by this time was handling Beck's personal legal affairs. On the trip over, Beck turned the tape deck up to speaker-rattling volume and sang along as he played a classic Shirelles song from the early 1960s. When "Tonight's the Night" ended, he flipped the homemade tape over, backed it up a bit, and played the Chiffons' "One Fine Day": "One fine day we'll meet once more / And you'll want the love you threw away before / One fine day you're / gonna want me for your . . ." The Chiffons finished the line with the word "girl" but Beck substituted "guy" and shouted it at the top of his voice. When "One Fine Day" ended Beck flipped the tape over again and played "Tonight's the Night" again. We must have heard each tune ten times.

As we neared Greenwich, Beck cut the volume and started talking about Vietnam. He told me a new tale, one he hadn't recounted at the Hôtel du Cap. He said that in the middle of the 1968 Tet offensive, his platoon was sent in search of a missing U.S. Army platoon in the Central Highlands. They found them all right, drawn and quartered and hanging from trees in a series of villages the North Vietnamese had passed through and leveled. In one village Beck came across a baby girl, no more than seven or eight months old. She was pinned between two corpses but appeared to be uninjured. Beck said he would never forget the look of relief in the baby's eyes when he picked her up. He strapped the child to his back and somehow managed to get her back to camp unscathed, where the whole company marveled at her survival. The baby was sent to an orphanage in Saigon. About six months later Beck was told that she had died, even though there were no apparent medical problems. One day her heart just stopped. No one could explain it.

The next morning, Easter morning, I was sitting at the kitchen table poring through Beck's files when he made his first appearance of the day. He looked even worse than on the Friday I arrived. He hadn't shaved in a couple of days and the gray in his beard nearly matched the pallor of his skin. He took a handful of pills at the kitchen sink and began pacing in front of me, sighing heavily.

Taking the hint, I said: "How do you feel, Jeff?"

"I'm getting weaker all the time, man," he said.

"You should get more exercise."

"No, it's not that." He stared out the window. "My fucking bones ache all the time now," he said.

"What do you mean? Is it serious?"

"Do you really want to know?"

"Well . . . yeah."

"Can you keep a secret?"

"Okay."

"Let's take a walk."

We went out the back door and strolled across the backyard toward the swimming pool, which had yet to be filled for the season. Swimming was out of the question on this dismal day. A light rain had been falling for hours and my shoes were soaked through after a few minutes. Beck put his hands in the front pockets of his blue jeans and trudged along with his head down as he struggled to find the words. By fits and starts, he backed into a disclosure that stopped me in my tracks.

About three weeks ago, his doctors had diagnosed him as having acute leukemia. They'd given him six months to live. The disease was so advanced, said Beck in a flat, emotionless voice, that chemotherapy was not likely to do any good. He'd tried one session of chemotherapy and had yet to decide whether to continue. For a moment, I thought —I hoped—that Beck was kidding, that he was setting me up for some kind of belated April Fools' Day prank. But as he talked his voice choked and his eyes filled with tears. He turned away from me and walked about twenty yards away and tried to pull himself together. I stood rooted to the spot, not knowing what to say.

Beck returned after a few minutes and said that he hadn't told anybody but me about his condition. Neither of us spoke for what seemed five minutes. I urged him to tell Margo and his sister immediately. He shook his head emphatically. "I don't want them to know."

"Won't it be even harder on them if they find out at the last minute?" I said. "How would you feel in their place?"

"I don't want anyone acting different just because they feel sorry for me," he said. "This is my problem."

We walked over to a tree with a tire hung by a rope from a high branch. Beck started swinging but didn't gain much altitude. He said that he felt exhausted all the time and that most nights his bones throbbed with such pain that he couldn't sleep. He said his doctors at New York University Medical Center had had a lot of difficulty diagnosing him and still weren't completely sure that it was leukemia. "These guys have never seen anything like it," said Beck, whose own theory was that whatever it was, his mysterious ailment was caused by exposure to Agent Orange, a chemical defoliant that had been used extensively in Vietnam.

"Why don't you go to the Mayo Clinic, get another opinion?" I said. My father was on the board of governors of the Mayo Clinic and probably could get Beck in without the usual wait.

Beck was appreciative but noncommittal. "I'm getting tired of getting poked with needles," he said. "If my time's up, it's up."

He said that before he died he wanted to rent out a dance hall somewhere and have a big, raucous rock-and-roll party and invite everyone he ever knew—friends and enemies alike. He stopped swinging. "Naaah, forget it," he said. "No one would show up. Would they?"

I would have showed up, which would have been only fair since, I would later learn, I was the only person whom Beck told of his impending death. During what were supposed to be his last six months, Beck kept pitching revised diagnoses my way, until finally, a few weeks before his scheduled expiration, he would tell me that the doctors had granted him a reprieve. Not that he was cured. The doctors didn't know exactly what was afflicting him, but they'd decided that it wasn't fatal.

While Beck had fabricated his own death sentence, he was indeed in pain—emotional pain so intense that it did in fact have physical symptoms, among them aching bones and joints, for which he sought medical treatment at New York University Medical Center. However, the pills I'd seen him taking over Easter weekend were Halcion, which had been prescribed by his psychiatrist to alleviate insomnia and depression. While Beck suspected that the pills might be aggravating rather than alleviating his depression, he was afraid to stop taking them. What if the drugs were indeed helping? Without them, he'd find himself in a hole so deep and dark that he'd never be able to crawl back out again.

If the double whammy of the Macy's nightmare and the dissolution of his marriage had pushed Beck to the edge this time, it was the increasingly intolerable psychic burden of his lies and fabrications that threatened to push him over. Beck's salary and bonus in 1987 had amounted to $1.2 million, which was what he'd earned the previous year and not nearly enough to cover the rate of inflation in the price of luxury goods. Instead of admitting to Margo that the money was running out, Beck turned his dilemma inside out, complaining of a surfeit of secret riches as the mid-1980s bull market added greatly to Rosebud's net worth. At one point, he told me that he was close to completing the negotiation of the merger of Rosebud into a major publicly held insurance company. Unfortunately, though, this company insisted on paying with shares of stock, which, given government disclosure regulations, would blow his cover by landing him near the top of the next *Forbes* 400 list. While selling to a private company would preserve his privacy, how many companies could afford to buy a colossus like Rosebud?

While Beck had been living with the risk of detection for years now, he'd greatly exacerbated the emotional burden of his masquerade by promoting under false pretenses both a movie and a book about himself. No doubt Beck must have realized that even if he fooled one or both of us, putting his lies into national circulation via *Mad Dog* and *Rainmaker* was almost certain to result in his being exposed as a fraud. And if there was a part of him that invited the cathartic effect of exposure, he must also have dreaded the consequences. However, he'd pushed his masquerade to the point where he couldn't pull out of the movie or the book without reneging on personal pledges that he'd made to two people whom he considered to be among his best friends, and his withdrawal might not be sufficient to kill either project, anyway. On the other hand, he must have realized that he would be doing Douglas and me a disservice by allowing to proceed to completion nonfiction works fatally compromised with fiction. In planting the ideas that grew into *Mad Dog* and *Rainmaker*, Beck in effect had chained himself, probably intentionally, to a ticking time bomb. The only question was when it would explode.

At Drexel one day, Max Liskin nearly made himself a human detonator. A weight lifter and marathon runner, Liskin was six foot one and built like a rock at 195 pounds. Liskin brought out the Mad Dog

in Beck, who showed his affection for the young banker by laying a
body block on him every now and then. One afternoon, Liskin came
across Beck talking to three junior bankers in the M & A "bullpen," an
open area on the floor where the department's associates were quartered. Beck was facing a quarter-turn sideways and thus failed to see
Liskin as he approached and put a muscular shoulder into his rib cage
a bit harder than he'd intended. Caught off balance, Beck stumbled
backward and slammed against a credenza, knocking books to the
floor.

Red-faced, Beck quickly gathered himself and charged as the trio of
bankers with whom he'd been speaking scattered for cover. Liskin,
though, was too horrified to move. "He had this look of blind rage that
I've seldom seen, even in the movies," Liskin said. Beck grabbed both
of his arms and flipped him to the ground. "You asshole," he
screamed. "I'm going to kill you, you motherfucker."

As Beck drew back his fist, Liskin shouted. "Jeff, come on," he said.
"What are you doing? We're friends."

A startled look flashed across Beck's face. He dropped his fist, released his grip on Liskin, and, without a word, ducked into his office
just down the hall. Dismayed at the absurd turn of events, Liskin
sheepishly entered Beck's office and tried to apologize. Beck refused to
speak to his young colleague other than to order him out of his office.
Liskin retreated and stood morosely in the hallway outside, convinced
that he'd be fired. Beck himself apologized in a few days.

During this period, all the symptoms of Beck's earlier crack-ups re-
curred: weight gain, nightmares, wild mood swings, quasi-catatonic
episodes. In all sincerity, he began telling Margo that the stress he felt
was reaching the point of threatening his life, that he feared that he
would drop dead of a heart attack as his father had at sixty-two. Beck
was only forty-one but found it quite conceivable that every year of the
fifteen that he'd spent on the Street had aged him two years, or thirty
years all told, making him forty-one by the calendar and seventy-one in
Wall Street time.

By the time Beck told me he was dying, he certainly looked the part
of a terminal patient. He made his impending death as real as he made
his Vietnam exploits. If nothing else, the sight of Beck crying was
enough to convince me of the truth of his words. Beck was in such
obvious pain—physical and emotional—that he probably came close
to convincing himself that he was doomed, if not from cancer then

from some stress-related ailment. Despite his condition, he said he intended to keep working at Drexel until it became physically impossible. When I asked him if he wanted to continue with the book, he insisted that the project was more important than ever to him and he urged me to accelerate my pace. Since Beck's decline inevitably would become a part of the book, I started noting our conversations in a diary. I kept this up for only a month or so, but the entries give a sense of the increasingly frantic, erratic quality of Beck's behavior. In his depression and emotional confusion, he was literally flailing about all over the world.

April 18, 1988: JB calls first thing in the A.M. from Beverly Hills, where he's attending Drexel's junk conference. He acts as if I'd left a message for him, though I hadn't. Sounds in better spirits than last time we talked. His voice isn't nearly as hoarse.

He says that one of his doctors had changed his diagnosis and is no longer sure it's leukemia. May just be an abnormal white count. Says he hasn't told Margo, who's back from Boston. They've decided to separate officially and he's looking at an apartment in the Museum Tower [in midtown Manhattan next to the Museum of Modern Art]. Met a woman at a dinner party thrown by Kirk Douglas to celebrate Michael's Best Actor Oscar for *Wall Street.* Cynthia Allison is her name. She's a reporter, covers Hollywood for a TV station in LA. Leads me to believe she was bowled over by his mere presence. Wonders aloud whether he should pursue her.

April 26: JB calls at nine-thirty P.M. Says he's in Paris and can't sleep. Been there two days working on some big deals of a mysterious nature. He also got a new assignment from Macy's but can't talk about it either. He says he feels pretty good. Not losing weight anymore. He asks about the Mayo Clinic. I tell him he can get in on one- or two-day notice. He's appreciative. Says he has to think about it. Says Pat Bromley from DLJ called him to say hello after talking to me. Wants to know who else I've talked to and what people are saying about him.

May 5: While I'm out in the evening, JB leaves two messages on my answering machine. Says it's urgent. He *must* talk to me. He sounds grim and very, very weary.

May 6: I call Barrett Farm first thing in the A.M. Margo and the governess answer simultaneously on different extensions. I ask for Jeff and Margo acts as if she doesn't recognize my voice. She's polite but very formal. "Mr. Beck has already left for work. May I take a message?" I say I'll call back later and can't hang up fast enough.

Later that afternoon, JB calls from his car on way to airport. Says he's going out to LA to spend some time with Allison. I ask him whether he trusts her and he gets very defensive. Is he doing something wrong? Why do I think he's doing something wrong? I tell him that all I meant was that he might fit into a story she's working on and that he might not want to be in it. Mentions that he is now officially separated, though still living with Margo at Barrett Farm. He and Margo are being "cordial and mature" about it all. Says he's thinking about going to the Mayo Clinic next week.

May 10: JB calls at seven forty-five A.M. from LA. Says he's decided to go to Tucson and check into a fat farm and clean himself out on some sort of diet before he goes to the Mayo Clinic. Says he feels awful physically, though he doesn't sound depressed. The latest medical theory is that excess weight may be screwing up his blood sugar.

He just talked to Sarah Lawson and told her about the book. Urges me to talk to her and gives me her LA number. There's a problem with Rosemary, though. She's a very private person and doesn't want to be interviewed. His sister will talk but not about early family stuff, which was rough for her. I ask a few questions about some Belushi-esque anecdotes he'd told me about his college days. He suddenly sounds queasy, says he doesn't want to come across as a buffoon in the book. I tell him the anecdotes convey rebelliousness, not buffoonery. He relaxes and tells me a few more wild tales of youth.

May 13: JB calls from airport while waiting to fly to Arizona. In a very ebullient mood. Tells two or three gross anecdotes about airplane mishaps, including chain-vomiting incident from Lehman days. We both laugh hard. Says he's decided to go to Europe for a while and will go to Mayo Clinic after—in three or four weeks perhaps. I tell him he shouldn't delay doing something that might save his life. Says he'll think about it but that he's sick of being poked with needles. Matter-of-factly describes the agony of having bone marrow extracted. He's in a very philosophical mood. "If my number's up, I'm going to go out laughing."

May 23: JB leaves a message on my machine. He's just read my last story for *Business Week,* a cover on Lazard Frères. Speaks in a gruff, hipster voice. "Hey, Bonkhead, nice cover, man. Why don't you give Jeffy a call at his office tomorrow, all right?" Modulates to a southern-sheriff voice. "You were supposed to come out here for the weekend, boy. I'll talk to you tomorrow, right, boy? You take care now, heah?"

May 24: JB returns my call in exuberant good humor. He checked out of the fat farm early because the generator broke down and it was 105 degrees in his room. He's leaving tomorrow on a trip to Paris, Sardinia, and Portofino. In Paris, he has to get some Rosebud matters squared away in case the doctors were right in giving him six months to live. Invites me to meet him in Sardinia to work on the book, but admits to potential distraction. Says that he's bringing the TV reporter with him.

JB takes ironic solace in the notion of death as his last great promotional stunt, since it would drum up interest in the book and the movie likely to be made from it. Mentions that *The New York Times* and *The Wall Street Journal* want to do profiles of him but that he intends to put them off till fall. Also, *The New York Times Magazine* wants to make him the centerpiece of a story on Vietnam vets who made good. Veterans' organizations are calling him up, urging him to cooperate, but he fears mention of his wealth will bring a barrage of people looking for handouts. He'd rather tell his story through *Mad Dog.* Filming will start next spring. I ask when it will come out. "I hope before I fucking die," he says.

On May 30 I flew off to meet Beck in the little resort town of Porto Cervo on the northern end of Sardinia. I landed at Olbia in the early evening and within an hour was in the lobby of the elegant Hotel Pitrizza, shaking Beck's hand. Tanned and well rested if still a bit blimpish, he looked to be in much better condition than on that gloomy Easter in Pound Ridge.

We retired to the terrace bar, where he ordered a double scotch. Beck was in a buoyant, talkative mood and I decided to press him on his Vietnam service, about which I was beginning to have my doubts. I'd been informed by the U.S. Army personnel center in St. Louis that there didn't seem to be any record of service corresponding to Beck's Social Security number. When I told Beck this, he was completely unruffled, and said that he'd put me in touch with a half-dozen men with whom he'd fought in Southeast Asia, mentioning each by name. He cautioned, though, that most of these guys were combat-scrambled wackos who were paranoid about contact with the press. He thought he might be able to persuade Charlie Beckwith to talk, though. Colonel Beckwith was the leader of Delta Force, an elite counterterrorist commando unit that had been created in Vietnam and was best known for its failed attempt in 1980 to rescue the American hostages held in Tehran after the Iranian revolution. Beck said he'd known Beckwith since 'Nam and worked closely with him, though never under his direct command.

I noticed a sharp rise in the drama of Beck's recollections whenever his new paramour was listening. Cynthia Allison was in her mid-thirties and pretty, poised, and intelligent, if somewhat given to dropping Hollywood names. While I failed to recognize half the people she mentioned, Beck seemed to know them all, at least within the context of the business of movies, and I couldn't help but be impressed at how quickly he seemed to have attained an insider's understanding of Hollywood. It was immediately evident that Allison's Hollywood credentials were critical to Beck's attraction to her; he was so fascinated by her career that he barely let her get a word in edgewise as he told the tale of how a nice Midwestern girl ended up on the big-time Hollywood glamour beat.

Allison was plainly smitten with Beck, or at least the man she thought she knew to be Beck. For his part, Beck seemed to swing every few hours between desire for Allison and a desire to ditch Allison, though not even at either end of this continuum was he confident in his opinion. He was forever taking me aside and asking my advice. Was he leading Allison on? Was she interested only in his money? Should he go back to Margo? Was he doing the right thing?

After a few days, Beck's manic ambivalence finally resolved itself into a brainstorm: Let's go to the Hôtel du Cap. The Hotel Pitrizza was too small to contain Beck's nervous energy, and there wasn't much to do in Porto Cervo, which Beck had originally selected because it was isolated and rather remote. I think what finally made up his mind, though, was the unreliability of the phone service; the thought that he might be missing deal calls from the United States infuriated him. We could have caught a commercial flight to Nice by way of Olbia and Rome the next afternoon. But the hellhounds were really nipping at Beck's heels, for he decided to charter a private jet the next morning and fly straight to Nice, where the Hôtel du Cap limousine was waiting at the airport for M. Beck and his guests. There was no perceptible diminution in the warmth with which Beck was greeted by the hotel staff, or in the courtesy that they showed him during my five-day stay, to suggest disapproval or even mild interest in the fact that he had taken up residence in the owner's villa with a woman other than his wife. This was France.

As had been the case at the Hotel Pitrizza, Beck seemed more restless and worn-looking with every passing day. One evening not long after sundown he excused himself and hobbled upstairs to bed, saying that he felt awful. A half hour later Cynthia and I were talking in the living room when we heard Beck begin moaning in apparent agony up in his bedroom. It was a mournful, pathetic sound. As we walked up the steps to check on him, it seemed to get louder. I knocked on his door but the moaning continued. We opened the door and looked in. He was sound asleep.

23

On a Sunday in September of 1988, Beck was holed up alone in the house at Barrett Farm, brooding over the mess he'd made of his life and vice versa. He couldn't have been any more miserable had he, in fact, been facing death in a month. Sitting in the glass-walled back porch, he was smoking cigarettes by the pack while keeping a glowering eye trained on his unwanted visitors. After long and fitful negotiations, he'd recently agreed to sell the place to Herb Wachtell, one of Marty Lipton's law partners. Although the contract wouldn't go to closing for another week or two, the Wachtells had come out today to show their kids around. Beck had given his permission for the visit, but now that the new owners were here actually poking around the property—*his* property—he could feel the anger and regret welling up inside him. He was getting a great price—$2 million, giving him a quick profit of $700,000 on a $1.3 million investment. But the money was small consolation for the ruination of the dreams that had inspired him to buy Barrett Farm in the first place. He'd come to the country in search of safe and lasting haven from the mounting lunacy of New York City; he'd moved hoping never to have to move again. Beck wanted finally to be settled, to be anchored by deep roots to one plot of earth where he and Margo would be able to measure out the remainder of their days not just by the clock and calendar but by the thousand subtle signs marking nature's procession of seasons.

But it was not to be, and now he felt a bit foolish for ever having believed in such a fairy tale. The reality was that he and Margo hadn't lived at Barrett Farm long enough even to complete the remodeling they'd begun after moving in. The dream was over—and so, apparently, was his marriage, though he hadn't completely abandoned hope of reconciling with Margo, nor she of reconciling with him. The two of them soon would be moving into separate apartments within a few blocks of each other on the Upper East Side. Katherine would live with her mother, though Jeff hoped and expected that she would be spending at least part of every weekend with him. For months, Jeff and Margo had been living at opposite ends of the house in growing discord. Now that he was confronted with the impending actuality of physical separation, Beck churned with ambivalence, swinging from relief at the prospect of an end to the incessant domestic strife of recent months to an almost panicky desire to somehow put his family back together again. The more Beck pondered his dismal marital history, while lying prostrate on the couch on the back porch, the blacker grew his mood. He'd compiled quite a line score: three marriages, two divorces, and a separation verging on divorce. And he was only forty-two. Plenty of time to stab more knives into his heart.

As he moped away this September day, Beck suddenly was roused from his reveries by the sight of the Wachtells at the pool—*his* pool, damn it—with his realtor, Craig Siano. Beck leaped up from the couch and yanked open the back door. "Siano," he shouted, his voice carrying across thirty yards of lawn to the pool like a cannon's roar. "Get in here."

Siano couldn't help but cringe a bit when he heard the sound of Beck's voice. This was exactly what he'd feared when he'd brought the Wachtells out here. All summer long, Beck had been throwing temper tantrums as he vacillated over whether to sell Barrett Farm. "He was raging against himself," Siano recalled. Finally, the realtor had importuned their mutual friend Michael Douglas to intervene on his behalf. "Don't fuck around with Craig," Douglas had told Beck. "Either the house is for sale or it isn't."

Siano left the Wachtells by the pool and walked up to the back door of the house. "Get those people the fuck off my property," Beck shouted at Siano. "Get them the fuck off! This place is not for sale."

"It's as good as sold, Jeff," Siano replied evenly.

Siano returned to the Wachtells and finished showing them around the property. The deal closed as scheduled on September 27, 1988, which, as it turned out, was close to the top of the market. By the time the last frantic gasp of 1980s takeover mania had ended, Barrett Farm's market value would have dropped along with Wall Street's profits, to the $1.4 million range.

Not long after Beck had moved back to the city, Siano was hanging out at Douglas's house when he happened to mention Beck. "Don't ever mention that guy's name again," the actor snapped. "I've found out that he's full of shit." In fact, Douglas was so chagrined by his association with Beck that he extended an unsolicited apology to Lynn Nesbit, the literary agent, for merely having introduced her to him. (Although by this time Nesbit had her own doubts about Beck's Vietnam legend, she was more sympathetic to Beck than angry at him, even though she, too, had put her professional reputation behind a project promoted in part on false pretenses.) Beneath the sensitive, laid-back persona that he projected through the press, Douglas prided himself on being a hard guy, just like his father. "I wouldn't be where I am today if I were as nice as everyone says I am," he told a reporter just after he'd won the Oscar for best actor in the spring of 1988. ". . . I can be a killer in business, and I love bearing grudges. I keep score, tit for tat. If I've been stabbed in the back, I don't forget. Bearing grudges gives you a lot of energy. I like finding devious ways to get back at people. Sometimes, it's almost as if I was sick."

My efforts to find out what had turned Douglas so bitterly against Beck were frustrated by the actor's refusal to speak with me. Bryan Burrough of *The Wall Street Journal* would later surmise (not having spoken with Douglas either, at least officially) that the actor had become infuriated when he learned in some unspecified way that the stories on which *Mad Dog* was based were false. According to Burrough, Douglas "called one of Mr. Kravis's aides and, in a rain of invective, denounced Mr. Beck as one of the vilest liars he'd ever met. 'He was never even in Vietnam!' Mr. Douglas is said to have shouted." While Beck's misrepresentation of his past certainly would have been reason enough for Douglas to dump Beck, there is something very fishy about this anecdote. Why would Douglas have called an aide to Kravis to denounce Beck? Yes, Douglas was a friend of Kravis's but he hadn't met Beck through him, nor had he asked the LBO king to vouch for Beck's credibility or involve himself in any way with *Mad Dog*. And if by some chance Douglas had felt like venting anti-Beck venom KKR's way, wouldn't he have aimed it at his old friend Henry instead of at an "aide"?

For his part, Beck insisted that his falling-out with Douglas had very little to do with *Mad Dog*, though he conceded that the movie project had been nothing but trouble from the outset. Beck was tardy in making the initial $22,500 payment called for under his contract with David Black, the screenwriter with whom Douglas had paired him. Black had signed his copy of their agreement and sent it on to Beck's lawyer in mid-January 1988, a few days before Beck threw himself into the scramble to find a white knight to contest Campeau's bid for Federated Stores. Having gotten no response by March, Black's agent asked Douglas to intervene as a last resort before taking the matter to arbitration. Nominated for his portrayal of Gordon Gekko, Douglas was anxiously awaiting the outcome of the Academy Awards voting, which would be announced in about a month. After leaning on Beck, Douglas told Black's agent that things "would go on schedule from now on" and indeed they did for a time. After sending Black a check, Beck twice met with the screenwriter to discuss the project, which, however, apparently died before it even reached the "treatment" stage. Beck could recall no angry confrontations with Douglas, no climactic showdown scene. Rather, the day came when he found himself unable to get his erstwhile best buddy on the telephone. In classic Hollywood fashion, he'd been frozen out.

According to Beck, he'd antagonized Douglas not by telling lies but by knowing too much truth about the actor. As self-described *"consigliere"* to Douglas throughout 1987 and early 1988, Beck had found himself in the midst of a nasty marital dispute between the Douglases and had become privy to secrets that contradicted Michael's well-tended image as Hollywood's Mr. Nice Guy. As Beck told it, Douglas was living in dread of the possibility that the dirt would find its way into print and, given the politics of the Academy, dash his chances at the Oscar. By midsummer, his market value having soared with his Oscar triumph, Douglas had finally succeeded in negotiating the terms of his withdrawal from Mercury/Douglas Films, which freed him to arrange financing for future film projects on terms far more favorable to himself. Instead of partnering with Beck, though, Douglas cut a production deal with Columbia Pictures under which the studio covered his overhead costs to the tune of $1 million a year in exchange for right of first refusal on his film projects. Once the Oscar was safely on Douglas's mantel and he'd secured his commercial future by extricating himself from Mercury/Douglas, he had no further need of Beck or Drexel.

Whatever its causes, the unraveling of the friendship left Beck nearly as embittered as Douglas apparently was. "I just felt like I was used," Beck said. "Hollywood is a seducer but Hollywood also is very easily seduced. If they think you're a pigeon with easy money, you can sit at the best tables at any of those Beverly Hills restaurants. I guess Michael's just not built to have a lot of close relationships. I can understand it. He got treated like a piece of meat for most of his career. In a world filled with users, you use someone before they use you."

At the same time, Beck's relationship with Kravis had all but come wholly undone as well. While continuing to take Beck's deal calls, Kravis had gradually phased the Mad Dog out of his social life. Only mildly insulted at his relegation to the back rows at Carolyne Roehm fashion shows, Jeff was bitterly disappointed when he arrived at a banquet honoring Kravis expecting to sit at one of the head tables with Douglas but instead was consigned to the ballroom equivalent of Outer Mongolia. He left in a huff. Beck was not the only one of Kravis's old acquaintances who found himself socially disenfranchised. It was on the occasion of Kravis's second Christmas party after his remarriage that Jeff and Margo first realized that Henry now had a B list and they'd been consigned to it along with many of the other 101 Dalmations. When Margo RSVP'd, she was asked to which event she was referring: the small sit-down dinner (for the Nouvelle Society élite) or the big cocktail party for *tout le monde.* What dinner? she said.

By the next year, the Becks would had been dropped altogether, their departure hastened by Jeff's inability to suffer Roehm's royal airs in silence. The denouement came one evening as they stood side by side chez Kravis, viewing some English sporting paintings that Henry had acquired recently. A little frown wrinkled Carolyne's brow. "Oh," she exclaimed. "They just don't speak to my soul." Beck snorted with derision. "Carolyne," he said, "you are just so full of shit."

From the isolation of Barrett Farm, Beck would only read about Roehm's and Kravis's greatest social triumph, a dinner party at the Metropolitan Museum of such sumptuous elegance that a leading society columnist dubbed it "the perfect party." For the hostess anyway, the climactic moment came during a performance by the Japanese violinist Midori. "One suddenly noticed that a single spotlight seemed to have been positioned to shine directly on Carolyne," wrote John Taylor in *New York* magazine. "Whether intentional or not, there she was, illuminated, her hands clasped together at her chest, a look of poised rapture on her face"—secure, no doubt, in the knowledge that never again would one of her perfect moments be spoiled by the howling rudeness of a certain Mad Dog.

While Carolyne luxuriated in her Nouvelle celebrity, society's crown rested uneasily on the head of "King Henry," as, to his annoyance, *Business Week* dubbed Kravis in 1988. Kravis took pains to justify his preeminence on the social circuit as an unwanted by-product of his wife's status as a celebrity designer. "When she gets her picture taken," he complained, "I get my picture taken, and we're in *Women's Wear* and the magazines. I don't like that." Indeed, *Women's Wear Daily* reported that Kravis was so upset by a *Daily News* item about him that he accosted Billy Norwich, its author, at a black-tie benefit at the New York Public Library, calling him an "asshole" and threatening to "break [his] kneecaps." Kravis denied threatening Norwich, who for his part insisted that *"Women's Wear Daily* is always accurate."

In business, too, Kravis's behavior seemed increasingly contradictory, even hypocritical, as he struggled to reconcile his compulsion to make deals with his carefully crafted image of respectability. Not long after KKR bear-hugged Beatrice into submission, Jerry Kohlberg split with his partners, citing "philosophical differences." Announcing the formation of his own firm, Kohlberg vowed to "stick with deals where reason prevails." Later, Kohlberg sued Kravis and Roberts, alleging in effect that his partners had chiseled him out of his fair share of the profits from several deals refinanced after his departure. The suit was settled out of court.

No longer constrained by Kohlberg's conservative scruples, Kravis and Roberts became ever more aggressive in their pursuit of big corporations, in terms of both tactics and the lavishness of their bids. After Duracell agreed to be acquired by Forstmann Little, for example, KKR unceremoniously barged in and outbid its archrival. KKR's seeming victory in a bidding contest for Macmillan was invalidated when a Delaware court ruled that the company had improperly favored KKR, which had offered several top Macmillan executives substantial equity positions. And even as Kravis was explaining the formation of E-II as an outgrowth of KKR's aversion to hostility, the firm was preparing to use the same sort of coercive strategy that Kelly would use against American Brands. In raising that giant LBO fund in 1987, Kravis and Roberts for the first time sought permission from their investors to secretly accumulate stock in companies before approaching management. KKR bought 9.9 percent of Kroger Company and, proclaiming its "outrage" when the company's management rebuffed its advances, hit the company with an unsolicited acquisition offer. However, Kroger refused to capitulate and KKR backed off, unwilling still to take the next step and launch a hostile tender.

The Wall Street Journal described Kravis's and Roberts's play for

Kroger as "probably the most forceful single action in KKR's history." It was indeed, and yet in a matter of weeks the Kroger contretemps would be all but forgotten as on October 20, 1988, the curtain lifted on the grand finale of the great 1980s takeover boom.

The battle for RJR Nabisco featured a Wall Street cast of hundreds, uniting all of the leading M & A players of the era for one last great orgiastic burst of greed and macho gamesmanship. At $25 billion, KKR's acquisition of RJR Nabisco was nearly twice the size of the previous record deal. In its scale and the ceaseless Sturm und Drang by which the action progressed, the RJR deal was positively Wagnerian. But the principals brought such ill-tempered pettiness to their roles that in the end the effect was far more comic than heroic. The RJR deal was *Der Ring des Nibelungen* directed by Mel Brooks and starring a collection of ornery, steely-eyed midgets in the guise of gangsters.

As documented in embarrassing detail in a barrage of articles and books, the battle began when RJR's management made a clumsy grab to buy the company on the cheap in alliance with Shearson Lehman, which had convinced itself that its survival depended on muscling its way into the LBO business. As RJR and Shearson were putting champagne on ice, Henry Kravis was in high dudgeon. How dare RJR steal his idea (he'd once had dinner with Ross Johnson, the CEO of RJR)! How dare Shearson Lehman not invite KKR to participate in history's largest buyout! Hadn't KKR tossed some juicy fees Shearson's way over the years? KKR assembled an unusually large band of prime-time M & A mercenaries, including Drexel Burnham, Merrill Lynch, Morgan Stanley, and Wasserstein, Perella. Kravis didn't trust Wasserstein but hired him so that no one else would. Before KKR had even made a bid for RJR, Wasserstein and Eric Gleacher went to Kravis and requested $50 million apiece for their services. Kravis was outraged; as a rule, KKR waited until after a deal before deciding on fees. Standing on principle, Kravis refused to discuss the matter (and eventually paid each $25 million). A few days after the RJR-Shearson group made its $75-a-share bid, KKR offered $90 a share—$20 billion—wholly subject to financing.

Now, it was Peter Cohen's turn to make like Dutch Schultz. Cohen, Shearson's CEO and an Aspen ski pal of Kravis, was outraged that a man whom he considered a friend would queer his best shot at belatedly making Shearson a force in buyouts. "I can't believe you're interfering in my deal," he told Kravis in refusing KKR's offer of $125 million to step aside. Kravis was unmoved. "I must be in this deal," he said. "I can't afford not to. It's my franchise." Kravis later denied ever invoking his "franchise," but to no avail. Gone was the humble, genteel image that Kravis had spent two decades creating.

At one point, the principal combatants—RJR/Shearson and KKR —worked out a peace treaty, only to see it unravel when Salomon Brothers, a relative newcomer to junk-bond dealing, refused to subordinate itself to its archrival, the hated Drexel. First Boston then jumped in, allied with the billionaire Pritzker family of Chicago. As Wall Street alliances shattered and re-formed and shattered again like so many waves pounding a beach, the battle for RJR escalated into a wild bidding contest reminiscent of the Campeau-Macy's battle for Federated. The per-share offer climbed from $75 to $90 to $92, $94, $100, $106, $108, $109 as the combatants lobbed lawsuits and shrill public accusations of skullduggery at one another. To Wall Street outsiders, all this seemed as incomprehensible—at once familial and viciously venal—as an intra-Mafia vendetta. Even for the see-no-evil free-marketers in Washington, RJR Nabisco was all a bit much.

For Beck, meanwhile, the RJR deal was a jumbo load of heartache. His voice was among the loudest of the chorus of Wall Street deal makers who greeted the news of RJR's surprise initial bid with howls of complaint at their exclusion. In this regard, Beck had a more legitimate beef than Kravis. Beginning in 1986, he'd laid a host of detailed restructuring proposals at Ross Johnson's doorstep—suggesting an LBO after Johnson rejected what Beck considered the best alternative, a master limited partnership. In fact, even before Johnson had vetoed the partnership idea, Beck was trying to interest Kravis in a buyout of RJR, sending him a detailed proposal in March 1987; this suggested a price of $75 a share, 30 percent above the market price (which, as it happened, was exactly the premium KKR was to offer in its initial $90-a-share bid a year and a half later). Kravis had his assistants start analyzing RJR. Using Don Kelly as an intermediary, Kravis invited Johnson to dinner at his apartment and laid his standard pitch on him. But Johnson was leery of running a debt-heavy company and told his financial staff to forget about an LBO with KKR or anybody else. "Let's throw some business Drexel's way for bringing us some of these ideas," he is supposed to have said, "but let's just take care of our own business now."

When Johnson changed his mind about a buyout in the summer of 1988, he decided that he didn't want to work with KKR, which would insist on control, or Drexel, which, *The Wall Street Journal* had reported, soon would be hit with charges by the government. If Drexel was a co-investor in a buyout, the government might end up forcing the liquidation of the firm's equity stake in RJR, destabilizing the company. Johnson turned instead to Shearson Lehman, with which he'd been working years before Beck entered the picture. The LBO bid that RJR unveiled in mid-October grew out of this assignment. Distracted though he was by his tempestuous relationships with his wife, with Allison, and with Douglas, Beck's deal radar remained acutely sensitive. Although James Welch, RJR's vice chairman, denied that a deal was in the works, Beck suspected otherwise and on October 3, 1988, told Kravis, "I think it's time to do something on RJR." Kravis doubted whether Johnson's opposition had softened but told Beck to go ahead and arrange a meeting with him. Not willing to rely solely on Beck, Kravis sent a second feeler to RJR through Steve Waters, Beck's old officemate at Lehman, who'd recently rejoined Gleacher at Morgan Stanley. Waters had no better luck than Beck in getting to Johnson.

KKR's decision to hire Drexel was only modest consolation to Beck since he was forced to take a backseat. Kravis turned first to Morgan Stanley for advice in structuring KKR's bid, and to Wasserstein when he needed a second opinion on deal tactics. What he wanted from Drexel was assurance that it could place the enormous junk-bond issue on which the financing of its bid hinged—and that was Milken's and Leon Black's province, not Beck's. Black never wavered in his insistence that Drexel would be able to engineer what would amount to the largest junk-bond financing ever, even though by this time the government had finally filed formal charges against the maverick investment bank. In early September, the Securities and Exchange Commission accused Drexel and Milken of fraud related to eighteen separate transactions from 1984 to 1986, all but two of them involving Ivan Boesky. In essence, the SEC alleged the existence of an intimate, secret alliance between Drexel and Boesky to manipulate stock prices. Although the SEC's civil complaint was damaging in itself, the bigger shoe was still to fall: the criminal case to be brought by the Justice Department, perhaps imminently.

Even though he played a secondary role in the RJR hostilities, Beck was back working almost around the clock as he not only helped out on RJR but was brought in by Pillsbury in early October to help defend it from a takeover attempt by the very determined and well-heeled Brit-

ish food and beverage giant, Grand Metropolitan P.L.C. Because Pillsbury also hired Wasserstein, Perella (plus First Boston and Shearson
Lehman), Beck found himself knocking heads with Wasserstein every
time he turned around. They clashed most vehemently over Pillsbury,
with Beck favoring a "Pac-Man" defense and Wasserstein urging management to "take the company into the swamp" of litigation. The
company followed Wasserstein's strategy, but lost the crucial court
decision and, eventually, its independence as well—though its shareholders got the consolation of a rich price. The most vivid image of
Wasserstein that Beck took away with him was the sight of his rival—
whom he described as "a knife and stiletto stylist"—finishing a glass of
fresh-squeezed orange juice and then rimming the pulp off the glass
with his tongue.

The RJR deal quickly turned into a full-fledged nightmare for Beck
when word of KKR's first bid was leaked to *The Wall Street Journal*
and *The New York Times*. Kravis assumed the source was Beck and
angrily called him on the carpet. Beck vehemently denied that he'd
been the source of the leak, but to no avail, as Kravis banned him from
further meetings. After ten agonizing days in exile, Beck was allowed
back into the deal after Kravis concluded that he'd been set up by
Wasserstein. (However, the leak controversy only seemed to have been
resolved. It would be revived—complete with a new twist—after the
RJR deal and would continue to haunt and infuriate Beck even after
he'd left Wall Street.)

After his release from Kravis's doghouse, Beck's spirits lifted from
altogether miserable to merely morose. For most of his career, deal
making offered respite from his private pain. But RJR was even worse
than Campeau/Macy's: the reckless bidding, the thuggish attitudes,
the blind greed, the keening, overbearing hysteria of it all. After a long
day spent dashing between the RJR and Pillsbury deals, Beck invited
himself over to Stan Pottinger's East Side apartment, where he lay
down on an oversized couch with an arm draped over his eyes and let
out enormous windy sighs. After a few minutes of this, Beck launched
into a long monologue about how depressed he was. "I gotta get out of
Drexel," he said. "I just gotta get out of that place."

One night in late November, I spent the evening interviewing Beck
in his new apartment, a sparsely furnished two-bedroom unit in a just-
opened luxury high-rise at Eighty-fifth and Madison. In a few days,
KKR would capture RJR Nabisco in a ferocious burst of last-minute
bidding, and the Wall Street middlemen involved in the transaction

would begin lining up to receive fees that totaled nearly $1 billion—the biggest payday of the decade. At ten-thirty a messenger arrived at Beck's apartment bearing Morgan Stanley's latest iteration of the numbers. Beck could barely bring himself to flip through the reworked deal book. "You'd think I'd be excited by the biggest takeover ever," he said laconically. "I'm not. I really don't care. I guess that says something."

"Yeah," I said. "It says you're burned out."

"No, it's maturity," Beck replied. "I'm just sick of assholes."

KKR's "victory" in the fight for RJR Nabisco exhilarated Beck only momentarily, for the more he thought about it the more he was convinced that the real winner was the man almost universally portrayed in the press as the big loser: Ross Johnson. In Beck's analysis, once KKR jumped into the bidding, as Johnson knew it would, the CEO's objective was not to buy RJR but to maximize the price he and his fellow shareholders would get for their stock. "I believe that Johnson would have done the deal for $80 to $85 a share," Beck said. "Once it got to $90, he was out and KKR was bidding against itself. In my studied opinion, Ross outfoxed KKR into paying as much as $5 billion more than RJR was worth. Five *billion*. Johnson is the most brilliant student of Machiavelli I've ever met. I saw him in London at Annabel's [a trendy nouveau-riche nightclub popular with Americans] months later and he was having the time of his life. He was laughing about the deal. He told me, 'I know you know.'"

RJR was the last great hurrah for both Beck and Drexel. A few weeks after KKR had captured its $25 billion prize, Drexel was thrown into chaos when Fred Joseph and the firm's board of directors crumbled under the prosecutorial pressure applied by Rudolph Giuliani, the U.S. Attorney for the Southern District of New York. Ever since Dennis Levine's arrest in early 1986, Joseph had proclaimed to the world that a series of internal investigations had uncovered no wrongdoing by Milken or his junk-bond minions. Of course, he'd also even more vehemently insisted to the press for years that he was in charge. In truth, Milken had always been a power unto himself, and indeed it was possible that Joseph, though he was both CEO and a Milken confidant, not only didn't know for sure what had gone on in Beverly Hills but had no way of finding out, lacking the subpoena powers of government.

The politically ambitious Giuliani had exploited the division in the

firm by prosecuting Drexel and Milken separately. While Milken ada-
mantly refused to even discuss settling with the government, Joseph
was willing to talk. Giuliani, who was as zealous a prosecutor as Milken
was a junk-bond dealer, threatened to slam Drexel with the full force
of the Racketeer Influenced and Corrupt Organizations Act (RICO).
Although RICO had been designed to combat mobsters and drug
runners, Giuliani saw in its draconian penalties the ideal prosecutorial
tool to break the resolve of securities firms reluctant to admit their
guilt. Under RICO, the government could take possession of Drexel's
assets at the moment of indictment. For a securities firm, confiscation
of assets was likely to bring instant death by prompting lenders to pull
billions of dollars in short-term credit lines used to finance securities
inventories. Giuliani also demanded that Drexel cooperate in the government's ongoing investigation to the extent of requiring its employees to waive their attorney-client privilege and thus enable the Justice
Department to prosecute Drexel people on the basis of information
they'd given the firm's lawyers in confidence.

Outraged by Giuliani's coercive tactics, Drexel's board on December 19, 1988, voted unanimously against settling. Coincidentally, that
night the corporate-finance department gathered for a Christmas party
in the ballroom of the Waldorf-Astoria Hotel. Beck watched about
eight hundred of his colleagues bang tables and scream with delight as
Robert Linton, the firm's chairman, appeared onstage to lead a defiant
sing-along of "Rudolph the Red-Nosed Lawyer." Like the vast majority of Drexel's highest-paid employees, Beck was vehemently opposed
to any settlement that included an admission of guilt by the firm. On
the basis of what he'd gleaned from the charges already filed by the
SEC and what he'd been able to pick up in conversations with Joseph
and with Drexel's lawyers, Beck thought there was a decent chance
that the government might not prevail in court. As a practical matter,
though, he was convinced that the quality of Giuliani's case didn't
much matter. In his opinion, Joseph faced a stark choice: Either stand
shoulder to shoulder with Milken, the man who made the firm—the
man who, for better or worse, *was* Drexel—and fight Giuliani all the
way to trial, or go out of business. It was that simple. For if Drexel
admitted guilt, Milken was likely to go to jail on the closely related
charges certain to be brought against him with a vengeance by Giuliani.

The next afternoon, Joseph got a call from Giuliani, who gave
Drexel until four P.M. the next day to settle or be hit with a RICO

indictment. That night Joseph and Drexel's chief outside counsel, Irwin Schneiderman, went to the U.S. Attorney's office and capitulated. Giuliani relented on the issue of attorney-client privilege but prevailed in almost every other respect as Drexel agreed to plead guilty on six felony counts, pay $650 million in fines, and assist the government in investigating its employees and customers alike. The board vote this time was sixteen to six in favor of settling. Joseph voted no in a symbolic protest that many employees considered an act of rank hypocrisy. Like many of his outraged colleagues, Beck suspected that Joseph had cut a deal to save his own neck. Joseph denied it, but Drexel's subsequent settlement of the SEC's civil charges did not contain so much as a wrist-slap for Drexel's CEO, who for years had boasted to reporters of his close relationship with Milken.

Although Joseph hung on to his CEO title, his authority was gone, destroyed by his loss of face. Milken, meanwhile, remained at Drexel for a few more months, resigning shortly after being hit with a ninety-eight-count felony indictment in March 1989. Milken's departure created a vacuum of purpose and power that Joseph tried to fill with money. In a misguided attempt to buy back the lost loyalty of the firm's remaining stars, Joseph guaranteed that their 1989 paychecks would amount to no less than 75 percent of 1988's compensation, which had been enormous. A month after Milken's resignation, his top junk-bond deputy, Peter Ackerman, was presented with a check for $107 million, largely for his work in orchestrating the $5 billion junk-bond offering to finance KKR's buyout of RJR. Joseph's generosity no doubt had something to do with Ackerman's threat to resign in the middle of the RJR financing in anger over the firm's decision to settle with the Justice Department. Joseph capitulated to Ackerman, as indeed he'd capitulated to Giuliani, rather than risk the abortion of an underwriting that would produce fees of $275 million, more than Drexel had made on any other transaction.

Although Milken's compensation had been unconscionable, at least it had been pegged to the profitability of his junk-bond group. In severing the link between pay and profits after Milken's departure, Joseph exacerbated the harmful consequences of the shrinkage in Drexel's franchise as the felony conviction convinced—or, in the case of many municipalities, forced—a growing number of its clients to take their business elsewhere. This lost revenue was not easily replaced, for the two businesses on which Drexel depended utterly—M & A and junk-bond dealing—were contracting sharply as the great 1980s takeover wave receded. Ronald Reagan had given way to George Bush, who, in contrast to his predecessor, was openly critical of the Wall Street nouveaux riches. Meanwhile, the spectacle of RJR had stirred a strong backlash on Capitol Hill, giving impetus to proposals to curb junk bonds and LBOs. While political pressure was effectively brought to bear against big commercial banks, many financiers were pulling back from takeover lending of their own volition as deal promoters resorted to ever-increasing leverage. Not long after Milken's retirement, junk-bond prices began a decline that turned into a full-scale rout as Integrated Resources, a major Drexel client, defaulted on its bonds and debt-laden Federated Stores started hemorrhaging. By the autumn of 1989, the specter of impending junk-bond apocalypse had so unnerved Wall Street that when an LBO of United Airlines was canceled for lack of financing, the Dow Jones average plummeted 190 points in a few hours, stirring memories of Black Monday.

In its eagerness to prove that its junk-bond might was intact, Drexel Burnham failed to submit to the dictates of a financial system in extremis. Rather than turn away high-risk financings, Drexel began lending its own money to a corporate client, either in the form of a bridge loan or by buying unsold portions of an underwriting for its own account, hoping to unload the bonds when the market strengthened. When the junk-bond market tanked instead, Drexel was caught holding $1 billion worth of paper that was trading at an ever-increasing discount to face value—to the extent that it traded at all. In October alone, the firm lost $86 million. Drexel's slide into the red had the perverse effect of intensifying the greed of its investment bankers. Late in 1989, Joseph approved bonus payouts totaling $260 million. When Black, who had rammed through the single most disastrous underwriting of Drexel's brief post-Milken era, learned that his pay for the year was only $12 million, he went raging in to see Joseph, who had every reason to hang tough—and, by his standards, did, coughing up only an extra $3 million to placate Black. Drexel thus earned the dubious distinction of becoming perhaps the first company in the history of commerce to agree on the eve of its bankruptcy to agree to pay $15 million to one employee.

Beck found 55 Broad Street so unspeakably depressing following what he considered to be Joseph's betrayal of Milken that he rarely went into the office. There wasn't much for him to do anyway. He'd specialized in cultivating a caliber of client that didn't *need* Drexel the way its infamous cadre of raiders had, that had plenty of alternative sources of financing. While Beck's relationships with Al Taubman, Arnout Loudon, Peter Grace, and most of the other clients to whom he was closest survived the government clampdown—Grace even attended the 1989 Predators' Ball, the firm's last—they were not about to throw any big assignments his way as long as he stayed at Drexel. Deal impotence was setting in on all fronts, though in the first half of 1989 Beck and some of his colleagues did manage to convince British media baron Robert Maxwell to take a close look at acquiring Paramount Studios—potentially, a $10 billion acquisition. This near-deal perked Beck up for a time, for he was intrigued with Maxwell, a flamboyant Czechoslovakia-born billionaire long rumored to have been involved in Cold War espionage. Beck was not alone in surmising that Marcel Bresson, the French raider-spy protagonist of David Aaron's novel, *Agent of Influence*, had been modeled after Maxwell, though Aaron himself never would comment on the matter.

Now officially separated from Margo, Jeff continued to spend much time in Los Angeles with Cynthia Allison and assorted denizens of the film colony. In the midst of the RJR bond sale, in fact, Beck flew off to Hawaii with Cynthia. Back in New York, meanwhile, Beck had begun seeing Mimi Russell, an eccentric, blue-blooded divorcée who'd founded her own construction company and raised three sons. Russell, who looked like a brittler version of Farrah Fawcett, was a daughter of Sarah Churchill and as a girl had lived for a time at Blenheim Palace. She was also descended from the famous Vanderbilts of New York and had gained a certain notoriety in society for her loopy irreverence. A true character, Mimi charmed and offended in equal measure and flitted in and out of society as it suited her moods. Like Beck, though for vastly different reasons, she simply didn't worry about the social consequences of speaking her mind. Although she was ambivalent about her pedigree, Beck gloried in it. "Mimi is the real thing," he often told me, by way of emphasizing the inauthenticity of Nouvelle princesses like Carolyne Roehm.

When Beck did manage to drag himself into the office, he stirred a boiling cauldron of discontent. As word filtered down through the ranks of the excessive compensation deals Joseph had cut with Ackerman, Black, and a few others, periodic explosions could be heard coming from Joseph's office as one managing director or another vented his indignation. None was more indignant than Beck, who argued that in light of his seminal contribution to the RJR deal he was shortchanged by at least $5 million when Joseph and Black set his 1989 bonus at

$3 million, the same as the year before. While morale was no better among the younger bankers, they couldn't complain about the politicization of compensation without risking their jobs. Beck became the younger set's mouthpiece, factoring in their grievances as he buttonholed Joseph regularly with unsolicited criticism on everything from his approach to pay and public relations to the firm's legal and business strategies. "Jeff was the only guy who said what he thought," said Jay Bloom, an M & A vice president who occupied an office next to Beck's for Jeff's last two years at the firm. "He reflected the thinking of a lot of the younger guys. We trusted him. You knew he wouldn't buddy-fuck you."

After the government appointed a federal judge to serve as an ombudsman for complaints lodged against Drexel by its employees, a young banker named Michael Gross presented Beck with a blue cap fitted out with gold military-style piping and the word "OMBUDSMAN " stenciled across the front. Beck used to wear the cap as he wandered the hallways looking for action. "If anybody has a problem," he'd bellow, walking down the hallway, "the ombudsman is in." Beck was kidding, but was touched and flattered when a fair number of younger bankers whom he knew only slightly did in fact come to him with their problems.

Seeking to make himself useful while securing his position within the firm, Beck volunteered to help reorganize Drexel's international-banking effort, which had never been up to snuff, in part because Joseph had used the area as a kind of quarantine zone for problem bankers from the domestic side of corporate finance. He was asked to write up a memo suggesting an approach, and did so, though nothing came of it. Joseph, however, did ask Beck to form a committee to think up new directions for the firm while improving the dissemination of information within the investment-banking group. Staffed with a dozen of the firm's best young bankers, this Strategic Investment Group met about once a month and was able to get some minor changes implemented, though nothing nearly dramatic enough to reverse Drexel's decline. As it became clear that Joseph was telling Beck what he wanted to hear but doing nothing of what Beck wanted him to do, Jeff began to court John Shad, who'd signed on as Drexel's new chairman after its settlement with the SEC. As a former chairman of the SEC, Shad had, ironically, overseen the launch of the agency's investigations of Drexel and Milken. Before answering Reagan's call,

Shad had been Joseph's mentor at E. F. Hutton and in fact had given him his first job out of business school.

Through a mutual friend, Beck introduced Shad, a widower, to Aline, the Countess of Romanones, an American beauty who had worked for the OSS (Office of Strategic Services, the forerunner of the CIA) and wrote *The Spy Who Wore Red* and *The Spy Who Went Dancing*. Beck also invited Shad to attend his Strategic Investment Group meetings. Shad showed good faith by attending, though he usually had little to say and at times fell asleep, which reinforced the widespread impression that he was merely a figurehead—or worse, a government functionary without portfolio. Beck nicknamed Shad "Catfish" because of his slow, ponderous manner and affinity for junk food, and to the amusement of his young colleagues gave the new chairman an enormously hard time during SIG meetings. "I truly felt sorry for John, who was in over his head," Beck recalled. "Shad was a captive of his own limitations and I believe that he took me on as his special project, to hold me in line with empty promises that all would be better at Drexel."

In midsummer of 1989 Beck broke his leg severely in a horse-riding accident in Bedford and stopped going to the office altogether. His leg was broken at the ankle in three places, requiring seven pins and two metal plates to fit the bone back together and many months of grueling physical therapy before he could walk without a cane. The accident jolted Beck into the belated realization that he had fallen in love with his (and Margo's) longtime riding instructor, Lisa Battey Stone. A thirty-four-year-old divorced mother of two, Stone had grown up in the area and ran her own business, which involved boarding horses as well as instructing their owners. Although she numbered many socialite riders among her clients, Stone herself was utterly without pretension and even a bit irreverent—sweetly so, to be sure. As Beck began spending weekends and then weekdays with Stone, he saw less and less of Russell.

During his recovery, Beck was more dependent than ever on the telephone, though some of the younger bankers kept him apprised of Drexel's continuing deterioration by periodically trooping up to his new Eighty-fifth Street apartment in search of career-damage-control guidance. Beck advised his young visitors to do as he was doing: Make plans to leave but don't actually depart until collecting past-due bonus payments. The long hours that he spent immobilized and blue in his apartment crystallized Beck's view of Drexel as the S.S. *Titanic* of Wall Street. Like the other creatures scurrying across its decks, though, he just couldn't bring himself to jump into a lifeboat as long as he saw any hope of extracting the millions due him for RJR. While battling Joseph over his 1989 bonus, Beck worked on his plans for the new deal firm he hoped to establish in partnership with some former RJR Nabisco people and a half-dozen colleagues from Drexel.

Predictably, plans for Checchi Beck Incorporated had come to naught when in mid-1988 Al Checchi decided the time had come to move on. For one thing, Checchi was tired of waiting. For two years now, every six months were to have been Beck's last six months at Drexel. Moreover, Beck's indecision seemed to Checchi to be symptomatic of deep psychological problems. Checchi let Beck down easy. "We have spent a good deal of time trying to get to know each other," Checchi observed in a "Dear Jeff" letter:

> We have shared, individually as well as collectively, both high and low comedy as well as moments of personal anxiety and, yes, "confusion." Throughout this period, I have to come to know (some) and like you (very much). . . . We simply operate differently and I think incompatibly. I would rather have a good friendship with you than a contentious partnership. I fear the latter would be the inevitable result of any further attempt to combine our business interests.

Beck had come to the same conclusion, and said so in his equally gracious responding letter. It was a most amicable parting, and Checchi soon made a very big splash by doing what Beck had urged him to do: "run something big." Checchi headed an international consortium that acquired Northwest Airlines in 1989 in a leveraged buyout valued at $3.7 billion, one of the largest transactions completed in the difficult deal year of 1989.

Beck interested some consultants to RJR executives in joining him and a half-dozen other Drexel investment bankers in a new merchant bank with a twist: The firm would invest partly in "social venture capital" and also contribute a portion of its profits to charity. Beck took this latest notion seriously and put much more effort into developing it than into any of his previous new-firm concepts. This time, Beck did in fact back up conversation with paperwork, as he enlisted Jack MacAtee's legal advice and the marketing help of a former partner of the Sawyer-Miller Group, a prominent Manhattan consulting

firm. The new firm, which Beck informally dubbed Creative Investment Associates (a play not only on "CIA" but on Michael Ovitz's
firm, Creative Artists Agency), was to begin with $1 billion in capital,
most of it put up by large institutional investors. While the bulk of this
money would be invested in companies Beck and his colleagues believed undervalued, 5 percent to 10 percent would be set aside for
equity investment in social causes. Beck was most interested in drug
rehabilitation and met several times with Dr. Mitchell Rosenthal, the
head of Phoenix House, a Manhattan drug-rehab organization that he
particularly admired.

Beck was deep into the work for CIA when he got a call from Bryan
Burrough of *The Wall Street Journal.* Burrough had interviewed Beck
at length for his book, *Barbarians at the Gate,* which was due out soon,
and wanted to profile him for the paper. While Beck craved attention,
he also remained mindful of publicity's dangers and made the rounds
of his friends asking their advice on whether he should cooperate with
Burrough. Beck told me and everyone else whose opinion he solicited
that Burrough had said his profile would be included in a series on
prominent 1980s deal men reviewing the past decade and looking
ahead to the 1990s. Two of the other stories were to feature Kravis and
Ted Forstmann of Forstmann Little. The idea of appearing in such
high-profile company appealed greatly to Beck, as did the opportunity
to present himself as a big-picture ruminator. Beck had skimmed
through the galleys of *Barbarians* at a dinner party and basically liked
how he'd been presented, though he wasn't quite sure what to make of
Burrough's description of him as "a cross between a stand-up comedian and an assassin." Russell advised Beck against talking, on the
grounds that he had nothing to gain from publicity at this stage and
much to lose if the story as written differed from the story as advertised.

Beck asked me whether he could trust Burrough. I'd never met
Burrough and knew nothing about him. While the idea of pairing
Beck with Kravis and Forstmann struck me as ungainly if not strange,
I advised Beck to cooperate if he were so inclined. Perhaps if I hadn't
been so preoccupied with my own investigation of Beck I might have
realized that he was about to walk into a trap.

24

The room was full of dignitaries and illuminated by bright lights, which emphasized the vaulted ceilings of the ornate hall. It was somewhere in Washington, perhaps the White House. Everyone was mingling and sipping drinks. Beck was discussing the latest leveraged buyout with someone who looked and acted important. It seemed to him that every pair of eyes was following his every move. Suddenly, the door opened and a hand holding a gun appeared and slowly extended into the room, which erupted in chaos as people scrambled for cover. Beck used his body to shield his important companion as the hand rotated the revolver from one side of the room to the other, searching for its target. When it found Beck, the gun stopped. It was pointing right at him!

Beck shouted, "Come out from behind the door." But his voice was drowned out by a thunderous gunshot that seemed to stop time itself, as if someone had thrown a freeze-frame switch on reality.

Mimi Russell rushed in from an adjoining bedroom and shook Beck awake screaming from this nightmare about six-thirty A.M. on Monday, January 22, 1990. As Russell comforted Beck, he related his dream to her. Then he arose, walked to the door of his apartment, and opened it. Lying outside was a real-life nightmare staring up at him from the hallway carpet. On the front page of that morning's *Wall Street Journal* appeared his own likeness under a headline that read:

TOP DEAL MAKER LEAVES
A TRAIL OF DECEPTION
IN WALL STREET RISE

Beck felt a sharp, stabbing pain in his chest, quickly followed by an adrenaline rush of pure rage. Unable to bring himself to pick up the newspaper, he bent over further from the waist until he could make out the next deck of the headline:

DREXEL'S JEFF "MAD DOG" BECK
DAZZLED MANY WITH TALES
OF WAR HEROICS, WEALTH

DOG BISCUITS AND A MOVIE ROLE

Finally, he forced himself to kneel down and pick up the paper. Retreating to his bedroom, he read with mounting horror an article that confirmed all of his worst fears about Bryan Burrough's intentions. Despite its length, the article skipped lightly over Beck's first dozen years on the Street and his activities at Drexel to focus on his discombobulation during his last crazy months at Oppenheimer & Company. Burrough's exposé was based mainly on Beck's claims of Vietnam heroism and hinged on quotes attributed to Beck's first wife, Sylvia Pfotenhauer, to the effect that the closest he ever got to military service was a few weeks in mandatory reserve training. "For a man who later claimed to be a war hero," wrote Burrough, "his first wife says Mr. Beck evidenced an ironic desire to escape service in the armed forces."

The jolt administered by the story was heightened by Beck's belief that he'd succeeded in gaining at least a temporary reprieve. Once it had become evident to Beck that Burrough was more interested in his biography than his views of the 1990s, he'd demanded a meeting with the reporter's editors at the *Journal,* claiming that he would provide them with documentary evidence of his military service. But if Beck was stalling for time, apparently so was Burrough. According to Beck, the reporter had agreed to set up a meeting with his editor but did not do so until the day before the piece appeared. That afternoon Beck called Burrough as Russell listened in on a second line. They heard Burrough say that he and his editor would meet with Beck at two o'clock the following afternoon. Like Beck, I did not expect the article that Monday, for Burrough had called me, too, over the weekend to ask whether Beck had gone to Vietnam. As a *Business Week* staffer, I was not about to give a *Journal* reporter the benefit of my reporting on Beck, nor did I want to tip my hand as to the content of *Rainmaker.*

The mere fact that Burrough had put himself in the embarrassing position of seeking confirmation of so fundamental a fact from a rival reporter convinced me that his story might never appear and certainly wouldn't see print as soon as it did.

But there it was, spread across seven columns of *The Wall Street Journal.* The story contained little of import that I hadn't uncovered myself, though I had to hand it to Burrough for locating Sylvia, whom I had yet to track down. (Months after the *Journal* story appeared, I finally found Sylvia, now Sylvia Seret, in Santa Fe. Her husband, Ira Seret, told me that Sylvia had no intention of ever again talking to a reporter about Beck. "She made that mistake once," Seret said.)

I'd just finished reading the article for the second time when Beck called about nine A.M. I'd expected him to be angry but instead he sounded eerily passive, almost anesthetized. However, his sense of humor was intact. "It could have been worse, man," he said. "They could have accused me of being a serial killer." He continued in a serious vein. "In a strange sense, I feel—it's not relief—but I'm just very calm about the whole thing," Beck said. "I guess you become calm when you know what the truth is."

I hadn't been able to completely satisfy myself that Beck had no CIA connection (and never would be able to, given the agency's standard policy of refusing to either confirm or deny things). But I was certain that his Vietnam combat career was imaginary and I was tired of the charade. "You know, Jeff," I said, "if there's any part of what you've told me that isn't true, now's the time to tell me."

He seemed to consider my offer momentarily, but was not ready to abandon the refuge of false heroism. To the contrary, given the ordeal of public disgrace that he was just beginning to endure, he needed it now more than ever. He assured me that his Vietnam stories were all true and that soon he would be able to provide me with documentary evidence.

After our conversation, Jeff called Margo, who hadn't read the story and, curiously, wasn't even mentioned in it. Beck was hurt that she didn't offer to rush over and sit with him in his hour of need, and offended, too, that her overriding concern seemed to be whether the article would damage Katherine's chances of admission to the kinder garten class at the élite Nightingale-Bamford School on East Ninety-second Street. Beck was only slightly less dismayed that none of his blood relatives other than his sister Judy called to offer sympathy. This might well have been the only day of his adult life that he actually wanted to hear from his mother. About eleven A.M., Jeff called Margo back and was thunderstruck that she hadn't yet gone out to buy a copy of the *Journal.* "You are truly on your own," Russell told him.

Beck spent all Monday holed up in his apartment with Russell, who was struck by her friend's seeming composure but stayed through the night to the next morning to make sure that he didn't do anything foolish. Beck was deluged with phone calls but had them all routed to his answering service, which later gave him a list of messages that ran on for pages and pages, constituting a surreal telephonic version of *This Is Your Life.* The first to call, about seven A.M., was Michael Douglas. Beck wondered where Douglas could be that he'd read the *Journal* at that hour, suspecting that wherever he was the actor must have known the story would appear today. Oliver Stone and Jack MacAtee also were among the first callers. All day long calls poured in from Drexel colleagues—including Leon Black, Donnie Engel, and John Shad—and clients, including Al Taubman, Terrence Daniels (who said that Peter Grace couldn't call because he was having hip surgery), Ross Johnson, Bill Spoor, Arnout Loudon. Henry Kravis left several messages, as did David Aaron, the only ex-Oppenheimer colleague with whom Beck was still on speaking terms. Kravis's ex-wife, Hedi, sent a note. A half dozen of the young Drexel bankers sent a cake that featured a big pair of breasts and the frosted legend "LOCK AND LOAD. " Among the 150 other callers were Al Checchi, Michael Ovitz, Eric Gleacher, and, from the old Coral Gables days, Jenny McGlannan, Steve Ernst, and others.

Mixed in with these personal calls were urgent inquiries from newspaper reporters working up their own quick-and-dirty versions of the *Journal* story. By early afternoon, telegrams from Hollywood producers were arriving, suggesting an immediate meeting to cut a deal for the rights to the Mad Dog's own story, and the big-time television newsmagazine programs—including *60 Minutes*—had joined the telephone queue. Then there were the comedians, amused by the fact that Beck's name was the same as that of one of the greatest rock guitarists. He got messages from "Eric Clapton" and "Rod Stewart" (both former bandmates of the other Jeff Beck). Other calls came flooding in from greedy strangers who wanted him to apply his rainmaking skills to make them rich; religious nuts offering to intercede with Jesus on his behalf; victims of assorted types crying real tears of empathy. The spectacle of his public ruination had made Beck a celebrity of sorts and his star glow was summoning forth a cross-section of crazies from the wormy woodwork of post-1980s America.

Once the initial ruckus receded, Beck began returning phone calls, but sparingly. He called Douglas at the actor's New York apartment. Diandra answered. "If I were you," she said, "I'd get a good book and go to the Caribbean."

Beck was in a surly mood. "I don't need your advice, Diandra," he snapped. "All I want to know is whether Michael has anything he wants to say to me."

"No, I don't think so," she replied.

"Great," he responded with mock joy and hung up. (Beck ended up unintentionally taking Diandra's advice. After Arnout Loudon of Akzo and his wife called to invite Beck along on their vacation to Anguilla, the Mad Dog spent a week in the Caribbean.)

Beck never heard back from Douglas, who later that day was spotted by Ed Novotny, a veteran Wall Street public-relations man, at Le Cirque, the tony Upper East Side restaurant where Jeff and Margo had held their wedding reception. Novotny walked up to Douglas. "You don't know me and I'm sure you don't want to hear this," he said. "But I'd just like to say two words to you."

Douglas looked puzzled. "What?" he said.

"Jeff Beck," Novotny said.

Douglas's eyes flashed with anger and his hand balled into a fist, crushing the breadstick he was holding.

About a week after the article appeared, Beck finally returned a call from Fred Joseph. In a mutually testy conversation, the Drexel chief declared himself happy to accept the Mad Dog's most recent resignation (which had been tendered on January twelfth) and Beck insisted that he was even happier at finally having been liberated from the Drexel "zoo."

Even so, Beck was devastated anew with both surprise and regret when on February thirteenth Drexel finished its own saga of self-destruction with the exclamation point of a Chapter 11 bankruptcy filing. Amid the many business collapses of the late 1980s, Drexel's was easily the most spectacular. This, after all, was a firm that had generated profits of at least $3.5 billion from 1983 to 1989 and, despite paying out the highest bonuses in the history of the world, had accumulated long-term capital of $1.4 billion by the end of 1988. Even after the government confiscated $600 million of that in fines, Drexel remained one of the best-capitalized firms on Wall Street. Ironically, though, the investment bank that more than any other had sold America on high-risk leverage was destroyed by its blindness to the risks it was itself taking. Like a poker player whose touch has deserted him, Drexel placed bets bigger than it could cover at a time when it should have passed instead of played.

History suggests that it is in the nature of financial markets to swing between excesses of optimism and pessimism by means of sharp, jolting transitions that always seem to occur when least expected. The RJR Nabisco buyout was a classic peak of speculative excess that marked a sharp reversal of fortune in the two intertwined businesses on which Drexel had enriched itself: junk-bond and M & A dealing. While every investment bank suffered the effects of the turning of the cycle, for Drexel it was the moment of truth. Faced with a choice between accepting a temporary end to prosperity while waiting for the cycle to turn again or persisting in its aggression in hopes that the downturn was only fleeting, Drexel rashly committed its capital in deals so risky that even Mike Milken would have recoiled in horror.

In November 1989, a favorite Milken whipping boy, the credit-rating agency Standard & Poor's, got revenge of sorts by lowering the rating on Drexel's commercial paper, short-term corporate IOUs that securities firms float in large amounts to finance their day-to-day operations. Unnerved by S & P's downgrading, investors refused to buy Drexel's paper when it came due, depriving the firm of $400 million in financing. At first, Drexel was able to keep itself afloat by borrowing from its own commodities-trading subsidiary, which in turn borrowed gold from foreign banks, sold the gold, and lent the cash to its parent company. Drexel began the new decade by losing $60 million in its first month, spooking its remaining creditors. As more and more banks refused to roll over the lines of credit Drexel needed to secure its remaining commercial paper, the firm needed more money than it could borrow from its commodities unit. In late January, about the time the *Journal's* exposé of Beck appeared, Drexel began draining its main securities subsidiaries of $400 million in capital, putting them in violation of minimum capital requirements. On February second, the New York Federal Reserve Bank got wind of these unreported transfers and alerted the SEC and other regulators, who intervened to block further such maneuvers.

It was about this time that John Shad and Leon Black visited Beck in his apartment to assure him of the firm's intent to provide him with a generous severance package. Shad had just come from the dentist, and Beck took it as a bad omen that he was bleeding heavily from the gums as he spoke optimistically of Drexel's improving financial condition.

In mid-February, Drexel had $400 million in unsecured debt coming due, with another $350 million scheduled to mature in March. Meanwhile, the commodities subsidiary needed its $650 million back to pay for the gold it had borrowed abroad. Joseph, who'd antagonized almost every other CEO on Wall Street over the years with his boasts and Establishment-bashing, began calling other investment banks looking for an emergency infusion of capital. He was everywhere refused. When Joseph called Peter Ackerman to seek his help in coping with the liquidity crisis, the $100 million man resigned from the board on the spot. Joseph hurriedly threw together a package of shaky bridge loans and private placements from Drexel's bulging inventories of unsold junk and offered it to a group of banks as collateral for a loan. Although Drexel estimated the value of these securities at $800 million, the bankers were less than impressed and, indeed, were angry, since they had previously refused to accept as collateral many of the very same securities included in the new package. Forget it, Fred, he was told. When as a last resort Joseph called the Treasury Department and the Federal Reserve Bank late on February twelfth, he was told to file for Chapter 11 the very next day or face a government liquidation. In its hour of need, Drexel Burnham was left with even fewer friends than Beck believed he had.

While Beck had no sympathy for Joseph, the firm's collapse only served to deepen Beck's misery, for he'd left the firm believing he was owed at least $60 million, including warrants in Beatrice and RJR that he claimed he'd been promised but not given. He knew, though, that he'd be lucky to get a fraction of the money due him, which he'd been counting on to help finance the divorce settlement that he and Margo had been negotiating in a state of perpetual ambivalence ever since they had separated in 1988. (They would not yet have resolved it by the end of 1990.)

As Beck's shock faded in the weeks after Burrough's story appeared, his pent-up emotions surfaced more explosively than ever as he veered between outrage and a despondence so utter that at times I feared for his life. The more Beck pondered the circumstances surrounding the *Journal* article, the more he convinced himself that it was the result of a conspiracy to destroy him that included many people he once considered friends. While Steve McGrath, Ron Peters, Sylvia, and the others who'd provided Burrough with damaging quotes were guilty by definition, there were other betrayers who, he was certain, had known the story was coming and yet failed to warn him. "Let's say the story was a hundred percent true, which it isn't," Beck said. "If I had a friend who got blasted in the press, I'd stick by him when he needed me. That's what really hurts. All the betrayals. I can't tell you how lonely it feels." After rereading *The Great Gatsby,* Beck was struck by the parallels between himself and Gatsby. "He's a guy from nowhere who creates an aura of mystery," Beck explained. "He bullshits his way into a moneyed society of big-time users, which sees him as a threat and wipes him out. Except that Gatsby was better off than me because they finished him off right away."

Beck's most constructive response to the depression and paranoia that now gripped him was to throw himself into a rigorous exercise program, setting the goal of competing in Hawaii's famous Iron Man triathlon, which consists of a 112-mile bike ride, a 2.5-mile swim and a 26-mile marathon back to back. Beck had begun working out with trainer Greg Gonzales, a triathlete who owned his own gym on the Upper East Side, as part of his therapy for his broken leg. "With the frustration and anger caused by the story about him, he picked up twenty percent in energy," Gonzalez said. As Beck's limp vanished, he not only lifted weights but adopted a near-daily triathlon-training regimen that included a run of six miles, a thirty-mile bike ride, and a one-mile swim. Gonzalez had to talk him out of doing more. "Jeff is like a wild horse," he said. "He has a tendency to overtrain. I called him the Animal." In July, Beck competed in a triathlon near Greenwich, Connecticut, and placed among the fastest 10 percent of the finishers. Having slimmed down to a rock-hard 167 pounds, he was in the best physical shape of his life.

As he huffed, puffed, and pumped himself into shape, Beck took some solace in knowing that he was not the only rainmaker on the run. By mid-1990, the volume of M & A announcements was 50 percent below the rate of the previous year, which itself was 10 percent below 1988's record total of $247 billion. The decline was mostly a function of the sudden disappearance of huge, highly leveraged deals of the sort epitomized by the buyouts of Beatrice and RJR Nabisco. While the vanishing of the mega-deal was obviously related to the demise of

Drexel and the contraction of the junk-bond market, the underlying reality was that the deal magicians had lost their magic. Banks, insurance companies, pension funds, and other custodians of the national wealth were no longer willing to wager billions of dollars on the ability of asset-shuffling wizards to carve a profit out of giant corporations before the loans incurred to buy them came due. What had begun as a long-overdue restructuring of American industry had segued into mass financial brinksmanship and had ended with mass default and bankruptcy. A deluge of profit had turned to drought, and Wall Street's rainmakers, who'd become rich and celebrated along the way, now were having their bellies ripped open. It was only natural. Those rainmakers who weren't accused by the government were attacked in the press. The discrediting of Beck was part of a larger backlash in which the Wall Street deal man was transformed from an icon of enterprise to an exemplar of greed and deceit.

Like Beck, most other rainmakers were chastened into hiding. Even Bruce Wasserstein shunned the press. Kravis, though, not only gamely maintained his high profile but tried to restore his lost luster with a burst of spin-doctoring. "Greed really turns me off," Kravis told *Fortune* magazine in the immediate aftermath of the RJR buyout. This comment was met with what *M* magazine called "general hilarity." Kravis also took the offensive in trying to head off the growing political backlash against LBOs, repeatedly flying down to Washington to lobby and testify. "I went down and said let's talk it through," Kravis recalled. "Would you rather have management that's entrenched, that's doing a terrible job and as a result causing us to lose our competitive advantage to foreign competition? Or would you rather have somebody like this come in and shake the management up and make this company more efficient?" In support of Kravis's arguments, KKR released a study purporting to show that its buyouts had produced $2 billion in additional federal tax revenues and created 37,000 jobs. But KKR's study was publicly blasted by scholars from the Brookings Institution and the University of North Carolina, who concluded that "the one KKR result that is verified by other post-LBO research is that LBOs yield high returns to investors."

Meanwhile, Carolyne Roehm was also retooling her image for the new decade. Only a year after appearing on the cover of *Fortune* as the embodiment of the "trophy wife," Roehm in mid-1990 told *Vogue*, "I feel differently about many things. I've been thinking about the fall of Michael Milken and the demise of Drexel Burnham, which stood for the junk bonds and the quick money"—not to mention the financing of KKR's largest deals. "I read all the criticism in the press. I thought about Donald and Ivana's divorce and Malcolm Forbes's death. I thought about the nineties and the Bush administration. And I vowed to stay home." As for the 1980s, said Roehm, indulging an apparent impulse to revisionism, she fingered Kravis as the social butterfly of the house. "We could have been out 365 days a year, four times a night. And if you're a couple, people always assume it's the woman who's keen. Actually, I want to stay home. But Henry's the most gregarious man on earth."

The unkindest cuts of all, though, came as KKR's reputation for deal savvy was tarnished for the first time by serious financial troubles at several of the companies it owned. SCI Television and Seaman Furniture missed debt payments and were forced into drastic financial restructurings that required KKR to make major concessions to bond-holders. However, KKR was unable to keep Hillsborough Holdings (formerly Jim Walter Corporation) afloat, as the big construction concern filed for Chapter 11 protection from its creditors. The filing came after major investors rejected Kravis's personal plea to accept a bond exchange offer. CRACKS IN THE HOUSE THAT DEBT BUILT read the headline on a *New York Times* story detailing KKR's woes. And that was before RJR Nabisco began staggering under the gargantuan load of debt it had to carry. Less than two years after the buyout, KKR eased RJR's short-term financial pressure (and sharply reduced its theoretical profit) by pumping another $1.7 billion of cash into its largest property. "If RJR went down," observed one of Kravis's rivals, "KKR might as well close up shop."

On June 7, 1990, Kravis was able to mix in a little good news with the bad as KKR announced that it finally had sold Beatrice. Conagra Inc. bought the company for $1.34 billion, which was far below KKR's 1987 asking price and too low to suit Don Kelly. "KKR just seemed determined to sell the company," said Kelly, who had urged Kravis to hold out for a higher bid. Having been billed initially as the decade's greatest deal and then as its greatest flop, the buyout of Beatrice ended up solidly in the middle.

In looking back on the buyouts of Beatrice and RJR from the lonely perspective of his exile, Beck, as usual, was contorted by ambivalence. He craved credit for having set in motion these mega-deals with his creativity and energy while just as emphatically wanting to disassociate himself from the ultimate results of his rainmaking efforts. On balance, though, Beck came to see both deals as personal defeats. "The bastardization of these deals was my greatest failing as a deal man," Beck said. "Well-thought-out ideas that could have worked out for greater long-run benefit of all concerned were perverted out of nothing more than ego and the desire for fees."

One of the few former colleagues that Beck remained in touch with after the *Journal* exposé was Mike Milken, who in April 1990 pleaded guilty to six felony charges. In exchange, the government agreed to drop all charges against his brother, Lowell. In a major anticlimax, Milken pleaded guilty not to supplying Boesky with inside information but to helping him file a false statement with the SEC and violating the minimum capital required of securities dealers. During the seven months he spent awaiting sentencing, Milken telephoned Beck with increasing frequency. They spoke for the final time a few nights before Judge Kimba Wood sentenced Milken to ten years in prison. Throughout the government's investigation of Drexel, Beck had given Milken blunt-spoken advice, which the erstwhile king of junk needed now more than ever. Moreover, Milken saw in Beck a kindred spirit of sorts. Although Beck had not been accused of a crime, his ordeal—like Milken's—took the form of an excruciating and very public crisis of identity.

While commiserating with Milken Beck tried to give focus and substance to his personal roster of grievances and vows of revenge by hiring one of the country's preeminent libel lawyers, John Walsh of Cadwalader, Wickersham & Taft. In what was perhaps the most celebrated libel case of the 1980s, Walsh had represented a top executive of Mobil Oil in suing *The Washington Post.* At the trial, Walsh won a surprise victory, only to have the guilty verdict overturned by an appeals court. Beck's hiring of Walsh wasn't the first time he'd jolted me into reappraisal just when I thought I had him all figured out. Beck said he'd shown Walsh the evidence that he would have provided to the *Journal* had they held the story—evidence to be provided to me, as well, as soon as he obtained official clearance—and indeed it seemed logical that Walsh wouldn't have taken on Beck as a client had the lawyer not been convinced that there were grounds for a suit. In any event, Beck never did show *me* any proof of military service.

To win a libel verdict, a plaintiff must prove "actual malice" on the part of the writer. The writer must be shown to have published false

and defamatory material knowing full well that it was false or, alternatively, the writer must be shown to have displayed "reckless disregard"
in not ascertaining whether the material was true or false. "Reckless
disregard" doesn't mean simply that the writer failed to research something thoroughly but that he failed to do so despite entertaining substantial doubts about the veracity of what he was committing to print.
This is a particularly onerous burden of proof for the plaintiff because
it speaks to the writer's motives as well as his actions. And since Burrough was correct in his basic assertion—that Beck had not fought in
Vietnam—the odds were stacked against Walsh, truth being an absolute defense against libel charges.

On the other hand, Burrough appears to have made some errors
that might have given Beck some hope of pursuing a suit. One involved Ross Johnson of RJR. "At their second meeting," wrote Burrough, "Mr. Johnson brought along a box of Milk Bone Dog Biscuits,
a joke on [Beck's] canine nickname. Then, while discussing strategy
with the chief executive of one of America's largest companies, Mr.
Beck ate the whole box."

After the *Journal* article appeared, at Beck's request Johnson provided him with a letter denying the incident. "As we both know,"
Johnson's letter stated, "and along with Jim Welch [at the time RJR's
vice-chairman] and the other Drexel personnel who know, under no
circumstances did you eat the box of dog biscuits." Beck also got a
Drexel colleague who'd attended the meeting to provide Walsh with a
letter denying that he'd eaten so much as a single Milk Bone.

Burrough also seemed vulnerable to legal attack over this anecdote:
"Mr. Beck's histrionics had endless uses," Burrough wrote. "When
Mr. Kravis's bid for Esmark was topped by Beatrice, a rival food company, Mr. Beck desperately wanted a fee for setting events in motion.
'You've got to do something for me; you've got to do something for
me,' he moaned, spread-eagled on the floor of an Esmark office in
Chicago. A mischievous Mr. Kelly, the Esmark chief, already persuaded to pay Mr. Beck, decided to play a trick. Called into Mr.
Kelly's office and told he wouldn't receive a fee, Mr. Beck went berserk, walking to the office window, opening it and shouting: 'I'm going
to jump!' Mr. Kelly, breaking up in laughter, yelled, 'Don't jump!'
then revealed his charade and gave Mr. Beck a $7.5 million fee for
Oppenheimer."

I happened to be in Kelly's office in Chicago a few days after the
Journal profile appeared. He said that he and Beck had never even

discussed the matter of Opco's fee for the Esmark-Beatrice deal. Later, when Beck called Kelly and asked him to send a letter for use in court, he obliged. "Don't jump!" his letter began. "It is difficult to find anything funny in some of the articles and stories I have read recently as they refer to Jeff Beck and Don Kelly. However, I must admit my somewhat perverted sense of humor was tickled by the report that you were going to open one of my office windows prior to jumping if I held back on your compensation. I have never had an office with a window that could be opened which makes the reported action even more remarkable. I also never remember you lying prostrate on the floor in my office or any other place which makes this wander through fairyland even more amazing."

Burrough told me that the anecdote had been supplied by a first-hand witness, whom he identified as Richard Beattie, the Simpson Thacher lawyer who had acted as Kelly's legal adviser on the deal. After I read Kelly's letter to Beattie, the lawyer massaged his eyes with both hands, turned bright red, and said the incident was accurate as Burrough described it. I then told Kelly that Beattie had confirmed Burrough's account. "Dick Beattie said that?" said Kelly, stunned that his own lawyer in effect was calling him a liar. Kelly paused and said, "In South Side Irish, that is one bullshit story."

What most enraged Beck about Burrough's article was its repetition of the accusations made in his book, *Barbarians at the Gate*, about the leak of KKR's offer for RJR Nabisco. In *Barbarians*, Kravis is quoted as first accusing Beck and then deciding that Wasserstein was the real culprit. "Months after the deal's completion, Kravis and [KKR partner Paul] Raether again amended their theory," wrote Burrough and his coauthor, John Helyar. "After checking Kohlberg Kravis phone records for that Sunday night, they claimed to have identified phone calls to reporters for *The Wall Street Journal* and *The New York Times*. Kravis came to believe there were dual sources for the leaks, Beck and Wasserstein, one for each newspaper. Beck's motive, they surmised, was pure ego: He wanted to take credit for the deal. Whatever the truth, both Beck and Wasserstein fervently denied being the source of any leaks."

Burrough, however, knew perfectly well who had leaked to the *Journal* since he'd been involved in reporting the story that contained the leaked information. Coyness aside, Burrough's account is flawed by a basic factual problem: Local calls are not itemized on phone-company billing records. "It's ridiculous, really," said Beattie, who was KKR's lawyer on this deal. "How could you figure out who made a call from billing records. What a silly idea. I think Paul Raether meant it as a joke. It fits in with his sense of humor. I thought it was written that way by Burrough—as a joke." Beattie also told Beck and Walsh that the phone records were "a joke."

Beck was not amused. And as he reread *Barbarians at the Gate* in the wake of his unmasking, it seemed to him that Kravis and his aides and associates were lurking everywhere in the tall reeds of the narrative —explaining this, alleging that, often behind the cover of anonymity. Out of a mélange of fact, circumstance, and suspicion, Beck drew the conclusion that Kravis, with Beattie's connivance, had decided "to take him out," as he put it, deliberately evoking the gangster mentality of the RJR deal. Idled by the combination of depression and a broken leg, he'd certainly outlived his usefulness to Kravis, and Burrough's article had said as much: "Investors like Mr. Kravis, who put up with Mr. Beck's half-truths and histrionics for years, kept him around for the simple reason that he had an incredible knack of sniffing out brewing takeovers." But what had he done to warrant execution? Beck had offended Kravis in so many ways over the years that he hardly knew where to begin in pondering this question. Yet the more he considered his fate, the more his suspicions hardened into certainty and the more avenging himself became an obsession.

The principal vehicle of his revenge was to be the libel suit. In connection with it, he intended to subpoena everyone whom he suspected and have Walsh grill them. It was a long list. Over the course of the next several months, Beck spent countless hours meeting with Walsh and his assistants, developing their case. Over and over again, he told me that he was days away from making a decision on whether to bring suit. Although he never admitted it to me or to his lawyer, Beck's reluctance to go to court was no doubt rooted in his dread of finding himself having to choose under oath between lying and admitting he hadn't fought in Vietnam. On the other hand, the *Journal*'s vulnerability on some points of fact explains in part why Beck took such protracted refuge in the idea of a libel suit and in the process running up huge legal bills at Cadwalader, Wickersham. It was fortunate for all concerned that libel cases in New York are subject to a one-year statute of limitations. As of January 23, 1991, Beck had to find some other way to fill the deal-emptied hours of his life.

* * *

While Beck immersed himself in the nuances of libel law, I was repeatedly pressing him for a resolution to the Vietnam mystery. Citing
my approaching deadline, I told him in countless ways: Either show
me proof or admit that you faked it. Unfortunately, my pressure had
the effect of pushing Beck even deeper into his masquerade, as he
insisted that he wouldn't be able to show me anything from the thirty
cartons of Vietnam-related material he had in storage unless he got
authorization from Washington. But one afternoon he nervously
showed me a photograph of himself with General Creighton Abrams,
who had succeeded General William Westmoreland as commander in
chief of all U.S. forces in Vietnam. A man who did indeed appear to
be General Abrams was standing in front of an airplane, surrounded by
a few South Vietnamese officers. Framed in the doorway of the plane
as he disembarked was a soldier who looked just as Beck must have
looked in the late 1960s. He was dressed in combat fatigues and carrying a big attaché case. To my admittedly inexpert eye, the photograph
did not look doctored, though it did strike me as odd that Beck was
the only one of the half-dozen men shown who was looking directly
into the camera, smiling shyly.

Beck said the photo had been sent to him unsolicited in an envelope
with a Washington postmark. He also showed me a copy of a letter,
which he said he'd received after the *Journal* story appeared, from one
Thomas E. Spencer, who claimed to have met him while working on a
top secret mission in Taiwan during the Vietnam War. Beck said he
didn't remember ever meeting Spencer and concluded, after talking
with him on the telephone and examining the materials he'd sent, that
he had indeed served in the U.S. Special Forces but was mentally
unstable. Beck rebuffed Spencer's suggestion that he fly up to New
York and talk over old times; he turned everything that Spencer had
sent him over to Walsh. Spencer wrote:

> I've always wondered what happened to you, the last time I saw you was
> at the O.K. Bar [in Taipei, Taiwan]. I want to thank you again for saving
> my life in Vietnam. I've spoken of you so many times over the years—ha,
> the stories we could tell! Those idiot newswriters obviously don't have any
> idea what "top secret" really means. At first I wasn't sure if it was you but
> then I knew—hell, I've worn a Seiko ever since. . . . I often remember
> those days in Vietnam and I'll never forget the time when we were covered
> with leeches; when I said I was hungry you told me to eat them. You always
> had a great sense of humour and I can see from reading *The Wall Street*

Journal article that you haven't changed a bit, you're still the old "Mad Dog."

I could go on and on about a lot of our times together but there were so many, and as you know, many of our Special Forces operations were classified. We signed statements that we would not reveal the true mission of many of our classified exercises because of the damage they would cause if revealed. I am very upset that *The Wall Street Journal* would do such a horrible thing to you. What they say about you they say about all of us. I still have so many documents about all those missions which, as you know, some are classified. They might be able to call you a liar, but they can't call me one. I've got the proof.

On the same day that he wrote Beck, Spencer also sent a letter to Burrough. It read in part:

Jeff saved my life in Vietnam and he was one of the finest, bravest and courageous Green Berets that served our country. If it wasn't for Jeff, I wouldn't be here today and my three sons would not have been born. If it wasn't for Jeff, ten years ago I would not have stood at the MGM Grand Hotel with over 30 general officers, the Sgt. Major of the Army, VIP's from the Pentagon, the official Army Drill Team, the Army Band, and the Old Color Guard. The Department of the Army was recognizing me for being one of the best. . . . I am very unhappy with your article. I was wounded in action, reported killed in action, and suffered many hardships along with Jeff and other Green Berets and I've got the proof.

However, Spencer's claims of certainty were undermined by a sentence that had been typed across the top of the letter and highlighted in Magic Marker: "***THIS MAY NOT BE THE SAME JEFF BECK I KNEW IN VIETNAM***." After speaking by telephone to Spencer, Burrough concluded that he was a crank.

Whether or not he knew Beck from Vietnam, Spencer does appear to have been a member of the Special Forces during the Vietnam years. In addition to news clips, Spencer sent Beck a copy of his ID card from "Forward Thrust," which apparently was a top secret operation in the late 1960s involving both U.S. and Taiwanese forces. Spencer was the latest in a series of Beck associates with an established or rumored link to intelligence activies, among them David Aaron, Peter Grace, the Countess of Romanones, and Robert Maxwell. Several months after the *Journal* article was published, Mimi Russell told me that she'd been snooping through Beck's briefcase while he slept one night in search of divorce papers when she'd come across some sort of document with CIA markings. While Beck might have put her up to this, I myself had once come across what appeared to be a undercover surveillance report lying on a table in Beck's apartment. Whether he'd mistakenly left the report there or created it somehow for the purpose of leaving it there for me to find, I'm not sure. All of it, including the photograph with General Abrams, added up to nothing in the way of proof of any tie between Beck and the CIA. On the other hand, none of it was easily explained away.

As I pondered these curiosities, I realized that I, like most people who knew Beck, had been assuming that if his elaborate tales of Vietnam combat had been fabricated then the whole superstructure of his identity as warrior-spy must come tumbling down like a building suddenly deprived of its foundation. However, even after Beck had explicitly recanted his Vietnam tales as fantasy, he remained unnervingly coy on the subject of the CIA. Whenever I confronted him with the direct question, "Have you ever had an affiliation with the CIA?" he'd smile cryptically and change the subject. There are two possibilities: Either Beck wanted to maintain one last inviolable sanctuary of fantasy or he was refusing to tell any more lies.

While I believe the former is far more likely, consider for a moment the hypothetical possibility that Beck's combat identity was not the foundation of his fantasy but a fabrication rooted in a covert but comparatively mundane reality. In the late 1960s, the CIA was actively recruiting on college campuses, especially conservative ones like Florida State University. Highly intelligent and bitterly alienated from his family and himself, Beck was a malleable young man in search of a romanticized identity to override reality—and, as such, was an ideal candidate for CIA recruitment. Although Beck was no superpatriot, deep down he may have been additionally compelled to public service by a need to atone for his father's transgressions. Joining the CIA would also have offered Beck the immediate comfort of forestalling the possibility that he would be shipped off to Vietnam as cannon fodder.

If Beck in fact had joined the CIA in college, that hardly means that he was the glamorous spymaster suggested by Beck's tale of Rosebud, which in the end he would admit was a fabrication. Despite the CIA's mystique of derring-do, most of its operatives are involved in intelligence-gathering activities no more dangerous than library research. They are analysts, not spies in the Hollywood mold. Perhaps, when Sylvia assumed he was off on a training exercise, Beck did go to Vietnam briefly, not to fight but to push a pencil as an junior analyst on some undercover project. Perhaps at Columbia he was part of the Nixon administration's misguided effort to spy on campus radicals. Perhaps, too, he was involved in the less thoroughly documented but nonetheless real infiltration by the CIA of Wall Street firms. Perhaps all those unexplained late-night phone calls and sudden disappearances that baffled Rosemary and Margo over the years did not involve other women but other duties. If this was the case—if Beck was some sort of CIA functionary—then perhaps his vigorous promotion of his fantasies in the mid-1980s was an escape not only from the increasingly burdensome realities of his private and professional life on Wall Street but from the antiheroic drudgery of his covert life as well. Perhaps.

Epilogue

My relationship with Beck reached its moment of truth one afternoon late in the summer of 1990 when I told him that I had uncovered the truth about his father. As I began speaking of those long-ago events in Pittsburgh, Beck seemed dumbstruck with surprise. It was quickly evident that I knew more about the details of what had transpired than he did, and so I went on at some length. I not only listed Lou Beck's convictions but explained the political context of his crimes—that in Pittsburgh in the Depression, the numbers racket was controlled from city hall almost as if it were a municipal utility; that the most distinctive thing about his father's criminal career was that he was the one white man accepted by the black numbers kingpins on the Hill; that somehow he'd offended the powers that be and gone to jail for something customarily dismissed with a slap on the wrist. After listening to my monologue with an expression of rapt queasiness, Beck got up from his chair at the dining-room table of his apartment, walked over to his couch, and lay down. Then he took his glasses off, covered his face with his hands, and wept bitterly.

When he recovered the power of speech, Beck said that he hadn't spoken a word about his father's crimes to anyone since the day twenty-eight years before when his mother had first mentioned them. He was so horrified at what he'd been told that he'd never made an effort to find out for himself what had actually taken place in Pittsburgh, attempting instead to obliterate the memory of his mother's words with action and fantasy. "Do you have any idea of the horror of waking up each day wondering if today is the day you'll be found out?" he said. After making a brief, halfhearted attempt to persuade me not to include his father's criminal history in this book, Beck said he was relieved that his secret would finally emerge. Over the next few weeks, Beck gradually let go of his fantasies, admitting that he hadn't fought in Vietnam and that Rosebud was a figment of his imagination. When I offered him the chance to explain himself in his own words, he leaped at it. What follows is, in effect, his psychological autobiography.

> "I have felt the wind of the wing of madness."
> —*Baudelaire*

What was the reality of Wall Street in the 1980s and what was the myth? The reality was that Ronald Reagan and George Bush opened the floodgates and set in motion the rampant speculation that occurred, with Mike Milken's access to the money at the vortex. The reality was that greed was not limited to Drexel but that all the other investment banks put their pursuit of fees ahead of their responsibilities to the country, to the economy, and often to their clients as well. The reality was that all of us who participated in the greed years of the 1980s on Wall Street were guilty of the same selfish thinking and should admit our failures and pay back in our own ways the system that we abused. The reality was that Wall Street needed more regulation, not less. What it got was the politicized justice of Rudolph Giuliani and his supporters, who crafted justice and used the press to suit their personal ambitions. The image makers cannot change these realities, for access to truth comes to individuals and societies only after they discard their false myths and understand the true content of what has happened to them.

But what was the reality of my life on Wall Street and how did I come to be successful in the opinion of others but not myself?

My earliest recollection of childhood was simply the desire to survive an unhappy home. To me, survival meant escaping almost daily from the harsh realities of my sadness. Escaping for me was to deny who I was, for so many times I was told that I was unworthy and not a planned addition to the family. While I do not wish to blame my mother, who had her own emotional baggage to carry, patterns of behavior are inevitably influenced by our parents and their parents and are molded through generations of behavior repetition. As fate would have it, my peculiar experience would be adaptive to a highly stressful and visible career on Wall Street, which became the ultimate escape.

The emotional havoc caused by the death of my father when I was fifteen years old and the almost immediate remarriage of my mother to a wealthy, albeit disturbed man gave me yet another reason to try to escape my sorrow at all costs. The inability to properly grieve has been with me for close to thirty years now and has affected all of my intimate relationships for the worse. It has been a constant fight to avoid the emotions that I felt for the loss of my father, who, given my mother's problems, had been my anchor. The rage and guilt associated with these bottled emotions were converted to an insatiable drive to be noticed and became the foundation for my unique form of self-destruction. At forty-four years of age, after fighting to survive through misdirected ambition and compulsive self-denial, I am finally mourning my father's death as if it happened yesterday. My beautiful daughter has given me the inspiration to change my behavior and to try to break the patterns of the past for her sake. I am as ferociously committed to achieving this as I was in any deal that I pursued. While I've experienced my share of depression and despair, for the first time recently I also have felt the glimmers of serenity and even joy.

From my background of pent-up rage and guilt converted into narcissistic drive, Wall Street became my candy store. When I came to the Street, it was evolving from a club of blue-bloods to a free-for-all revolving around one thing: the ability to be a money-maker. Each of us in the deal game fed the next person's ambitions to the point of insanity; we were all magicians creating wealth and power from thin air, for the benefit of the few at the expense of many unsuspecting victims. New identities and backgrounds were created daily and marriage vows even were exchanged to perpetuate the new identities. Existing personas were altered to fit the new imperialism, leaving the real persons like old dolls in a heap of rubbish. It was like going to a perpetual movie. For those of us who wanted to escape, to live vicariously by creating impressions like a picture show and never revealing who we were or where we came from, Wall Street was the best place in America to hide.

Truth about oneself or one's actions became secondary to the deal, in which there is no art but only random manipulations and opportunistic sensitivity. The specter of the Donald Trumps of the world really believing that they have artistic skills is as absurd as those lending institutions that watched their ballet and signed up for season tickets. Although I never thought of deals as an art form, deal making did become imagery, as opposed to the product of scientific, clinical analysis. For me, a transaction would grow out of my understanding of the authority figure who had the power or who was about to lose power over his enterprise. I would go to extremes to understand these people, utilizing my chameleonlike personality to gain the CEO's confidence while also establishing an intelligence network among his high-level subordinates. Hiding all the time behind my unpredictable, maverick personality, I inspired more trust and confidence in myself until my mosaic of the future was complete. I luxuriated in the intricacies not of the deal's financial structure but in the infinite variations and actions that corporate leaders and their directors could take. Coupling this with my ability to analyze events, I developed a rather consistent ability to predict changes of corporate control.

With success, I developed my own special form of hubris, weaving an intricate web of anecdotal curiosities about my background that became escapes, propelling me to create more transactions, to attend more black-tie affairs, and to live out selected fantasies about myself. I was convinced that I had to constantly promote my burgeoning reputation to any journalist who would listen. I began to believe that my vision and propensity to create large transactions would make me a conquering hero, eliminate discovery of my father's past, satisfy my mother's avowed desire for celebrity, satisfy the false image I had of my socially prominent wife, and give me the opportunity to have the biggest and best things. Everyone wanted to be my friend and, despite their pretensions, I fell for their sunshine because, like a drug, it took away my pain.

Spending money on apartments, charitable donations, country homes, vacations at the Hôtel du Cap, New Year's Eves in Paris, jewelry, designer dresses, private schools, chauffeurs, housekeepers, nannies, laundresses, antiques, interior decorators, and architectural designers was the outer manifestation of a personality out of control. It seemed that the more money I made, the less it sufficed. To make sure that my wife was more than adequately admired, I bought her baubles after every deal without ever being asked to do so. For myself, I would buy horses, naming them after deals, driving from my New York apartment to my country home in Pound Ridge in a chauffeured limousine to ride and jump these creatures on the weekends. I did this not because I loved horses—I'm actually scared witless of them—but because, alas, it was an impression I was creating. No one told me to stop, not one of my so-called friends, no member of my disjointed family. No one.

Everything was an impression, and my heroes became people like Henry Kravis. I bought a Dutch warmblood mare near Kravis's country estate and Margo and Carolyne Roehm watched me go through my paces. After buying the horse and naming her Beatrice (after "Henry's deal") the four of us had lunch and talked of Carolyne's plans for her new business, acquiring art, how good life was, and what geniuses we all were. It was an "I'm great, you're great" lunch. It was dining at court and I was one of many jesters. The only difference between me and the other jesters was that I knew that Henry and Carolyne could never become king and queen.

Still, I remember that day as golden. After lunch at Henry's estate, there ensued a gentle conversation between my wife and Carolyne on how Margo and I had met and, more important, how I was ensnared. As the sparkling autumn light penetrated the enclosed sunroom and glorified these two fragile women, I heard my wife exclaim, "I married Jeff because I loved him." This remark seemed to chill the vanishing warmth of the afternoon because I could tell that Carolyne was more interested in *how* to marry a man than *why* to marry a man. In the disjointed atmosphere of the 1980s, even marriage and love became a deal, it seemed, and were talked about in material terms rather than in terms of emotion. If marriage was not sacred, could anything be sacred? Everything and everyone, to the dealers of the 1980s, was a pretense for something else. In leaving Henry's house that afternoon I did not give what I had overheard a second thought, for I was as much a part of them as they were of each other. As the early shadows of night came down, I was comforted by the fee agreement I had with Kravis on Beatrice which made me richer and even more dangerous to myself, providing the first sparks slowly igniting my very own bonfire.

After the buyout of Beatrice was completed, I was really flying. I had risen from the dead and I was at Drexel, the most powerful investment bank on the Street. The ecstasy was short-lived, though, as I sank into postpartum deal depression. I was spent and felt that instead of doing something great I had helped to perpetuate a faulty system of corporate disassembly affecting thousands of hardworking employees. I was suspicious of Marty Siegel's and Ivan Boesky's role in Beatrice and, in fact, had suspected them of being in cahoots. Was I the only one on Wall Street who suspected him and Boesky? I doubted it and said so to reporters and other Wall Street types. Needless to say, these suspicions did not win me many friends. I became the in-house heretic at Drexel, feeling the distant gurgling of vendetta and perpetuating my own downfall with frontal attacks on the system to anyone who would listen. At the same time I accepted a fee from KKR of $4.5

million for initiating Beatrice, proving that while my vocal cords worked, my heart and soul were compromised by money. Actions really do speak louder than words.

I knew I could not escape forever but, like Captain Queeg in *The Caine Mutiny*, I was asking for help from all the wrong people. There was something in me that could not face the pain or the despair I felt. I did not want to face the abyss of my own grief because I knew I wasn't ready and I was scared of the pain that lurked beneath the surface and attacked me when there was a quiet moment in my brain, nibbling at the outer reaches of my soul. We all learn the hard way, though, and rather than stepping off the train, I stoked the engines.

Meeting Michael Douglas in the south of France opened the floodgates of fantasy as Hollywood made Wall Street look boring and tedious. After I went to the Academy Awards ceremony with Michael in 1987, he took me to Swifty Lazar's party at Spago, where the stars of Hollywood mixed with the stars of business and Wall Street. I was there with Jimmy Goldsmith, Michael Eisner, Sid Bass, Rupert Murdoch, and all the other fantasy explorers. The paparazzi made the entrance into an adoring sound-and-light show of cameras clicking and flashes illuminating the evening. The entertainment reporters were there to interview the wave of human fantasy purveyors and, yes, I was there on an orgasmic journey of total impression since there was no content. It was the greatest show on earth, the adult version of a Ringling Brothers circus. It was what I thought life was all about; to be there, to be seen, to be liked, to be worshiped; and money and power were the tickets to the ball.

Afterward, I accompanied Douglas to several movie premieres, him no doubt thinking of me as a money source, me thinking of him as access to a magical tour of the Hollywood kingdom—and both of us thinking of ourselves as actors. My stage was deal making on Wall Street and his was deal making in Hollywood. Who better than Douglas to star as Gordon Gekko, a lizardlike denizen of corrupted values? In watching Douglas's performance as Gekko, I saw many characteristics that he picked up from me: my laugh, my staccato style of deal speech, my arrogant swagger. We were both chameleons, both stars bringing our own fantasies of life to others. The only difference was that he was a professional actor known as such and I was in disguise as a Wall Street investment banker. His performance was a product of sound and light, mine of sound and darkness. We became the best of friends, each serving to bolster the other's fantasies, each of us unhappy with his past and trying to escape the present, each of us dislocating everything that really mattered.

For me, Wall Street and Hollywood became one, with Drexel's West Coast office providing nothing more for me than an excuse to be there. The more time I spent in Hollywood the more my unbridled ambitions and fantasies began to take the pain away. Sacrificing everything and everyone in the way of my great escape, my Hollywood experience took on a life of its own, as Michael and I danced to each other's tunes of self-destruction in the deadly embrace of make-believe. Through Michael came all of those who wanted to experience a little bit of star glow, who wanted to be with *me* because I was with *him*. The aphrodisiac of celebrity brought me a whole new level of pain relief. Getting to know the stars, the producers, the directors, the talent agents became even more interesting than analyzing CEOs because the Hollywood people dealt with fantasies every day and welcomed me like a warm blanket on a cold winter's day, spreading the warmth through my entire body.

The morning after Michael won the Academy Award I saw him in his suite at the Bel-Air Hotel and rejoiced with him in his accomplishment. I reveled in the attention my friend was receiving and was genuinely happy for him. That evening I attended a private party for Michael at his father's house and was struck by the similarity of father and son. Kirk was the old master, proud of his son but with a tinge of fatherly envy, having himself never received an Oscar, the perpetual glaze of anger in those riveting eyes, chin thrust forward, him showing me in his library seventy-five bound scripts, none of which had ever received the acclaim that his son got for *One Flew over the Cuckoo's Nest* or *Wall Street.* For that brief moment the reality of Michael's pain overcame me and I realized that, like me, he was driven to prove something to someone who primarily cared about only himself.

Douglas and I began to collaborate on the antiheroic story of a Vietnam vet nicknamed Mad Dog, a renegade who has problems with authority. He survives the brutality of the jungle but is court-martialed and committed to an army mental institution in San Francisco. After his discharge, Mad Dog travels from one coast to another viewing the sights and sounds of the late 1960s and finding redemption in life. Was the story of Mad Dog symbolically my own story or was it my attempt to search for what had actually happened to me in those furious years of deception and havoc? In any event, Douglas and I thought it was a story worth telling, and as I created it with a screenwriter (who took my money and wrote nothing, being enamored more with Douglas's involvement than with the story) I began to understand the pain of the character. Mad Dog was as real for me as Gordon Gekko was for Michael. That is why he won the Academy Award. But my award was yet to come and it obviously would not be a gold statuette but something much more meaningful to me: understanding and self-awareness, my realities for the future.

Trusting no one and becoming ever more isolated from my family, I turned to my own peculiar form of deal spinning at Drexel, concentrating on only a few accounts. I spent three years working on the probabilities of a massive restructuring or buyout for RJR Nabisco and Pillsbury. After all, I had to top the Beatrice transaction. I had my most productive year on Wall Street in 1988, working night and day on deals that had a total value of $40 billion, including Macy's, Pillsbury, and RJR Nabisco back to back. But the year became a living nightmare, as I grew more and more aware that I did not respect myself or those around me for what we were doing on Wall Street and that I'd played a large role in wreaking havoc on a family life that should have been my only priority.

The climax of this nightmare year came when Kravis accused me of leaking word of KKR's first bid for RJR to satisfy my own ego. Later, he conceded that he had overreacted and allowed me back into the transaction, which, after all, I'd helped to create. But I was never fully exonerated, and I began to wonder why I wanted to expose myself any longer to this world of malcontents and overblown egos perpetually craving more money and more acclaim. While I had the ability to predict major corporate events, I saw that my ideas were being subverted in the course of these big transactions as fee-lust turned them into auctions. I will never forget the cavalier attitude that existed at KKR's offices the night before it made its $90-a-share offer for RJR. Instead of discussing the merits of the business, the other bankers just wanted to get Kravis into the game as quickly as possible, and Henry fell for it. The RJR deal was the epitome of all that was wrong with the 1980s; paper-shuffling financial operators were taking control of corporations, in the process betting the nation's banking system on the outcome. I began to see Kravis and the others for what they really were —not great but insecure men driven to escape their own realities. I was no different, except that I could no longer play the game. Despite the monuments these people build to themselves, they will end up irrelevant footnotes to history.

My wife having virtually left me—and for good reason—I sank into an endless stream of lonely people, becoming the designated hero to some of the most bitterly dejected older women I have ever met. They created opportunities for me to escort them to fancy parties, to exchange my views on male-female conflicts, and to be both big brother and hero figure to them, without commitment. They vanished as quickly as they appeared, perpetuating their own forms of escape. Like so many vampires they seemed to come out only at night, returning to their lairs, with their bathroom mirrors reflecting too many parties, insincere relationships, and the daunting savagery of aging.

Cut off from my family and afraid to leave Wall Street, I no longer took pleasure from deal making, except as an escape. I listened to no one regarding my problems, thinking that I could overcome them myself. Feeling the numbing coldness of my own self-imposed isolation, I blamed anyone who was close to me for my own inadequacies. After I broke my ankle in the summer of 1989, I was relieved to absent myself from the Drexel vipers' nest. At times the pain in my left ankle left me drenched in cold sweat. In some strange way, though, my dedication to pushing through the physical pain relieved my mental pain, perhaps by giving me a clear goal to achieve. I tried to take refuge within myself, nursing my broken ankle and my tired mind. But it was hard to let go of the ego that always needed feeding, and I was still hurt by Kravis's treatment of me on RJR Nabisco.

On November 13, 1989, almost a year after KKR made its original offer, I hobbled into Kravis's "American Renaissance–style" offices and told him what I thought of him, his sycophantic advisers, his imperial life-style, and his obligations to his real friends and family. As I was speaking to the man that I'd assisted in creating his largest transactions, he suddenly seemed to be no one that I had ever known. After an hour of this, though, he invited me to dinner at the Japanese restaurant in the Waldorf-Astoria, changing his plans for the evening to continue talking with me. At dinner he reveled in his own glories, speaking of his plans for RJR Nabisco and telling me how grateful he was for my contributions to his success, but never apologizing for his treatment of me. The sensitive, meaningful topics between us were never discussed and I sensed a dark foreboding as we parted, me to my lonely apartment to recover, him to his coterie of idol worshipers.

The Christmas holidays have always been difficult for me since my father had died during this period. But I got through them, and afterward I flew to Miami to try to clear away the painful cobwebs of the past by seeing high-school friends I hadn't seen in twenty years. It was like going back in time. The primal memories that I had wanted to hide all my life came flooding over me as I resolved myself to try to cleanse away all the personality distortions of the 1960s. It was because I'd been unable to face these horrors that I'd spun my intricate web of convoluted backgrounds, destroying in the process all of the relationships that had really counted. This was distasteful to me but I didn't know how else to cope. Living in a world where there were no real heroes, I was compelled to create one within myself—a pain-drenched product of an era that left no one intact, a product of a war that coincided with my own internal war.

My inspiration was my older sister's first husband. A popular fraternity man at the University of Miami, he used to treat me like his little brother, driving me around in his new Chevrolet Impala. I missed him when he left to go to Columbia University, and after I was sent away to boarding school in Pennsylvania I would take a bus into New York City to see him whenever I could. When my sister for her own reasons had a love affair with another man, my brother-in-law was crushed. The last time I saw him was in 1962. He left bitterly heartbroken and joined the Special Forces. Years later, I came across some of his letters to my sister that illuminated the pain of their dissolution and his experiences as one of the early advisers to the South Vietnamese army. He was severely wounded and returned to the United States almost completely blind. He was the most important figure to me outside of my father and his torture became mine through a fantasy of transposition. To me, anyone who suffered as he had was truly important, and I made his importance mine. I hoped that one day I could see him again to share his pain, and he mine, so that I could finally bring it all to an end.

On Wall Street during the 1980s there were no boundaries to reality, and my creations took on a life of their own. It became a compulsion to never allow anyone to come close to the real me. Rather than confront the pain of my pitiful past, I decided to use my creative mind to convince people to believe in my false creations. While it became a challenge to my complex mind to keep reinventing this wheel of deception, I was also addicted to this escapist form of pain relief. The fight for survival against the deep depression led to more fantasy, ever deepening my fears and leaving me totally isolated from the world, like a spy who was truly out in the cold. The torment of hiding became overwhelming and ate away at me, devouring more and more of my free thought. The sanctuary of fantasy became a prison and I began to come apart as I tried to maintain the myths that I'd created while hanging onto the edge of sanity.

This is the state I was in when the *Journal* story appeared. In the aftermath, I have directed my rage into building a superior body while rebuilding and restoring my mind. Although the ability to overcome my problems has come slowly, the life of deception holds no more allure but offers me only sad memories of the moments when escape was still necessary to survive. However, I must say I still believe that *The Wall Street Journal* was influenced by powerful outside interests who, for their own reasons, wanted me silenced. Learning the intricacies of libel law has allowed me insight into how the power of the press can affect lives and how the arrogant abuse of the First Amendment can really threaten all of us.

In the meantime, my really good friends are still my good friends. All the others never counted anyway. They were so many fair-weather people who used me for sunshine when it suited them and discarded me when the story began to emerge. I have found solace in people who have nothing to do with Wall Street or New York City, who are honest and hardworking, raising families on a carefully planned budget. These, unfortunately, are the very people who will pay for all of the excesses of the Wall Street hotshots. These are the people who really understand me and accept me for me, warts and all. These are the good people who only care about real values and not the empty impressions created by self-indulgent people of the sort that I used to be. I will always be indebted to them and to Margo and my daughter, who have always tried to be there for me.

Like a magician, I thought for a long time that I was the only one who had the solution to my complicated tricks of identity. But I found that real people know a magician when they see one. To be a real person is to be responsible for your behavior regardless of the emotional traumas of the past, for it is not enough in the end merely to understand the damage inflicted in one's formative years. You have to act. As my behavior changes and the shrouds of depression and pain relief lift away, I hope that I have gained the wisdom to contribute my true thoughts, my true words, my true actions—my true life—to the search for the real explanations of what had gone on in America in the 1980s. I hope that I will never feel that "wind of the wing of madness" again, and I know that the Mad Dog in me has finally died.

Index

Personal Acknowledgments

While I am grateful to everyone who agreed to be interviewed, I'd like to single out those people who were particularly generous with their time, among them Don Kelly, Henry Kravis, Michael Milken, Don Engel, Ed Kelly, Ron Peters, Steve McGrath, Donald Goss, Phil Thomas, Mike Mc-Glannan, Jenny McGlannan, Rosemary Beck, and Margo Beck.

Special thanks go also to Peter Osnos, who acquired this book for Random House and whose enthusiasm and insight never wavered through occasionally trying times. Paul Golob brought great skill and diligence to the editing of the manuscript. Thanks, too, to Ken Gellman for promptly attending to everything.

Steve Shepard, the editor of *Business Week*, my professional home for the last decade, showed remarkable patience and understanding in awaiting my frequently postponed return. Ronnie Weil went above and beyond the call of duty in assembling the photographs, and Jessie Khatami provided invaluable research assistance. Two former *Business Week* colleagues also deserve thanks: Deborah Wise, for her reporting and wise counsel, and Sarah Bartlett, for her careful reading of the manuscript.

Last, though never least, I'd like to thank Jeff Beck for seeing through to completion a project that at times was agony for him. And my gratitude as well to his wonderful daughter, Katherine Beck, who was born about the time work on this book began and who, simply by existing, contributed as much to its completion as anyone.

About the Author

ANTHONY BIANCO is a senior writer for *Business Week* and has covered Wall Street for the magazine since 1982. He is a past recipient of the Amos Tuck Media Award for Economic Understanding, and has also written for the *Minneapolis Tribune* and *Willamette Week* in Portland, Oregon. A native of Rochester, Minnesota, Mr. Bianco now lives in Brooklyn, New York.